FIREPOWER

FIREPOWER

HOW WEAPONS
SHAPED WARFARE

———

PAUL LOCKHART

BASIC BOOKS
NEW YORK

Basic Books
Hachette Book Group
1290 Avenue of the Americas, New York, NY 10104
www.basicbooks.com

Printed in the United States of America

First Edition: October 2021

Published by Basic Books, an imprint of Perseus Books, LLC, a subsidiary of Hachette Book Group, Inc. The Basic Books name and logo is a trademark of the Hachette Book Group.

The Hachette Speakers Bureau provides a wide range of authors for speaking events. To find out more, go to www.hachettespeakersbureau.com or call (866) 376-6591.

The publisher is not responsible for websites (or their content) that are not owned by the publisher.

Print book interior design by Trish Wilkinson

Library of Congress Cataloging-in-Publication Data

Names: Lockhart, Paul, author.
Title: Firepower : how weapons shaped warfare / Paul Lockhart.
Description: New York : Basic Books, [2021] | Includes bibliographical
    references and index.
Identifiers: LCCN 2021010851 | ISBN 9781541672963 (hardcover) |
    ISBN 9781541672956 (ebook)
Subjects: LCSH: Firepower—Europe—History. | Military weapons—Europe—
    History. | Firepower—United States—History. | Military weapons—United
    States—History.
Classification: LCC U815 .L566 2021 | DDC 355.8/20903—dc23
LC record available at https://lccn.loc.gov/2021010851

ISBNs: 978-1-5416-7296-3 (print), 978-1-5416-7295-6 (ebook)

LSC-C

Printing 1, 2021

To Dad
with love

CONTENTS

Contents

PREFACE

This book is about weapons of war: the many ways that weaponry has influenced the art, science, and conduct of war, and how sometimes—surprisingly often—the evolution of weapons technology has had an impact on human life beyond the battlefield. Conversely, it's also about the forces that have shaped the progress of weapons design, and the complex interplay of war, politics, economics, and military technology.

These are topics that, for a variety of reasons, academic historians do not often address. That's not to say there are no good, serious books on the history of military technology. Indeed, there are many, some of which—like the excellent works by Jeremy Black, Max Boot, and Martin van Creveld, among others—inspired me to write this book. But these are broad surveys, and students of history looking for answers to narrower questions about weapons and war usually have to turn to another kind of literature altogether: specialist literature on weaponry. This niche genre includes books written about specific firearms, by collectors for collectors, and detailed accounts of individual warplanes, naval vessels, tanks, artillery, and so forth, written for military history buffs and wargamers. Because of their narrow scope, such books tend to be heavy in technical detail and light on the broader historical context. They can also be impenetrable to the uninitiated, with a highly specialized terminology and idioms all their own.

My hope is that this book can serve as a bridge of sorts between the broader studies of war and technology, on the one hand, and the specialist literature on the other. That too, as I've found in the process of writing this book, is no small undertaking. As a result, I've had to be somewhat selective in my approach. My chosen period is the epoch in which firearms were the dominant weapon type and the focus of innovation in military technology. This period stretches roughly from the end of the Middle Ages to the dawn of the atomic age at the end of the Second World War. My chosen geographical-cultural expanse is the West, because I feel that—at the very least, when it comes to warfare and military institutions—we can consider the West to be a distinct cultural, economic, and political entity, with its own distinct approaches to the conduct of organized violence. It should go without saying that the West does not exist, and has not existed, in a vacuum, and of course the military history of the Western states conditions its global relationships—and is in turn conditioned by them.

I should also issue the caveat, in advance, that this book is by no means intended to catalog all the significant or noteworthy weapons used by Western military forces over the course of half a millennium, nor does it flag every development in the evolution of weapons technology. Many weapons make an appearance in this book, to be sure, but as dizzying the variety might seem, it's only a minuscule fraction of the total body of weaponry used in European and American wars during the period in question. Human ingenuity is remarkably fecund when it comes to the invention of new instruments of death. But this selectiveness means that many readers will likely find that a favorite rifle or plane or battleship or tank has been omitted from this book. To those readers, I apologize in advance, and plead only that it is in the nature of surveys *not* to be all-inclusive. For the most part, the weapons discussed in this book are those that, I feel, best illustrate the broader points I want to make.

Preface

I've incurred many debts—mostly in the form of time, energy, encouragement, and support—in the years that I've spent working on this project and writing this book. While I can't possibly name them all, here are some of the more important acknowledgments. Family first. My wife, Mary Lockhart, deserves thanks most of all, for putting up with me as I wrote this, and for her unwavering support. My children—Kate, Nick, Paige, Phil, and Alex—have always been supportive, too. My youngest, my son Alex, undoubtedly felt the presence of The Book more than anyone else. It occasionally intruded upon my time with him, but because of his keen and wide-ranging interest in the subject matter—especially early twentieth-century naval warfare—he's also been both a sounding board for my ideas and a direct contributor to this book. Nick, Phil, and Alex have also been my partners at the shooting range for many years, and those experiences have been of great help to me as I worked on this book.

I can't possibly list all the historians, weapons experts, and grad students who have offered ideas, suggestions, fielded questions, and suggested further reading, but here's a selection: Mark Fissel, Rick Schneid, Rick Herrera, Art Johnson, Kim Wagner, Stuart Dempsey, Eric Bonekowski, Paul Dority, Evan Mason, Seth Marshall, Zach Jett, Dave Pridgeon, Dan Studebaker, Chad Kellersmith. The two colleagues who chaired the History Department at Wright State University during the time I was working on this book, Carol Herringer and Jonathan Winkler, deserve a great deal of thanks for a hundred little things, including accommodating teaching load requests, facilitating grants, and helping me to obtain a full year's sabbatical from 2017 to 2018. Thanks, too, to our infinitely resourceful history librarian at Wright State, Mr. Ran Raider.

Finally, I want to acknowledge my father, Newton F. Lockhart. It's to him that I dedicate this book. I first discussed it with him as soon as I knew I was going to write it, about six years ago, and I worked out the overarching structure of the book in conversations with him. He passed away not long after that. This will be the first book I've written that I won't be able to share with him. Still, I know that this book owes much to those early conversations with him, and to his loving support and evident pride over the years.

PDL
Washington Township, Ohio
5 February 2021

FIREPOWER

INTRODUCTION

THE AGE OF THE GUN

BICOCCA, NORTH OF MILAN, 27 APRIL 1522

The tenebrous morning fog that wreathed the high grass on the field west of Bicocca manor was just starting to burn off when the Swiss pikemen rolled forward, rank by rank, into battle. It was late April, and in Lombardy the mornings were still chilly. As the first rays of the sun warmed the dewy field, sending tiny tendrils of vapor skyward, the giant rectangles of tightly packed men tramped down the grass as they marched on toward the enemy. Most of them shouldered a long, slender pike, a spear about eighteen feet long, and their blocky formations looked very much like dense, spare, unnaturally upright forests on the move.

The men were in high mood, and they were noisy, too. There were several drummers in each pike block, pounding out the slow marching cadence, which was all but drowned out by the throaty cheers rising from the formations. Even the shouted orders of the officers were inaudible. The officers led from the front rank. The men, on the verge of mutiny the day before, had demanded that their leaders take their places in the front; the officers, having been elected by their men, weren't in any position to refuse.

One of the French lords commanding the army reined in his horse alongside one of the pike units. He implored the Swiss to halt until the artillery did its work, pummeling the enemy foot soldiers waiting at the other end of the field, softening the resistance to

1

make the assault easier. But the pikemen would not listen to the pleadings of a French lord in tiltyard armor. Their blood was up, and no one and nothing could stop them from charging straight at the enemy.

The Swiss were mercenaries, fighting only for pay, and these particular mercenaries were in the hire of the learned and bellicose French king, Francis I. Francis had inherited an expensive war with Spain from his father-in-law, who had in turn inherited it from his father, and since the beginning of that war in 1494 French and Spanish armies had sparred for possession of the lush valleys and rich city-states of northern Italy.

The French had two great advantages over their Spanish-Imperial foes: their numerical superiority, and the Swiss themselves. The Swiss were the most coveted mercenaries in Europe. Recruited from the towns and forests and mountain meadows of the Swiss cantons, they made a uniquely tough, well-disciplined, and ferocious infantry. They had become masters of simple weapons, like the pike, and found that if they held together and stood fast, they were nearly invincible—even when pitted against the cream of Austrian or Burgundian or French chivalry. Bristling with the sharp iron points of their pikes, a square formation of Swiss foot troops resembled nothing so much as a giant hedgehog. No knight on horseback, no group of knights, could break through the forest of pike points so long as the pikemen stood their ground. Even surrounded, the pike block could fight off attacking enemies on all sides. And when it went on the attack, the formation was equally irresistible, rolling over anything and anyone unwise enough to stand in its path. The Swiss had proven this again and again, and that knowledge gave them a strutting self-confidence. They rarely granted quarter to a defeated enemy, and they never asked for it.

On this damp April morning in 1522, the Swiss were to be the first element of the French army's assault against a polyglot enemy force representing the Habsburg prince Charles V, king of Spain and Holy Roman Emperor. Charles V's army—a mix of Papal, Imperial, and Spanish troops—numbered no more than eighteen thousand men; the French, under the command of Odet de Foix, vicomte de Lautrec, was at least half again as numerous. Even with the significant and favorable disparity in numbers, Lautrec hoped to avoid a fight. Battle killed soldiers, and soldiers cost money. The Swiss, though, wanted a battle, and they wanted it now. They had not been paid in weeks, and they were bored and restless, not having fought a battle or plundered a town for the entire campaign so far. Through their reluctant officers, they handed Lautrec an ultimatum the day before: fight a battle now, against the army in front of him, or else they would leave and find employment elsewhere. Lautrec could not afford to lose the Swiss, no matter how troublesome they were. He nodded his assent. He would give battle the next morning, and the Swiss would lead the attack.

Just before the first tentative beams of sunlight groped across the fields and orchards adjoining Bicocca's ancient manor house, the Swiss pikemen began the laborious task of forming themselves into pike blocks. Half of the Swiss contingent would be in the first wave, some eight thousand men, divided into two enormous formations, each roughly fifty men deep and eighty across. Once formed, they lurched forward. Lautrec, rightly, had thought it prudent to preface the assault with a brief artillery bombardment. But the Swiss would have none of it, contemptuously brushing the French gunners aside as they pushed on to glory, marching eagerly toward the enemy's earthworks.

The defenders of those earthen fortifications were the toughest foes the Swiss would ever face, but they were more than that: they represented the future of warfare. Their commander, seventy-year-old Prospero Colonna, had spent much of his career fighting against the French. He had served with the greatest soldier of the age, the Spanish general Gonzalo Fernández de Córdoba (1453–1513), and had been at his side precisely nineteen years earlier, when *El Gran Capitán* had dealt a stunning blow to another Franco-Swiss army in the battle of Cerignola. There, Córdoba's army had defeated a superior army—much like the one that confronted Colonna now—by making liberal use of the only kind of weapon that had a prayer of stopping a Swiss pike block: gunpowder firearms. Cerignola had proven that artillery projectiles could cut bloody swaths through a pike square; handheld firearms, such as the stubby, carbine-like arquebus and its longer, heavier cousin, the musket, could easily kill a man at a hundred yards. The densely packed pike formations presented rich targets, and they were nearly impossible to miss.

Gunpowder firearms were not new in 1522. Cannon had been profitably employed as siege engines since the mid-1300s. The arquebus—a primitive handheld firearm, short-ranged and slow to load—made its first appearance a little more than a century later. By 1522, arquebuses were a common sight in the armies fighting in Italy. Even the Swiss had made use of them, in small numbers, and the pikemen had felt their deadly sting before. Córdoba had seen great promise in the weapons, rearming much of Spain's native infantry with arquebuses. At Cerignola, the arquebus had proven its worth, helping to drive back repeated assaults by Swiss pikemen and French men-at-arms on horseback. That had been a sight to see, but what Colonna had in mind this day, here at Bicocca, was going to be much bigger.

As was the common practice at the time, the armies did not engage immediately upon making contact. Once they had de-cided to do battle, the opposing generals went about making their pre-combat arrangements, deploying their forces and allowing the men to get some rest. Colonna, then, had some time to prepare. He had good ground at his disposal and he made shrewd use of it. The old general had chosen a position that was well protected by roads and marshes on its flanks and rear, and by an ancient, heavily worn farm lane in front. Centuries of erosion and wagon traffic had gradually deepened the sunken road into a trench, and it was nearly as deep as a man was tall. Colonna directed his sappers to dig out the ready-made trench some more, making it broader and deeper, and to pile up the excavated soil behind them, on the south side of the trench. The dirt pile became a towering earthwork, some twelve feet high, protected in the front by the expanded trench. In the tall dirt parapet behind the sunken road,

Colonna's men built emplacements for the guns of the siege train. Ordinarily, siege guns were too heavy and cumbersome to be used in a land battle like this, but Colonna had time, and the big cannon were major assets.

Then Colonna deployed his troops. Spanish arquebusiers took position behind the high rampart, filling in the gaps between the gun emplacements. German pikemen—the flamboyantly dressed *Landsknechten*, professional rivals of the Swiss—took their place behind the arquebusiers. If Lautrec's pikemen were to try to take Colonna's position, they would have to either flank it or hit it head-on . . . and the latter would entail jumping down into the sunken road and scaling the sheer dirt wall that towered over them on the other side, all while enduring the fire of those arquebuses.

Neither Lautrec nor the Swiss knew the particulars of Colonna's dispositions, and it likely wouldn't have made any difference to the Swiss if they had known. They almost always won, and they were eager for a fight. After advancing past the French artillery, now silent, they crashed into a thin skirmish line of Spanish arquebusiers. The skirmish line easily gave way, the arquebusiers scampering back to their prepared positions to the south.

The Swiss were about three hundred yards out from the Spanish trench when Colonna's artillery opened up. Round shot, solid iron cannonballs, hit the ranks of the pikemen, plowing macabre furrows through the squares. There was no question of missing at this range. Each shot hit, each shot counted, each shot cut through the formations from front rank to rear. Round shot did not simply knock men down, or punch clean holes through them; it mangled them, tore them apart. The artillery barrage alone probably cost the Swiss a thousand men, a full eighth of their number, and they hadn't even reached the sunken road yet.

The Swiss were undeterred. The storm of iron only fueled their rage, and when the front ranks finally made it to the sunken road they were battle-mad. The first couple of ranks leaped down into the trench, and as the first men in tried to scramble up the steep slope of the parapet, more ranks crowded into the sunken road.

Soon it was filled with a milling mass of men unable to move forward, unable to extricate themselves.

The first volley rang out just then. On the rampart above, looking down on the Swiss, were Colonna's arquebusiers, three ranks deep. The men in the front fired, point-blank, down into the helpless mass of pikemen. Dense white smoke from the volley filled the trench and lingered over it, hanging heavily in the damp chill air. Even obscured by the white billows, there was no mistaking the impact of the volley. Screams and curses drifted up from below. Then a second volley, then a third, then a fourth.

It was said that the first ranks of the pikemen, officers among them, simply melted into the ground, falling as one in the face of that terrible volley. Every single banner had gone down, too, as did nearly all the officers. Still, the Swiss refused to admit defeat. They fought, or tried to, anyway, for a few minutes longer. A nimble few actually scaled the parapet, only to be impaled on the pikes of the *Landsknechten* and sent toppling backward onto the hillock of corpses that filled the sunken road.

What was left of the attackers eventually limped away, not in panicked flight but in admirably good order. But the pike units were a wreck. Eight thousand men had gone in; three thousand broken bodies lay in the trench and littered the field along the route of advance. There would be no second assault. The army had suffered a crushing blow, and Lautrec's heart was no longer in the battle. That evening, unmolested by Colonna's unscathed force, Lautrec withdrew north and left Milan to the enemy.

BICOCCA IS BARELY remembered today, one of a score of battles fought by the houses of Habsburg and Valois for control of Italy at the end of the Renaissance. It was a large and costly battle, though not decisive. It did not end a war, destroy an army, liberate a nation, bring down a tyrant; it met none of the requirements that we usually demand of a battle for being decisive. Bicocca was not the masterwork of a tactical genius, and while Colonna was a sharp and resourceful commander, his stratagem at Bicocca was straightforward, uncomplicated, and brutal. And the star weapon that makes Bicocca noteworthy—the matchlock arquebus, the first practical handheld firearm—was not new in 1522. Its basic properties, which were not all that impressive, were already well known.

The battle of Bicocca was not a turning point, nor even the beginning of an era, but it was a telling moment. The volleys of arquebus fire that thundered over the sunken road at Bicocca on that misty April morning showed the world—or Europe, at any rate—how firepower could be harnessed, and what awful destruction that firepower could inflict when unleashed. Bicocca revealed that even the humble arquebus could be transformed into a weapon of almost unimaginable power if used with purpose, imagination, and discipline. After Bicocca, there was no going back. The age of the gun was underway.

For the next four centuries, firearms—big and small, artillery and handheld arms alike—would dominate every aspect of warfare in the West. Strategy and tactics, logistics and military organization, even the role of the individual soldier and of leadership at all levels—all would be predicated upon the widespread and universal use of firearms. Firearms ushered in an age in which weapons technology, more than any other single factor, would shape the way in which armies and navies fought one another, the way they operated on campaign, and the way they prepared for war. Technology and the operational art of war would focus on achieving one deceptively simple goal: the effective, efficient, and overwhelming deployment of firepower against enemy forces. Firearms would be the nearly exclusive focus of weapons technology, and of military technology in general, from the Renaissance to the Second World War. And the killing force generated by those firearms—*firepower*—would be the exclusive concern of armies, navies, and their commanders. There was, of course, more to war than shooting, just as there was more to weaponry than firearms. Even so, those areas of military technology outside the realm of firearms were mostly concerned with the supply or use of firepower: the warship, for example, or the artillery fortress or the armored fighting vehicle or the warplane.

Even the dramatic advances in the field of military communications were meant, from the beginning, to be harnessed to the intelligent direction of firepower. Never before, certainly not in the history of the West, had weaponry acted as such a powerful determinant in the calculus of military operations, or had technology served as the principal factor in shaping the evolution of tactics and strategy.

The linkage between the operational art of war and the state of weapons technology was strongest in the area of tactics. Since tactics ("the art of handling troops," citing the succinct wording of a popular nineteenth-century military dictionary) involved combat at its most basic level, the impact of weapons technology (pun fully intended) was felt most keenly there. It was in the crucible of combat that disparities between competing weapons types revealed themselves: It was where generals and admirals—and often, unfortunately, common soldiers—learned the shortcomings of their equipment. It was the means by which commanders learned what kind of tactics best brought out the qualities of new weapons, what kind of tactics best countered the enemy's weapons . . . and what kind of tactics did neither. That relationship between weapons technology and the evolution of tactics was quite clear during the age of the gun, for advances in firearms technology were of the sort that could completely transform the essential parameters of combat very rapidly. Over the centuries, when firearms ruled the battlefields of Europe and the West, the range, accuracy, hitting power, and above all, speed of martial firearms improved continually and often dramatically. Tactics, then, had to follow suit.

The ripple effect emanating from developments in military technology didn't end at tactics. Changes in weaponry similarly affected all other facets of war making to some extent, including, for example, logistics. Firearms required much more care and maintenance than the earlier, simpler weapon types. Spare parts, portable repair facilities, and above all, powder and shot added huge physical burdens to an army's impedimenta. These supplements required additional transport, personnel, and of course draft animals, which themselves constituted another onerous burden in the form of such prosaic but herculean tasks as the supply of dry fodder and the removal of animal waste. And logistics, in turn, could not help but have a constraining effect on strategy, notably in land warfare. The burden of ammunition supply and (especially) the transport of large numbers of heavy artillery pieces severely limited the movement of armies, particularly when—as was the case in much of the history of Europe—roads were little more than dirt paths. They were suggestions of roads rather than the thing itself, often impassible when spring and autumnal rains turned them into bogs. Armies organized around the use of firearms simply could not venture overland wherever and whenever their commanders desired.

Events in the nineteenth century—namely, the Industrial Revolution, the rise of the entrepreneurial inventor and the engineering profession, the maturation of academic disciplines like chemistry, metallurgy, and physics—would alter and complicate the outwardly simple dynamic between weaponry and the art of war. That dynamic became more intentional, for one thing, as soldiers, government bureaucrats, engineers, inventors, and industrialists collaborated in the design and manufacture of munitions. Tactical change was no longer primarily a response to technological change; increasingly, the reverse prevailed. As the experience of combat revealed pressing tactical needs, these natural allies—governments, military establishments, industry, and academia—deliberately and aggressively sought solutions for improved weaponry. Innovation in weaponry became less a matter of serendipity and more a matter of purpose.

One result of this early incarnation of the military-industrial complex was an acceleration of the pace of change in the art of war. The Industrial Revolution encouraged and rewarded innovation, probably more in heavy industry and munitions production than in most fields of manufacturing. As a result, the rate at which new weapons designs appeared became almost exponentially faster after the middle of the nineteenth century. The parallel evolution of tactics and technology sped from a crawl to a sprint, to the point that not all the major players in the Western world were able to keep up.

That last observation—that the evolution of weapons technology accelerated so much that some Western powers were unable to participate—points to a surprising truth about the history of weaponry in the age of the gun: the implications of continual change in weapons technology were complicated and wide ranging, reverberating well beyond the narrow horizons of the battlefield. That impact can best be seen, and felt, in the closely related realms of politics and economics. The relationship between armaments and politics was, like that between weapons and tactics, reciprocal. Domestic political priorities would frequently exert weighty influence on weapons research and production. Militaristic states such as Wilhelmine Germany (1871–1918) were more likely to invest heavily in innovative firearms, and in their mass production, than states that maintained a less assertive stance in diplomacy and war. Maritime powers such as Britain, which placed greater emphasis on sea power for national defense (and to maintain their overseas empires), put greater store in the latest advancements in warships and naval gunnery than they did in the technology of land warfare.

Such reciprocal relationships are so patently self-evident that they scarcely need to be pointed out. Subtler, and more consequential, were the converse relationships, the effect of weapons technology on domestic and constitutional politics. For the most part, the critical factor here was cost, namely the heavy and unrelenting fiscal burden associated with developing and adopting new weapons on a massive scale. The most obvious European example of this phenomenon is the "military revolution" of the early modern period, from the fifteenth to eighteenth centuries. The introduction of gunpowder weapons during that period was one of several factors that favored the emergence of strong, centralized governments, optimized for making war.

But it was in the power relationships among the nation-states of the West—the international order, for lack of a more precise term—that the greater significance of weapons development would show itself most prominently. Technological sophistication and military might are, to be sure, not synonymous but closely connected, and military might is a vital factor in the calculus of international relations. Great powers tend to have great weapons, or at least a lot of really good weapons. Of course, that isn't always the case, and the interplay between weapons technology and military might was rarely as straightforward as that. Two consistent and complementary trends are visibly at work throughout the age of the gun: first, international rivalries spur innovation in weapons, and second, innovations in weapons spur international rivalries.

This interplay is the inescapable and circuitous logic of the arms race, a phenomenon that occurs several times during the age of the gun. We see an early naval arms race, starting with the first large artillery warships early in the sixteenth century, an arms race that never really came to an end but displayed an unusual intensity in the sixteenth, seventeenth, and eighteenth centuries. We see an arms race in the development of small arms—handheld firearms—rooted in the 1850s but picking up speed after 1870, not to slow down again until the outbreak of the Great War in 1914. This arms race closely paralleled a contemporaneous rivalry over artillery design. The naval arms race immediately preceding the Great War, especially between Germany and Great Britain, is better known—as is the renewed naval arms race of the decade before the next world war. The period between the world wars also witnessed a broad international competition over warplane design and a somewhat lower-key rivalry over the development of armored fighting vehicles and, of course, an overall massive buildup in military and naval forces, triggered mostly by the ascent of Nazi Germany and Fascist Italy.

In each of these cases, an arms race didn't mean a race only to build more . . . more ships, more rifles and machine guns and field guns, more fighters and bombers and close-support aircraft. "More" was important, to be sure, but the truly fevered aspect of those arms races involved research and design, to improve the effectiveness and superiority of individual weapons systems. Each of these arms races was also self-perpetuating, for while international rivalries, often rooted in insecurity, prompted governments and their military establishments to invest vast sums of time and money and resources into weapons development, the resulting advances in weapons design also served to intensify international rivalries.

It's no small thing that such trivial affairs as a race to build the superior infantry rifle in 1870–1900 could play a role in something so consequential as the fatal rivalry between France and Germany on the eve of Europe's great catastrophe. But the political repercussions of advances in weapons technology went much further than that. Perhaps the most momentous—and curious—effects of the evolution of weaponry during the age of the gun was its exclusionary quality. Before the factory system took root in Europe in the nineteenth century, military technology was simple enough and affordable enough that even lesser powers could maintain respectable armed forces. Any state, even powers of the second or third rank, could produce or purchase flintlock muskets and even artillery to supply an army of a hundred thousand men, and any state with a shipyard or two could build a fleet of wooden sailing warships. Because the pace of technological change was slow and steady, weapons systems did not obsolesce quickly, and therefore did not have to be replaced often.

That would all change with the industrialization of the West in the nineteenth century. The Industrial Revolution radically altered and shortened the process by which innovations moved from drafting table to production line to official adoption. As competition among states grew more intense, when an arms race was at hand, that process moved even more quickly, as military establishments actively encouraged and pushed for any innovation that might give them an edge over rivals and potential enemies. Innovation followed innovation, and weapons became outdated almost as soon as they went into production. But the mentality of the arms race compelled any nation-state that aspired to great power status to keep up with the pace of innovation anyway, because to lag behind in an arms race was to court existential disaster.

As if that were not enough of a burden for any nation-state to bear, the modern era also witnessed drastic growth in the size of military institutions, starting in the last decades of the nineteenth century. As the Western powers gradually embraced the universal military service obligation, armies (and navies) ballooned in size, and by the time of the Great War the larger armies of Europe—those of Russia, France, Germany, Austria-Hungary, and Italy—all numbered well over a million men each. Equipping armies of this size with the latest weapons required an enormous investment in energy, money, and resources; re-equipping them every few years to keep up with the latest and best weapons was well-nigh impossible.

The combination of numerically immense military forces, rapid technological change, and an often-fevered drive to compete was what gave the evolution of weapons technology its exclusionary quality. Increasingly, starting in the mid-nineteenth century and peaking in the era of the world wars in the twentieth, the ability to produce en masse became the most important benchmark of military might. Military power had come to equal industrial capacity. When the First World War erupted in 1914, only a handful of larger states could manufacture enough weapons to meet their own needs. Several of those states, the great powers of 1914, failed the test of war because they were unable to keep up with the demands of war making. When the Second World War broke out in 1939, the exclusive club of great powers had shrunk, and when that war came to an end, only two superpowers—the United States and the Soviet Union—could boast both world-class military forces *and* the capacity to keep those forces battle ready. Successive revolutions in military technology, in short, had helped to bring about something quite remarkable. They had significantly reduced the number of Western states that could act assertively in international politics, and reduced the states that could not into a condition of permanent deference.

But to see that story unfold, first we must turn to the distant origins of those revolutions, to another revolution half a millennium before—the gunpowder revolution in the West, at the twilight of the Middle Ages.

Book I

THE GUNPOWDER
REVOLUTION, 1300-1800

CHAPTER I

THE BOMBARD AND
THE FORTRESS

Philip the Bold, duke of Burgundy, was a warrior's warrior. Hawk-nosed, ambitious, and brash, Philip had been a soldier since childhood. He was still a smooth-faced boy of fourteen when he fought alongside his father, King John II of France, in the battle of Poitiers in 1356. Like King John, he was taken prisoner by the English when Edward, the Black Prince of Wales, vanquished the French on the field at Poitiers. A decade later, the duke, always looking for an advantage over the Englishmen who had invaded his country, embraced a novel technology: gunpowder. This mysterious Asian invention had been known in Europe for more than a century, and for nearly that long European armies had used it as a weapon of war—or, more precisely, as the substance that made another recent innovation, the cannon, work. So far, gunpowder artillery had not shown great promise. Cannon had been used as siege engines in European warfare at least as early as the 1320s. But for all the trouble and effort they demanded, they had not proven themselves to be much more effective than conventional siege weapons such as catapults and trebuchets, machines that used mechanical energy to hurl projectiles at castle walls. Certainly, the early cannon did not appear to be effective enough to justify their cost, which was substantial.

But Philip the Bold saw promise in the new weapons, especially the huge siege guns that came to be known as bombards, and in 1369 he began to invest heavily in them. France and England were then locked in the on-again, off-again series of dynastic conflicts known today as the Hundred Years' War (1337–1453). In 1377, when Duke Philip's brother and sovereign, King Charles V of France, ordered him to attack the English in the Calais region, the duke answered the call, bringing with him more than one hundred new cannon, including one monster of a gun that fired a stone cannonball weighing some 450 livres (around 485 pounds).

One of the duke's intended targets was the English-held castle at Odruik, built with stout masonry walls and surrounded by a thick layer of outworks. Odruik would be a tough nut to crack. Its defenders seemed to think so, too, and were confident that they could hold out against Duke Philip's army, even as the duke's men began to put their huge siege cannon into position in full view of the castle walls.

The first few shots from Philip's siege-battery hammered Odruik's outer walls into dust. Soon the stone cannonballs were sailing through the walls as if they weren't there; soon after that, the outer walls actually weren't there. After Philip's guns had fired a grand total of about two hundred rounds, much of Odruik's once-proud walls lay in ruin, and before the duke could send his men through the breach and into the castle, Odruik's defenders capitulated.

Philip the Bold's triumph at Odruik in 1377 was a harbinger of things to come, a revealer of unsettling truths. Gunpowder artillery had been used in sieges before, but Odruik was its first overwhelming and clear-cut victory over a castle. The siege of Odruik demonstrated that—when the guns were big enough, and when there were enough of them—cannon were more powerful than any siege engine yet invented, and could knock down castles in a matter of hours. What happened at Odruik would be repeated over and over again at castles throughout Continental Europe and the British Isles over the remainder of the Middle Ages and beyond.

Over the century to come, gunpowder began to leave its mark on the conduct of war in the West; access to superior siege artillery would make the difference between victory and defeat in land warfare. With artillery, the French would drive the English from their soil in the closing phases of the Hundred Years' War, turning defeat into triumph. With artillery, Christians in Iberia would drive the Moors from their last strongholds in Granada, ultimately creating Europe's first superpower: Spain. And in 1453, the Ottomans, also avid students of gunpowder artillery, would use their massive bombards to break down the walls of ancient Constantinople and destroy the last vestiges of the Roman Empire.

Plate 1. *Die faule Mette*, a giant bombard manufactured in the city of Braunschweig in 1411. "Lazy Mette" had a bore diameter that tapered from 80 to 67 cm from muzzle to breech, and fired a stone ball that weighed in excess of 400kg.

From C. W. Sack, *Alterthümer der Stadt und des Landes Braunschweig* (Braunschweig: F. Otto, 1861), p. 76.

After Odruik, artillery would spell both the end of the castle and the emergence of a new kind of warfare, based on firepower, that relied on the massed use of gunpowder weapons for siege, on the battlefield, and at sea. Within a century and a half of Philip the Bold's quick and noisy victory, very little about European warfare would even vaguely resemble what had come before. The weapons, the size and organization of armies, the role of fighting men and leaders—even the sounds, the smells, and the scale of the European battlefield—would be radically transformed by the advent of gunpowder weaponry. And the implications for life beyond the narrow horizons of the battlefield were even more profound. Artillery meant the end of the castle, an edifice that both symbolized the independence and power of local warlords in medieval Europe and gave those warlords a means of resisting the encroaching ambitions of central governments embodied in Europe's emerging dynastic monarchies. The cannon took down the autonomy of the old warrior aristocracy just as it did the walls of their castles; the onerous expense of making and maintaining cannon meant that only the wealthiest lords—the monarchs themselves—could afford to build up their arsenals of these terrifying new weapons. The cannon, in short, concentrated military force and political authority in the hands of the state at the expense of noble warlords.

WHAT MADE ARTILLERY possible was gunpowder, and gunpowder was the single greatest invention of the European Middle Ages, even if it wasn't actually European. It was first developed in China as early as the ninth century AD, and over the intervening centuries the Chinese had become proficient in its use. They employed the substance as an incendiary at first, only later discovering that it could also be used as an explosive and as a propellant, two related but distinctly different roles.

Just when gunpowder first came to Europe, and how it did so, remain mysteries. It may be that the Mongols, who used gunpowder weapons, unwittingly passed it along during one of their incursions into Europe's eastern borderlands in the thirteenth century.

The English scholar Roger Bacon mentioned gunpowder in his treatises *Opus Majus* and *Opus Tertium* (ca. 1267); a German cleric named Berthold Schwarz, likely mythical, has sometimes been given credit for conducting early experiments with the substance. In the end, it matters little. Like most debates over "who did what first" in history, disputes over the origins of gunpowder ultimately settle nothing. Suffice to say, the Chinese invented gunpowder and pioneered its use; in some fashion, Europeans acquired it from the East, and their use of it developed independently of Asia.

From the time of its first use in the Middle Ages until its replacement by better propellants and explosives in the nineteenth century, gunpowder went through a continual process of reinvention and reformulation. Its basic composition, however, remained the same throughout: roughly 75 percent saltpeter (potassium nitrate), 15 percent softwood charcoal, and 10 percent sulfur, by weight.

Gunpowder, also known as black powder, is neither an ideal explosive nor an ideal propellant, and its salient properties are unlikely to inspire much confidence. Black powder is volatile, easily ignited by spark or flame. But it is just as easily rendered neutral: water, even excess humidity, can make it useless. As originally formulated, black powder was a simple mixture, produced by combining the three ingredients with mortar and pestle.

Gunpowder doesn't actually explode when ignited. Rather it deflagrates—it burns rapidly—which means that it is better suited to its propellant role than to its role as an explosive. Black powder burns much faster than modern smokeless powders, and when used as a propellant with a projectile, it produces lower velocities than modern, slower-burning powders do. Black powder also burns inefficiently, creating two byproducts when ignited, both of them undesirable: smoke and fouling. Burning black powder produces clouds of acrid white smoke, enough to give away the position of a shooter with a single shot, enough to obscure visibility when fired from many weapons or from larger weapons. After combustion, black powder leaves behind hard carbon soot. In firearms, this residue—called fouling—can have serious and negative consequences. Prolonged firing of black powder in a gun barrel will result in the deposit of layer after layer of fouling, gradually constricting the interior of the barrel (the bore), making the task of loading difficult or even impossible.

Gunpowder may not have been an ideal propellant or explosive, but in 1400 it had no competitors, and for all its faults it was effective enough. It would not have to wait very long for a military application.

Gunpowder found that application in the practice of siege warfare. No form of land-based combat has been more commonplace than the siege, throughout the sweep of human history from the earliest known wars to the investment of Leningrad in 1941–1944. Pitched battles between armies or navies attract more attention, for they are suited to storytelling: battles are concise, they have movement instead of stasis, they have a narrative arc—battles are the stuff from which high drama is wrought. Yet the siege, for all its mechanical drudgery, is universal. Before the twentieth century, the siege was the principal kind of hostile interaction between opposing armies, and was far more common than the pitched battle. Sieges were also costlier, consuming more resources—men, materiel, and time—than pitched battles.

In the Middle Ages, the principal locus of the siege was the castle. Castles made their first appearance in Europe in the ninth century, rising up amid the fragmented remains of Charlemagne's empire. As the fortified residences of powerful lords, castles would become closely linked to, and emblematic of, the feudal system around which so much of Western European social and political life revolved. Castles functioned as seats of local authority and justice, a means of controlling and protecting the villages that sprang to life around them. They could serve, also, as focal points for rebellion. For a willful vassal who did not feel inclined to obey his lord or king, a castle was a sanctuary and a power base. In the emerging kingdoms of the High Middle Ages, castles strengthened the power of the noble landowning class, often at the expense of royal power.

Castles, in short, had a significance that went far beyond their military function, but first and foremost they were fortifications. In the Holy Land, the great castles of the Crusaders—such as the imposing Krak des Chevaliers in Syria—allowed European invaders to maintain a near constant presence in the region, to defend the fragile Crusader states, and to mount offensive operations. English military operations in France during the Hundred Years' War revolved around the construction and possession of castles. As with any technology whose useful life spans centuries, the design of the castle was constantly evolving. The motte-and-bailey fortifications of the tenth century would seem puny and impotent when compared to the stone-built castles of the thirteenth.

From a military standpoint, the castle proved to be such an enduring technology because it was very good at fulfilling its main purpose: to keep hostile forces out, and to keep the people within safe. High walls and fortified gates guarded against forced entry; masonry walls were impervious to flame; and towers with loopholes—thin vertical firing slits for archers—gave a modicum of protection, making it potentially costly for a besieging army to move close. So long as the defenders were adequately provisioned and had ready access to water, a castle could hold out indefinitely. For a besieging army, if a castle could not be taken by storm, or its garrison intimidated or starved into capitulation, then it would have to be reduced.

Reducing a castle was an uncomplicated process, and quite literally mechanical, in the sense that it involved the use of machines or siege engines. While it was possible to bring down an outer wall by sapping—that is, by tunneling under the very foundations of the castle, causing the walls to sink and hopefully to collapse—breaching a wall by means of siege engines was the preferred method. Medieval siege engines, or "mechanical artillery," had changed little since late antiquity: a mechanical force—torsion in catapults, counterweights in trebuchets, and human brawn in onagers—powered a heavy throwing arm that could hurl a heavy projectile, like a large stone, and send it crashing against the castle's outer walls. Though simple in concept, the act of smashing walls with such weapons was laborious and time-consuming. It could be costly in lives, too, if the crews operating the machines were exposed to archery, which was likely because the range of catapults and trebuchets was quite short. A heavy trebuchet could not toss a large stone much further than *two hundred yards*, within effective longbow range. Consequently, the results were often long in coming.

This is where gunpowder came in, but not as an explosive—which, perhaps surprisingly, was almost an afterthought. It wasn't until late in the fifteenth century that European soldiers began to use gunpowder in so-called mines: massive quantities of gunpowder packed in tunnels dug beneath the castle walls. When detonated, such subterranean mines could collapse the sturdiest wall in moments. Instead, gunpowder found its first serious employment as a propellant in a primitive gun. That technology—compressing a charge of gunpowder in a tube that was closed at one end and open at the other, so that the expanding gases from the deflagrating powder would push out a projectile with great force and speed— was also a Chinese invention. In Europe, when gunpowder arrived, the knowledge of primitive firearms arrived with it.

The first major use of firearms in the West involved truly big guns, what we know as gunpowder artillery. That might appear counterintuitive. Small, logically, should precede big. But small arms, handheld firearms, were later additions to the European arsenal. The first functional firearms in the West were cannon.

A cannon, or bombard, might seem like the simplest of weapons, but in the Middle Ages metallurgy and metalworking had not yet advanced to the point where it was possible to cast a large tube in one piece, at least not in any metal sturdy enough to withstand the shock released by the deflagrating gunpowder. The first cannon were of "hoop-and-stave" construction, products of the cooper's art rather than the iron-founder's. Long wooden staves were laid together in parallel around a central core, and were then bound together and reinforced by hoops of wrought iron. Soon iron bars replaced the wooden staves. The resulting tube was open at both ends, and so the first European cannon were breechloaders—the powder and projectile were loaded not from the muzzle, where the projectile exits the barrel, but from the opposite end. A separate breech-piece acted as a powder chamber; it was attached to the open breech-end of the tube, and was then secured in place with a wooden wedge.

There was not much about such a weapon to inspire confidence. Even ignoring the many serious deficiencies of gunpowder, the cannon themselves had plenty of problems of their own. Hoop-and-stave construction is inherently weak. The earliest pieces burst frequently, and were nearly as dangerous to their gun crews as they were to their intended targets. And because it was impossible to create an airtight seal between the open-ended tube and the breech-piece, there would always be a gap between the two. Hot gases would leak from the gap when the gun was fired, bleeding off some of the energy of the deflagrating powder and potentially burning anyone unwise enough to stand close to the gun.

These early gunpowder monsters were crude weapons, to be sure, and their performance reflected it. In all the ways that we assess firearms—range, accuracy, rate of fire, reliability—the bombards came up short. But in the fourteenth century, there was simply nothing better to which they could be compared. The first guns were eminently useful because there was nothing else like them, and because for all their shortcomings they were the best and most powerful siege engines yet devised. Their range was limited, but they needed only to outrange an arrow or a crossbow bolt so that their crews could work safely outside arrow range. Their accuracy was poor, but their targets were anything but small; they needed only to be able to hit the towering outer walls of a castle. Their projectiles flew slowly, but they only needed enough force to shatter brick or stone masonry. They were slow to load and fire, but siegecraft demanded patience, not speed.

In short, to justify its existence and the not-inconsiderable sums of cash and materials that it consumed, gunpowder artillery only had to be better and faster at smashing castle walls than the catapult and the trebuchet. Even in its earliest, crudest, most primitive forms, the bombard met those criteria. Besides, the catapult and the trebuchet were the late-generation offspring of a venerable, mature technology, at the apex of their potential, unlikely to be improved upon. Gunpowder was yet in its infancy. There was nowhere for it to go but up.

And up it went. Between the mid-1300s and the early 1500s, gunpowder artillery advanced rapidly, or as rapidly as any technology would before the modern era. During this period, cannon would assume most of the characteristic features that would carry the weapon through to the nineteenth century. Advances in metallurgy and the metal-founder's craft account for most of those advances. European artisans learned to cast cannon out of iron and bronze—solid, in one piece, much as church bells were cast. Bronze, an alloy of copper and tin, was the preferred material; cast bronze wore better and longer than cast iron, and cast-bronze cannon were thought to be less prone to bursting when fired. Cast iron, on the other hand, was cheaper and slightly less dense. The two materials would predominate in artillery manufacture until the advent of mass-produced steel, later in the nineteenth century.

The greater expense of cast-metal cannon tubes was worth the investment. They were infinitely more stable than the early hoop-and-stave guns. That was a great advantage in itself, but there was more to it. Solid-cast cannon had to be loaded from the muzzle, since the cast gun would by definition be closed at the breech-end. Powder and projectile would have to be inserted from the muzzle and then rammed down the length of the bore. A narrow vent, drilled through the breech into the bore, allowed access to the main powder charge after it was loaded, so that it could be ignited from the outside of the barrel via a priming charge inserted into the vent. To modern eyes, this transition—from breech-loading, a common feature of nearly all modern firearms, to muzzle-loading, which seems quaint and old-fashioned—appears retrograde. But it was actually a great leap forward. A cast, muzzle-loading cannon does not leak gas at the breech. The inherent strength of its construction meant that it could tolerate heavier charges, heavier projectiles, and more powerful powders without bursting.

That added strength came in handy, for gunpowder too was evolving. The constituent elements and their proportions would remain essentially the same for a long time, but the method of processing the ingredients was becoming more sophisticated. The original formulation of gunpowder, popularly known as serpentine, was compounded dry, the ingredients ground together to make a fine dust. When jostled in transport, the charcoal, saltpeter, and sulfur tended to separate, so the gunpowder would have to be reblended before use. That was a tricky and hazardous chore, one best left to an experienced gunner.

At the end of the Middle Ages, though, European powder makers had stumbled upon the process of corning. Corned powder was made by moistening the mixed serpentine, usually with water, sometimes with other liquids; artisans passionately debated the relative virtues of wine and urine for corning. The dampened powder was pressed into cakes, allowed to dry thoroughly, and then milled into "grains" or "corns." Corned powder didn't separate, didn't have to be reblended before use, and gunners found that it burned more efficiently and predictably than serpentine. Soon powder makers were producing specialty powders: slower-burning, coarse-grained powder for artillery, finer powders for small arms, the finest powder for priming. Gunners discovered, too, that the corned powder was more powerful, and for that cast guns were perfectly suited. Hoop-and-stave guns were nowhere near sufficiently robust to handle the new formulations, and they began to fade away.

Cannon tubes cannot stand on their own. They require a carriage or mount, for transportation and for aiming. The earliest mounts were simple wooden beds to which the gun tube could be strapped. Wheeled gun carriages, which first appeared in Europe early in the sixteenth century, were far more mobile, and made the process of aiming simpler and more precise. When combined with a new design feature called the trunnion—a pair of solid metal cylinders projecting from the sides of the cannon barrel just forward of the tube's center of gravity, cast integral with the barrel—the wheeled carriage was nothing short of revolutionary. Trunnions held the gun more securely to the carriage, and—most important—they made it so the gun could be elevated or depressed, tilting the muzzle up or down so as to increase (or decrease) the gun's range. Ultimately, the wheeled carriage would make possible the first truly mobile field artillery, cannon that could be used on the battlefield alongside infantry and cavalry, and deployed as necessary. That day, though, was still some ways off. For now, cannon were too bulky to play an important role outside of the siege.

Artillery ammunition was simple. The most common form at the time of the Renaissance was the solid shot, a simple sphere, which in the early days of gunpowder artillery was usually made of chipped stone. Stone balls had a few advantages over cast-iron: they could be produced on-site during a siege, for instance, and they were typically lighter than cast-iron balls of the same size. Cast-iron shot, on the other hand, tended to hit harder and travel farther than stone, but their greater weight required a heavier powder charge and therefore were more stressful on gun barrels. But once cast-metal guns became available, the cast-iron solid shot caught on.

What made iron shot practical was an innovative and novel concept: standardization. Here, history has given the lion's share of the credit to a remarkable team of brothers, Jean and Gaspard Bureau. The Bureau brothers were not soldiers so much as they were professional artillerists, and until the eighteenth century European artillerists considered themselves members of an elite, highly technical craft guild rather than military men. The Bureau brothers, as manufacturers and professional gunners, understood cannon inside and out. During the last two decades of the Hundred Years' War, they served as commanders of the French artillery train.

Their king, Charles VII (r. 1422–1461) of France, trusted the Bureau brothers and allowed them much latitude, and the brothers put that trust to good use. They encouraged gun-founders to use cast iron instead of the more expensive cast bronze, and they promoted cast-iron shot over stone. By far their greatest achievement was the reduction in the number of types of cannon to a few standard models. In the fifteenth century, long before manufacturing introduced the notions of interchangeable parts and precision measurement, standardization was a pretty loose concept. Cannon were still individually crafted, as everything was. The Bureau brothers' standardization was at a more basic level. Rather than leave the dimensions of cannon tubes up to the gun-founders, as had been the practice before, the Bureaus set rough universal measurements to which all makers had to adhere. Guns of a particular class would all be roughly the same length and the same weight, of the same materials, and use the same carriage. More important, they would all have the same bore diameter, which meant that they could all fire the same shot.

ARTILLERY EVOLVED FASTER than any other military technology in Renaissance Europe. Even so, with vastly improved durability, power, and portability, it still was not practical for open battle. The smaller guns were too heavy to be truly mobile. Cannon could accompany armies on the march, but not with any celerity, and only if a navigable river coursed close to the line of march if the roads were not dry and firm. In autumn and spring, when regular and heavy rains turned what passed for roads in premodern Europe into impassible quagmires, cannon could be transported only by water. Their weight and bulk meant that it took hours to set them up on the battlefield, and once set up they could not be repositioned quickly. Cannon were, in short, something just shy of being useless impedimenta on campaign. Worse than useless, in fact, because in a precipitous retreat they would have to be abandoned, and the big guns were too valuable to leave behind for the enemy.

Instead, artillery found its first real niche in the less dramatic, but more critical, world of siege warfare. In this role, the cannon excelled, and it wasn't very long before they became an indispensable component of a besieging army's toolkit. When Charles of Valois used hoop-built cannon to reduce La Réole in 1324, they were a strange and frightening spectacle; two decades later, bombards were a common sight. French armies in particular made heavy use of siege guns in the Hundred Years' War. At first, they shared the stage with the tried-and-true siege engines. When John, duke of Normandy, invested the English-held castle at Aiguillon in 1346, he used both cannon and trebuchets to breach the walls. But within a very few years the medieval siege engines were out, and the cannon was the siege engine of choice.

The first guns were marginally better than mechanical artillery; the cast-metal, muzzle-loading guns of the fifteenth century were far superior, in range, firepower, and overall effectiveness. Though the cast-metal guns were available in a wide variety of sizes, the real star of late medieval artillery was a specialized gun designed expressly for bashing down castle walls: the bombard.

The bombard, as a species, predates cast construction. The first bombards were hoop-and-stave beasts, made to use serpentine powder. The introduction of cast construction and corned powder, late in the 1300s, made the bombard truly dangerous. By 1400, the bombard had evolved into a genuine monster of a weapon. Perhaps the most famous of all is Mons Meg, built in Hainault in the Low Countries in 1449 and given to the king of Scotland five years later. Mons Meg was built in the old way, with bars of iron fused together longitudinally and hooped, and with a powder chamber fastened directly onto its breech with locking lugs. With a bore diameter of nearly twenty inches (520mm), it could hurl a cast-iron ball nearly a mile, or a chipped stone ball double that distance. Mons Meg was hardly the biggest of its breed. The Flemish bombard Dulle Griet had a 25-inch bore; the cast-iron Faule Mette (Lazy Mette), made in the German town of Braunschweig in 1411, threw a 29-inch ball. The stubby *Pumhart* of Steyr boasted an awe-inspiring 32-inch bore.

Individually, cannon were hard to move; moving a siege train of many cannon, including ammunition, tools, apparata, and draft animals, was a major logistical enterprise. When a Flemish army marched against the city of Bruges in 1382, its three hundred cannon and accompanying gear required about two hundred wagons for transport. The baggage for the entire Flemish army and its provisions, by contrast, took up only seven wagons. And these were mostly smaller cannon. The great bombards required much more support and planning and sheer muscle than that. One of the bombards that the Turks brought with them to the walls of Constantinople in 1453 allegedly weighed nineteen tons, requiring sixty oxen and two hundred men to drag it on the march. During the Spanish Reconquista, Queen Isabella of Castile found it necessary to employ six thousand laborers to build a road for the sole and express purpose of hauling her great siege pieces to bombard the Moorish town of Cambil.

Were the results worth the trouble? Certainly those who built up the large siege trains—like Charles VII of France, or Ferdinand and Isabella of Spain—thought so. Artillery helped Charles drive the English from France, and artillery helped Ferdinand and Isabella claim Spain for Christ and themselves. The trouble was enormous, of that there can be no doubt, but the results could be dramatic. Using mechanical artillery, it could take weeks, months even, for a besieging army to reduce a well-maintained and garrisoned castle. The bombard cut that time down to days, and sometimes mere hours. A bombard, preferably a group of them, could crush a castle's outer walls to dust in a day.

Modern experiments have confirmed what contemporaries thought of these brutes and their raw power. Researchers have shown that a bombard like Mons Meg could have thrown a 160 kg stone ball at a muzzle velocity of about 315 m/sec, or just slightly under the speed of sound. The amount of damage that such a projectile could cause when fired against a masonry wall would have been astonishing; iron shot, even at a reduced velocity, would have done even more. According to legend, Mons Meg's first shot fired in war, during James II of Scotland's siege of Threave Castle in 1455, passed straight through the castle's outer walls and continued well into the interior. The story is likely apocryphal, but it rings of some truth. Castles were not built to withstand that kind of pounding, and artillery was only growing more powerful and more numerous with each passing decade. Even if a single bombard couldn't pierce a castle's masonry skin with a single shot, there was little doubt that a small group of bombards, hammering together in concert against a small stretch of wall, could breach the outer defenses in no time at all.

The bombard's reign was brief. Smaller cast-iron and cast-bronze guns could withstand higher internal pressures, meaning that they could use corned powder and cast-iron shot. Such guns could do nearly as much damage as the big bombards, but they were much more portable and could keep up with armies on the move without most of the logistical hassles that bombards demanded.

At the end of the fifteenth century, the advantage in siegecraft lay with the attacker. No castle, no matter how densely fortified, could withstand an artillery bombardment for very long. Likewise, possession of an artillery-based siege train proved to be a—if not *the*—critical factor in determining the outcome of land campaigns. French prowess in artillery design and manufacture, and the willingness of the French crown to invest time and capital in artillery, gave French forces the decisive edge over their English foes in the last phase of the Hundred Years' War. Farther east, Ottoman artillery—remarkably similar to European guns in form and function—bashed their way through the walls of Constantinople to conquer old Byzantium. Artillery, quite literally, reshaped the European continent in the Renaissance.

Artillery had become so vital to the conduct of military operations on land that its presence was what made an army an army. The cannon was no longer a helpful tool in siegecraft; it had itself become the essence of the siege. Cities were known to capitulate as soon as it was confirmed that an approaching enemy army had artillery. The mere reputation of artillery was enough to compel great cities to fall.

IF THE CASTLE was fundamentally useless, what kind of fortification would replace it? Whatever form it took, it would have to be artillery-proof, and for a fortification to be artillery-proof, it would have to meet a few basic requirements. First and most obvious, the outer walls would have to be sufficiently resilient to withstand direct artillery fire for more than a few hours at least. Ideally, the outer walls would be canted or rounded so that incoming projectiles would not strike them at right angles, instead hitting a glancing and less destructive blow. Those inside the walls should also be capable of fighting back. Since the only weapon with sufficient range to target siege artillery was artillery itself, that meant that this ideal fortress could be equipped with cannon, to (hopefully) destroy the besieger's guns and keep enemy soldiers from approaching the walls. A fortress designed for modern warfare at the end of the Middle Ages, then, would be built for artillery use: with broad, deep platforms atop the ramparts, galleries inside the walls, and loopholes or embrasures through which cannon could fire. The guns would have to be positioned so that there was no dead space—areas that could not be swept with the fortress's artillery fire—close to the outer walls.

Medieval castles clearly had none of these features, and so the looming threat of siege-by-bombardment demanded a radical departure in military architecture. Sometimes it was possible to retrofit existing castles with modern features, which was cheaper—and therefore more attractive—than razing older castles and rebuilding them completely. Edward III of England, for example, added gunports and cannon to many of his castles, fearing French and Scottish invasions of English soil.

But the first serious experiments with gunpowder architecture took place in France and the Low Countries, where siege warfare was a constant feature of everyday life. Early in the 1400s, French kings Charles VI and Charles VII took a direct and personal interest in fortress design, understanding that the development of artillery-based fortifications was a matter of grave national concern. Two promising innovations emerged from this fertile mix of military necessity and royal support: the boulevard and the artillery tower.

Boulevards were outworks, low-lying supplementary fortifications placed outside the perimeter of the castle to guard vulnerable spots, like gates. Constructed from timber and packed earth, boulevards could be thrown up quickly and easily, or they could be made more permanent and reinforced with stone. A characteristic feature of boulevards was the presence of artillery platforms, where cannon could be positioned. Because of their low profile, they were difficult for siege guns to target, but they could make life miserable for any besieging army brave or foolish enough to approach the castle from that direction. The artillery tower, in contrast, made no pretense at subtlety. Built with thick walls, frequently round in cross-section, and bristling with cannon, artillery towers were frequently built near or attached to the flanking walls of existing castles.

The next generation of castles began to incorporate these supplementary features. The newfangled castle at Dijon, erected after 1477 on the orders of King Louis XI of France (r. 1461–1483), barely resembled the castles of the previous century. Dijon's four massive walls were joined at the corners by four equally massive artillery towers. Gunports dotted every tower and wall, while boulevards bolstered the defenses on the fortress's western and southern faces. Dijon was built to withstand artillery bombardment *and* to fire back on its attackers.

There was no single architectural solution to the challenges posed by siege artillery. Fortification styles in the artillery age varied greatly from region to region and from decade to decade, but some managed to attract broad international interest. Perhaps the most popular and widely adopted solution first arose in the city-states of northern Italy at the tail end of the Renaissance, when Italy first encountered, close up, the face of modern warfare.

In September 1494, Charles VIII of France (r. 1483–1498) invaded northern Italy, intent on forcing his family's tenuous dynastic claim on the throne of the Kingdom of Naples. No ordinary dynastic scuffle, the invasion was a landmark event of the first order in the history of the West. The act inaugurated six decades of bloody wars between Valois France and Habsburg Spain, and it marks the moment when Italy fell under foreign subjugation, where it would stay for the next three-and-a-half centuries. The French invasion was the beginning of the end of the High Renaissance and, paradoxically, the means by which the splendors of Renaissance literary and artistic culture would spread north of the Alps, via the agency of thousands of young noblemen drawn to Italy from all over Europe during the Italian Wars.

The 1494 invasion was a signal event in the history of warfare, too. The army that Charles VIII led into northern Italy that September was unlike any military force ever seen on European soil. It was at least twenty thousand strong, and possibly larger; half of that number consisted of infantry, and most of that infantry were pike-armed Swiss mercenaries. And because King Charles meant business, and knew that he could not possibly avoid a siege or two on his long trek south, he brought along an enormous siege train of great cannon.

Artillery was not unknown in Italy, though there were clearly some eyewitnesses to the 1494 invasion who had never seen them before. The Florentine diplomat Francesco Guicciardini found the spectacle of the French king's siege train positively terrifying:

> The French brought a much handier engine made of brass, called cannon, which they charged with heavy iron balls . . . and drove them on carriages with horses, not with oxen, as was the custom in Italy . . . attended by . . . clever men. . . . They were planted against the walls of a town with such speed, the space between the shots so short, and the balls flew so quick, and were impelled with such force, that as much execution was done in a few hours, as formerly, in Italy, in the like number of days. These [were] rather diabolical than human instruments. . . .*

---

*Simon Pepper and Nicholas Adams, *Firearms and Fortifications: Military Architecture and Siege Warfare in Sixteenth-Century Siena* (Chicago: University of Chicago Press, 1986), p. 11.

So equipped, the French invasion force progressed with breathtaking speed through the peninsula. Town after town fell to the invaders. But some Italian cities were better prepared for the onslaught than others, having already devised a style of fortification intended to withstand the kind of firepower the French had at hand. The angled bastion, a native Italian creation, was simple and brilliant. It was nothing more than an elongated projection, characteristically diamond-shaped, incorporated into a fortress's walls at the corners. Like the round artillery towers, bastions were meant to be furnished with artillery. Unlike those towers, they were relatively squat. More important, the inward-looking facets of the bastions provided overlapping fields of fire covering all approaches to the walls.

When combined with defensive artillery and a perimeter ditch, the bastion gave rise to a new species of fortress, known by its place of birth: the *trace italienne*, or Italian trace. The typical Italian trace fortress was purpose-built as an artillery fortress, in that it could both withstand artillery fire and deliver it. An Italian trace could take on many shapes—squares, rectangles, and pentagons predominated—but the attachment of bastions to each angle gave Italian trace fortresses a characteristic star shape. The walls themselves were low and thick, as a rule, with much of their bulk hidden from view by the fortified ditch surrounding the walls. At the core of the walls lay a base of packed earth, far superior to masonry in three ways: it was inexpensive, easy to work with, and above all able to absorb cannon-shot, where masonry tends to shatter when hit. Masonry was still a key component, though. Walls were faced with brick or cut stone, if for no other reason than to retard erosion and discourage vegetative growth. Few things could destroy an earthen fortification more thoroughly than tree roots and heavy rains.

Although cannon could still destroy an Italian trace fortress— for all its virtues it was not artillery-proof—it was, however, artillery-resistant. Artillery fire could not smash through it in a matter of hours, and if the fort itself was adequately armed, then the defenders could keep the attackers at bay and make their job

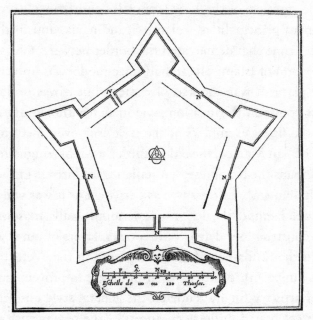

Plate 2. A bastioned artillery fortress.
From *Les Practiques du Sieur Fabre, sur l'ordre et reigle de fortifier, garder, attaquer, et defendre les places* (Paris: Samuel Thiboust, 1629), p. 49.

much more difficult and costly. In short, the Italian trace fortress restored the balance between besieger and besieged to its earlier, medieval condition: neither side had a clear or unbridgeable tactical advantage over the other. Sieges remained the most common form of hostile encounter between armies, but now they were far more complicated and demanding than before. Laying siege to a fortified town now required a much larger commitment in time, resources, cash, and of course firepower . . . plus healthy doses of patience and good fortune.

As the 1494 invasion dragged on, and a state of perpetual war descended over Italy, Italian trace fortresses began to sprout from the fecund soil of the peninsula, surrounding every town that could afford to invest in rebuilt fortifications. They caught on quickly elsewhere, one of Renaissance Italy's many gifts to the rest of Europe:

along the frontiers of the Low Countries and France, throughout the German principalities, Poland, Scandinavia, and in the tenuous buffer zone that demarcated the border between Christendom and the world of Islam. The Italian trace model was universal, and in some places it was adopted piecemeal, but it was undoubtedly the most common fortification style in sixteenth-century Europe. One of the finest exemplars of the style isn't even in Europe: the Castillo de San Marcos, the old Spanish fort in St. Augustine, Florida, is perhaps the best-preserved Italian trace fortress in the world.

The Italian trace fortress was as persistent as it was widespread. The basic elements of the design—low, sloping walls, masonry-faced earthen construction, defensive firepower, layers of outer works—remained the fundamentals of fortification in the West until well into the nineteenth century, when dramatic improvements in the power of artillery finally rendered the general style obsolete. Even the most celebrated military engineers of the seventeenth century, Sébastien de Vauban and Menno van Coehoorn, built on these very same structural elements. Vauban-era fortresses are larger and more layered with outer works than their sixteenth-century antecedents, but in form and function the Vauban fortress is a refined version of the Italian trace. Even the taller, casemated seacoast forts of the nineteenth century—like Alabama's Fort Morgan or any of the other double- or triple-tiered Third System forts built in antebellum America—were not radical departures from the Italian trace.

NONE OF THIS technological change was cheap. Cast cannon, especially guns large enough for siegework, were major expenses, and they were not even permanent. No matter how well cast, no matter how well maintained, cannon did not last forever. At some point they wore out. Bores eroded through use and corrosion; repeated stresses, especially from firing, weakened the barrels and led to their eventual failure. And cannon became obsolete or went out of style, just as hooped bombards gave way to cast guns. Likewise with fortifications. Fortifications designed to endure artillery fire were costly to build. Even if they did not have to be rebuilt or reworked periodically to withstand more powerful guns, they too required maintenance. Masonry had to be dressed and pointed periodically, matters of erosion and foundation settlement corrected, and vegetation—the bane of earthen forts—had to be removed or kept under control at all times.

In medieval Europe, most nobles of the middling and higher sorts could afford to build at least modest castles, making use of local labor and local building materials. Most could also afford to go to war, provided they had a sufficient network of clients or vassals. But warfare, especially siege warfare, became a much more expensive proposition in the fourteenth and fifteenth centuries. Few members of the noble estate, anywhere in Europe, could mobilize the resources and the labor needed for the construction of a large artillery fortress. Fewer still could shoulder the financial burden of keeping a modern siege train at hand. Cannon carried a price tag that only the wealthiest landed lords could afford, even in small quantities. By the dawn of the sixteenth century, if not earlier, only the vast resources at the disposal of the larger political units, the kingdoms and principalities of Europe, could afford both the construction of Italian trace fortresses *and* enough heavy artillery to both defend those fortresses and equip a siege train in the field.

The gunpowder revolution, then, had both rewritten the rules of warfare and drastically changed existing patterns of land warfare. Gunpowder also threw the strategic advantage to the kings of Europe, to the centralized governments of the emerging dynastic states, and took away much of what had made the nobility so powerful during the Middle Ages. But the death of the castle, and its reincarnation as the artillery fortress, was only the first step in what would prove to be a directional shift of unimaginable proportions in the conduct of war.

CHAPTER 2

THE SHIP-KILLING SHIP

Artillery had proven itself to be the most useful—and the most disruptive—innovation in military technology in the history of the West thus far, even if only the wealthy and powerful could afford to take advantage of what it had to offer. If all it could do was to bash down castle walls, it would have been enough, but creative minds found other applications in short order. Slightly smaller, lighter, more mobile cannon could follow armies on campaign, and as early as the fifteenth century, artillery sometimes played a role in land battles other than sieges. And at about the same time, someone had the brilliant idea of mounting cannon aboard ships.

The two technologies, ships and artillery, were natural partners, and the idea of transforming an oceangoing vessel into a floating gun platform was not a complicated one. That's not to say that the creation of artillery-based navies happened overnight. There were matters of naval architecture and ship design that had to be worked out first. More immediately, there were as yet no navies, no organized collections of combat vessels that could employ cannon. And there was no naval combat, either, not in the sense that we would understand it today. Except in the Mediterranean, combat at sea was a trivial component of medieval warfare, barely worthy of mention.

At the dawn of the Renaissance, the Mediterranean was Europe's beating heart, the first locus of culture, commerce, and learning.

Europe's ties with the East, tenuous as they were, ran through the Mediterranean, and the exotic spices and silks that the European elite grew to crave made their way to European markets in the holds of Italian merchant ships. As the primary dividing line between Christendom and the world of Islam, the Mediterranean was also the most dangerous transcivilizational flashpoint in the West. The conflicting ambitions of the states that ringed it, Christian and Muslim, and the constant presence of pirates who preyed on the region's rich commercial traffic, meant that the Mediterranean was in a perpetual state of low-intensity war.

Perhaps the most remarkable thing about Mediterranean warfare in the Middle Ages was how little it had changed since classical antiquity. The technology, and the tactics, used by European and Ottoman navies were much the same as those of the Phoenicians, Greeks, and Romans. At the center of that way of war was the oared galley.

The late medieval galley was well suited to its native environment. Long and slender, it could sprint over short distances under oar-power alone, though most galleys had a mast (or several) to harness the wind via sail whenever possible. A shallow draft allowed galleys to work close in to shore, or even to be beached and refloated when necessary—a quality that made them ideal for amphibious operations. Galleys had little space for cargo or for crewmen off duty, but then they rarely needed it. Speed was the main design imperative.

Exactly when it was that someone, shipwright or otherwise, first had the idea of arming ships with cannon is impossible to say. Shipbuilding, like most forms of medieval high tech, was a craft, meaning that it was not governed by any principles we would regard today as being scientific. Ships were built from plans that existed only in the head of the shipwright, not from blueprints or detailed models; proportions and measurements were determined by experience and instinct instead of exacting calculations. Innovations—like adding guns to a ship, for example—generally went unrecorded.

We do know that early in the fifteenth century, the first shipboard artillery made its appearance in the Mediterranean. These were not big guns, though. Bombards were too large and heavy to fit aboard a gracile, lightly built galley. The first naval guns were breech-loading cannon of hoop-and-stave construction, bolted directly to the deck; or they were swivel guns, light pieces the length of a man's arm, mounted on swivels atop rails along the upper deck. Breech-loading cannon were much more practical aboard ship than muzzleloaders, which were hard to service in cramped spaces.

The placement of these guns was critical. They could not be mounted "in broadside," along the sides of the hull, at right angles to the vessel's centerline. In a galley, the oarsmen took up nearly all that space. To make space for guns, the new generation of galleys featured reinforced, raised decks, located at the bow and in the stern, that were strong enough to bear the weight of guns, ammunition, and gun crews. Over time, these superstructures, called castles, grew stouter and larger, as heavier cast-bronze and cast-iron guns replaced the fragile hoop-built breechloaders.

This new kind of galley, which reached the peak of its development in the mid to late sixteenth century, was a decidedly different animal than the galleys of classical antiquity. It retained the sleek lines and oar-driven propulsion of its predecessors, but the massive gun towers were jarringly novel. Yet even with the castles, the galley did not make a very good gunship. Galleys were built for speed, not for bearing heavy loads or withstanding great stresses, nor—assuming that they would engage with other cannon-armed vessels—were they built to absorb damage. Besides, only so many cannon could be stuffed into the castles, both fore and aft.

Yet the prospect of a warship that could batter, cripple, and destroy enemy ships at a distance—a ship-killing ship—was so alluring that it soon pushed naval architecture into a different direction entirely. In the Mediterranean, that took the form of a galley redesigned around artillery. This new vessel, commonly called a galleass, was first built by Italian shipwrights in the mid-sixteenth century. More stoutly constructed than galleys, galleasses had the built-up fore- and aftercastles of the gun-carrying galleys *plus* heavily reinforced gun decks that ran over the heads of the oars-men. They had many times the available firepower of the galley, and when they first went into action against conventional Mediter-ranean naval vessels they quickly proved their worth. The outcome of the most famous clash of early artillery warships in the Med-iterranean, the battle of Lepanto (7 October 1571), was in large measure the work of the galleass. Six Venetian galleasses were the centerpiece of the allied Christian fleet when it was attacked that day by Ali Pasha's larger Ottoman fleet, in the Gulf of Patras off the Ionian Sea. The Christian fleet was better led and organized than its Ottoman opponent, and its lopsided victory owed much to those advantages, but the first devastating volleys from the heavily gunned galleasses threw Ali Pasha's initial advance in dis-array, so when the two fleets made physical contact, the Christians were in much better shape to withstand a knock-down, drag-out fight. Though most of the battle was fought at close quarters, as Mediterranean sea battles usually were, the initial volleys from the Venetian galleasses shook the Ottoman fleet at the outset of the clash, and throughout the day Christian superiority in shipboard artillery kept the Ottoman vessels from drawing close enough to turn Lepanto into a typical sea battle that was mainly hand-to-hand combat.

Both the galley and the galleass persisted, even flourished, in the Mediterranean, where they were born, where they were in their element. Giant galleasses were seaworthy enough to accompany Philip II's Spanish Armada on its fateful journey to the English Channel in 1588. In the Mediterranean, and even in the sheltered waters of the Baltic, cannon-armed galleys and galleasses remained in occasional use well into the eighteenth century. But elsewhere in Europe, where heavier seas and longer sea-lanes required a much sturdier, resilient, less elegant kind of vessel, a shift in naval archi-tecture was already underway. That technology, and not the galley, would lead directly to the modern battleship and a whole new way of making war.

SOMETHING TRULY REMARKABLE happened to European trade during the Renaissance: the commercial center of the Continent shifted north and west, from the ancient sea-lanes and sun-drenched ports of the Mediterranean and the Adriatic to the new maritime states emerging along the Atlantic seaboard. The advantage, and the momentum, lay with these emerging new commercial powers. These states would come to dominate European trade, finance, and dynastic politics in the sixteenth century. They stole the exclusive access that Italian merchants had once had to the alluring riches of the East by finding direct sea routes to India and the Spice Islands. They managed to outline the African coastline, previously unknown to Europeans, to find the Americas and then to carve out the New World and exploit it mercilessly. Europe had entered its first, furtive age of imperialism, and the Atlantic would be its principal highway.

The great economic shift to the Atlantic world would shape the history of the modern West, and the history of the modern world, too, so profoundly that it's all but impossible to comprehend the scope of what it wrought. The great powers of the Western world stepped forward because of the shift: first (and very briefly) Portugal, then a newly united Spain, Europe's first superpower; then, in the next century, England, France, the Dutch Republic, Denmark, Sweden, Poland, the Hanseatic League, and Muscovite Russia. In this realigned configuration of European military might, a new way of fighting war at sea emerged early in the 1500s and continued—unabated and mostly unchanged—for three-and-a-half centuries.

In Atlantic Europe around 1500, gunpowder artillery gave rise to both a new kind of war *and* a new kind of fighting force: the navy. The technological breakthroughs that brought about the creation of navies and of the ship-killing ship came together not by design, but entirely by serendipity. The marriage of gunpowder artillery to naval architecture was, of course, a deliberate choice, but the evolutionary paths that ship design and artillery followed were purely coincidental. Gunpowder artillery was becoming commonplace, and becoming lighter and more lethal, at the same time that naval architecture was moving in the direction that would allow ships to carry big guns, and lots of them. Innovations in ship design—hull profile, sail and rigging plans, construction methods—were maturing at the end of the fifteenth century. The initial purpose of those innovations was not martial, but by coincidence they served martial purposes well.

The archetypal medieval cargo vessel, the cog, was very unlike the Mediterranean galley, for they filled different roles and sailed in different seas. The cog's round, plump hull was double-ended, pointed at both bow and stern. It was built using lapstrake, or clinker-built, construction: long rows of planks were applied horizontally to the ship's skeleton, overlapping one row over the next. A single mast, mounting a single sail on a single spar, provided the propulsion; a large sweep oar served as the steering mechanism. Cogs were ungainly but capacious, well suited to carrying bulkier cargoes, and their deeper draft gave them some stability in the rougher waters of the storm-tossed North Atlantic.

The ravages of the Black Death, which in Europe were worst between the mid-fourteenth and mid-fifteenth centuries, predictably put a damper on seaborne commerce, but trade came roaring back to life at the end of the fifteenth century. Portugal's first bold attempts to find a sea route to Asia via the southern tip of Africa, which paid huge dividends after Vasco da Gama's momentous voyage to Calicut in 1497–1499, ushered in a prolonged period of exploration by sea. Neither galleys nor cogs were up to the challenges posed by long voyages and rough seas. But European shipwrights rose to meet those challenges, and new designs were just around the corner.

And so the carrack came to be, first in the shipyards of Genoa and Venice, then revised and improved upon in Atlantic ports in the Low Countries and the British Isles. The carrack was built to carry heavy cargoes in heavy seas, a capacious design with plenty of room for provisions and fresh water—an absolute must when sailing to unknown shores across vast expanses of uncharted ocean. The carrack was nothing at all like a galley and very little like a cog:

it was larger, for one thing, and though the carrack could hardly be called sleek, it was proportionately long. Carracks were carvel-built, meaning that the planks that formed the outer hull were butted up against one another instead of overlapping. The bow had a distinct rake, or forward tilt, while the stern was almost flat. A hinged rudder replaced the cog's steering oar. The carrack's size required more than one sail, so carracks typically shipped three or four masts, square-rigged on the foremast and mainmast, lateen rigged (that is, with triangular sails) on the mizzen and after-mizzen—meaning there were ten sails on the carrack to the cog's one. The carrack was the first true ship-rigged sailing vessel.

With the carrack came the potential for a different mode of naval warfare. Fighting at sea wasn't unknown in northern Europe, but it was rare. Over the century-plus span of the Hundred Years' War, there was only one naval engagement of note: the battle of Sluys, fought between English and French "fleets" on 24 June 1340. The tactics used at Sluys weren't fundamentally different from those used in Mediterranean warfare. It was a land battle fought at sea, using bows and spears and swords, only with cogs rather than galleys as the fighting platforms. But the carrack, large and stable, opened up new possibilities. For the carrack was born to carry artillery.

Almost as soon as the carrack made its debut in northern waters, sometime in the fifteenth century, somebody decided to arm it. The first war-carracks were armed much like galleys and galleasses, with most of their guns concentrated in castles, both fore and aft. But the gunport, another late-fifteenth-century invention, made the carrack into a true artillery platform. The gunport was a simple but brilliant idea: nothing more than a hinged door covering an aperture cut in the side of the hull, allowing cannon to be mounted on the lower decks and fired through the hull. Its primary value was as a safety feature. When the guns were not in action, the gunports could be closed, sealed with caulk, and made watertight, so that the ship could roll in heavy seas without danger of taking in water through open gunports and making a quick trip to the bottom.

Now it was possible to mount guns in broadside, along the sides of the ship, on the top deck and on the decks below, something that could not be done with an oared fighting vessel. This was not a deliberate rejection of the "land battle at sea" school of tactics; that idea was too deeply engrained to be dismissed so quickly. There was a universality to the understanding of how battles were fought. Whether on land or at sea, combatants used missile weapons to thin out the enemy and break his will, then got close and went at it with bladed weapons or polearms. The only real difference between land and sea battles was the means by which you closed with the enemy. Smaller cannon, which made up the armament of the early carracks, were best suited to this kind of warfare. They were not big or powerful enough to smash through a ship's hull, but they could sweep a deck of soldiers.

But what if one were to mount a few larger guns on board? Heavy guns could do real damage to the hull structure of an enemy ship, even at a modest range. Such an armament would allow for a completely different kind of tactical approach. Cannon could be used to fend off an attacker, especially if attacking on the port or starboard sides, or to soften up an enemy prior to closing with him and boarding. With big guns in broadside, it would be possible to damage, disable, or even destroy an enemy ship without making physical contact. Victory could be achieved at a distance, and all by firepower.

The ship-killing ship was born.

IN THE EARLY 1500s, as shipyards all over Europe were laying down carrack after carrack, the Continent was descending into a state of continuous war, a condition that would soon come to be the normal state of affairs in the West. That's not to say that the Middle Ages weren't violent. Of course they were, and shockingly so, but for the most part warfare—organized violence—tended to occur more at the local or regional level. There was very little interstate violence, as we would understand it today, or even as it was understood in the sixteenth century, before the Hundred Years' War. The central governments of Europe's emerging kingdoms were fully occupied with power struggles closer to home, such as with their own nobilities, and thus had no spare cash, resources, time, or energy to spend pursuing political goals outside their borders.

But by the dawn of the sixteenth century, those same kingdoms had coalesced around well-established dynasties whose wealth and resources—and, as we have seen, access to siege artillery—put them on an entirely different playing field from the nobles with whom they had formerly competed. The dynastic states of the Renaissance era—Valois France, Tudor England, Spain and the Holy Roman Empire under the Habsburgs, Poland under the Jagiellonian dynasty, Oldenburg Denmark, Vasa Sweden—were much more aggressive about pursuing national and dynastic interests abroad, and using military force to accomplish it. Charles VIII's landmark invasion of Italy in 1494, with the explicit goal of claiming the throne of Naples, heralded a new age in international relations in the West: an age in which territorial aggrandizement and the application of brute force for the sake of naked dynastic self-interest would become the common currency of European international politics.

Amplifying the hypercompetitive atmosphere of the European political scene after 1494 were the aftershocks of the Reformations. The creation of the new Protestant confessions concentrated even more power, wealth, and influence in the hands of European monarchs. For those princes who broke with Rome, "reform" meant confiscating Church lands, monasteries, cathedrals, and all the wealth accumulated within, even the incomes that rightfully belonged to the pope in Rome. It meant that secular rulers controlled their churches, that clergy were now civil servants, hired and fired and told what to do by their monarchs; it meant that the pulpit could now become a font of princely propaganda as well as of the Word of God. Catholic rulers benefited, too, mainly because the Church in Rome desperately needed their support in the battle for the soul of Europe.

But more important, the Reformation provided European sovereigns with both an excuse and a reason to fight wars even more frequently. Though often the religious divide served as nothing more than a justification for wars fought over territory or prestige or some other more worldly matter, religious identity genuinely divided the European states great and small, and religion acted as a lens through which all Europeans—even great kings and queens—viewed the world. The resulting atmosphere was genuinely apocalyptic, as even the most clear-eyed statesmen of the 1500s and early 1600s truly believed that the End of Days was nigh, and that their opponents fought on behalf of the Antichrist. A climate of fear—fear bordering on paranoia—pervaded Europe between 1550 and 1650, adding exponentially to the bellicosity of the age.

The end result, predictably, was war, perpetual war, to the point that at any time during the period 1500 to 1700 at least a couple of European powers were fighting it out. During those two centuries, there were, perhaps, only twenty-four months of peace in Europe in aggregate.

That kind of intensive, high-stakes competition between the European kingdoms just about guaranteed an arms race, the first of many in the history of the West. The dramatic growth in the size of armies was one symptom of that race; so was the compulsion to improve infantry firepower, and to fortify national frontiers with thick layers of modern artillery fortresses. But the biggest, costliest, and most visible manifestation of that arms race was the growth of state navies ex nihilo. Navies, as permanent institutions with their own infrastructures, simply did not exist in Europe before 1500. By the end of that century, all the major players in European politics—England, Spain, France, Poland, Denmark, Sweden, Venice, even the independent German cities that made up the Hanseatic League—had permanent naval establishments. That meant more than just a lot of warships. There had to be large infrastructures, too, which included both bureaucracies and physical facilities. Unlike armies, navies couldn't simply be dismissed when not in use, nor could warships be stowed away for later. Navies required continuous management, upkeep, and physical maintenance. For a fleet royal in the sixteenth century, that meant shipyards, drydocks, ropewalks, not to mention the management of supply in the countryside—the harvesting of timber and hemp, the manufacture of tar and pitch. Denmark's naval facility at Bremerholm in Copenhagen, which included all these elements plus warehouses, a ropewalk, living quarters for officers and men, and even a brewery, was not atypical.

The arms-race mentality was also on full display in the ships themselves, as the new royal navies built up their inventory. The war-carracks of the early sixteenth century were built to truly ludicrous proportions. Scotland's *Great Michael* (1507), commissioned by King James IV, displaced a thousand tons and carried more than sixty guns. Henry VIII, never one to be upstaged by his northern neighbor and rival, in response ordered construction of two giant carracks, *Mary Rose* (1510) and *Henry Grace à Dieu* (1514). *Henry Grace à Dieu*, probably the most powerful European warship of its day, was a tad smaller than *Great Michael* but more heavily armed: more than forty cannon on two gun decks, plus a large complement of smaller swivel guns.

Many things drove this compulsion for building ever-bigger warships. But above all, it was fear, the fuel that always feeds arms races: fear that not keeping up with enemies, or with potential enemies, would be disastrous if war were to break out. But thirst for prestige was just as compelling. From their beginnings in the early sixteenth century, the European fleets were intimately connected to the monarchs themselves, in a highly personal way. The fleets were the creation of the kings of Europe, built at their insistence and initiative, maintained and built up under their close supervision and patronage. In almost every instance where a European navy went through a period of intensive expansion and reform during the sixteenth century, a king or queen was behind it: Francis I and Henry II in France, James IV in Scotland, Henry VIII and Elizabeth I in England, Philip II in Spain, Gustav Vasa and Erik XIV in newly independent Sweden, and Frederik II in Denmark.

And with good reason. The great ships were weapons, to be sure, but they also served another purpose: they were visible, tangible, portable tokens of royal power and prestige. This was, after all, the beginning of the age of splendor at court, of heightened opulence in royal living spaces. The warships were, like palaces, a canvas on which the monarchy's legitimacy and ambitions could be painted, a pedestal on which his or her wealth and martial might put on public display. The sheer size of the capital ships was impressive enough, but increasingly shipwrights festooned the great warships with elaborate carvings, colorful paintings, and decorations wrought in gold and silver. The gold used in the decoration of Charles I's *Sovereign of the Seas* (1637) would have been sufficient to have paid for the construction of another similar ship.

Artillery warships, then, were gigantic investments. It's difficult to exaggerate just how costly such ships were. There is simply no analogue to present-day investment in a single piece of military hardware.

There were, to be sure, cost-cutting alternatives, like the substitutions of armed merchantmen for purpose-built warships. Merchantmen carried sizeable armaments themselves, for protection as they ventured into pirate-infested waters. Such vessels could serve as a naval militia in wartime without burdening the state treasury in peacetime. Purpose-built warships were demonstrably superior to merchantmen, built as they were to absorb punishment and to carry nothing more than guns, men, and provisions. But that superiority came at a price, because warships had to be built to different standards, able to tolerate the crushing weight of artillery, ammunition, and larger crews, and to sustain damage without sinking.

Warships were major capital investments, but they tended to be short-lived. They wore out, they obsolesced, and they succumbed to bad weather and dry rot. Naval technology advanced faster than any other variety of weapons tech, far outpacing the rate of change in firearms design. It helped that naval technology had other uses besides war. The technology of naval warfare was also the technology of seaborne commerce.

In less than a century, the carrack was outdated. Carracks were better artillery platforms than any other European vessel type that had come before, but they were hardly ideal. The massive war-carracks like those in Henry VIII's fleet royal had execrable sailing qualities—their towering artillery castles fore and aft compromised their speed and stability. Instability, in this case a pronounced tendency to roll in high winds, was probably what caused the sinking of King Henry's carrack *Mary Rose* in the Solent in 1545. And by then shipwrights were already improving on the design.

The universally accepted solution by the mid-1500s was the galleon. The galleon's origins are unclear, but it first appeared in Iberian shipyards, likely a blending of Spanish, Portuguese, and Mediterranean shipbuilding traditions. The design caught on fast, spreading to the ports of northern Europe in a matter of years. Though the name *galleon* may evoke images of lumbering, cumbersome ships carrying Spanish gold across the Atlantic from the New World to the Old, galleons were quite sleek. They featured starkly reduced forecastles to reduce drag, a slightly lower aftercastle, a prominent beakhead on the bow, and a pronounced "tumblehome," meaning that the sides of the hull above the waterline sloped inward toward the center of the ship, a feature that added greatly to stability. The galleon was built for both strength and speed.

It was also a remarkably adaptable vessel. With a few minor adaptations, the galleon would remain the most common trans-oceanic cargo transport for the next two centuries, and the war fleets of sixteenth- and seventeenth-century Europe would be built around it. From roughly 1550 to 1650, a flurry of improvements would transform the galleon into the penultimate form of the Western sailing warship.

First, armaments. Even the great war-carracks of Henry VIII's fleet were haphazardly armed with a bewildering variety of muzzle-loading and breech-loading cannon. Most of them were light anti-personnel weapons. The more stable war-galleons were better suited to the greater weight of the large cast-iron or cast-bronze muzzle-loaders. Such guns were readily available by the mid-1500s, when the galleon superseded the carrack.

Another invention, seemingly minor, made the use of the big muzzleloaders more practical aboard ship. Gun carriages were nearly as important as the gun tube itself, doubly so for naval guns. The mount mattered a great deal in the cramped spaces 'tween-decks in a man-of-war: it absorbed recoil and permitted aiming. And recoil—the backward-driving energy when a firearm is discharged—was a big problem aboard ship. The weight of the heavy guns was already a tremendous strain on a ship's frame, but the stresses created by the guns leaping back from recoil was worse still. On land, a gun could be allowed to roll back freely on a wheeled carriage, but not aboard ship. Even when not being fired, cannon were safety hazards. On a ship rolling and pitching violently in heavy seas, cannon—if not properly secured—could be tossed about, crushing men as if they were twigs, and inflicting grave damage to the ship's hull from the inside. A "loose cannon" could quite literally sink a ship without firing a shot.

One solution was to bolt cannon to the deck. That solved the problem of rogue cannon bouncing about on the gun deck, but it did nothing to buffer recoil, as it transferred the stress directly to the deck planking instead. Fixed guns could also be difficult to load. The old-fashioned, breech-loading cannon worked adequately on a fixed mount, but not the more powerful muzzleloaders, not if their muzzles protruded over or through the ship's hull. At the battle of Gravelines (29 July 1588), where the fleet of Elizabeth I soundly beat the Spanish Armada, Spanish gunners were observed serving their muzzle-loading pieces outboard—in other words, by hanging over the ship's side to load and ram powder and shot into the cannon's muzzle.

In this regard, the English fleet at Gravelines had an undeniable advantage: the truck carriage. The truck carriage was a heavy wheeled mount built for large naval guns. It was squatter than a field carriage, for it was not meant to travel by road; the wheels—either two or four per carriage—acted only as rollers to facilitate backward movement from recoil. For the truck carriage was not intended to stop recoil abruptly. Instead, a breeching rope—a massive hemp cable, which attached the cannon's breech directly to the ship's frame—held the gun in check. When the gun fired, it leapt back, slamming hard against the breeching rope, which arrested its rearward flight just at the point where the muzzle was inside the gunport. Then the gun crew could go about its business—swabbing, loading, ramming—safely within the confines of the ship. Once the gun was loaded, the gun crew could easily move the gun back into battery (firing position) by pulling on the side tackles. Then it was ready to fire again. The truck carriage was simple genius: it harnessed the energy of recoil to make it possible to load the gun safely.

Hull design, and rigging, too, went through a continual process of improvement. Conventional Spanish galleons, like those that made up the core of the 1588 Armada, were far from the lumbering, massive beasts that tradition has made them out to be. The

Plate 3. A 24-pounder naval gun mounted on a truck carriage, 1805. In this illustration, the gun is not ready for action, but is instead stowed for travel, lashed firmly in place to prevent any movement while the ship is underway.

Image courtesy of Nationalmuseet, Copenhagen, Denmark.

first generation of galleons were noticeably smaller than their carrack ancestors, and not until the next century would larger warships become the fashion again. Meanwhile, in the shipyards of
northern Europe, a refined kind of galleon had begun to take form,
around 1570 or so. Called race-built galleons—so named because
their castles had been reduced, or "razed"—they were longer, lower
to the water, and sleeker than earlier galleons. A reduced forecastle
and a more pronounced beak reduced drag and improved handling
in high seas, while a deeper hull improved stability. These were
the qualities that allowed the race-built English galleons—like
Sir Francis Drake's *Revenge* (1577) and Sir Walter Raleigh's *Ark
Royal* (1587)—to all but run circles around the less lithe Spanish
ships. That, plus the heavier armaments of the English ships, with
muzzle-loading guns mounted on truck carriages, put them head
and shoulders above their Spanish foes.

These innovations spread rapidly throughout the Continent.
Sweden and Denmark, with two of the largest fleets in northern
waters, followed with their own versions of the race-built galleon,
and by 1600 the streamlined, midsized galleon, with heavy cast-
bronze guns ranged on one or two gun decks, had become the
standard man-of-war in all European navies outside the Mediterranean. That rapid pace of technological improvement owed much
to the uniquely sophisticated infrastructure of the European fleets
royal. Spurred by the first great wave of colonial expansion, and
by concerted, state-directed efforts to cleanse the major sea-lanes
of pirates, the major European navies developed permanent bureaucracies and all that went with them. Navies served as a kind
of intermediary between those who sailed warships and those who
built them, which all but guaranteed a speedier path from concept
to experimentation to accepted practice.

THE GUIDING PURPOSE behind the transformation of the
galleon was tactical. Navies may have been organized, in an administrative or structural sense; naval officers were mostly consummate professionals, for it took a lifetime of experience to command

and manage something so complex as a warship. But while armies were already creating tactical doctrines and standard practices, and seeking to impart uniformity and regularity through drill, navies did no such thing. There were no ship types or classes as we know them today, and beyond a few broad trends there was great variation in dimensions, design details, and the size and number of guns carried shipboard.

There were also no established schools of thought when it came to tactics. Battles at sea were usually chaotic affairs, with neither side attempting to maintain any kind of prearranged formation. Closing with the enemy ships and boarding them, essentially fighting a naval battle with soldiers, was still a tactic very much in favor, but most sixteenth-century naval battles were swirling maelstroms of ships, as individual captains maneuvered their vessels as their instincts and the conditions in their immediate vicinity dictated. They did not make much of an effort to act in concert with their comrades.

Yet a basic tactic was emerging, for which the war-galleon and its armament were well suited. As the Anglo-Spanish battles in the Channel showed all too plainly, superior firepower could keep an enemy at bay, no matter how determined. And even if cannon fire couldn't smash enemy ships to splinters, it could at least fend off attempts to close and board. The new formation, later known as line ahead, took advantage of this. In line-ahead formation, the fleet would arrange itself in a single-file line, the ships following one another bow to stern. While in formation, they would sail past the enemy, parallel to him and within easy cannon range, firing their guns in broadside as they passed. Then they would double back and do it again, wind permitting. In the right circumstances, if the wind cooperated and the individual captains kept to the plan and stayed in place, then the prolonged, concentrated firepower of a fleet ranged in line-ahead formation could be devastating. Of course, if the enemy were just as well prepared, it could be devastating for both sides. The tactic worked best when employed against a passive, static, or disorganized enemy.

The tactic was known before 1600. None other than the famous Portuguese mariner Vasco da Gama used a version of line ahead in 1502, soundly defeating a Muslim fleet off Calicut. Dutch admiral Maarten Tromp formed his modest squadron of twenty-nine men-of-war into line ahead when he drove off a much larger Spanish fleet in the Action of 18 September 1639. Soon line-ahead tactics were standard operating procedure among the European fleets.

Line-ahead tactics were clear-cut and simple in concept, but it was a demanding simplicity to execute. They required a degree of discipline, cooperation, and communication that did not come naturally to ship's captains, who were inclined to be independent in thought and action. They also demanded a well-defined command structure, and something entirely novel: a means of signaling from ship to ship at a distance, so that fleet or squadron commanders could pass along orders in the midst of battle. Flag signaling emerged in the seventeenth century as the principal means of transmitting orders.

Line-ahead tactics put even bigger demands on the ships themselves. Not every warship possessed the special qualities needed to fight in the line. Speed and maneuverability were admirable qualities in any sailing vessel, of course, but in the line they were secondary. The truly necessary virtues were, first, heavy armament, and second, a strong and forgiving build. Smaller, faster warships had many roles to play, but service in the line wasn't one of them.

And hence, the birth of a new class of vessel—not one based on a new rig or a new hull design, but a general class derived from the war-galleons of the early seventeenth century: the ship of the line. Perhaps influenced by the nature of naval combat in the late 1500s—like the Channel battles of the 1588 Armada, or the clashes between Danish and Swedish fleets in 1563–1570—European navies were already leaning toward bigger, stouter, more heavily gunned ships. The next generation of royal "prestige ships" led the way. The vanity men-of-war of the seventeenth century—*Tre Kroner* (Christian IV of Denmark, 1601), *Prince Royal* (James I of England, 1610), *Sovereign of the Seas* (Charles I of England, 1637), the ill-fated *Vasa* (Gustavus Adolphus of Sweden, 1628)—were even more ridiculously overwrought, overgilded, and overfestooned with carved and painted figures from mythology. But beneath the layers of dazzling paints and gold leaf were thoroughly modern warships, packed with big muzzle-loading, ship-killing guns . . . on *Vasa*, two full decks of guns, and on *Sovereign of the Seas*, three.

Those royal vanity ships were the very first ships of the line. That's what the type came to be called, and its meaning was quite literal: a ship that had enough firepower and structural integrity to engage in a protracted slugging match with other large ships. The mania for prestige ships would fade toward the dawn of the eighteenth century, but the type did not. The typical ship of the line

Plate 4. The Danish warship *Tre Kroner*, 1601. Built at Flensburg by the prolific Scottish shipwright David Balfour, *Tre Kroner* was an ornately decorated "prestige ship," serving in the navy of King Christian IV of Denmark.

Image courtesy of Nationalmuseet, Copenhagen, Denmark.

Plate 5. American ship of the line USS *Ohio* (1820). *Ohio*, one of the very few true ships of the line in the US Navy, was rated at 74 guns. Currier & Ives print, 1847.

Image: Library of Congress.

of the period 1660–1830 was plainer, even unadorned, business-like. It was ship-rigged (square-rigged on all three masts), massive but sleek, carrying in excess of sixty big guns; the guns ranged in broadside on two or three gun decks. The elevated forecastle was all but gone, as were the "chasers," the cannon placed to fire directly ahead or astern. There wasn't much need for them anymore. The broadside armament was what counted.

Ships of the line were not identical, and by the eighteenth century most European navies found it advantageous to maintain several different sizes, or classes, of line ships simultaneously. Well into the 1700s, ships that carried in the neighborhood of sixty-four guns were the mainstay of the big battle fleets; in Britain, these were known as third-raters, using a size-category system that had been in place since the reign of James I. The largest warships—the first-raters in British service—often carried well over one hundred heavy cannon, but their great expense kept their numbers down.

The transition from war-carrack to galleon to ship of the line took only a little more than a century. By the standards of the age, that was breathtaking speed for a shift of such magnitude and expense. Political circumstances, domestic and international, favored both the rapid growth of fleets and the development of warship design. In an age of intense constitutional conflict, pitting ambitious monarchs against their noble elites, powerful standing armies could be divisive things, for it was easy to see in a strong army, answerable to the monarch, a potential tool of royal despotism. Navies carried no such political baggage. Still, European monarchs took an intense personal interest in their fleets, much in the same way that they obsessed over royal residences and opulence at court. And for much the same reason, too: prestige. Warships exalted the ruler's authority, reputation, and ambition in ways that muskets or cannon could not, displaying them for all the world—and for the king's own subjects, as well. Enthusiastic support from the monarchs themselves—plus the calculus of the great European arms race, the escalating frequency of war, and the intensifying competition for overseas empire—provided the motivation for continual improvement in warship design.

Those factors—prestige and power—were the necessary impetus; and a new way of thinking about naval architecture made improvements possible. Shipbuilding had been, like most forms of construction, a craft trade and not what we would consider a technical or engineering field. In this sense, naval architecture wasn't much different from the architecture in general in the Middle Ages: building plans, such as they were, existed entirely in the mind of the architect, and considerations related to stability, stress, and so forth were determined by experience and instinct, not by scientifically derived models. That seemed to work, for the most part, into the Renaissance. But the unique challenges of building warships, with their heavier construction and massive loads of ordnance and men, could not always be reliably met by instinct and feel.

As the demand for more heavily armed warships mounted, so too did the need for a less haphazard approach to naval architecture.

One of the most infamous naval disasters of the seventeenth century, the sinking of the Swedish great ship *Vasa* on the first day of its maiden voyage in 1628, was in large part a direct result of the improvisational nature of warship building. *Vasa*, a very early two-decker warship, was built in the old way—without plans or drawings, based instead on the instincts of the shipbuilder and some basic specifications set down by Gustavus Adolphus. In the case of *Vasa*, the builder, Henrik Hybertsson, had no experience with ships of this size—with two full gun decks—and the resulting design was notably unstable. This instability was obvious even as the ship sat moored in Stockholm harbor: just by having a few sailors run across the deck from port to starboard and back again, *Vasa* could be made to roll almost uncontrollably. When it did set sail, it was still within sight of Stockholm when a sudden squall heeled it over, letting seawater flood into the open gunports of its lower gun deck. That only made the ship lean over farther, taking in more water, and within a matter of minutes *Vasa* sank to the bottom.

The lesson of *Vasa* was clear: bigger, heavier ships required more careful engineering. By the end of the seventeenth century, the craft of shipbuilding had become markedly more scientific and exacting, with ships being built according to drawn, carefully modeled plans.

The new fleets royal of the seventeenth and eighteenth centuries were more carefully planned in another way, too: they were designed as fleets. The degree of forethought that went into the long-range planning of fleet composition put navies of the late seventeenth and eighteenth centuries head and shoulders above their predecessors. The ships of the line were the center of attention, to be sure, but they were not all-purpose warships. They were expensive to build, expensive to maintain, and required enormous crews to keep them in fighting trim. More important, perhaps, the capital ships were not very fast and not suited to independent action, for they were designed explicitly for slugging matches. Supporting them were the true workhorses, the myriad smaller vessels that were far more critical to the day-to-day operations of the fleet. Some of them served very specialized purposes. Bomb-ketches, ketch-rigged two-masters designed to carry one or two heavy siege mortars, came in handy when it was necessary to bombard coastal forts. Other two-masters, small and fast—brigs, brigantines, snows, sloops, and in American waters, schooners and tops'l schooners—were useful whenever speed was required, such as when running dispatches between ships, chasing smugglers, or patrolling for pirates close to shore.

The most useful of the smaller warships was the frigate. The term first appeared early in the 1600s, and at the time it referred to a fast warship of modest proportions. A century later *frigate* meant something very specific. The classic frigate in the age of Napoléon was a ship of the line in miniature, carrying its main armament only on the upper deck. Its sailing qualities allowed it to outrun or outmaneuver a ship of the line, and its armament was heavy enough so that it could almost hold its own in a firefight with a larger vessel. Some of the later super-frigates, most famously the American frigate *Constitution* (1797) and its sisters, could actually outfight and overpower larger enemies. And because frigates were capacious enough to carry adequate provisions for long voyages, they were ideal for long-range patrols, operating independently of and far away from the main battle fleets.

By the last decades of the 1600s, the technology of the sailing warship had just about reached its peak; the era of the sailing warship, though, would continue for another century and a half, well into the 1800s. That's not to say that naval technology was completely stagnant over the course of that century and a half. A host of minor improvements, in ship design and in armaments, emerged during that time. Copper sheathing, first applied to ships' bottoms on a broad scale in the 1780s, did wonders for the longevity of wooden ships. More expansive sail plans, with greater surface area of canvas, permitted greater speeds. Ships grew gradually in size, and in the numbers and size of guns. In British service, first-raters carrying more than one hundred heavy guns would become commonplace by the time of the Napoleonic Wars; twelve- and eighteen-pounder guns gave ground to much bigger 32s and 42s. A new addition to the naval arsenal, the carronade, made its debut on warships late in the eighteenth century. Originally built as a cheap alternative to full-size naval guns, carronades were stubby and lightweight, produced in really large calibers. For long-range gunnery they were next to useless, but at point-blank range they were perfect, and they weighed only around one-quarter to one-third the mass of a cannon of comparable caliber.

Important advances, to be sure, but nothing revolutionary. The typical Western warship of 1800 was superior to its counterpart from 1660; of that there was no doubt. But in the essentials, in the ways that counted, there really was very little difference between a ship of the line from the time of Louis XIV (r. 1661–1715) and another from the time of Bonaparte, except a slight discrepancy in size. Nor did combat methods evolve very much over this same time interval. The appearance, function, and combat methods of the sailing warship remained essentially frozen in time in all but the most superficial or trivial forms.

What *was* revolutionary was the existence, the very notion, of the navies themselves. Of all the great transformations of warfare that took place in the period from 1400 to 1800, nothing surpassed the creation of centrally organized state navies in terms of overall impact. The artillery warship, the extension of firepower to war at sea, opened up another theater of war, another *dimension* of war, one hitherto unknown in the West outside the Mediterranean. Possession of a fleet was an enormous asset to a sovereign state, one with which non-maritime nations simply could not compete. Sea power, wielded through fleets of artillery warships, conferred the ability to protect commerce, to guard coastlines, to carry out blockades and wage commercial warfare; besides taking on other European naval forces, a fleet could raid enemy commerce and do something about piracy on the high and narrow seas.

A fleet, in short, gave a state the ability to project power, both economic and military, over long distances. This was what made Western imperialism possible. Without navies, the contest for empire in the Americas, Asia, and Africa would have taken on a very different form, if it had happened at all; it is hard to imagine the great colonial conflicts of the seventeenth and eighteen centuries, above all the American Revolution, without the added dimension of naval power. The European kingdoms that became global powers were able to do so because they could project military might in far-flung places, and in terms of grand strategy that capacity to project power meant more than having a top-notch army. Britain's army at the time of the American Revolution was hardly the best, or the largest, in Europe, and one would be hard-pressed to find a reason to think it superior to the land forces of France, Austria, Russia, or Prussia. But the size and the range of the Royal Navy meant that Britain had the ability to strike at will, almost anywhere in the world, and to supply and sustain military forces abroad for extended periods of time. This was a power that none of its Continental rivals, save perhaps France, could boast.

The rise of the ship-killing ship thoroughly rewrote the rules of warfare and redefined the nature of power in Europe before 1800. The creation of state navies also helped to bring about the single most momentous political development of the preindustrial West. Ships cost money, lots of money, and every year those costs escalated, as Europe's pre-1800 arms race compelled maritime states to expand their fleets, build bigger ships, and equip them with bigger guns. Navies were the biggest line items in state budgets, demanding huge and steady investments in cash, timber, hemp, linen, iron, men, real estate, and infrastructure. Those costs did not diminish appreciably in peacetime. No other form of technology, no other form of organized violence, was as financially burdensome as navies were. By forcing European governments to mobilize resources on an unprecedented scale, the ship-killing ship helped to create the modern, centralized, bureaucratic state.

Invaluable as navies were, and regardless of the amount of attention lavished upon them, armies and land warfare ranked higher in the estimation of European princes than fleets did. Sailor-kings were a rare phenomenon—Christian IV of Denmark

(r. 1596–1648), who led Danish fleets to battle more than once, is notable in this regard—but the tradition of the warrior-king was old and universal, and very much the norm in medieval Europe. But the nature of armies, just like the nature of navies and of the siege, was also in flux, and in this realm, too, gunpowder would be the agent of change.

CHAPTER 3

PIKE AND SHOT

W hen Prospero Colonna's arquebusiers swept the Swiss pike blocks from the field at Bicocca in 1522, gunpowder was already an established fact in Europe. Artillery had shaped the art of the siege for nearly two centuries, and big guns were just then going to war at sea, as well. Both of these types of warfare, naval and the siege, were arguably more important in the grand scheme of things than the land battle, the open clash of armies. Still, the land battle was the chief focus of the art of war, the wellspring of martial honor, the ultimate expression of bellicose impulses. The Hundred Years' War was won by superior French artillery and siegecraft, but we don't remember the sieges. What we remember is young King Harry and his archers at Agincourt on St. Crispin's Day in 1415—a dramatic moment, to be sure, but of less consequence than most individual sieges of that war.

Firepower created the modern navy; firepower rewrote the rules of siege warfare and military architecture. Its effect on land warfare, or rather on the art of the land battle, was equally profound but less immediate. The most consequential change in the art of war at the end of the Middle Ages was the shift from feudal armies based around heavy cavalry—the mounted, armored, nobly-born knight—to mercenary armies made up of foot soldiers of common birth. Gunpowder did not make this happen; the dominance of infantry was already assured well before muskets and arquebuses made their first appearance in numbers.

Yet the use of gunpowder firearms—or, to be more specific, gunpowder handheld weapons, or small arms—completely transformed the nature of that dominance, the role of infantry in battle, and the nature of armies themselves. Once assimilated into European land warfare, the musket and its smaller cousin, the arquebus, became part of a complex and highly effective tactical system, one that required a great degree of organization, coordination, and professionalism on the part of the armies that made use of them. Though the process of integrating firearms into warfare was longer and more complicated for land forces than it was for navies, gunpowder would create the first modern armies in the West.

IN MEDIEVAL EUROPE, and in those places where Europeans fought outside the Continent—like the Holy Land during the Crusades—the basic unit of any military force was the knight. The predominance of the mounted, armored heavy cavalryman was as much a matter of social and political necessity as it was military. The knight was the linchpin of feudal society, and since the time of Charlemagne it was the warrior aristocracy that enforced the law, governed the land, and in times of military emergency took up sword and lance when called to do so by their liege lords. A knight owed his lofty place in society to his service "in advice and deed," as an administrator, magistrate, constable, and fighter. Infantry, foot troops, were also part of medieval armies, but they were regarded as auxiliaries and not highly valued. Little thought was given to infantry tactics, and rarely did foot troops play a decisive role in battle.

That is, until they proved that they could.

Mounted troops, it was believed, were superior to foot troops for many reasons. They were socially superior, of course, and it was a commonplace that the nobly-born were inherently better than the peasants and the townspeople of the lower estate. But there was a compelling tactical reason, too: namely, that foot soldiers couldn't stand up to a determined charge by cavalry. It takes an extraordinary amount of physical courage to stand one's ground when a horse and rider are bearing down at a gallop, even more when the rider is couching a lance, even more when the horse is one of the huge destriers specially bred for bearing the crushing weight of an armored knight, and even more still when there is not one knight, but hundreds, in the charge. It goes against every sane instinct to stand fast when under attack by mounted troops. A mounted charge, in other words, can break an infantry unit's *cohesion*, that vital military quality that allows soldiers to stifle or master their fear in combat, and to stick with their comrades.

By the fourteenth century, that basic assumption about infantry—that they simply could not withstand a mounted attack—was itself coming under attack. Foot troops would demonstrate, repeatedly, that they could hold their own against feudal heavy cavalry. In July 1302, a band of Flemish militia on foot administered a stinging defeat to a superior French army outside the town of Courtrai in Flanders. Armed mostly with short, stubby pikes called *goedendags*, the Flemings repulsed charge after charge of the French horse, ultimately forcing them to retreat in disarray. The feat would be repeated, again and again, by other armies of commoner infantry fighting off other armies of mounted chivalry. At Bannockburn in 1314, a Scots army under Robert the Bruce held its own against the more conventional (and superior) army of Edward II of England by forming its pikemen into densely packed rectangles called *schiltrons*.

And then there were the Swiss, the vanquished of Bicocca. The Swiss cantons—poor, largely bereft of nobles and horses, and therefore lacking feudal heavy cavalry—developed local militia bands for self-defense. Their weapons were primitive: the Lucerne hammer, the halberd, a primitive spiked club called a morning star (*Morgenstern*), and the pike. The halberd—a polearm that integrated an axe blade, a spearpoint, and a sharpened hook into one staff-mounted weapon—may have been the iconic Swiss weapon, but it was with the pike that the Swiss earned their reputation as the most obdurate, most brutal, toughest, and bravest foot soldiers in Europe.

The Swiss pike blocks that rolled forward into oblivion at Bicocca in 1522 had been around for nearly two centuries by that point, and it was without a doubt the most effective kind of infantry ever encountered in Europe after the fall of Rome. Densely packed and symmetrical, the pike block could not be overrun or flanked, and was equally deadly on each of its four sides. For it to function correctly, though, it required precisely the same virtues that the Swiss pikemen showed at Bicocca: discipline, the ability of the men to keep their cool under stress, and to be able to move their bodies and weapons in unison when ordered to do so. That kind of discipline only came from training, and lots of it. Whatever the requirements, the Swiss mastered them, and when they clashed with stronger but more traditional enemies, it was usually the Swiss who came out on top. At Morgarten in 1315, a ragtag Swiss force ambushed and virtually annihilated a superior Austrian army of mounted knights and foot troops; at Laupen in 1339, and again at Sempach in 1386, Swiss pike units repulsed and routed larger, better-trained, better-equipped enemies.

Another, much different kind of infantry emerged in England at roughly the same time. During his conquest of Wales late in the thirteenth century, King Edward I (r. 1272–1307) first encountered the Welsh longbow. Bows were nothing new, but the Welsh longbow was different. Its greater length permitted a long draw, and consequently greater range and more penetrating power than its contemporaries. Edward I and his grandson, Edward III (r. 1327–1377), both encouraged its use in England, so that by the time of the Hundred Years' War, English armies in France could field a good solid body of trained longbowmen. There were drawbacks to the weapon—competent use required years of training, unlike the more easily mastered crossbow, and the sheer force required to draw the bow could tire out a man's arm in minutes—but the advantages far outweighed the steep learning curve. A good archer could easily loose six to eight shots per minute, and the arrow was still dangerous at ranges well past two hundred yards. It could penetrate heavy clothing, leather, and chain-mail armor, some of its proponents claiming that it could even drive through plate armor at short distances. The latter claim is dubious but immaterial: the longbow could fire fast and hit hard, and in that regard it had no peer. It was the most effective personal missile weapon of the Middle Ages, and in English hands it yielded victory after victory. At Crécy (1346), Poitiers (1356), and most famously at Agincourt (1415), English longbowmen helped to win unlikely victories against larger and more sophisticated French feudal armies.

The longbow did not win these battles alone. Foot soldiers armed with spears, swords, and other conventional shock weapons were just as vital to the success of English arms. But the longbow contributed something novel. The high rate of fire, long range, and penetrating power of the longbow made it a devastating weapon when employed en masse. Archers could let fly a withering fire against advancing foes. Contemporary accounts describe "clouds" of arrows darkening the skies over Crécy and Agincourt. Even when armor could deflect direct arrow hits, some arrows—just through sheer volume of fire—would invariably find their way to vulnerable spots, like eye-slits in helmet visors, and at Crécy in particular the arrow cloud caused great slaughter among the less-protected horses. At the very least, the unrelenting barrage of arrows would have been a great distraction and nuisance, sowing confusion and sapping morale, ultimately breaking the cohesion of the attackers.

In England, the longbow would persist long after the introduction of firearms. English archers continued to train with the weapon well into the sixteenth century, and as late as the English Civil War in the 1640s some military writers clamored for its return. The weapon did not inspire imitation outside Britain; it required a lifetime of training to master it, and for this reason alone was hardly an ideal weapon for general issue. But still, it bequeathed a legacy of no small significance. The longbow showed the potential of missile weapons when used in large numbers and with intentional coordination. Employment in large numbers meant more hits, and therefore more casualties. But when used in numbers the longbow, much like the machine gun in a later century, had tactical properties that transcended the mere increased incidence of casualties. Coordination, direction from above, ensured that the cloud of arrows could be unleashed at just the right time, at just the right distance, and at just the right target, to achieve the maximum disruption. This concept, known in a later century as fire discipline, would be a critical feature of firepower.

The Swiss pike and the English longbow did not make infantry more powerful—discipline, training, and organization did that. Those qualities transcended specific weapons, and without them neither the longbow nor the pike would have meant much of anything. The pike and the longbow became such powerful weapons because they were wielded by men who had training, discipline, and organization. And within a generation of the archers' victory at Agincourt, those same virtues—above all discipline—would boost another weapon to greatness, increasing the power of infantry far beyond the level where the Swiss and the English had taken it. Only a century after Agincourt, gunpowder firearms had come to replace the longbow.

IN THE EARLY years of gunpowder weaponry, the big guns— the siege pieces, the bombards—evolved first, because they fit a clear need. Smaller guns did not, but they persisted anyway. Sometime in the fourteenth century, the very first handheld firearms emerged, and occasionally they put in an appearance in battle. The late medieval "hand gonne," as it was often called in English, was simplicity itself. It was nothing more than a small, close-ended tube, resembling a miniature cannon, fashioned from wrought or cast iron. It could be mounted on a rough wooden gunstock, or have a wooden shaft fitted into a socket at the breech-end. It operated like a muzzle-loading cannon, too. The gunner would pour a measured powder charge down the barrel from the muzzle, insert a ball—usually cast lead—and ram powder and ball down the barrel to the breech with a wooden ramrod. When ready to fire, the gunner tucked the wooden stock under an arm, gripping it in his armpit, pointed the weapon in the general direction of the target, and inserted a glowing-hot wire into the venthole to ignite the powder charge in the breech.

All other defects of black powder aside, the hand gonne was not a promising weapon. It required an awkward firing posture. The weight of the barrel would quickly tire the gunner's arms. Clamping the stock into the crook of the armpit meant that the barrel was nowhere near being level with either eye, even with the gunner's head tilted to the side, so the weapon's inherent inaccuracy was made worse by its inability to be aimed properly. And a source of fire had to be kept near at all times.

There was no question about where the hand gonne ranked as a missile weapon, either: it was distinctly inferior to the longbow and the crossbow, the most common personal missile weapons of the age. Bow weapons were more accurate, less temperamental, and had a higher rate of fire than the hand gonne. But the hand gonne did indeed have a few things going for it. The smoke, flame, and noise of the gonne were enough to terrify men and horses unaccustomed to firearms. The soft lead balls used as projectiles hit their targets with great force, enough to penetrate most kinds of armor at close ranges. And when they hit unprotected human flesh, the wounds were ghastly and difficult to heal.

Most important, perhaps, was that firing a hand gonne took very little training. It took years, decades even, to make a longbowman. A hand gonner could learn the basics in minutes.

There must have been something alluring about the primitive firearm, for Charles the Bold of Burgundy made heavy use of them in his armies in the middle of the fifteenth century; the Swiss mercenaries and their crosstown rivals, the *Landsknechten*, sometimes brought them into battle, too. The weapon evolved with use, and by 1500 it took on a more familiar, more useful, form. Two forms, actually, differing only in length and weight: the arquebus and the musket, the first general-issue infantry firearms in the history of the West.

Two main design features distinguish the arquebus and its larger cousin, the musket, from the late medieval hand gonne. First was the design of the stock. The hand gonne's shaft served two important purposes: it kept the barrel safely away from the gunner's face, and it gave him something to hold on to besides the naked iron barrel, which would grow scorching hot after a couple of shots. Arquebus and musket stocks were far more sophisticated. They ran underneath the barrel for nearly its full length, so that the arquebusier or musketeer could grip the weapon almost anywhere without fear of burning a hand. Earlier arquebuses were meant to be tucked under the arm, like the hand gonnes, but soon gunstocks developed a flared butt end that was intended to be held *against* the body instead of next to it. Some were designed to be anchored against the center of the chest, aligning with the center line of the shooter's body, but the most common solution was the one most familiar today: to place the weapon against the right shoulder. That allowed the thicker musculature in the shoulder to absorb the impact of recoil when the weapon kicked back in firing, and with a slight tilt of the head the shooter could line up his right eye with the upper surface of the barrel. It could, in other words, be aimed and not merely pointed.

The ignition system was the other difference. Gunpowder has to be ignited through direct application of flame or spark. The hotwire method commonly used with the hand gonnes was distracting to say the least; it would have been impossible to keep an eye on the target *and* on the ignition of the powder simultaneously. The invention of the first ignition system—the matchlock—changed all that.

Like gunpowder itself, the matchlock likely did not originate in Europe. There is evidence to suggest that it was in fact an Ottoman invention, perhaps back as far as the late fourteenth century, and it appears to have been adopted by Europeans late in the 1400s. It substituted a length of slow match—cord, often hemp, impregnated with a saltpeter solution so that it burned slowly and steadily—for the red-hot wire. On a matchlock firearm, a priming pan, a small metal dish, was affixed to the side of the barrel just below the venthole. Adjoining the pan, mounted on the right side of the stock, was a "lock," a simple mechanical device that handled the task of ignition. The lock included a pivoting iron arm, called a serpentine or cock because of its resemblance to a pecking chicken. On one end, the cock fastened to the lock-face; on the other end was a small vise, tightened with a thumbscrew. The entire lock assembly fit into a cavity mortised into the wooden stock.

The loading process sounds complex but was actually quite simple. The arquebusier would first pour a small quantity of gunpowder into the priming pan. A sliding metal pan-cover prevented the powder from falling out during the rest of the loading process. The arquebusier then "cast about" the weapon, lowering it butt-first to the ground, and while in that position he poured a premeasured powder charge into the muzzle, fetched a lead musket ball from a ball-pouch on his hip, and then rammed them down to seat them securely in the breech.

When he was ready to fire, the arquebusier would raise his weapon to breast height, hold it level, and retrieve a length of slow match, already lit and smoldering. Holding the burning cord was one of the less reassuring aspects of the process; commonly, it would be held in the fingers of the left hand, which did most of the work of holding, rather than loading, the weapon. The arquebusier would then refresh the match by blowing on it, getting rid of any surface ash. Then he cocked the match, fitting it into the vise-end of the cock, rocking it gently backward to ensure that the match was properly aligned with the priming pan. When ready to fire, the soldier brought the weapon up to his shoulder, slid open the pan-cover to expose the priming powder, and slowly pulled the trigger. There was no "snap" because the serpentine was not spring-loaded. Pulling the trigger slowly forced the serpentine to descend, also slowly, until the lit end of the match touched the priming powder in the pan.

If all went well, the lit match ignited the priming powder. The priming would go up with a bright flash and an upward plume of white smoke, and in theory—*in theory*—some of that flame would flit laterally through the venthole and reach the main charge. The main charge would detonate in turn, and the expanding gases would send the lead ball racing down the barrel and toward its target.

Plate 6. Musketeer blowing on his match, from Jacob de Gheyn, *Wapenhandelinghe van Roers Musquetten ende Spiessen* (The Hague: Robert de Baudouz, 1607). The sliding pan-cover, which protects the priming powder in the pan atop the lock, is closed. Note also the forked rest, which the musketeer holds together with the musket in his left hand, and the bandolier worn from left shoulder to right hip. Each of the wooden bottles dangling from the bandolier held a single charge of gunpowder, while the powder used to prime the musket would be stored in the flask hanging down along the soldier's right leg.

Author's collection.

Without much reflection, even someone unfamiliar with fire-arms should be able to identify half a dozen things that could go awry with this process. Priming powder doesn't always detonate, even when in direct contact with flame. A matchlock can hang fire, meaning that the priming powder detonates several seconds after the match touches it, or that the main charge detonates inexplicably several seconds after the priming powder ignites. If a speck of fouling blocks the venthole, the flame from the priming might never actually reach the main charge, resulting in a specific kind of misfire, called a "flash in the pan." A strong wind could blow the priming powder out of the pan before the match touched it, or even while in the process of igniting. Damp powder does not ignite; thoroughly wet powder renders a weapon completely useless. A truly driving rain could even extinguish slow match.

Those were the worst-case scenarios. There were dozens of other points in the loading and firing process where just a minor error or mishap could result in failure. When everything did go as planned, there was no guarantee the shot would be effective. A matchlock could not be fired on command, instantaneously. There was always prefiring preparation to be done, and the lag time—the interval between trigger pull and discharge—was unpredictable. Because of its brightly glowing match, stealth was next to impossible, especially at night. Matchlocks were inherently clumsy and awkward to operate while on foot, and nearly impossible when mounted and holding the reins.

The ballistic qualities of the arquebus and musket also left much to be desired, though they were probably nowhere near as abysmal as historians have been inclined to believe. Smoothbore muskets and arquebuses were not accurate. Modern rifles, or even primitive rifles for that matter, are accurate because of the feature that makes them rifles: rifling—the spiral grooves cut into the bore, the inner surface of the barrel. When a projectile fits the bore tightly enough to engage the rifling grooves, the rifling imparts a spin to the projectile corresponding to the twist of those grooves. The projectile continues to spin in flight, and as long as that spin isn't too fast, it stabilizes the bullet in flight and gives it much improved accuracy, range, and penetration. With a smoothbore, the projectile has no spin, and if the bullet or ball fits loosely enough, its flight path may be erratic.

The speed of the bullet as it leaves the weapon, its muzzle velocity, was also significantly lower in arquebuses and early muskets than it is in modern high-power rifles, which use modern smokeless propellants and smaller bullets. The muzzle velocity of a modern AR-15 rifle firing the 5.56mm/.223-inch caliber round tends to run in excess of three thousand feet per second (fps). A black-powder arquebus or musket, firing a soft lead ball of, say, around .75-inch diameter, would likely achieve a muzzle velocity of right around one thousand fps, just under the speed of sound. For reference, this muzzle velocity is much closer to what's generated by modern pistols. But the spherical shape of the musket ball—unlike modern elongated bullets—is aerodynamically unsound, and the velocity of a musket ball bleeds off very quickly once it exits the muzzle.

The result was that neither the arquebus nor the musket was a long-range weapon, its effective accuracy extending to only very short ranges. In the hands of an experienced soldier, a smoothbore musket stood about a fifty-fifty chance of striking a man-sized target at which it was aimed, one hundred yards distant; at fifty yards, it was much more accurate. At anything over one hundred yards, though, the ball's flight path was unpredictable. Beyond two hundred yards, there was little chance that the ball would hit, much less seriously hurt, a human target, and at three hundred yards it would be harmless.

So, were these first infantry firearms powerful and accurate? Obviously, from a twenty-first-century standpoint, the answer is a resounding "no." But accuracy is a relative concept, and the term is all but meaningless when it's divorced from the context in which a weapon is used. If the arquebus and the musket seem inaccurate and weak, their loading process overly complicated and overly long, it is because we judge them from the perspective of our time. Taken on their own merits and seen within the context of sixteenth-century (and earlier) warfare, they appear much different. They were powerful and accurate enough. The range of the longbow was not that much greater than that of the musket, and medieval combat took place face-to-face more often than not. Perhaps a shot fired from an arquebus was likely to miss an individual man at one hundred yards, but then battles weren't fought between individuals at one hundred yards—they were fought between armies, between large groups of individuals. As long as armies operated in anything resembling closed formations, then the arquebus and the musket were unquestionably effective weapons. If a shot from an arquebus hit the man it was aimed at or a man standing five yards to either side of him, it made no difference. The target was the enemy, not *an* enemy.

The perceived weakness of musketry is similarly deceptive. Regardless of the projectile's low velocity, muskets and arquebuses were cruelly effective weapons. A musket ball could penetrate most kinds of armor better than an arrow could, and they did more damage to human targets—more damage, even, than modern bullets from high-powered firearms. Modern bullets are smaller in diameter and are normally jacketed—that is, the bullet is encased in a thin layer of a harder metal, usually copper. Jacketed bullets do not deform in flight or even upon hitting a soft target, like a human body, unless they're explicitly designed to do so. They create smaller wound channels when they strike a human body, and often they perforate, meaning that they pass in and out of their targets. But musket balls and other early bullets weren't jacketed. They were made of pure, soft lead, weighing more than an ounce, and they deform drastically when they hit. They flatten on impact, forcing their way into a human body with a massive entry wound, dragging clothing and skin (and filth) into the wound, thereby practically guaranteeing infection and likely death.

Their large size and low velocity meant that musket balls rarely had the energy to pass all the way through a human target. Inside the body cavity, they would bounce around, wreaking massive organ and soft-tissue damage. They shattered bone into hundreds of tiny shards, rendering limbs irreparable. Military surgeons of the premodern era are often faulted for what is perceived as their hamfisted, ignorant brutality in dealing with gunshot wounds, indiscriminately lopping off shattered arms and legs because they didn't know how to do anything else. Ignorant they may have been as a group, but their zeal for amputation was grounded in stark and bloody reality. A major leg or arm bone hit by a soft-lead musket ball was destroyed, shattered into scores of splinters and fragments, beyond reconstruction or healing by even modern surgical methods. Amputation was the only viable option to obviate infection and long-term suffering.

Simple to use, cheap and easy to manufacture, accurate enough to hit a body of troops at moderate distances, capable of inflicting horrific, crippling wounds, the musket and the arquebus were truly revolutionary weapons. Combined with the ascendancy of infantry, they rewrote the tactics of their time. Firepower had become the focal point of warfare on land, the central tactical factor in pitched battles as well as in the siege.

THE MATCHLOCK WAS a resilient technology. From the time it began to appear in European warfare, early in the 1500s, to the beginning of the eighteenth century, it dominated the battlefield—nearly two full centuries, longer than any other variety of small arms, and longer still if we look outside Europe. Its origin was the Ottoman world, then the technology made its way to Asia, including Japan, where Portuguese merchants introduced it sometime in the mid-sixteenth century. During those centuries, the weapon went through remarkably few changes, not because there wasn't anything worth improving, but mostly because the early modern attitude toward technology was much different from our own. Military art and science in the Renaissance did not look for constant technological change and improvement, and artisans did not go looking for a solution when there wasn't an obvious problem to be solved. The matchlock was effective at what it did, and there was no reason to replace it with something else. Besides, change was disruptive and costly. Nothing proved that point better than the upheaval in military architecture.

Not that there weren't alternatives to the matchlock, whose major weakness was the matchlock ignition itself—temperamental, unreliable, and incapable of being hidden. Sometime during the sixteenth century, European gunmakers found a superior alternative: the wheellock. Wheellock ignition replaced the slow-burning match with a carefully engineered machine. The wheellock's lock mechanism, like the matchlock's, had a movable cock or serpentine, but this cock held in its jaws a piece of iron pyrites, beveled to a sharp edge. Below the priming pan was a spring-driven, serrated steel wheel that was wound with a spanner, much like a clock. Like a clock, it was complicated inside but simple to use. Once the weapon was loaded and primed, and the wheel spring wound, all the shooter had to do was to lower the cock—so that the iron pyrites rested atop the toothed edge of the steel wheel—and pull the trigger. The wheel spun, the pyrites sparked against the wheel's edge, the priming powder ignited, and the gun went off. Ignition was almost instantaneous.

The wheellock was infinitely more reliable than the matchlock, and it was much handier, too. It was the first gunpowder weapon that could be carried ready to fire, and it was easier to use when on horseback. These qualities alone made the wheellock ideal for less savory uses, like armed robbery; a wheellock pistol could be carried concealed, in a holster or a pocket, drawn, and fired immediately. But it was also delicate and expensive, not desirable traits in a military weapon destined for hard service. A sophisticated piece of technology, the wheellock required a sophisticated artisan's hand, so it was mainly found in weapons made for royalty and nobility—hunting weapons, mostly. Still, its value for mounted troops was not lost on anyone, and through the sixteenth and seventeenth centuries the preferred firearm for cavalry was the wheellock pistol.

The wheellock was by far the superior weapon, but the matchlock was better suited to war and tight budgets, and so it remained the principal shoulder arm of European armies. The only significant design change to emerge during its long life was its size. The arquebus, shorter and lighter, was better suited for mounted troops, a role that its descendants—the caliver, the musketoon, and the carbine—would fill for some time to come. The musket replaced the arquebus as the infantryman's firearm. Muskets tended to be longer and of a larger caliber than arquebuses. The bigger, heavier projectile it threw presumably made more debilitating wounds, and it was believed that a longer barrel resulted in greater accuracy, power, and range. In its seventeenth-century form, the musket was heavy enough to merit the use of a rest—in German, a *Gabel*, or fork—a long wooden pole, shoulder-high, with an iron bracket at the end. The rest took some of the burden of holding a twenty-pounds-plus musket off the musketeer.

When the matchlock made its combat debut on European battlefields early in the 1500s, the timing was perfect. Infantry had just established itself as the dominant military arm, and soldiers throughout the Continent were searching eagerly for a way to counteract the tactical superiority of the Swiss pike block. Could firearms defeat the Swiss?

The answers came, at first, from the great testing grounds of Renaissance warfare: Italy, where the armies of Habsburg Spain and Valois France battled it out after 1494. They were the pioneers of firepower-based tactics in Europe, but the Spanish most of all. Under the leadership and tutelage of the greatest soldier of the age, *El Gran Capitán* Gonzalo Fernández de Córdoba, the Spaniards tried in earnest to find a tactical advantage over the Swiss. One early solution involved the use of sword-and-buckler men, specially trained light infantry armed with short swords and small round shields (bucklers), who could penetrate the Swiss pike formations once they were locked in close combat with Spanish pike troops.

But the pike block's greatest weakness was its vulnerability to firearms, something that was demonstrated several times before the carnage at Bicocca. At a modest range, the pike formations presented a target that couldn't be missed. Artillery could make short work of densely packed infantry units, as French armies demonstrated in the battles of Ravenna (11 April 1512) and Marignano (13–14 September 1515). But artillery wasn't a practical solution. Field artillery did not yet exist, and siege guns were too cumbersome to be maneuvered about in battle.

This was a job for the arquebus and the musket. A one-ounce lead ball couldn't take out as many men as a twelve-pound iron shot, but a field army could deploy thousands of arquebusiers and musketeers, and they could fire faster than cannon. Most important, they were mobile and could be moved around the field just like any other infantry. The 1522 slaughter at Bicocca was only one of several instances where massed infantry firepower decided the outcome of a battle.

Bicocca taught many lessons. It taught that firepower could break up enemy formations at a distance, even the heretofore almost invincible Swiss pike block; it could stop an assault dead in its tracks; it could shatter the morale of the survivors, compromising their cohesion as a unit. Bicocca showed, too, that timing mattered, and that when it came to infantry firepower there was something especially devastating about volley fire.

The concept of volley fire was, and still is, a misunderstood one. Military historians often claim that firing by volley was a way of compensating for the dreadful inaccuracy of the musket. While it is true that muskets were inaccurate, the argument is nonsense. Whether a musket is fired individually, or together with other muskets, its chances of hitting a target are the same. Firing by volley doesn't magically improve the accuracy of smoothbore weapons. Volley fire is no deadlier than uncoordinated, unsynchronized fire. But volley fire is more damaging and more efficient. The roar of a grand volley, of hundreds or thousands of firearms discharging almost simultaneously, is jarring and disorienting, doubly so in a society—like that of premodern Europe—unaccustomed to loud sounds and high levels of ambient noise. The wreckage it produced was more shocking still. The sight of so many soldiers being struck down at precisely the same moment, the visual impression of an entire rank melting into the ground, was calculated to trigger a feeling of hopelessness and panic in those who survived.

Then there was the matter of command and control, and in particular of fire discipline. As experienced infantry officers would learn, long before the advent of military psychology, foot soldiers armed with firearms, when under direct attack—either from an advancing enemy or even an enemy at a distance, firing on them—will tend to fire back. Or, to be more precise, they will feel compelled to fire at their tormentors even if doing so doesn't help them at all, even if it's counterrational to do so, even if they can't even see the enemy who is firing at them. Training in volley fire compels soldiers to wait to fire until they have heard the spoken command of their officers. Then, presumably, the officers can judge the exact moment when a well-placed volley would have maximum effect, rather than leaving that decision up to nervous or even panicky troops.

Bicocca also offered up a caution: firepower was important, critical even, but it was not and could not be everything. Overwhelming superiority in firepower *helped* to win battles, *helped* to disrupt an enemy, *helped* to push that enemy aside, but it did not in itself achieve victory. Firepower could stop an advancing enemy, maybe even cause him to flee, but it could not take ground. At Bicocca, the withering fire of the arquebusiers blunted and shattered the Swiss pike charge, but what ultimately drove the Swiss back were the enemy pikemen.

That would be the basic formula, then, of the standard infantry formation—and of the land battle itself—for a century and a half after Bicocca. The pike and the musket were specialty weapons, neither one on its own capable of delivering victory, but the strengths of the one compensated for the weaknesses of the other, so they worked well together in concert. The arquebusiers and musketeers would chip away at enemy cohesion and will to fight from a distance, through superior firepower; once that cohesion had been sufficiently shaken, then the pike units could roll forward and finish the work begun by the firearms. And if the tables were turned, and the enemy attacked, then the arquebus-musket units would endeavor to blunt the enemy advance through firepower, leaving the task of close-quarters combat to their own pike units.

But the kind of coordinated action needed to pull off those tactics was a tall order, far more complex than it appeared on its surface. Ordinary soldiers had to know their places in the battle formation, and officers had to know how to get them there without wasting precious hours doing so. Complicating this was the fact that "pike and shot" tactics only worked with large numbers. A pike block was effective, at defense or offense, when it was big and heavy; its physical impetus and mass were its most important qualities. And muskets were only intimidating in their hundreds or their thousands. Only a large volley of musketry made a visible impact on the enemy, and if a commander wanted to reserve the fire of some of his musketeers—to hedge his bets against some unforeseen tactical emergency—then he couldn't afford to let his musketeers all fire at the same time. How could this be done? How to arrange pikemen and musketeers so that they supported one another without getting in each other's way? How, exactly, could you coordinate fire and shock?

The answers came from Spain, probably the greatest military innovator of the sixteenth century. Sometime in the middle of the century, generals in the Spanish service came up with a solution for their tactical quandary: a formation called the tercio. Meaning "one-third," as in a third of a regular field army, the tercio was a combined-arms unit intended to function on its own or as part of a larger force. It would take many forms over the course of its useful service life, but its core elements remained the same: a large, squareish formation of pikemen surrounded by a thick layer of arquebusiers (or, later, musketeers). That layer of firepower ran all the way around the central pike square, and was supplemented by smaller, rectangular subformations of musketeers, placed at each corner of the pike/musket mass. Viewed from above, the tercio closely resembled a *trace italienne* fortress.

The tercio was a milestone in military history, unjustly forgotten today. It was, among other things, the first modern military unit. The tercio consisted of several subunits, including a permanently assigned complement of officers, staff, and musicians; it camped together, marched together, trained together, fought together. It was both an administrative unit and a tactical unit, and it did not have to be cobbled together on the battlefield. From a tactical standpoint, it was capable of both offensive and defensive action without changing shape or form. Its symmetry was an asset: it could generate the same volume of firepower on all four sides. The tercio could not be flanked because the tercio had no flanks.

But the tercio was also massive and cumbersome. A typical tercio of the late 1500s might number as many as 3,000 officers and men, and the process of shifting the individual subunits from a marching column into tercio formation could take hours. Its depth, like that of the Swiss pike blocks, made it a rich target for enemy artillery, too, and that was a liability in another way: when fighting the enemy from the front, which was typically the case, much of the firepower on the flanks, and all at the rear, was completely wasted.

THE PACE OF technological change between 1550 and 1800 was quite slow. The arquebus of Córdoba's day was fundamentally the same as the musket used by Louis XIV's armies a century and a half later, differing only in detail—granted, significant detail—from the general-issue infantry weapon of Napoleonic armies a century and a half after that. Before the Industrial Revolution of the nineteenth century, the means for technological advancement were more restricted, and not just because of the absence of factories capable of mass production. One of the key innovations of the industrial age was the advent of engineering as a discipline—as the application of scientific principles to practical, everyday problems—and this way of approaching weapons design was truly a development of the nineteenth century. Until then, there was not necessarily a common scientific language, or even a theoretical framework, that would allow disciplined research into weapons design. Before the nineteenth century, for example, Europeans had not yet developed anything approaching a modern understanding of ballistics, and hence of the factors that might influence the flight path of a projectile. So experimentation with weapons was mostly done blindly, as a result of almost random trial and error.

The means of technological advancement were lacking, and so too was the incentive. Early modern European society did not view change, even what we might perceive as being change for the better, as an unqualified good. There was always a price to be paid for change, and it was the balance between that price and the benefit that was critical. When it came to innovation in weapons technologies, that price was obsolescence. New weapons meant that older, established technologies would have to be discarded, as one technology displaced another. That could be a very costly proposition when it involved the manufacture of, say, tens of thousands of muskets. The will to innovate, in other words, was not always there, even if the immediate benefits of innovation were understood and appreciated. The states of early modern Europe were already hard-pressed to mobilize sufficient resources to equip and sustain large military forces in the field from campaign to campaign, and re-armament could prove to be too great a strain on those material resources that were already stretched to the breaking point.

Tactics, though, *did* evolve, as generals sought to get the best possible results from the technologies available to them. The Spanish tercio was one attempt to create a formal system of infantry tactics, one that played on the virtues of the musket and compensated for its weaknesses. Spain's enemies, conversely, tried their best to out-tercio the tercio. And on the way, they did something extraordinary: they invented the modern soldier.

That process began at the end of the sixteenth century, in the middle of Spain's war to subjugate its rebellious subjects in the Low Countries, an area roughly analogous to the modern-day kingdom of Belgium and the Netherlands. The Dutch Revolt, as we know it today, flared into a hot war in the late 1560s, a product of both religious factionalism and local chafing at expanding Spanish authority. Despite the overwhelming odds set against them, the rebels held on tenaciously under the guidance of William the Silent, prince of Orange, the principal leader of the revolt. As international Protestant support for the war against Catholic Spain flooded in, it seemed as if the Dutch rebels might actually have a chance at victory. Still, Spain was Europe's superpower, and King Philip II was bound and determined to reduce his willful subjects in the Low Countries to obedience.

When William the Silent fell victim to an assassination plot in 1584, his son Maurice of Nassau took his place at the head of the Dutch rebels. Tutored at Leiden by the famous Neostoic scholar Justus Lipsius, Maurice had come to admire the military institutions of ancient Rome, developing a deep familiarity with the works of the tacticians Aelian and Vegetius.

That kind of admiration for ancient Roman authors was hardly unusual for an erudite young man like Maurice. It was, in fact, the very hallmark of Renaissance learning, often to the point of slavish imitation of what Renaissance humanists liked to think was the greatest civilization in the history of humankind. None other than Niccolò Machiavelli, author of *The Prince*, penned a treatise on land warfare inspired by his study of Roman military institutions. But where Machiavelli expressed his reverence for antiquity with slavish imitation, calling for a return to Roman tactics and weaponry, Maurice looked instead for timeless principles that he could glean from the Roman experience and apply to warfare in his own day.

What Maurice learned from his study of Roman warfare was this: Roman infantry was so effective, so flexible on the battlefield, and so precise an instrument in the hands of a skilled commander because of the discipline and intensive training of the common soldiers as a group. But it was not the kind of training to which medieval knights dedicated themselves, cultivating individual martial skills with sword and lance. The Romans, instead, trained their soldiers to execute several simple actions, further breaking down each action into a small number of minor movements that could be performed by the entire group in unison, as one man, to a cadence. If practiced often—for hours every day, preferably—then the soldiers would respond to voiced commands without thinking, carrying out their synchronized movements reflexively and in perfect coordination with their comrades.

Maurice of Nassau had rediscovered drill.

Maurice and his cousin, Willem Lodewijk of Nassau, took the Roman idea and adapted it for their own infantry and their own weapons: pike, musket, and arquebus. Each and every movement of the pike—sloping it on the shoulder for the march, leveling it for attack or defense, swinging it to the rear or the sides to guard against a sudden threat—was reduced to two or three equally timed motions. The voice command for each of these "postures" was given in two parts: a command of *preparation* and a brief command of *execution*. With the command of preparation, the soldiers knew precisely what movement was coming next, and were ready for it; with the command of execution, sharply given, they acted, performing the order at the same time, at the same pace, with machine-like precision. With a weapon like the pike—long and cumbersome, easily tangled up when hundreds of men carried them within a confined space—such precision was vital, preventing the myriad mishaps and even injuries that were bound to occur if their movements were not regulated.

For firearms, drill was just as important. The detailed loading procedure, broken down into a dozen or more individual motions, ensured that new recruits would learn the loading process properly, without skipping steps or getting them out of sequence. But drill was more than just an effective learning mechanism, teaching complex tasks by rote. Even with veterans, drill served a valuable purpose. Left to their own devices, a hundred musketeers would load their muskets at a hundred different speeds, and be ready to fire at a hundred different points in time. Drill guaranteed that they would load quickly, expeditiously, and—perhaps most important—in close coordination with one another. Their commander, the one whose job it was to know the best exact moment to unleash a volley, would know when his men would be ready to fire, down to the second.

Nor was drill just meant for the coordination of weapons. Its most basic elements were very simple concepts, like the measured, cadenced, coordinated step. If each man stepped off at a gait and pace of his own choosing, a closely ordered formation would quickly devolve into muddled chaos once it started to move. When each man stepped at the same time, and took a step of the same length, as all the other men in the unit, then the formation could stay together. Even minor details mattered. The "left, right, left" cadence of a military march, mindless though it may seem, was absolutely vital to any kind of movement in close order, for without it the men would be continuously treading upon the heels of the unfortunates placed in front of them in formation. All these details— the coordinated step, the particulars of how to face to the side or to the rear, and of course of how to manipulate the weapons—turned an otherwise unruly band of armed men into a tool, a machine, that responded to the bidding of its commander. When the commander combined the individual commands in the right sequence, he could make that machine do what he wanted, move it where he wanted it to go, as efficiently as could possibly be done.

Drill was, without a doubt, the single most important innovation in Western land warfare between the introduction of gunpowder and the development of rapid-fire weapons in the nineteenth century. True, it was a recycled idea, like so many of the notions promoted by Renaissance humanists eager to bring back the vanished glories of Rome. It was not unique to Europe, developing independently in Japan, China, and Korea, too. It is even possible that drill, after a fashion, had been practiced in Europe before Maurice. The existence of the Swiss pike formations and the tercio imply the use of some basic coordinated movements. Without the cadenced, measured step, for example, the movements of these earlier close-order formations would not have been possible.

If Prince Maurice's innovations had ended with drill, that would have been more than enough to earn him a place in the pantheon of great Renaissance generals. But there was so much more: a reduction in the size of the basic infantry unit, from the two-to-three-thousand-man tercio to the five-hundred-man battalion; a dramatic increase in the proportion of officers and non-commissioned officers (NCOs) to enlisted men; the introduction of a harsh but uniform and consistent code of military justice; and the disbursement of pay on a consistent schedule, a practice that obviated all sorts of disciplinary problems common in other armies. Yet when it came to the art of war, drill was the thing, and the greatest of the Nassau reforms.

THE GREATNESS OF drill came from its ability to maximize the combat performance not only of the men but of the technology—their weapons—as well. Paradoxically enough, drill, rigid and inflexible, imparted a tactical flexibility that simply wasn't possible in a less regimented system. Prince Maurice sought to reduce the depth, the bulk, and the vulnerability of the tercio, and to increase its firepower, by elongating it. Drill allowed him to do just that. He transformed the blocky tercio from an elaborate square into a thick line. A line of battle, even a deep one, took up more frontage than a tercio. Best of all, it could generate more firepower in battle. So much of a tercio's arquebuses and muskets were distributed along the flanks and rear of the formation, essentially useless there unless the tercio was threatened on all sides. But in a line, all the missile weapons could fire to the front, or to the rear if necessary. When attacked from the front, fewer than half of a tercio's firearms could be trained on the advancing enemy, and probably close to one-third or even less, but with a line *all* the firearms could be brought immediately into action.

Line formations have their disadvantages. Compared to a tercio, a line has less tactical weight, the quality that allowed the tercio or the Swiss pike block to steamroller opponents in their path. A line is more vulnerable on its flanks, for a tercio—being symmetrical—has no flanks. Maurice took this into consideration, and for the comforting and secure bulk of the tercio he substituted the tactical flexibility imparted by drill. His infantry units could alter their formations, making abrupt changes in direction or face, in a matter of moments. Maurice's battalions were meant to be dynamic, changing orientation and formation as needed to meet evolving conditions on the battlefield.

An example of this newfound flexibility—and of how tactics were evolving to work with the new weaponry—was a movement called the countermarch. The musketeers in a Dutch infantry battalion were ranged in line of battle, ten ranks deep. When ordered to fire, the men in the first (front) rank would discharge their muskets in a volley, then face to one side or the other and march single file to the rear of the formation. There they would reform as the rear, or tenth, rank, and begin the process of loading and priming their muskets. As they did this, the rest of the formation would move forward one pace in unison, so that what had been the second rank was now the front rank. These men would fire, peel off, file to the rear, and form the new rear rank, while the rest of the formation repeated the process. By the time that all ten ranks had fired and moved off, the very first rank was back in its original position, its muskets loaded and ready to fire. The ten-rank depth was not arbitrarily chosen; the time it took for all ten ranks to go through this exercise was just enough to ensure that the first rank was ready to fire again when it resumed its place at the front of the formation. The countermarch allowed for a continuous succession of musket volleys, while ensuring that at least one rank was ready to fire at all times.

Maurice and Willem Lodewijk went a step further: they codified drill in print form. Gutenberg's printing press was not new in 1600, but the breadth and depth of its impact on the European world were only just beginning to be understood. The press allowed for the transmission of ideas across time and physical distance, and that was as momentous a development in the art of war as it was in any other field of endeavor. Hence the drill manual.

The first iteration of the drill manual was primitive. Maurice hired a Dutch engraver, one Jacob de Gheyn, to illustrate the postures of the pike, arquebus, and musket, with sparse accompanying text giving the commands of preparation and execution. It went into print in 1607 as *Wapenhandelinghe van Roers Musquetten ende Spiessen* (*The Exercise of Arms for Arquebuses, Muskets and Pikes*). *Wapenhandelinghe* takes the prize as the first printed drill manual, but it was soon supplanted by a much more detailed and useful successor. Johann Jacobi von Wallhausen, a professional soldier who taught tactics at a military academy in the northwestern German town of Siegen, published his *Kriegskunst zu Fuss* (*The Art of War on Foot*) in 1615. Wallhausen knew the Dutch system well—he had fought in the Dutch Revolt, and his patron, Johann VII, count of Nassau-Siegen, was a distant cousin of Maurice's—and his *Kriegskunst* reflects that. *Kriegskunst zu Fuss* contained everything that was in *Wapenhandelinghe*—now rendered in German—plus a great deal more. Every movement was described in voluminous detail, down to the precise placement of hands and fingers when performing the manual of arms. And unlike de Gheyn's brief work, Wallhausen's book gave instructions, in writing and in diagrams, on how to form companies into battalions, or battalions into brigades, how to shift an infantry battalion from column of march into line of battle, and so forth. Translated into a host of languages, Wallhausen's *Kriegskunst* was the first modern drill manual, providing the means for spreading the new firepower-driven tactics to the rest of Europe.

The first drill manuals were milestones in the history of the art of war. They were also emblematic of a sea change in the composition and nature of armies, harbingers of the most basic—and most disruptive—development in the history of war in the West: the rise of the professional soldier. True, mercenary armies had existed before, and hence war was both a trade and a way of making a living in medieval Europe. Knights, the basic building blocks of feudal armies, were career warriors in the sense that they trained throughout their lives for war. Military service was the indirect source of their income and their privileges; fighting justified their elite status.

But the professionalization of armies from the seventeenth century onward was of an entirely different nature and magnitude. For military leadership, this meant that officers came to rely upon study as well as practical experience to learn their increasingly complex trade. For common soldiers, the shift was more dramatic still. Drill, after all, did not build up individual martial skills, at least not overtly. Drill built up communal martial skills. It broke down individuality. Drill transformed soldiers, with minds and thoughts and impulses of their own, into conscious automatons. The fighting man was no longer an individual, but part of a team, a cog in a machine, and that machine functioned well only so long as the cog did what it was supposed to do, what it had been commanded to do, without question. The fighter, in short, had become a soldier.

The growing prominence of foot troops on the late medieval battlefield showed the importance of organization and discipline. The rapid growth in the size of field armies, evident at the very end of the 1400s, made forethought, planning, and systematic movement essential. But it was the widespread adoption of the new weapons technology, the arquebus and the musket, that completed the transition from the semiorganized bands of medieval infantry into the unit-based, hierarchical, hyperorganized armies of the seventeenth century. The close cooperation between individual infantry units when musket and pike were combined demanded the kind of regimentation that drill taught. Directly or indirectly, gunpowder was the catalyst that—in the West—invented the modern soldier, the modern notion of military discipline, and the modern army.

CHAPTER 4

MUSKET, BAYONET, AND FIELD GUN

I n 1600, war was the normal state of affairs in Europe. The great
dynastic contests of the sixteenth century—between Habsburg
Spain and Valois France, between Tudor England and both Spain
and France, between Denmark and fledgling Sweden—spilled
over, unresolved, into the seventeenth, complicated and intensified
by the religious divisions opened up by the Protestant Reformation and its aftershocks. The clashing ambitions of European kings
and their mutual, reciprocal fears about religion came together in
Europe's first continent-wide conflict, the Thirty Years' War (1618–
1648). At first a civil war within the German principalities, triggered by a religious and constitutional uprising in Bohemia, the
Thirty Years' War quickly expanded into a vast international mael-
strom that engulfed just about every polity in Europe. It was the
most destructive man-made cataclysm in European history before
the First World War, depopulating vast swaths of the continent,
bankrupting its participants, triggering revolt and social upheaval
in nearly every state that had been dragged into the fray. Even
when it was over, the map of Europe redrawn, and all the combatant states exhausted, Europe did not remain at peace for long.

A new series of wars plagued Europe in the last third of the
seventeenth century, most of them closely tied to the unbridled

aggression of France under the Sun King, Louis XIV. Though interstate violence was decidedly less commonplace after Louis XIV's death in 1715, old dynastic rivalries kept peace from lasting for very long, and the rapidly escalating competition between the major imperial powers—in particular, Spain, the Netherlands, France, and Britain—extended the boundaries of European warfare well beyond Europe. The War of the Austrian Succession (1740–1748) and the Seven Years' War (1756–1763) were simultaneously conflicts fought over conflicting dynastic interests on the Continent and wars fought between European armies overseas.

In 1600, on the battlefield, infantry was king. Except on the eastern fringes of the Continent, where tradition and terrain favored mounted troops, foot soldiers—about evenly divided between musketeers and pikemen—made up the bulk of armies in the field. Cavalry had not disappeared, nor had it become irrelevant. Instead, cavalry had been transformed, serving the needs of the infantry rather than the other way around, performing functions that infantry simply could not. That included anything that required speed or stealth, like long-range scouting, foraging, raiding, and screening troop movements from a vigilant enemy. When armies dragged artillery with them, as they usually did, it was primarily with siege warfare in mind.

Those basic features of tactics and army organization would not change radically for the next two hundred and more years. What would change was the role of firepower within that basic framework. Advances in firearms design increased the musket's rate of fire, and therefore the potential volume of firepower that a given unit of infantry could deliver in combat. Advances in metallurgy and gun-founding made possible the manufacture of light, portable artillery—the field gun—that was mobile enough to move at least as rapidly as infantry. By 1700, the soldier with a firearm had displaced the soldier with a long spear, artillery had gone from being an occasionally useful auxiliary to a vital and integral part of any field army, and gunpowder weaponry had come to be the exclusive expression of military power.

PIKEMEN WERE STILL a vital component of any European field army in 1600. No serious soldier would have suggested otherwise. The pike complemented the musket, on the offensive and on the defensive. And pikemen were considered something of an elite, although not in the sense that they were any more or less socially acceptable than musketeers. Soldiers, after all, ranked at the bottom of society, by virtue of what they did for a living, no matter what weapon they carried in battle. Rather, it was believed that the proper use of the pike called for the best soldiers, men of above-average intelligence, fortitude, and upper-body strength. Not for nothing were pikemen called, in German armies, *Doppelsöldner*—double-pay men—because of the higher wage they typically collected. But a musketeer? Anyone could learn to use a musket, so long as he was taught the drill each and every day for hours, his lessons reinforced with occasional beatings.

Still, firepower was the thing, and commanders in the Thirty Years' War obsessed over it. They gradually reduced the ratio of pikemen to musketeers from roughly 1:1 to 2:3, or even 1:2, by war's end, retaining only the bare minimum of pikemen needed to protect the musketeers. Clearly, in the estimation of soldiers of the time, the pike's usefulness had waned.

The physical characteristics of the pike changed, too, to the point that it was no longer a pike at all. The pikemen of the Spanish tercios wielded an instrument not much different from the medieval Swiss weapon: a slightly tapered shaft, usually made of ash, eighteen or more feet in length, with only minor variations in the shape and profile of the iron point. The length was both a virtue and a liability. A longer pike was more intimidating, and in the infantry formations of the pike-and-shot era, musketeers could always take shelter from a direct attack by throwing themselves under the cover of their pikemen. But the long pike was also hard to maneuver. Marching with an eighteen-foot pike through any kind of broken or difficult terrain, especially forested areas, could be a frustrating chore. In true wilderness, like that which the first European settlers in North America encountered, long pikes proved to be worse than useless. Pikes figured prominently in the arms inventories of the early English settlements in New England and Virginia, but soon they all but disappeared. The pike had no place in the kind of "ranging" warfare that Europeans fought against indigenous peoples.

The pike still had a part to play in conventional European warfare, but experience proved that a shorter pike did the job just fine at a fraction of the inconvenience. The pike shrank to sixteen feet, then to twelve, then shorter. The Swedish army, the most innovative in Europe at the time of the Thirty Years' War, introduced a truly novel idea: a musket rest that doubled as a short spear, often called a *Schweinfeder* (pig feather) in German. It appears to have seen very limited service despite some promising reports on its use in combat.

While the *Schweinfeder* didn't catch on, it did raise a compelling prospect: What if the musketeer didn't need the pikeman? What if each musketeer could be his own pikeman, combining shock and missile weapons in the hands of each soldier? What if it were possible to have only one kind of infantry soldier? The idea was not quite so far-fetched as it might have seemed in the days of the tercio, and in fact it soon became reality with a very simple invention: the bayonet.

The notion of fixing a blade to the muzzle-end of an infantry longarm was neither new nor exclusively Western. The Chinese were already making primitive bayonets at the dawn of the seventeenth century, though there is no evidence to suggest transmission of the idea from East to West. But there are reports of plug bayonets in the French army as early as the closing battles of the Thirty Years' War, and their use during the reign of the Sun King, Louis XIV, is well documented.

The plug bayonet was the earliest incarnation of the weapon, and it worked as its name suggests: it attached to the muzzle of the musket by plugging it. It looked like a short, straight sword, thin and flat in profile, mounted on a soft wooden grip of just the right diameter to fit into the muzzle. The faults were obvious. If the wooden grip was too dry, it would shrink, fitting loosely and easily falling out; if conditions were too damp, the grip could swell and be nearly impossible to extricate from the muzzle without a herculean effort—a distinct liability if done in the midst of combat. Worst of all, the musket could not be fired with the bayonet affixed. In the battle of Killiecrankie during the 1689 Jacobite rising, loyalist Scottish infantry, unable to fix bayonets quickly enough after firing their last volley into the rapidly closing enemy, suffered tremendous losses when charged by Jacobite rebels.

Still, the idea had promise. By the 1680s, plug bayonets were in common use throughout Europe. Minor improvements greatly enhanced their utility. The ring bayonet did away with the wooden plug handle and relied instead on a pair of iron rings that slid over the muzzle. Since the bayonet didn't block the muzzle, it was possible to fire the musket with the bayonet attached, but it was not a robust attachment. The socket bayonet, introduced at the beginning of the eighteenth century, solved that problem. A tubular sleeve, welded or brazed to the bayonet blade, slid over the muzzle; a slot cut into the sleeve fit over a lug on the exterior surface of the musket's barrel at the muzzle. The lug-slot configuration kept the bayonet from working itself loose in combat, and made it possible to extricate the blade from the body of a victim. The shape of the blade evolved, too, from the swordlike blade of the socket bayonets into the more familiar triangle-profile blade, often fluted along its length to save material and make it stronger. In this form—the triangular socket bayonet, with a blade length between fifteen and twenty inches—the bayonet would serve in the armies of the West for nearly two centuries.

The bayonet was, without question, a compromise. A musket with a bayonet affixed was not a pike. It did not have anything approaching the reach of a pike. In British practice, well into the nineteenth century, the overall length of musket and bayonet was kept at six feet, six inches, a far cry from the twelve- to eighteen-foot pike. The bayonet couldn't quite match the pike's power to intimidate, nor could it hold off charging cavalry as well as the pike

could. To use the bayonet, whether for intimidation or actual killing, the infantryman would have to get much closer to his enemy,
which required greater resolution and physical courage on his part.
And the proper use of the bayonet demanded additional training.
Like the pike, it was not a weapon for amateurs.

But the advantages more than made up for everything. A bayo-
neted musket was far handier than a pike. From both a tactical and
administrative standpoint, the elimination of the pike must have
been an enormous relief. Commanders no longer had to worry
about the proper way to combine pike and musket, or maintaining
the ideal ratio between the two types of infantry, or supplying and
paying two different categories of foot soldiers. Soon, very soon, infantry would split into a multitude of specialized troops for specialized roles: light infantry, line infantry, heavy infantry, grenadiers,
voltigeurs, chasseurs, and tirailleurs. But in its most basic sense, all
infantry was the same, armed with the same weapon.

EUROPEAN COMMANDERS IN the seventeenth century
somehow managed to find ways to increase the volume and rate of
missile fire. As Maurice of Nassau had proven, discipline, drill, and
the clever tweaking of formations went a long way toward expanding firepower. One consequence of this trend was elongation. If it
were possible for musketeers to load and fire their weapons faster,
then the formations could be made thinner and more muskets
could fire at once. One of the greatest generals of the seventeenth
century, the Swedish warrior-king Gustav II Adolf (Gustavus Adolphus, r. 1612–1632), accomplished this very thing only a few years
after Maurice first rolled out the ten-rank countermarch. Gustavus
Adolphus managed to wring a slightly faster loading speed from
his highly trained native infantry, allowing him to reduce his musket formations to a mere six ranks. Understanding the crushing
physical and moral impact that massed firepower could have on
enemy cohesion, the Swedish king also introduced the concept of
multiple-rank volleys. For emergency situations, like when an advancing enemy was too close to permit more than one final volley

before closing, Swedish infantry was trained to fire in volleys of two or three ranks. In extreme cases, all six ranks could fire at once, a desperate tactic called the grand salvo.

But such tweaks could only go so far. There was a logical limit imposed by the technology itself, a ceiling on the matchlock musket's rate of fire, and no amount of drill or discipline or elaborate countermarching could transcend that. The musket did go through some minor optimization during the 1600s, to be sure, which made it overall a better weapon. Smaller calibers, it was found, actually had better ballistic performance than larger ones, without sacrificing killing power, so bore diameters tended to decrease over time—not a serious change, but one that reduced barrel mass and therefore weight, and meant that individual musket balls became lighter, too. Later muskets tended to be shorter as well, and in the last half of the 1600s muskets became significantly lighter, so much so that musketeers could dispense with the forked musket rests that had been a part of their standard equipage for generations.

One seemingly minor innovation had a measurable impact on the musket's rate of fire: the self-contained cartridge. This, too, came from the fertile military culture of Gustavus Adolphus's Sweden. The widespread adoption of gunpowder small arms in the 1500s and 1600s had presented a whole new set of problems relating to supply and transport, for now armies required vast quantities of black powder—volatile, touchy, unpredictable black powder. Typically, it was packed in casks, separate from musket balls and artillery solid shot, and it was issued loose. For most of the musket-and-pike era, musketeers carried their powder in small wooden bottles suspended from a bandolier worn across the chest, each bottle holding a single charge of powder. Musket balls were carried in a separate ball-pouch, worn on the hip, and powder for priming the musket went into a special priming flask. The advantage of the arrangement was that the musketeer did not have to measure out individual charges of powder; the disadvantage was that he was limited to carrying about a dozen charges on his person, and once he ran out of ammunition he would have to refill his bottles manually—a task both inconvenient and potentially hazardous.

The self-contained paper cartridge was a simple, cheap, and much safer alternative, and in a way a mini-revolution in weapons technology. A small piece of sturdy paper was rolled into a tube, twisted and tied off at one end, and then filled with a musket ball and a full charge of powder. The open end was then creased and folded shut. It took seconds to make, and using it was simplicity itself. The musketeer simply tore off the folded end, usually with his teeth, tipped the open cartridge into the muzzle of the musket, poured the contents down the barrel, and packed it down firmly with the ramrod. The paper could be used for wadding, rammed home atop the ball. The process was slightly faster than loading with a bottle and loose shot. Plus it was far safer, and it was much easier to transport and distribute ammunition if it was already packed in cartridge form. The longevity of the paper cartridge as the common and universal form of small-arms ammunition—from the early 1600s to the late 1800s—attests to its simple genius.

The paper cartridge would survive for a long time, but the matchlock's days were numbered. Other ignition systems were available, and they were faster and more reliable than the matchlock but cheaper and sturdier than the fragile wheellock. Soon after the Thirty Years' War the matchlock began to fade from the scene.

Since the Industrial Revolution, we in the West have become accustomed to the omnipresence of engineers and the notion of research and development, the constant application of scientific inquiry to practical problems. In few areas of modern life is that connection between science and technology so obvious and so open to public view as it is in weaponry. In the premodern era, before industrialization, an understanding of science was definitely emerging, but that understanding had little to do with engineering. Science, in the age of Copernicus and Brahe and Kepler, was the objective study of the physical world, freed from the constraints imposed by the medieval Church and the shackles of tradition in a society that was anything but secular.

But the pursuit of scientific knowledge was not inspired by a concern for the pragmatic. Science wasn't intended to solve problems. The earliest European scientists wanted to satisfy their curiosity about the world and the universe around them, because they sought to understand God's creation. There was no such thing as a weapons designer or a ballistics engineer; in fact, there was no such thing as a science of ballistics, because—outside of architecture, which was still more art than science—there was no such thing as engineering. There was not even an intellectual framework for comprehending the physics of a projectile in flight, because an understanding of motion and the forces that act upon it was just not there before Sir Isaac Newton. Craftsmen, not engineers or scientists, designed firearms, and so innovations were more the result of accidental discoveries or eccentric experimentation, not of planned research. Even as the dynastic states of post-Renaissance Europe were already in the throes of building large and complex bureaucracies, including vast military establishments, this did not translate to government involvement in weapons technology. Ordnance officers, such as there were, inventoried weapons but did not study them. Governments did not invest in weapons research, and neither did they encourage innovation. Innovation, like all change, was disruptive. Innovation was costly.

But innovation happened anyway, if unlooked-for and by accident, and the matchlock gave way to a superior ignition system. This system, the most dramatic improvement in small arms technology from the introduction of gunpowder up to that point, was already known in Europe as early as the sixteenth century. It bore many names, and had many variants over time and distance, but the one that seems to have persisted the most was *firelock*.

The firelock wasn't a single mechanism, but an entire family of them, all operating on the same principle: flint striking steel and igniting powder with sparks rather than by the direct application of flame. In its most basic form, which first appeared in the German lands around 1540, the firelock consisted of a cock, much like the cock on a wheellock. A vise on the striking end of the cock held a specially knapped piece of flint gripped within its jaws. Unlike the matchlock's serpentine, which pivoted freely in the lock, the firelock's cock was powered by a strong straight leaf spring—called the mainspring—inside the lock. The mainspring linked directly to a notched tumbler at the base of the hammer; a sear, attached to the trigger, rested on the tumbler. When the cock was pulled back, or cocked, the sear caught in one of the notches on the tumbler, compressing the spring but restraining the hammer.

There was still a priming pan, integral with the barrel, situated just below the venthole and immediately forward of the cock. A sliding pan-cover protected the priming powder when not in use. A steel striking surface—in English, a frizzen—was mounted into the lock so that it could rest atop the priming pan and pivot forward, away from the pan. In every regard other than ignition, the loading procedure was the same as with a matchlock.

To fire, the shooter first pulled back the hammer to the full-cock position. When he pulled the trigger, it pushed up on the sear inside the lock, which released the spring-powered hammer. The hammer came down with great force, and as it did the beveled front edge of the flint in its jaws struck the sparking surface of the steel frizzen. As the flint scraped down the surface of the frizzen, it struck a shower of sparks just as the frizzen rotated forward on its pivot, tilting up the pan-cover with it as it moved, exposing the priming powder in the pan. Thus the powder was exposed at the precise moment when the shower of sparks fell into it, and those white-hot sparks did the rest. They ignited the priming powder, and the resulting flame shot through the venthole and into the breech, igniting the main charge and expelling the musket ball.

Described in this way, the firelock mechanism seems complicated, and when compared to the matchlock it certainly was. But it was also much more reliable than the matchlock, with a substantially smaller chance of misfire, and there were fewer things that could go wrong. Most important, the firelock was far more convenient. It didn't require the constant maintenance of a lit match, for one thing. Firelocks could be kept loaded and primed, ready to fire on an instant's notice, without the time-consuming preparations that a matchlock demanded, and there was no telltale glow of a slow match to reveal the shooter's whereabouts if stealth was a concern.

An added bonus was that ignition was *almost* instantaneous. If all went according to plan, and it usually did, the pull of the trigger was followed by a distinctive mechanical *clunk* as the flint hit the frizzen, followed immediately by the flash of ignition and the boom of discharge.

The firelock would go through an evolution of its own. In the earliest types, like the so-called *snaphaans* or *snaphaunce*, the frizzen and pan-cover were two separate parts, linked together so they moved as one. In later variations, like the English lock, the doglock, the Spanish (or miquelet) lock, and the French lock, the frizzen and pan-cover were one L-shaped component. The new ignition system introduced other noteworthy innovations, such as the very first safety mechanisms; one of them, seen in the French lock, was a specially designed tumbler with a built-in safety catch. Pulling back the cock one "click"—half-cock, as it was called in English—set the safety; pulling it back one more click put the weapon at full cock, meaning it was ready to fire. Like most safeties, ancient and modern, it was not mechanically foolproof, and it could fail. It's from the French lock mechanism that we get the idiom "to go off half-cocked"—to act prematurely.

With the introduction of the French lock—which came to be known as the true flintlock—the infantry musket attained its penultimate form. The flintlock, muzzle-loading, smoothbore musket, with triangular bayonet, would remain the main weapon of the European (and American) infantryman from the early 1700s to around 1840. This was not so long a service life as that of the matchlock, but an impressive reign nonetheless, and the tactics of some of the West's greatest battlefield commanders—Marlborough, Eugene of Savoy, Frederick the Great, George Washington, Napoléon Bonaparte, Winfield Scott—revolved around the strengths and limitations of this remarkable weapon.

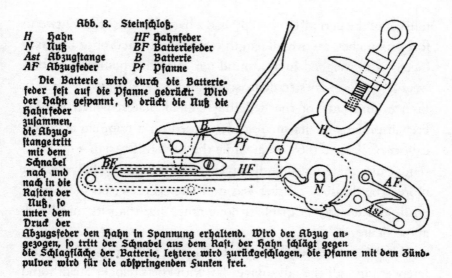

Abb. 8. Steinſchloß.

H   Hahn   HF Hahnfeder
N   Nuß   BF Batteriefeder
Ast Abzugſtange   B   Batterie
AF Abzugfeder   Pf Pfanne

Die Batterie wird durch die Batteriefeder feſt auf die Pfanne gedrückt: Wird
der Hahn geſpannt, ſo drückt die Nuß die
Hahnfeder
zuſammen,
die Abzug-
ſtange tritt
mit dem
Schnabel
nach und
nach in die
Raſten der
Nuß, ſo
unter dem
Druck der
Abzugsfeder den Hahn in Spannung erhaltend. Wird der Abzug an-
gezogen, ſo tritt der Schnabel aus dem Raſt, der Hahn ſchlägt gegen
die Schlagfläche der Batterie, letztere wird zurückgeſchlagen, die Pfanne mit dem Zünd-
pulver wird für die abſpringenden Funken frei.

Plate 7. Diagram of the interior of a mid-eighteenth-century flintlock. The mechanism is somewhat simpler than it appears. Drawing back the hammer or "cock"—here shown in the position of "full cock," ready to fire—rotates the tumbler (part N) clockwise, compressing the flat cantilever spring known as the mainspring (part HF). The sear (part AST), under pressure from the sear spring (AF), catches in a notch in the tumbler, preventing it from moving. The deep notch is "half cock," the "safety" position. Pulling the trigger pushes up on the back end of the sear, releasing the spring-loaded tumbler and slamming the hammer down. The flint (not pictured here) then scrapes along the vertical surface of the frizzen or "battery" (B), producing a shower of sparks just as the frizzen tilts forward and exposes the priming powder seated in the pan (Pf).

Image from R. Weiss, *Die Handfeuerwaffen, ihre Entwicklung und Technik* (Leipzig: B. G. Teubner, 1912), p. 13.

In ballistic terms, the flintlock performed at about the same level as the old matchlock, because in most regards they were the same weapon. A lead musket ball fired from a smoothbore barrel with black powder, after all, is a lead musket ball fired from a smoothbore barrel, whether that black powder is ignited by slow match or by sparks. Even the dimensions were roughly similar, though smaller muskets came into vogue as time passed. A typical infantry musket of the period 1750–1830 had a barrel length of forty-two to forty-six inches, an overall length (without bayonet) of nearly sixty inches, and weighed in at around ten to twelve pounds. Calibers were large by today's standards; the armies of eighteenth-century France (and later of the fledgling United States, which favored French designs for its small arms) settled on a nominal standard caliber of close to 0.69-inch, while the British, Russian, and Prussian armies preferred slightly larger bore diameters of 0.75-inch or more. The flintlock musket was no more accurate, no more powerful, and no more capable of long-range fire than its matchlock antecedent.

Yet there were differences between the two weapons, big differences, and all the advantages lay with the firelock. Stealth and ease of operation were two of them. The firelock required little preparation once it was loaded and primed; one click of the hammer and it was instantly ready to fire, with no smoking match demanding attention—or, even worse, drawing attention to the firer. These were advantages in any context, but in what was called *petite guerre*—"little war," or guerrilla warfare, where ambushes and raids were common currency—that kind of stealth was critical. In the wars between European colonists and indigenous peoples in North America, for example, that quality was highly prized, and the matchlock fell from favor in the colonies much faster than it did in Europe. English colonial forces carried mostly matchlocks during the Pequot War (1636–1638), but by the time of King Philip's War four decades later the matchlock had all but faded from use, and firelocks of various types predominated. In America, the difference between matchlock and its descendant was literally one of life and death.

The decisive advantage, the one that compelled European armies to cast aside an old, familiar, reliable technology in favor of something new, was the flintlock's greater capacity to generate firepower . . . firepower measured, in this case, by rate of fire. Here the flintlock clearly came out on top. To load a flintlock, the foot soldier withdrew a paper cartridge from the leather-and-wood cartridge box he wore on his hip, tore off the tail end with his teeth, and poured a small amount of powder into the open priming pan. Slamming the pan shut to hold the priming powder in place, he then "cast about" the musket so that it stood upright before him, muzzle-end up, and loaded the rest of the cartridge into the muzzle. He withdrew the ramrod from its pipes beneath the barrel, reversed it, inserted it into the muzzle, and forced the load down the barrel to the breech, tamping it down firmly. Then the soldier brought the musket up to his right shoulder, drew back the hammer to the full-cock position, and he was ready to fire. For an experienced musketeer, the whole process of loading and firing took twenty seconds or less, making possible a rate of fire of about three (or more) rounds per minute. It was just that fast.

To a modern generation all too painfully familiar with military rifles that can fire hundreds of rounds per minute, with interchangeable magazines that can be swapped out in seconds, calling a flintlock musket fast must seem quaint or ridiculous. But it *was* fast, because in the three or four centuries that handheld firearms had existed, there was nothing that could be loaded and fired as quickly as a flintlock musket. If we assume that a matchlock musket could be loaded and fired once per minute—a *very* generous estimate, which under the stresses of combat would likely be unattainable—then three rounds per minute represented a volume of firepower roughly *triple* what had been possible with a matchlock. This was no mere matter of shaving off a few seconds. It was not trivial in the least. The flintlock gave infantry the ability to generate an overwhelmingly higher level of firepower.

It was possible to fire even faster than three rounds per minute, at least so long as the musket remained clean. French soldiers were trained to fire four to five rounds per minute with their flintlocks. In Prussia at the time of the soldier-kings Frederick William I (r. 1713–1740) and his more famous son Frederick the Great (r. 1740–1786), speed loading became an obsession. The Prussians introduced a double-ended, heavy iron ramrod for their muskets, sparing each soldier the awkward motion of twirling the ramrod over his head before inserting it into the muzzle, and thereby saving maybe a second or two in the process. In the 1780s, they introduced a musket with a conical venthole, so that powder from the breech could actually flow backward through the vent and into the priming pan—a self-priming musket, in other words. So it's possible that eighteenth-century musketeers could fire as fast as five rounds per minute—the musket loaded, raised, aimed, and fired in the space of twelve seconds—but that could hardly be sustained in combat. It was one thing to load and fire that fast when on the parade ground before awestruck spectators—who, presumably, didn't return fire—and quite another to do so on the battlefield, under enemy fire. Once muskets began to foul with carbon, loading became much slower. Three rounds per minute is probably a good overall estimate. The transition from matchlock to flintlock was fast, though not entirely without reluctance; the Austrian army, for example, initially replaced its matchlock muskets near the close of the seventeenth century with hybrid muskets that incorporated both ignitions systems into one clumsy weapon. But the superiority of flintlocks was so obvious, and the potential military costs of ignoring the technology so great, that the switch was complete by the very first decade of the eighteenth century. The course of events in Europe in the late 1600s made that transition essential. Even after the experience of the Thirty Years' War, the European states were soon at it again, and the second half of the century was even more bellicose than the first. As Louis XIV of France began one war of aggression after another, the entire continent was yet again engulfed in conflict. In this hostile environment, the tactical advantage conferred by the flintlock musket was not one to be casually dismissed.

THE ARMIES OF the eighteenth century could generate a great deal more firepower than their predecessors a half-century earlier. The flintlock musket was in part responsible, but so too was the growing prominence of artillery. There was nothing new about artillery in the seventeenth and eighteenth centuries, except in size, but the reduction in bulk and weight of artillery pieces dramatically expanded the roles that artillery could play in European land warfare. Prior to 1600, nearly all artillery was to be found aboard ship, or atop the ramparts of fortresses, or in the siege train. But soon a new kind of cannon emerged: the field gun.

It was common knowledge that artillery could play a decisive role in land battle. If artillery was good at knocking down walls, it was even better at tearing large formations of soldiers to bloody shreds. It had been done before: in the Habsburg-Valois wars over Italy, and in several battles of the Thirty Years' War, well-sited artillery batteries had been able to achieve spectacular results in a very short time.

Then why wasn't artillery used in battle more often? The issue was simply one of mobility. Small, mobile cannon were little more effective than muskets, but much heavier, and hardly worth the trouble of lugging them around. Cannon big enough to do real damage were too cumbersome to be moved easily. It was one thing to arrange them in a siege battery, where the pace of combat was slow, but it was another thing entirely to deploy them in battle. It wasn't impossible to use siege guns in battle; it simply took a large measure of planning and preparation. Since most battles of the seventeenth century and earlier were set-piece battles—meaning that the opposing armies made contact, halted, set up their prebattle dispositions, and often waited for the next day to engage—a judicious commander would have time to identify the best positions for siting his cannon, and maybe even dig rudimentary field fortifications to protect his gun emplacements.

But once deployed, the larger guns were semipermanent fixtures. They could not be moved hastily in the midst of battle. If the flow of combat took the battle in an unanticipated direction, then the carefully placed guns might prove to be useless. Or worse—if a turn of bad luck made it necessary to beat a hasty retreat, then there could be no waiting for the gun crews to rescue the pieces. Artillery was more easily captured than it was withdrawn. When the army of Christian IV of Denmark took to its heels at the catastrophic finale of the battle of Lutter-am-Barenberge in August 1626, every single gun in the king's invaluable artillery train—abandoned by their crews—fell into enemy hands. Given the exorbitant costs of cannon, such losses were unbearable.

If artillery were to be a reliable partner for infantry and cavalry on the battlefield, if it were to contribute to an army's firepower in any significant way, it would require two things thus far lacking in artillery: physical mobility and tactical organization. The first of these was the most obvious, and even before sophisticated metallurgy and better casting techniques made more portable cannon feasible, there were tantalizing hints about what truly mobile field artillery might be able to achieve.

One of those hints came from the ever-fertile military culture of Gustavus Adolphus's Sweden. In the 1620s, the Swedish army experimented with a light cannon, known forever after as the "leather gun." The idea was not too far off from the hoop-and-stave construction of medieval cannon. At the center of the leather gun was a lightweight tube of rolled copper, wrapped tightly in several layers of heavy leather, thoroughly wetted. As the leather dried, it shrank, bonding it tightly to the copper tube. The gun was indeed light but weak, and it could withstand only light loads without bursting from the internal pressures. Though a major disappointment, it spurred the Swedes to experiment with small, conventionally cast cannon, light enough to be manhandled by a few men. The result was the "battalion piece," so called because these guns were meant to be used individually, with each gun attached to a separate infantry battalion.

Did the battalion pieces work? It's hard to say, because there's little evidence to suggest their effectiveness one way or the other. They could not have had the range or impact of the larger guns. But they introduced the notion of mobile field artillery. On the march, the battalion pieces would travel much like any cannon—pulled by horses—but unlike their larger cousins, the lighter guns could go forward with the troops, or retire to safety, or focus their fire on individual targets, all as the changing conditions of battle warranted.

Fashion and technology, specifically metallurgy, caught up with the notion. Earlier cast-iron and cast-bronze cannon were excessively heavy because of casting imperfections and impurities; making the cannon extra thick at the breech, where the internal pressures were greatest during firing, was a way of compensating for poor-quality castings. During the seventeenth and eighteenth centuries, gun casting techniques matured to the point where it was possible to reduce barrel thickness substantially. Ornamentation diminished, too. Artillery pieces could be gaudy things. They were significant investments, after all, and objects of pride for the monarchs who commissioned them, so it was not at all unusual for medium- and larger-sized guns to be festooned with elaborate royal crests, inscriptions, and mottoes, or even with complete genealogical tables. Other features added to the barrel weight: wide, flaring muzzles; heavy knobs and built-up sections at the breech; and massive handles placed just over the center of gravity, called dolphins because they were often cast in the shape of stylized dolphins or fish. Barrel reinforcements could serve a structural purpose, but in the main these were unnecessary and ornamental features, and could be dispensed with. As the eighteenth century wore on, one by one the decorative elements fell by the wayside.

The net result of this streamlining was an appreciable reduction in weight. Western armies classified artillery pieces by the weight of the solid shot they threw. A six-pounder gun, for example, was so called because it fired a cast-iron shot weighing six pounds, almost three and two-thirds inches in diameter; a twelve-pounder threw a ball that was just over four and a half inches. The difference sounds trivial, but it was actually quite substantial, so that a six-pounder was far more portable than a twelve-pounder. But the design changes of the eighteenth century helped to fix this, so that larger guns could be made to be as manageable as their smaller brethren. The tube of a twelve-pounder gun from the time of the Thirty Years' War, early in the seventeenth century, could tip the scales at nearly 4,000 pounds; a French twelve-pounder of the Vallière system (1732) weighed around 3,300 pounds; a French twelve-pounder from the Gribeauval system (1765) weighed about 2,100 pounds. In the artillery systems—families of artillery pieces of standardized sizes, accessories, and component parts, a characteristic feature of field artillery in the rapidly professionalizing armies of the eighteenth century—the smaller guns were still the most prominent. Six-, eight-, and nine-pounder guns would predominate in field batteries through the Napoleonic wars. But bigger—and therefore more destructive—guns could now be taken on campaign with no loss of mobility.

Gun carriages were in for their share of revision, too. From a distance, a field gun carriage from the eighteenth century looks much like one from two hundred years before. All the basic elements are there: heavy oaken construction; iron fittings; a pair of iron-shod, spoked wooden wheels; a large tailpiece, called a trail, that was usually two separate pieces of sturdy oak. Reduction in size of the cannon barrel allowed for a lightening of the carriage, but the parameters were otherwise the same, except in one important regard: the mechanism for elevation. When a fieldpiece went into action, its gun crew began with the process of aiming, known as "laying on." The first subtask of laying on was adjusting traverse, the lateral positioning of the barrel: the gunner identified the target, sighting down the barrel, and the crew rotated the entire piece, right or left, using handspikes to push or pull the trail.

Adjusting for elevation was trickier. In the days before optical rangefinders, gunners had to estimate distance-to-target by gut instinct and experience, and then adjust the cannon accordingly. Many things influenced the shot's range—wind, atmospheric conditions, and of course the size of the powder charge—but elevation was the main factor that lay within the gunner's control. A gunner's quadrant helped estimate the angle of elevation of the barrel, but actually getting the piece to angle upward (or downward) at the requisite angle was problematic. Prior to the late eighteenth century, elevation was adjusted with a quoin, a wooden wedge that sat underneath the cannon's breech. Hammering the quoin in, toward the gun, raised the breech and depressed the muzzle;

drawing it out had the opposite effect. It was a time-consuming process, taking far longer than the loading process itself, and it was impossible to be precise. The introduction of the elevating screw, sometime around 1760, changed all that. The elevating screw was a massive threaded bolt that screwed into a vertical metal socket in the carriage right below where the cannon breech rested. Turning the bolt handle rotated the screw up or down, raising or lowering the breech, allowing for quick and precise elevation.

In these early years of field artillery, the majority of artillery pieces were guns, a term that had a much different meaning than it does today. We use *gun* as a generic reference to all firearms, but not that long ago it had a more specific military meaning. So, too, did the word *cannon*, which was a synonym for gun. A gun was an artillery piece with a long barrel and a straight bore (meaning that the bore diameter was the same at the muzzle as it was at the breech), designed to fire solid shot along a relatively flat trajectory. *Relatively* flat, for until the introduction of improved propellants late in the nineteenth centuries, even guns threw their projectiles with a very high arc. British experiments with field guns showed that a solid shot fired from a nine-pounder gun at zero degrees elevation—the barrel perfectly level—would drop to the ground at four hundred yards. To hit a ground target at nine hundred yards, the same gun would have to be elevated two degrees . . . and the shot would reach a zenith of around thirty feet before arcing back to earth.

Until the twentieth century, guns outnumbered all other types of artillery pieces put together. A second kind of artillery piece, the howitzer, started to appear in European field batteries in the eighteenth century. Originally a siege weapon, the howitzer was a compromise between a gun and a mortar, very much a special-purpose weapon. Howitzers differed from field guns in dimensions, construction, and performance. They were stubby weapons, shorter than guns of the same caliber, and unlike guns—which had a straight bore—the breech-end of a howitzer's bore was smaller in diameter than the rest of the barrel. This constricted end acted as a powder chamber, for howitzers used smaller powder charges than guns of equivalent bore diameter. They were much shorter-ranged than field guns, because they were not intended for the same purpose. Like mortars, howitzers could fire common shell, the very first type of explosive ordnance, and their high, plunging trajectory made them ideal for *indirect* fire against enemy targets.

Artillery ammunition also evolved to meet the special requirements of open battle. Until the eighteenth century, siege guns relied almost exclusively on solid shot, because their purpose was to batter. But on the battlefield, "hard" targets, like structures, were rare. Solid shot was useful against field fortifications, even if packed earth tended to absorb cannonballs. For counterbattery fire—focusing artillery fire on the enemy's artillery—solid shot was essential, because of its superior qualities for smashing things. But shot was less effective as an antipersonnel round. That's not to say that it was useless, though. Even a relatively small shot, like a six-pounder (about three-and-a-half inches in diameter) could tear a man in half, and unlike a musket ball its flight would not be stopped by a single victim. In a densely packed or deep formation, a solid shot could inflict horrific damage by going through one man after another, from the front of the formation to the rear. Its chief value was as a weapon of terror: a bounding solid shot was unnervingly visible to soldiers standing in its path, and few sights on the battlefield were more unsettling than that of horses or men reduced to mangled flesh and viscera by a cannonball.

Solid shot were also inefficient killers, in that they could kill or disable only a limited number of enemy soldiers individually. There were much more efficient ways of killing men with artillery, and by the eighteenth century specialized antipersonnel ammunition was in regular use in Western warfare. Grapeshot, a few cast-iron balls clustered around a wooden spindle attached to a disk-shaped base, was already well known to European naval gunners. Its more common army equivalent was case shot, also known as canister. Canister followed the same basic principle as grapeshot but on a different scale: a large number of lead shot, between forty-one and eighty-five for a six-pounder gun, contained in a lightweight metal cylinder. Canister transformed a field gun or howitzer into a giant scattergun. After exiting the barrel, the balls broke free from the cylinder and spread out quickly. It was purely a short-range round, ineffectual past five hundred yards, for the balls spread far (roughly thirty feet for every one hundred yards of range) and rapidly lost velocity. But canister wasn't meant for long distances; it was intended to break up infantry or cavalry assaults as they drew close, and within one hundred yards canister was absolutely devastating. A single solid shot, fired at an infantry formation three ranks deep, could at most take out three men, regardless of range; canister, at short range, could take down dozens at a time.

That kind of power, that ability to cause massive casualties and shatter morale, was what made artillery worth the trouble of hauling it along on campaign. They were a lot of trouble, after all, given the number of men and draft animals required to move and service them, and all the gear and supplies that went into moving big guns around the countryside: food and fodder, ammunition and spare parts, special gear for blacksmiths and farriers. But the new field-pieces of the eighteenth century were much lighter than their predecessors, easier to transport, more useful in combat. They required fewer (and smaller) draft animals to draw them on the road. Oxen were the artillery draft animals of choice in earlier centuries, but the lighter pieces could be pulled with horses instead. Typically, it took a team of four to eight horses to pull a field gun and its limber, the two-wheeled cart to which the gun was hitched. While horses were finicky and fragile as compared to oxen, they could pull a lot faster, and that speed was an invaluable asset. Smaller teams of smaller animals meant less dry fodder, less veterinary care, less of all the logistical burdens that come with military animals. Now artillery could move as fast as infantry, or even faster. Later in the eighteenth century, the Prussian army introduced the first horse artillery units. In horse artillery—also called flying artillery—the gun crews and all attendant personnel rode either on battery vehicles or on horseback, so they could zip around the battlefield nearly as fast as cavalry could.

Lighter guns and better transport helped to make artillery a viable part of a field army; drill did the rest. Drill was at least as important to functioning artillery as it was to infantry. A well-drilled gun crew could unlimber a fieldpiece and manhandle it into position in seconds, and load it faster than an experienced infantryman could feed his musket. Even with the extra time involved in laying on, a veteran gun crew could easily load and fire twice in a minute, three times if in a hurry, as when desperately shooting canister into a rapidly advancing enemy.

An immense, even decisive, advantage came from speed, and it dramatically increased the value of artillery in battle. Artillery had now, in the eighteenth century, become a dynamic asset and not a static one; it did not have to be put in position the night before a battle to be useful. Truly mobile artillery gave Western armies an additional and often decisive layer of firepower, which could be more flexible than infantry. Artillery batteries—in Europe, the basic tactical and administrative unit, with four to eight guns and their support vehicles—could be shifted about the battlefield as necessary to meet new or changing threats. Batteries could be dispersed throughout the battlefield or concentrated into ad hoc "grand batteries" to focus their massed fury on a single target at a decisive moment. By the mid-1700s, no sane general would even think of going on campaign without an adequate complement of field guns.

The numbers show plainly the rapid ascent of the field piece. At Blenheim (13 August 1704), one of the largest engagements in the bloody War of the Spanish Succession (1701–1714), the allied army of 52,000 men had 66 guns, while the opposing French army (56,000 men) had 90 guns. The aggregate guns:men ratio was roughly 1:692. Fifty-five years later, that proportion had nearly tripled. At Minden (1 August 1759), in the Seven Years' War, the aggregate armies numbered 81,000 men and 343 guns, or a ratio of 1:236.

THE INCREASED KILLING power of eighteenth-century firearms, and the disappearance of the pike, translated into new battle tactics. There was no single abrupt or dramatic break with the past, but rather a smooth, incremental transition, along developmental lines that had been discernable since the days of the tercio. Artillery rose in importance, cavalry diminished, infantry ruled the battlefield, and tactical units became longer and thinner. Generating firepower was no longer the exclusive province of specialist troops; firepower was now the focal point of tactics.

Eighteenth-century battles were infantry battles. Infantry made up the bulk of the armies, and it was infantry that did most of the fighting, killing, and dying. Though there were innumerable variations upon the basic theme, infantry battles were quite simple at their core. Two armies met, on purpose or by chance, and then deployed from marching column into line of battle. While in line, the opposing forces used their artillery to disrupt the enemy's deployment, or to neutralize enemy artillery, or both, and the infantry closed to within musket range. There they would trade volleys, until one commander or the other decided that the enemy's cohesion had been sufficiently compromised and an infantry assault was possible.

Once launched, that assault could not stop. Speed and steadiness were key, because the faster the assault moved forward, the fewer the volleys the defending enemy could unleash against it, and the greater the chance of success. Speed, however, didn't mean that the troops could run. Running could exhaust the attacking troops before they got close to the enemy, and running was the enemy of steadiness and cohesion. The defender, for his part, would attempt to fire as many volleys of musketry as possible, knowing that shattering the attacker's cohesion was the only hope he had for blunting or repelling the assault. The most critical volleys were those fired in the very last moments of the attack, in the last fifty yards, when every shot hit home and found a target.

All depended on speed: speed of movement, rate of fire. And speed required training, in the form of hours and hours of drill. From the time of Maurice of Nassau at the dawn of the seventeenth century, drill had been the most valuable investment of an army's time, and since Maurice's day the infantryman's fire-power had increased dramatically. This permitted shallower and shallower formations: ten ranks of musketeers under Maurice, six under Gustavus Adolphus, four by 1700, when the flintlock was in its ascendancy, and three ranks by midcentury. In the American Revolution, where the field armies were comparatively puny, two-rank formations prevailed.

To the modern eye, there are few things in the history of Western warfare that appear more ridiculous than the spectacle of linear tactics in the eighteenth century. The tactics look stiff, formal, even suicidal. Casual students of war like to point out the absurdity of armies trading volleys at close range. Why didn't soldiers take cover, relying on individual initiative and marksmanship, instead of standing up in the open?

Contrary to outward appearances, linear tactics were eminently practical and were grounded in contemporary reality, taking into account the nature of both the weapons and the soldiery. Keeping the men in tight formations made them easier to control and command. As combat-experienced officers knew, men under fire tended to bunch up anyway, even if it was counterrational to do so, because in the stress of combat green troops in particular sought out the comfort and security of physical closeness to their comrades. Firing by volley gave officers greater control over the direction and timing of fire, both critical. And assaulting in formation ensured that the men would keep going, without stopping to fire back at the enemy as their instincts told them to do, and hit the enemy with the bayonet all at once, in one massive blow.

Nor were "frontal assaults" always frontal assaults. "Turning movements" became all the rage in the mid-eighteenth century, made popular by the much-admired warrior-king Frederick the Great of Prussia (r. 1740–1786). A turning movement was nothing more or less than a combined diversion and flank attack. While a portion of the attacking force made a demonstration—a feint—somewhere along the enemy's line, another attacking force went around to hit the enemy on a vulnerable flank, rolling up the flank before the surprised defender had time to react and shift his forces accordingly. The textbook case of this was Frederick's defeat of a much superior Austrian army at the battle of Leuthen (5 December 1757), during the Seven Years' War. Frederick's army of just over thirty thousand hungry and bone-weary veterans destroyed an Austrian force more than twice its size. The battle of Bunker Hill (Breed's Hill, 17 June 1775), usually touted as an exemplar of why frontal assaults do not work, was actually a British attempt at a turning movement gone horribly wrong.

Even after the smoothbore flintlock musket and the light field gun became the standard weapons of the eighteenth-century battlefield, the tactics were continually evolving—and always with an eye toward maximizing firepower and speed of maneuver. Among French military commanders in particular—probably the most intellectually engaged officer corps in Europe—there was a very active debate about tactical reform. Some officers, arguing that the deep, blockish formations of the seventeenth century had a tactical weight and impetus that shallow linear formations couldn't match, called for a return to infantry formations that looked a lot more like tercios (the *ordre profond*, or "deep order"); others, admiring the prodigious musketry of Frederick the Great's armies, preferred shallow linear formations to emphasize firepower over weight (the *ordre mince*, or "thin order"). And some, like the brilliant young French tactician Guibert, advocated for flexible infantry units, which could transform from one formation to another as the tactical situation warranted—shallow lines for firepower, deeper assault columns for the offensive. Linear tactics were anything but ossified, and an increasingly professional European officer corps experimented constantly with tactical formations that best took advantage of the weaponry of the age.

Linear tactics weren't the only option available to eighteenth-century commanders, nor were they always advisable. The flintlock musket lent itself to many different approaches to land warfare, approaches that wouldn't have been possible with the matchlock. The growth of Western empires outside Europe, and the extension of European political control into the periphery of the Continent, meant that starting in the seventeenth century, European armies came into increasingly frequent contact with irregular forces, enemies who did not fight in the European manner and had no intention of doing so: Native Americans, for example, or Scottish Highlanders. Rather than dismissing indigenous fighting methods out of hand, European soldiers readily adapted to them, integrating unique native tactics into their own ways of war. By the last quarter of the eighteenth century just about every army in Europe had adopted some form of light infantry, trained to fight irregular wars, in and out of formation. Light infantry could mean many things. The British were the real pioneers of the concept. In their army, irregular warfare included the kind of informal woodland tactics known in colonial North America as "ranging." Their light infantry also included elite units of soldiers, handpicked for their intelligence and resourcefulness, trained to fight as conventional infantry in closed order, or as skirmishers and scouts in open order. Contrary to what Americans like to believe about their Revolution, the British were exceptionally good at the practice of wilderness warfare.

THE FLINTLOCK, SMOOTHBORE, muzzle-loading musket fit all of these roles, and in that sense it was the first universal infantry weapon in the history of Western warfare. There was no need to supplement or coordinate it with any other kind of infantry. Because of the flintlock musket's rate of fire—substantially higher than that of the matchlock—musket-armed infantry was far less vulnerable to attack than it had been at the time of Córdoba and Maurice and Gustavus Adolphus, and the addition of the socket bayonet gave musketeers the ability to defend themselves in combat at close quarters. The musket-bayonet combination couldn't match the pike in its ability to intimidate, but it was a satisfactory enough substitute. Musketeers could now attack as well as defend, take ground as well as hold it, without needing the assistance of auxiliary or supporting troops. Infantry tactics could be simplified somewhat as a result, now that maneuvering foot troops on the battlefield no longer involved an intricate dance between pike-men and musketeers. Field artillery did not bring about any revolutionary change in battlefield tactics, but reinforced the greatly augmented firepower of the all-musket infantry. Now that artillery could move at least as fast as infantry, and now that infantry was no longer encumbered by the inherent complications of the pike-musket partnership, European armies could aim for a kind of tactical flexibility that simply wasn't possible with the blocky, dense infantry formations of the pike-and-shot era. That flexibility extended into irregular warfare, too. The unconventional tactics of frontier warfare in the eighteenth century—emphasizing stealth, speed, and individual initiative—could not have been carried out with the matchlock. The flintlock changed the way armies fought.

In other ways, though, firearms hadn't evolved much from the end of the Middle Ages to the time of the American and French Revolutions. Ballistically speaking, a musket is a musket; flintlock ignition had no effect on the weapon's range, or accuracy, or penetrating power. The technological evolution of gunpowder firearms—small arms and artillery both—had been quite modest over the span of the preceding four hundred years. But in a flash, only a couple of generations after the end of the American Revolution, the technology of firepower would change drastically, as flintlock musket and smoothbore, muzzle-loading artillery would be replaced by radically different weapons. The armies of the West would have to adapt, and in a big way.

War itself did not bring about this sea change in weapons technology. Instead, it was an upheaval in the European economy, a shift that favored and rewarded innovation, that would change the tools and art of war forever.

CHAPTER 5

THE MILITARY REVOLUTION

War in 1800 looked nothing like war in 1400. There was, literally, no resemblance at all, not a tendril to connect them. In 1800, the European states, great and small, had standing armies of uniformed, professional soldiers, organized into permanent military units, numbering in the hundreds of thousands. Their commanders had all (or mostly all) gone down one avenue or another of formal military training, and many of them took their professions quite seriously. Their cavalry, infantry, and artillery all used weapons of standardized patterns; serving their needs was a vast and growing support network of auxiliary personnel: staff officers, quartermasters, commissaries, paymasters, ordnance officers, and artificers. The men were paid regularly, usually monthly, and trained daily, in accordance with the regimen and tactics laid out in regulation drill manuals and standard operating procedures, procedures that governed nearly every aspect of a soldier's daily life.

Many of those states also had navies, large, complex, growing institutions, highly professionalized, with even more expansive bureaucracies than those of the land forces. Navies entailed a grand investment in, and commitment to, those physical facilities without which a fleet could not survive for very long. As with the growth and increasing centralization of land forces, navies represented not only a vast expansion in military might under the purview of the state but also a great, onerous, even crushing burden in expense.

In 1400, none of these things existed. Armies were raised ad hoc when needed, and only when needed. There was no uniformity of dress, equipment, weapons, or even tactics. Even tactical units themselves were transient, assembled on the field of battle, and did not exist outside of that realm. There was no permanent and hierarchical command structure in place, and certainly no auxiliary or support systems to aid in the daily functioning of an army in garrison or on campaign. None of these things existed, because armies as we understand them did not exist. Firearms, on the contrary, did exist, but not in sufficient numbers to matter, and they were still in the nebulous zone between dangerous novelty and useful tool. Navies did not exist either, and indeed the notion of wedding gunpowder artillery to sailing ships was still far off in the future.

Between 1400 and 1800, the European states—and the United States—had developed and nurtured recognizably modern military establishments. Those establishments were predicated on the conviction that a sovereign state had to be ready to go to war at all times, and were to be paid for with the confiscated wealth of its subjects—taxes, in other words. That belief was not pervasive in 1400s Europe, nor was taxation a regular source of state income. But soon these things would come to pass, and that had everything to do with the rise of modern military institutions.

The impact of the technological revolution that started with the introduction of gunpowder weaponry in medieval Europe was broad and deep. Gunpowder firearms drastically transformed military architecture and the art of the siege. Gunpowder was the main precondition of the rise of the ship-killing ship, and therefore the creation of the first state navies; it took a preexisting development, the rise of infantry, and accelerated it, until the tactics of land warfare revolved exclusively around the organized and coordinated use of firearms. But that technological revolution also lay behind some of the most profound developments in the history of the West.

IN 1953, AN English-born historian named Michael Roberts delivered his inaugural lecture at Queen's University Belfast.

Roberts was known primarily for his works on Swedish history, and especially a massively researched biography of the warrior-king Gustavus Adolphus. In his work on early modern Sweden, Professor Roberts couldn't help but notice the intimate connections between the growing sophistication of military institutions and practices, the greater frequency of warfare, the size of military establishments, and the burgeoning of state power in Sweden. And Sweden, he noticed, fit into a general European pattern, one that earlier German historians had been pointing out for a while: that war and state development were inextricably linked, that the conduct of war and preparation for war prompted the expansion of political authority—that war, in short, created the modern state.

So when Roberts delivered his lecture at Belfast, he chose this broader topic as his focus, and he called it "The Military Revolution." It was a history of European warfare and state development painted with a very broad brush. Like any set of complex ideas illustrated at this level, it wasn't perfect; some strokes of the brush were too broad, some misplaced, some that ought to have been there missing entirely, but taken as a whole the portrait Roberts painted was a brilliant one. New weapons and new tactics, mostly centered on the rise of infantry and the introduction of firearms, brought into being a way of war that was bigger, more complex, and more expensive than warfare had been earlier in the Middle Ages. Armies and navies grew larger, navies emerging ex nihilo, and the pace of expansion and change accelerated as an arms-race mentality, fueled by religious differences and emerging dynastic rivalries, spread across the Continent. The new kind of warfare reduced the power of the nobility, transforming it from the class of elite, independent warriors it had once been into a class that mostly served the state, to the benefit of the central governments of Europe's dynastic states.

But those same states, well into the sixteenth century, still operated with simple, modest bureaucracies and infrastructures. Such bare-bones administrations had been perfectly adequate to handle the tasks that medieval monarchies were called upon to perform, such as the occasional collection of taxes, but they were unequal to the burdens imposed by war and military institutions. Ultimately, from the strivings of the state to mobilize resources for war and to command military forces at war, and from the predictable struggles that came with political transformation, the modern state—strong, its authority exuding from a single government, its continued existence sustained by the lifeblood of taxation—emerged from the growing pains of the "military revolution."

As historical theories go, Roberts's idea was a hit. It still is. It explains so much, above all the origins of modern states; it ties the history of warfare to social, political, and economic history, demonstrating the relevance of military history to an academic establishment skeptical of the value of studying war. The military revolution immediately attracted adherents within that same establishment. Few historical theories have found such widespread acceptance, and in multiple fields. The concept of RMAs (revolutions in military affairs), rooted in Roberts's original thesis, has permeated the modern disciplines of security studies and geopolitics.

There have been detractors, too, and a healthy and vigorous debate over Roberts's thesis. Some critics have pointed out that Roberts based his observations largely on the experience of northern, predominately Protestant, Europe, and that he overlooked the somewhat different experience of war and politics in southern, Catholic Europe, especially Spain. Others have insisted that while there were definitely revolutions in war and politics, the truly big developments—in the size and complexity of military institutions and the governments that built them—came later, in the eighteenth century. Medievalists, justifiably aggrieved when nonmedievalists make sweeping and inaccurate generalizations about their time period, have taken Roberts to task for overstating the primitive nature of medieval bureaucracies and armies, and found medieval antecedents for developments that Roberts claimed for a later era. More recently, the Roberts argument has been at the heart of a debate between historians of Europe and those of the larger world. The military revolution, it's been claimed, was the basis of Western supremacy in the use and projection of force—an argument that historians of Asia and the Middle East have pointedly refuted, proving through their research that China, India, Korea, and the Ottoman Empire had military revolutions of their own.

Valid points, every one of them. But none detracts from the validity of Michael Roberts's main idea: that, at the end of the Middle Ages, changes in the conduct of war helped to bring about a sweeping political and social transformation in Europe, that many if not most of the salient characteristics of the modern state can be traced directly to military factors, and that the emerging dynastic states were entities geared first and foremost toward war making.

This is not to say that the gunpowder revolution was the *cause* of the military revolution, and therefore the root factor in the rise of the centralized state. That would be technological determinism, the idea that technology drives the development of every other aspect of society, politics, and culture. Nor can we argue that gunpowder was the thing that gave the states of the West a power advantage over all other civilizations around the globe, for clearly other cultures and other states—Ottoman, Chinese, and Indian—exploited gunpowder technology as thoroughly as Europe did. But we can, and should, acknowledge that those technological advances did indeed help to effect the transition of the European states into the modern age.

With those caveats in mind, how then did new weaponry at the dawn of the modern age help to create the modern state?

THE AREAS OF the greatest change in land warfare during this time of transition were, first, the shift from cavalry-based to infantry-based armies, and, second, the evolution of the European fighting man from warrior to soldier, the latter understood to be a member of an organized tactical unit, training to fight as part of a team and not so much as an individual. The introduction of black-powder firearms did not cause either of these developments. Infantry was already supplanting feudal heavy cavalry, and the shift toward infantry was already well underway when the first handheld firearms began to trickle into European combat.

More sophisticated tactical organization also predated firearms. To function correctly—to assemble in formation, to move about on the battlefield, to launch an assault or hold fast against an enemy attack—the Swiss-style pike block required a set of standardized procedures, and therefore, de facto, drill of some sort, even if not actually codified into written procedure. Such formations also required an internal command hierarchy of some sort—officers and noncommissioned officers (NCOs), in other words. Coordinated movement is simply not possible without a critical mass of officers and subordinates, and the larger the unit, the larger the requisite command structure.

When firearms entered the scene in force, early in the sixteenth century, the need for organization, professionalism, and hierarchical structure grew. Volley fire and its intended product, fire discipline, were simply out of reach without the fulfillment of these basic requirements. Within a few decades, the norm for infantry organization in Europe was the tercio or something very much like it: tactical units that combined both firepower and shock, musket (or arquebus) and pike, into a single group. That combination demanded coordination on a level not imagined necessary before. Forming a tercio for battle involved moving the individual sub-units, separate companies of pike and musket, out of marching column and into the tercio battle formation, a complicated process that would have been impossible without an adequate number of experienced officers and NCOs. Successive tactical systems after the tercio—Dutch and Swedish infantry tactics, improved tercio formations in the early 1600s, and then the linear tactics of late seventeenth- and eighteenth-century armies—required these same things, only more, plus a greater degree of professionalism on the part of the commanders, and an ability of the enlisted men to function together as a well-oiled machine. That ability came only from intensive training via the constant application of drill. Infantry tactics—and artillery and cavalry tactics, too—in the eighteenth-century Age of Reason were more orderly, efficient, and flexible *only* because organization, professionalism, and training made them so. And those were attributes that only a permanent military establishment, a standing army, could achieve; half-trained levies, no matter how motivated, simply could not. For a European state in the late 1600s and 1700s, that meant keeping an army on a wartime footing at all times, even when it wasn't immediately needed, and *that*, in turn, meant a big financial commitment and a permanent budget.

That financial commitment would, in turn, mushroom as time went on. First of all, there was the matter of scale involved in the tactics of land warfare, especially with infantry. The weapons of medieval combat were, mostly, the weapons of individual combat, meaning that their use could be taught and learned individually, and they were weapons intended for one-on-one fighting. The weapons of the new infantry formations were not. An eighteen-foot-long pike, no matter how deftly wielded, is too awkward for single combat. Muskets, similarly, were more effective when employed in large numbers, and when used in a coordinated way. The tools of the new infantry, then, necessitated that they be used in larger tactical units, and not by lone individuals or in very small groups.

The arithmetic of gunpowder infantry, the numerical requirements of the new weaponry, drove the increase in size of armies. This was the universal trend in Europe at the time. But an even weightier influence was the arms race mentality that permeated European international politics after 1500. The destruction of a united Christendom, the legacy of the Protestant Reformation, heightened international tensions after 1550, resulting in something like a state of constant war. The religious divisions between and among the states, great and small, made it even more difficult to resolve international disputes peacefully. And when the European states stepped back from the edge of the abyss after 1650, intentionally if only tacitly rejecting religious differences as a reason to go to war, competition over empire quickly took religion's place. Army size grew steadily as a result, in some cases with a tenfold increase between 1500 and 1700. Spain's collective military manpower in 1500 probably numbered little more than twenty thousand men; in the midst of the Thirty Years' War, it was close to three hundred thousand. There were likely fifty thousand men in France's armies at the close of the wars in Italy in the 1550s, but during the reign of Louis XIV, a century and a half later, that number reached nearly half a million.

The revolution in other forms of warfare, at sea and at the siege, carried similar implications. The new artillery fortresses of the sixteenth century were expensive to build, but soon governments perceived that they were vital for guarding frontiers and strategic points, and so modern forts went up in their hundreds. Construction wasn't the only expense, for regular maintenance was necessary to keep fortresses from falling victim to wind and rain. Much the same could be said of navies, but on a much larger scale. To keep a navy was to commit to an unrelenting fiscal burden. Ships required constant maintenance, just like forts. While they could be put up "in ordinary," something close to the twentieth-century practice of mothballing, ships could not just be neglected when not in use. They had to be crewed, too, and constantly. Navies had to be permanent, standing institutions. And by the end of the 1500s it had become clear that ad hoc solutions—like relying on armed merchant vessels—just did not work very well. Purpose-built warships were invariably superior.

BESIDES THE OBVIOUS implications for the nature of combat, on land and at sea, the growth of armies and navies also reset the balance of political power and social prestige within European society. The old nobility, born from the unique political conditions of the European Middle Ages, was losing ground as a result of the Military Revolution. Prior to the fourteenth century, the nobility's collective prestige, power, and privilege stemmed from its traditional role as the warrior class; nobles trained for war as individual warriors, and it was this warrior class that formed the backbone of medieval military forces. As armies began to depend more and more on foot troops, recruited from the commoner classes, and cavalry fell back to a supporting role, the nobility lost much of the justification for its ancient claims to privilege. Instead, military service became a career option for young noblemen, and not an identity that was their birthright by virtue of their bloodlines. They still enjoyed preeminence in military leadership, and they came to dominate the officer corps of most European armies. They were no longer independent warriors but were transformed into a service nobility, dependent on the largesse of the state for their livelihood and status. The revolutions in military and naval architecture amplified this trend. The obsolescence of the castle robbed the European nobility of their power bases in the countryside. Navies, which depended from the very beginning on a narrow kind of technical expertise, drew much of their leadership from the ranks of the unprivileged. Ship's captains were rarely noblemen, for noble families as a rule did not gravitate toward maritime trades. Navies opened up a world of opportunities for the humbly-born to advance socially.

But the broader impact of the Military Revolution, and therefore of the sea change in military technology, was felt in the treasury. The thread linking all the technological changes together was cost. Medieval states did not have to have very sophisticated budgets, nor—since extensive interstate conflicts were uncommon in the Middle Ages—did they have to worry overmuch about the funding of wars. But the sudden expansion of armies and navies after 1500 changed that. The typical European state of the sixteenth and seventeenth centuries carried administrative and fiscal burdens that had not been common in centuries prior, and which it was not equipped to manage. The "defense budget," to use a hopelessly anachronistic concept, was all but nonexistent in the Middle Ages, but with the Military Revolution it became the single biggest chunk of state expenditures, claiming the lion's share of state revenues.

And preparing for war was not just a matter of paying troops and buying war materiel, but of allocating all sorts of resources:

iron, grain, the elements of gunpowder, leather, horses, oxen, dry fodder, cloth—in short, *everything* an army or navy needed. This was an especially pressing problem with navies, for they consumed vast amounts of material resources, many of them highly specialized and not always conveniently available. Masts required tall, straight pines, the kind that grew in abundance in the Scandinavian Peninsula and in the forests of the Baltic rim, and in North America. Framing timbers and hull planking required good, stout oak, sometimes deliberately misshapen so that key components could be milled from a single piece of wood. That kind of attention to resource allocation demanded not only ready cash, but also infrastructure, and lots of it. Naval bureaucracies mushroomed in size during the seventeenth century, almost to the point of being absurdly convoluted, and there was a good reason for this.

The costs of war, the costs of preparing for war, and therefore the regular annual costs of maintaining the state itself all exploded in the sixteenth and seventeenth centuries. And the European way of war became overall much more sophisticated during this time. Yet the European way of governance did not keep pace. The technology of war and the art of war moved ahead of the state's ability to pay for war; military establishments were growing, not shrinking, and armed conflict on the Continent was increasing in frequency, not decreasing. Without having developed mechanisms for raising cash and mobilizing strategic resources, European monarchs and their power elites were in something of a bind. States fought wars on credit, borrowing vast sums of money from the great European banking families, and usually at interest rates that would seem terrifying today. Of course, loans have to be paid back, and because there were so few breathing spaces between wars this was a difficult prospect. For a state like Spain, Europe's greatest power during the sixteenth and much of the seventeenth centuries, payback was sometimes entirely out of the question. Even though Spain had an enviably steady income stream accruing from its silver mines in the Americas, its war-related costs were so crushing that the crown more than once mortgaged future silver shipments in order to secure loans. Another alternative was to declare state bankruptcy, default on loans, and then begin again with a fresh batch of borrowed money. During the reign of Philip II alone (1557–1598), the Spanish crown did this no fewer than five times.

An army could save the state a great deal of money and trouble by supporting its own existence. Until the middle of the seventeenth century, most armies were recruited not by the state, but by military enterprisers, private venture capitalists who raised armies for hire. Thus the state was initially insulated against the start-up costs of mobilization: recruitment, clothing, equipment, weapons, provisions, shelter, and pay, the latter including—sometimes— enlistment bonuses to entice men into service. The military enterpriser took care of those costs, receiving his own compensation in a lump sum from the government that hired his services. The system had its advantages, but from the hiring state's perspective it was costly and inefficient. Army costs while on campaign could also be defrayed. During the Thirty Years' War, many commanders engaged in what would become known as the "contribution system." Armies would live off the land in an organized way, promising not to pillage towns in return for regular payments in kind—whether that was beer, food, or cash. The contribution system was, in essence, a racket, a form of highly systematized extortion. At best, it kept armies fed and civilians safe from the worst excesses of plundering at the hands of a rapacious soldiery.

The contribution system was not an effective long-term solution. Absent any other kind of friction—like crop failures, for example—armies quickly bled entire provinces dry in a matter of weeks, for few areas of Europe were sufficiently fecund to support campaigning armies for more than a very short span of time. Still, the notion—which Gustavus Adolphus immortalized with the pithy phrase "*bellum se ipsum alet*" (war feeds itself)—persisted until the middle of the 1600s. After the massive destruction of the Thirty Years' War, though, the European states began to reconsider how best to supply their armies in the field.

When it came to finance, though, in the end the solution was clear and decisive: taxes. Taxation increasingly came to be the lifeblood of the state, the means of supporting the state at war and in all its other endeavors. Regular, routine taxation had not been a hallmark of European life in the Middle Ages, and taxes were mostly levied when a rare emergency—like war—rendered the ordinary income of the crown, or the kingdom, inadequate. Tradition and law enjoined monarchs to "live of their own"—that is, from the proceeds of the lands they owned, plus sometimes additional lesser sources such as tariffs and import-export duties. But these were not enough to maintain military forces for any length of time. During the Thirty Years' War, participant states (and those that chose to remain out of the conflict but prepared for war anyway) resorted increasingly to tax levies to meet their financial obligations. Because this was a novelty, and an unpleasant one at that, taxation met with fierce resistance just about everywhere, from the towns as well as the peasantry, and often with outright insurrection.

Taxation wasn't the only focus of domestic strife brought on by the drastically increasing costs of war. The relationship between central governments, as represented by their monarchs, and their noble power-elites became strained, violently so, in the first half of the seventeenth century. Kings wanted the power to tax, to make war and peace, and to make policy without having to consult with their nobilities; noble elites wanted to keep royal power in check when it came to state finances and taxation. War and its costs were the main factors behind constitutional fractures in nearly every state in Europe: between Cardinal Richelieu and the French nobility; between Cardinal Mazarin and the French nobility, culminating in the prolonged rebellion known as the Fronde (1648–1653); between Charles I and his Parliament, leading up to the English Civil Wars; between Christian IV of Denmark and his aristocratic Council of State during the Thirty Years' War.

In England, of course, that struggle for political supremacy ultimately ended in favor of Parliament and the advocates of limited monarchy, to the detriment and diminishment of the king. But elsewhere in Europe the clash between monarchs and nobilities usually concluded differently—with the triumph of monarchy, and the gradual creation of a political system that we've come to know—rightly or wrongly—as "absolutism." Even where absolute monarchy did not take root—as in England—the constitutional impact of the military revolution was essentially the same: not representative government, not anything even vaguely resembling parliamentary democracy, but the creation of a strong, centralized, bureaucratic state.

THAT TRANSFORMATION—FROM DECENTRALIZED medieval kingdoms to centralized bureaucratic states—was perhaps the most enduring legacy of the military revolution. German historian Otto Hintze called this new species of polity "the sovereign power-state," which existed solely for the purpose of making war. Every policy, every tax, every branch of the bureaucracy, and nearly every penny it spent—everything—was ultimately bent toward the wielding of organized violence. Hintze, no doubt, overstated his case. Like Roberts, he ascribed too much influence to changes in tactics, to the size of military establishments, to the evolution of military technology. We know now that, in creating the modern bureaucratic state, there were many other factors at work, ranging from religious identity to international commerce to political culture. But warfare stands out above all the others, and the transformation that it wrought in the sovereign states of Europe went far beyond a reordering of taxation and bureaucracy. It fundamentally altered the nature and scope of governmental power. Effective taxation required something that previous European governments simply did not have: extensive, detailed information about their populations. To tax—or to conscript—meant that the state needed to know who its subjects were, where they lived, what religion they practiced, how much they owned, what they did for a living, how many people their households supported. The authority of the state, in short, had become intrusive in a way that was utterly unprecedented, its relentless probing eye now peering in on the private details of its subjects' lives. The juggernaut of the modern bureaucratic state—invasive, not recognizing limits on its authority—was born from the omnipresence of war, and indirectly from the revolution in military technology that contributed to it.

Some components of this new arrangement, of sovereign states ruled by powerful monarchs and vast bureaucracies, would be swept away in the eighteenth and nineteenth centuries. The twin Atlantic revolutions, American and French, would eventually overturn the old order of society, undermine the legitimacy of the nobility, and make the idea of popular sovereignty the new norm in Western politics. But the prominence of war, the permanence of military institutions, and the costs of military technology would not go away. If anything, over the course of the nineteenth century, those trends would accelerate, propelled by a revolution in the very nature of technology itself.

Book II

THE AGE OF
REVOLUTIONS, 1800–1870

CHAPTER 6

WAR AND TECHNOLOGY IN THE AGE OF REVOLUTIONS

On 20 September 1792, French and Prussian armies clashed in the pouring rain near the village of Valmy, some 120 miles east of Paris. Only three years had passed since the French revolutionary experiment in popular government had begun, and already it was in danger of being extinguished by a foreign invasion. French armies, chaotic and inexpertly led, had suffered a string of disappointments, and the force facing the Prussian invaders that September was dejected, its strength and morale sapped by defeat, dysentery, wet weather, and too much pointless marching. But at Valmy that day, the French army not only held its own but triumphed. Under the command of the Revolution's first two soldier-heroes, Charles Dumouriez and François Kellermann, that army—an unconventional mix of inexperienced volunteers and white-coated soldiers from the old royal army—pummeled the Prussians with artillery fire, silencing the enemy guns. Then, with General Kellermann leading them on, they charged at the Prussians with the bayonet, the inspiring words of "La Marseillaise" ringing in their throats as they drove the hated invaders from the field.

News of the victory at Valmy hit Paris like a lightning bolt. The French had triumphed over the Prussian army, once the most feared fighting force in Europe. True, it wasn't *that* big a victory;

casualties were comparatively light on both sides, and the enemy was able to retreat unmolested. But the proud legions of the Hohenzollern kings limped back toward the Germanies in humiliation, and Paris had been saved. The animating spirit of the Revolution soared in Paris, and the National Convention—the brand-new, popularly elected legislature of the radical Jacobin government—boldly marked the occasion by proclaiming the death of the ancient monarchy and the birth of the French Republic. Valmy was, if only symbolically, the birth of a nation.

It was also the birth of a new kind of war—or, more precisely, of a new kind of army. Most European armies of the period, like the Prussians at Valmy, were made up of long-serving professional soldiers, often foreign-born, who had volunteered for service—not usually from a sense of duty to king or nation, but because soldiering offered a secure living, a modicum of adventure, and perhaps escape from unpleasant circumstances at home. When France went to war in 1792, it drew on another source of recruits: men motivated by patriotism and love for the Revolution, whose enthusiasm partially compensated for their lack of training. But there were not enough of these eager "Volunteers of '92" to meet France's manpower requirements, and so a few months after Valmy, the newborn French Republic resorted to a desperate and unpopular measure: conscription.

The concept of compulsory military service was not new when the Jacobin government introduced it in France in 1793. Sweden, cash-strapped and surrounded by enemies, had built its military might on the draft, and Prussia supplemented its recruited regiments with conscripts. But the *Levée en Masse*, the military draft instituted by the Jacobins, went further than any of its antecedents. "Henceforth, until the enemy has been driven from the territory of the Republic," it proclaimed, "the French people are in permanent requisition for army service. The young men shall go to battle; the married men shall forge arms and transport provisions; the women shall make tents and clothes . . . the children shall turn old linen into lint; the old men shall go to the public places to . . . preach the unity of the Republic and the hatred of kings."

The language was high-flown but the meaning was clear: in a free commonwealth, such as the French Republic purported to be, the inhabitants were citizens, not subjects. As citizens, they were guaranteed basic rights, a kind of equality before the law, and a voice in their destiny. But the price of those freedoms was eternal vigilance and—more important—a blood-debt owed to the Republic, payable on demand. The concept, however imperfectly executed, radically and permanently altered the underlying relationship between government and governed, the foundational meaning of the nation. The *Levée en Masse* introduced what we have come to know as total war, a condition in which a nation's entire population, its last ounce of material resources and energy, are bent toward the needs of the state at war.

In a purely military sense, the universal service obligation would have profound and immediate repercussions. Armies of the eighteenth century and before had filled their ranks with men who could best be described as dispensable: men who either contributed nothing of value to society or were actually a burden upon it, such as the landless younger sons of peasant families or day laborers without families or the "undeserving" poor or chronic debtors or men hoping to outrun the law. But drawing on the entirety of the adult male population opened up a much larger pool of available manpower. In February 1793, the French army numbered some 360,000 men in service, a respectable, typical number for an army of that time; one and a half years later, the ranks had swelled to some 1.1 million men under arms—by far, the largest army ever seen in Europe.

But numbers weren't everything, and a huge army wasn't necessarily a superior one. Conscripts were notoriously unwilling to serve. Desertion rates among conscripted troops were high, and in some areas—most famously the Vendée region on the Atlantic coast—reluctance turned to resistance and then escalated quickly into violent counterrevolution. That, in turn, demanded a forceful response from the authorities in Paris, meaning that combat troops had to be diverted from elsewhere so that they could punish counterrevolutionaries and enforce the draft.

Even if conscription had been a popular measure, there would always be a plethora of physical constraints. There was no way to train such huge numbers of raw soldiers with any alacrity, and the Republic's ability to clothe, arm, and feed its massive citizen armies could not possibly keep up with its ability to mobilize manpower. Entire battalions of half-trained, half-armed, indifferently clothed troops would be sent haplessly into battle against armies of much better equipped troops. Casualty rates were predictably frightful.

Still, the ideal of the nation in arms was here to stay. It helped to make possible the stunning, improbable victories achieved by French forces during the Revolutionary wars of the 1790s; it allowed Napoléon Bonaparte to amass the vast legions with which he conquered most of continental Europe before 1810; it allowed France to take on the Western world almost single-handedly, and win. Yet the nation in arms was more than a method of managing and regimenting human resources for state service. It was also a manifestation of something else, a cultural and political phenomenon that was just now taking root in France and would soon permeate the entire Western world: the concept of nationalism.

FEW EVENTS IN the history of the West have done so much to shape the nature of war and warfare as the French Revolution. The wars that flowed from that revolution, and those fought by Bonaparte in its name, recoded the software of war. The social makeup of armed forces, the size and complexity of military establishments on land and at sea—these things were markedly different after 1815 and the end of the Napoleonic era. Even the aims and purposes of war had shifted, and not subtly. Most eighteenth-century wars had been fought over the conflicting interests of rival dynasties or clashing imperial ambitions. Revolutionary France fought not only to protect itself and its new and fragile experiment in governance against foreign invaders—and for territorial gain, too—but also to spread an ideology. Its opponents fought just as hard to contain and destroy that ideology. Though overweening personal ambition lay behind Napoléon's hunger for conquest, his legions still carried revolutionary notions—equality before the law, for example, or universal manhood suffrage—with them into Austria, the German states, Italy, the Low Countries, and Iberia, forcing them on conquered populations at bayonet point.

Those same legions brought nationalistic fervor with them, a fervor awakened and nurtured by the Revolution. With no small trace of irony, French revolutionary nationalism awakened counternationalisms, as France's enemies sought to tap into the latent nationalistic passions of their own populations as a means of fighting back against their invaders. In staid, conservative Prussia, that meant social, political, and military reforms that gave newfound power—and newfound opportunity—to subjects outside the noble elite.

But nationalism was frightening. It was—as it is today—as irrational, unpredictable, uncontrollable, and potentially destructive as it was inspiring and creative. Nationalism was, and is, reductionist, eschewing nuance in favor of broad generalizations based on stereotypes and age-old prejudices. Nationalism was, and is, a passion, after all, and hence not a reasonable or rational way of looking at the world, for in trumpeting the unique virtues of the People it also devalues those outside the national group. In more practical terms, nationalism toppled legitimate political regimes, inflamed popular passions, and caused wars. Recoiling at the bloody chaos caused by the Jacobins in their Reign of Terror, repulsed by the sheer destruction that followed in the wake of Revolutionary and Napoleonic armies, after 1815 the European kingdoms did their best to turn the clock back to 1789 and restore what they could of the Old Regime.

For a while, the architects of the new old Europe succeeded. They restored pre-Revolutionary dynasties, such as the Bourbon in France, to their rightful places; disassembled the constellation of satellite states built up by Napoléon over the years; and from 1819 to 1848 crushed dozens of insurrections across the length and breadth of the continent—insurrections inspired by the twin political forces of the new century: nationalism and the new ideology of individual liberty, liberalism. But those new forces proved to be unstoppable, the old order not wholly restorable. By 1848, the Year of Revolutions, liberalism and nationalism were beginning to make a significant impact on political life in Europe: liberalism in the development of constitutional monarchies in, for example, Britain and Denmark, and the dissolution of monarchy in France; nationalism in the resurgence of France under Louis Napoléon, and the growing power of national unification movements in Germany and Italy.

So, too, with the institutions of war. The reactionary regimes of post-1815 Europe sought to take warfare back to eighteenth-century norms, with small armies of long-serving professionals replacing the massive conscript armies of the Revolutionary age. The motivating concern was as much fiscal as it was ideological. Small armies were cheaper and easier to maintain. But the cat was out of the bag, so to speak, and the concept of the nation in arms would not go away willingly. The midcentury would witness a tentative return to conscription and citizen armies in the American Civil War and in the German wars of unification, and then universally throughout the West by the end of the century.

And that was indeed the greatest change in the art and conduct of war to emerge from the Revolutionary and Napoleonic era: the scale of war. Field armies were larger, on average, after 1792, and consequently battles were bigger. Napoleonic battles could be massive affairs. At Borodino (7 September 1812), the single bloodiest day of fighting in the Napoleonic wars, Russian and French forces totaled some three hundred thousand men. Opposing French and Allied armies at Leipzig—the "Battle of Nations," 16–19 October 1813—numbered well over half a million.

The increased size of battle presented generals with a whole host of challenges. Everything scaled up as a result, and simple tasks were rendered complicated. More soldiers meant more provisions, more ammunition, more uniforms, more shoes, more weapons, more medical supplies, more horses and fodder and tack—more of all the materiel required by an army on campaign. Even before the notable growth in army size, few regions in Europe could boast the agricultural productivity necessary to sustain a smaller army for more than a few days, and only at certain times of the year. An army of one hundred thousand or more combat troops, plus camp followers and assorted noncombatants, simply couldn't be kept alive on local resources. Efficient logistical arrangements were more vital than ever before, and transportation became a thornier issue.

When armies formed up for battle, their greater size meant that they took up more room. The environment of land battle—the *battlescape* for lack of a more precise term—expanded accordingly. Battlefield communications became exponentially more problematic as armies, and therefore formations, swelled in size. The flow of information between a commanding general and his immediate subordinates, between those subordinates and individual units, or between reconnaissance troops and the main body of an army, was only as fast and secure as an expendable young lieutenant on a horse, carrying handwritten dispatches from point to point. Such a link was easily severed, disrupted, or delayed, and the information it conveyed frequently misconstrued. That was difficult enough to pull off with an army of forty thousand men and a battlefront half a mile wide. With an army of two hundred thousand, a front that might stretch for several miles, and reserve units in the rear adding depth to an army's formation, the seemingly simple task of communicating orders or relaying on-the-spot intelligence became impossible in the swirling chaos of battle. The complexities of battlefield communications would bedevil armies and limit their actions until the introduction of field telephones and wireless radio in the twentieth century.

There were ways of coping with the challenges of communications, movement, and logistics for larger armies. One solution, first used in the eighteenth century, was the employment of tactical divisions or corps, advocated by the French military theo-rists Jacques-Antoine-Hippolyte, Comte de Guibert and Pierre de Bourcet late in the eighteenth century. Both Guibert and Bourcet advocated dividing large field armies into several roughly equal sub-units, which would move on the commanding general's intended target along a broad front, following parallel routes. Each of the subunits was, on its own, far less cumbersome than a single large body, and less likely to get bogged down by the kind of mundane mishaps that could block a road or disrupt a march. The subunits would be far enough apart so that the enemy would be left guessing as to the army's true and specific intention, and therefore unable to react decisively until the last moment, when the subunits coalesced on their chosen target. But the subunits would also be close enough together, maybe a couple hours' march distant, so that if any one of them encountered the enemy the other subunits could rush to its aid. Napoléon's reliance upon such tactical divisions was a hall-mark of his generalship on campaign.

But in other ways, warfare in the Revolutionary era, and af-ter, was more distinguished by continuity than change. There were changes in battlefield tactics, to be sure. Napoleonic armies, for example, made heavier and more aggressive use of field artillery, as with the so-called artillery charge: highly mobile field batter-ies would be thrown far forward to engage enemy troops, beyond range of the enemy's muskets but comfortably within close range for the cannon. Unless the enemy parried with counterbattery fire, the artillery could pound the enemy with impunity and bru-tal effectiveness. If threatened or hard-pressed, the guns could be limbered quickly and withdrawn to safety. Heavy battle cavalry—wearing breastplates, helmets, and depending on sabers as their primary weapon, as Napoléon's cuirassiers did—enjoyed some-thing of a rebirth in the French wars, and they figured prominently in Napoleonic battles. All armies of the period made heavy use of light infantry, fighting in open order as skirmishers rather than in closed ranks.

None of these features could be considered an innovation. Light infantry fighting in open order was a development of the Seven Years' War and the American Revolution; heavy battle cavalry had once been a common feature of European armies that had only recently fallen into disuse. The tactics of Revolutionary warfare were not revolutionary. They were the logical developments of trends that had been in place for a half-century or more. Much the same could be said of fortifications, siegecraft, and war at sea: nothing new here. Fleets still clashed in line-of-battle formations; smaller craft, like frigates, still conducted long-range patrols and occasionally fought one-on-one duels, using tactics that would have been comfortably familiar a century before. Ships had grown in dimensions and firepower, even in the surface area of sail, but not in purpose or use or overall design. From a tactical perspective, Napoleonic warfare was eighteenth-century warfare writ large, slightly bloodier, and with different uniforms. There was nothing to be seen at Waterloo that would have stood out as being remarkable to a soldier from 1750 except the size of the armies engaged.

Why, then, wasn't there a revolution in tactics? The answer, in large part, must be found in technology—or, more properly, in the stagnancy of technology. The infantryman's weapon, in 1815 as in 1756 as in 1709, was a smoothbore, muzzle-loading, flintlock musket, firing a soft lead ball of roughly .70-inch caliber, mounting a triangular bayonet. Cavalry relied on the same weapons as in the previous century: smoothbore, muzzle-loading flintlock carbines and pistols, sabre, and lance. Artillery pieces were virtually the same in weight, caliber, and construction as they had been for decades. In just about every way that mattered, the hardware of Napoleonic warfare was functionally identical to the hardware of battle in the age of the Sun King.

Yet within the space of another generation after 1815, the battlefield would become a different place, and that had everything to do with technology. After a century without significant improvement in the tools of war, and three full centuries with only minor tweaks, Europe and the West would witness in the nineteenth century a giant leap forward in the complexity and efficiency of military technology: in the killing power of weapons, certainly, but also in supply, transport, and communications. This technological revolution, unlike the gunpowder revolution that preceded it, was not the product of a single innovation. Instead, it came about because for the first time in the history of the Western world, the producers and consumers of military hardware—manufacturers, entrepreneurs, inventors, and engineers in the first group, armies and navies in the second—worked closely and continuously together to improve military technology, and to adapt innovations from civilian life to military purposes. This partnership between the private sector and the state, between the making of weapons and the institutions that used them, came about entirely because of the most earth-shattering event in the history of the Western economy: the Industrial Revolution.

THE INDUSTRIAL REVOLUTION wasn't so much an event as it was a development, one that had neither a discrete, discernable beginning nor a definite ending. As early as the mid-1700s, the first stirrings of the new factory-based economy were visible in Britain, where conditions were just right for industry: abundant raw materials and sources of energy, navigable interior waterways, and a large pool of displaced rural labor, made possible by dramatic (and ruthlessly executed) improvements in the efficiency of farming. More important, Britain's emerging middle class had a mindset that was perfectly suited to entrepreneurship: ambitious, acquisitive, competitive, and open to technological solutions that increased efficiency and therefore profits.

Not all of the West benefited immediately from industrialization, at least not at once, and the factory economy spread unevenly and sporadically. Britain's reign as the industrial powerhouse of Europe, and indeed the world, went unchallenged until the middle of the 1800s, when France emerged as a major competitor. By the end of the century, two relatively new states—Imperial Germany and the United States—had surpassed Britain in most areas of heavy manufacturing. Other great powers, soon to be *formerly* great powers, fell behind. Russia would not become an industrial giant until Joseph Stalin forced it to, at incalculable human cost, between the world wars. Austria (and Austria-Hungary), Italy, and Spain would never even come close to becoming industrial powers.

The impact of industrialization was enormous, and in every conceivable way. The French Revolution had begun the inexorable process of tearing down the old social order and the dominance of the nobility; the Industrial Revolution replaced it with a new dominant class, the bourgeoisie, which gradually came to take the lead in Western economic and political life. Industrialization changed where and how the laboring classes lived and worked, not usually for the better; it created cities where there had been none before, and swelled older cities to the point of bursting. Industrialization rebuilt the structure of the family, the collective experience of time and life, work and leisure, and rewove the social fabric.

The influence of the factory on warfare was just as profound and enduring. Its impact was visible on the world stage: it reordered the global balance of power. Soon, the factory system gave to Europe and the United States a decisive technological advantage over the rest of the world, in terms of sheer might and the ability to project that might. Prior to the industrial age, Western civilization could claim no great technological superiority, including and especially in weaponry, over China, or Japan, or Korea, or the Indian subcontinent. Industrialization upset that parity. By 1900, perhaps even as early as 1850, European weapons were far deadlier and European transport and communications were much faster. Most important, the West's productive capacity to manufacture these technologies had rapidly outstripped the collective productive capacity of Asia or Africa. In short, the West could now produce better weapons, in greater quantities, and deploy them more effectively, than any other part of the world.

Certainly, the imperial powers of the West—after 1870, that meant nearly every nation, great and small—would take advantage of that superiority. That the great wave of Western imperialism began in earnest in the mid-nineteenth century is no accident: it was a direct consequence of that technological and productive edge. And though there were many motives at play in Europe's fevered grasp for empire in the half-century before the First World War, industrialization itself was a motive. Industry was dependent on a range of raw materials that could only be found, or were best found, in Asia or Africa: gutta-percha, rubber, and soon, very soon, petroleum. Industry made large-scale imperialism work, but industry also required imperialism.

The global legacy of the Industrial Revolution, then, was nothing less than Western supremacy in the world—not a permanent state of affairs, by any means, but one that would last well into the twentieth century. The local implications of that revolution, the impact of the factory on warfare in the West, were just as profound. Industrialization shaped the conduct of war in three complementary ways, all directly tied to technology.

First is the matter of productive capacity, or how much stuff can be produced within a given period of time. The factory system increased, exponentially, the ability of individual states to provide for their own military needs, and even to realize the strategic goal of self-sufficiency in armaments. The nation in arms meant very little without the productive capacity to back it up, as the armies of the tsar would learn, tragically and at great cost, early in the First World War. It was a brutally simple formula: more workers in more factories meant more firearms, ammunition, uniforms, railroad rolling stock, aircraft, tanks, processed food, and battleships. Perhaps the French Revolution put the idea of a people's army into practice for the first time in European history, but it was the Industrial Revolution that made it possible to keep such armies in the field, fed, supplied, and equipped. Hence a nation's industrial output was just as important as its ability to recruit or conscript manpower, and a nation's labor force was just as vital to victory as were its men on the front lines. Industrial power equaled military might.

Second, the Industrial Revolution was also a transportation and communications revolution. The steam engines patented by Thomas Newcomen and James Watt later in the eighteenth century helped to fuel, quite literally, the growth of industry in Britain. Steam engines made it possible to power factory machinery without direct access to moving water and hydrokinetic energy. Soon steam engines propelled cargo vessels and warships, and then an entirely new kind of land transportation: the railroad. Industry gave birth to the steamship and the railroad, and the steamship and the railroad in turn bolstered industry. The invention of the telegraph, which spread with the dramatic growth of rail lines in the 1850s and 1860s, was another civilian technology rich with applications for warfare. Railroads could move men and supplies in a matter of hours across distances that would have consumed weeks of travel by foot. The telegraph made it possible for armies, their high commands, and their governments to exchange information in minutes rather than days.

Both were mixed blessings. Railroads and telegraphy gave generals more operational freedom than they had ever had before, but they could also restrict and tether, too. Instantaneous communication was a two-edged sword, especially so when armies were in regular contact with the regimes they served: telegraphic connections sped urgent requests—like calls for reinforcements or resupply. But they could just as easily become a conduit for meddlesome and uninformed political authorities, and in this way they could also stymie or discourage independent thought and action by commanders in the field.

Railroads and telegraph lines were also very demanding. They required constant attention and care, and therefore manpower and resources. As lifelines to supplies and intelligence, railroads and telegraph lines were vulnerable and tempting targets in wartime, and hence had to be guarded—and repaired—continuously. The twin technologies also amplified a perceptible trend in the evolution of military institutions: a shift in the balance of combat troops and support personnel. Before the nineteenth century, the vast majority of personnel in Western armies (and navies) consisted of fighting men, and such rudimentary support services as did exist—like cooking, laundry, and transportation—were performed by camp followers and teamsters, all civilians attached to the army. As armies grew in size, complexity, and organizational uniformity, increasingly those roles fell to enlisted military personnel, and the scope of those support services broadened with each passing decade. As the American and Prussian armies would discover in the 1860s, the railroad realized its full potential as a military resource only if it were fully integrated into the planning and execution of military operations. As the technology of combat evolved and became more complex, the proportion of support personnel in armies and navies ballooned, and that of frontline combat troops diminished.

Third—and most relevant to martial weaponry—industrialization forever altered the process that led from invention to manufacture to use. The primary consumer of weapons was, of course, the state. Though there was an overall drawdown in the size of military establishments after the fall of Napoléon in 1814–1815, most states retained armies and navies of respectable size, and while there would not be another general war until the fateful summer of 1914, war and preparation for war would be common enough throughout the nineteenth century. The demand for war materiel might have its peaks and lows, but over the long haul war was a reliably steady source of business. Though the desultory nature of that demand could present risks—in the form, for example, of production orders canceled when peace treaties made them unnecessary—government contracts for weapons were highly profitable.

The result of that heavier demand for weaponry was a relationship that was already at the heart of the factory system in the nineteenth century: a close partnership between engineers, inventors, manufacturers, professional soldiers, and government officials. That partnership was the origin of research and development as we know it today. Inventors seeking fame or fortune patented and promoted new weapons, or refinements to existing weapons; factory owners and engineers built prototypes and tested them; military professionals and government representatives supervised the research and testing, adding their own combat-derived expertise to the process and ultimately deciding whether or not to adopt those technologies for official use. That process, formal or informal, was for the most part conducive to efficiency and progress, because the main considerations for weapons technology—ease and cost of manufacturing, ruggedness and practicality, usefulness and performance—could be discussed and compared by those who were best able to assess those qualities.

The partnership between those who designed, produced, and used military weaponry heralded something darker, as well. When US President Dwight D. Eisenhower warned Americans about the insidious power of the "military-industrial complex" in his 1961 farewell address, he was referring to a trend that had begun more than a century before. The intimate ties between war and business, always a component of organized violence, tightened dramatically with the beginning of the factory system. Granted, that tie, and its potential for harm, was perhaps not readily apparent in 1815, or even in 1870. What would become evident in the five or so decades following the fall of Bonaparte, rather, was the speed with which the technology of killing could evolve when soldiers, inventors, and captains of industry worked together to advance their individual interests. After two or more centuries of relatively slow-paced change, the technology of combat would take off after 1800, dramatically increasing the killing power of individual weapons and therefore the striking power of armies and navies.

CHAPTER 7

THE RIFLE AND THE BULLET

The morning of 3 July 1864 dawned sparkling clear and warm over the tiny village of Lundby, in the rolling farmland near the northern end of Denmark's Jutland peninsula. A world away, in the divided United States, a larger struggle was still raging on after three years of bloody battles, but Denmark had its own troubles and its own war. A united Austro-Prussian army had invaded Denmark five months earlier, acting on behalf of German nationalist rebels in Danish-ruled Schleswig and Holstein. Danish defeat was a foregone conclusion. The Austrian and Prussian armies had bashed their way through the formidable defenses on the Danish frontier, and the king of Denmark's enthusiastic but pitifully small army retreated north.

Lundby had, so far, been comfortably distant from the seat of the war many miles to the south. But Prussian forces were sweeping rapidly northward, fanning out across the breadth of the Jutland peninsula, on the hunt for retreating Danes, and here, in the villages south of the harbor town of Aalborg, the hunters became the hunted. A Danish detachment, marching all day on 2 July and through the following night, had been tracking one of these Prussian columns, and with the help of Danish farmers along the way they caught up with the Prussians at Lundby, just as dawn was breaking over the village's U-shaped farmsteads and the Prussians were rousing themselves from sleep.

The Danish force was small, a single company of the 1st Infantry Regiment, but—unlike the Prussians they had cornered—they were veterans. They were tired and hungry, certainly, but they were also spoiling for a fight, eager to drive the Prussian invaders from their homeland. With their commander, Lieutenant Colonel Hans Charles Johannes Beck, they approached Lundby, quickly and silently, from the south. The green Prussians lounged around their campfires, just starting to prepare breakfast, oblivious to the oncoming Danes. Most of the Prussian soldiers were several hundred feet from where their rifles were neatly stacked. They were not ready for battle.

Just after dawn, Col. Beck's column crested the Kongehøj, a modest grassy rise overlooking Lundby. A dog in the village, more vigilant than the Prussians, caught wind of the approaching soldiers and barked. A Prussian sentry looked up, and the Danes were discovered. The Prussians abandoned their breakfast and ran for their rifles, so thoroughly surprised and unprepared that to one Dane they looked "like sheep pursued by a dog." Col. Beck, understanding the urgency of the moment, didn't bother to deploy his marching column into line of battle. There was no time. Instead, he sent his men rushing headlong at the double-quick, still in a column ten men across and sixteen ranks deep, bayonets fixed. With a shout, they lunged toward the Prussians, but kept their formation perfectly in order, a model of discipline and precision. "They looked," one Prussian soldier recalled afterward, "as if they were drilling." The race was on: the Prussians to improvise a defensive line in the few moments left to them, the Danes to hit the Prussians before they could do so. The odds were with the Danes.

But the Prussians had one decisive advantage, and the Danes were unaware of it. While the Danish infantry, like soldiers in most Western armies in 1864, carried state-of-the-art rifle-muskets, the issue weapon in the Prussian ranks was the *Zündnadelgewehr*, or "needle-rifle." Patented by German gunmaker Johann Nikolaus von Dreyse back in the 1830s, it was a marvel of modern technology. From a distance, it looked like every other military longarm of the period: long, festooned with brass hardware, bulky and solid like all Prussian weapons. But closer inspection would reveal that it was something radically different. At the breech-end, it resembled a modern bolt-action rifle, and indeed that's exactly what it was.

A heavy iron bolt handle protruded from the right side of the Dreyse's breech. To operate the rifle, the soldier would first cock the firing pin with his thumb, turn the bolt up and draw it back, revealing the open breech. He would then insert into the breech a fresh paper cartridge, which contained black powder, an elongated lead bullet, and a percussion cap inserted into the base of the bullet. The soldier would then push the bolt forward, pushing the cartridge into place in the rifle's chamber, and then down, locking the bolt in place. When the trigger was pulled, the firing pin—actually a long, thin iron needle—shot forward, penetrated the cartridge and detonated the percussion cap, in turn igniting the powder charge. That was it. The whole process of loading and firing took approximately four seconds, for a rate of roughly fifteen aimed shots per minute—five times the rifle-musket's rate of fire.

The Dreyse's superior qualities wouldn't count for much if the Prussian soldiers didn't actually have them in hand. The officer commanding at Lundby, one Captain von Schlutterbach, somehow managed to restore some semblance of order in the Prussian camp. With about seventy-five of his riflemen, he took up position behind an old earthen dike right in front of the rapidly advancing Danes. The Prussians got there just in time. The Danes would soon be upon them.

Callow troops, when caught in the press of combat, have a tendency to fire at the enemy when under attack. It doesn't matter if their shots are ineffectual; it doesn't matter if the enemy isn't even visible. It's a natural response to the unbelievable stress of being shot at, something that drill, training, and combat experience—experience above all else—can eventually mitigate. It was all that Captain von Schlutterbach could do to keep his nervous men from firing at the Danes, still a few hundred yards away but advancing fast. Yet the Prussians held their fire. Only when the head of the

Danish column crested a small rise directly in their front, about two hundred yards out, did Schlutterbach shout the command: "In the name of God, fire *now*!" Seventy-five Dreyses fired in a volley, hitting the Danes hard, every bullet likely finding a mark at that range. For a moment it looked as if the entire column had gone down, for even those who were not hit threw themselves to the ground when they heard the volley ring out. But in an instant, the survivors were back on their feet again and running straight at the Prussians.

If the Prussians had had conventional muzzleloaders, the Danes might have been able to close the distance fast enough to fall upon the Prussians without having to endure more than one more volley. But these weren't muzzleloaders, and the Prussians let loose volley after volley, with only a few seconds separating each deadly burst of flame, smoke, and lead. The Danes pushed on, despite horrific losses. "God in heaven, how frightful was the action," one Prussian veteran recalled later. "But these brave men . . . did not become disordered as they fell. They closed up tighter, and with a 'Hurrah!' they kept going."

Bravery wasn't enough to compensate for the Dreyse's formidable firepower, and there was only so much of a beating the Danes could endure before breaking. A few of them made it to within twenty-five yards of the Prussian line before they, too, were cut down. The officer leading the attack, Captain P.C.C. Hammerich, gave the order to fall back. The Prussians considerately held their fire, allowing the wrecked Danes to retreat unmolested. Strewn on the field behind the pitiful remnants of Hammerich's command lay thirty-two dead and forty-four wounded—more than 50 percent of the original force, all shot down in less than twenty minutes time.

LUNDBY WAS A tiny episode in a mostly forgotten war. Fewer than three hundred soldiers fought at Lundby, and the entire action lasted less than half an hour. The losses were trivial, too, especially when compared to the much larger, much bloodier, much more consequential battles that flanked it in the timeline of war in the 1860s: the third day of Gettysburg, the day of Pickett's immortal charge, was precisely one year to the day before Lundby; and two years later on the same exact date, the Prussian army—rebuilt by the "Iron Chancellor" Otto von Bismarck and Field Marshal Helmuth von Moltke—would destroy an entire Austrian field army at Königgrätz, one of the biggest battles of the entire century. Lundby was small potatoes by comparison.

But European professional soldiers found Lundby to be at least as interesting as, perhaps even more so than, the larger and bloodier battles of the American Civil War (1861–1865). The major European powers were far more likely to be involved in a war with Prussia or Austria than with distant America, an ocean away, and anyway there was a feeling—not entirely unjustified—that the armies of Europe had little to learn from the half-trained citizen armies of the North and the South. More important, perhaps, Lundby had a significance that belied its size. It wasn't bloody in absolute terms, but in proportional terms it was a ghastly slaughter: while the Prussians emerged practically unscathed, with a loss ratio of less than 2.5 percent, the Danes suffered a casualty rate greater than 50 percent. Such casualty rates were by no means unheard of in European warfare, but in such a short interval, within the space of a few minutes, the statistics were astonishing. In article after article in professional military journals, soldier-scholars picked apart the Lundby skirmish detail by detail. While they disagreed on the tactical implications of the battle, they all knew exactly why the battle had been such a lopsided victory for the green Prussians, and why the bayonet charge that should have worked didn't work. It had everything to do with the Prussian Dreyse rifle. Though the Prussian high command had adopted the Dreyse back in 1841, it had seen only very limited use since then, and its capabilities were largely a mystery outside the German kingdom. The Prussian government liked it that way, and did its best to hide the Dreyse from prying foreign eyes. It was, to all intents and purposes, a state secret.

The Dreyse represented something remarkable: after a long period of stagnation in the development of handheld firearms, which were only marginally improved in performance in 1850 over what they had been in 1550, firearms technology had taken a quantum leap forward. The ballistics of the Dreyse, admittedly, weren't very impressive. Its accuracy, while better than that of the smoothbore musket of the previous generation, was no better than that of less advanced rifles from the same period; its range was slightly inferior to other rifles. The Dreyse's principal virtue was its high rate of fire, which was easily five times that of a conventional, muzzle-loading infantry musket. And rate of fire, as experienced soldiers knew, trumped accuracy and range any day. Firepower was the essence of land combat in the modern era, and in the delivery of firepower the Dreyse excelled.

What made the Dreyse needle-rifle and its competitors feasible was the Industrial Revolution. So complex a firearm, requiring precision machining to fine tolerances, could not have been manufactured in quantity without a factory-based firearms industry. Nor could it have been conceived without an industrial economy. The very fact that the *Zündnadelgewehr* came to be known by its inventor's name was a sign that firearms design and production had come to be a much different affair from what it had been before industrialization. This was the age of the engineer and the inventor-entrepreneur. In the firearms industry, a growing number of self-taught engineers came to be the rock stars of the world of technology. Some of those names have lived on to the present day—Colt, Remington, Winchester, Mauser—but there were hundreds more, maybe thousands, who made innumerable contributions great and small to the evolution of firearms.

As a result, change came fast in the arms industry after 1800, much faster than ever before, and the variety of firearms available to armies in 1870 was infinitely greater than it had been only thirty or forty years earlier. And on average, the performance of the new firearms was infinitely better than that of their predecessors. Firepower made a huge leap in the years 1830 to 1870, and that forward movement would only accelerate in the fifty years that followed 1870. The flip side of rapid progress was rapid obsolescence. As the

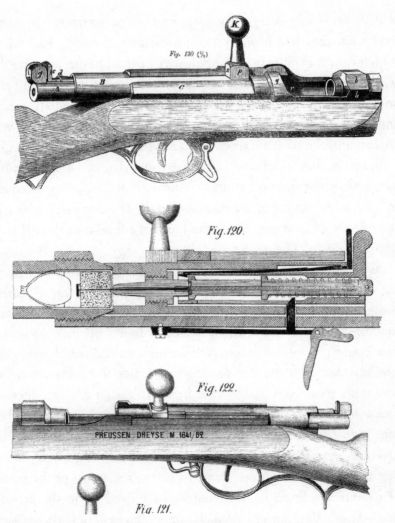

Plate 8: The Dreyse *Zündnadelgewehr*, or "needle-rifle." Top view is of the Dreyse action, with the bolt open, exposing the breech so that a fresh cartridge could be inserted. Pushing the bolt forward and down closed the action. The middle view is a cross section of the rifle after the trigger is pulled; the long, spring-loaded iron needle has already been released by the trigger pull, and has penetrated both the base of the cartridge and the primer. The powder charge is behind the primer, the egg-shaped bullet in front of it.

Images from Josef Reiter, *Elementar-Waffenlehre zum Gebrauche der k.k. Divisions-Schulen* (Triest: Lloyd, 1868), p. 109; Herrmann Weygand, *Die modernen Ordonnanz-Präcisionswaffen der Infanterie* (Berlin/Leipzig: Luckhardt, 1878), Tafel V.

nineteenth century wore on, new weapons—rifles and cannon in particular—replaced older models with ever-increasing frequency.

The Dreyse was one of a new generation of rapid-firing small arms, and while something of a surprise in 1864, the appearance of these first practical rapid-fire weapons was not an overnight development. It was, however, *nearly* overnight, and the result of a demand for greater accuracy without sacrificing rate of fire, a demand that came from professional soldiers. That was the main motivation behind the search for a better military rifle. What made that search possible was a pair of developments, seemingly disconnected, that favored the rapid evolution of weapons technology after about 1830.

First, the military establishments of the European nations and the fledgling United States had grown, if not in raw numbers, certainly in administrative complexity and sophistication. The bureaucracy of nineteenth-century armies and navies outsized and outclassed those of the previous one hundred years. Part of that growth was the creation of modern ordnance departments, bureaucratic divisions concerned solely with the design and supply of weapons and ammunition. Professional ordnance officers took a keen interest in weapons design and performance, and through their ties with engineers, inventors, and private industry, they could help facilitate the advancement of new ideas. And since the nineteenth century was also a period of explosive growth for government-owned arsenals and armories—St. Étienne, Châtellerault, and Tulle in France, Potsdam in Prussia, Springfield and Harpers Ferry in the United States come immediately to mind—the connection between soldiers, engineers, and manufacturers encouraged experimentation with weaponry, with official support and sanction.

Second was the Industrial Revolution itself, which put a premium on invention and innovation ... especially if that innovation brought greater profits. Few realms of technology promised greater profits than the tools of war, so it was natural that so many inventors were attracted to the prospect of developing the next great rifle, cannon, or projectile. Industrialization resulted not only in expanded productive capacity but also in greater speed and consistency of manufacture, too. Since the time of the Bureau brothers in fifteenth-century France, standardization had been a much sought-after goal, primarily in order to simplify logistics. It was an elusive goal, especially with small arms. Conventionally, manufacturers who accepted government contracts to make, say, muskets, would be given a government-approved "pattern piece," a fully functional model musket, which the manufacturers would then use as a basic guide when manufacturing their own.

Muskets contracted this way were notionally interchangeable, in that they looked the same as the pattern piece, and sometimes larger parts—like barrels or stocks—would fit together with parts made by another contractor. Smaller parts would still have to be hand-fitted, and screws were rarely made to a standard pitch and thread—you could not, in other words, replace a breech-tang screw on one maker's musket with a screw made by a different contractor, even if the two muskets were technically of the same model. Eli Whitney, the American who invented the cotton gin, is often credited with the concept of true interchangeability of parts, but even that is not exactly true. Whitney's many contract firearms— he manufactured several varieties of martial muskets and rifles for the US government—were interchangeable with each other; that is, a part from a Whitney-made musket was certain to fit another Whitney-made musket. But Whitney was, at the same time, one of the worst contract violators in the history of American military weaponry. He all but ignored the government pattern pieces he was given, changing the overall design of his weapons as he chose and without official consent. Parts from Whitney-made firearms only fit into other Whitney-made firearms.

Manufacture by machine, though, made true standardization, and true interchangeability, feasible. The advantages in supply and in firearms maintenance were patently obvious. Though there were some notable outliers—British small arms still used hand-fitted parts well into the 1850s—the practice of standardization was becoming commonplace before the middle of the century.

The Rifle and the Bullet

FIREARMS DESIGN IN the nineteenth century was a frenzied thing, populated by engineering geniuses and eccentrics by the hundreds. There were so many inventors trying their hand at radically new designs, so many thousands of patents issued in all nations of the West, that it appears as if industrialization had blown open the creative floodgates. But there was focus and purpose to the apparent chaos, and nearly all the inventions of the period, successful or not, fall into one of three basic categories. First was the search for a reliable means of *ignition* to replace the ancient flintlock. Second, inventors sought to improve the *accuracy* of small arms through the use of rifling, but without sacrificing rate of fire. Third, the pioneers of the modern arms industry looked for ways of improving *rate of fire*, especially through the use of breech-loading mechanisms.

Ignition was the simplest issue and the first to be solved. The flintlock had proven its worth over the centuries, having unequivocally forced the matchlock out of the picture entirely, within Europe at any rate. It was infinitely more reliable than the matchlock, but it was still not reliable. Too many things could go wrong: hang fire (delayed discharge) and flash in the pan (no discharge) remained common occurrences. And while the flintlock was more weatherproof than the matchlock, it was only by degrees; the flintlocks were hardly impervious to the elements.

The flash of creative genius that eventually supplanted the flintlock came from an unlikely source: a Scottish Presbyterian parson named Alexander John Forsyth. Forsyth, an avid hunter, was unhappy with the delay between trigger pull and ignition on his flintlock fowler. The delay was so long, he noticed, that when he went bird hunting near his village of Belhelvie, the mechanical *clunk* of the flint hitting the frizzen was enough to alert and flush his intended prey. He wanted a faster and more reliable means of ignition, and he found it in chemistry—his other calling.

Fulminates—chemical compounds that detonate with friction or percussion—had just recently been discovered. Forsyth was aware of this, and he tried chlorate of potash fulminate, or

163

potassium chlorate. A small drop, when hit with a hammer, exploded with a loud bang and a tremendous flash. The good reverend attached a nipple-shaped cone to the venthole of his fowler, and replaced the flint cock with a small hammer. He stored the fulminate in a small flask—Forsyth called it a "scent bottle" because of its outward resemblance to a perfume container—mounted to the lock near the nipple cone. Tilting the priming bottle deposited a small drop of the fulminate atop the nipple. When the hammer struck the nipple, the flame from the exploding fulminate raced down the touchhole and into the main charge, igniting it instantly. There was virtually no lag between trigger pull and ignition.

That was in 1805. The following year, Reverend Forsyth took his invention to London, managed to get an audience with the king's master general of ordnance at the Tower of London, and to his great surprise was met with an enthusiastic response. For a while, he worked at the Tower, perfecting his invention and finding a way of converting old flintlock muskets to the new system. His second career as a weapons designer came to an abrupt end when a new master general, who did not share his predecessor's enthusiasm for the project, fired him. Forsyth continued to work on his own, but he would never receive a penny from the British government during his lifetime.

Forsyth's basic idea—of igniting the main powder charge by striking a chemical compound—came to be known as percussion ignition. The idea spread quickly. Napoléon Bonaparte himself, it was rumored, offered Forsyth a huge sum of cash for it. Soon other inventors and gunmakers took up where Forsyth left off, crafting more practical and efficient means of packaging the ignition compound. Fulminate of mercury, far less corrosive than potassium chlorate, became the detonating compound of choice, and subsequent incarnations of the percussion system used single-use detonators rather than a bottle. The final and enduring version was the percussion cap. A small pellet of fulminate of mercury was affixed to the underside of a small, hat-shaped "cap," fashioned from a thin sheet of a malleable metal such as copper or brass. Fitted to the nipple-cone, the cap helped to contain and focus the explosion of the fulminate, sending a searing jet of flame down the vent. Several inventors, including the British-born American artist Joshua Bell, claimed credit for the percussion cap and scrambled to substantiate their claims with patents. Most likely, the real "winner" in the race was one of the better-known London gunmakers, like Joseph Egg or Joseph Manton, in the late 1810s.

The percussion cap would take several forms. The Austrian army would later adopt a percussion tube, designed by Giuseppe Console and Vincenz von Augustin, which fit into a peculiar pan/anvil contraption that lay alongside the venthole. A Washington, DC, dentist, Edward Maynard, patented the Maynard Primer: individual charges of fulminate of mercury inserted into a long, thin paper ribbon, almost exactly like children's roll caps of a much later generation. A special device attached to the lock fed the ribbon along the top of the nipple, so that each time the hammer was cocked, the ribbon moved precisely far enough forward so that a fresh cap was set atop the nipple. It worked, and marginally increased rate of fire, but it was complicated and expensive. Only the United States adopted it for a handful of weapons, and with the outbreak of the Civil War the Maynard Primer would all but disappear.

But the hat-shaped cap prevailed, and it was (nearly) an instant success. Since it shot a jet of flame into the vent—in contrast to the flintlock's brief flash of flame next to the vent—it was far more certain and reliable, as well as faster, than a flintlock. Though fumbling with tiny caps might be a challenge to soldiers with clumsy or winter-chilled fingers—and all but impossible while wearing gloves—the process of grabbing a cap and placing it atop the nipple-cone was still faster than the task of priming a flintlock. And there was no telltale flash and plume of smoke to betray the shooter's position. The only real drawbacks had to do with supply and manufacture. Flints could be knapped by hand, but caps required precision machinery, for they had to be made in huge quantities to tight tolerances. This was a minor concern, though, as Europe was in the process of industrializing, and the benefits of percussion ignition outweighed the complications. Slightly higher rate of fire, instantaneous and more reliable ignition—there was simply no denying that the percussion system constituted a great improvement on the flintlock.

Professional soldiers thought so, too, for it was adopted nearly everywhere and within a remarkably compressed timeframe. Britain's first general-issue percussion muskets went into production in 1838; Prussia followed suit the following year. The US Army formally adopted the percussion system for its Hall carbines and rifles in 1833, and for infantry muskets in 1842. Sometimes common soldiers proved hesitant to accept the new technology. On at least one occasion, US regular army troops bound for the war in Mexico in 1846 outright refused to accept the unfamiliar new muskets, threatening to mutiny if not allowed to keep their now obsolescent—but familiar and reliable—flintlocks. But the percussion system was here to stay.

Not for very long, though. Every Western army had adopted percussion-ignition small arms by 1845; two decades later, percussion itself was obsolescing. In 1870 it would be gone almost entirely, percussion weapons having been replaced by breechloaders firing metal-cased ammunition. The flintlock musket dominated every battlefield of the eighteenth century, and for most of the first half of the next century. Percussion weapons were to be found only in a handful of wars over the course of the 1840s, 1850s, and 1860s: the Mexican-American War, the Crimean War, the Franco-Austrian War, the Schleswig-Holstein wars, the wars of the Italian Risorgimento, the American Civil War, the Seven Weeks' War, and the French campaigns in Mexico. But those were not small wars, for the most part, and even when percussion ignition faded into obscurity the cap continued to live on in other forms. The primers used in modern cased ammunition, for example, were direct descendants of the percussion cap.

The percussion system would prove to be only a minor episode in the history of firearms technology, likely forgotten if it had not been revived when shooting vintage weapons became a popular pastime in North America later in the twentieth century. Yet there was something peculiar about the manner of its adoption by European and American armies, something unprecedented and unheard of, a radical break with the past, soon to become the norm. Before the advent of percussion ignition, the armies of the Western states did not eagerly embrace new technologies, and they rarely went looking for them intentionally. Innovation was expensive and potentially troublesome, after all, and prior to the Industrial Revolution there was no prevailing notion that innovation could be considered a good thing.

But with the percussion system, those armies went out of their way to adopt the new technology, without dwelling overly long on the budgetary costs of the shift. If anything, most of those armies rushed to introduce percussion ignition with something resembling recklessness, abandoning any appearance of fiscal responsibility. In the United States, for example, though the Army had officially gone over to percussion small arms by 1842, it had also approved in 1835 a new pattern flintlock musket, which did not go into production until 1840. The two models of musket, one flintlock and one percussion, were being manufactured simultaneously in the mid-1840s. In the meantime, since it was a simple matter to retrofit flintlock muskets with percussion locks, the American government converted tens of thousands of its older flintlocks to percussion ignition.

The US Army, like the armies of Britain and France and Prussia and Austria, understood that the advantages of the new ignition system were so great, and the potential strategic or tactical costs of *not* adopting the new technology so high, that there really was no option. Thrift took a back seat to security; technological progress had become an existential issue. The arms race mentality, the mindset that encouraged improvement in weaponry to keep up with possible enemies regardless of the price tag, had begun to take hold.

Ignition wasn't the only challenge bedeviling ordnance officers and inventors in the first half of the nineteenth century. While they were assessing the effectiveness of the percussion cap, they were also wrestling with a much older, much more vexing matter: the technology of rifling.

Rifling is a very old technology, nearly as old as handheld firearms themselves. The practice of cutting parallel grooves into the interior surface of a weapon's barrel, usually in a slightly spiral pattern as they ran lengthwise from breech to muzzle, was familiar to European gunsmiths as early as the sixteenth century. The theory behind rifling was simple, and its effectiveness easily demonstrable. If the projectile fit tightly into the bore, tight enough that the rifling "grabbed" it, then the rifling would impart a spin on the bullet as it traveled down the barrel. The bullet would continue to spin in flight, and that spin made all the difference. A ball fired from a rifled weapon might have a slightly reduced muzzle velocity when compared to a round ball shot from a smoothbore weapon, but it traveled farther and straighter, and it hit harder. Rifling made just about any firearm deadlier, shot for shot, and far more precise.

The technology was available, in other words, even as the smoothbore musket came to dominate the European battlefield in the seventeenth century. So, if the rifle was superior to the smoothbore musket, if it could hit a smaller target at a greater distance, then why weren't rifles in general use? Were European soldiers that shortsighted?

For all the virtues of the rifle, its shortcomings outweighed its merits, at least within a military context. One of those shortcomings was cost. Rifling a barrel, in the days before rifling machines, took a great deal of effort, specialized tools and specialized skills, and therefore rifles were costlier and more time-consuming to produce. But the main issue was actually performance—not in accuracy or range, but in speed of loading and therefore rate of fire. In order for rifling to be effective, there had to be a tight fit between bore and bullet. The outside surface of the bullet had to engage the rifling grooves, meaning that the bullet had to be slightly larger in diameter than the diameter of the bore, as measured across the *lands*, the raised surfaces between the grooves. Introducing the bullet into the muzzle would be challenging enough; ramming it down the entire length of the barrel, from muzzle to breech, would require great strength, a sturdy ramrod, and possibly a hammer. And that was with a clean barrel with no obstructions. Once a black-powder weapon had been fired, it began to accumulate hard carbon fouling along the length of the barrel, residue from the burned gunpowder, and that effectively constricted the bore—making it even more of a chore to ram a lead ball home.

There were solutions. One was to use a patch, a small piece of lightweight leather or heavy cloth, generously coated with grease or tallow. Wrapped around a slightly smaller ball, it helped engage the bullet with the rifling while also easing the passage of the ball, courtesy of the grease. Even in this way, though, the muzzle-loading rifle's rate of fire could not possibly match that of smoothbores. With smoothbores, fit was not a concern, and indeed a tight fit was less than desirable. Conventionally, musket balls were cast (or pressed) in a diameter that was significantly smaller than the actual caliber of the musket for which they were intended—usually around 0.05 to 0.1 inch smaller, which is a larger difference than it appears at first glance. That difference between ball diameter and bore diameter, called windage, was important. It helped to account for irregularities in manufacturing, for one thing; a musket that had a nominal caliber of 0.75 inch might have an actual bore diameter as large as 0.80 inch, or as small as 0.72 inch. There was an even more pressing reason for windage: it made up for the fouling that inevitably built up in a musket barrel after it was fired. As the bore constricted because of hard carbon deposits, it became more and more difficult to load. A slightly subcaliber musket ball headed off those potential difficulties, keeping the rate of fire reasonably steady. It also meant that if a loaded musket were tilted muzzle-down, the ball might just roll out again, but that's where wadding came in. The paper envelope of a standard musket cartridge, crumpled up and rammed into the barrel atop the musket ball, served just this purpose. Windage, however, did not work with a rifle at all. A subcaliber ball would not engage the rifling, and a rifle thus loaded would perform no better than a musket.

The rifle's accuracy depended almost as much on the user as it did on the tool. In this sense, it was much like the Welsh-English longbow. The proper and effective use of a rifle demanded much skill, acquired over many years. Sights were very primitive, closest to what today we would call open irons: the rear sight was a simple iron V, brazed to the top of the barrel over the breech; the front sight was a post or blade mounted atop the muzzle. Such sights could not be adjusted for distance, or made to compensate for the effects of wind on the bullet's flight path, so hitting a target at any distance required a keen sense of how the rifle performed, and that, in turn, required hours and hours of training *with that particular rifle*. And since the rifle's range and trajectory would vary widely with different powder charges, a capable rifleman would have to have the kind of experience with a single firearm to know how it behaved with different powder charges. Maybe, in fact, the rifle was a less effective weapon than the longbow, because while effective use of the longbow also demanded much experience, it still had a high rate of fire. The rifle, no matter how experienced the rifleman, was still slow.

Simply put, professional soldiers understood that the key to effective firepower on the battlefield was rate of fire, not the accuracy of individual weapons, and in this regard the smoothbore musket was the hands-down favorite.

Yet the rifle still had a purpose, and during the eighteenth century the rifle experienced a rebirth of sorts. In British North America, though most colonists still preferred smoothbore muskets and fowling pieces, on the fringes of the frontier the rifle was often the weapon of choice. American frontiersmen and the gunsmiths who catered to them developed several distinct regional variations, most famously the Pennsylvania-style long rifle: long-barreled and slender, their stocks carved from highly figured, native hardwoods such as maple, usually of a smaller caliber than was typical of muskets. In hunting game, the musket's greater rate of fire was still not high enough to be an advantage. A miss on the first shot would frighten away the intended prey, which would be long gone by the time a second shot could be reloaded—even with a musket. A kill on the first shot was a necessity, and so the more accurate rifle was better suited.

Rifles figured prominently in North American warfare during the eighteenth century. Perhaps the most remarkable units in Washington's Continental Army during the American Revolution were the rifle companies recruited from the backwoods of Pennsylvania, Maryland, and Virginia, who ultimately formed a Continental rifle corps under the command of the colorful Daniel Morgan. They were no substitute for line infantry armed with muskets, but they were a valuable ancillary nonetheless, capable of picking off individual soldiers at astonishing ranges. Such was the reputation of the rifle—and of its users—even before the Revolution, that when the Second Continental Congress announced the creation of the Continental Army in June 1775, the very first units it authorized were ten companies of riflemen.

The armies of the individual German states that made up the Holy Roman Empire also made use of a homegrown rifle tradition. Professional foresters, commonly employed on noble and royal estates in Germany to manage populations of wild game, relied on a native style of rifle: short, thick-barreled, and of a larger caliber than its American cousins, heavy but handy in thick, tangled undergrowth. The foresters—dead shots, inured to backcountry life, skilled at tracking game—made perfect light infantry. Soon the German armies began to incorporate entire battalions of these *Jäger* or *Feldjäger*—huntsmen. German mercenaries fighting for British pay in the American Revolution included substantial numbers of *Jäger* units. Their American opponents feared and admired them, so much so that their name—and their rifles, too—became part of the early American lexicon.

The rifle grew slowly in popularity at the beginning of the next century. The British came to embrace the concept, building up their own rifle units in the wars against Napoléon. Well before midcentury, the practice of including specially trained rifle companies in each infantry battalion had become nearly universal practice in the armies of the West, and accordingly arsenals and gunsmiths produced the first standard-issue rifles, made specifically for combat. The British adopted the stubby, robust Baker rifle in 1800; and though it had a tiny army, America followed suit with its own native design in 1803.

There was no intention, not at this stage, of replacing the musket with the rifle as the main-issue infantry weapon. Rather, the rifle filled a niche; it was a specialized weapon meant for specialized troops. The rate of fire was no better than it had ever been. At the ranges that were typical for infantry combat, usually between fifty and one hundred fifty yards, the rifle had no advantages at all over the smoothbore musket, and a distinct disadvantage in the reduced firepower and requisite investment in training.

But what if the rifle could be made to fire as fast as the musket? Maybe the improved accuracy wouldn't pay off in a short-range firefight, but it could increase the range of that firefight, so that armies could engage at two hundred or three hundred yards. And having a weapon with that kind of range could give an army a huge advantage over an opponent armed only with smoothbores, even if the riflemen were not expert shots.

That was the motivation for arms designers and ordnance officers in the first half of the nineteenth century, the inspiration for the hunt for an improved infantry weapon. So the race began: to make a rifle that could be loaded and fired as fast as a smoothbore musket.

The challenge, of course, was the friction between bullet and bore. It all boiled down to that. If that could be overcome, then there was no reason that a rifle couldn't achieve the same speed of loading as a smoothbore. There were really only two ways to obviate that friction: either cut down the distance that the bullet had to travel down the barrel during the loading process, or make the bullet smaller.

The first of these options was both simple and complicated. How to arrange it so that the bullet didn't have to travel far down the barrel? The answer was simple: make the rifle a breechloader. If the breech could be opened, the ball could be inserted into the barrel from the rear. No ramrod, no ramming, no long push home. Even if the chamber, where the ball or cartridge would be inserted, could be made just a little larger than the diameter of the bore itself, it would still work; the explosion of the gunpowder would force the soft lead projectile into the rifling. And breechloaders could be loaded and fired even *faster* than smoothbore muzzleloaders!

The breechloader, as we have seen, wasn't exactly a new idea. Many early cannon were breechloaders, and breech-loading small arms were not unknown, either. They were seen as inferior, and with good reason, because their faults—notably gas leakage at the breech—made them unsuitable for military use. But a new generation of breechloaders, made possible by the Industrial Revolution, endeavored to change that.

One of the first breechloaders to see combat was a flintlock rifle invented during the American Revolution by a Scottish officer in the British army, Major Patrick Ferguson. The Ferguson rifle gave access to the breech via a threaded breech plug—essentially a large vertical screw attached to the inside of the trigger guard—that was lowered away from the breech by pivoting the trigger guard. When the rifleman rotated the trigger guard, the breech plug unscrewed from the barrel, dropping down to expose the breech-end of the barrel. Once the breech was exposed, the rifleman inserted powder and ball, screwed the breech shut again, primed the pan, cocked, aimed, and fired. The accuracy and range were a significant improvement over a smoothbore musket, but the rate of fire was the truly astonishing thing about the Ferguson: seven shots per minute, more than double the smoothbore musket's rate of fire, and close to seven times that of a muzzle-loading rifle.

On the other side of the Atlantic, the American-born inventor John H. Hall—an engineer by avocation, originally a tanner by trade—developed a simpler design. In the Hall rifle, first patented in 1811, the breech-end of the barrel was a separate piece, hinged so that it could pivot upward. Pushing a small lever, located on the underside of the rifle just forward of the trigger guard, released a catch and raised the breechblock, allowing a paper cartridge to be inserted directly inside. Push the breechblock down to seat it against the barrel, prime it, cock it, and the Hall was ready to fire. As with the Ferguson, the Hall rifle delivered an impressive performance: an effective killing range of more than a thousand yards, and a rate of fire of eight or nine shots per minute.

There was no question about it: the Ferguson and the Hall—and others like them—were superior weapons, superior in power, accuracy, range, and rate of fire, superior in just about every way but three: cost, complexity, and comfort. The Ferguson cost around four times as much to manufacture as the British infantry musket of the time—the Short Land Pattern, one of a family of muskets commonly called the Brown Bess—and took much, much longer to make. The Hall was not quite so costly, and Hall's sophisticated rifle works at Harpers Ferry, Virginia, helped to keep production costs down. Neither rifle was difficult to operate, but they were complex enough to require special cleaning, and like all breechloaders they would quickly become inoperable if not cleaned and oiled after use. And breechloaders like these were also not as robust as muzzle-loading muskets, the Ferguson in particular being susceptible to breakage.

The comfort issue was a matter of simple mechanics. With the Ferguson it was a lesser disadvantage, but with the Hall it was a real cause for concern. In the Hall rifle, the pivoting breechblock simply butted up against the breech-end of the barrel. There was no rubber gasket, no gascheck or seal of any kind, only metal on metal. Even if the juncture where breechblock met barrel were perfectly sealed, eventually the iron parts would wear with time, use, and corrosion. Once that happened, the breech lost its integrity. So when the rifleman fired the Hall, a thin jet of searing-hot gas could shoot up through the minuscule gap in the breech, dangerously close to the rifleman's face. This was a problem inherent in just about every breech-loading design: no matter how it worked, it was impossible to ensure a tight seal at the breech, and gas leakage was the result.

The British army dumped the Ferguson after a very short while; the Hall persisted in American service into the Civil War, having seen some prior service in the Second Seminole War and the Mexican-American War. The Hall's survival in American service owed mostly to its usefulness as a weapon for mounted troops, for it was far easier to load a Hall while on horseback than it was to fumble around with the ramrod of a muzzle-loading carbine.

The qualified success of systems like the Hall did not discourage inventors and engineers. If anything, it encouraged a tidal wave of inventions and patents in Europe and America. Some were quite successful, like the rifles and carbines of Christian Sharps, perhaps the most commonly used breechloader in the American Civil War, and the repeating pistols and longarms patented and manufactured by Samuel Colt. The breechloader would not be going away anytime soon. But there was no getting around certain design limitations, especially when it came to simplicity and cost, and so ordnance officers searched for solutions elsewhere.

HENCE THE NEXT approach: What if it were possible to make rifles faster to load and fire, not by changing the rifle, but by redesigning the bullet? Would it be possible to make a bullet that was smaller in diameter than the bore, so it would load into a muzzle-loading rifle as easily as a musket ball in a smoothbore, and then somehow get the bullet to expand in the bore before it was fired?

As it turned out, it *was* possible, and European engineers found several ways to accomplish this. One was to make bullets that fit the rifling mechanically—in other words, they fit into the rifling perfectly when loaded, and did not have to be forced to engage the rifling by sheer muscle. The so-called Brunswick rifle, adopted for light infantry use by the British army in 1837, was one such design. The barrel of the Brunswick was rifled with two deep grooves, diametrically opposite one another. The bullet it fired was a "belted ball"—a sphere, much like a musket ball, but with a single raised belt around its circumference, so that it almost resembled the planet Saturn in profile. The ball did not have to fit the barrel tightly, so long as the belt fit into the two rifling grooves. Loading it was much easier, and therefore faster, than loading a conventional muzzle-loading rifle. The Brunswick's rate of fire, roughly three rounds per minute, was comparable with that of a smoothbore musket.

Unfortunately, the bullet itself was not ideal. Its flight path was slightly erratic, for—as it turned out—the belted ball was not especially aerodynamic. Its flight path was consequently erratic, so its accuracy and range—while better than those of a smoothbore—did not compare well with those of other rifles. British riflemen complained about the unnerving screech that the Brunswick bullets emitted as they flew through the air, and the fact that after a few rounds it was very difficult to load the rifle; the deep rifling grooves, as it turned out, acted as a magnet for fouling. The Brunswick rifle was not a success, though the British stubbornly held on to it until the early 1850s. There was nothing inherently wrong with mechanically fitted bullets. Two of the most famous, and most accurate, target rifles of the period—the hexagonal-bore Whitworth and the four-grooved Jacobs—employed the concept, and proved to be extraordinarily accurate. The Whitworth was prized as a sniper rifle during the American Civil War, and the Jacobs became a popular choice for big-game hunters. But they were as slow to load as any muzzle-loading rifle, and thus not suitable solutions.

A more promising approach came from France: the manually deformed bullet. Henri-Gustave Delvigne, a former French army officer turned inventor, patented in 1826 a radically different rifle. Delvigne's weapon was still a muzzleloader, but it had a powder chamber: the last couple of inches of the barrel at the breech were smaller in diameter than the rest of the barrel. The smaller cavity was large enough to fit a full charge of powder, and the point at which the bore narrowed formed a "shoulder." When the rifleman loaded a subcaliber ball and rammed it down, it stopped at the shoulder. Using a heavy iron ramrod, the rifleman would then hit the soft lead ball hard, mashing it against the shoulder of the powder chamber. As a result, the bullet expanded radially and fit into the rifling. Delvigne later improved upon his design by substituting a cylindro-conoidal bullet (an elongated projectile with a flat base, shaped like a cylinder topped by a rounded cone) for the round ball. A few years later, another French army officer, Louis-Étienne de Thouvenin, revised Delvigne's design. Thouvenin's *carabine à tige*—"pillar rifle"—got rid of the powder chamber and instead employed an iron pillar that jutted up from the base of the breech. When loaded, the powder charge would fit around the pillar, and the bullet would rest atop it. A few sharp blows from the iron ramrod would mash the bullet into the rifling.

The two systems, Delvigne and Thouvenin, performed remarkably well. Accuracy was much better than with a smoothbore musket, as was range and penetration, and the loading time was only slightly longer. French army leadership was sufficiently impressed with the Thouvenin system that it adopted the pillar-breech as the official weapon for rifle units in 1846. It would go on to see service in the Crimean War (1853–1856), the Franco-Austrian War (1859), and—in small numbers—in the American Civil War. No doubt Mssr. Thouvenin's status as a general played no small role in the rifle's official adoption. The *carabine à tige* had its virtues, no doubt, but the deformed bullet solution had significant flaws. No matter how carefully the rifleman hammered on the bullet with his ramrod, he could not be sure that he was hammering evenly, so more often than not the smashed bullet was lopsided, unevenly engaged in the rifling, and therefore likely to be erratic in flight. In the heat and stress of combat, such an issue could only get worse. And both Thouvenin's and Delvigne's weapons were difficult to clean—especially the Thouvenin rifle, since getting a brush or a rag into the tight spaces between the pillar and the bore was a hopeless task. Extensive corrosion at the breech-end was the inevitable result.

The manually deformed bullet didn't entirely do the trick, but Thouvenin and Delvigne had hit upon something. The main problem with both designs was the human factor, in this case the inability of the rifleman to deform the bullet uniformly. The next solution sidestepped that issue by eliminating the human factor and letting the weapon—or, more precisely, the gunpowder—do the work. There were several inventors working this angle, but one of them stands out above the rest. Claude-Étienne Minié was a French infantry officer who had fought in the North African campaigns of the 1830s and 1840s, and he knew something about rifles. Sometime before 1846 he came up with the idea of a self-expanding bullet, a projectile that used the energy produced by the burning gunpowder to make the bullet expand radially as it was traveling down the barrel. A traditional round ball obviously wouldn't suffice for this, so Minié instead designed an elongated, cylindro-conoidal bullet with a hollow base. In Minié's original design, the base cavity was shaped like a truncated cone, flaring outward from the center of the bullet to its open bottom end. At the bullet's base, the walls of this cavity—frequently called skirts—were quite thin. Minié inserted an iron cup into that cavity.

The bullet, being smaller in diameter than the rifle's bore, would slide easily down the barrel, just like a musket ball. But when the rifle fired, the expanding gases rammed into the iron cup, forcing it upward into the bullet's cavity and causing the skirts to expand in diameter and engage the rifling. Soon Minié discovered that the iron cup was unnecessary, and that the bullet expanded just fine without it. In fact, sometimes the iron cup would blow straight through the soft lead bullet, leaving a troublesome (and potentially dangerous) ring of lead stuck in the bore.

Other inventors were at work on the same problem, either improving upon the Minié design or coming up with alternatives. British and American ordnance experts added their talents to Minié's basic idea. In British service, a softer plug, of clay or boxwood, replaced Minié's iron cup, obviating the problem of blow-through. Soon it became apparent that the bullet did just fine without any kind of plug, the gas itself being more than sufficient to expand the bullet's skirts. The Austrian army adopted the Wilkinson bullet, which worked on a slightly different principle. The Wilkinson was a compression bullet: it had a solid base, without the cavity of the Minié, but with deeply inscribed rings encircling its base. The weakened base, when hit by expanding gases upon discharge, was

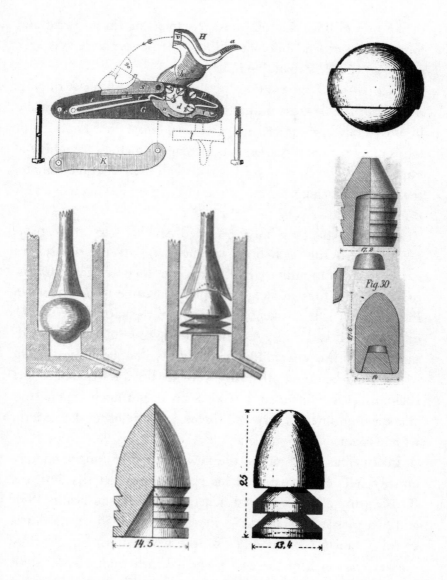

Plate 9. Inside view of a percussion lock; cross section of rifle breeches using Delvigne (chamber) and Thouvenin (pillar) systems; rifle-musket projectiles: Brunswick belted ball, the Minié and Pritchett expanding bullets, the American Burton, the Austrian Wilkinson compression bullet.

Images from: Reiter, *Elementar-Waffenlehre*, p. 60; Weygand, *Die modernen Ordonnanz-Präcisionswaffen der Infanterie*, Tafeln II and III; J. Scoffern, *Projectile Weapons of War and Explosive Compounds; including some New Resources of Warfare, with Especial Reference to Rifled Ordnance* (London: Longman, Brown, 1859), pp. 237–239.

driven upward into the solid nose, compressing the soft lead and forcing it to expand into the rifling. The performance was very similar to Minié's expanding bullet.

That performance was nothing short of astonishing. A rifle firing one of the new expanding bullets demonstrated dramatically improved range, accuracy, and power. And it sacrificed nothing in terms of rate of fire. Because of its windage, which was roughly the same as that of a conventional musket ball used in a smoothbore, the expanding, elongated bullet was just as easy, just as fast, to ram from muzzle to breech.

The new expanding bullet breathed new life into an old technology. The resulting hybrid weapon was markedly superior to every musket and military rifle that had ever come before. It was, indeed, a new firearm altogether, one that came to be known in English as the rifle-musket. As confusing as the name can be to the uninitiated, it had a very specific meaning to soldiers in the mid-nineteenth century. Traditionally, military rifles were shorter than infantry muskets, and often they were not fitted for bayonets. The rifle-musket was intended to serve as an all-purpose weapon, suitable for both line infantry and riflemen, a rifle of musket length, with a bayonet, like a musket.

Like percussion ignition, the new technology caught on very quickly. Minié first patented his expanding bullet in 1846; the British army adopted its first general-issue rifle-musket in 1851, and first took it into combat in the Crimea in 1854. In the battle of Inkerman (5 November 1854), the new pattern Enfield rifle-musket got much of the credit when British troops repulsed an overwhelming Russian assault. A reporter for *The Times* of London fairly crowed over the Pattern 1851 Enfield, "the king of weapons," and its performance at Inkerman: "The volleys of the Minié cleft them like the hand of the Destroying Angel, and they fell like leaves in autumn before them."*

---

* Harold L. Peterson and Robert Elman, *The Great Guns* (New York: Grosset and Dunlap, 1971), p. 196.

The Rifle and the Bullet

The legend of the "Minnie musket" was born at Inkerman. Most armies were already making plans to upgrade their smoothbore muskets, flintlock or percussion, to the rifle-musket, but that process accelerated after news of the British victory in the Crimea. By 1855, nearly every first- or second-rate army in the West—those of Austria, France, the United States, Bavaria, and most of the German states, the Scandinavian kingdoms, the Netherlands, Belgium—officially approved the rifle-musket as the new standard. This was an enormous undertaking, particularly for the major powers like Britain or Austria, where the task of rearming hundreds of thousands of infantrymen with modern rifle-muskets must have put an onerous burden on both manufacturing capacity and state finances.

But the rifle-musket was also a flexible technology, and not a radical departure from previous small arms; that it could be applied—or, rather, retrofitted—to obsolete weapons certainly eased the path for its introduction. Old smoothbore muskets could be rifled and provided with long-range sights; flintlock muskets could be fitted with percussion locks and then rifled. The rifle-musket did not have any peculiar features, because the modern technology was in the bullet, not in the firearm itself. Under the capable direction of Jefferson Davis, US secretary of war in the 1850s (and later president of the southern Confederacy), American arsenals converted hundreds of thousands of flintlock muskets to percussion, and smoothbore muskets to rifle-muskets. When the American Civil War broke out a few years later, these were the weapons that armed the hordes of volunteers who flocked to the colors on either side. The supply of newly made rifle-muskets was nowhere near large enough to meet the needs of the Federal and Confederate armies, and rifle-muskets did not fully supplant smoothbores until more than halfway through the war.

The transition from smoothbore musket to rifle-musket was faster than just about any change of weaponry in a Western army up to that point. Industrialization made that transition possible, as it had the switch from flintlock to percussion; it was something that would not have been conceivable or doable before the mid-1800s. More telling is the fact that the move from smoothbore musket to rifle-musket was done by a studied, conscious, deliberate effort. Soldiers and inventors devoted their energies and their professional lives to craft a superior weapon; armies, and their governments, willingly invested time and cash into testing the new designs. And once they found an advantageous new technology, they acted swiftly, conscious of but unconstrained by the attendant costs. For "cost" entailed more than mere cash, the vast sums required for the manufacture of tens of thousands of new rifle-muskets. It also involved new ammunition, too, millions of rounds of it, new gear for carrying that new ammunition, and new manuals and training regimens to account for the performance of the rifle-musket. Even with all those additional complications and expenses, the armies of the Western world pounced on the rifle-musket. They put modernization and international competition ahead of frugality. In this sense, more than any other, more than the tactical implications associated with it, the adoption of the rifle-musket was a milestone in the history of military technology.

FOR ALL THAT trouble, the rifle-musket was a remarkably short-lived weapon, lasting little more than a decade in service. It was only slightly shorter-lived than percussion ignition, which was one of its component technologies. The rifle-musket made its debut in the Crimean War and played a starring role on the battlefields of the Franco-Austrian War and the American Civil War. By 1866 it was already a relic. That compressed lifespan was symptomatic of a pattern in the evolution of firearms that would become all too familiar in the decades to come. An apparent revolution in weapons technology—revolutionary enough that all the Western armies spent vast amounts of money and went to extraordinary lengths to adopt it—was rendered obsolete by a subsequent leap forward almost immediately afterward.

During its brief life, the rifle-musket saw action in some of the biggest battles of the century—Balaclava, Solferino, Gettysburg,

Königgrätz—and yet it did not appreciably change the art of war. Perhaps that assertion appears counterintuitive; if the rifle-musket was such an improvement over the smoothbore that preceded it, if it indeed was a deadlier weapon, then surely the nature of infantry combat would have to change accordingly to accommodate the rifled weapon's greater range and accuracy. To argue the rifle-musket's minimal impact is also to go against the grain of American national mythology, in particular the way that Americans understand the military significance of their Civil War. This, in fact, is the rifle-musket's primary claim to fame, at least in the United States. American historians have long contended that the Civil War was the first "modern war," a comfortably vague claim, and that it was uniquely bloody. The unusually high casualties exacted by Civil War combat, we are told, was the result of a fatal mix of unimaginative and incompetent leadership, old-fashioned tactics, and revolutionary new weaponry—including, and especially, the rifle-musket.

Civil War generals, so the argument goes, were firmly grounded in Napoleonic warfare, and Napoleonic tactics were in turn based on the capabilities and limitations of the smoothbore musket. The longer-ranged, much deadlier rifle-musket rendered the linear tactics and bayonet charges of the Napoleonic era obsolete, but Civil War commanders were unable or unwilling to perceive this. Instead, in battle after battle, commanders north and south continued to rely on these dangerously outmoded tactics, lining up their armies to trade volleys at close range before launching useless bayonet assaults against one another. The result was a slaughter, and especially so for the Confederacy, whose generals seemed to be least aware that the rifle-musket vastly increased the power of the defensive over the offensive in land warfare. Whether at the Hornet's Nest in the battle of Shiloh (April 1862) or at the Sunken Road during the battle of Antietam (September 1862) or Pickett's Charge on the last day of Gettysburg (July 1863) or Grant's advance at Cold Harbor (May–June 1864) or John Bell Hood's repeated assaults at Franklin, Tennessee (November 1864), the rifle-musket proved that the day of the bayonet assault was over. Hence the (alleged) hyperbolic costliness of the American Civil War: the weapons, as Shelby Foote drily observed in Ken Burns's magisterial television documentary *The Civil War*, "were way ahead of the tactics." And the rifle-musket was to blame.

It's a flawed argument, demonstrably wrong on several counts. The Civil War was not uniquely bloody. True, more Americans lost their lives than in just about all other American wars combined, but that was a function of scale, not of casualty rates. Losses in Civil War battles were—proportionately measured—no greater than in battles of the Revolutionary War or the War of 1812 or the Mexican-American War. More men died in Civil War combat because more men fought in Civil War battles because the armies were significantly larger, and not because the weapons were so advanced or the tactics so out of date. In fact, for much of the Civil War, the competing armies continued to carry obsolete smoothbores, even some flintlock muskets, into battle. It was not until the middle of the conflict that the supply of modern rifle-muskets—either from domestic production or via European imports—kept up with the demand, and rifle-muskets predominated in combat.

Supply wasn't the only factor limiting the effectiveness of the rifle-musket. The rifle-musket was only as good as the man using it. Without extensive training in marksmanship—or at least some—the accuracy of the rifle-musket didn't amount to much. Only target practice would accustom a soldier to the relatively primitive sights with which most rifle-muskets were equipped, and target practice was a rarity in American Civil War armies as in most European armies. Moreover, clouds of black-powder smoke obscured the battlefields of 1854–1866 as much as they did those of the eighteenth century, and accuracy meant little when it was impossible to see the target very well. That's not to say that the rifle-musket had no real advantages—in combat, and in the hands of a less than proficient marksman—over its smoothbore predecessor. The rifle-musket's longer range was a distinct plus. Even if the average infantryman couldn't pick out or hit a man-sized target at five hundred yards, he could at least hit *something* at five hundred yards, provided he elevated his weapon correctly; nothing short of divine intervention could make a smoothbore musket throw a ball much more than half that distance. It was no longer safe to position field artillery within three hundred to four hundred yards of enemy infantry, a common practice in Napoleonic warfare. But in every other regard, an ordinary infantryman with a rifle-musket wasn't much deadlier than an ordinary infantryman with a smoothbore musket.

There was another limitation, too, a quirk in the rifle-musket's ballistics that rendered it less deadly than its theoretical performance would indicate. The trajectory of the rifle-musket's elongated bullet was distinctly parabolic. To hit more distant targets, as with almost any missile weapon, the rifleman would have to elevate the muzzle, meaning the bullet would loft well above the line of sight. When aimed, with correct elevation, at a man-sized target three hundred yards away, the bullet would follow a high arc and then plunge as it neared its target. Over the length of that flight path, the bullet would traverse two killing zones: one close to the shooter, as it ascended, and the other just a few yards in front of the intended target. But in between those two killing zones was a safe zone, where the bullet went above the height of an average man. A man standing midrange, in this case at 150 yards, would be perfectly safe, even if the rifle-musket seemed to be aimed straight at him: the bullet would travel well over his head.

This was no big secret, no arcane knowledge; the existence of the rifle-musket's "safe zone" lay at the heart of infantry tactics at the time of the American Civil War. The French, probably earlier than anyone else, understood the tactical implications. Though the increased range and accuracy of the rifle-musket would *seem* to have made bayonet charges obsolete, in truth they had not, and the keys for the attacker were speed and discipline. If the attacking force attacked quickly, it was possible to get through the killing zones quickly and stay in the safe zones. Because of the plunging trajectory of the Minié bullet, the killing zones were relatively shallow, and if the defender overestimated or underestimated the distance

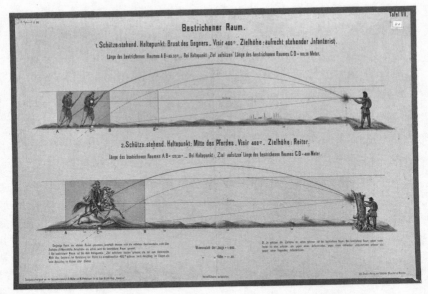

Plate 10. The ballistics of black-powder military rifles. This chart, published for the Bavarian army after the unification of Germany in 1871, shows the parabolic nature of the rifle-musket's trajectory. The rifleman—in order to hit an enemy soldier some 400 meters away—must elevate his rifle so high that the bullet soars to nearly double a man's height at the halfway mark. This Bavarian soldier undoubtedly has a M1869 Werder breech-loading rifle, but the trajectory would be the same with a rifle-musket of the 1850s and 1860s.

Image courtesy of Nationalmuseet, Copenhagen, Denmark.

to the attacking force, most bullets would either fall short or sail safely over the attackers' heads. Moving fast made it difficult, or more difficult, for the defending riflemen to correctly gauge the distance separating them from the forces attacking them. Would the attacker suffer losses? Undoubtedly, and especially in the last fifty yards or so of the assault, as the rifle-musket's trajectory was not an issue and just about every shot by the defending riflemen would hit home. But even if the attackers suffered significant losses, most of them would be upon the defenders, with bayonets leveled to kill, in a flash.

Discipline was necessary, too, the kind of discipline that kept the attacker moving forward without stopping, without pausing to fire back at the enemy. That was easier said than done, of course; one lesson that infantry commanders had learned from the earliest days of the musket era was that soldiers under fire felt an almost irrepressible urge to fire back on their tormentors. To cross over a few hundred yards of open ground at a fast pace, without stopping to fire back, without succumbing to dismay as their comrades fell around them, straight into the face of an enemy force—such feats required training and discipline, and a great degree of physical fitness, too.

The French army had that discipline and that measure of fitness, or rather it inculcated those qualities in its soldiers. The French soldiers who fought against the Austrians in Italy during the Franco-Austrian War (1859) certainly did, and it showed in their combat performance, as they consistently executed successful bayonet assaults against Austrian troops armed with modern rifle-muskets, as at Magenta (4 June 1859). But American Civil War armies were not made up of French soldiers. True, American military intellectuals studied and practically worshipped the French. The prevailing infantry manuals copied shamelessly from French tactical doctrines; even trends in American martial clothing came largely from French fashions. But American soldiers were not trained like the French were; they were citizen-soldiers and not long-term professionals like their French counterparts, and hence they could not fully emulate the French approach to infantry tactics. In Civil War battle after Civil War battle, bayonet charges quickly devolved into short-range firefights, as the attacking infantry stopped moving, went to ground, and succumbed to the urge to shoot back.

It didn't have to be that way, of course, and there are examples of American forces carrying out French assault tactics correctly. On 10 May 1864, Col. Emory Upton—a rising star in the US Army—led an attack column in an assault against the Mule Shoe salient at Spotsylvania Court House, with his handpicked men moving quickly on the Confederates without pausing to fire.

Upton's assault was a dramatic success, and in the end the attack failed only because his superiors did not properly support him or follow up on his breakthrough.

The rifle-musket was a revolutionary new weapon—revolutionary in its accuracy and power, in the sense that it was almost immeasurably more accurate and more powerful than the smoothbore muskets of the previous generation. But it was not revolutionary in the sense that it had any noticeable impact on the art of war, except, maybe, in that it highlighted the need for extensive marksmanship training for aspiring riflemen. The rifle-musket's unexceptional performance in combat also helped to reinforce the notion, current for a long time among experienced professional soldiers, that accuracy and range were lesser qualities in a firearm. What made the most difference, what counted the most in combat, was rate of fire. Bayonet charges still worked against rifle-muskets because rifle-muskets were slow to load.

FOR THAT VERY reason, experimentation with breech-loading firearms did not end with weapons like the Hall rifle. In fact, research and development in the arms industry during the 1840s and beyond centered mostly on the design of breech-loading small arms, reaching peak feverishness in the United States during the Civil War. That war brought forth hundreds of designs, many of which went into production, for the Federal and Confederate governments were desperate to snap up any rifle or carbine that could be thrust into the hands of a young recruit. The Federal government, keen to supply breech-loading carbines to its cavalry, and blessed with a better-developed firearms industry, adopted dozens of unique, patented designs. The Merrill, Gallagher, Burnside, Maynard, Starr, Cosmopolitan, Smith, Sharps, Spencer—all these models, and more besides, found their way into the hands of Federal troops throughout the war. The resulting multiplicity of ammunition types proved to be a logistical nightmare. Cavalry units received the lion's share of these newfangled breechloaders; infantry, by and large, relied on cheaper and more reliable rifle-muskets.

Despite the apparent variety, the individual designs differed only in appearance and minor details, for the most part. Most of them—like the Hall—either made use of the breechblock that rose up or dropped down, exposing the breech so that a cartridge could be inserted (Sharps, Burnside, Starr); in others, the barrel pivoted forward or down to open the breech (Maynard, Gallagher, Smith). Some, like the popular and reliable Sharps, chambered a soft cartridge encased in combustible paper or linen, but a growing number made use of cartridges cased in hard, durable materials, such as brass or vulcanized rubber (Gallagher, Maynard, Smith).

There was no doubt that breech-loading carbines had a greater rate of fire than their muzzle-loading cousins, and that therefore a Federal cavalry regiment in the Civil War generated much more firepower than an equal number of infantry—keeping in mind that the carbine was less effective, shot for shot, than the rifle-musket at longer distances. The success of John Buford's Federal cavalry on the first day of Gettysburg (1 July 1863), holding off superior numbers of Confederate infantry for hours, attests to this. But what made the world sit up and take notice, or—more important—to act on the recognition that breechloaders were superior, was a battle fought three years after Gettysburg, and a world away.

In 1866, the kingdom of Prussia went to war with Austria, while the rest of Europe watched breathlessly. Only two years before, the two German powers had been allies, invading Denmark together in 1864. But the Prussian chancellor, Otto von Bismarck, wanted to unify the German states around Prussian rule, and for that to happen Austria would have to be pushed forcefully out of the way. Austria would not do that, not without a fight, and the odds were with Austria. Though it had taken a beating at the hands of Napoléon III's army in Italy in 1859, Austria had one of the most powerful military establishments in Europe. Prussia was an upstart, an unknown quantity.

We know now, in the perfect light of retrospect, that the Prussian army was first-rate, that in the ways that mattered it was superior to every other army in the West. Prussian military leadership, inspired by the use of railroads in the American Civil War, had been exploring the logistical and strategic possibilities offered by an organized military railway service. Prussian artillery was the best in the world. Both of these things would become widely known in 1866. But the difference that made a difference, the thing that the Prussian army most prided itself on, was its infantry rifle: the Dreyse.

Because the story of the Danish defeat at Lundby in July 1864 had been splashed all over European military science journals, the Dreyse's strengths were no secret, nor were its flaws. It suffered the same shortcomings that plagued all early breechloaders, plus a few that were entirely its own. Lack of a tight seal at the breech meant gas leakage, and it was said that Prussian infantrymen preferred to fire from the hip so as to avoid burning their faces—hardly a recipe for accurate shooting. The slender iron firing needle that detonated the Dreyse rifle cartridge rusted easily and broke frequently. Its range was noticeably shorter than that of the standard Austrian rifle-musket, and its accuracy was no better.

But when Helmuth von Moltke's Prussian army crashed into the Austrians at Königgrätz in July 1866, it was the Prussians who came out on top, and the Dreyse was one of the reasons why they did. True, the Prussians were better organized, had better leadership, better artillery, and better logistics, and the superior Prussian use of railways to get troops and supplies to the seat of the war went a long way toward accounting for Prussia's startling victory. But eyewitnesses on both sides couldn't stop raving about the Dreyse and the superior firepower of the Prussian infantry. The overall superiority of the breechloader to the rifle-musket was already a matter of common knowledge; Lundby, and the entirety of the American Civil War, had made that point plainly enough.

What Königgrätz revealed—or what it was believed to have revealed—was a more sobering truth: that breech-loading rifles were no longer an option, but an imperative. No matter how modest a nation's strategic and political goals were, whether it cherished some hope of significance in international power politics or simply wanted to be able to defend its borders, then it would have to rearm its infantry with breech-loading rifles immediately. It didn't matter that the rifle-musket was less than two decades old in 1866, or that most Western armies had begun the process of mass-producing rifle-muskets for general issue no more than fifteen years before. Austria had fallen behind Prussia in firearms technology, and in 1866 it paid a heavy price.

The next major war in the West, less than four years away, would pit the French army of Napoléon III against the allied armies of Prussia and the lesser German states. The Franco-Prussian War of 1870 would be the first war of any consequence to be fought entirely with breech-loading rifles. The muzzle-loading infantry long-arm was dead and buried.

And very soon, so too was the Dreyse. It was already showing its age in 1866, and by the time of the war against France in 1870 it was well past its prime. There were newer and much better rifles available then. Now it was Prussia's turn to rearm or risk defeat. The rapid pace of weapons development, and the corresponding rapid pace of weapons obsolescence, triggered a renewed arms race in the West—not only in rifles but in artillery and warships, as well.

CHAPTER 8

SHOT AND SHELL

As with small arms, so too with artillery: industrialization and the accelerated pace of technological innovation drastically altered the performance of firearms in a very short period of time, and those nations unwilling or unable to keep up would quickly feel the sting. The Ottoman Turks learned this harsh lesson the hard way in November 1853, when a Russian fleet approached the Turkish port of Sinop (Sinope) on the south rim of the Black Sea. Only a few months before, the Russian tsar had goaded the Ottomans into a declaration of war over a number of grievances—most stemming from conflicting territorial ambitions and Russian concern for the fate of Christian minorities in the Ottoman-ruled Holy Land—and so far the Turks had given a good account of themselves. Turkish armies, supplied from bases like Sinop, had performed well against Russian forces along the Danube River and in the Caucasus. The Russian government decided to push back. It was not a decision taken lightly, for the British and French governments had made it clear that if Russia were to show any aggression toward the Turks, then the two Western nations would intervene on Turkey's behalf.

But the Turks had to be taught a lesson, and something had to be done to weaken their forces encroaching on Russian territory. Sinop would be an appropriate target. After an initial reconnaissance of Sinop and its defenses, Russian admiral Stepanovich Nakhimov led his fleet in a direct attack on Sinop. No one in Nakhimov's command expected much of a fight, for the Russian Black Sea Fleet outnumbered and outgunned the Turkish warships at Sinop by a wide margin. The Russians had six ships of the line, including two 120-gun first-raters, wielding more than 700 big guns altogether, plus a few smaller warships. Against this, the Turks could only muster about a dozen vessels, mostly frigates, lightly gunned by comparison. There were a couple of shore batteries ringing the harbor, but still the disparity between Russian and Turkish weaponry was not negligible.

As Nakhimov's fleet closed with the Turkish ships on 30 November 1853, the Russian admiral used a slight variation on the time-honored line-ahead formation, sending his ships in so that they trapped the Turkish warships between the Russian fleet and the shore batteries, partially shielding the Russian ships from shore fire. Not that it was necessary. The Russian advantage in firepower was so completely overwhelming that the Turkish fleet was annihilated in a matter of hours. One of the six Turkish frigates was sunk, the other five ran aground and were in flames. Only one Turkish ship, a small steamer, managed to escape the conflagration. Once the ships had been taken care of, the Russians trained their guns on the shore batteries and destroyed them, too. The Turks lost nearly three thousand men; the Russians, around 270.

The Russian triumph at Sinop would prove to have tragic consequences, and not just for the Turks. It triggered the entry of Britain and France into the conflict, and few wars of the nineteenth century can rival the Crimean War for incompetence and hamfisted butchery. The victory of Sinop itself, though, was a foregone conclusion. Nakhimov's warships could have been a century out of date and the result would still have been, statistically, the same. But the way in which the Turks had been defeated, with most of their fleet not just battered and leaking but actually ablaze—was something new and unsettling.

That dramatic ending owed entirely to a new kind of artillery, patented three decades earlier. This new gun was the brainchild of a middle-aged French artillery officer and ordnance expert, Henri-Joseph Paixhans. Paixhans was a firm believer in the power of explosive ammunition, what was commonly referred to as shell, and he designed a cannon explicitly around the concept. The Paixhans shell gun, first developed in 1822, was unlike any cannon ever seen before, though its mass was evocative of the bombards of an earlier age. It was massively built so that it could fire a large-caliber explosive shell using a heavy powder charge. The size of the shell meant that more powder could be stored within, for a bigger explosion; the larger powder charge meant that the shell would fly with a flatter trajectory, and at a high velocity, which in turn meant more penetrating power. Against a wooden ship, Paixhans predicted, the effect would be devastating. The high-velocity shell would penetrate the wooden sides of all but the stoutest first-raters, and then explode *inside* the ship—and for a wooden ship, that would be very bad indeed.

Nakhimov's first-raters shipped a larger number of Paixhans guns, in which the Russian fleet—oddly, given the navy's reputation for parsimony and overall backwardness—had invested heavily. These were what had set the Turkish ships afire; these were what had lit up the sky and set the dark waters at Sinop aglow on a dark November night in 1853. Sinop had shown the world a frightening new aspect of artillery. For five centuries, the big guns had been capable of doing only one thing effectively: battering. Whether it took the form of a single round shot or a stand of grape, artillery had fired mostly solid projectiles, and explosive shell was a barely effective rarity. But the Paixhans gun was capable of something else entirely. It could project an explosion. The new shell guns threw projectiles that could be made to explode remotely, over a target, or against it, or inside it. Sinop announced to the world that the days of the wooden warship and the brick masonry fort were numbered, and that from this moment on the power of artillery would be enhanced by the explosive force of the projectile itself.

The invention of the shell gun was the first in a series of inventions that would transform artillery in the industrial age. Great forward strides in metallurgy, chemistry, and engineering, combined with the enhanced productive capacity of the industrialized West, transformed the big guns into something almost unrecognizable when compared to their ancestral technologies from the Renaissance. By the dawn of the twentieth century, artillery would become the deadliest family of weapons in the Western arsenal, the ultimate expression of firepower.

TO BECOME DEADLIER, artillery had to overcome the physical constraints imposed by its structure and the nature of the ammunition it used, much as with small arms of the same period. The first, and arguably the most dramatic, improvements were in the design of artillery ammunition. In the Napoleonic wars and before, a gunner had two basic options when it came to ammunition: a single solid projectile, or a group of solid projectiles. Time had proven their usefulness and versatility. Solid shot was indispensable in siege warfare, for smashing through walls; and in naval warfare, for battering wooden ships. When used by field artillery on the battlefield, solid shot could serve both as an anti-materiel round, to smash objects—in counterbattery fire, for example, to knock out the enemy's guns and artillery vehicles—and as an antipersonnel round. Of course, a single solid shot could kill or maim only a few soldiers at a time, and even then only if it hit a deep, densely packed formation. The greater value of solid shot on the battlefield came from its impact on morale. Cannonballs were large enough to be visible in flight, and the sight of a solid shot arcing through the air or bounding along the ground was enough to unnerve even veteran troops. The sight of artillery casualties, human or horse, was horrific. When a nine-pounder ball took away the head of Asa Pollard, the first American to die in the Revolutionary War battle of Bunker Hill (17 June 1775), the bloody spectacle nearly sent the entire American force into a panic.

The other kind of ordnance readily available to artillerists before the Napoleonic age were the short-range, dispersing projectiles: grapeshot and canister. The underlying principle of the two types was one and the same. Grapeshot consisted of a load of small round shot, usually iron, bound together around a spindle fixed to a wooden sabot, or base. Netting wrapped around the assemblage held the shot in place, and the whole thing resembled a cylindrical cluster of grapes—hence the name. With canister, a larger quantity of smaller shot, usually lead musket balls, was placed in a metal can. Either round turned a cannon into a giant shotgun, spraying shot over a wide front. Grapeshot allowed for slightly longer ranges, and could do heavier damage to hard targets; canister was strictly a close-range round, but it threw more projectiles and consequently could take down more men per shot. At ranges of less than one hundred yards, canister was brutally effective.

There were also a variety of special-purpose rounds, mostly for naval use. Chain shot and bar shot, for example, were valued for their ability to shred sails and slice through rigging. Hot shot— ordinary solid shot, heated red hot—could wreak havoc with sailing ships and wooden structures. But hot shot required a special furnace, and therefore its use was restricted mostly to coastal fortifications.

It wasn't long after the first appearance of the big siege guns in the fourteenth century that artillerists began to wonder if it might be possible to make cannonballs explode. Theoretically, it could be done: cast a hollow iron sphere with a single hole in it, pack it with gunpowder, insert some kind of fuse in the hole. Simple, yes, but deceptively so, for there were serious challenges involved. Make the chamber too big, then the outer walls could be too thin; when fired, the shell was likely to be crushed by the explosive force of the main charge before it could so much as exit the muzzle. Make the chamber too small and the walls too thick, and the explosive charge might not be enough to even crack the shell when it detonated, let alone generate enough force to cause much damage.

But the biggest challenge was ignition. How would it be possible to light the shell's fuse with some degree of safety? Gunners learned that the firing of the cannon itself could light the fuse, the flames licking through the windage between the inside of the barrel and the outside of the shell. The problem was that there was no telling which way the fuse would face—a spherical shell, once inserted into the muzzle, will roll, and there would be no way of controlling its position when it came to a halt atop the powder charge. If the fuse pointed toward the breech, toward the powder charge, then disaster would be all but inevitable. The explosion of the main charge would blow the fuse into the shell, likely detonating it while it was still in the barrel.

The earliest attempts at addressing the ignition problem were quite primitive. The first fuses were nothing more than lengths of slow match, plugged into the shell's fuse-hole. The gunner would light the fuse immediately before loading it, then force it down the barrel and hope for the best—a tricky, uncertain, and very dangerous practice. With short-barreled mortars, the process was less fraught with danger, as the loaded shell was close enough to the muzzle to be aligned manually. But if there were any delay in igniting the main charge, the gun crew would be in deep trouble.

Still, there were solutions to these problems, and over the course of the seventeenth and eighteenth centuries European gunners gradually found them. First, the fuse itself. Plug fuses, usually wooden tubes packed with a quick-burning substance, like antimony, replaced the slow match. Experience taught that plug fuses could be cut down at predetermined intervals, thereby adjusting the burn time of the fuse. An expert gunner, if he was capable of estimating the range of his intended target and calculating the shell's time-in-flight from muzzle to target, could cut the fuse so that the shell would burst at precisely the right distance—over the heads of infantry or cavalry, for example. And strapping the round shell to a wooden sabot, a disk of roughly the same diameter as the shell itself, kept the ball from rolling down the barrel, ensuring that the fuse would be facing toward the muzzle.

This projectile, the simple shell, led to more complicated designs. One of these, the brainchild of an aspiring British lieutenant, combined shell with canister. Rather than relying on the clunky, jagged fragments of the shell's body for its killing power, this new hybrid contained both a concentrated bursting charge and as many small lead or iron balls as could fit inside the shell. If timed correctly, the fuse would ignite the bursting charge right over the target, showering it from above with musket balls at high velocity. It performed, in other words, like long-range canister. The hybrid ammunition was a brilliant idea, and it was quickly adopted throughout the Western world in the first half of the nineteenth century. Formally, the new shell—and its more recent descendants—was called "case shot" or "spherical case," but gunners came to refer to it by the name of its young inventor: Lieutenant Henry Shrapnel. Today, we use the term shrapnel to refer to almost any kind of shards produced by almost any kind of explosion, but in its original and proper context it meant a very specific type of antipersonnel ammunition for artillery.

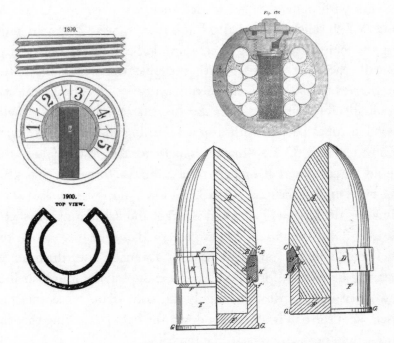

Plate 11. Innovations in artillery ammunition; The Bormann time fuse; spherical case or shrapnel; Hotchkiss patent shell, 1861.

Images from Park Benjamin, *Appletons' Cyclopædia of Applied Mechanics* 2 vols. (New York: D. Appleton, 1888), 2:891; Reiter, *Elementar-Waffenlehre*, p. 195; US Patent 32293, issued 14 May 1861.

Early in the nineteenth century, the explosive shell was part of the artilleryman's conventional toolkit. It was the preferred round for field howitzers, for the howitzer's arcing trajectory was peculiarly suited to lofting shells onto troops protected by trenches or walls. The shell was really the only practical choice for mortars, whose sole purpose was to toss projectiles over obstructions. But explosive shells could also be used in field guns, too, and the further refinement of fuses made it easy to do so accurately. The Bormann fuse, a Belgian design from the middle of the nineteenth century, took much of the guesswork out of gunnery. The lead and tin Bormann fuse easily screwed into a threaded fuse-hole in the shell, and its soft zinc face was marked off in time intervals, measured in increments of quarter-seconds. Once the gunner determined the distance of his target, he consulted a chart to calculate the shell's time in flight, and using a special tool he punctured the fuse face at the appropriate time marker.

If explosive shell was useful in land warfare, it was doubly so in naval combat, at least so long as warships were wood-built. Here mortars and howitzers were less satisfactory, though of course bomb-ketches, armed with mortars, came in handy when bombarding shore fortifications. Ship-to-ship action, the kind of combat that navies were primarily designed for, required direct fire, flatter trajectories, and greater penetrative power, so conventional naval guns were more in order. But that presented a quandary when it came to using shell. For a shell to be truly effective at ship killing, it had to be big enough to hold a substantial explosive charge of gunpowder and still have sturdy, thick walls. If it were not to bounce harmlessly off the thick oaken sides of a man-of-war, the shell would have to be fired at a high velocity, but it would also have to be substantial enough to survive both the shock of the cannon firing *and* its initial contact with its target. The guns that made up the bulk of naval armaments in 1800, mostly twenty-four- and thirty-two-pounder cannon, were not quite big enough.

Enter Henri-Joseph Paixhans and his shell gun. What was noteworthy about the Paixhans gun was that it took already existing technologies and recombined them into a novel weapon—or, more accurately, into a familiar weapon with a different and specialized purpose. A conventional howitzer was adequate for land warfare, where the shell merely had to reach its target and then explode. But for ship-to-ship action, the Paixhans gun was far superior. Its massively thick, "built-up" construction allowed it to withstand truly large powder charges, and the resulting flatter trajectory and high velocity meant that it could send a shell crashing through the thick sides of a first-rater before the shell exploded. The Paixhans gun's huge caliber—the original Paixhans had a bore diameter of 22mm, or nearly nine inches—meant that the shell packed a lot of explosive force.

Plate 12. 9-inch Dahlgren gun, aboard a US Navy gunboat—possibly the USS *Miami*—during the American Civil War. The distinctly bottle-shaped Dahlgren was part of the second generation of naval shell guns, an improvement upon the French Paixhans shell gun.

Image: NH 61933 courtesy of the Naval History & Heritage Command.

As was beginning to become the pattern in the industrial era, the new technology moved fast, from idea to execution to testing to adoption. Paixhans first proposed the design in 1822; in 1824, he was given the opportunity to demonstrate his prototype guns, including a series of test-firings against the condemned ship of the line *Pacificateur*. The Paixhans guns made short work of *Pacificateur*, whose shredded hulk convinced French naval authorities to order more shell guns. Time and again the Paixhans guns proved their worth in combat. A small French squadron, armed partly with shell guns, easily overwhelmed the Mexican citadel of San Juan de Ulúa at Veracruz late in 1838, with well-aimed shells touching off the fort's powder magazines in short order. During the Three Years' War (First Schleswig War, 1848–1851), Schleswig-Holstein's rebellion against Danish rule, the Paixhans gun scored its first victory against a warship. In an engagement in the Eckernförde near Kiel (April 1849), rebel shore batteries—armed with Paixhans guns—set the Danish two-decker *Christian VIII* afire, which subsequently exploded. And then there was the terrifying spectacle of Sinop. But the major navies of the West did not need any more convincing than that. They were already sold on the concept well before the Ottoman fleet had been reduced to cinders. Britain, France, the United States, Russia, all were eager to embrace the use of explosive ammunition at sea, even if that very act doomed the wooden warship to immediate obsolescence.

The first American trials of homebuilt shell guns, in the 1840s, would give rise to a tragic scandal. An experimental US Navy warship, the steam-powered screw sloop USS *Princeton*, carried an equally experimental armament. Aboard *Princeton* were two American shell guns. One, dubbed Oregon, was designed by a team of engineers, including a young Swedish prodigy named John Ericsson, who had also played a critical role in designing *Princeton* itself. Oregon made use of a brilliant construction method of Ericsson's design. It was a built-up gun, meaning that the wrought-iron barrel was wrapped with several successive iron bands around the gun's breech, each applied while still very hot so that it shrank as it cooled. The result was a very heavy gun, but the breech-bands allowed the wrought iron barrel to withstand the enormous chamber pressures generated by the huge powder charge needed to throw the shell. Ericsson arranged for the gun to be built at the Mersey Ironworks in Liverpool and shipped to the States. The rival shell gun had been designed by *Princeton*'s captain, Robert F. Stockton. At twenty-seven thousand pounds gross weight, Stockton's gun, Peacemaker, was even more massive than Ericsson's. Peacemaker's bore was a full twelve inches in diameter, and it fired a solid shot weighing over two hundred pounds. It must have been an impressive sight; one group of learned visitors hailed Peacemaker as "beyond comparison [to] the most extraordinary forged work ever executed." But that did not mean it was any better. On the contrary—Stockton's shell gun was far less reliable, because the bands girdling the breech of Stockton's Peacemaker were welded in place, not shrink-cooled, the feature that made Oregon phenomenally strong. And while Ericsson had insisted on a thorough proofing of Oregon, Stockton's Peacemaker was all but untested.

One fine February day in 1844, *Princeton* slipped its moorings at Alexandria, Virginia, embarking on a short demonstration cruise along the Potomac, arranged for the benefit of a small crowd of visiting dignitaries. Aboard were the president of the United States himself, John Tyler, his daughter, much of his Cabinet, former First Lady Dolley Madison, and a mixture of politicians, diplomats, and their families. Stockton, an inveterate self-promoter, insisted upon a test-firing of his gun, despite repeated warnings from Ericsson that Peacemaker hadn't been adequately proofed and was likely dangerous. The elegantly dressed throng aboard *Princeton* clapped and cheered when Peacemaker boomed its first round over the Potomac, and the sight was so thrilling that Stockton—by popular demand—had the gun crew reload and fire again, and again, and again.

It was on the fourth shot when Peacemaker burst. The entire left side of the "monster gun" blew out in a shower of jagged hot iron and flame. One huge chunk of iron struck Secretary of the

Navy Thomas Gilmer, Secretary of State Abel Upshur, and three other men, killing all five instantly. Seven died altogether, and another dozen or so were wounded. President Tyler was below deck at the time of the explosion—as he told Stockton, "I don't like firearms"—and escaped unscathed.

Tyler's reaction to the terrible accident was measured and gracious; rather than seek to punish any of those involved in the construction of Oregon and Peacemaker, he reminded Congress that, sometimes, accidents happen, and especially so in military service. It was a generous and pragmatic sentiment to be sure, but Tyler inadvertently made an important observation: in an age of such unprecedented progress, of such breathtaking speed in the introduction and implementation of warlike inventions, failures were to be expected, and sometimes people would get unintentionally hurt.

Neither Stockton nor Ericsson would be punished, though the fault lay with Stockton if it lay with anyone. Stockton went on to fame and glory and power, as a naval officer and then as a politician; that California would become part of the Union owed in no small measure to Stockton's actions as commander of the US Navy's Pacific Squadron in 1846–1847. Ericsson did not suffer for his part, nor should he have, but neither was he rewarded for all the work that went into the pathbreaking ship *Princeton*. He was not even paid what he had been promised. For that he held a grudge, toward the US Navy and toward the federal government, but fortunately for the United States he did not nurse that grudge forever. The Navy would call upon him in a moment of grave national peril, and Ericsson—reluctant or not—answered the call. He had, with *Princeton*, designed and helped construct what was possibly the most advanced warship in the 1840s, and the most advanced naval gun, as well. In 1861, he would step forward with an even more radical design, and the most advanced fighting ship of its day: the USS *Monitor*, the forerunner of all turreted battleships.

FOR ALL THE spectacle of its first uses in combat, the Paixhans gun was seriously flawed, although for the most part those flaws were understood from the beginning. For naval shell to be effective, it had to be large enough to carry a big explosive charge; for the shell to be large enough to do that, it needed a big gun to fire it. The Paixhans guns were, therefore, elephantine in proportions: the original model was over nine feet long and weighed more than four tons. Aboard ship, the weight wasn't an insurmountable problem, but the vast bulk of the Paixhans guns didn't allow ships of more modest size to mount very many. As more than one naval officer noted, too, the Paixhans guns were single-purpose weapons. They could throw an explosive shell, quite well in fact, but they were not designed to fire shot. Shot, being solid iron, was heavier than shell of the same caliber, and generated greater chamber pressures when fired. Plus, shell did not render shot obsolete. Even Paixhans himself, a fervent advocate for shell, did not dispute that. That meant that naval vessels would have to line their gun decks with two different types of cannon, at a time when naval engineering favored the concept of standardizing everything.

The Paixhans guns were just emerging from novelty status when their replacements began to appear, guns that were large enough to hurl a shell into the side of a wooden warship but strong enough to handle shot as well. The built-up construction seen in John Ericsson's Oregon was one, and though Ericsson did not get much credit for it—nearly everyone associated with the *Princeton* disaster suffered a diminished reputation for it, deserved or not—other entrepreneurs-engineers took up the concept and ran with it. The cannon designs patented in the 1850s and 1860s by Sir William Armstrong and Captain Theophilus Blakely in Britain, and by Robert Parker Parrott in America, all relied on the application of reinforcing bands applied hot around the breech of the cannon tube.

More promising results came from advances in metallurgy, specifically new methods for casting and working iron. In the United States, where national security policy rested heavily on the protection afforded by the vast oceans that separated North America from potential rivals in Europe and Asia, it was the fleet and the seacoast forts that acted as the main bulwark against foreign invasion. Consequently, while American land forces were pitifully small when compared to those of even the middling European states, the American navy and forts were first-rate, and both required big guns. Early in its history, the US Army developed a class of super-cannon, which came to be known as columbiads. They were reminiscent of the bombards of old but intended to defend fortifications rather than bash them down.

In the 1840s, less than two decades before the outbreak of the Civil War, a career army officer and inventor—no longer an unusual hybrid—named Thomas Jackson Rodman tackled the problem of making big guns smaller, leaner, and tougher. He was something of an unsung genius among geniuses, his fame and fortune likely constrained by his sense of duty to country, because he was at the center of several key inventions that made fortress artillery more powerful. One of his inventions was a new kind of gunpowder. It featured compressed, shaped grains that burned slower and more consistently than conventional artillery powder, resulting in greater velocity and range. But Rodman's real gifts were in cannon design. Rodman was stationed at the Fort Pitt Foundry in Pittsburgh, and for a full decade he experimented with new ways of casting iron cannon. By the mid-1850s he had come up with a promising casting technique, the so-called wet chill method. The cannon would be cast hollow around a specially designed core. Hollow-cast cannon were not unusual, but the core was. While the cannon was being cast, chilled water would be forced through an array of pipes in the core, while hot coals were piled up around the cannon's exterior. Cooling from the inside first, rather than from the outside in, made all the difference. Impurities were forced to the surface—the outside of the barrel, that is—and the thickest material gravitated toward the center of the barrel. The metal on the outside gradually shrank against the rapidly cooling interior. The result was a barrel that resisted the massive chamber pressures created by huge powder charges, making it practical to construct cannon of (almost) unprecedented size and power. The Rodman columbiads, which went into production right at the outbreak of the Civil War, came in 8-, 10-, and 15-inch calibers. Toward the end of the war, Fort Pitt made a 20-incher, a monster that tipped the scales at nearly sixty tons and fired a 763-pound shell. While the 20-inch Rodman never emerged from the experimental stage, the more practical 15-inch columbiad saw widespread use during the war, and it was an impressive performer. Using a charge of 40 pounds of gunpowder, the 25-ton behemoth could hurl a 350-pound shell nearly three miles. Yet the construction was amazingly durable; Rodman guns almost never burst.

The Rodman wet chill method was equally applicable to smaller guns. Another American officer used wet chill to make an improved naval gun as a replacement for the Paixhans. The son of a Swedish diplomat in Philadelphia, John A. Dahlgren became the leading American expert on naval artillery. He helped to establish the US Navy's weapons office, the Ordnance Department, in the 1840s, and devised a percussion lock that could be used to fire a shipboard cannon with an ordinary musket cap. American sailors sent ashore as landing parties had vastly increased firepower thanks to the line of easily portable boat howitzers that Dahlgren designed for naval service.

But Dahlgren's big contribution was a new shell gun. He had studied the American-made Paixhans guns that were in service by the time of the war with Mexico, and found them wanting—mostly, he later wrote, because they couldn't fire solid shot. After a few years of experimentation, at roughly the same time as Rodman was working at Fort Pitt, the first Dahlgren guns went into production, in 1855. The wet chill method gave the Dahlgrens the same sturdiness as the Rodmans, only on a smaller scale; the most popular calibers were nine and eleven inches. In common parlance, they became known as Dahlgren shell guns, but they were just as capable of hurling shot.

THOUGH ARTILLERY AND small arms were closely related technologies, they filled different roles, and they followed divergent paths of development. For small arms, rate of fire was the most important attribute, closely followed by simplicity, cost, durability, range, and accuracy. For artillery, range and power were the design imperatives.

The Paixhans gun and its derivatives, such as the Rodman, Armstrong, and Dahlgren guns, elevated artillery to a new plateau in range and power. It was only natural, though, that artillery experts might ponder if the great ballistic innovation in nineteenth-century small arms—rifling—would produce parallel effects in the ballistics of the big guns. There was nothing at all far-fetched about the idea, and in fact artillerists had been experimenting with rifled cannon since at least the seventeenth century. As with small arms, the obvious challenge was getting a tight fit between projectile and bore, so that the projectile would engage the rifling, a challenge made steeper by the greater size of the weapon and the hardness of the projectile—artillery ammunition tended to be made of iron, rather than the soft lead of small-arms bullets.

What made rifled, muzzle-loading artillery possible—as Claude Minié and his contemporaries had discovered—was a major redesign of the projectile, rather than the gun itself. Elongated artillery projectiles, like rifling, were not new; Paixhans, among others, favored elongated shell, even for smoothbore guns, for elongated projectiles simplified the fuse problem. If the fuse was put in the nose of an elongated shell, there was no danger of the fuse facing the powder charge if it was loaded correctly. Elongated shells even suggested the possibility of using percussion fuses. Percussion fuses, which detonate when the projectile physically strikes its target, only work if the projectile hits that target nose-first, which is impossible to arrange if the projectile is spherical. An elongated shell, in theory, will strike its target nose-first. But when fired from smoothbore artillery, there was always a chance that an elongated projectile might tumble in flight, end over end, and there was no telling what part of the projectile would hit the target first—or, for that matter, that it would hit anywhere near the target, since a tumbling shell was hardly an accurate thing. Rifling eliminated those problems. By imparting that all-important spin, rifling guaranteed that an elongated projectile would fly straight, true, and on target.

There were almost as many approaches to rifled artillery design as there were to bullet design. Some, like the field guns of the French La Hitte system, used mechanically fitted projectiles. Shells and bolts (a common synonym for elongated solid shot) for La Hitte guns were fitted with lugs along their sides, which fit directly into the deep rifling grooves in the bore. Other designs, like many used in the American Civil War, were more similar to the expanding bullets used in rifle-muskets. The Reed patent shell, for example, featured a soft iron cup bolted to the base of the cylindrical iron body; just like with the Minié bullet, expanding gases from the charge forced the cup into the rifling upon discharge. The Hotchkiss-pattern projectiles, also commonly used in the American Civil War, relied on compression instead. The Hotchkiss shell consisted of two iron segments, front and rear, connected by a thick leaden belt. The shock of discharge forced the rear iron section into the forward section, compressing the lead belt and squeezing it into the rifling.

The first combat-tested affirmation of rifled artillery's superiority came in the 1859 Franco-Austrian conflict in Piedmont. The French had just adopted the so-called La Hitte system of rifled bronze muzzleloaders, and had rifled many of their smoothbore guns—such as the 1853 model *Canon obusier de campagne de 12cm*, later to become famous in America as the model for the "twelve-pounder Napoleon," arguably the most ubiquitous cannon on Civil War battlefields—so that they could fire the La Hitte system's special studded projectiles. The guns were so new, in fact, that as the French army prepared to move on Italy in April 1859 the emperor's artillery batteries mustered in with empty gun carriages, the tubes themselves not being issued until the army reached Genoa. The French gun crews were unfamiliar with the La Hitte rifled guns, but they gave a stellar account of themselves in battle. The La Hitte guns—principally the Model 1859 *Canon de campagne de 4 La Hitte*, a lightweight 86mm-caliber gun that fired a 4kg shell—was vastly superior to the Austrians' smoothbore field guns. The

La Hitte pieces consistently outranged and outshot the Austrian artillery, knocking out entire Austrian batteries before they could even deploy for action. The La Hitte cannon fired only explosive shell and canister—the French did not issue solid shot for their rifled guns—and their fuses were comparatively primitive. But even given these shortcomings, there was no doubting that rifled artillery was the wave of the future.

By the time the American Civil War broke out two years later, most Western armies had made big strides toward rearming with rifled field guns. The Austrians very nearly copied the French design that had so tormented them at Magenta and Solferino. The American army, conservative as it was, already had rifled guns in service before the outbreak of hostilities against the southern Confederacy.

Interestingly, the rifled guns never completely replaced the old smoothbores in either Federal or Confederate service. In part, that was because—as with smoothbore muskets—there were still so many of them sitting around in federal and state arsenals at the beginning of the war; and in part, that was also because smoothbores still had their uses. In heavily wooded country, the greater range and accuracy of the rifled guns did not count for much; and the smoothbores, usually bigger than comparable rifled guns, often packed a bigger punch. The 4.62-inch bore diameter of the twelve-pounder Napoleon could fire a lot more canister than a 3-inch rifled gun, and a twelve-pounder shell could hold a significantly larger explosive charge than a 3-inch elongated projectile.

Where the rifled guns really showed to advantage, though, was in their greater accuracy, and the bigger the gun, the greater the gap in performance between rifled and smoothbore. The American experience of 1861–1865 made that point clear. In the spring of 1862, Federal forces invested the Confederate-held stronghold of Fort Pulaski, a modern masonry-and-earth fortress guarding the sea approaches to the vital port of Savannah, Georgia. Fort Pulaski was in good shape, well armed, and surrounded by swamps and tidal marshes that made it all but impossible for a besieging force to get close. None other than Confederate general Robert E. Lee, an engineer by training, deemed Pulaski impregnable. "They cannot breach your walls at this distance," he assured the fort's commander.

The Federals sought to prove otherwise. After careful preparation, their siege batteries opened fire on Pulaski on 10 April 1862. The Federal siege batteries included an eclectic mix of old and new: smoothbore columbiads, gigantic siege mortars, and a variety of rifled guns—thirty-pounder (4.2-inch caliber) banded Parrott rifles and several James rifles, older smoothbore guns of large caliber that were modernized with rifling. The largest of the James guns was an old forty-two-pounder gun, which after its conversion to the James system threw a sixty-four-pound shell (or an eighty-one-pound bolt) seven inches in diameter. The mortars did very little to damage the fort or its garrison, but the more powerful rifled guns chewed it up. In the very first day of the siege, the Parrott and James rifles, firing from about a mile away, clawed a breach in Pulaski's massive seven-and-a-half-foot-thick walls. The Confederates fought back tenaciously, but eventually had to accept the inevitable. On 12 April, after less than two days' bombardment, Pulaski surrendered to its besiegers. There was no denying the object lesson: rifled artillery spelled the end of the masonry fort.

Already asserting itself on the battlefield, artillery was once again on the verge of bringing sweeping, even revolutionary change to warfare. But change moved fast in the industrial age, and within the span of a generation after the fall of Fort Pulaski, the guns of the midcentury—Paixhans, Rodman, Parrott, all of them—would be swept onto the rapidly growing heap of curiosities and antiques. Taking their places would be bigger, faster-firing, more accurate guns, making use of more powerful explosives, more efficient propellants, more durable metals. By the end of the century, artillery would rule the battlefield.

And not just rule the battlefield, but transform it as well. Nowhere was this more evident than in war at sea, where the shell gun demanded a major and drastic shift in warship design.

CHAPTER 9

IRONCLAD

The shell guns that savaged the Turkish fleet at Sinop in 1853 were one of four innovations that collectively brought the era of the sailing warship to an abrupt end. Wooden-hulled ships simply could not stand up to the shell gun, even if they were equipped with shell guns themselves. The other three innovations—the marine steam engine, the screw propeller, and the use of iron and steel in shipbuilding—were just as critical. All four came to be in the half-century after Lord Nelson's victory at Trafalgar in 1805; all four came together for the first time in combat in 1855, in the closing act of the Crimean War. But the first truly stunning exhibition of what the new naval technology could achieve came a little more than six years later, in one of the most fraught moments of the American Civil War—and one of the most dramatic moments in the history of naval warfare.

On 8 March 1862, a Confederate naval flotilla steamed from its home port at Norfolk, Virginia, and into Hampton Roads, where the mouth of the James River meets Chesapeake Bay and, ultimately, the Atlantic. The mouth of the Potomac is only some eighty miles to the north; to the west and north, up the James, lies Richmond, then the capital of the Confederacy.

As the Union had focused its war effort in this particular theater on the capture of Richmond itself, and because Washington, DC, was not all that far away up the Potomac, there were Federal naval forces in and about Hampton Roads. Numerically, at least, they were far superior to whatever force the rebels could muster. Here in the roadstead there was ample evidence. Two fifty-gun steam frigates, *Roanoke* and *Minnesota*, with two sailing frigates, *St. Lawrence* and *Congress*, swayed at anchor, just off the mouth of the Elizabeth River. A sailing frigate, USS *Cumberland*, was also anchored just off Newport News, closer to the James River. *Cumberland* was a veteran, almost forty years old, but it carried a powerful battery of Dahlgren shell guns. The Confederates, on the other hand, had almost no navy to speak of.

But on this morning, a ragtag assortment of vessels flying the Confederate naval jack was making its way north into the roadstead, brazenly heading straight for the Federal vessels, which sat on guard, gunports open, black cannon muzzles protruding menacingly. The Federal sailors were not alarmed, not at first, for the rebel squadron looked harmless: three small gunboats—nothing more than half-broken-down harbor tugboats, each carrying a cannon or two—and a couple of paddle-wheel steamboats with a few light guns. The Federal ships could have blown all of them out of the water in a matter of minutes.

And then there was *that thing*.

It really didn't look like a ship at all. Most of its hull was, apparently, underwater, and its only deck rode so low that it was just about totally awash. Above the water stood only its superstructure, a barn-like object, black and gleaming dully, rounded fore and aft, with a small cone-like pilothouse attached to the top. A single funnel belched black smoke. There were no masts and no rigging, but there were gunports, visible on both sides and on the ends.

None of the officers watching from the quarterdecks of the Federal men-of-war had seen it before, but they all knew what it was, for the hype had long ago preceded the thing itself. It was an ironclad ram, built up from the charred remains of what had once been the steam frigate USS *Merrimack*, destroyed when the Federals torched Gosport Navy Yard before abandoning it to the rebels in the first days of the war. The rebels had reclaimed the wreck, burned almost down to the waterline, and resurrected it as some kind of ironclad behemoth. Reports from Federal sympathizers in the area indicated that it had a massive iron ram bolted to its prow.

The other Confederate ships were irrelevant. The only one that wasn't entirely worthless, besides the former *Merrimack*, was the armed steamer *Patrick Henry*—and a few well-placed shots fired from a Federal shore-battery burst its boiler and put it out of commission. But the armored ram kept coming. *Minnesota* got underway to confront the strange object, and promptly ran aground.

The ram went after *Cumberland* and *Congress*. Both ships fired on it, but with no effect, the huge projectiles from *Cumberland*'s 10-inch Dahlgrens simply bouncing harmlessly from the ram's armored sides. The ram didn't move very fast—its top speed was less than nine knots—but it descended on *Cumberland* without hesitation. Even as the *Cumberland*'s crew pounded the strange vessel's casemate with shell after shell after shell, the ram crashed straight into *Cumberland*'s starboard side. The massive cast-iron ram tore a terrible gash in the frigate, below the waterline, and in seconds the wounded ship began to list to starboard as water gushed into its lower decks. It almost took the ram with it, as the ironclad struggled to extricate its prow from *Cumberland*'s hull. Finally the ram sheered off of the ironclad's bow, the Confederate ship was free, and the *Cumberland* sank to the bottom, taking more than one hundred twenty of the crew with it into the depths.

Now it was *Congress*'s turn, and *Congress* had exhausted its options. It had run aground in the shallows of the Roads. The damaged ironclad no longer had a means of ramming, so its commander contented himself with shelling *Congress* from a modest distance. The rest of the Confederate squadron joined in on the kill, and soon *Congress* was in sorry shape. *Congress*'s captain was down, as was much of the crew, and with no apparent hope of rescue the surviving officers struck their colors in surrender. The ironclad's skipper, a curmudgeonly old salt named Franklin Buchanan, made arrangements to ferry *Congress*'s survivors off the battered ship to safety. But Federal shore batteries, unaware of what was transpiring in the channel, fired on Buchanan and his crew, and an infuriated Buchanan ordered *Congress* destroyed. A few hot-shot rounds fired into *Congress*'s hull set the frigate ablaze. Sometime very late that night, the fire spread to the magazine, and a tremendous explosion ripped *Congress* apart.

Minnesota would have been next. It, too, had run aground, and the other Confederate ships had already begun to trade shots with it. But darkness approached, and it didn't seem likely that the stricken Federal ship was going anywhere. With the ironclad in the lead, limping slightly from the loss of its ram, the Confederate squadron reversed course and steamed back to anchor off Sewell's Point.

It had been a historic day, the first battle between ironclad and wooden warships, the first battle within recent memory between sailing ships and a mastless, sail-less, steam-powered vessel. The Confederate ram, known officially as CSS *Virginia* even though more famous to posterity as *Merrimack*, had done very well on its first combat mission. It was a flawed design, to be sure, built on a damaged hull with damaged engines; *Virginia* was so ungainly that the simple act of executing a 180-degree turn under full steam consumed a full thirty minutes. Yet even with those handicaps it had managed to destroy two well-armed warships and frighten away several more.

The next day, when Buchanan intended to bring *Virginia* back to the roadstead and pick off the remaining Federal vessels, would turn out to be a historic day, too. For the US Navy's answer to *Virginia*—a smaller, lighter, much less substantial looking ironclad—had arrived on the scene like a miracle in the night.

THE ART AND technology of war at sea followed the same pattern as war on land in the age of revolutions: while the wars with Napoléon had been fought with the technology of the eighteenth century, industrialization thereafter radically altered the pace of innovation and technological change, and truly jarring advances in the tools of war were the result. Naval engagements of the period

1792–1815 were identical to those of a century before, except in scale. Whatever brilliance we can ascribe to the likes of Lord Nelson, he was still an eighteenth-century admiral fighting eighteenth-century battles with eighteenth-century warships.

With the downfall of Napoléon in 1814–1815 came a predictable downsizing of European armies and navies, as kingdoms large and small transitioned to a peacetime footing and prepared to meet the manifold challenges of the postwar order. There was a perceptible if subtle shift in the balance of naval power, and in the relative ranking of the great fleets. Britain still held the top spot, and would do so for the century to come. Defeated or not, France would remain Britain's chief competitor, the two nations engaging in a low-intensity arms race through much of the subsequent century. The Russian fleet grew in size if not quality, and the upstart United States—though still young and weak—began to develop a respectable fleet. Some navies that had once been great, like those of Spain and Denmark, began to slip into insignificance.

But naval technology itself was stagnant, firmly rooted in the established notions of naval architecture, weaponry, and tactics that had prevailed since the universal acceptance of line-ahead tactics. The only perceptible trend was a general increase in the size of both ships and guns. Thirty-two- and forty-two-pounder guns replaced the eighteens and twenty-fours of Nelson's day. First-raters grew to ridiculous proportions. Lord Nelson's flagship, HMS *Victory*, was considered enormous when it was launched in 1765; the 226-foot-long vessel displaced over 2,100 tons and carried 104 guns on its three decks. By contrast, the French ship of the line *Valmy*, one of the last all-sail warships ever built in the West (1847), displaced close to 6,000 tons and was armed with 120 guns, more than half of them shell guns of Paixhans's design. Even the Americans, who relied on ships of more modest proportions, got in on the game. On their frigates, like the USS *Constitution* (1797), they stuffed as many guns as possible onto the gun deck; *Constitution* had the proportions of a 44-gunner, and was rated as such, but it actually carried 56 guns and carronades. The US Navy even departed from its budget-conscious reliance on frigates to build its own ships of the line, such as the USS *Ohio* (1820, 64 guns) and the USS *Pennsylvania* (1837, 130 guns). The warships of the early nineteenth century, in short, packed a slightly bigger wallop than their immediate ancestors, but the roles they played, the tactics they followed, the nature of the armaments they carried, and their sailing properties had changed very little.

Each of the four technological innovations in naval warfare—the steam engine, the screw propeller, the shell gun, and the use of iron and steel—was a ground-shaking invention in its own right. Put together within the space of two or three decades, the result was quite literally a sea change in the purpose, significance, and even the politics of navies. And even then, this new age of iron ships and powerful guns would only be a passing phase, a mere taste of the fevered sprint for technological superiority, brute strength, and unthinking national pride that would mark the naval arms race that preceded the First World War.

It's difficult to say which one of these four innovations was most important. They came together too quickly to allow us to assess the impact of one without the other three, and they were so closely related. Steam power made armored and iron-hulled ships possible; the shell gun made them necessary. But steam power came first, and its potential for travel by water was tested before it was first successfully applied to land-based locomotion.

That realization—that the steam engine could be applied to water transportation—came right on the heels of the invention of the steam engine itself. Thomas Newcomen patented his "atmospheric engine," designed to pump water out of flooded subterranean mines, around 1712; the first patents for steamboats that used the Newcomen engine as a means of propulsion were issued in the 1720s. A Newcomen engine powered the first working steamboat, Claude de Jouffroy's *Pyroscaphe*, when it made its maiden voyage on the Saône River in France in 1783. The American inventor James Fitch demonstrated his steamboat *Perseverance* to delegates attending the Constitutional Convention in Philadelphia in 1787. Jouffroy and

Fitch were not alone. There were dozens of inventors working on dozens of prototypes, in Britain, France, and the United States in particular. The concept was not a difficult one, but the execution of it was costly, and the expense deterred many would-be inventors. Steamboats were pricey things, and it wasn't immediately obvious that they held any commercial potential—the main motivator for innovation in the industrial age. Their power plants and their fuel load took up too much cargo space. Plus they were slow, unreliable, noisy, sooty, and, well, weird.

But James Watt's smaller, more efficient steam engine (1776) ameliorated most of these issues. It was far better suited to maritime purposes than Newcomen's had been. In Scotland, William Symington used a Watt engine to power his ship *Charlotte Dundas* (1803); in the United States, Robert Fulton's *North River Steamboat*, more familiar as the *Clermont*, was also powered by a Watt. Fulton was able to prove to his rapt audiences—who lined the banks of the Hudson River to watch in wonder as *Clermont* made the 150-mile journey from New York City to Albany in thirty-two hours—that steamboats had many uses, some of them lucrative. Within a decade, steamboat companies in the United States and Britain were providing regular ferry and passenger service.

Short-run steamboat journeys were one thing, long-distance or overseas travel quite another, but transferring the new technology to larger, oceangoing vessels was a simple step regardless. The only thorny issue was fuel load. The early steamboats and steamships were paddle-wheel driven, meaning that their steam engines—placed centrally in the hull—powered a lateral drive shaft that ran across the ship's beam, in turn moving large paddle wheels on either or both sides of the ship. The engines took up a lot of valuable real estate, and they had a voracious appetite for fuel, as much as sixteen tons of coal per day. That was perfectly all right for local steamboat services along rivers or confined to harbors, as a source of fuel was never far away. But for a voyage across the vast span of the Atlantic, for example, there were no fuel stops, and since an Atlantic crossing could take weeks to complete, carrying enough fuel for that journey was simply not practical. Small wonder that steam was at first seen as an auxiliary to sail, not the main source of power. When a ship was becalmed, or when it was navigating into or out of a harbor, the steady, predictable power of a steam engine was an invaluable asset. But on the open sea in a fair wind, the funnel went down and the sails went up. Except for rivercraft, steamships were hybrids that incorporated both traditional rigs and marine engines.

That didn't stop the steamship pioneers from attempting longer voyages, even transoceanic passages. In 1819, the American steamship *Savannah*, a ship-rigged three-master retrofitted with a steam engine and a paddle wheel, crossed the Atlantic from Savannah to Liverpool in twenty-nine and a half days, cruising for much of the voyage under steam. *Savannah* was not a great commercial success, no matter how astonishing its transatlantic crossing might have been. Within two years, the ship would be sold, stripped of its engines, and wrecked off Long Island. But in 1819 *Savannah*'s celebrity status was undeniable. It was a star. President James Monroe inspected the ship before its departure for England; the tsar of Russia and the king of Sweden, plus untold numbers of foreign dignitaries and naval officers, visited the ship as it toured northern European ports after its reception in Liverpool. The excitement it generated was no less intense than the fascination that gripped Europe when Charles Lindbergh flew the *Spirit of St. Louis* across the ocean little more than a century later. The advantages of steam-powered sea travel were probably more apparent in 1819 than the advantages of long-distance air travel in 1927. *Savannah* showed the world that a ship could make a voyage of several thousand miles without danger of being set back or left stranded by wind.

Among those who visited *Savannah* during its long European sojourn were naval officers by the score. Doubtless they saw the martial potential of a steam-driven warship. Such a ship could make better time overall on long-distance voyages, but even better were its advantages in combat. In battle, a steamship would not be dependent on the speed or direction of the fickle winds. It could move where its skipper wanted it to move, when he wanted, and having the "weather gauge" over the enemy—the advantage of being upwind—would no longer matter.

Savannah gave the steamship the publicity it needed, and European naval officers bought into the idea of a steam-powered, conventional warship—but not *all* European naval officers. In Britain, the Board of Admiralty looked upon the possibility of a steam-powered navy with something akin to abject horror, the First Lord making the bizarre claim in 1828 that—if adopted—the steam engine would bring about the obsolescence of the existing fleet and therefore "strike a fatal blow at the naval supremacy of the empire."

Maybe the reaction of the Admiralty to technological progress was risible, but still there were legitimate objections to the use of steam in warships. So far, the only viable propulsion mechanism to be combined with the steam engine was the paddle wheel. The *Savannah* was a paddle wheeler, as was the very first steam-powered warship, Robert Fulton's *Demologos*—a clumsy, underpowered, barely seaworthy floating battery built to defend New York Harbor during the War of 1812. Paddle wheels worked well enough, but they took up an enormous amount of space. On a conventional warship with guns mounted in broadside, the massive wheel and its housing—not to mention the engines—would occupy space ordinarily used to mount guns. So steam propulsion entailed a reduction in shipboard armaments, something that no naval commander wanted to contemplate. And paddle wheels were quite fragile. There was no effective way to shield them from shot, and their placement on the outside of the vessel meant they were easy targets. One or two well-placed hits from a shell gun and a paddle-wheel steamship would be dead in the water. When the British and French navies began to incorporate steam power, it was used mostly for unarmed utility vessels like harbor tugs and supply ships, and only later for small, lightly armed gunboats.

Solutions were already underway. Since the 1810s, European and American engineers had been experimenting with what would become known as the screw propeller. Screw propellers were an ancient invention, usually attributed to the Greek philosopher-scientist Archimedes of Syracuse in the third century BC, and are the basis for all modern marine and aircraft propellers. Several angled blades were mounted around a shaft; when the shaft was rotated along its axis, the blades transformed the rotational energy of the shaft into linear thrust. By 1830, screw propellers had already shown themselves to be superior to paddle wheels in every way. One of the engineers working on the screw propeller was the ubiquitous Swede John Ericsson, but he was only one; the propeller seems to have been invented by several individuals, working independently at roughly the same time.

Early trials with screw propellers were highly encouraging. The French dispatch vessel *Napoléon* (1842), which used a screw designed by the engineer Frédéric Sauvage, clocked a speed of 12.4 knots while under steam power alone. In 1845, the British Admiralty, having shed its resistance to steamships, sponsored a series of competitions between two steamships, one a paddle wheeler, the other powered by a screw. In every race, the screw-driven *Rattler* handily beat the paddle sloop *Alecto*, and a tug of war between the two confirmed what those watching already understood. After a few minutes of deadlock, the *Rattler* began pulling the hapless *Alecto* backward, eventually hauling it stern-first at a speed of over two knots while *Alecto*'s paddle beat furiously at the water.

It was settled: the steam engine coupled with the screw propeller was the wave of the future. The Americans took the first big step with the launching of USS *Princeton* in 1843, but *Princeton*'s cursed existence did not encourage an immediate follow-up in the US Navy. The French navy, less hidebound than the British and better funded than the American, took it from there. The first steam frigate—or, more accurately, the first sailing frigate with a steam engine and a screw propeller—was *Pomone* (1845). Five years later, the first steam-powered ship of the line, the French first-rater *Agamemnon*, astonished the world with a top speed of fourteen knots under steam power without sails.

By the 1850s, the rest of the major Western fleets had begun to catch up with the French. There were still all-sail warships, and paddle wheelers too, but the steam-powered, screw-driven, three-masted hybrid warship was both the apex and the norm of modern naval architecture.

Not for long.

STEAM POWER HAD become the standard technology of propulsion just as the large-caliber shell gun had become the established standard for naval weapons. The ships of this new generation of screw frigates were nearly all heavily armed with guns of the Paixhans variety. This was true even before the massacre at Sinop in 1853. Sinop did not introduce shell guns to the naval world; it merely justified prior investment in the technology.

The destructive power of the shell guns highlighted the inherent weaknesses of wooden fighting ships. Steamship and sailing warship were alike in this way: no matter the source of their energy, be it steam or wind, the Paixhans gun could burn them all. Adopting steam propulsion had been a choice—a good choice, clearly, but not something that was forced on Western navies by necessity. But the power of the Paixhans guns at Sinop made it clear: modern warships would have to accommodate the shell gun—to be protected against them and to carry them—if they were to survive a single hostile encounter.

Once again, the French—overall the real pioneers of naval and military technology in the nineteenth century—led the way. Shortly after Sinop, the French government commissioned and hurried into production five ironclad "floating batteries," with the first sliding down the ways at Cherbourg in late 1854. Despite the name, the *Dévastation*-class ironclads were fully functional ships, each with three masts and a steam engine capable of moving the ironclad along at a top speed of four knots. But their main purpose was bombardment—both giving and receiving. Their sides were covered with a coat of iron plate, four-and-a-half inches thick, backed by seventeen inches of wood. Each was armed with sixteen fifty-pounder shell guns, and the first three of the class—*Dévastation*, *Tonnante*, and *Lave*—were finished in time to see action in the Crimean War. French paddle frigates towed them to the Black Sea, where in October 1855 they participated in the bombardment of Russian coastal forts at Kinburn.

The French ironclads were ugliness incarnate. In form they resembled large cast-iron bathtubs more than anything else. But they performed wondrously. The ironclads did most of the heavy work in reducing the main Russian fortress at Kinburn to rubble and knocking out its guns, collectively firing over three thousand rounds from their shell guns. And while the Russian guns frequently found their mark, they left few visible scars on the ironclads. *Dévastation* was hit seventy-two times, *Tonnante* sixty-six, and the total casualties between the three ironclads amounted to two killed and twenty-one wounded. French observers noted with satisfaction that Russian solid shot bounced harmlessly off the sides of the ironclads; shells lobbed from Russian shell guns burst against the armor plate but inflicted no damage whatsoever.

Kinburn made it plain: the antidote to the shell gun was armor. It was a timely lesson, as more powerful shell guns—the bottle-shaped Dahlgrens and the built-up Armstrong rifled guns—took the place of the aging Paixhans. Some navies assimilated that lesson faster than others. There is probably no more jarring example of the gap between old and new than two new major warships launched at roughly the same time. On 12 November 1859, the brand-new first-rater HMS *Victoria* slid down the ways at Portsmouth. A wooden three-decker carrying 121 guns, *Victoria* was both the largest warship in the world and a throwback to an earlier age. To be sure, *Victoria* was a steamship—or rather a steam-sail hybrid—with a 4,403 horsepower engine driving a massive screw propeller, but in every other regard it was an oversized relic of the age of sail. It was also so big as to be impractical. Heavy iron strapping reinforced its hull from the inside, but the vibrations from the steam engine and propeller were enough to shake its seams open from time to time.

Twelve days later, the newest French warship made its public debut in the harbor at Toulon. This was *Gloire*, the masterpiece of naval architect Henri Dupuy de Lôme, and it was nothing at all like *Victoria*. Its low-slung, plain black hull was sleek and unadorned, its bow bluff and not at all graceful. Like *Victoria*, it carried a full complement of sails on its three masts, but the 2,500 hp trunk engine was its main source of power. *Gloire* carried a mere thirty-six guns, big 6.5-inch rifled muzzleloaders of a new French design, all ranged on a single gun deck. *Victoria* dwarfed *Gloire*, but *Gloire* was light-years ahead of *Victoria* in every possible way.

The thing that really set *Gloire* apart from *Victoria*, and from every other warship that came before it, was its armor. Covering the entirety of the outer hull was a coat of iron plate, 4.7 inches thick, backed by seventeen inches of wood. Months before *Gloire* slid down the ways at Toulon, ordnance experts had tested the armor. Even at point-blank range, they found, the biggest naval guns in the world could neither penetrate nor significantly damage *Gloire*'s armored belt. And even with all that weight, *Gloire* could reach a speed of 13.5 knots under steam—a full two knots faster than *Victoria* with its much larger engine.

Gloire was the first armored seagoing warship in history, and it wouldn't be too much of a stretch to call it the first modern battleship. Still the French did not rest easily, and over the next six years they added three more ships of the *Gloire* class to their fleet, ten more of a slightly improved design, and finally two ironclad ships of the line, *Magenta* and *Solferino*, two-deckers bristling with modern shell guns and rifled cannon. By 1865, France had the world's most powerful, and most modern, battle fleet.

Britain wasn't far behind. It produced a milestone of its own: the very first iron-hulled warship, HMS *Warrior*, in 1860. The idea of building a ship's hull entirely from iron had been around for some time, and the British acted on it before anyone else, with the first iron-built vessel (the barge *Vulcan*, 1819) and the first iron-hulled steamship (*Aaron Manby*, 1822). The notion had merits beyond the extra protection that iron afforded in combat. Steam engines were getting progressively bigger and more powerful, and naval guns much heavier; soon it became apparent that traditionally built wooden hulls were not up to tolerating the increasing weight and stresses. The French recognized this, too, and had actually begun to build their own iron-hulled, ironclad warship—*Couronne*, one of the improved *Gloire* class—but *Warrior* was finished first.

Together, *Gloire* and *Warrior* set a new standard in naval construction. Curiously, though, they did not usher in a new age in the

Plate 13. The ironclad warship CSS *Stonewall*, at anchor off Washington Navy Yard, 1865–1867. Built in Bordeaux in the middle of the American Civil War, *Sphinx* (its original name) had an interesting career that included stints in the Danish, Confederate, US, and Japanese navies. *Stonewall* was a typical oceangoing ironclad of the *Gloire–Warrior* generation, with a wooden hull covered with iron armor between 3.0 and 4.5 inches thick.

Image: NH 43993 courtesy of the Naval History & Heritage Command.

tactics of war at sea. Contemporaries marveled at the great leaps forward, the technology built into the hulls and armaments of the new iron ships, but there was no sense that combat at sea would be any different—bigger, louder, more expensive certainly, but essentially the same. What else were warships, with their guns mounted in broadside, supposed to do? *Gloire* and *Warrior*, and the scores of imitators and improvements that followed, were built to trade broadsides in line-ahead formation, in the ways that European men-of-war had fought for two centuries or more. They were just built to be better at it.

Almost four thousand miles away, on the other side of the Atlantic, some much smaller, less conventional warships were pointing toward a possibly different future.

ARMORED SHIPS HAD yet to fight against one another, in ship-on-ship combat, when the ironclad ram CSS *Virginia* steamed into Hampton Roads in March 1862. *Virginia*'s confrontation with the screw frigates of the US Navy's blockading fleet was brief, brutal, and convincingly one-sided. When it was all over and *Virginia* was returning to port, the Federals had lost two ships and well over two hundred men had been killed. *Virginia* had suffered some light surface damage and a leak in the bow, inflicted when the ram was wrenched off during the fight with *Cumberland*.

As advanced as *Virginia* may have appeared to the Federal sailors who fought against it that March, the ship's futuristic design owed more to the unconventional nature of the American Civil War, and to the desperate straits in which the Confederacy found itself, than it did to an intentional break with past technologies. The US Navy had a respectable fleet of wooden warships, a combination of modern screw sloops and screw frigates, paddle-wheel warships from the 1840s, and older, all-sail ships of the previous generation. At the beginning of hostilities, the Navy pressed into service anything that would float and carry a cannon or two, because the North's grand strategy of strangling the South by means of a blockade—covering all Southern ports from Virginia to Texas—demanded a very large fleet. But as the vast majority of America's shipyards were situated in Northern ports, the Union's shipbuilding industry was a formidable one, able to keep up with wartime demands.

The South, on the other hand, had no conventional navy to begin with, few shipyards, few marine engines, few ironworks capable of producing marine engines, and few naval architects. But the Confederacy could not simply shrug off its lack of a navy. It was dependent on its vital lifeline to European ports, where it could trade its cotton for war materiel, medicines, and other essentials.

Confederate naval strategy therefore focused on three priorities: keeping the major ports—Charleston, Savannah, Pensacola, Mobile, New Orleans, Galveston—out of Federal hands, breaking the Federal blockade, and using wide-ranging commerce raiders to divert Federal attention away from the coasts. For the first two priorities, the Confederacy's almost vestigial navy did not need frigates or ships of the line. It needed small, fast craft that could be cobbled together in a hurry and with minimal resources, skilled labor, and shipbuilding facilities.

Virginia, built upon the ruined hulk of a burned-out Federal warship, was an act of desperation. Everything above the waterline, though, was brand-new construction. A single, flat, lightly armored deck surmounted the *Merrimack*'s lower hull, and atop that rose the casemate. This flat-topped, barn-like structure, wrapped in a blanket of four-inch-thick armor, housed the ship's armament of ten heavy guns. It was low in profile, and the utter lack of masts, spars, and sails added to the ship's futuristic, otherworldly appearance.

For the remainder of the Civil War, the Confederate navy poured most of its limited resources into the construction of more ironclads. Some were unique, even bizarre designs: the turtle-like, single-gunned *Manassas*—built atop a former icebreaker-tugboat, for example—or the clumsy paddle-wheeler giant *Baltic*. The rest, the vast majority of Confederate armorclads, followed *Virginia*'s basic design. These so-called casemated warships varied greatly in size, quality, and effectiveness. They were simple enough in construction that they could be built just about anywhere, even at improvised river shipyards deep inland, like the homemade iron-clads *Neuse*, *Albemarle*, and *Arkansas*. Indeed, it was the homemade ironclads that probably did the most damage relative to what they cost to build, the *Albemarle* and the *Arkansas* causing more than a few headaches for the Federal high command.

But the inferiority of Confederate shipbuilding and heavy man-ufacturing was truly telling. Perhaps most crippling was the lack of a native source of marine engines. Most of the power plants for rebel ironclads were scrounged from decrepit harbor ferries and tugs, and they were invariably underpowered. The ironclad rams *Chicora* and *Palmetto State*, the backbone of the CS Navy squadron defending Charleston Harbor, had engines so weak that even at full steam they could barely stem the outgoing tide.

Federal armored warship design was more varied, less consis-tent, and overall of higher quality. In the campaigns along the Western rivers, the Federal brown-water navy relied heavily on sev-eral types of ungainly casemated ironclads, broader and bulkier than their Confederate counterparts. This armored gunboat fleet was absolutely critical to Northern successes along the rivers, such as U. S. Grant's victories at Forts Henry and Donelson in 1862, and his conquest of Vicksburg on the Mississippi in 1863. The US Navy even adopted two broadside ironclads that approximated Eu-ropean designs, closely related in form to the *Gloire*, but neither was a great success. The thinly armored *Galena* was nearly shot to ribbons when it attempted to force a passage of the James River in 1862, while the more redoubtable *New Ironsides* proved to be unstable and sluggish.

But the most common ironclad model in Federal service during the war, the one whose form came to represent Union naval supe-riority, was the weirdest and most unlikely of all, the most radical departure from the established norms of naval architecture. John Ericsson's *Monitor* was built in response to the first rumors of *Vir-ginia's* construction. The design was very nearly rejected by Federal authorities; only the direct personal intervention of President Abra-ham Lincoln, who had a surprisingly keen interest in unconventional weaponry, saved *Monitor* from oblivion. The construction process itself was remarkable, in speed if nothing else. Solid intelligence suggested that *Virginia* was about to turn loose its fury on the Federal blockading squadron, and rumors abounded that it would sail unopposed up the Potomac to shell and burn the Capitol and the White House. Urged on from above, Ericsson and his subcontractors in New York City finished *Monitor* in less than five months.

Monitor's design did not initially inspire confidence. Its iron hull was topped with a single, heavily armored deck, but there was no casemate, and *Monitor* did not carry guns in broadside. Instead, *Monitor*'s sole armament—two big Dahlgren 11-inch shell guns— was mounted in an armored, circular turret, twenty-one feet in diameter and nine feet high. The turret rotated on a central axle, powered by a pair of steam winches. The only other structure of note above deck was a small pilot house, located near the bow.

Turreted guns are hardly novel today, but in March 1862, when *Monitor* was ready for battle, they were entirely new. Critics hailed *Monitor* as "Ericsson's folly" or, more descriptively, as the "cheesebox on a raft." But when it went into action against *Virginia* at Hampton Roads on 9 March 1862, the doubts quickly dissipated.

The arrival of *Monitor* that night, mere hours after *Virginia* had broken off from its battle with the wooden ships of the Federal blockading squadron, must have seemed providential. Actually completed before *Virginia*, *Monitor* had been hurried to the scene of the action, towed by a tug through heavy seas in a taxing two-day voyage. But it arrived intact, and when the Confederate flotilla returned to Hampton Roads the next morning at dawn, *Monitor* was there, blocking the way and protecting the remnants of the Federal squadron. As the unconventional vessel first came into view, Confederate sailors had no idea what they were looking at. *Virginia*'s new commander, Lieutenant Catesby ap R. Jones, thought he saw a boiler being removed from USS *Minnesota*, only to discover that what he thought was a boiler on a barge was actually *Monitor*. Jones and his opponent, *Monitor*'s skipper John L. Worden, squared off, and the first duel between ironclads began.

The *Monitor-Virginia* battle was technically a draw, with neither ship doing serious damage to the other. But though *Virginia*, mounting six Dahlgren shell guns and four heavy Brooke rifled cannon, was by far the more heavily armed, *Monitor* was much more nimble. Despite a few minor setbacks—a turret malfunction or two, the disabling of one of the two heavy iron gunport shutters—*Monitor*'s two guns scored as many hits on *Virginia* as *Virginia*'s ten guns did on *Monitor*.

The battle could have turned out much differently. *Virginia*'s guns were supplied only with explosive shell; with solid shot, the powerful Brooke rifles might well have been able to penetrate *Monitor*'s armor. And on John Ericsson's recommendation, Lieutenant Worden ordered that *Monitor*'s two Dahlgrens use powder charges of fifteen pounds, even though the guns could have been safely loaded with as much as thirty pounds per shot. If the full thirty-pound charges had been used, the velocity and penetrating power of the Dahlgrens' 11-inch shot would have been much greater. *Monitor* likely might have smashed *Virginia* to bits.

Monitor was the hero of the hour among the general public and in the US Navy, and soon shipyards throughout the North were churning out new and upgraded monitors, as the class quickly came to be known. The new monitors were superior to Ericsson's vessel, with bigger guns, more powerful engines, thicker armor; some were even double-turreted. Monitors served with the brown-water navy, and they were instrumental in naval operations against Confederate ships and forts at Charleston, Savannah, and Mobile Bay. After the battle of Hampton Roads in 1862, monitors only tangled with Confederate ironclads on a couple of occasions, and the turreted warships always came out on top. When the *Passaic*-class monitor USS *Weehawken* squared off with the stoutly built Confederate ram CSS *Atlanta*, *Weehawken* disabled its opponent with five shots—blowing the roof off *Atlanta*'s pilothouse, severing its steering chains, and knocking out two of its guns.

The monitors were not miracle weapons; they had their limitations. Though Ericsson predicted that *Monitor* would be able to

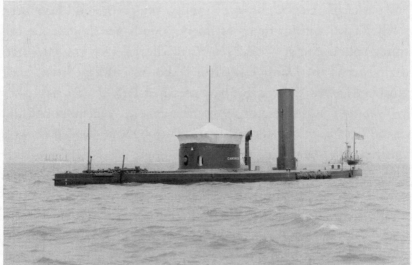

Ironclads of the American Civil War.

Plate 14a. USS *Atlanta*, formerly the CSS *Atlanta*. *Atlanta* was typical of Confederate "casemated" ironclads. It was captured after a brief but decisive duel with the monitor USS *Weehawken* in June 1863.

Plate 14b. USS *Canonicus*. Armed with two 15-inch Dahlgren shell guns in its powered turret, the monitors of the *Canonicus* class were among the best ironclads of the American Civil War. *Canonicus* remained in active service into the beginning of the twentieth century.

Images courtesy of the Library of Congress, Detroit Publishing Company photograph collection, 1907.

ride out big ocean waves "like a duck," the truth was that monitors were not designed to weather heavy seas. *Monitor* itself sank in a storm off Cape Hatteras before it was even a year old. But that was almost immaterial. *Monitor*'s greatest contribution to military technology was not its general design, but its powered, armored gun turret.

Even the gun turret, as practical as it was, did not catch on immediately. European military leaders tended to regard the many novelties of Civil War combat with a mixture of amusement and skepticism, convinced that in most regards the nature of combat in America was of little relevance to European warfare. This applied to naval warfare, too. Monitors were invaluable when the main fighting was taking place in harbors and along inland waterways, but they were not capable of sea travel and did not have a place in the line of battle. True, the powered armored turret could be combined with a more stable, more conventional hull design—but why? Turrets restricted the number of guns that a ship could carry. How could an armored, ocean-going warship mounting only two, or four, heavy shell guns possibly be superior to a more conventional armored ship carrying several dozen in broadside?

Strange as it may have seemed in 1865, within two decades the turreted capital ship would become the gold standard in Western navies, and the age of the modern battleship would begin.

Book III

THE REVOLUTION IN FIREPOWER, 1870-1918

CHAPTER 10

THE GREAT ARMS RACE AND THE GREAT WAR

The great European arms race of 1870–1918 was more compact, more intense, and more dangerous than any previous arms race in the history of the West. The stakes were higher, the fears more febrile. There was a new and unprecedented complication in the form of nationalism, that most dangerous of populist passions, for now national prestige was no longer the exclusive province of kings and ruling elites. Ordinary people were also quite conscious of their nation's standing in the world and—through the vote— they felt that they had a stake in that standing. The evolution of weapons technology during this period also tightly bound to nationalism. If anything, the fear that drove the arms race was rooted at least as deeply in the intrinsic performance qualities of each weapon as it was in the size of rival armies and navies. The arms race leading up to and including the Great War was as much about quality as it was about quantity.

In the fifty-year span between the Franco-Prussian War and the end of the First World War, weapons technology advanced further and faster than it ever had before. In some ways, that breakneck pace of advancement would never again be repeated. It was a period of profound, rapid, even violent change in the killing potential of weaponry, made possible by the confluence of brilliant engineering, great leaps forward in the academic disciplines of chemistry and physics, and—perhaps more important—an arms race propelled by governments aggressively seeking out every possible advantage they could steal on their enemies, neighbors, and rivals.

The weapons of 1860 were much closer, in function and effectiveness, to their eighteenth-century predecessors than they were to the weapons of 1880. Military firearms of 1918 were in a different category altogether than those of four decades earlier. Small arms became infinitely more powerful, longer ranged, accurate, and faster firing; so, too, did artillery, and artillery ammunition became far deadlier. At sea, the wooden-hulled sailing warship gave way to the all-steel, turreted battleship. And then there were the brand-new technologies that simply had no equivalents before 1900, like the warplane, the armored fighting vehicle, and the torpedo-launching submarine. All this within the space of fifty years.

The pace of that change was dizzying, unsettling. And disruptive. Admirals, battlefield generals, and military theorists struggled to construct new tactics that took the vastly advanced weaponry into account; staff officers wrestled with the logistical challenges presented by increased demand for ammunition, the mass use of motor vehicles, and—another feature of the period—much larger armies. These were no easy tasks. Soldiers in the late nineteenth century had received their training and formative martial experiences while the art of war was still very much under the long shadow cast by the legacy of Napoléon Bonaparte. That legacy was still germane to warfare in the 1860s, for Waterloo and Leipzig were still part of the recent past; but the disparity in weapons effectiveness between 1815 and 1915 was so great that the Napoleonic experience had about as much relevance in 1915 as the campaigns of Scipio Africanus did.

The new firepower forced a major shift in the conduct of war on land and at sea, which in turn introduced two new theaters of war: in the skies and beneath the waves. It transformed tactics, strategy, and logistics, admittedly in a very uneven way at times; the art of war did not always keep step with the rapidly evolving weaponry. This was a reciprocal relationship, though. The conduct of war, or more precisely the practical experience of combat and military operations, also helped to shape the progress of weapons development. That reciprocity was not in itself new, but its speed and intensity were. More than ever before, the battlefield was an invaluable testing ground for new technologies, and the feedback from combat performance cycled directly back to the drafting table and the factory with remarkable immediacy.

Further complicating the disruption caused by the new firepower was the matter of scale. The size of armies and navies, and therefore of battles, grew by leaps and bounds in the last half of the nineteenth century. The opposing armies at Solferino (1859) had numbered about 260,000 men, at Gettysburg (1863) around 200,000 men, at Königgrätz (1866) 460,000 aggregate; but in the months-long Battle of the Somme the opposing forces came close to three million combatants. The new scale of warfare would do as much as the new weaponry to transform the conduct of combat.

The implications of the firepower revolution extended far beyond the battlefield, the factory, and the supply chain. The connections between weapons development and bigger matters—diplomacy, statecraft, grand strategy, geopolitics, the economy, and the irresistible sweeping force we call nationalism—were never more obvious, or more complex, than they were in the decades up to and including the Great War of 1914–1918. As with tactics and operations, these were two-way relationships. Imperialism, international competition, and nationalism exerted a major guiding influence on weapons technology, just as weapons technology helped to drive the cutthroat competition of the Western powers in Europe and abroad. And the fevered pace of weapons development could not help but have jolting economic repercussions. New inventions cropped up in such profusion that they obsolesced almost as soon as the factories tooled up to make them, but the brutal and inescapable logic of the post-1870 arms race meant that armies and navies had to pounce on every new weapon as soon as it passed muster. Weapons technology was no longer an arcane subfield of engineering that mattered only within the confines of the military profession. The firepower revolution after 1870 left an indelible impact on every facet of life in the West.

WHAT, PRECISELY, WAS the nature of that tangled web of connections between weapons development and life in the West? Those relationships were least complicated, predictably, in the immediate realm of tactics, logistics, and the nature of war. The upshot of the revolution in weapons technology was that the firepower of modern armies and navies, more specifically the killing power of firearms on land and at sea, vastly increased. That, in turn, demanded a corresponding revision of army and naval battle tactics: the range at which armies, for example, engaged one another, how and when they launched assaults, how they defended themselves against attack, how armies gathered intelligence on the battlefield, how they communicated information and orders from headquarters to the constituent elements of a field army. Naval commanders still dreamed of, and planned for, fleet actions that weren't much different from those of Lord Nelson's day, but now they would have to do so at much greater distances from one another—and now they would have to reckon with, thanks to the torpedo-armed submarine, the possibility of attack from beneath the waves. The battlescape was transformed into something much larger, much more complex, much more unknowable, than what generals of the eighteenth and early nineteenth centuries had to deal with. Modern communications technology, in the form of the field telephone and wireless radio, made it *possible* for generals and their staffs to perform in the much-expanded physical space taken up by military operations on land, but communication was nonetheless a challenge of a magnitude not previously known in Western warfare.

Naval and military theorists would have to address these issues as they developed tactical doctrines for the next century, rooted in the enhanced performance of the new weaponry. These revised tactics unfolded gradually, as armies experimented with them and worked them out in combat. The First World War would be the ultimate laboratory for these innovations. Yet between 1870 and 1914 there would be plenty of opportunities to sample what the new weapons could do. In the East, longstanding Russian territorial ambitions combined with rising Balkan nationalism to bring on the Russo-Turkish War (1877–1878), and the First and Second Balkan Wars (1912–1913), which collectively deprived the Ottoman Empire of its foothold in Europe and heated up the already dangerous rivalry between Russia and Austria-Hungary. The rise of Japan as a major regional power in the Far East led to clashes with China (the Sino-Japanese War, 1894–1895) and with Russia (the Russo-Japanese War, 1904–1905). Most other conflicts of this half-century arose from competing Western imperial ambitions in Africa and elsewhere: the Italo-Turkish War in Libya (1911–1912), the First and Second Boer Wars (1880–1881, 1899–1902) between Britain and the Dutch republics in South Africa.

One thing was obvious about the changing nature of war, even before the outbreak of the First World War in 1914: the role of the soldier, and of the sailor, was changing. Naval personnel in the age of the sailing warship had to master a specialized toolkit, one that embraced both the physical operation of the ship and its rigging *and* of the ship's ordnance. Now sailors had to be intensively trained to handle specific tasks in a complex vessel. For soldiers on land, more complicated weapons required more extensive weapons training, just as more accurate weapons demanded more time spent on the range in live-fire exercises. Volley fire was still taught to recruits, but it became a curiosity in practice after 1900.

The common soldier also looked completely different after 1870 or so. He now carried a much heavier load of gear, much of it directly related to evolving weapons technology. A typical infantryman in the eighteenth century, in heavy marching order, might carry a musket and bayonet, a leather cartridge box, a bayonet scabbard and shoulder belt, a short infantry sword (hanger), a simple cloth breadbag for rations, a water bottle or canteen, a knapsack or haversack, a blanket, and possibly a few bulkier extras: spare shoes, cooking gear, leather polish, and perhaps a greatcoat in wintertime. Heavier items traveled with the regimental baggage.

Armies of the Industrial Age issued much more impedimenta to their troops: bandages and first-aid kits, rifle-cleaning tools, a variety of hygiene and grooming items, and some sort of combination poncho/ground cloth/shelter-tent, like the German *Zeltbahn*. After 1880, the soldier would also lug around a personal entrenching tool, such as the patented Linnemann spade; after 1915, a gas mask with accessories would be added to the small mountain of personal gear, as would a steel helmet. Perhaps the worst offender was ammunition. The much higher rate of fire of modern rifles dictated that individual soldiers would have to carry a lot more ammunition in their ammo pouches.

The new gear reflected the brutal realities of the modern battlefield. So, too, did the contemporaneous shift in military clothing. Uniforms had become much less ornate after the end of the Napoleonic wars, characterized by more muted colors and looser, more comfortable cuts, but they were still highly visible at long distances in clear weather—and hence made excellent targets. Well before 1914, Western armies had (mostly) learned the value of dull, earthtoned uniforms. Prussian blue gave way to German *Steingrau* (stone gray) and *Feldgrau* (field gray), Austrian white to pike gray, British madder and scarlet to khaki. It was not always an easy transition to make, for uniforms were emblematic of martial glories past and were therefore powerful symbols of national identity and pride. In France, efforts to replace the prewar army uniform—dark blue tunics and coats, bright red breeches, and red *képis*—with something less visible met with fierce resistance from older, more conservative officers and scorn from the general public. It took only a brief exposure to combat against the Germans in the opening campaigns of the Great War for the folly of that sentimentality to sink in, and early the next year the French metropolitan troops debuted a new uniform of pale, dull blue. And in headgear, the soft forage caps and tall shakoes of the mid-nineteenth century gave way to steel helmets in 1915–1916.

So the sweeping changes in weaponry paralleled, and to some extent caused, corresponding changes in the appearance, function, and role of the individual fighting man. The new weaponry changed the experience of being a soldier or sailor, especially the former, and what it meant to serve in an army.

WEAPONS DEVELOPMENT HAD global implications, too. Imperialism was not new to Europe and the United States in the late nineteenth century. Spain and Portugal had worked assiduously to build up their overseas empires in the Americas and Asia since the close of the fifteenth century. And the subsequent three centuries saw Britain, France, the Netherlands, and even some of the lesser European powers, endeavor to build viable colonies outside Europe. For all the advances in European military technology during that period, during the age of the military revolution, the West did not collectively establish military superiority—in technology, tactics, or organization—over established states in India, China, Japan, and even Korea. Indeed, the Ottoman Empire was at the very least on parity with the European powers for much of that time. The "gunpowder empires" of the East were more than a match for European martial strength—even if the European powers would have made common cause and worked together, in itself an impossibility.

The Industrial Revolution, though, gave the West a formidable technological lead over the rest of the world, one not easily or quickly bridged. Advances in transportation and communications effectively shrank the globe. The advent of the telegraph, and then the telephone, allowed for rapid communications between far-flung parts of the world and Europe; messages that, only a century before, would have moved by means of sailing ship and taken weeks or even months to transmit, now could be sent by telegraph from one end of the globe to another in minutes. The new generation of steam warships made it possible for the maritime powers of the West to project overwhelming military might just about anywhere, and the weaponry of the machine age—like the machine gun, the magazine-fed rifle, and high explosive—all but guaranteed victory when Western forces clashed with non-Western forces, at least in conventional warfare. Only on rare occasions and in exceptional circumstances, or when vastly outnumbered, were European or American military forces unable to overcome their non-Western opponents. Such incidents—for example, the dramatic British defeat at the hands of a Zulu army at Isandlwana in 1879—stand out because they were so unusual.

The new technology, in short, enabled the new imperialism, and imperialism in turn helped to shape technological change. Western expansionism served an insidious purpose: it provided a testing ground for new weapons and tactics. European imperialism, especially in Africa, offered innumerable opportunities to give new weapons a try against human—though not White and European—targets. Hiram Maxim's machine gun, for example, would have its first significant combat testing at the battles of the Shangani River (1893) and Omdurman (1898).

European soldiers weren't sure how to evaluate the evidence that came from colonial warfare, given that indigenous forces did not use European tactics and only sometimes used European weapons. Sure, the Maxim gun could cut down Matabele or Mahdist warriors by the hundreds or thousands, but did that prove that Russians or Germans or Frenchmen would fall victim to the hail of bullets in the same way? Or was it a weapon to be used only against the "uncivilized," or against warriors armed only with spears? These were vexing questions, and until the opportunity arose to use them in battle against Western opponents, there was no way to be certain. Those opportunities, though, would appear soon enough.

Conversely, European soldiers and political leaders were under the impression that race made a difference, and that colonial warfare might require different tools than conventional warfare against a Western opponent. Non-Christian "savages," in their eyes, were so very different from "civilized man." Sir Winston Churchill, for example, favored the use of the infamous "dum-dum" bullet in colonial warfare. The dum-dum was a partially jacketed bullet with a soft point and an incised top, so that when it struck the human body it expanded dramatically, causing massive tissue and bone damage, leaving behind giant, gaping exit wounds as it left the body. The favor shown the dum-dum in the British army came from this particular variety of racism: that Africans and Asians did not feel pain the same way that rational, civilized Europeans did. Motivated by fanatical and atavistic impulses, it was argued, non-Europeans continued to fight even when badly wounded. Fighting them required weapons that caused wounds that were instantly fatal or crippling.

However repugnant it is to us today, that distinction—between what was acceptable for killing Western soldiers and what was acceptable for killing non-White, non-European "savages"—signaled another novel issue associated with military technology: a sincere if strange fussiness over the ethical questions raised by the deadlier weapons of the age. Among Western military commanders and politicians, there arose a growing conviction that there were moral boundaries to weapons effectiveness, and that progress in weapons technology must not be allowed to proceed unchecked. To prevent modern warfare from descending into blood-soaked barbarism, Western governments were willing, sometimes even eager, to impose legal limits on the technology of death—to put constraints, by fiat, on the conduct of war. The Hague Conventions of 1899 and 1907, initiated by Russian tsar Nicholas II and American president Theodore Roosevelt respectively, endeavored to create internationally recognized laws governing the conduct of war for the modern age. Much of the work done at The Hague focused on procedural matters—how to treat prisoners of war humanely, for example, or what kind of courtesies to extend to hospital ships—but the participating nations also addressed specific weapons-related issues. The first Hague Convention, for example, outlawed the use of dum-dum and soft-point bullets, poison gas deployed via artillery shells, and any kind of firearm or explosive fired or dropped from a balloon. A few of those reservations stuck; Western armies religiously shunned the dum-dum when fighting each other. But nearly everything else in the do-not-do lists compiled at The Hague had become a normal part of conventional warfare before the First World War was over.

The Hague Conventions pointed to something else, even more disturbing than the thought of dum-dum bullets and poison gas. They were a sign that war—a big war, a general European war—was on the way. Nobody could say with any precision where and when it would happen, or which one of a score of national rivalries and grievances was most likely to set it off. But war was coming, and soon, and this too was inextricably intertwined with the firepower revolution.

WE ALL KNOW when and where and how that general war started: with an assassination in Sarajevo in that last glittering summer of 1914, followed by more than four years of the bloodiest and most destructive conflict that the Western world had been compelled to endure since the Thirty Years' War three centuries earlier. Many factors led Europe to the brink of catastrophe in 1914, but the increasingly heated rivalries between the European powers stand out as being critical. There were the conflicting ambitions of the Romanovs and Habsburgs over the Balkan lands recently separated from the decaying Ottoman state; the mutual hatred between newborn Italy and Austria-Hungary over *Italia irredenta* (unredeemed Italy); and the naval rivalry between Britain and upstart Germany.

The new wave of Western imperialism that escalated after 1878, above all the "scramble for Africa" at the end of the century, added greatly to the hostile climate, as well. Proponents of Western expansion into the non-Western world often claimed that imperialism was a healthy alternative to war: by allowing the European powers (and, increasingly, the United States) to jostle with one another safely distant from the civilized world, the contest for empire would actually diminish the likelihood of a European war. Of course, competition over empire did nothing of the sort. In the hypernationalistic political atmosphere that prevailed in the age of Bismarck, imperialism did not reduce or relieve interstate tensions; it exacerbated them. But towering above all other rivalries was the legacy of 1871. Reeling from the Franco-Prussian War, the French public ached for revenge on Germany, whose very existence was a painful reminder of that humiliating defeat; and in Germany there lingered a corresponding and all-too-justified fear of French revenge.

One predictable result of that unrelenting rivalry and competition was militarism. Not militarism in the way that the term is used by journalists and political pundits today, as a vague reference to an aggressive foreign policy or a strong commitment to maintaining formidable military forces. Rather, this was militarism as historians understand it: when the needs of the military *are* the needs of the state, when public policy prioritizes the military establishment above all other constituents, when that establishment is the centerpiece of the regime and the focal point of national pride, when everything in everyday life is somehow subordinated to the well-being of the army and navy. Europe in 1914—Europe in 1890, for that matter—was militaristic in this way.

Militarism was evident in a whole host of ways. It was evident in the hundreds of inflexible war plans that the armies of the great powers concocted before 1914, detailed contingency schemes that treated strategy as science, with all its variables being known quantities. It was also evident in the nineteenth-century compulsion for universal military service. After the French Revolution, most European armies reverted to the practice of building armies out of long-serving volunteers, but the war-obsessed powers of *fin de siècle* Europe revived the Jacobin practice of the nation in arms. In nearly every European state—with the notable exception of Britain—the practice of drafting *all* adult males for military service became the norm. The basic model of the universal service obligation was quite simple. The German model illustrates the principle quite well. At age twenty, all men would begin a two- or three-year stint as active duty soldiers, living in barracks and training every day, and after their time was up they were discharged to live their lives as they pleased. But until late middle age they were still considered soldiers, part of the reserves, liable to be called up in time of war. In Germany, service in the army and the active reserves (the *Landwehr*) was followed by a few years in the inactive reserves, the *Landsturm*. While the older men in the *Landsturm* might not be physically capable of serving as combat soldiers, they could fill secondary roles, like guarding prison camps and supply depots, freeing up the younger men of the army and the *Landwehr* to fight. The advantages were obvious, and the unanticipated triumph of Prussia's citizen army over Austria in 1866 highlighted the wisdom of the system. By century's end, Austria-Hungary (1868), France (1872), and Russia (1874) had adopted the universal military service obligation in one form or another. Europe was fast becoming an armed camp.

The main advantage—and the main challenge—of this kind of mass conscription was the potential for explosive army growth in very little time. Germany's active-duty army immediately before the declaration of war in August 1914 numbered around 808,000 men. Twelve days later, the mobilization of the reserves brought that total up to more than 3.5 million—trained, uniformed, armed, already organized into regiments—more than quadrupling the size of the army in less than two weeks. The proportion of men in uniform to those who stayed at home was accordingly, and shockingly, high. During the course of the Great War, nearly 80 percent of military-age men in France and Germany would serve in uniform.

Putting logistics and transportation issues to the side for the moment, those hyperbolic numbers could not help but have an impact on the conduct of war, or at least of land-based war. With armies numbering in the millions, conventional assumptions about the scale of warfare were all but irrelevant now. Battles during the Great War would be accordingly bigger: more men, more food, more ammunition, supplied more regularly; a larger battlescape; greater distances between commanders and subcommanders, and hence more daunting challenges for communications—and more death. Such matters of scale presented complications for which no European general could be prepared. How could they be? There was no parallel, nothing in Western military history up to this point, to which the vast scale of the coming Great War could be profitably compared. This, more than the new technology of the age, would be the tallest tactical, strategic, and logistical hurdle facing ground commanders in the First World War: how to fight, maneuver, and support armies as vast as those of 1914–1918.

Here's where the weapons come in. The intensive rivalries and bitter resentments that coursed like dark threads through the fabric of the European state system—rivalries that were heightened, not diminished, by the burgeoning size of armies and navies after 1870—also determined the nature of the arms race that preceded the First World War. Like all arms races, the participants sought to outdo one another in the aggregate size of their military and naval forces, but this race was just as much about the pace and scope of weapons design as it was about crude quantities.

In this environment, fraught with peril and secrecy, a single well-timed technological advance could give one potential combatant nation a significant tactical advantage over a rival—the kind of advantage that might, if and when it came to battle, spell the difference between victory and defeat. Innovation could not be ignored or go unanswered. German and French engineers raced neck and neck to build a better infantry rifle between 1870 and 1898; German and British fleets competed to construct capital warships that were faster, more heavily gunned, more heavily armored than those of their opponent. Over nearly every weapon, nearly every piece of gear, there was bitter competition to improve performance: machine guns, artillery pieces, ammunition of all kinds, even things as seemingly trivial as entrenching tools and personal gear. The competition was as relentless as it was fast-paced, and it was still going strong when war erupted in 1914.

The implications of the prewar arms race were enormous, not least that the competition itself—with its accompanying and not invalid fears of international espionage, sabotage, and idea theft—only served to fan the flames of current resentments that were burning bright enough already. But there were two aftereffects, each of them largely hidden from view at the time, which pointed up the increasingly complex relationship between technology, politics, and society in the twentieth century. The first was the impact of the arms race on the distribution of military power across the nation-states of the West. While its vastly increased industrial capacity finally gave the West an insurmountable military advantage over the larger empires of the East, within the West the Industrial Revolution exacerbated the disparities in power among the larger military states. The First World War would confirm what generals and statesmen had already begun to suspect: that industrial power *was* military power. The American Civil War had dropped more than a few hints of this, but even in that conflict the Southern Confederacy had done pretty well absent any major industry, and by conflict's end had even managed to improve domestic production of weapons and vital military goods. But increasingly this was the exception and not the rule.

To maintain competitive military and naval forces, nations required *both* the intellectual wherewithal to innovate *and* the productive capacity to equip their armies and navies with state-of-the-art weaponry and equipment—and to be able to do so on a regular basis, since the technology itself was evolving so quickly in the last third of the nineteenth century. And that rapid evolution was entirely a function of the condition of the industrial economy in each major polity. Britain, France, Germany, and the United States, the industrial giants of the period 1870–1918, could compete in this arena. They, and they alone, could afford to rearm their troops with new rifles and new cannon and new battleships every time a major advance emerged. Other states, notably Russia, Austria-Hungary, Spain, even Italy, simply could not keep up. Maintaining an army of, at most, half a million men, armed with nothing more sophisticated than a flintlock musket or a bronze six-pounder, was one thing; maintaining an army of millions, and keeping them equipped with magazine-fed rifles and recoil-suppression artillery, was quite another. Even though the United States had a ridiculously small and inexperienced army in 1914, over the long haul it was still more than a match for the outwardly superior forces of Austria-Hungary, because the industrialized United States had the capacity to keep its factories operating continuously. The mediocre-to-poor performance of Russia and Austria-Hungary in the Great War had more to do with their inability to keep their armies supplied and fed than it did with incompetent generalship.

That's not to say that the major industrial powers could readily absorb the attendant costs of the arms race without trauma. The costs of innovation per se weren't all that high. All the Western states, even the smaller ones, engaged in weapons R & D on a regular basis. The costs of implementation, on the other hand, were high. When, as was the case with France and Germany, a new rifle design or field gun recommended itself every few years, and the generals in charge decided that those new designs could not be ignored, the decision to adopt the new weapon was a messy process. Adopting a new rifle, for example, would usually entail retooling the production lines at government arsenals and at private arms manufactories with government contracts; existing contracts for the now-antiquated earlier models would have to be canceled or settled. Then the new rifle would have to be put into production.

For a country that practiced the universal service obligation, as most of them did, that meant equipping not just the several hundred thousands (or more) of the active army, but also the tens of millions more who made up the reserves . . . millions of rifles, then, while millions of the previous model would have been made obsolete. For Germany, which adopted a new service rifle in 1871, in 1884, in 1888, and in 1898, that could become a very expensive proposition. A new service rifle could also mean a new bayonet, new ammo pouches, new cleaning kits, new slings, and new ammunition, all of which had to be produced in quantities just as vast. The constant turnover in weapons and gear raised another matter, too, one which up to this point had not been a very serious issue: the fate of military surplus. While it was always a good idea to hang on to at least some of the previous model of rifle or field gun, in case production of current models was not enough to supply an expanded army in wartime, outmoded weapons soon piled up, and the disposition of surplus war materiel became a genuine administrative headache. In the next century, it would get far worse.

Military surplus was the most obvious symptom of the second aftereffect of the prewar arms race: its prodigal wastefulness. The social costs of rearmament must have been enormous. The late nineteenth century, after all, was not only the age of exaggerated militarism; it was also an age of social and political progress in the West, at least throughout western and central Europe. The growing acceptability of trade unions and of social democratic political parties meant that the working class enjoyed prosperity and privilege on a level that would have been beyond its wildest dreams before. France, Britain, the Low Countries, the Scandinavian kingdoms, and even Imperial Germany had become more responsive to the needs and wants of their laboring classes, even to the point of investing heavily in social welfare programs developed with the working class in mind. But so much tax money, so many resources, were instead bent to the needs of burgeoning military institutions, resources that could have been invested elsewhere. This was militarism in its truest form.

Soon, very soon, those new weapons and those swollen armies would be put to use. While professional soldiers knew, in theory, what those weapons were capable of, no one could have foreseen what would happen when such lethal weaponry was put in the hands of vast armies of millions.

CHAPTER 11

THE RIFLE AND
THE BULLET REVISITED

The Franco-Prussian War of 1870–1871 was a milestone like few others in the history of the West. It was one of the most important international contests of the century, ranking with the wars against Napoléon Bonaparte—shorter and smaller, to be sure, but with aftershocks that were just as unsettling. Granted, its political significance would not be apparent for another generation or two, but in retrospect it's easy to see why it was such an important moment. For the war of 1870–1871 accomplished two things that would help to define the twentieth century: the birth of a unified Germany, and the start of the long-standing mutual hatred between the new German Empire and humbled France. The victory over France brought the German states together like no previous experience, with Prussians shedding blood alongside their Saxon and Bavarian brethren, and Prussian chancellor Otto von Bismarck seized upon the nationalistic sentimentality of the hour to create a German state built upon Prussian rule. The act created, instantaneously, a new great power, whose population, resources, capacity for industry, and collective military might outstripped those of nearly all its rivals.

But Prussia's—and Germany's—triumph was also France's moment of national humiliation. There would be a long road to recovery ahead for what had been Europe's greatest military powerhouse, but through all the conspiracies, crises, and scandals that bedeviled the French Third Republic after the war, there thrummed a steady undercurrent of nationalism of the most dangerous kind, demanding *revanche* against Germany and the restoration of lost national pride. What made that sentiment truly dangerous was the fact that Germans—both the broader public and their leaders—recognized it, feared it, and expected it to materialize some day in the form of a rematch. It was precisely that recognition that drove Bismarck's notoriously intricate web of international alliances during the 1870s and 1880s, the whole purpose of which was to ensure that France would not have a reliable ally. Bismarck reasoned that if France were to be kept diplomatically isolated, then Germany would be safe, for the French would not dare to attack without an ally or two in its corner. Bismarck's project, as it turned out, was a gargantuan failure. The breakdown of his carefully crafted alliance system was one of the preconditions to the onset of a general war in the summer of 1914. But it all began with 1870, with the creation of a powerful Germany and a powerful hatred.

To professional soldiers and students of war, the Franco-Prussian War was also a milestone, even while it was happening. The contest couldn't have been any more dramatic, because of who its antagonists were: France, long established as Europe's premier military power, whose army was deemed worthy of emulation even in the United States; and Prussia, the newcomer, whose glory days under Frederick the Great were long past, but which had pulled off the astonishing feat of having all but destroyed Austria's* much-vaunted military might in a single campaign only four years before. France had a veteran army of long-term, seasoned professionals; Prussia, an army of native-born, short-term conscripts, supplemented by

---

*The Habsburg dynastic state was still commonly called Austria until the Ausgleich of 1867, which elevated the constitutional position of Hungary. After the Ausgleich, the Habsburg state became Austria-Hungary, which would last until the end of the Great War and the dissolution of the Dual Monarchy.

the less impressive armies of the other German states. France had a tradition of inspired and brilliant generalship; Prussia had in its general staff a planning organization of proven efficiency, with an unmatched understanding of military railroads. From a military professional's standpoint, it was a clash worth watching closely.

Not least among the features that drew the attention of the armies of the West was the technology of the war. Both France and Prussia had been hard at work rebuilding their respective arsenals, incorporating new and innovative designs in small arms and artillery. When it came to weaponry, this would be a war of firsts on multiple levels, but the technology that attracted the most rapt attention was the ordinary infantry rifle. Amid all the advances in small arms technology in the middle third of the nineteenth century, this war would be the first major conflict fought entirely with breech-loading small arms.

THE RIFLES CARRIED by French and German infantry in the war of 1870–1871 were not the products of cutting-edge technology; they were not the most advanced in the world, or even in Europe. The Prussian army still clung to the Dreyse, now beginning to show its age only six years after its first significant public appearance in the war with Denmark. It was the same rifle as it had been back then, as it had been when first introduced in 1841, with the same attendant faults and problems. Its greatest flaw, as combat experience had demonstrated, was its propensity to leak hot gases from the breech when fired, which both reduced the muzzle energy of the weapon and made it difficult and uncomfortable to fire from the shoulder.

The French had already found a solution to the leakage problem. Their answer to the Dreyse was in fact inspired by the Dreyse, and was the brainchild of Alsatian gunsmith Antoine Alphonse Chassepot. It operated on the same basic principle as the Prussian rifle: a single-shot breechloader, opened by a rotating bolt, using a long firing pin to detonate the primer inside a paper cartridge. But there were several critical differences that made the Chassepot a far superior weapon. It had a smaller bore diameter—11mm caliber as opposed to the Dreyse's 15.4mm bore—and used a heavier powder charge. Most important was the addition of an obturator in the form of a rubber gasket affixed to the front face of the rifle's operating bolt. When the rifleman slammed the bolt forward after loading the Chassepot, the bolt compressed the obturator inside the breech, sealing the gap between bolt and breech so that no gas leaked out. Eventually the rubber obturator would become hard and brittle, but it could be easily and quickly replaced. The Chassepot was a gigantic improvement over the Dreyse. Smaller bullet, heavier charge, less gas wastage thanks to the obturator—all these things added up to a firearm that was far more powerful than the Dreyse, with a higher velocity (almost by a full third), a flatter trajectory, and double the range: around 1,300 yards maximum effective range, as compared to the Dreyse's 600 yards.

Driven by fear of Prussia after its jaw-dropping victory over Austria at Königgrätz in 1866, the French had rushed the Chassepot into production immediately. They ditched their old Minié rifles, now completely outdated, and managed to rearm the regular army within a couple of years, in itself an almost unimaginable feat. When Chancellor Bismarck goaded France's Napoléon III into a declaration of war in July 1870, the French army—or at least its infantry—was ready.

In the end, having a superior rifle did not save the French. The French lost despite the marked superiority of their infantry weapons, which was not enough to compensate for poor organization in command and control, an officer corps that exhibited less initiative than its Prussian counterpart, clumsy handling of railway transport, and distinctly inferior artillery. Those factors ultimately doomed the legions of Napoléon III to defeat in the six-month war.

The Franco-Prussian War yielded important revelations about weapons and tactics. The Prusso-German victory was fast, no doubt, but it was not without cost. Until the Germans learned how best to exploit the virtues of their excellent Krupp-made field guns, and to coordinate artillery fire with infantry movement, the massed fire of the longer-ranged Chassepots took a terrible toll in German lives. But the Germans did learn. They learned to use their advantage in artillery to silence the French field batteries and suppress enemy rifle fire; they learned to avoid making massed frontal assaults with infantry. That tactic had still worked in the compressed heyday of the rifle-musket, not that long ago, but the Chassepot had changed the rules of the game. Prussian commanders, instead, learned to send their infantry forward in small assault units, taking advantage of cover, trying to flank the enemy rather than meet him head-on.

There was another lesson to be taken in from the war with France: the day of the Dreyse was over. The Chassepot was a better rifle, and it too was fast becoming obsolete. Oddly, the French and Prussian armies—by nearly all measures, the best armies in Europe—did not have the most up-to-date rifles. Just about every other army in the West, even that of the United States, had already taken the next great leap forward in rifle technology. They had adopted for general military use what would prove to be one of the most consequential inventions not only in the history of firearms, but in all of world history, since the introduction of gunpowder: the self-contained, internally primed, metal-cased cartridge.

THE METAL-CASED SMALL-ARMS cartridge was not new in 1870. The advantages of encasing powder and bullet in a cylindrical metal case were obvious. The metal case was robust, while paper or linen cartridges were prone to breakage, and could be easily bent or deformed. Metal-cased ammunition was almost impervious to moisture, while even indirect exposure to water could ruin paper cartridges instantly. The soft cartridges were also less safe. Sometimes the discharge of the weapon did not burn up all the paper, leaving smoldering embers in the breech—hardly a good thing when the next fresh round was inserted or rammed down. Paper or cloth cartridges could be rendered "combustible" by soaking the casing in a flammable solution, so that it quickly burned down to a fine ash when fired, but such cartridges were expensive and hardly foolproof. But metal-cased cartridges obviated all these problems, and more besides.

The greatest single advantage of the metal-cased cartridge was that it made breechloaders much more practical. For mechanical reasons that should be obvious, a metal-cased cartridge could only be used with a breechloader, since it would be next to impossible to extract a spent cartridge case from a muzzleloader. But in a breechloader, a metal-cased cartridge did something that a soft cartridge simply couldn't: it acted as its own obturator. The case itself effectively sealed the breech when it was closed, blocking even the most minuscule gaps and preventing gas leakage. That seal, as the performance of the Chassepot showed, meant more power and range, and fewer singed faces.

The first metal-cased cartridges appeared almost simultaneously with the percussion cap. Swiss-born gunmaker Jean Samuel Pauly, while working in Paris in 1812, patented a self-contained cartridge, cased in brass or heavy paper, containing primer as well as bullet and powder charge. By a fateful coincidence, Pauly's assistant at the time was a promising young German engineer named Johann Nikolaus von Dreyse. And Dreyse, in turn, borrowed Pauly's idea when designing his needle-rifle.

Two decades later, another Parisian gunsmith, Casimir Lefaucheux, developed the pinfire cartridge. Like Pauly's cartridge, the pinfire round—encased in a brass cylinder, closed on one end—contained powder, bullet, and primer, but also a firing pin: a stubby brass nail, protruding out of the sidewall of the cartridge case, its sharp end resting atop the internal primer. It required a specially designed firearm with a slot cut into its breech, so that the pin would stick up from the barrel; a sharp blow from the gun's hammer drove the pin into the primer, setting it off. The design caught on, though its popularity was restricted to Europe, where it found a niche market for revolvers and shotguns.

The Pauly, Dreyse, and Lefaucheux cartridges were brilliant but limited designs. The Dreyse cartridge did not obturate (or seal off), and the pinfire was finicky. Enter the Americans. In the early

1850s, the Massachusetts-born entrepreneurs Horace Smith and Daniel Wesson formed their own eponymous firearms company—the iconic Smith & Wesson—to produce a radical new rifle design, dubbed the Volcanic. The Volcanic, a distant forerunner of the later Winchester rifle, proved to be clever but impractical and unprofitable, and soon the partners shifted their focus to a more reliable technology and a more lucrative market: revolvers for civilian use. Samuel Colt's patent was due to expire in 1856, and Smith & Wesson was one of many companies primed to take advantage of the growing American obsession with handguns. Colt's revolvers still made use of traditional soft-bodied cartridges and percussion caps.

Daniel Wesson's revolver would be substantially different from Colt's, and the difference was in the ammunition. Wesson designed a cartridge specifically for his revolver. The rimfire cartridge, as it came to be known, had a brass cylindrical case, its closed rear end featuring a hollow rim circling the base. A small amount of priming material was spun into this rim, the cartridge was filled with powder and then topped off with an elongated bullet. A sharp blow to the rim, anywhere around its perimeter, detonated the primer and ignited the powder charge. Smith & Wesson's first product line, the S&W Model 1 (1857), fired Wesson's brand-new .22-caliber Short cartridge. The S&W factory in Springfield, Massachusetts, couldn't keep up with the demand—the new revolver and its unique cartridge were such a hit with the American public that they flew off store shelves nationwide. Other arms designers and entrepreneurs took notice, and by the time the Civil War began in 1861 new rimfire guns crowded the market.

The rimfire cartridge design was flexible, and it lent itself to all kinds of small arms—not just pistols, but rifles, too. And the rimfire cartridge also made something possible that gunmakers so far had only been able to dream about: a weapon that held multiple rounds in reserve, in a storage device called a magazine, and which could be fired rapidly several times in a row before being reloaded—the repeater.

PRACTICAL REPEATERS WERE already in existence, in the form of the revolver. A revolver, by definition, is a repeating, breech-loading firearm, in which the magazine is also the breech—a cylinder, closed at the rear, open at the front, with multiple chambers clustered around a central axis. One round is loaded into each chamber; when the cylinder is rotated, each chamber can in turn be aligned with the open breech-end of the single barrel, which is fixed in place. Samuel Colt's revolver, the first truly practical one, was superior to earlier revolvers in that it was mechanical. Pulling back the hammer not only cocked the weapon, but it also rotated the cylinder precisely the distance of one chamber, so that the next shot was ready to go when the hammer was cocked. Colt's revolvers met initially with a lukewarm reception, but they took off in popularity in the late 1840s. By 1860, the revolver had all but pushed single-shot pistols out of the civilian market and military use as well.

Colt's revolvers had their limitations. Before the end of the Civil War, they were all "cap and ball" guns, which made them very time-consuming to load. They also had a disturbing tendency to chain fire, meaning that an accidental flash from one shot could ignite all chambers in the cylinder simultaneously, destroying the revolver and possibly hurting the operator. That was bad enough with a pistol; with a rifle, a chain-fire incident would be likely to shoot off the rifleman's left hand. Colt's revolving rifles and shotguns consequently never sold very well. Ironically, Samuel Colt's greatest contribution to the Union war effort in 1861–1865 was to make tens of thousands of conventional muzzle-loading rifle-muskets for the Federal government.

The rimfire cartridge made the revolver faster to load and safer to shoot, but it also opened up all sorts of other possibilities for repeaters that transcended the revolver. Bright, ambitious gunsmiths were quick to pick up on them. Two of the most successful were Americans who patented their inventions on the eve of the American Civil War. Benjamin Tyler Henry worked for Smith & Wesson, and then for the aspiring young businessman Oliver

Winchester; Christopher Spencer started out his career at Colt's Hartford, Connecticut, factory before striking out on his own. Both of their repeating rifles, the Henry and the Spencer, were built around—and made possible by—the new rimfire cartridge, and both used what would come to be known as tube magazines. In a tube magazine, cartridges are loaded in a metal tube, end on end. A powerful spring, called a follower, exerts constant pressure on the cartridges, pushing them toward the breech mechanism (the "action"). In the Henry rifle, the tube magazine was slung below and parallel to the barrel, with the follower pushing the cartridges backward; in the Spencer, the tube magazine fit into a recess in the buttstock, the follower pushing the cartridges forward.

Although the internal mechanisms of the Spencer and the Henry were quite different, they were very similar to operate. In both models, the trigger guard, hinged at the front, acted as the operating lever. When the rifleman pushed the trigger guard down and forward, the breech opened, automatically extracting and eject-ing the spent cartridge case from the previous shot. The follower pushed the next fresh round from the magazine toward the now-empty chamber. The return stroke of the trigger guard chambered this cartridge and closed the action. On the Henry, the hammer cocked automatically when the operating lever was cycled, while the Spencer's hammer had to be cocked manually in a separate motion, giving the Henry a marginally higher rate of fire. Eventu-ally the magazine would be empty. The Spencer's tube magazine held seven rounds, the Henry's fifteen. But refilling the magazine was much easier on either rifle than it was on a revolver. The result was a rifle that could be loaded and fired as quickly as the rifleman could work the lever back and forth, take aim, and pull the trigger. With the Spencer, that meant a cyclic rate of *twenty aimed shots per minute*—about five shots per minute faster than the Dreyse, and six to seven times the rate of fire of a rifle-musket.

The advantages of the Spencer and Henry rifles were mani-fest, and they won over many converts. Abraham Lincoln himself was one of them, spending a memorable day in 1863 test-firing a Spencer alongside Christopher Spencer near the partially completed stub of the Washington Monument. The US Army purchased several thousand M1860 Spencers for cavalry use. They quickly proved their worth in battle. At the battle of Hoover's Gap (24–26 June 1863), a Federal brigade armed with Spencers held off repeated assaults by a superior Confederate force, inflicting such heavy casualties that the rebels were forced to withdraw. The reputation of the repeaters was such that individual units, even individual soldiers, purchased the rifles and ammunition with their own pay. But neither the Spencer nor the Henry, regardless of their popularity, ever became general-issue weapons. Neither replaced the trusty muzzleloader.

That the new repeating rifles of the 1860s did not see more widespread use in the American Civil War shouldn't be surprising. For the Confederacy, the reason was simple: it lacked the industrial

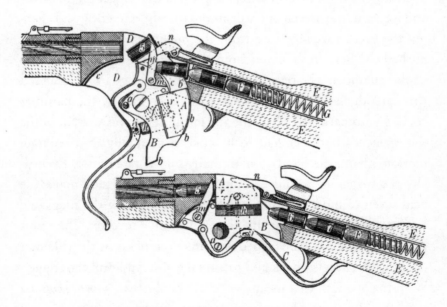

Plate 15. Spencer rifle action. In the upper diagram, the lever has been pushed down and forward, extracting and ejecting the spent casing (5), while the follower spring (G) inside the tube magazine (F) pushes a fresh round toward the chamber.
Image: Weiss, *Handfeuerwaffen*, p. 47.

capacity to make any weapons in quantity, let alone something as complex and so demanding of precision as a Spencer or a Henry, or their ammunition. For the North, the matter was more complicated. It's often argued that conservative army officials, unwilling or unable to see the genius behind the repeating rifles, stubbornly folded their arms and stood directly in the path of progress, deliberately opposing the widespread adoption of repeaters. But the plain truth was that those authorities recognized the general inadvisability of effecting a major shift in technology in the middle of a war. Because the repeaters fired much faster than the rifle-musket and other muzzleloaders, ammunition consumption per soldier would increase accordingly. Soldiers would have to carry more ammunition on their person while on campaign, adding to an already back-breaking and ill-balanced burden of gear—and military surgeons were taking note of the debilitating effects of that burden on soldiers' physical health. Soldiers were notorious for firing carelessly when in the midst of combat, and for discarding extra ammunition when on the march. If their new rifles could be fired faster, and if they were carrying larger and larger quantities of heavier ammunition, how much worse would the wastage be once the repeaters became standard-issue weapons?

These were not unreasonable concerns. But the real issue, the one that made the complete replacement of muzzleloaders with repeaters impossible at that moment, centered on supply. Northern factories were capable of producing Spencers and Henrys *in limited quantities*, but to bend Northern industry to the task of re-equipping all (or most) Federal infantry with repeating rifles would have constituted an insurmountable challenge. As it was, the demand for rifle-muskets already strained the North's productive capacity. The American Civil War was already half over by the time the single Federal arsenal (at Springfield, Massachusetts) and the score of firms building rifle-muskets under contract managed to make enough longarms to meet the demands of the Union armies in the field. And that was with rifle-muskets, an established technology, relatively simple to manufacture. If the US Army had tried to switch over from rifle-muskets to repeaters, in the middle of a war, the results would have been disastrous. The limitations of the factory economy, and not some kind of stodgy, conservative resistance to new technology, were what would delay the large-scale use of repeating rifles in combat.

That fact highlighted what was fast becoming a salient feature of the firepower revolution that was just beginning around 1860–1870. Adopting new weapons was costly, in time and resources and money; adopting new weapons in quantities sufficient to be meaningful—like enough to rearm entire armies and navies—was costlier still; discarding those weapons once they obsolesced, then replacing them with the innovation of the moment . . . well, that was profligate. And yet that's exactly what the great powers of the West sought to do, time and time again, in the half-century before the end of the First World War. As it turned out, not all nations were up to the task of re-equipping their armed forces every few years. Great powers without significant industry, like Austria-Hungary and Russia, would find it impossible to keep up with the frantic pace of continual rearmament at the dawn of the twentieth century. The new technology, instead, favored the more robust industrial economies, like those of Britain, France, Germany, and the United States. And even for those industrial powerhouses, keeping pace with technological change would prove to be a difficult and risky proposition.

BUT EUROPE WAS engaged in an arms race after 1870, so economic logic and fiscal responsibility didn't necessarily apply. Arms races, after all, have a logic all their own. Having access to more and superior military might than one's enemies and potential enemies was the paramount concern. It was, in fact, an existential concern, or at least it was perceived as existential by those states that participated in the arms race, and the perception was all that mattered. That competition between the Western powers—infinitely more concentrated, fevered, and intense than the European arms race of the military revolution period—drove all sorts of decisions relating to military policy, and it drove the development of weapons technology, too. In the realm of small arms, that meant that the armies of the West actively sought out rifles (and pistols, and machine guns) that were faster, more accurate, more powerful than those of their neighbors and rivals. They eagerly grabbed at innovations almost as soon as they could, with lots of testing but relatively little reflection, even if that meant scrapping millions of perfectly good, serviceable firearms of the next-latest pattern—rendered obsolete by their newly assimilated replacements. Sometimes those new weapons systems so outperformed their predecessors that their adoption made perfect sense; on most occasions, though, the gains achieved by modernization were trivial, not enough to justify the gargantuan sums of money expended on them. Having a better infantry rifle was hardly a guarantee of victory. The French Chassepot, after all, was markedly superior to the Prussian Dreyse, but it wasn't France that celebrated victory in 1871.

Nearly every Western nation took part in the race to build a better rifle, even the smaller states that didn't stand a chance of protecting their borders in the event of a general European war. But the primary drivers of this arms race were the two nations whose industrial capacity and mutual hatred made their rivalry the most dangerous: France and Germany. Their development of the modern repeating battle rifle after 1870 is the arms race in microcosm.

In 1871, there was no question that the breech-loading rifle was infinitely superior to the muzzle-loading rifle-musket. The difference between the two, just measured by rate of fire, was too great, and Austria's defeat in 1866 had proved it beyond a doubt. After 1866, in fact, Western armies—and some in the East, too, notably Japan—scrambled to rearm themselves, but as most of them had only just recently invested in rifle-muskets, they hoped to spare some expense by converting, rather than discarding, their rifle-muskets. A whole host of designs emerged in the 1860s and 1870s, all of them retrofitting the rifle-musket to take advantage of the new metal-cased ammunition.

At the same time, a further development in ammo design emerged. The rimfire cartridge would survive, even thrive, into the present day; the .22-caliber "Long Rifle" rimfire round remains the most popular small-arms cartridge in the history of modern firearms. But rimfire was hardly perfect, and right after the American Civil War it ceded its primacy to a better design. The centerfire cartridge, the basic form of nearly all modern ammunition, was not the work of a lone inventor, but rather appeared in several countries at roughly the same time. Early in the American Civil War, for example, a South Carolina businessman named George W. Morse patented an ingenious breech-loading carbine that fired a centerfire cartridge of Morse's own design. Morse's factory would make a small number for Confederate service, but—as in so many areas of military technology—the South simply did not have the resources to invest heavily in Morse's invention.

The centerfire cartridge had a single primer, much like a percussion cap, embedded in the base of the cartridge case, opposite the rear of the bullet. A firing pin—stouter and sturdier than the needle in Dreyse's rifle—would strike and detonate the primer, igniting the charge. It was more reliable than rimfire cartridges, and easier to manufacture, too. The two most common variants—invented independently by the American rifle-advocate Hiram Berdan and the Englishman Edward Boxer—received patents in 1866 and were available for sale immediately after.

European and American armies responded quickly, converting their not-so-old rifle-muskets into single-shot breechloaders, and then producing improved, newly made rifles based on those designs. Right after the Civil War, the US Army started converting its Springfield rifle-muskets to the Allin "trapdoor" breechloader, firing an underpowered .58-caliber rimfire round; the rifle's considerable deficiencies, and the sudden availability of centerfire ammunition, led to its immediate replacement with an improved trapdoor, the M1866, which chambered a new .50-caliber centerfire cartridge. Britain similarly transitioned to the .577-caliber Snider breechloader; Russia converted its rifle-muskets to the centerfire

Krnka breechloader; the French—before adopting the Chassepot in 1866—recycled many of their muzzleloaders into the Tabatière model breechloaders. By 1870, the Dreyse needle-rifle looked positively old-fashioned.

The perception of progress at the time must have been astonishing. In the 1840s, most armies were just beginning to put aside their flintlock, smoothbore, muzzle-loading muskets; two decades later, they had breech-loading rifles firing self-contained metallic cartridges. Astonishing, yes, and costly too, even if it was possible to recycle some of the old rifle-muskets as a stopgap measure.

But the pace of innovation in small arms design did not slacken. It actually accelerated, faster than the armies of the West could convert their existing stocks of rifle-muskets into breechloaders, faster than ordnance officers and gun-industry experts could keep up with the flood of new models. France and Germany had slipped behind the rest of the West, but the fear that boiled out of their mutual bitterness and suspicion prompted both states to search aggressively for new weapons. The Germans made the first move. Even before the war with France, the Prussian high command had already begun the search for a new infantry rifle, and was already leaning toward a design that was both very conservative and very promising.

The Mauser brothers, Paul and Wilhelm, came from a gun-smithing family. Their reputation was solid but not scintillating. Paul had designed a new rifle-musket for his native Württemberg in the 1850s, and while it was a solid rifle there was nothing about it to hint at any great genius. Nor, at first glance, was there anything remarkable about the prototype breech-loading rifle that his brother Wilhelm tendered to the Prussian government. It looked very much like a slimmed-down Dreyse. But it was not based on the Dreyse, and in fact the two rifles were quite different. The Dreyse's bolt had no *locking lugs*. In a modern bolt-action rifle, a locking lug is a steel lug that protrudes from the round sides of the rifle bolt, which fits into a matching channel machined into the interior surface of the rifle's receiver, where the bolt rests when closed. The lug helps hold the bolt securely in place, so that when the rifle is fired the bolt does not fly backward in response to the violent explosion that occurs right in front of it. The Dreyse did not have this feature; the only thing holding the bolt in place was the handle itself. The locking lug meant that the Mauser action was much, much stronger than the Dreyse, which allowed the Mauser to use a more powerful round—and that, in turn, meant higher velocity and longer range.

The locking lug was, perhaps, the most important thing that Wilhelm Mauser brought to the table. Another advantage of the Mauser was the firing pin. The Dreyse used a long, slender iron needle to detonate its paper cartridge; it had to be long, because it had to travel all the way from the rear of the cartridge to the primer at the base of the bullet. Mauser's rifle used a short, almost stubby firing pin, far more resilient than Dreyse's needle, to set off the primer on the base of its brass-cased, centerfire cartridge.

Mauser's rifle easily won an official design competition for the Dreyse's replacement, and one of the first acts of the new Imperial German army was to adopt the rifle as the *Infanterie-Gewehr* (Infantry Rifle) M1871. Within a year, it was in full production, and three years later it was in the hands of all active-duty troops in the German army—except for the Bavarian regiments, who clung to their own homemade rifle. This was a tall order, for the German army was quite large. But it was just the beginning, the opening salvo in a tech war with France.

Up until now, the French had had the better rifle. The Chassepot was perhaps the pinnacle of paper-cartridge firearms, but Mauser's *Gewehr* 71 was better. Its 11mm centerfire cartridge offered slightly improved ballistics over the Chassepot, but the brass-cased Mauser round loaded more quickly and smoothly, leaving behind less residue in the chamber after firing. Less residue meant fewer misfires, fewer jams, and better performance overall.

The Germans were ahead, again, and that wouldn't do. The French could not let that stand. National pride and security dictated otherwise. The Chassepot was still a pretty good rifle, not

The Rifle and the Bullet Revisited

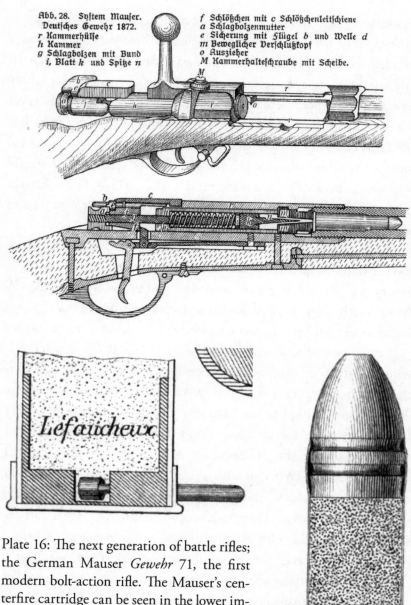

Plate 16: The next generation of battle rifles; the German Mauser *Gewehr* 71, the first modern bolt-action rifle. The Mauser's centerfire cartridge can be seen in the lower image, in the chamber and ready to fire; cross section of the base of a Lefaucheux-patent pinfire cartridge; rimfire cartridge for the M1860 Spencer rifle and carbine, cal. 56-56.

Images from Weiss, *Handfeuerwaffen*, p. 43; *Die modernen Ordonnanz-Präcisionswaffen der Infanterie*, Tafeln III and XIII.

significantly inferior in range or accuracy, but soon French engineers were back to the drawing board. Postwar France was a tangled mess of political factions and economic malaise, not in any condition to spare the vast sums necessary to build a whole new rifle, and there were hundreds of thousands of perfectly good Chassepots in the arsenals. Army officer and ordnance expert Basile Gras came up with both a new rifle—which looked an awful lot like the Chassepot—and a method for converting the Chassepot into a new rifle. The new model, the M1874 Gras, fired a brass-cased 11mm centerfire round, almost identical to the 11mm Mauser cartridge in performance.

The race was on, and the rest of the world tried to keep up, too. Britain dropped the Snider and embraced the quirky Martini-Henry with its odd, bottle-necked .450 centerfire cartridge; the US Army stuck with its tried and true trapdoor rifle, now in .45-70 Government caliber;* Russia scrapped the Krnka after its lackluster performance in the Russo-Turkish War (1877–1878), replacing it with two different American rifle designs patented by Hiram Berdan. With the exception of the second-model Berdan rifle, these were not bolt action like the Mauser and Gras rifles. With the early Berdans and the American trapdoor, a hinged breech-piece pivoted upward to expose the chamber; the Martini-Henry, the rifle that accompanied red-coated British soldiers all over the Empire, had a "falling breechblock" that pivoted down when the trigger guard was forced downward. Denmark adopted a different American design, the so-called rolling block patented by the Remington firm.

All of these were single-shot breechloaders; there was not a single repeater among the entire crop of European military rifles circa 1875. But repeaters were not forgotten. They had proved their qualities on a limited scale in the American Civil War, and—more recently and closer to home—during the Russo-Turkish War of

---

* The .45 Government cartridge adopted by the US Army in 1873 contained a 405-grain, .45-caliber bullet, and a propellant charge of 70 grains of black powder. Properly it should be the ".45-70-405," but it is conventionally called the .45-70 round.

The Rifle and the Bullet Revisited

1877–1878. Even if repeaters were slower to load when empty, even with the added task of filling a magazine after several shots, the advantage in overall rate of fire more than compensated. Having several rounds in reserve at a critical moment, like when under attack, was a potential lifesaver. During the siege of Plevna, during the Russo-Turkish conflict, the otherwise unimpressive Ottoman army was partially armed with American-made Winchester repeaters, the direct descendants of the Henry rifle. The Winchesters couldn't compete with the Russian Krnkas and Berdans for range and power, but they could be fired with blistering speed. Armed with Winchesters, the defending Turks, vastly outnumbered, made the tsar's troops pay a terrible price for every inch of ground they took at Plevna.

Plevna brought the lesson home in a way that the American experience had not, and the quest for a rugged and reliable repeater became the next big thing in small arms engineering. The tube magazine, used in the Spencer, Henry, and Winchester rifles, was simplest and most familiar; the bolt action—the overarching design of the Dreyse, Chassepot, Mauser, Gras, and later Berdan rifles—paired well with it. It was a natural combination, the bolt-action and the tube magazine. Bolt-action rifles were mechanically stronger than, say, lever-action rifles like the Winchester, and other actions just couldn't be adapted to work with a magazine.

The Austrian engineer Ferdinand Früwirth first combined the tube magazine with a bolt-action breech, and an Austrian general—Alfred, Ritter von Kropatschek—improved upon it. The Kropatschek's tube magazine ran underneath and parallel to the barrel, encased in the rifle's wooden stock for protection. A follower spring exerted constant pressure from the muzzle-end, pushing cartridges back toward the action. When the rifleman rotated the bolt up and drew it back, it extracted and ejected the spent case and cocked the firing pin; at the same time, the follower spring pushed a fresh cartridge onto a pivoting elevator, called a lifter, below the bolt, and the lifter tilted the cartridge up into the breech. As it moved forward again, the bolt caught on to the fresh round on the

269

lifter and pushed it, straight and firm, into the chamber. Filling the magazine with ammo took a few seconds, but with a Kropatschek a rifleman could load and fire as fast as he could work the bolt, without pausing to grab a new round every shot, for a rate of fire roughly two to three times that of the Mauser. There was no doubt about it: the Kropatschek was a better rifle.

In 1878, the French navy officially adopted the Kropatschek as its service rifle. Six years later the French army followed suit, and in doing so stole a lead over Germany—a big lead. Predictably, the German army could not sit still and let the French rearm with a repeater, so Mauser revised the *Gewehr* 71, adding a tube magazine and a lifter similar to those on the Kropatschek. The new rifle, dubbed the *Gewehr* M1871/84, succeeded its single-shot predecessor, and France and Germany were at parity again. For the moment.

THAT STATE OF affairs didn't last for long. Neither France nor Germany wanted it to. This was a struggle for supremacy and advantage, not parity and *détente*. If there was any way to enhance the killing power of their small arms, then German and French engineers would find it, and the rest of Europe would follow along because, in an arms race, there is rarely a satisfactory alternative to participation.

The next stage in the small-arms race came about as a result of a breakthrough in the science of ammunition—one might well say *the* breakthrough, the one single development that changed everything about firearms. The German chemical industry was more sophisticated than that of France, and German chemists were the leaders of the discipline, but the French had more narrowly focused their efforts on the chemistry of weapons, specifically propellants. In the 1870s, nearly every basic element of firearms technology had changed drastically from what had come before—every basic element, that is, except for the propellant. Black powder was still the all-purpose explosive and propellant of choice. Engineers and chemists had been working on alternatives for some time, focusing more on explosives than on propellants. Explosives had more applications in civilian life, notably in mining and in railroad construction, for controlled explosions saved a lot of time when it was necessary to tunnel through a mountain of rock. Nitroglycerine, the first high explosive, made its debut in the 1840s; trinitrotoluene (TNT) was patented by the German chemist Julius Wilbrand in 1863. But these were explosives, ill-suited to work as propellants. While black powder deflagrated, nitroglycerine and TNT exploded fast and forcefully—they were too powerful to be contained safely within a steel rifle barrel. Nitrocellulose, commonly known as guncotton, showed more promise as a propellant. The Austrian army adopted guncotton for its rifle-musket ammunition, but only temporarily.

The big break came in 1884, when a brilliant young French chemist named Paul Vieille compounded nitrocellulose with ether and paraffin, producing a whitish-colored powder that could be formed into flakes or pellets. It was not unstable or volatile like gunpowder, not overly sensitive to moisture, and it was more difficult to detonate than black powder—a desirable quality, since Vieille's compound was far easier to make and to handle safely. It deflagrated more slowly than gunpowder, but overall it was more powerful—up to three times more powerful by volume. That burn rate could also be adjusted, Vieille found, simply by varying the size of the grains into which it was formed. And it burned more efficiently. *Poudre blanche* (white powder), as Vieille called it— the French army gave it the official label Poudre B—left virtually nothing behind in the barrel when it burned. Poudre B deposited no hard carbon fouling in the barrel; it didn't gum up the moving parts of a breechloader. Most surprising of all, Poudre B produced only tiny amounts of smoke. It was, indeed, a smokeless powder, but it was so much more.

Vieille's invention was the first modern projectile propellant, the senior member of the family of smokeless powders. Its advantages did not end with the absence of smoke or fouling. Its ballistic properties, especially when paired with a slightly smaller bullet, were simply astonishing. Bullets fired with a charge of Poudre B traveled farther, faster, and with a much flatter trajectory than was possible with large-caliber elongated bullets and black powder. Their killing range could now be measured in miles rather than in thousands of yards; the flat trajectory meant that the "safe zone," a ballistic peculiarity of the previous generation of ammunition, was drastically reduced. Smaller powder charges, and smaller bullets, meant lighter ammunition. Everything about Poudre B was superior to black powder. Everything.

Keeping Vieille's discovery a closely guarded secret, the French army quickly got to work designing a rifle worthy of the new propellant. Such innovations were no longer left to chance, no longer entrusted to private industry or independent inventors. The state of military technology had become, in the militarized political climate of post-1870 Europe, an issue of existential importance, too sensitive to be left to serendipity or the unpredictable fecundity of individual genius. In France, as in Germany, weapons design had become a form of institutionalized research, conducted by committees of engineers, scientists, and career soldiers. In France, Vieille's new powder was handed off to the army's Repeating Firearms Commission (Commission des Armes à Répétition). A recent addition to the commission, a veteran colonel named Nicolas Lebel, designed a new cartridge around Poudre B, and the commission designed a rifle to use the new ammo. In 1886, under great pressure from the War Ministry to come up with a prototype, the commission finally approved a new rifle for general issue, officially called the Fusil Modèle 1886 dit "Fusil Lebel"—the Infantry Rifle M1886 called "Lebel Rifle."

It was appropriate that the new French battle rifle would be known by the name of the man who had invented its ammunition, because that was the most important thing about it. The Lebel rifle was not remarkable in itself. It was a bolt-action repeater with an eight-round tube magazine, little more than an updated Kropatschek. It had a stronger bolt than its predecessors, with multiple locking lugs, because Poudre B generated much stronger chamber pressures than its black-powder antecedents.

What made the Lebel rifle a head-turner wasn't so much the rifle itself as it was the eponymous cartridge. Col. Lebel's cartridge, officially dubbed Balle M, combined all the most modern elements: smokeless, high-velocity Poudre B; a centerfire cartridge configuration; and a long, flat-topped bullet of 8mm caliber. The bullet's flat top was an important safety feature. Since the centerfire cartridges rested end-to-end in the Lebel's tube magazine, the bullet point of one cartridge would be nestled against the primer of the cartridge in front of it; a pointier bullet, it was feared, stood the chance of accidentally detonating the primer of the next cartridge if the rifle were subjected to a sharp blow, causing a disastrous and likely fatal chain explosion in the magazine. The smaller caliber of the bullet was the truly radical departure from established norms. Conventional wisdom held that you needed a massive bullet to stop a determined soldier; but the ballistics, especially the range and the accuracy, of the smaller 8mm bullet were so much better than those of the .40 to .45-caliber bullets of the Lebel's contemporaries.

It was also discovered that lead, the traditional material for bullets, was too soft for the high velocities generated by the new smokeless powder; a lead bullet could soften, even partially melt, during its brief journey down the barrel and out the muzzle, deforming the bullet in flight and seriously compromising its accuracy. But in 1882, a Swiss army officer named Eduard Rubin had discovered that by coating the bullet with a thin layer of a slightly harder metal—a process called jacketing—the resulting projectile would be soft enough to engage the rifling and hard enough to retain its shape after being fired. Lebel incorporated Rubin's discovery into his Balle M; the Lebel bullet was covered with a "full metal jacket" of copper and nickel.

This was no mere tweak in small arms design. Because of its cartridge, the Lebel was in a class all by itself. It outranged every other rifle in service, anywhere in the world; its accuracy was unparalleled; its trajectory was almost flat; its muzzle velocity was double that of the M71/84 Mauser. Tests later performed by the German army revealed that the Lebel was faster, too: although both rifles were bolt-actions with tube magazines, German experts assessed the Lebel's rate of fire at forty-three rounds per minute, as opposed to the M71/84's twenty-six. In one stroke, every other military rifle in the world was rendered obsolete.

If France could have rearmed its entire infantry and cavalry branches with the Lebel before the Germans could come up with an effective countermeasure, the German army would have found itself facing a technological gap that no amount of superior training or tactical doctrine or logistics could have bridged. It was not a ridiculous fear. In France, a strident anti-German nationalism was very much on the rise in the late 1880s, and that combined with the technological achievements of the French military gave Chancellor Bismarck substantial cause for alarm. According to conservative German estimates, France would have completely rearmed its troops with Lebels by 1889—only a year and a half after Germany produced enough M71/84s to equip its army. One German general considered the French technological edge to be so decisive that, if it came to war with France, German infantrymen "will all be shot down like a nation of partridges."*

That the invention of a superior rifle and cartridge could be regarded in Germany as a national emergency seems curious, and yet for Germany that's exactly what the Lebel round represented. The German analog of France's Commission on Repeating Firearms, the GPK (*Gewehr-Prüfungskommission*), had been working with private industries in hopes of developing improved propellants, but without much luck. About the best they could come up with was Max Duttenhofer's Rottweil Cellulose Powder, a wood-based "nitro" propellant that delivered slightly higher velocities than black powder but was unstable and, worse, produced clouds of smoke when fired.

---

*Eric Dorn Brose, *The Kaiser's Army: The Politics of Military Technology in Germany during the Machine Age*, 1870–1918 (Oxford: Oxford University Press, 2001), 46–50.

The Rifle and the Bullet Revisited

When the French army revealed the Lebel rifle and Balle M to the world, the reaction in German military circles was surprise infused with panic. Even though Germany's great statesman, Chancellor Otto von Bismarck, had been doing all he could to keep France diplomatically isolated and therefore unlikely to risk a war with Germany, there was still much concern that if the French were able to find a military advantage great enough, then war between the two powers might ensue immediately. After all, the French minister of war who had lobbied hard for the adoption of the Lebel was none other than Georges Boulanger, the scandal-ridden general-politician whose populist appeal was based almost entirely on his furious calls for *revanche* on Germany. It didn't matter that the entire German army was still in the middle of transitioning from the single-shot *Gewehr* 71 to the magazine-fed *Gewehr* 71/84, a rifle that was all of two years old when the Lebel went into service. Germany's survival depended on catching up with French military technology.

The Germans did catch up, and quickly, owing mostly to serendipity. Only a year after the Lebel went into service, an enterprising French army deserter made his way into Germany with his Lebel and some ammunition, hoping that he could turn a quick profit when he surrendered to German authorities. Bismarck, hearing of the incident, made sure that it was given the attention that it was due. The German high command immediately terminated Duttenhofer's experiments with nitrocellulose and shamelessly reverse engineered the French ammo that had fallen into their hands. And because they were engrossed in a life-and-death arms race, the Germans added improvements of their own, upping the game in the process.

First, the rifle. The GPK, under great pressure to respond to the French, weighed a couple of options: redesigning the *Gewehr* 71/84 so that it could work with a high-pressure, small-caliber cartridge like Balle M, or starting from scratch. The officers serving in the GPK opted for the latter; they would not be content with merely equaling the French. They would stick with a trusty bolt action, but here they had a few choices. Other nations, and other inventors, had gotten in on the bolt-action game, so Mauser and Kropatschek no longer enjoyed an exclusive lock on the type. Germany's ally Austria-Hungary had just adopted a promising bolt-action of native design, the brainchild of engineer Ferdinand Mannlicher. The M1886 Mannlicher rifle fired a conventional black-powder cartridge, and in this sense was a step backward from the Lebel, but what attracted the attention of German arms experts was its magazine. The Mannlicher did not use an under-the-barrel tube, but rather a box magazine, placed right under the action, just in front of the trigger guard. The box magazine was simpler and better than the tube. Ammunition was loaded straight down through the open breech, the cartridges stacked one upon the other in a single row. A spring-loaded follower pushed them up from the bottom of the magazine, so that the round on top was always ready to be loaded into the chamber.

Simpler, stronger, easier to clean and repair, but best of all it was *faster*. Herr Mannlicher had devised an ingenious way to fill the magazine in a fraction of the time it took to fill a tube magazine. Five cartridges could be preloaded into an open sheet-metal container, called an *en bloc* (or stripper) clip. Rather than load the cartridges one at a time into the open magazine, the rifleman merely had to insert an entire clip directly through the open breech into the magazine. It took one quick, smooth movement, and the rifle was fully loaded. The clip itself remained inside the magazine until it was empty, then dropped to the ground via an open port in the bottom of the magazine, and the rifleman could shove another clip into the magazine. Clip-loading meant that a soldier could now fire his rifle without any appreciable interval between shots, vastly increasing the rate of fire.

So far, so good. The GPK was off to a promising start. Next the cartridge. Balle M was quite good, and the combination of a small-caliber, jacketed bullet with high-velocity powder was unquestionably revolutionary. But the Lebel round's profile was disadvantageous. It was trimmed down from the 11mm Gras cartridge, so the brass case tapered sharply from a wide base to a very narrow neck, and a large rim protruded from around the circumference of the base. The large rim could be helpful—it was easy to extract from a hot chamber—but the pronounced taper was a distinct liability. Because they were wider at the base than they were at the tip, the cartridges couldn't be stacked side to side in a straight line, and would require a curved magazine. So the GPK reworked the profile of the cartridge so that it had practically no taper at all, not even a rim. The new German round, the *Patrone 88*, could be stacked in a straight pile.

Little more than a year after discovering and dissecting the Lebel, the German army announced the arrival of its new cartridge and rifle, the *Gewehr* M1888—like the Lebel, a rifle designed by committee. Ballistically it was the rough equal of the Lebel, but its new magazine system was a clear improvement on the Lebel's tube magazine. Germany was in the lead again. There was no hesitation and precious little debate about the change, because that was never an issue; there was no question that Germany had to adopt a new rifle. It didn't matter that the German army hadn't yet rearmed completely with the *Gewehr* 71/84, which was still quite new. Fire superiority over France was an imperative that could not be impeded by petty concerns about frugality.

The race to build the world's best battle rifle did not end with the *Gewehr* 88. Two years later, the French adopted a new bolt-action rifle with a box magazine and *en bloc* clip, the Berthier. The Berthier was a mediocrity, hardly the contribution to firearms history that the Lebel had been. Overall France did not manage to keep up with Germany in the 1890s.

The rest of the Western world, and those nations who followed its lead, struggled to keep up with Europe's two most advanced armies. And they did so, for the most part, without too much consideration given to cost. For smaller states without arms factories, that usually meant buying rifles abroad, for example from the Mauser factories in Oberndorf or the ŒWG (Österreichische Waffenfabriksgesellschaft) in Steyr. Overall, though, there was

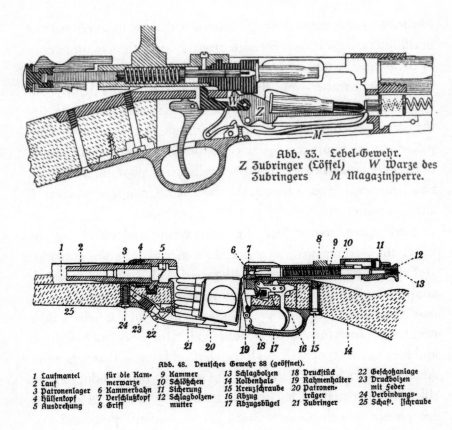

Abb. 33. Lebel-Gewehr.
Z Zubringer (Löffel)   W Warze des
Zubringers   M Magazinsperre.

Abb. 48. Deutsches Gewehr 88 (geöffnet).

1 Laufmantel	für die Kam-	9 Kammer	13 Schlagbolzen	18 Druckstück	22 Geschoßanlage
2 Lauf	merwarze	10 Schlößchen	14 Kolbenhals	19 Rahmenhalter	23 Druckbolzen
3 Patronenlager	6 Kammerbahn	11 Sicherung	15 Kreuzschraube	20 Patronen-	mit Feder
4 Hülsenkopf	7 Verschlußkopf	12 Schlagbolzen-	16 Abzug	träger	24 Verbindungs-
5 Ausdrehung	8 Griff	mutter	17 Abzugsbügel	21 Zubringer	25 Schaft. [schraube

Plate 17. The revolutionary rifles of the smokeless era: the M1886 Lebel action. Note the tube magazine (right side) and the cartridge lifter (Z); the 1888 German *Kommissionsgewehr* (Gew88). Note the "clip" holding five rounds together inside the rifle's box magazine.
Images from Weiss, *Handfeuerwaffen*, pp. 49, 83.

a preference for homegrown rifles, chambered to use specialized ammunition, produced domestically. That impulse was both an expression of nationalism—perhaps the most consistent thread in European politics at the time—and of the perceived need to be self-sufficient in strategic resources.

Austria-Hungary adapted the redoubtable Mannlicher rifle to the new smokeless powder in 1895. Russia in 1891 went with a rifle that combined a native bolt-action (from its own Sergei Ivanovich

Mosin) and a magazine (by Belgian gunmaker Léon Nagant); the resulting hybrid, the Mosin-Nagant Three-Line Rifle would go on to become perhaps the most commonly used bolt-action rifle in the history of the world. Italy adopted the Carcano system, a Mannlicher variant, also in 1891, while Japan issued a native-born, Mauserlike rifle, the Arisaka, starting in 1898. The British stuck loyally by their single-shot, black-powder Martini-Henry breechloaders until 1888, when they began to phase in a new series of magazine-fed bolt-action rifles: the Lee-Metford (1888), the Lee-Enfield (1895), and then the iconic SMLE (Rifle, Short, Magazine, Lee-Enfield), affectionately called the "Smelly" by British soldiers.

The United States was, as usual, anachronistic, odd for a nation with such a well-developed arms industry and a rich history of firearms genius. The black-powder trapdoor rifles, which went through several iterations between 1866 and 1892, served the frontier Army well enough, but by the 1890s even the cost-conscious Americans understood that they could no longer afford to put off modernizing their weaponry. After rejecting both Mauser and Mannlicher models, an Army board charged with rifle selection settled on the current Danish service rifle, a bolt-action magazine rifle codesigned by Norwegians Ole Krag and Erik Jørgensen. The Krag-Jørgensen—the "Krag" in American parlance—went into US service in 1892, and it was a curious choice. In most regards it functioned about as well as any other European infantry rifle of the 1890s, but its five-round magazine was an oddity. It opened via a hinged, springloaded access door on the right side of the receiver. It functioned smoothly but could only be filled one round at a time, not with clips like just about every other military rifle of its vintage.

The US Army's principal attraction to the Krag was a minor feature called a magazine cutoff, which with the flick of a switch blocked the magazine from feeding fresh rounds into the chamber. The cutoff appealed to leaders—mostly older and senior—who feared ammunition wastage, and saw the magazine more as an emergency backup than anything else. The Krag could function, in other words, both as a single-shot breechloader and as a modern magazine rifle. The Krag proved to be an unfortunate choice, and its brief combat career in American service only served to bolster the arguments of those who advocated an aggressive approach to assimilating new weapons technologies. During the war over Cuba (the Spanish-American War, 1898), American troops found, somewhat to their dismay, that their Spanish foes were better armed overall. The Spanish service rifle was the M1893 Mauser, a clip-fed bolt-action rifle chambered in 7mm Mauser caliber. Using clips, the M1893 could be reloaded much faster than the American Krags, and on top of that the Mauser cartridge was more powerful and longer-ranged than the American .30–40 Krag round. The clearly inferior performance of the Krag proved to be its demise in American service, and within a few years the Army replaced it with a Mauser-like rifle, the soon-to-be-famous M1903 Springfield.

There were dozens of different rifle models in service at the time of the First World War, but Mauser ended up as the winner. The Mauser became the most popular rifle in the world, as engineers at the Mauser factories in Oberndorf came up with model after model, mostly for foreign sale, starting in 1889. Belgium, the Ottoman Empire, Spain, Sweden, Mexico, Argentina, Peru, Brazil, Siam, Persia—all of them adopted one of the new, improved Mauser models. Even Germany, whose *Gewehr* 88 was still a very modern and serviceable rifle, couldn't resist the temptation to re-arm with the slightly modernized Mausers. Likely Mauser's best design, the M1898—or *Gewehr* 98 in German service—became the German service rifle and would be the basis for the main infantry rifle of the Wehrmacht in the Second World War.

THE PACE OF innovation in rifle design, and the feverish drive to build a superior infantry shoulder arm, slackened a bit as the new century began. Other, more urgent priorities emerged; France and Germany locked horns over yet another area of weapons tech— namely, field artillery—and the naval race between Britain and Germany heated up dramatically. But while the pace of innovation in rifle design slackened, it did not abate entirely. Mauser invented a new kind of ammunition clip—the charger clip—cheaper than and superior to the en bloc clip used in Mannlicher-type magazines. And just before the dawn of the new century, one by one the European armies adopted a new kind of bullet for their centerfire cartridges. Extensive testing on the range revealed that sharply pointed bullets—known in German as *Spitzgeschoß* or "spitzer" bullets—were more accurate than the blunt- or flat-nosed bullets in common use before 1900. A spitzer with a "boat-tail," a gradual inward taper at the rear end of the bullet, was even better. This entailed, perhaps surprisingly, a not-trivial expense because longer bullets often meant that rifles had to be altered to chamber them. When Germany adopted the *Spitzgeschoß* in 1905, the army had to alter the receivers of all its 1898-model rifles, and many of its old *Gewehr* 88s, to accept the new ammunition.

By 1905, if not earlier, every army in the West—and many non-Western armies with a heavy Western influence, like those of Japan, China, and the Ottoman Empire—had armed its foot troops with modern bolt-action, magazine-fed rifles, firing centerfire ammunition using smokeless powder. To be sure, there were hitches. Industry could not always keep up with demand. Germany was largely self-sufficient, but most of the major participants relied on foreign-made rifles to supplement insufficient production at home. Well before the United States joined the Great War as a belligerent in 1917, American firms supplied the armies of the Allied nations—France, Britain, and especially Russia—with rifles and ammunition, among other things. Both Remington and New England Westinghouse, for example, manufactured exact copies of the M1891 Mosin-Nagant rifle for the armies of the tsar, while Winchester produced a specially built lever-action military rifle (the M1895 Winchester Musket) chambered for the Russian 7.62mm rifle cartridge.

When war erupted in 1914, there weren't quite enough modern weapons to arm *all* the men in uniform, reservists included, and sometimes rear-echelon troops had to make do with obsolete, oddball, or foreign rifles. A gray-bearded German reservist in the

Landsturm might be compelled to carry an old *Gewehr* 71 while guarding a railway depot; Russian frontline troops not infrequently used Japanese-made Arisakas; Ottoman troops relied heavily on German-manufactured rifles. But the frontline troops had modern rifles. And as much as modern-day collectors might quibble about the relative merits and demerits of Mosin-Nagants and Mausers and SMLEs, they were all pretty much the same in terms of performance. None was markedly superior to another. After all the frantic competition over rifle design after 1870, no one had actually won the rifle race. The only real question about the new battle rifles in 1914–1918 was which nations had the long-term industrial capacity to meet wartime demand, and which did not.

As impressive as they were, as far as they had come in the span of two or three generations, the new battle rifles were not the biggest news in firearms technology. An entirely new class of small arms was just beginning to make itself known, and in the Great War it would make itself heard.

CHAPTER 12

FULL AUTO

One hot evening in early summer 1883, an American expat living in East Central London was toiling away in the basement of the house he had rented at 57D Hatton Garden. His name was Hiram Maxim, and though he hardly fit the mold of American inventors in the pioneering days of industry, he rivaled even Thomas Edison in his creativity and success. Indeed, he considered himself to be Edison's actual rival. At forty-three, Maxim was a bear of a man, a native of Maine, entirely self-educated, not at all bookish, but a genius all the same. Outgoing and loud, Maxim was possessed of a self-confidence that bordered on braggadocio. He was a notorious womanizer, possibly a bigamist, and he worked alone.

By the time he left the States for Britain in 1881, Maxim had invented an automatic sprinkler system, a steam-powered flying machine, and a menthol inhaler; Maxim was chronically afflicted with bronchitis and other respiratory ailments. He claimed to have invented an incandescent light bulb, and he did in fact install the first electric light system in New York City, for the Equitable Life Building on Broadway. But in doing so he ran afoul of Thomas Edison, and Maxim decided to try his luck in Europe.

Maxim had since turned his attentions to firearms. He would later claim that while in Vienna he had made the acquaintance of another American, who had given him some very blunt career advice. "Hang your chemistry and electricity!" he exclaimed to

Maxim. "If you wish to make a pile of money, invent something that will enable these Europeans to cut each other's throats with greater facility." The story may be apocryphal, but Maxim took the sentiment to heart.

And here, in his lab on Hatton Garden in 1883, Hiram Maxim was doing exactly that. His present task was something wholly unprecedented, something that no other inventor was currently working on: a firearm that used the energy unleashed by the detonation of the propellant to automatically reload—and then fire—itself. As a child, he would recount later, he had once fired a rifle, and the recoil was so strong that the backward shove from the rifle bowled him over. The experience impressed upon him just how much of the firearm's energy was directed back at its operator. He would, he hoped, find a way to harness that energy, so that it would operate a mechanism to load and fire the gun, which would in turn reload and fire and reload and fire, again and again. A firearm that was fully automatic, a firearm that was also a machine, and the fuel for that machine was the ammunition itself. A machine gun.

Maxim's prototype gun was still quite primitive in the summer of 1883, but on that one evening it functioned well enough to prove that he was on to something. He loaded several rounds of modern centerfire ammunition into the fabric feed-belt that substituted for a magazine, threaded the belt into the prototype gun, cocked the charging handle, and pulled the trigger. Six rounds blasted out in rapid succession, six empty brass cases flew out of the weapon and bounced, clanging metallically, on the floor—with only one squeeze of the trigger.

And with that simple and successful experiment in 1883, the nature of the battlefield, of military firearms, and of firepower itself changed forever.

HIRAM MAXIM WAS not the first inventor to dream of the notion of a truly rapid-fire weapon. Upping the rate of fire, for small arms and artillery alike, was the overarching goal of the arms industry in the nineteenth century. There were some successes, and decades before Maxim ran his first successful machine-gun experiment, there were rapid-fire guns in use on the field of battle.

First and simplest were the volley guns, multibarreled weapons in which all barrels are fired simultaneously or in rapid succession. The Billinghurst-Requa Battery (1862), the joint invention of a Rochester, New York, dentist and a gunsmith, was one; its twenty-five .52-caliber rifle barrels were arranged in a single layer, in parallel, atop a light artillery carriage, and were fired simultaneously with a single percussion cap. The somewhat better-known French volley-gun actually saw significant, if short-lived, combat use. A refinement of a thirty-seven-barrel design by Belgian gunmaker Joseph Montigny, the French Reffye *mitrailleuse* volley gun (1866) had twenty-five parallel barrels, arranged in a five-by-five grid and housed in a tube, so that from a distance it closely resembled a light field howitzer. To fire the Reffye, a plate holding twenty-five 13mm-caliber centerfire rifle cartridges, arranged in a grid to match the corresponding pattern of the barrels, was dropped into the open breech. Closing the breech pushed the cartridges into the cluster of barrels; a turn of the hand-crank mechanism fired off the barrels one by one. The rate of fire was therefore dependent on the speed with which the gunner turned the crank, but with a well-trained crew the Reffye was easily capable of firing off one hundred rounds per minute.

But even if reliable, as the Reffye certainly was, volley guns were bulky and heavy. The Reffye tipped the scales at just under a ton. It had to be employed as artillery. Although its volume of fire was impressive, its performance in combat—during the Franco-Prussian War—was not. The French generals never fully understood how best to take advantage of the Reffye's potentially withering volume of fire. Placed too close to enemy infantry, its exposed crew—who had to stand out in the open while serving the weapon—could easily be picked off; placed too far away from the enemy, it wasn't nearly as effective. The Reffye's size and weight strictly limited its combat role.

True rapid-fire guns shared that bulkiness, and on top of that they were much more complicated mechanically than the volley guns. The American Civil War—which seems to have inspired twice as many ridiculous designs as it did workable, practical weapons—witnessed a couple that actually managed to make the leap from patent model to functioning firearm. One was the Union Repeating Gun, whose unusual appearance prompted Abraham Lincoln to call it the "coffee-mill gun" when he got to see it in operation. It faded into obscurity after some limited (and highly unsatisfactory) action early in the war. Its contemporary, the Gatling gun, did not.

Dr. Richard Gatling, a North Carolina–born inventor and physician, patented his mechanical marvel in 1862. The Gatling design was outwardly simple: a ring of barrels, grouped in a circle around a central axis, spun by means of a hand-crank mechanism. As the operator turned the crank, the breech-end of the topmost barrel lined up with a hopper-filled feed mechanism, which fed (by gravity) a small steel tube into the breech-end. The tube acted as a cartridge case; it contained a .58-caliber rifle-musket cartridge, and at its rear end a priming cap rested atop a nipple. The Gatling's hammer, cocked by the hand-crank, released, hit the cap, detonating the cartridge, and as the barrel rotated away again the empty steel cartridge-case dropped clear, and the process began all over again. Rate of fire was variable, and could get as high as 200–250 rounds per minute. That all depended on the operator and the strength of his arm.

In its original 1862 incarnation, the Gatling was hardly an ideal weapon. Black-powder fouling was bad enough in a musket that fired three rounds per minute; in a rapid-fire weapon with a delicate breech mechanism and a lot of moving parts, that fouling was bound to gum up the works, causing misfires and jams. The reusable steel cartridges did not obturate the breech, and hence there was significant gas leakage during firing. Later versions of the Gatling—like the 1865 model, which took advantage of the new rimfire cartridge, and even later models that used smokeless powder—were more reliable. But the main issue with the Gatling was not reliability, but weight. Like the volley guns, it was exceedingly heavy and required a light artillery mount for service in the field. Like the Reffye, the Gatling was an artillery piece called upon to fill an infantry role, or an infantry gun that had to act like artillery.

Yet the Gatling had its virtues as well. The multibarrel design was one. For Dr. Gatling had, in his quest for high-speed fire, solved one of the thorniest problems in engineering rapid-fire weapons: how to keep the barrel cool. Rapid-fire weapons heat up and wear down quickly. High rates of fire are especially hard on barrels. But the Gatling design obviated that problem. The interval between the time a barrel was fired and the time that it was back in battery again, loaded and ready to fire, might have been brief, but it was enough to allow air to circulate through and around the barrel, cooling it. That cooling was crucial: it prevented heat-related mishaps and extended the service life of the barrel.

The Gatling worked better than any of the other early experiments with rapid-fire weapons. Its role in the Civil War was tiny, with only a very few being purchased by Federal forces, much to the dismay of Dr. Gatling himself. Gatling firmly believed that deadlier weapons would somehow spare lives and make war less costly—a common delusion among those who invent terrifying new weapons. But its insignificance in the Civil War was wholly predictable: the Gatling was anything but a proven technology, and anyway it was unclear what role it would, or could, fill in combat. After the war, though, the Gatling found its niche and its enthusiastic advocates. It went through iterations, including a larger naval version intended to serve as a "deck-sweeping" antipersonnel gun.

Once adapted to modern, smokeless, centerfire ammunition, the Gatling became truly useful. Although already rendered obsolete by the first generation of "true" machine guns by then, the Gatling proved itself in high style during the Spanish-American War of 1898. A detachment from Lt. John Henry Parker's Gatling battery took part in the American assault on Cuba's San Juan Hill on 1 July, softening Spanish defenses atop the heights prior to the attack. A few days later, the Gatlings participated in the siege of

Santiago, at one point knocking out a heavy Spanish fortress gun and annihilating its crew—from two thousand yards away. American officers attributed the success of those operations in large part to Parker's Gatlings, but none so effusively as a thirty-something American volunteer who had fought near the Gatlings throughout the campaign, a bespectacled lieutenant colonel of cavalry named Theodore Roosevelt.

The Gatling could never fill the role that would be taken—or created—by machine guns. The nature of the design was such that it could never be made truly portable, a small arm that could be deployed with infantry. But the Gatling never entirely faded into obscurity. Its core concept—achieving a high rate of fire through the successive firing of individual barrels in succession—caught on with other inventors. In the 1870s, the British navy adopted the multi-barreled Nordenfelt, a Swedish design, as a light deck-mounted gun for its warships large and small. Richard Gatling himself initiated what would prove to be the most valuable, and most enduring, iteration of the gun that bore his name. He understood that the greatest limitation on the performance of the Gatling was that imposed by human strength and endurance: misfires and jams aside, the Gatling could only be fired as fast and for as long as a man could turn the crank. The external source of energy, then, was key to the weapon's performance. In 1893, Dr. Gatling paired his gun with another recent invention, the electric motor, and the results were shocking: a rate of fire that nearly reached three thousand rounds per minute. Strangely, the coupling of these two technologies did not find the audience it deserved until after the Second World War. It came to life again in 1959, in the form of the M61 Vulcan rotary cannon. The motor-driven Vulcan, which can fire 20mm explosive shells at a breathtaking six thousand rounds per minute—one hundred rounds *every second*—became one of the most effective and ubiquitous aircraft armaments of the late twentieth century.

IMPRESSIVE AS THE Reffye and the Gatling might appear from our vantage point in the twenty-first century, they did not have an appreciable impact on the conduct of war. The Reffye could have, perhaps, had the French army—which had so enthusiastically embraced the *mitrailleuse*—actually found a way to integrate it into its tactics. The Gatling never had a chance, not in land warfare, because it didn't really have a niche, as the balance of bulkiness, range, and rate of fire did not work in its favor. It's easy to succumb to the temptation, as many armchair ordnance experts do, to see the Gatling as yet another promising technology cast to the side by unimaginative, hidebound conservatives who were dismissive of anything new. The Gatling never had a chance because there really was very little it could add to the tactical potential of armies at the turn of the century, certainly nothing that would justify the expense and trouble. To be truly effective, rapid-fire small arms would have to be portable in a way that the cannon-sized Gatlings were not.

Enter Hiram Maxim and his invention, brilliant and terrible.

The Maxim has to rank at the very top of historic weapons designs by virtue of its sheer simplicity and sophistication. Maxim took out a flurry of patents before he publicly debuted his prototype gun, and that act alone proves the depth of his understanding of firearms technology. The American expat perceived, with enviable clarity, that the energy unleashed by the detonation of ammunition in a firearm could be collected and redirected in more ways than one. Maxim discerned three ways in particular. First there was the "recoil-operated" action, which used the retrograde motion of the barrel—recoil—to power the gun's loading and firing mechanism. Closely related to recoil operation was what is known today as a "blowback" action, harnessing the energy created by the propellant at detonation, the same energy that would propel a spent case out of an open breech. Finally, there was the energy provided by excess gas moving forward behind the bullet, venting out the muzzle when the bullet left the barrel. Weapons that use this surplus gas are said to be "gas-operated." Maxim patented designs to use each of the three. He was an entrepreneur, after all, and rightly or wrongly he felt he had been cheated out of the wealth and acclaim that he believed were rightfully his but stolen by Thomas Edison.

The Maxim gun was recoil-operated, and it was simplicity itself. The ammunition fed into the gun via a fabric belt, much like a soldier's bandolier, with the rounds held in place—parallel to each other—with fabric loops. The belt entered the gun through the feed block, mounted immediately above the breech-end of the weapon's single barrel. Behind the barrel was a steel box, the receiver, rectangular in cross section, which housed the operating mechanism. Inside the receiver, a set of rails ran along the right and left sides, and on those rails rested the truly critical element, the lock. The lock was a device that simultaneously acted as the breechblock, the housing for the firing pin and the spring that threw the pin forward, and the extractor-ejector for spent cartridge cases. The lock could move back and forth along the internal rails, but a strong coil-spring (the "fusee spring") pressed the lock firmly against the breech-end of the barrel.

When the Maxim gun was loaded and ready to go, a round would be in the chamber, the lock holding it in place; the firing pin would be cocked and its spring compressed; an extractor plate on the front face of the lock, which could slide up and down, gripped both the unfired round in the chamber *and* a fresh round in the ammo belt, located directly above in the feed block. When the operator pulled the trigger, the mechanism released the firing pin, firing the centerfire cartridge in the chamber. The barrel—which floated freely, and therefore could move back and forth—moved violently backward with the recoil of the shot, and that backward motion was the key to the whole operation. The barrel, flying back, "unlocked" the lock and threw it back along its rails, compressing the fusee spring as it did. During that motion, the lock, truly the marvel of the mechanism, accomplished several tasks in a fraction of a fraction of a second: gripping the fresh round in the feed block and the recently fired cartridge case in the chamber, it extracted both when the lock flew backward; it cocked the firing pin; and once the pin was withdrawn into the lock, the extractor plate dropped just enough so that the fresh round, recently extracted from the feed block, lined up perfectly with the now-empty chamber, and the spent round was aligned with an ejection port, located right below the chamber. Once the lock reached its rear limit, the compressed fusee spring threw it forward again. The lock slammed against the breech and locked in place, secure against the next firing; the fresh round entered the chamber, and the spent case went flying through the ejection port and outside the gun to the ground. A feed pawl in the feed block advanced the fabric ammo belt exactly one round's distance, as the extractor plate rose again, hooking on to a fresh round and the round currently in the chamber. So long as the gunner was still depressing the trigger, the firing pin flew forward, fired the chambered cartridge, and the entire process began anew.

The entire process consumed just a hair over one-tenth of one second.

Hiram Maxim's new gun would evolve over the next decade. Cooling would be a major obstacle, as it would with any single-barrel, rapid-fire weapon. Maxim's solution was straightforward if inelegant. He surrounded the barrel with a water jacket, a cylindrical water tank that could be filled via an intake port on top (and drained through a drain cock on the bottom). A hot barrel would soon heat the water to boiling, which meant that it had to be replenished regularly, but it was also possible to recycle the resulting steam by venting it through a rubber hose and into an external condensing can, where the vapor could be cooled, condensed, and recycled back into the jacket. Without the coolant, the barrel would overheat very quickly and likely jam or otherwise become inoperable, possibly damaging the barrel permanently; but with the water jacket kept full, the Maxim could be fired almost indefinitely—what would be called today a sustained-fire weapon.

Maxim's prototype gun was designed for black-powder ammo, since smokeless powders were not yet available in 1883. But the new ammunition technology, featuring smokeless powders and jacketed bullets, proved to be a boon for the machine gun. Smokeless powders didn't foul the mechanism as black powder did, and once Maxim adapted his invention to the higher chamber pressures generated by modern ammunition, he found that the absence of

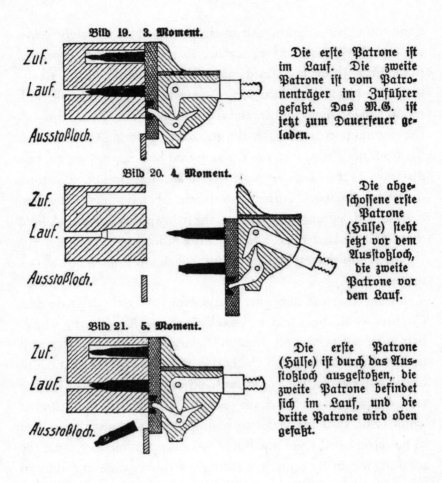

Bild 19. 3. Moment.

Zuf.

Lauf.

Ausstoßloch.

Die erste Patrone ist im Lauf. Die zweite Patrone ist vom Patronenträger im Zuführer gefaßt. Das M.G. ist jetzt zum Dauerfeuer geladen.

Bild 20. 4. Moment.

Zuf.

Lauf.

Ausstoßloch.

Die abgeschossene erste Patrone (Hülse) steht jetzt vor dem Ausstoßloch, die zweite Patrone vor dem Lauf.

Bild 21. 5. Moment.

Zuf.

Lauf.

Ausstoßloch.

Die erste Patrone (Hülse) ist durch das Ausstoßloch ausgestoßen, die zweite Patrone befindet sich im Lauf, und die dritte Patrone wird oben gefaßt.

Plate 18: The firing cycle of the Maxim gun. These three diagrams show the workings of the brilliantly simple Maxim action. "3. Moment": The lock (right) is closed against the breech (left). The lock is gripping a fresh round from the feed-belt (top, black cartridge) and the chambered cartridge that is about to be fired. "4. Moment": The gun has now fired; the retrograde motion of the barrel from recoil throws the lock back, away from the breech. The lock-face drops, so that the fresh round just drawn from the belt is now opposite the chamber ("Lauf," or barrel) and the spent casing is opposite the ejection port ("Ausstoßloch"). "5. Moment": The lock, powered by the fusee spring, slams forward again, chambering and firing the fresh cartridge as it hurls the empty out of the ejection port. The lock-face slides up and the process begins again.

Image: Friedrich von Merkatz, *Unterrichtsbuch für die Maschinengewehr-Abteilungen Gerät 08* (Berlin: R. Eisenschmidt, 1915), pp. 94–95.

fouling made for a far more reliable weapon, capable of truly sustained fire.

The modern centerfire cartridge was perhaps the most critical invention of the nineteenth-century revolution in firearms technology, for it made so many other advances possible. But Hiram Maxim's bullet-powered machine has to stand out as the most remarkable innovation in weaponry in the past two centuries. Indeed, it has made such an indelible—and awful, in all senses of the word—impact on our world, on our wars and our society and our culture, that it could be ranked among the most important of *all* inventions of the modern era.

It's impossible to exaggerate the gape-mouthed surprise with which the military community, and the general public for that matter, greeted the Maxim gun. It was a popular sensation long before any major army officially adopted it. It's easy to see why. Even in an age of engineering marvels, the machine gun stood out. The increase in the firepower of the individual infantryman, in the range and volume of the firepower at his very fingertips, was already remarkable in itself. A musket-armed infantryman in 1850 could fire three rounds a minute, and he could expect to be able to kill at one hundred yards, sometimes at two hundred if he was firing at a large group of enemies and had luck on his side. A rifleman in 1890 could fire twenty rounds a minute, and his rifle could kill at five hundred yards or more, provided he could see to hit something that far away. But the machine gun's killing potential strained credulity in comparison. Using ordinary rifle ammunition, the range and accuracy of the machine gun were no less than those of a rifle, and probably better, for machine guns tended to be solid firing platforms and so were less subject to operator error. And then there was that incredible rate of fire. With a Maxim, that rate was somewhere between 450 and 600 rounds per minute, or seven and a half to ten rounds *per second*. This was, admittedly, the cyclic rate, the theoretical rate of fire and therefore a high average. Few machine guns could, in practice, ever live up to their cyclic rates, to fire for a full minute uninterrupted. But with the water-cooled

Maxim, the cyclic rate was very close to the practical rate. It took only a few seconds to load a new belt of ammunition into the feed block, and hence the Maxim could zip through belt after belt after belt with scarcely a pause.

The British military theorist J.F.C. Fuller capably summarized the Maxim gun's importance in one simple, pithy, and chilling phrase: it was the concentrated essence of infantry.

MAXIM'S NEW GUN didn't catch on quite as quickly as, say, smokeless powder did, perhaps because—unlike smokeless powder—the invention was the product of an inventor-salesman and not of a concerted government-directed effort. Maxim himself made a public demonstration of his prototype in London in October 1884, and he quickly drew a crowd of investors, prominent among them the British steel magnate Edward Vickers. Only a month later, Maxim and Albert Vickers, Edward's son, formed the Maxim Gun Company. Maxim, a consummate showman, hawked his new gun not only to the British but to armies all over Europe, and by the close of the decade his hard work had paid off. Professional soldiers worldwide came to recognize the new weapon's potential. The army of Austria-Hungary put in the first order, in 1888, and the British tentatively followed suit. The armies of Germany, Russia, and Belgium all succumbed to the Maxim's deadly charms over the course of the 1890s. That enthusiasm, however, never crossed over into the kind of manic, fevered urgency that was the nature of the rifle race; nobody ever seemed to have thought that ownership of the machine gun was an existential matter. The machine gun, after all, was still an unknown, or imperfectly known, quantity. At most, it was thought that the machine gun would be a useful ancillary to rifle fire; at least, a curiosity, like the Reffye had proven to be not that long before. The machine gun had yet to prove itself, but that would soon change.

The British army, whose colonial entanglements presented plenty of opportunities to try out new weapons and tactics, put the Maxim to use first, during a military expedition into Gambia in

1888. That didn't attract much attention, but the next incident—the battle of the Shangani, in October 1893—did. A large force of Matabele warriors, around five thousand strong, attacked a small British column under cover of night, near the Shangani River in what today is Zimbabwe. The British force, a fifth or less the size of the Matabele, had set up a fortified camp, complete with four or five Maxim guns. Without the Maxims, the British would not have had a chance; the Matabele, armed with spears and British Martini-Henry rifles, should have been able to make short work of the British column, overwhelming it by sheer force of numbers. But the Maxims stopped them short. The stuttering machine guns mowed down the Matabele in waves, and the terrified remainder fled, leaving some 1,500 dead behind on the battlefield. The Maxim starred in an even more prominent role five years later, when Lord Kitchener defeated the Mahdist army at the battle of Omdurman in September 1898. There were myriad reasons, tactical and technological, behind Kitchener's lopsided victory over the Mahdi. But it was the Maxim that made the newspapers.

Even as the Maxim established itself as the gold standard of rapid-fire weapons, other inventors rushed to match or surpass the American's achievement. If there was one lesson that the post-1870 firearms revolution taught, it was that obsolescence came fast, and that for every breakthrough in weapons design, there was bound to be a better one right around the corner. Plus there were reasons, some of them quite sound, not to commit fully to a foreign design—matters of patent law and licensing, for example. National self-sufficiency in arms production remained a high strategic priority when Europe was in the grip of a frenetic arms race.

This second wave of machine-gun designs produced a flurry of new models in a very compressed timespan. Austria-Hungary developed, and ultimately adopted, two very different homegrown machine guns, the Salvator-Dormus "Škoda" (1893) and the 1907 Schwarzlose—heavy, water-cooled guns like the Maxim, but blowback operated. Another Austrian, the Baron Adolf Odkolek von Augezd, patented what was likely the first gas-operated machine gun. In the Augezd gun, a port in the barrel bled off excess gases, funneling them to drive a piston that operated the action. It was more complicated by far than Maxim's recoil-operated action, but it worked reliably as long as it was kept clean, and Augezd's design had something else to recommend it: an air-cooled barrel. It could not be fired quite as long without overheating as the water-cooled machine guns, but it was much lighter, more portable, and didn't require access to water. Those features were enough to convince the French army, which adopted it for colonial use in 1897. It was manufactured in Paris by the Hotchkiss Company, and would become the primary automatic weapon of the French army in the Great War. Incidentally, the Hotchkiss Company had been founded by another New England expat, the Connecticut-born gunsmith Benjamin Hotchkiss (1826–1885)—the very same Hotchkiss who manufactured rifled artillery projectiles bearing his name during the American Civil War.

Americans, in fact, were at the forefront of automatic weapons design and manufacturing. One of those Americans was John Moses Browning, a Utah-born Mormon who would become one of the most famous and enduring names in the world of firearms. Browning, like the Baron von Augezd, had been experimenting with gas-operated systems since the late 1880s. By 1889, John Browning and his brother Matthew had constructed a working machine-gun prototype; a patent followed three years later, and then the Colt firearms concern purchased it, putting it into production as the M1895 Colt-Browning. In the Colt-Browning gun, the gas vented from the barrel near the muzzle, forcing down a pivoting arm that in turn pushed an operating rod. If the gun were placed too close to the ground, the pivoting arm could easily embed itself in the dirt, earning the Colt-Browning its unflattering nickname: the "potato digger."

The potato digger was not Browning's last design, and it was certainly not his best. It could not approach the Maxim for rugged reliability or capacity for sustained fire. But it functioned well enough to attract a devoted following in the US Navy. It became standard equipment on American combat vessels during the Spanish-American War, and the Marines took a section of them ashore when they fought in Cuba in 1898—the very first American troops to use a machine gun in combat. As late as 1918, an improved version—the M1917/1918 Marlin—could be found mounted on American fighter planes patrolling the Western Front.

By the turn of the century, the machine gun was standard equipment in nearly every army in the Western world. Only one major Western nation held itself aloof from the machine-gun mania, and that, with compelling irony, was the United States, the native land of Richard Gatling, Hiram Maxim, John Browning, and Benjamin Hotchkiss. America had little use for the weapons. The army, which still functioned mostly as a frontier constabulary, was pitifully small when compared with the gargantuan conscripted armies of Germany, France, Austria-Hungary, Russia, and Italy. The US Army ranked, purely in terms of manpower, closer to the smaller armies of Latin America and the new Balkan states. America didn't need anything bigger. The nation had no European ambitions, and Army leadership didn't consider the likelihood of war against a European opponent to be very high. When American forces finally did go up against a European army—the Spanish army in Cuba in 1898—they found themselves seriously outclassed in weaponry. Spanish rifles and artillery were overall superior to their American counterparts. The handful of Colt-Browning machine guns that saw service with the Marines gave a mediocre performance, subject to frequent jamming, probably more the result of half-trained operators than any fault on the part of the guns themselves. Col. Theodore Roosevelt, who watched the potato diggers in action, was singularly unimpressed, while he was full of admiration for the Gatling guns. Roosevelt's opinion carried a great deal of weight, and it was widely shared.

But America was the exception. Everywhere else, the machine gun found itself fully integrated into the infantryman's arsenal. Even the most conservative professional soldiers, men who had learned their trade in Napoléon's shadow, had to admit that this was no passing fad. Machine guns would clearly play a role. But *what* role, precisely, and *how* that would change the tactics of land warfare remained unclear. Before the end of the nineteenth century, the Maxim had only been used against non-European opponents in non-European contexts, and in ways that played directly to the Maxim's obvious virtues as a primarily defensive weapon. At the Shangani River, at Omdurman, men densely packed and in great numbers had rushed directly at the well-placed Maxim guns, and the Maxims had mowed them down. But could the Maxim, or any machine gun for that matter, be used in an offensive capacity? Was it fated to become another kind of artillery, like the Reffye or the Gatling? And, more to the point, what would happen if the men facing the Maxim's devastating firepower *didn't* rush headlong into that field of fire?

The answers would come soon enough. The first significant encounter between European (or European-style) forces came at the very end of the century, in the Second Boer War (1899–1902), Britain's conflict with the Boer republics of South Africa. The British Maxims were modern weapons, firing smokeless, high-velocity ammunition, but they didn't have quite the effect that British leadership had anticipated. Because their Maxims were mounted on tall, wheeled carriages, the gun crews had to work in the open, standing upright, exposed to enemy fire. The Boers, renowned for their skill as marksmen, could make quick work of the Maxim crews. Plus the Boers had Maxims of their own: the Transvaal republic had purchased the latest product from the Maxim-Vickers factory, the so-called Pom-Pom gun, a giant Maxim-designed autocannon that could fire a one-pound, 37mm explosive shell at the rate of nearly 450 per minute. Maxim crews standing in the open didn't have a chance. Much like the Reffye *mitrailleuse* of a generation before, the Maxim could not function both as artillery and as an infantry weapon. The solution was obvious: don't put machine guns on artillery carriages.

The next time that two European-style armies came to blows— in the Russo-Japanese War of 1904–1905—the machine gun's role would be much different, and its possible uses much clearer. Both Japan and Russia had embraced machine guns just before the outbreak of the war in 1904, and by war's end both were employing them in increasing numbers. Japan had gone with the French Hotchkiss, Russia with the Maxim. Relatively lightweight and fired from a low-profile tripod mount, the Hotchkiss was among the most portable machine guns at the time. The tsar's army was Maxim's most loyal customer; Russian and Soviet armies would keep the Maxim in service through the Second World War. The Maxim was much heavier than the Hotchkiss, thanks mainly to the water jacket, but was sturdier and more capable of sustained fire. The first Maxims in Russian service were issued with artillery-type field carriages, as the British had used earlier.

The Russo-Japanese War held European military observers in rapt attention. As a war between a slightly backward giant and what was seen as a Western-influenced upstart, its political and strategic implications were inherently interesting. More to the point, it was a war that pitted modern, largely untried technologies against one another, both on land and at sea. The war did not disappoint, for there was much to be gleaned in a very short span of time—including, as it turned out, in the tactics of the machine gun. The previous, mostly British, experience with machine guns did not give either the Russians or the Japanese much useful guidance, so both armies made it up as they went along.

The Russians, for their part, explored the defensive qualities of the Maxim. As casualties mounted among Maxim crews, the soldiers began to improvise their own low-to-the-ground mounts. Eventually, near the end of the conflict, the army officially scrapped the high-profile carriages and introduced the M1905 Sokolov mount, a low-slung two-wheeled carriage, heavy but easily moved about, with folding legs that allowed it to be used as a tripod. Using their Maxims mostly to break up Japanese assaults, the Russians found that their Maxims delivered. On one grisly occasion, two well-placed Maxims in a Russian trench made short work of four hundred Japanese infantry who were caught out in the open as they tried to attack the Russians. Once the Maxims opened up, the Japanese tried to get away from the hail of bullets that enveloped them, unable to advance or retreat without being shot down. "The Maxims did their work as only Maxims can," an observer noted laconically, as the panicked Japanese soldiers "were wildly fighting to get away, trampling on the wounded, climbing over piles of corpses. . . ."

The Japanese pioneered a much different role for their light machine guns. As they were frequently on the tactical offensive, they found ways to incorporate their Hotchkiss guns into infantry assaults, using concentrated and focused bursts of machine-gun fire to suppress Russian defenses, then moving their infantry forward between the bursts. The portability of the Hotchkiss guns meant that the Japanese machine-gun crews could move forward with infantry on the assault.

The Russo-Japanese War changed the tone of the small-arms race at the dawn of the twentieth century. Before 1904, there were still a few senior soldiers who saw in the machine gun "a weapon for use against Hereros and Hottentots," an instrument of colonial control over indigenous populations rather than a serious weapon for conventional Western warfare. The Russo-Japanese War proved them wrong and removed all doubts. From 1906 to 1914, the armies of Europe scrambled to beef up their automatic arsenals, and to incorporate the machine gun into their tactical doctrines. Those armies that had not yet committed fully to their use did so; those which had already adopted machine guns in the 1880s and 1890s upgraded their guns and mounts after they picked up a few pointers from the Russo-Japanese War. Imperial Germany adopted the Maxim as the MG 08, with a unique sled-like mount; Austria-Hungary settled on the 1907 Schwarzlose; and Britain went with the Vickers, an improved Maxim design patented by Maxim's old business partner. Those armies that dragged their heels—like those of the United States and Italy—did not do so because they failed to recognize the weapon's importance, but out of parsimony.

AS THE THREAT of war loomed ever more menacingly over Europe in the summer of 1914, it was an accepted fact that the machine gun would play a major role in land warfare. And so it did. Like the gas mask and the tank, the angular, unattractive silhouette of the Maxim gun came to represent all that was impersonal and inglorious about war in the industrial age, a machine that killed mindlessly, without remorse or compunction.

And the machine gun came to symbolize something else about the First World War, a perception of combat that is so deeply rooted in our historical consciousness that it shapes our collective understanding of the tragedy that was the Great War: the failure of leadership and the victimhood of ordinary folk. The machine gun was the mechanization of death personified, and—so we are told—it was the failure of the generals to appreciate the lethality of the machine gun that led directly to the mass slaughter on First World War battlefields. Nothing better illustrates the futility of war—of *any* war, but especially of 1914–1918—than the blithe willingness of generals on all sides to send wave after wave of young, innocent soldiers "over the top" and straight into the bloody maw, as the clattering machine guns reaped them like ripe grain.

There's a kernel of truth to this argument, but only a kernel. As historian Paul Cornish has pointed out, the machine gun was part of a "triumvirate of death" in the Great War, three technologies that contributed most to the death toll: quick-firing artillery, high explosives, and automatic firearms. Of these, the combination of quick-firing artillery with high-explosive shell was the deadliest, and by a wide margin. Among small arms, though, the machine gun was king, deadlier even than the latest infantry rifles, which the great powers had gone to such pains to modernize.

The machine gun's astronomically higher rate of fire was, of course, the key to that deadliness. Its ballistic properties aside from speed are often forgotten. Contrary to the way they're often portrayed, machine guns were (and often still are) precision instruments. The typical machine gun of the Great War—water-cooled, heavy, bolted down to an equally heavy mount—was quite stable.

When locked in place on their mounts, machine guns did not move, and their sights were generally of a much higher quality than the open iron sights typically found on military rifles. They were quite accurate out to remarkably long distances, and their sturdy weight meant that they could be laid on a target and left alone. By its very nature, the machine gun was less subject to operator error than the infantry rifle. A rifle in the hands of a weary, hungry, stressed, likely frightened soldier was anything but steady, but a machine gun was stable.

The machine gun, though, was more than just a highly accurate, fast-firing rifle. The differences between the machine gun and the bolt-action magazine rifle transcended speed, even if they fired the same ammunition. The Russo-Japanese War gave Western soldiers a taste of the machine-gunner's craft and the weapon's potential, but it was in the First World War that these transcendent properties first came to light. One of them was completely unexpected yet invaluable: the tendency of machine-gun fire to create a "beaten zone." Not all bullets followed exactly the same flight path, even if the gun itself remained perfectly still while being fired. Nor did those flight paths vary wildly in direction or range. Tiny, imperceptible differences between each shot—affected by the temperature of the barrel, slight variations in the weight or profile of the bullet or the weight of the propellant charge, or the impact of external forces like wind—could create slight changes in direction, just fractions of a degree. But when firing at long range those fractions of degrees translated into a hit a few feet forward, or back, or left or right from the intended target. This was the "cone of fire," as the bullets landed in a roughly circular pattern around the center of the target. A single machine gun, in other words, could make an entire area dangerous, as the bullets in that cone of fire slammed into the ground circumscribed by the cone—the beaten zone. By saturating the air around the beaten zone with bullets, the machine gun could make an entire area uninhabitable, denying enemy troops the opportunity to occupy it. Like the bayonet and the pike, the machine gun could accomplish tactical objectives without actually killing anyone.

The machine gun was no ordinary small arm, nor was it artillery. It was neither; it was both; it had unique properties that field artillery and conventional infantry firepower could not mimic. Whatever it was, the machine gun was a specialized instrument, meriting specially trained handlers. The German army recognized this essential fact first, putting its gunners through a different and more rigorous training regimen than that for ordinary riflemen, and supplying them with their own manual and tactical doctrines—another first. While the other armies of the Great War divided their machine guns into very small detachments, sprinkled among the infantry units, the Germans grouped all their machine guns into larger units commanded by specialist officers. They could be dispersed among smaller infantry units, or they could operate together to focus their massed fire on important targets. And the machine-gun units were always under the supervision of an officer who knew fully automatic weapons inside and out.

Combat experience in the Great War quickly bore out the wisdom of the German approach. No one used machine guns to greater effect than the Germans, and the Allies rushed to follow their lead. The British formed their own elite Machine Gun Corps late in 1915; the French consolidated their machine-gun crews, formerly dispersed throughout the infantry, into autonomous machine-gun companies; the American Expeditionary Forces (AEF) included three machine-gun battalions in each division, in addition to machine-gun companies in each infantry regiment. As the factories churned out more and more machine guns, the individual armies drastically increased the numbers of automatic weapons in the field and the proportion of machine guns to combat troops.

As the numbers and experience grew, the tactics evolved. Contrary to received wisdom, most combat commanders in the First World War quickly came to appreciate the unique qualities of the machine gun and readily adopted tactics that played to its strengths. They could shore up a defensive line; they could be used as fire support for infantry assaults, provided the ground permitted them to fire over the heads of their own assault troops. For the men carrying out the assault, the sound and feel of bullets zipping right over their heads could be more than a little unnerving, but over time they learned to appreciate the value of good fire support. Machine guns, like artillery, were capable of indirect fire at long range—firing on targets not in direct line of sight—by estimating the range and direction of enemy positions via map and compass. The "machine-gun barrage," a technique that involved concentrated fire from massed machine guns, could be nearly as effective as the more conventional artillery barrage in clearing ground, suppressing enemy fire, and preparing the way for an assault.

In these roles, the machine gun performed admirably. Though it worked just fine at medium and close range, just like a rifle, it wasn't necessary to place machine guns in the forward trenches for them to be effective. They were long-range weapons and could fulfill many of their tasks from a distance, which made sense anyway because machine-gun crews were prime targets for enemy artillery and sniper fire. Artillery, of course, was deadlier, and had greater range, but the machine gun was just as effective a deterrent to infantry assault. The Maxims defending the German positions on the first day of the Somme (1 July 1916) reaped a terrible harvest of British soldiers. Though the ghastly death count—the deadliest single day in British military history—was the result of many factors, British and German observers alike gave the lion's share of the credit to German machine-gun fire. Conversely, the machine gun could also aid in the offensive. On the very first day of the Allied assault on Vimy Ridge (April 1917), the nearly three hundred machine guns of the Canadian Corps carried out a massive creeping barrage, slaughtering the defending Germans by the thousands and helping to prepare the way for the Canadian infantry to move forward and attack.

Together with the modern magazine-fed rifle, the machine gun finally accomplished something that firearms—including the much-vaunted rifle-musket—had thus far failed to do: make direct assaults, over open ground and against an entrenched enemy, suicidal or something very much like it. The tactical stalemate from 1915 on along the Western Front and elsewhere was in no small measure a consequence of the heavy use of machine guns by both sides in the Great War.

THE MACHINE GUN put an enormous volume of firepower into the hands of individual foot soldiers, but that firepower still wasn't very portable. Heavy, bulky, water-cooled guns—Maxim, Vickers, Browning, Schwarzlose—could be moved from position to position with a crew of two or three men, but they could not accompany fast-moving infantry on the assault. Even the air-cooled, relatively stripped-down French Hotchkiss tipped the scales at over fifty pounds.

But what if machine guns could be made portable? What if machine guns could lend their firepower to the infantry assault, not from a distance, but from right up front with the assault troops themselves? What if infantry could carry their machine guns all the way up to the enemy's defensive positions? The benefits of such a weapon were manifestly obvious, and while the Great War raged on, the creation of light automatic weapons became the focus of small arms design.

There were all sorts of reasons to make machine guns lighter. Military aviation, for one. When aircraft began to take firearms aloft for self-defense, the machine gun was the obvious choice, but the relatively weak motors and delicate airframes of the early aeroplanes did not pair well with the weight of Maxims and Vickers. For aerial combat, the lightened machine gun would prove to be a necessity.

The prospect of a light machine gun for infantry use was even more alluring. Fortunately, such weapons were already available. Danish engineers Julius Rasmussen and Theodor Schoubue patented the first true light machine gun in 1896, and their design— the Madsen *rekylgevær* (recoil rifle)—went into production two years later. The Madsen had a complicated but surprisingly reliable action, and best of all it could be used *almost* like a rifle: it had a shoulder stock, a conventional trigger, and used a twenty-round box magazine mounted on top. It could be fired from the shoulder, like a rifle, but it also had a folding bipod near the muzzle that made firing prone a simple matter. At twenty pounds, the Madsen wasn't exactly light, but it was a small fraction of the weight of a Maxim and its mount. A single man could carry the Madsen, plus several spare magazines, and operate it himself, though the process was a lot smoother if the gunner had an assistant. The Danish army adopted it, as did the Russians, who issued their Madsens to cavalry units.

But most armies simply weren't interested in light automatics beyond aircraft use. They were seen, not incorrectly, as less robust and less dependable, and early experiences with them were not reassuring. In 1909, the US Army, not normally a risk-taker in weapons design, adopted a modified Hotchkiss, known in the American service as the Benét-Mercié Machine Rifle. Its first test in combat, against Pancho Villa's raiders outside Columbus, New Mexico, proved an abject failure. The machine rifles jammed and broke down repeatedly after very little use. Later examination revealed that the guns themselves were just fine, the problems stemming entirely from operator error on the part of poorly trained gun crews. But the bad reputation stuck anyway. Besides the Madsen, the only other light machine gun that found a ready audience was the American-designed Lewis gun, invented by army officer Isaac Newton Lewis in 1911. The gas-operated Lewis gun, fed by means of a high-capacity (47- or 96-round) rotary magazine, was solid and reliable, and at twenty-eight pounds much more portable than the water-cooled guns of the time. It did not find a warm reception in the United States, but the British and the Belgians liked it well enough to place substantial orders just before the outbreak of the First World War.

For the most part, though, the major armies were skeptical of light automatics and were reluctant to embrace them. From the beginning, it was clear that light machine guns were not at all like their heavier cousins, and that in most regards they were distinctly inferior. They were not capable of sustained fire, for one thing. Box magazines could not hold anywhere near as much ammunition as a 250-round belt. Air-cooled barrels overheated much faster than water-cooled ones, so an air-cooled gun could not be fired indefinitely. Gas-operated mechanisms were less bulky than the recoil-operated actions of the Maxim and Schwarzlose, but they were also less reliable, more likely to jam, and more likely to be deranged by a handful of dirt. A Lewis gun, in short, was a poor Vickers.

But that's the thing: A Lewis gun is *not* a Vickers, just as a pistol is not a rifle. It's a different kind of beast altogether, with a different purpose and a different range of applications. The lighter guns were inferior to the heavy guns in performance, but they could do all sorts of things that a heavy gun simply could not. Their more manageable weight meant that they could be carried with the infantry, rather than deployed separately, and could keep up with the infantry in attack or retreat. Since the light automatics could be deployed and open fire within seconds, with a crew of one or two men, they could be used to apply their firepower as immediate circumstances demanded.

The significance of those virtues might not have been apparent when the armies first clashed in the summer and fall of 1914, but even in those first campaigns the usefulness of the light automatic became clear. The light automatic was at the heart of a new kind of assault tactic, popularly known as the *feu de marche*—"marching" or "walking fire." In a walking-fire attack, infantry would rely less on artillery support or even on speed, but would instead fire continuously on the enemy *while* they were advancing. This couldn't be done unless the attacking troops could deliver a volume of fire so withering that it forced the defending enemy to seek cover, thereby suppressing his defensive fire, and bolt-action rifles could not generate that kind of firepower. It would only work if many, if not most, of the attackers carried machine guns. Maxims and Vickers were unsuitable for such a task. The main French light machine gun, the M1915 Machine Rifle CSRG or Chauchat, was designed explicitly for this purpose. At twenty pounds unloaded, the Chauchat was still a beast to carry, let alone fire offhand, but its shoulder stock and left-hand grip meant that it could be wielded like an ordinary rifle. Its low rate of fire (240 rounds per minute, less than half that of the Maxim) made it easy to control, an advantage in a light machine gun. Sadly for the French, their factories couldn't possibly produce enough Chauchats to arm more than a small fraction of their troops, and the design was heavily flawed anyway. The Chauchat became the main machine gun of the American Expeditionary Forces in 1918, and the doughboys found it to be an utterly execrable firearm.

By war's end, the light machine gun was a common feature in most of the combatant armies. British and Commonwealth troops stuck with the reliable Lewis gun. Americans were initially cursed with the Chauchat, but later adopted one of the most enduring light machine gun designs of the century, John Browning's M1918 BAR (Browning Automatic Rifle), which would go on to serve with American forces in the Second World War and even in the Korean War. The Germans proved to be singularly unimaginative. Their idea of a light machine gun was to take the standard heavy machine gun, the MG 08 Maxim, and reduce its size, adding a shoulder stock and a pistol grip, and substituting a bipod for the bulky "sled" mount. The MG 08 weighed, with its mount and a jacket full of water, a ponderous 152 pounds; the stripped-down version, designated the MG 08/15, was around 40 pounds. Much lighter, yes, but it was still a 40-pound, water-cooled machine gun, and it still needed a two-man crew to operate.

The walking-fire concept, for which the light machine gun was originally intended, was never implemented to the extent its pre-war advocates had expected or hoped. In the very last campaigns of 1918, as American, French, and British troops gradually pushed the beleaguered German forces eastward toward their homeland, the light machine gun did perform this duty; BARs and Lewises and Chauchats kept up with the rapidly advancing infantry as the Allies drove the Germans toward armistice. That was a critical moment in the history of the machine gun. The heavy machine gun, as represented by the Maxim, had proven its worth well before the assassination at Sarajevo, and it would remain a staple weapon in

Machine guns of the Great War:

Plate 19a. The German *Maschinengewehr* Model of 1908 (MG 08).

Image: Library of Congress.

Plate 19b. Soldiers of the 16th US Infantry practicing with the Fusil Mitrailleur Modele 15 CSRG, more infamous to American doughboys as the Chauchat.

Image: Courtesy National Archives, photo no. 86707272.

the Western arsenal for years to come, but the light machine gun was the firearm of the moment in 1918. If mobility were to be restored to ground warfare, as 1918 hinted it could be, then the firepower provided by a portable machine gun would have to be an essential component of infantry tactics in the future.

CHAPTER 13

HIGH EXPLOSIVE

Artillery had come a long way by 1870. Breechloaders were beginning to replace muzzleloaders, rifled guns were taking the place of smoothbores, and cast steel had superseded iron and bronze. Explosive ordnance, like shell and shrapnel, once an unreliable rarity, was now as common a sight on the battlefield as solid shot, and precision fuses gave gunners the ability to time shell explosions to a fraction of a second. The new technology didn't win over everyone at once; sometimes the advantages were not immediately apparent. For all their extra expense and trouble, breech-loading cannon were not that much faster to load and fire than muzzleloaders. Some critics were concerned that breech mechanisms in breech-loading guns were not capable of handling powder loads as heavy as those used in muzzleloaders. And rifled guns were not *always* more effective than smoothbores. In the otherwise lopsided Second Schleswig War of 1864, the Prussian army's more modern rifled artillery could not destroy Danish earthworks, while the Danes' older smoothbore guns took a respectable toll in Prussian lives.

But in a very short time, those objections evaporated. Rifled guns were still more accurate and more powerful than smoothbores. The merits of breechloaders were as clear, overall, for artillery as they were for small arms. Breechloaders were also safer. In 1879, one of the two huge 12-inch muzzle-loading rifled guns aboard the turreted battleship HMS *Thunderer* burst when its gun crew—somehow unaware that the gun had misfired during a gunnery exercise—inadvertently rammed a second charge and a second shell atop the earlier, unfired load, still intact in the breech. Double-charged and double-shotted, the thirty-eight-ton monster burst when fired, killing a dozen sailors and maiming three times that many. Whatever else could be said about the new guns, it was all but impossible to accidentally double-load a breechloader.

Still, in 1870, most armies (and navies) of the West were in no particular hurry to make cannon bigger, more powerful, faster to load, or better. Within a couple of years that would change. Between the Franco-Prussian War and the First World War, artillery would experience an evolutionary arc very similar to, and in fact almost exactly parallel to, that of the battle rifle. Before the outbreak of the Great War in 1914, new artillery designs, combined with the new propellants that replaced black powder in the 1880s, resulted in cannon with far greater accuracy, range, and rate of fire. But there was another development alongside these, and it came from the increasingly sophisticated discipline of chemistry. Smokeless powder spelled the end of black powder as a propellant; a new family of chemical compounds, collectively called high explosive, did the same thing for black powder as an explosive substance. Combat in the First World War revealed the results: artillery had become the supreme killer on the battlefield.

SURPRISINGLY—OR PERHAPS NOT—THE motivating factor behind the fast-paced evolution of artillery technology was also the same one that had propelled the rifle race after 1870: the bitter, deadly rivalry between humbled France and newcomer Germany. Thus far, before 1870, Britain and the United States had led the world in artillery research and development. But quietly, behind the scenes, the Prussian army began to steal the lead in cannon technology, just as it had done with the infantry rifle. The Prussians had come to rely heavily upon the brilliant engineering skills of Alfried Krupp and the manufacturing capacity of Krupp's steelworks in Essen. Alfried and his father, Friedrich, were able to improve upon the revolutionary Bessemer process for casting steel, a technique that the Krupps applied to cannon tubes as early as the 1840s. Rifled steel breechloaders came next, in the late 1850s, and by the time that Chancellor Bismarck got the war he wanted with Austria, in the summer of 1866, the Prussian artillery arm was in the process of transitioning from muzzleloaders to breechloaders. The Prussian army that struck the Austrians at Königgrätz in July 1866 used three different field guns of three different calibers: a twelve-pounder smoothbore muzzleloader and two Krupp-built breech-loading rifles made from cast steel.

The new Krupp field guns—primarily the 91.5mm C/61 (six-pounder) and the 78.5mm C/64 (four-pounder) breech-loading rifles—were clearly superior to the main Austrian guns, which were four- and eight-pounder rifled muzzleloaders. The Krupp guns had greater range, fired bigger projectiles (the Prussian four-pounder shell was, oddly, heavier than the Austrian six-pounder, and the Prussian six-pounder heavier than the Austrian eight-pounder), and had a higher rate of fire. Paradoxically, that technological edge wasn't enough to make up for the Austrian superiority in tactics. The Austrians had taken a pounding at the hands of French artillery in Lombardy in 1859, and the experience taught the Austrian high command the virtues of highly mobile artillery that could be massed in giant "grand batteries." And Prussian artillerists, in turn, learned from their Austrian foes in 1866.

When Prussia next went to war, this time against France in 1870, it was with a completely revamped artillery arm. The older smoothbores still in service in 1866 were withdrawn right after the Austrian war, as were the overly heavy C/61 breechloaders, and the field batteries were re-equipped with the C/64 and its improved successor, the 78.5mm C/67. These were innovative designs, well ahead of anything else in service in any other Western army. They employed a special Krupp-patented breech mechanism, the *Doppelkeilverschluss* (double-wedge closure): the breechblock consisted of two opposing steel wedges, held together by a breech-closing screw that ran between them. Mechanically simple, it nonetheless proved to obturate, or seal off, the breech effectively, since gas leakage was as much of a problem with breech-loading cannon as it was with breech-loading rifles. And it was superior to anything the French had.

Seeing the writing on the wall after Moltke's crushing defeat of the Austrian army at Königgrätz in 1866, Emperor Napoléon III and his generals roused themselves from their longstanding complacence and did their best to prepare for what many believed was an inevitable clash with Prussia. The French, though, devoted the greater part of their attention to small arms, and in this they were spectacularly successful. There was little doubt that the French Chassepot was the Prussian Dreyse's superior in every way, and the fact that French arsenals were able to churn out a million of them between 1867 and 1870 was a minor miracle. Artillery reform was not ignored, but it was an intentional afterthought. Only months before the outbreak of the war with Prussia, the French army had adopted a modern rifled breechloader, the 85mm M1870 7-pdr field gun. The cast-bronze M1870 boasted advanced features, but it was developed too late to play much of a role in the coming war. A couple hundred of the new guns went into service before the 1870 war, but not enough. The French artillery in 1870 consisted of a hodgepodge of conventional muzzleloaders, both smoothbore and rifled, and the new breechloaders.

Much to the surprise of foreign observers, it was the Prussian artillery that won the war, and it made up for the serious deficiencies of the Dreyse. Absent massive artillery support, Prussian infantry assaults were cut down by rifle fire from the Chassepots before they could get very far. But the Prussian artillery completely outclassed the French guns. The Krupp C/64 and C/67 guns could throw an explosive shell 3,800 meters with great accuracy, and the shells exploded reliably, thanks to precision fuses. Even the best French guns couldn't hit anything more than 3,100 meters away, and the fuses for their explosive shells were much less functional. The technology was only part of the story, though. After some experimentation in the field, forward-thinking artillery commanders, such as Prince Kraft zu Hohenlohe-Ingelfingen, one of the great artillery theorists of the age, developed a two-stage "artillery battle" for supporting infantry assaults. First, the field guns would be massed into grand batteries of many guns. Well out of range of the French guns, the Prussian grand batteries could concentrate their fire on the enemy artillery, silencing it. Then, and only then, the grand batteries could disperse, moving forward with the infantry, then targeting French infantry once in range. Their firepower, and not that of the Dreyse needle rifles, would do the necessary work of softening up the enemy and preparing the way for an infantry assault. Prussian gunners, much better trained than they had been in 1866, were even able to pull off a particularly tricky battlefield maneuver: to provide covering fire for their own infantry while the foot soldiers were advancing to attack French positions, firing over their heads to suppress French defensive fire. It was a tactic that required both highly skilled artillerists and infantry with nerves of iron.

The new line of Krupp field guns was not a big state secret, the way that the Dreyse had been prior to 1864. Its qualities were known in military circles throughout Europe, and the French were painfully aware going into the war that their own artillery could not match that of their enemies. But the combination of superior technology, superior organization, and a superior understanding of what massed but tactically flexible artillery could accomplish turned heads. While still intent on optimizing small arms design and performance—and while throwing vast sums of cash and time into battleship technology—the major European powers steadily worked at improving their artillery arm over the next four decades.

Within a couple of years after the final French defeat at Sedan in September 1870, muzzle-loading cannon just about disappeared from Western armies, even if they hung on a while longer in the early turreted battleships. The new generation of breech-loading guns, starting with the Krupp guns of 1870, were vastly better than the earlier Armstrong guns and their contemporaries. Their breech mechanisms, like the locking wedge of the Krupp C/64, were stronger than those in previous breechloaders, permitting the use of heavier powder charges, which translated into greater power and range. They were also simpler and faster to manipulate, which meant a higher rate of fire.

And they only got better. Leading the pack, ironically, was France. France was forced to rebuild its artillery arm after 1871; much had been destroyed in the Franco-Prussian War, and the rest had been carted off as booty by the victorious Germans—there was quite literally nothing left. More important, the French military—and indeed popular opinion—smarted from the humiliation of 1870–1871 and ached for revenge. What is often forgotten, though, is not only that France had been until very recently Europe's greatest military power, but that it had long enjoyed a reputation for producing fine engineers. Justifiably so, for in armaments design, the French excelled over both Britain and Germany. In Eugène Schneider, the French government had an industrial partner equal to the Krupps.

The Franco-Prussian War was barely over when the Schneider-Creusot steelworks began churning out new models of field guns, designed by the artillery officers Henri Périer de Lahitolle and (the aptly named) Charles Ragon de Bange, and the prolific superintendent of the government cannon-works at Meudon, Jean-Baptiste Verchère de Reffye, the very same Reffye who had invented the underappreciated *mitrailleuse* volley gun. The Reffye, Lahitolle, and de Bange guns incorporated features that put them way ahead of the Germans, and everybody else in the West for that matter. All made use of an interrupted-screw breech, which in terms of operation meant that the gunner could unlock and open the breech merely by rotating the breech lever a quarter-turn, resulting in a higher rate of fire than was possible with the earlier breechloaders. On top of that, the French applied the principles of small-arms ammunition to artillery ammo: propellant, projectile, and primer were kept together in a brass casing. As with rifles, the brass casing acted as an obturator, or gascheck, effectively sealing the breech, and it was much faster to load a breech-loading cannon with fixed ammunition than it was with separate powder and shot. The French, in other words, had invented what would become known as the quick-firing field gun. Quick-firing, indeed: while a trained gun crew could be expected to fire perhaps two rounds per minute with the previous generation of breech-loading field guns, the new quick-firers with cased ammo could be fired as fast as seven rounds per minute, more than tripling the firepower of field artillery.

IN THE 1870S, France leaped far ahead of the competition in artillery design, and up to the outbreak of the great European war in 1914 it never surrendered its lead. Every landmark innovation in the evolution of cannon during this time, between 1870 and 1914, came from French factories and French engineers. The creation of the quick-firing gun, which was quickly imitated by France's neighbors and rivals, was only the first of several milestones in the pre–Great War artillery revolution. That revolution, if anything, was more dramatic, more profound in its implications, than the parallel and contemporaneous explosion of small arms technology—the machine gun, of course, excepted.

But the tactics of the land battle were evolving, too, in response to the greater speed, range, and accuracy of firepower. From the time of the American Civil War, military thinkers and tactical theorists were coming around to the view that the new firepower, on the whole, favored the defense over the offense. That's not to say that conventional infantry assaults, even frontal assaults across open ground, were a thing of the past. They could be done, and done well, but they required speed, discipline, and maybe a little bit of stealth. Union Col. Emory Upton's lightning-strike assault on the Confederate lines at Spotsylvania (10 May 1864) clearly demonstrated that the rifle-musket could not stop a determined and rapid bayonet charge, properly executed. But the tactical defensive, all other things being equal, was superior to the tactical offensive, and as rate of fire for both small arms and artillery rose, the disparity between offense and defense only grew wider.

The common tactical response to this was to dig in. Field fortifications were nothing new in 1914 or 1904 or 1877 or 1864, but the readiness with which battlefield commanders resorted to digging trenches in semipermanent positions was. Starting with the American Civil War—and especially the last twelve months in the Eastern theater of that war, where Generals U. S. Grant and Robert E. Lee slugged it out over the approaches to Richmond—the construction of impromptu earthworks became a common feature of battle tactics. This was not necessarily a product of new and more powerful weaponry. In the American Civil War, for example, infantry firepower was not significantly greater than it had been in the Napoleonic era, or in the eighteenth century; rather, digging in was a logical approach for less experienced, less disciplined armies. Often, the digging of impromptu field fortifications was not a deliberate tactic initiated by commanders, but something done on the initiative of individual soldiers. During the Civil War, observers frequently noted that veteran infantrymen would drop to the ground and start to carve out foxholes—using bayonets, tin plates, spoons, whatever tools they had at hand—as soon as they came under enemy gunfire.

The necessity of building rough fortifications on the spot prompted the invention of one of the most ever-present and enduring pieces of military gear ever devised. In 1864, near the conclusion of the Second Schleswig War, a middle-aged Danish infantry lieutenant named Mads Johan Buch Linnemann came to the conclusion that digging in was so important that each soldier needed to carry some kind of digging tool on his person. Three years later, he presented his solution to the world: the Linnemann spade. The eponymous tool was nothing more and nothing less than a small shovel, less than two feet in length, perfectly balanced so that it was easy to wield, short enough so that a soldier could hang one from his waist belt without impeding his movement. Linnemann's idea was that roughly every other foot soldier would carry one, the rest making use of picks, mattocks, and fascine knives. But the Linnemann tool was so obviously useful that soon it became part of the standard equipment that all soldiers routinely wore on duty. The Danish army adopted it first, in 1870; the Russian and Austro-Hungarian armies took it up next, manufacturing it under license. Germany and France refused to recognize Linnemann's patent and manufactured their own versions. Linnemann was rewarded with a substantial fortune and a knighthood, and the ordinary soldier had an extra piece of heavy gear to carry.

Perhaps the most surprising thing about the mania for field fortifications was just how durable they proved to be. Of course, they provided effective cover against small-arms fire; that was what prompted their use in the first place. But they also seemed to be quite resilient even when pounded with artillery fire. The Prussian army had discovered this, much to its frustration, when it invaded Danish territory in 1864: though the Danish defensive works along the Dannevirke and at Dybbøl were unremarkable, simple earthen fortifications, the heavy Prussian rifled cannon were unable to destroy or even breech the Danish works. The earthen walls simply absorbed artillery projectiles, whether solid shot or explosive shells, and shells that buried themselves deep in the dirt walls before exploding were all but harmless.

Even better evidence came from the brief-but-bloody Russo-Turkish War of 1877–1878. Little known as the war is to military buffs today, the Russo-Turkish War was scrutinized like few conflicts in European history—not only for its geopolitical significance, for on the war hinged nothing less than the future of Ottoman rule in the Balkans, but also for what lessons it could teach about the new military technology. It was the first European conflict of any size since the Franco-Prussian War seven years earlier, and much had happened in weapons technology over the intervening years. There was much to observe, but the thing that attracted the most comment was the role of field fortifications. Though the Turks ultimately lost the war (and most of their Balkan possessions besides), under the brilliant leadership of Osman Pasha they held on to the city of Plevna (present-day Pleven, Bulgaria) for five months, against overwhelmingly superior Russian-Romanian-Bulgarian forces. It helped that the Turks had better rifles and better cannon—modern Krupp breechloaders purchased from Germany—but in the main it was their reliance on fortifications that counted. Noting the Ottoman soldiers' affinity for digging in, a British observer noted that "it was the nature of the Russian soldier when he stops for a month to instal himself, in the matter of fortifications, as if he would remain for a day; whereas the Turk, stopping for a day, instals himself as if for a month."* The prolonged combat at Plevna, characterized by repeated, unsuccessful, and bloody Russian infantry assaults, was—far more than the better-known trench warfare at Petersburg in the American Civil War—a taste of what was to come in 1914–1918.

From an artillerist's point of view, the Russian experience at Plevna was somewhat concerning. Though Russian artillery was shorter-ranged than the Turks' Krupp guns, it still consisted of modern breech-loading rifled guns, firing explosive shell. Yet no matter how many guns the Russians pressed against the Turkish works outside Plevna, the artillery hardly seemed to make a dent. Artillery barrages did not do significant damage to the earthworks, just as the Prussians had discovered at Dybbøl a decade earlier. It must have been a confusing lesson. The combat experience of the Franco-Prussian War, only a few years before, had demonstrated the potentially devastating power of rapid-fire field artillery in conventional, open battles. The Prussians had won, in no small part, because of their superior artillery. Now, it appeared, after a brief period of battlefield supremacy, artillery was no longer quite so vital. Good earthworks reduced its effectiveness.

The French had a solution in the works for that, too. Throughout Europe, engineers and chemists had been experimenting with new propellants and new explosives since the 1850s and the first promising trials of guncotton (nitrocellulose). But the French government was more assiduous about the matter. Paul Vieille's invention of the

---

*William McElwee, *The Art of War, Waterloo to Mons* (Bloomington: Indiana University Press, 1974), p. 204.

first smokeless powder—Poudre B, or pyrocellulose—in 1884 was as important for artillery as it was for small arms, for the virtues of Poudre B benefited guns big and small. The much-improved ballistic properties were the same as for rifles: higher velocities, greater range, greater penetration, flatter trajectories. The advantages that came from the near elimination of fouling were greater for cannon than they were for rifles. Gun crews no longer had to scour barrels to extinguish every last remaining spark and ember left in the breech between shots. And, of course, commanders no longer had to contend with the billowing clouds of smoke that batteries of black-powder artillery produced. Cannon smoke obscured battlefields, and also revealed the most carefully concealed gun emplacements. American gunners would discover this the hard way, in the war with Spain in 1898, when their antiquated black-powder guns gave away their positions to Spanish snipers and counterbattery fire, at a high cost in American lives.

It was typical of the age that, after Vieille's invention, a host of new smokeless propellants emerged from laboratories from around Europe in rapid succession. Alfred Nobel, already famous for dynamite, patented ballistite in 1887; two years later, an official British commission on explosives developed cordite, patented by Sir Frederick Abel and Sir James Dewar; American chemists, often working with the giant chemical firm DuPont, developed several smokeless powders during the 1890s and 1900s. Though they were all different formulations with different properties, in their essentials they were strikingly similar: they burned more slowly than black powder, they produced little smoke or fouling, and they imparted higher velocities and flatter trajectories to the projectiles they propelled.

The new smokeless powders made outstanding propellants but poor explosives. Certainly they exploded, but not predictably or controllably, and hence were ill-suited for artillery shells. Pyrocellulose was sensitive to shock, so it was entirely possible that an explosive shell loaded with the substance could explode before it exited the barrel.

Once again, enter the French arms industry, and a whole new family of explosive compounds.

High explosives are compounds that, when detonated, produce a blast that moves faster than the speed of sound. While smokeless powders deflagrated more slowly than black powder, high explosives burn much, much faster. They do not make very effective propellants, but they are far more destructive and powerful than black powder.

Although the first true high explosive, liquid nitroglycerine, was first synthesized in 1847, it was far too unstable for most practical applications, and another forty years would pass before high explosives were tested with artillery ammunition. In 1885, French explosives expert Eugène Turpin discovered that picric acid—whose explosive properties were first discovered by the Anglo-German chemist Hermann Sprengel—could be used for many applications once it was pressed and cast. Since it was less sensitive than smokeless powders, not volatile like nitroglycerine, and yet far more powerful than black powder, it seemed like a perfect candidate for use in artillery shells. The French government adopted picric acid for just this purpose, combining it with guncotton to form an explosive they manufactured under the trade name Mélinite (1887).

What Poudre B was to black powder the propellant, Mélinite was to black powder the explosive: infinitely superior in every way. More stable, less volatile, less vulnerable to heat and moisture— and far, far more powerful. Black powder's greatest shortcoming as an explosive was that it took a large quantity of the stuff to produce a respectable and deadly blast; as a consequence, only the largest cannon—fortress and naval guns—could fire a shell that packed a large enough blasting charge to cause any significant damage within a blast zone more than a few feet in diameter. The shells thrown by field guns, with bore diameters four inches or smaller, simply weren't big enough to carry a significant explosive charge of black powder. But with high explosive, a little bit went a long way. Small charges had unprecedented blasting power. A high-explosive shell thrown from even a relatively small piece, like a 75mm field gun, could kill by blast alone, and over a larger area. The shards of steel flung at supersonic velocities by the bursting charge caused even more death and destruction.

Between 1884 and 1887, the French had stolen a huge lead in firepower, in all its major forms, over friend and foe alike: the first high-velocity smokeless powders, the first modern battle rifle, then Mélinite, the first high explosive designed specifically for military use. The trio of advances threw a lit match into an already highly combustible arms race, causing palpable consternation in military and diplomatic circles across the continent. Britain, Germany, and Austria-Hungary raced to catch up. It didn't take them long. Talented chemists were everywhere, and so too were spies.

NEARLY EVERY SALIENT feature of the early cannon had been transformed in the space of two decades between 1860 and 1880. In 1860, the cannon was essentially the same as it had been three hundred years before: muzzle-loading, fashioned from cast iron or cast bronze, probably smoothbore. Now cast steel replaced iron and bronze, rifled tubes replaced smoothbore, breech-loading mechanisms replaced rammer and sponge, elongated shell replaced round shot, smokeless powder and high explosive replaced black powder. There was really only one frontier remaining to be conquered, and it was no mystery, for every artillerist knew what it was: recoil. Recoil was the thing that most compromised a cannon's performance, especially its rate of fire, and eliminating it was the priority of weapons engineers as the nineteenth century drew to a close.

In fortresses or aboard ship, recoil could be an ally. It propelled guns backward so that they could be safely loaded from the muzzle within the confines of a fortress casemate or a ship's gun deck. But for a crew serving a mobile fieldpiece on land, recoil was most assuredly a foe. The wheels that made the gun carriage mobile also sped its violent retrograde motion, and a recoiling cannon could not be stopped safely by hand. On level, dry ground, an ordinary field gun would recoil several feet when fired. That didn't prolong loading time, but it required the gunner and the crew to haul the piece back "into battery" and "lay it on"—aim it—all over again. The gun's elevation might have to be adjusted, but there was no getting around the task of re-aiming. Recoil was the time-thief in artillery fire.

Weapons engineers throughout Europe went after the problem of recoil suppression aggressively. Most of the proposed solutions involved a free-floating gun barrel that could move backward and forward along a slide, mounted to the gun carriage, with the barrel's movement regulated by springs or hydraulic shock absorbers. But none of them worked well enough to merit adoption.

One design came close, though. A brilliant—and terribly unfortunate—young engineer working for Krupp, Konrad Haussner, submitted to his employer in 1888 a lengthy and detailed proposal for a hydraulic recoil-suppression system of his own design. The authorities at Krupp, no longer the visionary weapons engineers they had once been, rejected Haussner's idea out of hand. Haussner left Krupp, patented his invention on his own, raised the necessary capital to have a prototype built, and then presented it to the German army. It was rejected again. Krupp's leading competitor, Heinrich Ehrhardt, caught wind of Haussner's work, hoping to acquire it for his new company Rheinische Metallwaaren- und Maschinenfabrik—since famous as Rheinmetall. Ehrhardt worked with Haussner to secure another audience with the military authorities in Berlin. Once again, the conservatives prevailed, and Haussner faced rejection. When the Kaiser's army adopted a new field gun in 1896, it went with a tried-and-true, rigid-mount gun, without any kind of recoil absorption device.

But the French had been paying close attention all along. The senior French artillery officer, General Charles Mathieu, got hold of Haussner's design and seized the opportunity to benefit from it. The French were more eager than anyone, certainly more eager than Krupp, to solve the recoil problem. France's foremost expert on gunnery, Hippolyte Langlois, had stressed the need for truly quick-firing artillery. Langlois, who was professor of artillery at the Paris École de Guerre—the very same school where Napoléon himself had learned the art of gunnery—envisioned a more aggressive use of field artillery, with large numbers of highly mobile quick-firing guns overwhelming enemy artillery and infantry units with targeted but brief, furious, intensive barrages from hundreds of guns at once. This tactic, referred to in the French service as the *rafale*, required cannon that could be loaded and fired almost as fast as a bolt-action rifle. Such a cannon, though, did not yet exist. Recoil stood in the way.

Inventing such a gun was a tall order, but General Mathieu's subordinates and engineers delivered. Mathieu entrusted the task to Lt. Col. Joseph-Albert Deport, from the state arsenal at Puteaux. Working in great secrecy, Deport and his team started with Haussner's design, and between 1892 and 1897 they built a new field gun. The French army eagerly adopted the new cannon in 1898; on 14 July 1899, it was finally revealed to the world in the annual Bastille Day parade.

The new gun deserved all the secrecy and hype. Officially dubbed the Matériel de 75mm Modele 1897, it was mostly a mélange of design features from previous French guns, now brought together in a package that was unlike anything in any other European arsenal at the close of the century. The gun and carriage incorporated loads of progressive features: integral steel seats for crew members, a rectangular steel shield to protect the crew from small-arms fire, and a telescopic sight called a collimator. The breech mechanism, invented by the prolific Swedish engineer Thorsten Nordenfelt, was smooth and rapid. Gas escaping from the breech was not an issue—the Mle 1897, like the previous generation of French field guns, used self-contained, metal-cased ammunition, which acted as an obturator; after being fired, the breech mechanism automatically opened on recoil, ejecting the spent case, and the gun was ready to be loaded again. A simple half-turn of the handle locked the breech and made the gun ready to fire again.

But the revolutionary thing about the French field gun—which would become known to French *poilus* in the Great War as

Mademoiselle Soixante-quinze and as the "French 75" to everyone else—was its recoil suppression system, based heavily on Haussner's brilliant patent. Upon firing, the barrel moved backward on rollers along its slide; a system of oil- and gas-filled tubes above and below the barrel slowed the movement and gently halted the recoil; compressed nitrogen gas in the recuperator tube pushed the barrel back into battery. The entire process, from discharge to return to battery, took less than two seconds. The recoil suppression system absorbed virtually all the recoil. A trail-spade, quite literally a shovel-like appendage at the very rear end of the carriage that could be dug into the ground, firmly anchored the gun in place and took care of the rest.

What all this meant was that the French 75 did not have to be re-aimed with each and every shot. Once on target, it stayed on target, so the gun could fire as fast as the crew could feed it shells, without having to pause to realign or re-elevate the piece. It could throw a Mélinite-packed, high-explosive shell as far as 8,500 meters—more than five miles—with astonishing accuracy, and it could do so twenty to thirty times per minute. Even in an age of technological marvels, the performance of the French 75 field gun seemed almost inconceivable. Small wonder, then, that the French went to extraordinary lengths to keep their amazing new field gun secret, even intentionally circulating false data about the 75 to mislead German spies. Even after the 75 went public in 1899, its properties remained a mystery . . . until 1901, when it first went into action, during the Boxer Rebellion in China. In one especially dramatic episode, a mere two 75s provided covering fire for a handful of elite Zouave light infantry assaulting a village defended by two thousand rebels. The two quick-firing guns were able to so thoroughly suppress the resistance that the Zouaves took the village all but unscathed.

Every other model of field gun in Europe was rendered immediately obsolete.

As with every other great leap forward in weapons technology in the fraught years at the turn of the century, whatever advantage

Plate 20. Matériel de 75mm Modele 1897, better known as the French 75mm field gun, Model 1897.

Courtesy National Archives, photo no. 45523753.

came from exclusive possession of it didn't last long. Word of the French field gun's superior properties spread fast, and the rest of Europe frantically sought to catch up. Britain and Norway purchased significant quantities of Haussner-designed guns from Rheinmetall, and artillery engineers throughout the West went to work on modern fieldpieces of their own. The German army was put in the uncomfortable position of discovering that its brand-new cannon, the M1896 77mm field gun, was already obsolete. Even worse: that France had once again stolen a giant lead over Germany in a critical military technology, and—by rejecting Haussner's design not once but repeatedly—they had only themselves and Krupp to blame. But soon the Germans, too, accepted the new reality, and starting in 1905 they sent their new M1896 guns back to Krupp and Rheinmetall to be retrofitted with a new carriage and hydraulic-spring recoil system. By the time the First World War broke out, just about every army of note—even the noticeably backward American army—had officially adopted some type of limited-recoil, quick-firing gun.

The tactical implications were enormous. The combination of smokeless propellants, high explosive shell, and recoil suppression meant that artillery could kill more men, faster, and dominate more ground than would have been dreamed possible in 1860. The field gun had become, at least theoretically, the deadliest weapon on the battlefield, and artillery the deadliest combat arm. Artillery officers understood this better than anyone. In the days of the *ancien régime*, the so-called technical branches—engineering and artillery—had drawn their leadership from the increasingly prosperous, ambitious, and well-educated middle class, while more honorable posts in the infantry and cavalry tended to be reserved for noblemen. True to their bourgeois roots, artillerists were perhaps more open to change and innovation than the authors of infantry and cavalry tactics. They understood that artillery could now, in 1900, achieve much more than it had even in the Franco-Prussian and Russo-Turkish conflicts, where field guns had played the starring role; and they understood, more willingly than their colleagues in the other service branches, that they would have to abandon most of the notions that had guided artillery tactics thus far.

The great test lab for modern artillery was the Russo-Japanese War (1904–1905), just as it was for weaponry from machine guns to battleships. The land forces of Russia and Japan were well equipped, or at least equipped with modern weapons. Their artillery, as it stood in 1904, wasn't quite up to the admittedly high standard set by the French 75, but still modern. The main Russian field gun, the 76mm M1900, consistently outranged the Japanese Type 31 76mm gun by as much as one thousand meters, and it had a slightly more advanced recoil-suppression apparatus, but both were of the quick-firing type, using smokeless powder and high-explosive shell. Both the Russians and the Japanese also had access to the first generation of field phones, still primitive and touchy but nonetheless invaluable in combat.

It was the Japanese, with their inferior guns, who proved to be the tactical innovators. Russian gunners continued to cling to old-fashioned notions of artillery tactics, sending their guns into the open to engage the Japanese batteries—and getting slaughtered in the process. The Japanese took a much different approach. Their battery commanders were accustomed to working and problem-solving together, giving the entire field artillery arm a tactical flexibility and cohesion that the Russians lacked. Unburdened by Napoleonic traditions of machismo and physical courage in the artillery, the Japanese made up for the lesser qualities of their field guns by masking their batteries, placing them well out of sight on the reverse slopes of hills, or digging in, and making use of netting, foliage, and shadow to camouflage their positions. That attention to concealment, plus use of smokeless propellants, meant that the Japanese guns were all but invisible to their foes.

The Japanese had learned, before anyone else, the principle of indirect fire, of bombarding targets not in the gunner's direct line of sight. It was still a novel idea in 1904; European observers, early in the war with Russia, mocked the Japanese for what seemed to be a measure born from cowardice. But it would become one of the defining features of modern gunnery, and it began with the Japanese. Firing on an invisible target was about as difficult and demanding as it sounds. The tactic required a third party, an observer, who could watch the target and place it accurately on a map; it also required that the gun crews follow their observer's guidance exactly, adjusting the elevation and traverse of their gun according to his directions. Indirect fire also required some means of rapid communication. Semaphore would work in a pinch, field phones would be ideal, but the young expendable lieutenant on horseback, for centuries the most common medium of battlefield communications, would no longer suffice.

The contrast between Russian and Japanese artillery tactics could not have been any starker. At the battle of the Yalu River (April–May 1904), the first major land engagement of the war, Japanese artillery played a crucial role in driving the Russians off the field. The Russian batteries, given the task of preventing a Japanese crossing of the Yalu, were posted in the open; the main Japanese battery, some thirty-six field guns and twenty howitzers, was dug in and camouflaged. The Japanese had gone so far as to dig up trees and transplant them immediately in front of the gun emplacements, to screen the muzzle flashes from enemy eyes. Artillery observation posts, set up on high ground to the rear, communicated with the batteries via field phones. When the Japanese artillery opened up on the Russian positions early in the morning of 29 April, they easily destroyed the Russian field guns in half an hour. "The Japanese were invisible and comparatively invulnerable, the Russians were conspicuous and everywhere most vulnerable," noted Sir Ian Hamilton, who tagged along with the Japanese as an official British observer.

The Russo-Japanese conflict gave European soldiers and military intellectuals much to think about. It had given a brief and compelling glimpse into the twentieth-century battlefield, and into the combined effects of quick-firing guns, modern propellants, and high explosive. Nothing, though, could prepare the armies of the West for the vast scope, scale, and power of artillery operations in the Great War to come.

High Explosive

ARTILLERY WAS THE principal killer of the First World War. It had many rivals, some of which we tend to associate with the manifold horrors of the 1914–1918 battlefield: poison gas, the flamethrower, the tank, the machine gun. But it was the common artillery piece that took the most lives. Undoubtedly, many more rifle- and machine-gun bullets were fired than rounds of shell and case shot, but the combination of quick-firing cannon, high-explosive, and precision sighting proved to be exceptionally lethal. Just under 60 percent of Germany's combat deaths in the Great War can be attributed to artillery fire.

Artillery played the main role, but that role wasn't exactly what professional soldiers had anticipated, just as the near immobility of the main armies on the Western Front (and more often than not on the Eastern Front) wasn't what professional soldiers had anticipated. In fact, the two features were closely related: it was the relative absence of mobility that exaggerated artillery's prominence in battle. Because the armies were static, the artillery could be reasonably static, too, allowing artillery units to devote more time to camouflaging their positions, to pay more attention to observation and communications. As the experience of the Russo-Japanese War had suggested, most artillery fire was not line of sight but indirect, with targets identified and artillery fire monitored by remote observers.

Unlike in the Russo-Japanese War, battery commanders could rely upon an entirely new and very promising resource for fire control: military aviation. Military aviation, while yet in its infancy in 1914, evolved rapidly during the Great War, and of all the functions it came to perform—pursuit, reconnaissance, close support, even strategic bombing—arguably the most important and the most fruitful was artillery spotting. Aerial observers, either in two-seater reconnaissance planes or stationary observation balloons, could get views of the battlefield that were impossible to acquire by any other means. The only weak link was communication from aerial observer to fire-control officers on the ground. From balloons, this could be done by wired field phone or telegraph. From an airplane in flight, transmission and reception were somewhat trickier but by no means impossible. Air-to-ground wireless telegraphy was a common practice throughout the war, and in 1915 the British successfully conducted experiments with voice-to-voice transmissions. Wireless telegraphy, though perhaps awkward for the observers who had to key in their reports from the open cockpit of a rickety biplane, made the connection between aerial observer and gunner practically seamless.

But the trench-bound nature of combat in the Western—and often the Eastern—theaters also dictated that the specific role of artillery would be a bit different from what it had been in the Russo-Japanese conflict. There, the field guns, hidden or not, had done most of the work, and it seemed to vindicate the prewar focus on light quick-firing guns. The state-of-the-art field guns of 1914, though, were not quite so effective when combined with trench warfare. As powerful as high explosive shell was, as rapid and precise as the French 75 was, small-caliber shell did only limited damage to well-built trenchworks. As long as soldiers in the front lines could find shelter in an underground bombproof, they were relatively safe, physically at least, from the effects of bombardment. That same lack of mobility, though, made it possible to use larger pieces—the kind of artillery that ordinarily would have been reserved for siegework—in nearly all operations. Here the Germans were way ahead of their enemies going into the war. Believing that a war with France would require quick reduction of French and Belgian concrete-built forts, German artillery designers had developed very good 105mm and 150mm howitzers. Those big guns could do a lot more physical damage to earthen fortifications, not to mention human bodies.

The flat trajectory of high-velocity field guns was also not well suited to trench warfare; unless firing from a higher elevation than the target, it was exceedingly difficult to drop a shell into a trench. Howitzers were a different matter, as were mortars. The plunging trajectories of howitzer and mortar rounds made them ideal for trench warfare, because howitzers and mortars could drop high explosive rounds into trenches rather than firing into or through them.

The Great War breathed new life into the mortar as a conventional weapon. Previously, mortars had been reserved for siege-work, at which they were quite effective. The Federal army had used mortars in large numbers during the American Civil War, but they were hardly mobile pieces. Thanks to the comparative weakness of black-powder shells, it only made sense to produce mortars of a large caliber, and that made for an unwieldy weapon. The American M1841 10-inch seacoast mortar tipped the scales at just under three tons, the 13-inch mortar at eight-and-a-half tons, and accordingly they saw action only in long-term siege operations like those at Charleston, Petersburg, and Vicksburg.

With all the focus devoted to the quick-firing field gun, the armies of the West seem to have forgotten all about mortars in the late nineteenth century. Not so the Germans. German observers in the Russo-Japanese War had seen mortars in action and were impressed by their effectiveness. In 1910, the German army adopted the first of several models of *Minenwerfer*—literally "mine thrower"—a 250mm-caliber monster that could lob a 214-pound high-explosive "bomb" over four hundred yards. Lighter, more portable models followed. There were only a handful available at the outset of the war in 1914, but as soon as the fighting in France devolved into trench warfare, those few mortars quickly proved their worth, and the Germans rushed them into mass production.

Other armies followed suit, and by the middle of the war the large-caliber mortar was a common sight on the battlefield. But the most interesting response to the initial German edge in mortars came from Britain, and specifically from a civil engineer who had been tapped for service with Britain's Ministry of Munitions, one Frederick Wilfrid Scott Stokes. Stokes had spent most of his career designing railroad bridges and cranes, not in armaments, but in 1915 he came up with a brilliant counter to the German *Minenwerfer*. The Stokes trench mortar was a strikingly uncomplicated weapon in an age of mechanical marvels: a simple smoothbore tube, three inches in diameter, mounted upright on a heavy base. At the bottom of the tube a striker, or firing pin, sat upright on the base. It fired a special 3-inch round, which incorporated a high-explosive shell, its propellant charge, and a primer at the base. To fire the Stokes mortar, the gunner simply dropped a mortar round, base first, into the tube. Gravity did the rest. The shell fell to the breech, the primer in the base striking the stationary firing pin, then detonation and explosion—and the propellant carried the shell in a high arc as far as eight hundred yards, depending on the elevation of the tube. Adjustable legs allowed the mortar crew to change elevation, and thus range. The rate of fire was quite high—as fast as twenty-five rounds per minute. The whole assembly weighed a total of 104 pounds, and could be broken down into three easily transportable sections. It had few moving parts and was cheap to manufacture. It packed the punch of a much larger field gun into a tiny package that could be used by just about anyone, just about anywhere—even by infantry on the attack—with no complicated gear.

The British high command initially resisted the Stokes mortar—its specially designed shell was bound to become a logistical and manufacturing burden—but eventually they caved, thanks in no small part to the personal intervention of David Lloyd George, the future prime minister. During the second half of the Great War, the Stokes mortar saw heavy use, and Stokes was knighted for his contribution to the war effort. Other armies caught on to the idea, too, for it was too good not to copy, but most of these Stokes-inspired mortars appeared too late to see much action before the Armistice in November 1918. It would be in the next war that the mortar would play a much larger role, as the principal form of mobile light artillery. Nearly all the infantry mortars used in the Second World War were close approximations of the Stokes 1915 design.

Artillery, mortars included, took on unusual and unprecedented tasks in the Great War. Artillery proved to be the most effective means for delivering poison gas. The Germans pioneered this creative if ghastly expedient. At the battle of Bolimów (31 January 1915), they fired shells filled with xylyl bromide—a kind of tear gas—on Russian troops, with little effect, thanks to very low temperatures and contrary winds; three months later, in their spring offensive, they launched a barrage of chlorine gas shells at French positions near Ypres. The French and British scrambled to catch up, and from 1916 to war's end poison gas became a routine if horrific part of a soldier's daily life, and it was almost always delivered via artillery.

The revolution in artillery firepower brought about by smokeless powder, high explosive, and more durable steel similarly reset the basic design and qualities of the truly big guns, like coastal and naval artillery. Though not as prominent in military operations during the Great War, except at sea and on those few occasions—as during the Dardanelles campaign of 1915—when warships bombarded land targets, the range and power of the heaviest artillery increased almost exponentially. The United States and Britain especially invested huge sums into big guns. Britain's priority was, after all, its navy, where huge guns were the main tools of the trade; the US, on the other hand, needed coastal artillery to arm its new generation of reinforced-concrete harbor fortifications, including the so-called Endicott forts that dotted the Atlantic, Pacific, and Gulf coasts.

Some of the largest examples of heavy ordnance ever devised put in a battlefield appearance or two, thanks to the notion of "railway artillery"—mounting supersized guns on railcars so that they could be transported *and* put into firing position by train. France, Britain, Austria-Hungary, Russia, and above all Germany used railway artillery at one point or another. Most successful were the German *Langer Max* 38cm naval guns. First employed early in 1915, these 270-ton cannon could lob a 1,600-pound shell, packed with well over a 100 pounds of high explosive, close to twenty-five miles. The *Langer Max*, though, couldn't match the star appeal of perhaps the most famous cannon of the twentieth century. The *Kaiser Wilhelm* gun, better known as the Paris Gun or—incorrect but most popular—Big Bertha, was a 256-ton, 112-foot-long siege gun capable sending its 238mm shells as far as seventy-five miles. The Germans used it to shell Paris, where it caused some consternation but little actual damage. Just as with all the super-guns of the Great War, the time, energy, and resources expended on the Paris Gun were not justified by the unimpressive results.

THOUGH MUCH WAS expected of them, the railway guns were mere novelties, as most super-weapons turn out to be eventually. It was in the day-to-day combat operations of the light and medium artillery, shelling enemy positions daily, that artillery did its most important and deadliest work in the Great War. In the eyes of the generals, artillery, as an integral and vital component of the infantry assault, was the key to breaking the tactical stalemate imposed by trench warfare. Only infantry could take and hold ground, but artillery, it was believed, could beat that ground into submission first, sparing the infantry the prospect of heavy casualties. The generals may have been right in thinking so, but it took the expenditure of much time, ammunition, and blood for the combatants to develop artillery tactics that served the purpose of restoring mobility and maneuver to warfare.

Early in the war, artillery support for ground assaults against fortified enemy positions usually took the form of what the French called *rafale*—a furious, intensive artillery bombardment of the enemy's front lines. The rationale behind the rafale was that it would not only reduce enemy defenders and demoralize the survivors, but that it would also render trenches uninhabitable, wreck machine-gun positions, and flatten or blow apart barbed wire obstacles. The logic behind the rafale was unassailable, except by bitter experience, which demonstrated that such bombardments rarely achieved any of these things. Defending troops could simply take shelter underground in heavily reinforced bombproofs, emerging after the bombardment was over, while reinforcements from the rear could move into position as soon as the rafale ended. And since the entire purpose of such a profligate expenditure of ammunition was to soften up the enemy prior to an assault, the rafale had an unfortunate tendency to tell the enemy precisely where he could expect to be attacked soon.

Probably the most famous cannonade of the war proved these very points: the British artillery assault that kicked off the first day of the 1916 Somme offensive. Over the course of a week, over 1,500 British guns hurled more than 1.6 million shells at the German lines. Though it did wreak havoc with the German trenches, the shelling neither neutralized the German barbed wire defenses nor eliminated German opposition. It's hard to say if the pre-assault cannonade helped or hindered the infantry assault that followed, but that assault—on 1 July 1916, the single bloodiest day in the history of the British army—was a disaster. The artillery fire had churned up the ground over which the British advanced, making it virtually impassable in places, and the barbed wire defenses had suffered only light damage. The butcher's bill—over nineteen thousand killed, fifty-seven thousand overall casualties, nearly half of the attacking force—proved quite eloquently that even with its vastly improved firepower, artillery alone could not simply destroy a determined enemy or break his cohesion.

A more precise kind of bombardment, the barrage, superseded the rafale. Barrages could take many forms, but their defining characteristic was that they were precise and carefully planned, and their targets well chosen. A barrage could hit the enemy's front lines, then "lift" or "leap" to target areas beyond the frontmost trenches, to destroy reinforcements coming up or prevent them from moving forward. Perhaps the best-known variant was the creeping barrage, in which artillery fire accompanied an infantry assault. As the infantry moved forward, the artillery fire would move in front of them and with them, hopefully suppressing enemy opposition until the assault troops reached their objectives. It required impeccable timing and great care: if it moved too slowly, it courted the possibility of falling short and hitting friendly troops; if too fast, or if the infantry failed to keep pace, it would allow the enemy sufficient time to recover and reform their lines before

Plate 21. British BL 6-inch Mk VII naval gun, employed as a field gun on the Western Front in the First World War. Though the armies of pre-1914 Europe focused on field guns, especially after the unveiling of the French M1897, the big guns and howitzers were found to be far more effective, at least within the context of trench warfare.
Image: Library of Congress.

the assault troops could take their positions. But if properly coordinated, a creeping barrage could—and often did—achieve stunning results. The remarkable successes of the Canadian Corps in its assaults on Vimy Ridge (April 1917) owed much to the effective cooperation between Allied artillery and Canadian infantry.

In the rafale and the barrage, artillery firepower was a crude tool, a blunt instrument, no matter how much careful planning went into its use. It was brute force unrefined, designed to bludgeon and obliterate. And it was the opposite of stealth, for even a precision barrage openly announced to the enemy that an attack was in the offing, and just where the main assault would likely hit. The power, the sheer raw power, of artillery in the First World War was a direct result of the industrial age. But the technology of the industrial age also imparted to artillery qualities that went beyond power—range, precision, speed, and the ability to fire on targets that could not be directly seen, via the assistance of advanced optics and range-finding apparatus. These latter qualities allowed artillery to play a role that was vastly subtler.

Though it's become standard fare in any interpretation of the First World War that generals were unimaginative dunderheads who mindlessly sent their soldiers straight into certain death in futile assaults against enemy trenches, the plain truth is that most European commanders fully understood the tactical challenges facing them and were actively working to overcome them with varying degrees of success. The slaughter of British infantry in the first day's assault at the Somme, tragic as it was, was not the result of criminal negligence, indifference, or incompetence on the part of the British generals, but rather it was a failed experiment, a miscalculation. It was a costly miscalculation, the cost tallied in thousands of lives, but it was not a ridiculous miscalculation. British assault tactics, on paper at least, made perfect sense, and they were based on a reasonable understanding of modern weaponry and time-tested assumptions about the nature of offensive battle. For all its pathos and bloodiness, the Somme offensive in 1916 taught a valuable lesson: however powerful artillery was, even the heaviest pre-assault bombardment was not in itself enough to shatter enemy cohesion. Something more than bludgeoning was called for.

But even as the tragedy at the Somme unfolded, elsewhere other, more promising solutions to the stalemate of trench warfare were emerging, and all of them cast artillery in a leading—but much different—role. One of these new approaches came from the Brusilov offensive of 1916, Russia's greatest military success and one of the most promising Allied operations of the entire war. In the midst of a dismally bloody campaign, in the spring of 1916, General Aleksei Alekseyevich Brusilov proposed a truly audacious summer offensive against Austro-Hungarian forces in Galicia: a surprise attack along a wide swath of the enemy's front lines, three hundred miles in breadth. The attack involved stealthy but massive infiltration attacks against weak and thinly held sectors in the enemy's front lines. That in itself was a cardinal sin against the legacy of the great Bonaparte, who was still very much worshipped by general officers; Napoléon, after all, had opined that one should always hammer on the enemy's strong points, and the rest will fall. Brusilov would bypass and seal off those strong points, letting them atrophy from isolation as the main attacking body forced itself through the gaps punched in the weak points.

But even in Brusilov's tactics, artillery was key, and less was more. There was no heavy, hours-long barrage before the attack; that would only signal to the enemy where and when the hammer-blow would fall, and give him time to react, to send up reinforcements, to prepare. There would be no creeping barrage, because that would chew up the ground across which the attack would take place, slowing down the first wave when speed and stealth were critical. Artillery would serve a much different role. Several days prior to the actual assault, brief artillery barrages against seemingly random targets, at seemingly random times, for seemingly random durations, would sow confusion, not clearly signaling where or when an assault would happen—or if it would happen at all. Pre-assault barrages would be brief and accurate, not allowing any time for the enemy to recover or react. The infantry did the heavy work, but artillery prepared the way, physically and psychologically.

The Germans had also been working assiduously, since 1915, on combined-arms approaches to achieving a breakthrough in trench warfare. One of these approaches was not dissimilar to Brusilov's, and it emerged in 1917–1918 as "stormtrooper," or *Stoßtruppen*, tactics. Pioneered by a veteran infantry captain named Willy Rohr, promoted and further developed by General Oskar von Hutier, stormtrooper tactics focused on stealthy infiltration of enemy lines by light assault infantry (*Stoßtruppen*), who were specially trained in close-quarters combat. As the stormtroopers infiltrated enemy frontline trenches, conventional infantry would follow up on their successes, much as in Brusilov's offensive. Again, artillery played a crucial role. A preferred tactic, known as the "fire waltz" (*Feuerwalz*), involved a general bombardment of enemy positions, not directed specifically at the intended targets of the assault—those goals were not to be given away—but aimed mostly at targets in the rear: roads and road junctions, ammo dumps, communications centers, reserve trenches. The idea was not so much to pummel the front-most enemy defenses, but to paralyze the enemy's ability to react, to prevent reinforcements from making their way to the front, and to compromise or completely cut off communications between front and rear.

THE NEWFOUND DEADLINESS of artillery fire, accomplished between 1870 and 1914, was the result of a coming together of many technological breakthroughs that occurred at roughly the same time: smokeless propellants, high explosive, high-quality cast steel, cased ammunition, quick-firing breech mechanisms, recoil suppression, indirect fire control by aerial observers, and wireless communications. Mechanization, despite claims to the contrary, had little to do with it. Gas- and diesel-powered tractors did indeed haul artillery pieces during the course of the Great War, but horse-drawn guns were much more common during that conflict—horse labor far exceeded horsepower. Of all the relevant factors, the invention of high explosive was arguably the weightiest. The speed and precision of artillery fire stemmed from the properties of the gun itself, but high explosive had so many applications besides artillery, including demolition, that it proved to be a more universal innovation. High explosive put much greater firepower into the hands of infantry by war's end, via the Stokes mortar and its imitators.

High explosive served infantry in yet another way, transforming close-range combat in the First World War and redefining small-unit tactics for the century to come. The hand grenade, an ancient weapon of questionable usefulness, experienced a rebirth in the Great War. Hand grenades were nearly as old as gunpowder itself, though they were almost always improvised devices and rarely very effective. Mostly they were small iron spheres—sometimes small-caliber shell was drafted for this very purpose—filled with gunpowder and detonated with a length of quick match, which the user would have to light manually before throwing. In the late seventeenth and early eighteenth centuries, it became fashionable for European armies to equip their largest and sturdiest infantrymen with grenades; hence the term *grenadier*, a designation that continued into the nineteenth century, long after grenadiers had stopped carrying grenades. Grenades tended to appear most often in sieges, as a weapon that could (presumably) clear an enemy trench of its human inhabitants, and often grenades were the handmade products of bored soldiers with time and gunpowder on their hands. A British officer in the Crimea recounted how his men would fill soda water bottles with gunpowder and nails, topped with a fuse, and lob the lit improvised bombs into Russian trenches during the siege of Sevastopol; even he admitted that the weapon was no more than an annoyance to the enemy. The American Civil War witnessed the use of both improvised grenades, like hand-thrown six-pounder cannon shells, and a new generation of patented hand grenades. The most famous of these, the Federal-made Ketchum Grenade, was an oblong cast-iron shell with a finned tail at one end and a large plunger at the other. When it hit a hard surface, the plunger in theory pushed inward and detonated a percussion cap, which in turn ignited the charge inside—provided that the grenade landed on its nose.

The early grenades were clumsy, weak, and ineffective, hardly worth the effort of making them. The advent of high explosive changed all that. The very concept of hand grenades had long since gone dormant, with a nearly universal consensus that they were antique curiosities, until European observers saw them in action during the siege of Port Arthur in the Russo-Japanese War. Russian and Japanese soldiers alike made their own improvised devices by stuffing high explosives—dynamite and picric acid were favorites—into any containers they could find, like meat tins, lengths of iron pipe, and cut-down artillery casings. These homemade devices were no mere distractions from the tedium of life during a siege, but serious and deadly weapons of war. Soldiers from both armies used them to clear enemy trenches during raids, and even to sweep enemy-held buildings in close-up, house-to-house combat.

High Explosive

The Russo-Japanese War aroused some interest in grenades, but there were only a few designs available when war broke out in 1914, most of them unsatisfactory. The main British model, the No. 1, Mk. 1 grenade (1908), used an impact fuse, meaning that it detonated when it hit the ground—or anything, for that matter, and proved to be too sensitive for safe use in the trenches. Once the war settled down into a trench-based affair, early in 1915, soldiers predictably began to make their own makeshift explosives, but new designs were in the offing. By 1915–1916, the first "safe" grenades went into service—notably the French F-1 and the British No. 5 Mills bomb. Safe grenades did not have to be lit with a match, and they did not employ impact or percussion fuses, which were too prone to detonation by accident. Although varying in the mechanical details, safe grenades used a time-delay fuse, connected to a handheld lever, or "spoon," which was itself restrained by a safety pin. The user held down the spoon while gripping the grenade with his throwing hand, then pulled the pin. When thrown, the spring-loaded spoon flew up, igniting the fuse, and the explosion came around four to seven seconds later. There were two basic types of grenades: fragmentation and blast. Fragmentation grenades, called defensive grenades in British service, were wrapped in an iron sleeve, which threw fragments and shards at a high velocity in all directions when the grenade exploded. Blast grenades relied on the blast force of the high explosive itself, which was enough to kill within a limited radius and at least stun nearby troops outside of that kill radius.

The early safe grenades had their problems, as one might expect of a new weapon tested in the midst of war. They were potentially dangerous to the user and those near him, even if used correctly. The British Mills bomb, for example, was slightly overpowered. The British army reminded servicemen that the maximum throwing distance for the Mills bomb was around thirty meters—in practice, it was probably closer to fifteen—but that the explosion was potentially lethal at one hundred. The thrower would have to take cover immediately after tossing the grenade if he didn't want to become a victim, as well.

But thanks to the invention of high explosive and the time-delay fuse, the hand grenade did something remarkable: it put the power of a small artillery piece into a small package that could be carried, and delivered, by anyone. Its true value became apparent in close combat, during trench raids, and especially during the German *Kaiserschlacht* offensives of 1918. German *Stoßtruppen* relied on melee weapons including pistols, daggers, trench clubs, entrenching tools, and grenades. A few grenades tossed into an enemy trench during the assault were more effective than anything else at smashing resistance in one blow. In the next world war, when mobility was the byword and close-up fighting in urban environments a common occurrence, the hand grenade would come into its own.

High explosive was *the* defining combat technology of the First World War, and would remain so for some time to come. It was without a doubt the deadliest: it exerted the greatest influence on tactics of land warfare, and more than any other feature of the Great War, it shaped the day-to-day experience of the ordinary soldier in the trenches. The combination of high explosive, smokeless powder, and the quick-firing gun vastly expanded not only the raw destructive power of artillery of all kinds but also the usefulness and versatility of it, too, as the big guns began to take on previously unimagined roles. And at sea, the steel-shattering might of these guns initiated the greatest, and last, developmental stage in the history of the ship-killing ship.

CHAPTER 14

DREADNOUGHT AND U-BOAT

T he great Western arms race and the revolution in the technology of firepower went hand in hand. Competition among
the great powers fueled the drive for research, development, and
constant improvement in armaments; constant improvement in armaments, conversely, amplified that competition, with each new
weapon fairly demanding an immediate response from the other
powers whose weaponry had just been rendered obsolete. And not
only in one area of military tech, but in many: small arms ammunition, rifles, machine guns, explosive compounds, artillery.
The cumulative effect of this inescapable cycle of development-
and-rearmament was to consume vast—and constantly growing—
quantities of resources and cash at a time when the nation-states of
the West were investing heavily in popular domestic amenities—
infrastructure, public education, and social welfare programs
aimed at placating the increasingly vocal working class. In that
context, the arms race was an onerous burden to bear, but one that
could not be casually tossed aside without existential risk.

In that hypercompetitive environment, the impact of navies
was greater than that of land forces. Navies had more permanence
than armies, and they were costlier, hence the political stakes were
higher. Large armies, for example, could be easily reduced in size to
save costs, but a commitment to building more—or more modern,
or larger and more powerful—warships was a long-term one. A

larger army, within reasonable bounds, could always be justified, at home and abroad, as a self-defense measure; large navies, with powerful capital ships, implied either an ambitious foreign policy or imperialistic designs or both. Building up a modern navy looked like a more aggressive act than building an army. And though capital ships were no longer ornamented like royal palaces, they were still prestige items just as much as they had been in the sixteenth century. Warships were visible tokens of a nation's power, and mobile, too, able to display the state's military might far away from home waters. There was no better way to signal interest in establishing a colony, or in getting involved in a diplomatic dispute, than to send a squadron of battleships or cruisers to a disputed region. Warships were visible at home, too, as objects of veneration, and ordinary folks could take nationalistic pride in seeing a great steel, oceangoing behemoth flying the banner of their country.

The five decades that began with the anticlimactic *Monitor* versus *Virginia* fight at Hampton Roads in 1862 were a period of continual innovation in the technology of warfare at sea. The differences—the superficial, outward differences at a minimum—between a capital ship in 1800 and another in 1850 were minimal, and extended mostly to propulsion and armament. But the differences between that 1850 ship and its analog from 1900 were so vast that a sailor would be hard-pressed to find any parallels at all between the two vessels. To the untrained eye, a screw frigate looked very much like a sailing frigate of Nelson's day, but a predreadnought from the turn of the century would seem like something that had emerged from the pages of a Jules Verne novel.

No naval officer would have suggested after 1865 that a wooden warship was anything other than a relic. True, most navies still had a few sailing warships in service, and wooden-hulled, screw-propeller-driven warships made up a preponderance of vessels in most navies worldwide until the 1870s. It would be a while before that last generation of wooden ships, outmoded though they were, would be cycled out of service and replaced by more modern designs. Still, that was the goal. The lessons taught by the ironclads in the American Civil War—like the homemade, mediocre iron-clad ram *Virginia* defeating an entire Federal naval squadron on its own, or the two big guns of the turreted monitor *Weehawken* crippling the Confederate ironclad ram *Atlanta* with only half a dozen shots—could not be dismissed or ignored.

The armored warship was here to stay. The American experience in the Civil War, especially the performance of the late *Monitor* models, had made that clear. European naval officers were so impressed by the performance of the monitors that they soon adopted the type for riverine squadrons and for harbor defense. But the great fleets were intended to fight at sea, not in narrow waters, and so monitors could never aspire to be anything more than ancillary vessels. The next generation of European capital ships, then, consisted mostly of vessels more like Britain's iron-hulled *Warrior* than the American *Monitor*: iron-hulled screw ships, armored, carrying modest numbers of powerful guns mounted on deck, not in turrets. Ships, in other words, that looked like ships.

There was one matter on which the American Civil War offered absolutely no guidance whatsoever: tactics. How would such warships actually fight in groups? There were no true fleet actions in the Civil War. Only the Federal naval assaults on New Orleans (1862) and Mobile Bay (1864) even vaguely resembled fleet battles, in that the Confederates managed to cobble together groups of vessels that might generously be called naval squadrons, and in both cases these impromptu squadrons were quickly and easily overwhelmed by superior Federal strength. So, what would an action like, say, Trafalgar look like if most of the ships were like *Warrior* or the French ironclad frigate *Gloire*? And if all the ships were heavily armored, rendering them shell-proof, how could one side hope to damage the other, let alone prevail in a decisive way?

One answer, not wholly satisfactory, came from the Adriatic. In the tumultuous summer of 1866, as Prussian armies marched to an unexpected victory over Austria, the nascent Kingdom of Italy attempted to wrest control of Venice from its Habsburg overlords. The Italian fleet swept up the Adriatic to support amphibious operations against the fortified island of Lissa (present-day Vis, Croatia); a hastily assembled Austrian fleet moved to confront it. The Italians, surprisingly, had the advantage both in numbers and in technology: their fleet included no fewer than a dozen modern ironclad warships—built in Italian, French, American, and British shipyards—armed with modern rifled guns, supplemented by seventeen unarmored warships. The Austrian fleet was smaller— seven ironclads, eleven wooden warships—and at a distinct disadvantage in the number and size of their guns. But the Austrians had in Wilhelm von Tegetthoff one of the most astute naval tacticians of the age, and that was more than enough to compensate for the Austrian fleet's physical deficiencies.

Lissa (20 July 1866) was a confusing swirl of a clash, not the neatly ordered passing of line-ahead formations that was still taught as the ideal sea battle. Tegetthoff hurried to close with the enemy quickly, to deny the Italians the chance to pummel the Austrians with their superior guns from a longer range; the Italians, for their part, were disordered and unprepared. The battle devolved into a bewildering series of ship-on-ship actions, more akin to chaotic sea battles of the grand fleets in the century before line ahead became the fashion. From a tactician's point of view, there were few lessons to be derived from the battle. Italian superiority in guns and armor did not win the day; superior technology did not equal a clear-cut advantage. It almost appeared as if a battle between fleets of ironclads, much like the duel between *Monitor* and *Virginia* four years earlier, would conclude as an anticlimactic draw, as even the biggest guns afloat proved to be incapable of effecting a decision. For all the noise and smoke and fury, for all the shots fired in the engagement, only two ships—both of them Italian—were sunk in the battle.

One episode at Lissa stood out to contemporary observers as being instructive. In European naval circles, there lingered a strong conviction that, as armor reduced the effectiveness of big naval cannon, ramming might be the only way to sink a heavily armored warship. The example of *Virginia* ramming and sinking

Cumberland in 1862 bolstered this suspicion, regardless of all the other failed Confederate attempts at ramming Federal warships during the Civil War. Most European ironclads, including those at Lissa, were equipped with heavily reinforced rams built into their prows, just below the waterline. Both of the Italian ships lost at Lissa were victims of ramming. Tegetthoff's flagship, *Erzherzog Ferdinand Max*, rammed the Italian ironclad *Palestro* repeatedly, setting it afire and ultimately causing it to explode and sink. More dramatically, *Erzherzog Ferdinand Max* struck the American-built ironclad *Re d'Italia* square on its port side, ripping a hole eighteen feet wide beneath the Italian ship's waterline. *Re d'Italia* reeled from the impact, and when Tegetthoff's flagship reversed engines and backed off, *Re d'Italia* rolled back on its port beam. A torrent of seawater rushed into the huge gash made by the Austrian ram, and in less than ten minutes *Re d'Italia* went to the bottom with nearly all hands.

The clash at Lissa fueled a renewed interest in rams. For the next two decades, rams remained a common feature in warship architecture. But navies and shipbuilders did not lose faith in the big guns, and the fast pace of innovation in artillery between 1870 and 1900 would justify that faith.

Overall, the evolutionary arc of the Western battleship from the time of Lissa to the First World War was a radical one. Until well into the 1870s, though, Western navies were reluctant to dispose of some of the basic elements of warship design that dated back to the first days of the ship-killing ship. One of those elements was the presence of masts and sails. Most American ironclads of the Civil War era were outliers here, with no sailing rigs at all, but for oceangoing vessels the venerable three-masted configuration was remarkably persistent elsewhere. Sail power, now an auxiliary to steam and not the other way around, did have the practical advantage of saving fuel on long voyages, but for the most part sailing rigs held on because of plain, unvarnished conservatism. Those who commanded fleets and made naval policy in the 1860s and 1870s came from the last generation of pre-steam sailors, to whom steam power was still a novelty, not to be entirely trusted. But soon that generation would fade away, and in their place came naval officers who had been trained from the start to be engineers as well as sailors. Masts were still a common feature in battleship design and would be until after the First World War, because they did fill practical roles: observation and communication. But spars, and sails, and the intricate web of standing and running rigging that went along with sail power—those were all gone shortly after 1880.

Broadside armament was the next design feature to recede into the past, but much more gradually. The reason for the persistence of broadside guns was part practical, part traditional. Guns had been placed in broadside since the days when war-carracks ruled the European Atlantic, because broadside mounting allowed for the largest possible armament. Line-ahead tactics, still the ideal, favored the broadside. Gun turrets like those on the *Monitor* allowed for only a very limited armament. More was better when it came to naval artillery, and simpler was better, too; the mechanisms for rotating turrets promised the additional disadvantage of potential breakdowns in combat. Besides, broadside mounting went hand in hand with sailing rigs. Turrets did not function at their best when their field of fire was occluded by masts and partly netted in with rigging.

That didn't stop naval architects from trying to combine turrets with sailing rigs, but the results were less than ideal. One especially notorious incident involved the British warship HMS *Captain*, an otherwise conventional iron-built screw steamer. The ship's designer, Cowper Phipps Coles, added two gun turrets of his own design to *Captain*'s main deck, but retained a full ship-rig on three masts. *Captain*'s freeboard was quite low but its center of gravity was high, meaning that in heavy seas the ship would be highly unstable. Only five months after *Captain* was commissioned (April 1870), it capsized and sank in a violent storm off Cape Finisterre on the Spanish coast, taking Cowper Coles and most of the crew with it. Turrets and sail power, apparently, made for a dangerous combination.

While sail power remained popular in commercial vessels, it faded away rapidly after the *Captain* incident, but *Captain's* fate did not dampen enthusiasm for armored turrets. Oddly, the legacy of the battle of Lissa helped to promote turrets. If ramming were to be the preferred offensive tactic in battle at sea, then forward-firing guns were at least as important as guns mounted in broadside. Two distinct variations of turret emerged: barbette turrets, in which the guns sat on a rotating platform and fired over an open-topped armored enclosure; and true turrets like those on most American monitors, which were fully enclosed circular structures. Either way, the new fashion was to eliminate or reduce broadside guns and cluster the main armament, the big guns, in a central "citadel" aligned along the ship's center axis. The world's first mastless battleship, HMS *Thunderer* (launched 1872, completed 1877) led the way, and by 1880 the turreted, armored, steam-only battleship had become the European norm.

THE SIZE AND power of the big naval guns was increasing rapidly, so rapidly that armor could barely keep pace. The French Paixhans guns had given way to the powerful shell guns and rifled muzzleloaders of the 1850s, which were in turn outperformed and replaced by the big rifled Armstrong guns of the 1860s. The British held on to their reliable Armstrong muzzleloaders well into the 1870s, until the explosion of an Armstrong aboard HMS *Thunderer* in 1879 convinced them otherwise. The French and the Germans were by then already relying on the huge cast-steel breechloaders manufactured by Schneider and Krupp, and in the 1880s such guns became standard equipment on Western capital ships.

The invention of new propellants in that same decade, cordite in particular, had even greater significance for naval warfare than it did for field artillery. Cordite generated much higher velocities than black powder, and resulted in flatter trajectories, greater range, and greater penetrating power, even against iron and steel armor. Then came the first armor-piercing projectiles: at first, solid elongated shot, called bolts, with "chilled" or hardened points; later came hardened shells with modest bursting charges, designed to penetrate armor and *then* burst inside the target. Combined with the power of cordite, the new armor-piercing ammunition was devastatingly effective, and by the end of the century such projectiles could smash through just about any kind of armor in use at the time.

The new naval ordnance could fire faster, too, paralleling developments in field artillery. Regardless of size, artillery was artillery, and the rapid succession of patents and mechanisms for breech-loading artillery thoroughly revamped naval guns, too. Obturating, semiautomatic breech mechanisms, using self-contained cased ammunition—just like in field artillery—increased the rate of fire dramatically. Improvements in steel casting allowed for the construction of bigger and bigger guns, capable of tolerating heavier explosive charges. By the end of the 1880s, a 6-inch naval gun, a caliber once considered huge, was now a smaller gun.

The designers of naval armor struggled to keep up. The 4.5-inch wrought iron plate that had made the French floating batteries invincible at Kinburn during the Crimean War in 1855 was pathetically inadequate ten years later. Nine-inch-thick wrought iron plate was the armor norm for capital ships in 1868, 12-inch in 1871, 14-inch in 1875. Soon the armor had become so thick as to be almost unworkable. The British battleship *Inflexible* (1876) was girded with a belt of 24-inch-thick iron armor at the waterline, composed of two 12-inch belts sandwiching layers of teak, and single-layer iron armor plate of 22-inch thickness came into use by 1880. It was almost a pointless exercise, for the biggest naval guns of the period (in one test case, a 17.7-inch caliber rifle) could perforate 22-inch iron plate and shatter 22-inch steel plate. Guns, in short, were beating armor.

Eventually that would change. New construction methods and treatments made it possible to armor a ship without resorting to iron plates of ridiculous thicknesses. Armor plate got progressively stronger: compound armor, first developed by two British firms at Sheffield, in which steel plate was welded atop iron plate; and oil-tempered steel and 5 percent nickel steel, both developed by the Schneider works in France in the early 1880s. The use of cast-steel and hardened cast-steel artillery projectiles temporarily rendered most armor useless by the end of the 1880s. But in 1891 H. A. Harvey, an American inventor from Newark, New Jersey, came up with a process of carburizing steel armor, a manufacturing method that created a superhardened, high carbon "face" on the steel plate. The final product was far more resistant to penetration by steel projectiles. For three years or so, "Harveyized" armor reigned supreme, until it too was rendered obsolete by a series of discoveries made by engineers at the Krupp works, discoveries that collectively created a degree of face hardening in nickel-chrome steel that easily outperformed the Harveyized armor. The Krupp process, which was soon widely imitated internationally, would remain the international standard for battleship armor well past the end of the Great War.

Between advances in metallurgy and in firepower, the pace of innovation in naval armaments was so rapid that it became impossible for any of the world's major navies to keep up after 1880. Battleships were already obsolescing as soon as they were laid down. It was only natural that naval officers, and their political bosses, would want to have the best technology at their disposal, and in the context of the 1880s and 1890s that meant the biggest battleships with the most powerful guns and the most resilient armor—and the largest number of those ships, too. But the deepening international rivalries that bedeviled the European state system in the age of Otto von Bismarck demanded more, turning the desire to adopt the newest and best naval technology into a compulsion, and then into a strategic imperative. For Britain in particular, committed to the so-called two-fleet standard—meaning that Britain would endeavor to maintain a fleet that was at least as large as the next two largest fleets combined—the tyranny of modernization was truly onerous. Before, the Admiralty had only to worry about the French and a handful of much smaller European navies, but after 1870 the emergence (or re-emergence) of so many powerful fleets—German, Italian, Russian, Austro-Hungarian, American, and French—gave much cause for alarm. Germany in particular. The formal unification of Imperial Germany in 1871 created, in an instant, Europe's newest superpower, with an industrial capacity that rivaled or surpassed Britain's—and soon, very soon, with a will to challenge Britain's self-proclaimed command of the seas.

That kind of arms race, far more compressed, urgent, and expensive than any that had preceded it, was barely sustainable for great or wealthy powers like Britain or France or Germany. For other, smaller states, with fewer resources and more modest means, it was absolutely impossible to keep up. Spain, the Netherlands, Denmark, Sweden—all these states once had first-class fleets. The Dutch still retained a respectable naval force, necessary because of their extensive colonial possessions in Asia, but it was hardly comparable to the Dutch fleet that had once ruled northern European waters in the seventeenth century. Denmark kept up a surprisingly high-quality fleet as late as 1864, when its navy managed to keep the combined sea forces of Prussia and Austria at bay, but the small state had neither the industry to build great battleships nor the wherewithal to purchase them abroad; nor, for that matter, did it have much use for a big fleet.

Not all experts believed that a big fleet of big ships was necessary. In fact, a growing number of younger naval officers were coming to the conclusion that the exclusive focus on big-gunned capital ships was a mistake. The big ships were lumbering beasts, after all, and their sluggishness was a weakness that could possibly be exploited by smaller, faster, and far cheaper vessels. None other than the great Paixhans himself had envisioned a fleet of small, fast gunboats carrying a small number of big guns. Maybe his idea wasn't quite so practical in the days of the heavily armored giants, but a weapon that made its debut in the 1870s gave some real substance to the notion of a small-boat navy.

WE THINK OF torpedoes as swift-moving underwater bombs, usually launched from a submarine at periscope depth, slicing almost gracefully through the water toward an unsuspecting ship, but until the end of the 1860s that wasn't what the term meant. Robert Fulton, of early steamboat fame, first used the term, and soon *torpedo* was applied to any underwater explosive device, including what today we would call naval mines. Underwater mines had existed for quite some time, and they are known to have been used on a few rare occasions since the seventeenth century, if not earlier. But though the prospect of sinking ships stealthily and remotely was an attractive one, the engineering problems involved were daunting. Often, naval officers did not regard them—understandably—with anything other than revulsion and horror, as an underhanded and dishonest way of fighting a war. Still, mines saw some limited use, mostly as an act of desperation. Americans used mines as a means of defending their harbors from British invasion during the War of 1812; Russians used them to protect the Gulf of Finland from the Anglo-French fleet during the Crimean War. In the American Civil War, torpedoes flourished. It was the Confederacy, lacking conventional naval forces, that relied on torpedoes and mines as part of its defensive naval strategy to slow Federal advances into the South's larger harbors—and even to go on the offensive.

In this, the Confederates had some notable success. Underwater mines did indeed hamper Federal operations in narrow waters, and though they did not stop the inexorable advance of Northern forces, they certainly exacted a toll in tonnage and lives. In one of the most dramatic moments of the war, the monitor USS *Tecumseh* hit a Confederate mine and sank like a stone as it rushed into Mobile Bay at the head of the Federal naval assault there in August 1864—the very thing that prompted the Federal admiral commanding, David Farragut, to (perhaps apocryphally) give the order, "Damn the torpedoes! Full speed ahead!"

But the torpedo did not have to be either stationary or defensive. Its most impressive early use was as a ship-mounted weapon. In the American Civil War, the Confederate navy had some success with "spar torpedoes": a percussion-fused torpedo fixed on the end of a long pole, protruding from the bow of a small boat so that it could be rammed into an unsuspecting enemy vessel at night. Of course, the Union adopted these techniques, too. In October 1864, a young US naval lieutenant named William B. Cushing sank the troublesome Confederate river ironclad CSS *Albemarle* using a spar torpedo affixed to a steam-powered launch. Occasionally effective, spar torpedoes were dangerous to deploy, because when they exploded—*if* they exploded—close to their crews, spar torpedoes could be just as damaging to friend as to foe. Lieutenant Cushing's launch sank when it rammed the *Albemarle*, and only part of its crew survived. But the concept persisted. In 1877, the *Rândunica*, a British-built torpedo boat in the Romanian navy, attacked and sank an Ottoman monitor with a spar torpedo.

A solution to the obvious shortcomings of the spar torpedo was already in the works, thanks to the Austrian navy: a self-propelled or "locomotive" marine torpedo. In 1866, a collaborative effort between Giovanni Luppis, a Croatian-born officer in the Habsburg navy, and the British engineer Robert Whitehead paid off. The first *Minenschiff* (mine ship) was disappointingly erratic, but Whitehead tweaked it until it worked. Whitehead's improved torpedo was driven by compressed air and incorporated a hydrostatic valve that allowed it to run below the surface at a steady depth. The first Whitehead-Luppis torpedo could push a warhead loaded with eighteen pounds of dynamite at approximately six knots for a few hundred yards. The performance steadily improved over the next few years. By the 1880s, the self-propelled torpedo was no longer a novelty, but a vital addition to the European naval arsenal, and soon Whitehead's factory in Britain was struggling to keep up with the orders that came in from all over Europe. The torpedo had become a truly marvelous weapon by the end of the century: sixteen feet long, weighing half a ton, ranging nearly a kilometer at speeds as high as thirty knots. More conventional engines replaced the compressed air, and gyroscopic steering devices (after 1898) ensured stability and accuracy.

Whitehead's invention quickly proved its worth. First used in combat in 1877, the torpedo claimed its first victim the following year, during the Russo-Turkish War, when the Russian warship *Velikiy Knyaz Konstantin* sank the Ottoman steamer *Intibah*.

European navies were quick to embrace the new technology. To some, it was a godsend. The iconoclastic naval experts of the French school of thought known as *Jeune École* (Young School) believed that the future of warfare at sea belonged to fast, highly maneuverable craft and not to the heavyweight battleship. Paixhans's dream of a fleet of small gunboats was laughably quaint now; armor and the superguns of the later nineteenth century made it so. But the locomotive torpedo . . . that would be the equalizer. All ships were vulnerable to sinking by torpedo, and unlike heavy naval artillery, torpedoes did not require a large, stable firing platform. France's navy had been of little use when the Second Empire succumbed to the German invasion of 1870–1871, and Germany—not yet a major naval power—was the principal threat to French security. So the kind of fleet that the *Jeune École* wanted actually made sense, doubly so in cash-strapped postwar France.

The French navy, and then the British, introduced the first torpedo boats in the late 1870s. The early torpedo boats were very small, designed to be carried aboard battleships and used only for stealth attacks in sheltered waters. But in the 1880s there emerged a much more substantial species of torpedo attack craft: larger, ocean-going boats, capable of zipping about at speeds in excess of twenty knots and carrying multiple torpedo launch tubes in their bows.

The French embraced the torpedo boat enthusiastically. The British navy was more reticent, many of its officers seeing in the tiny warships a desperate measure for inferior nations. Eventually, though, the British followed the example of their cross-Channel rivals and made torpedo boats a regular part of their fleet. All the major navies adopted them, and most of the minor navies, too. For states like Denmark and the Netherlands, nations with strong maritime traditions but limited resources and no illusions about their ranking in the world, the torpedo boat offered strategic options that hadn't existed before. Big-gunned battleships were beyond the reach of the smaller states, but those same states could turn out dozens of fast torpedo boats in no time at all, each of them capable of taking down a battleship in the right circumstances. Such craft were well suited to coastal and harbor defense. They might not be able to defeat a hostile battleship fleet, or even hold it off indefinitely, but they could sting in a way that would make a potential aggressor think twice. In an age in which technology was—because of its expense—restricting military power to a smaller and smaller circle of nations, the torpedo boat was one of the very few new weapons that actually favored the smaller and weaker.

Naval officers actually feared the torpedo boat, and rightly so, for it threatened the supremacy of the battleship, and battleships were big investments. Even the fastest battleship could not outrun a marine torpedo. The torpedo boat demanded a response, and a Spanish naval officer, Fernando Villaamil, provided one. With the approval of his superiors in Madrid, Villaamil designed a special warship for the purpose of guarding against, and hunting down, torpedo boats. His ship, the *Destructor* (1887), was fast and sleek, able to get to nearly twenty-three knots, but heavily armed for its size. Its armament—a 90mm-caliber breechloader, plus a handful of quick-firing 57mm and 37mm guns—could in no sense compete with larger warships, but then *Destructor* wasn't designed for that. The quick-firing guns, plus the two torpedo tubes built into the bow, were more than capable of making short work of lightly built torpedo boats. Villaamil dubbed his creation a "torpedo-boat destroyer." It proved to be a valuable warship in its own right, superior in most ways to the torpedo boat and yet able to fulfill most of the same functions. The torpedo-boat destroyer, known by 1914 simply as a destroyer, would become the workhorse of even the largest fleets.

The broadside, wooden ship of the line had evolved into the armored battleship with its main armament housed in center-line turrets. The brigs, sloops, and other coastal craft of the age of sail were reincarnated as the torpedo boat and the destroyer. What about the middling sort of warships, the frigates, which had proven themselves more valuable in day-to-day naval operations than the biggest three-deckers? They evolved, too. Oddly, frigates persisted in their old form—wooden-hulled, three-masted, ship-rigged—longer than any other kind of Western warship. They were hopelessly anachronistic by the 1880s, though, and soon they re-emerged as a new class: the armored battlecruiser. In form, they looked like mini-battleships, with a turreted main armament and smaller, quick-firing guns mounted in broadside, armored heavily enough to protect against all but the largest naval guns of the 1880s and 1890s, rifled guns of 12-inch bore and larger. The battlecruisers were not designed to engage in one-on-one combat with true battleships, nor in fleet actions against them. Their main defense against heavier enemies was speed. Just like the frigates of the previous century, their forte was, well, "cruising": long-range, independent missions, patrolling thousands of miles away from home, reserving the battleships—as true ships of the line—for fleet actions and the like. For a navy on a budget, like that of the United States, the battlecruiser was an adequate and much less expensive substitute for the battleship.

FOR ALL THE vast, sweeping changes that naval technology went through in the half-century after the first ironclads, Western navies did not really know what their warships, or their weapons, could do. Extensive testing could show how strong armor was, or what kind of damage a cordite-powered armor-piercing shell could do to the hull of an enemy battleship, but not what would actually happen in combat. Naval experts could make educated guesses, based on largely outdated experience and a theoretical understanding of modern weapons and ship construction. They could guess at how turreted battleships would function in a fleet action, or if the line-ahead formation was even still practical given the drastically different technology of the Belle Époque. The widespread popular faith in science that was characteristic of the age didn't make up for the fact that no one really knew how the steel sea monsters would behave once let loose against one another.

And that was because, for all the ferocity and strutting nationalism and posturing of the naval arms race, there was very little actual naval combat between Lissa in 1866 and the Russo-Japanese War of 1904–1905. What little there was, Western naval observers watched with unwavering intensity, trying to wring every last ounce of meaning from what they saw. And no pat, easily digestible lessons were forthcoming. In September 1894, a modern Japanese fleet trounced a badly outdated Chinese fleet in the battle of the Yalu River, but there were no useful lessons to be derived from the clash; the disparity in quality between the two fleets was too great. And though the US Navy played a critical role in the American victory over Spain in 1898, the Spanish-American War at sea offered little conclusive evidence about the implications of the new technology.

When Russia and Japan went to war in 1904, though, heads turned. Some European observers dismissed the war, and its combatants, out of hand: the Russians because of their poor leadership, morale, and organization; the Japanese for reasons that mostly boiled down to overt racism. But both were well equipped with the latest generation of battleships, battlecruisers, destroyers, and torpedo boats, and so the rest of the West sat up and paid close attention.

What the war revealed was quite surprising. Japanese torpedo attacks on Russian ships at anchor were disappointing. In the opening engagement of the war, the Japanese surprise night attack on the Russian fleet at Port Arthur (8–9 February 1904), Japanese destroyers scored three hits out of sixteen torpedoes launched, damaging two battleships and one protected cruiser but not sinking anything.

But what European naval observers really wanted to see was how the new technology affected the big battle fleets, and here they were not disappointed. On 10 August 1904, the Russian and Japanese navies clashed in the inconclusive Battle of the Yellow Sea, an all-out slugging match between the two main fleets ranged in line-ahead formation. The battle uncovered some unexpected truths about modern naval guns. The medium-sized, quick-firing guns (around 6-inch caliber), found in large numbers on the capital ships, did virtually no damage to warships on either side. Only the large main guns of the bigger battleships, the 12-inchers, did any real damage. Even then, long-range gunnery proved, counter-intuitively, to be more effective than short-range attacks. At longer ranges, the large-caliber shells plunged downward onto their targets, hitting the relatively unprotected decks, while at shorter ranges the trajectories were flatter, and shells tended to hit the heavily armored sides. The catastrophically decisive battle of the Tsushima Strait (27–28 May 1905), in which Japanese admiral Togo Heihachiro's ships utterly destroyed the Russian Baltic Fleet, confirmed the lessons of the Yellow Sea battle, but with more drama. The Japanese proved their superiority in all sorts of ways: they had better rangefinders, their gunners were better trained, their armor-piercing, high-explosive shells were of a higher quality. And as at the Yellow Sea, the secondary guns proved themselves to be utterly useless in a fleet action.

In the high-stakes world of naval affairs, these lessons reverberated like a gunshot. It no longer made sense to stuff battleships indiscriminately with guns of several calibers. Only the big guns mattered. Speed mattered, too, because one of Togo's great advantages at Tsushima was that his battleships were markedly faster than the tsar's.

For the British in particular there was no time to waste. In the eyes of the Admiralty—and in the eyes of the public, too—the arms race was a life-and-death matter, and the greatest threat to Britain's security was that emanating from the new, powerful German Empire and its erratic leader, Kaiser Wilhelm II. The Russo-Japanese conflict highlighted the dangers of falling behind in technology. With the support and guidance of Admiral Sir John "Jacky" Fisher, a new kind of battleship took shape in the royal dockyards at Plymouth, its characteristics revised in accordance with the lessons taught by the battles of the Yellow Sea and Tsushima Strait. Jacky Fisher's ship, to the inexpert eye, didn't look that much different from the battleships of the previous generation—of course, in the world of battleship design, the "previous generation" was only five years before. The new ship would carry a main armament of 12-inch guns only, mounted in double turrets, meaning two guns per turret. Fisher's engineers had determined that a modern battleship needed to mount at least eight big guns; the new ship would have ten, placed in five armored turrets.* The secondary armament was mostly eliminated, but not entirely; a couple dozen quick-firing guns were kept aboard to defend the ship against torpedo boats. Girding the hull was a belt of steel armor eleven inches thick; twelve-inch armor protected the turrets. Even the decks were armored.

And that was just the beginning, just the external features. Inside, too, the new ship was a significant departure. Fisher's battleship took advantage of another new development in marine engineering. All battleships of the time carried large reciprocating steam turbine engines as their power plants. Reciprocating engines powerful enough to push a hulking battleship through the water had to be gigantic, and the resulting strains on engine and hull alike were barely tolerable. On long-distance cruises they frequently broke down, so prudent skippers avoided running their ships at full speed for more than very short sprints. Even Togo, at Tsushima Strait, warned his captains not to exceed the modest speed of 15 knots as they steamed into battle.

But recently, the Royal Navy had begun to experiment with a new compound steam turbine devised by engineer and entrepreneur

---

*The minimal number of guns was determined by the aiming process. Even with sophisticated rangefinders, direct hits on the first shot were rare, and it was up to fire-control officers—usually stationed as high as possible in the battleship's superstructure, very often in an enclosed position atop a mast— to "correct" the gunners' aim. They did this by looking for the splashes in the water surrounding the targeted vessel. If the splashes fell short, then the gunners would be instructed to increase their elevation; if they went long, to decrease elevation. It was ideal when the shots "straddled" the target, meaning that they either fell on both sides or made a direct hit. But it was taken as a given that it was only possible to make accurate adjustments to long-range fire if the big guns were fired in salvos of four. So eight guns meant that four could be used for finding the target, while the other four were being readied and loaded.

Charles Parsons in 1884. On smaller ships, the Parsons turbine performed flawlessly: the steamer *Turbinia* (1897) easily cruised at 34 knots, and the turbine-driven destroyer *Viper* (1899) achieved a world record speed of 36.6 knots. Soon the Parsons turbine was adapted to larger vessels, most famously the doomed Cunard liner RMS *Lusitania*, which could make 25 knots—almost unimaginable for such a bulky ship.

Fisher adapted the Parsons engine—or, rather, four Parsons engines, plus eighteen boilers—to his new battleship. There were also auxiliary steam and diesel engines to power the ship's electrical systems (which in turn powered hoists, pumps, winches, lighting, and telephones). Topping it all was an integrated fire-control system, which allowed observers to transmit range and aiming information to each of the turrets by voice pipes. It's difficult to conjure up a starker contrast between Fisher's battleship, state of the art when it launched in 1906, and a comparable ship from a century earlier, like Nelson's *Victory*. Outside of the fact that both were naval vessels built around artillery, there was hardly a single point of similarity; the two technologies they represented were jarringly unrelated. To a navy man, the differences between Fisher's battleship and its immediate contemporaries were pretty big ones, too, though of course on a completely different order of magnitude.

A few months after its launching in February 1906, Fisher's project was ready for sea, and it was commissioned with the name HMS *Dreadnought*. *Dreadnought*'s performance was nothing short of extraordinary. In its first sea trials, *Dreadnought* clocked a jaw-dropping 21 knots—impressive indeed, given the ship's imposing size, heavy armor, and heavy armament. But even more important, this was a sustainable speed. An earlier battleship with conventional reciprocating steam engines, like Togo's flagship *Mikasa* (1902), could get up to 18 knots, but it wouldn't be able to maintain that speed for very long for fear of breakdown or permanent damage. With the more resilient Parsons turbines, *Dreadnought* could travel at high speed for days without worry of engine failure. On one voyage early in its career, *Dreadnought* covered seven

The revolution in battleship design:
Plate 22a. HMS *Dreadnought* (1906), the ship that started it all.
Image: NH 61017 courtesy of the Naval History & Heritage Command.
Plate 22b. USS *Pennsylvania* (BB-38), an American superdreadnought launched in 1915. Note the super-firing turrets.
Image: NH 63562 courtesy of the Naval History & Heritage Command.

thousand miles nonstop, at an average speed of 17.5 knots, without ever experiencing engine trouble.

Fast, powerful, so heavily armored that it could resist the most powerful artillery of its day, with every system aboard more sophisticated than anything that could be found in any of its contemporaries, *Dreadnought* was truly revolutionary. From the moment it launched, all other battleships became instantly obsolete. Soon its name would find its way into general usage, referring to the new apex predator of the seas, and to the era that brought it forth.

All the other maritime powers took note, took a deep breath, and the race began anew.

THE TURBINE-POWERED SUPER-BATTLESHIP set a new standard for capital ships, but it also kicked the naval arms race into a new, more dangerous, costlier phase. Germany, at a critical moment in its bid for naval power and prestige, had just been outmatched at sea, just as France had stolen a leap forward with the Balle M cartridge, the Lebel rifle, and the Mle 1897 field gun. Germany would react, predictably, because it *had* to; the logic of arms races, of nationalistic pride and militarism, required that it do so, without hesitation and without much mindfulness about the price tag. So, too, would any nation that cared about its military standing in the community of Western nations. All—France, Italy, Austria-Hungary, Russia, the United States, Japan—would follow Britain's lead, but the race to watch was that between Britain and the Kaiser.

The Germans went to great lengths to make sure that they could build ships even more redoubtable than *Dreadnought*. Their first step was to build new dry docks, larger than those of their British competitors, to accommodate ships larger than anything that had yet been launched. They broadened the Kiel Canal, so those future giant dreadnoughts could pass quickly back and forth from the North Sea to the Baltic without having to pass through Danish territorial waters. And by 1908, when the first German dreadnoughts were laid down, the Kaiser's navy had vowed to exceed British tonnage in capital ships in about a decade. This was a serious threat to

Britain's vaunted, self-proclaimed mastery of the seas, and not least because the Germans didn't even have to match the British ship-for-ship to achieve numerical supremacy. Britain's imperial obligations meant that the Royal Navy had to disperse its ships all over the globe, while the Germans only had to focus theirs on the North and Baltic Seas, meaning that the Royal Navy would have to be at least as large as the German fleet in local waters *plus* whatever forces its presence elsewhere in the world demanded.

These were prospects that raised the alarm not only in the Admiralty, but also with the British public in general, who demanded—regardless of party sympathies—the expansion of the fleet so as to surpass Germany once again. At this, Britain did in fact succeed: in 1914, the Royal Navy had twenty dreadnoughts and nine battle-cruisers; Germany had fourteen and four, respectively. But numbers were only one part of the renewed arms race. The dreadnought race was also a matter of technological one-upmanship, with each new subgeneration of dreadnought, separated from each other by only a year or two, introducing some new or improved feature. Fire-control systems, already advanced on the original *Dreadnought*, became entirely electrified, so the fire-control officer could transmit targeting information to all turrets simultaneously. Most of the upgrades, though, involved armor, armament, and size. Armor belts on hull and turrets grew in thickness. Twelve- and 14-inch guns were the standard main armament, but the numbers and the positioning changed. The US Navy—which followed, surprisingly, closest on Britain's heels with its *South Carolina*–class dreadnoughts—introduced superfiring turrets, an arrangement in which a second turret would be mounted just above and just behind a deck-mounted turret, doubling the armament on that part of the deck with only a small additional investment in real estate.*

---

*Of all the dreadnought-type battleships laid down between 1906 and the Washington Naval Treaty a decade and a half later, only one still exists today: the American *New York*–class battleship USS *Texas* (BB-35), launched in 1912, now a museum ship near Houston, Texas.

Only a few years after *Dreadnought* first went to sea, this new species of amped-up dreadnought, the so-called superdreadnought, set an even higher standard for capital ships. Superdreadnoughts took their place at the head of fleets all over the world; even Brazil and Argentina had them, purchased from shipyards in the United States and Britain. As a class, they featured larger guns—14- and even 16-inch guns—and more of them, heavier armor, and greater bulk. The British *Orion*-class of superdreadnoughts, dating from 1910, were significantly bulkier than *Dreadnought* and could boast a weight of broadside—the collective weight of projectiles that could be fired simultaneously—twice that of its predecessor. This was how fast, and how manically, the naval arms race moved: only about five years after *Dreadnought* took to the seas and made all other battleships irrelevant, *Dreadnought* itself was obsolete.

The naval arms race extended to cruisers, too. The Russo-Japanese War had proven that anything smaller than a full-sized battleship had no business fighting in the line of battle. Building fleets of small battleships, with smaller guns and reduced armor, was a pointless endeavor unless they possessed some other virtue to compensate for their weaknesses in combat—like, for example, speed. There was little use, as Admiral Fisher himself pointed out, for a warship that could neither fight nor run away, and most cruisers at the beginning of the twentieth century could do neither. Hence a new class of battlecruiser, developed post-Tsushima by the British, German, and Japanese navies. The new battlecruiser was meant to be as powerful as a dreadnought but faster. The power came from dreadnought-sized guns, the speed from the combination of turbine engines and reduced armor.

These vessels—the dreadnought, the superdreadnought, and the battlecruiser—formed the core of the major fleets at the outset of the Great War. The superdreadnought, brand new in 1914, was the physical representation of military and naval might, and individually the most expensive weapon in any nation's arsenal. Like the possession of an overseas empire, dreadnoughts were prestige items. Having a fleet of them was a symbol of power, a badge of membership in the exclusive club of great nations.

For the dreadnought revolution had repercussions that went far beyond naval combat. The undeniable superiority of the dreadnought and its immediate descendants had the effect of restricting access to naval power—not only the unfettered ability to project military might at a distance, as Britain did and Germany aspired to, but even so basic and unambitious a goal as the ability to defend national coastlines and guard against invasion from the sea—to a mere handful of nation-states. The superdreadnought made naval warfare unaffordable for all but the largest, wealthiest, most populous, most industrialized states. But were they worth the investment for those states that could afford them? That's a difficult question to answer, even in retrospect, because the mechanics of an arms race aren't necessarily bound by the logic of the balance sheet. Once an arms race begins, shrinking from it, or choosing to remain aloof from it, are not realistic options for aspiring great powers, because doing so would allow potential enemies and rivals to move forward and create an unbridgeable technology gap—one that could well mean rapid, humiliating defeat in war. Arms races, once begun, tend to justify themselves.

Beyond the undeniable prophylactic value of keeping rival fleets at bay, though, the huge capital ships didn't exactly earn their keep in the First World War. True, sometimes they came in handy in a supporting role, as when they lent their firepower to the Allied amphibious landings at Gallipoli, at the entrance to the Dardanelles, in 1915. But large fleet actions in the old style, the kind of engagement for which the dreadnoughts and superdreadnoughts were intended, were very rare. The largest, and last, of the fleet-on-fleet actions were the battle of Jutland (31 May to 1 June 1916) and the Action of 19 August (19 August 1916). The very magnitude of Jutland alone—with roughly 250 ships engaged—almost compensated for the dearth of fleet battles in the Great War; the British lost some 6,000 sailors and fourteen ships, including three new battlecruisers, while the German fleet lost one battlecruiser, ten smaller or older vessels, and about 2,500 men. Big or not, Jutland could hardly be called decisive, and apart from demonstrating that the more heavily armored, compartmentalized German ships were able to absorb more damage than their British counterparts, it had few lessons to impart. For the most part, the dreadnoughts accomplished very little in the Great War.

THE REAL ACTION, instead, was beneath the surface.

Judged by the attention and resources poured into the great fleets prior to 1914, the First World War at sea should have been a dreadnought war. Instead, though wholly unanticipated, it turned out to be a submarine war. The submarine is another iconic weapon of that conflict, emblematic of what was so horrific and unsettlingly impersonal about the new face of war in the twentieth century. Submarines held a solemn significance for the Allies, especially for Britain and France, because the technology of undersea warfare was directed primarily at them, and they suffered most from it. Germany's practice of unrestricted U-boat warfare was one of the ways in which civilian populations were explicitly targeted, and indeed was nearly the sole cause of American civilian casualties in the war.

Submarine warfare was made possible by a series of innovations in naval architecture that appeared, in rapid succession, in the last few decades before 1914. The idea of making underwater warships, though, was quite old. During the American Revolution, a Yankee inventor named David Bushnell built a one-man, acorn-shaped submarine, which was used in 1776 in an unsuccessful attempt to fasten a bomb to the hull of the British flagship HMS *Eagle* in New York Harbor. Robert Fulton, the American mechanical genius and proponent of steam propulsion, built a slightly larger submersible, the *Nautilus*, testing it successfully on the Seine River near Paris in 1800. Sail-powered while running on the surface, powered by a hand-cranked propeller while submerged, *Nautilus* was promising but slow, achieving a maximum speed of two to three knots underwater. A Bavarian engineer named Wilhelm Bauer built a couple of similar boats for Prussia and Russia in the 1850s. And the American Civil War, that wellspring of novel weapons both revolutionary and ridiculous, predictably birthed more than one submarine. The US Navy formally accepted a French-designed, Philadelphia-built sub, USS *Alligator*, in 1862; the following year, Confederate lawyer turned amateur engineer Horace L. Hunley built his third and most famous submarine, the *H. L. Hunley*.

Each one of these submarines was quite clever, but they could not aspire to be anything more than curiosities. They lacked an effective means of underwater propulsion; they lacked a suitable offensive weapon. Nothing shows this better than the brief and tragic career of Horace Hunley's eponymous submarine. The Confederacy was desperately seeking ways of breaking the Federal naval blockade of its ports, which was slowly strangling the South. The Confederate navy relied mostly on homemade ironclad warships, but the army was willing to try more radical methods—like small cigar-shaped torpedo boats called Davids. The Davids, although they rode low in the water, were surface vessels, but Horace Hunley's boat was actually submersible. Hunley was part of a design team that had built prototype submarines in New Orleans and Mobile, and in 1862 he funded a solo effort. The *Hunley*, made of cast iron, held a crew of six men and two officers, who powered the sub by turning a hand-cranked propeller, giving it a top speed of some four knots. On the night of 17 February 1864, the *Hunley* and its crew attacked the Federal screw sloop USS *Housatonic*, on post just outside Charleston Harbor. Its spar torpedo exploded on contact with the *Housatonic*, blowing a large hole in its hull beneath the waterline and sending the Federal ship to the bottom. The massive explosion, only twenty feet from *Hunley*'s bow, also sank the submarine and likely killed its crew instantaneously. Clearly, contact weapons, like spar torpedoes, were not a good match for a submarine.

Those were the challenges: a form of engine that worked well, or at least worked, underwater, and a weapon that could be used from a distance. Those challenges were met in surprisingly short order, and incrementally—one small step at a time—the modern submersible warship emerged. Propulsion was the most daunting issue. As early as 1863, Siméon Bourgeois and Charles Brun, a French naval officer and engineer respectively, designed and built the *Plongeur* for the French navy. *Plongeur* used a reciprocating engine powered by compressed air to power its screw propeller while cruising beneath the surface. It was a clever idea, but not very practical; *Plongeur* couldn't travel any faster than *Hunley*, and its range without being recharged was a mere five nautical miles. Steam power, the norm for surface vessels, was not really an option; coal-fired boilers needed oxygen and ventilation to function, and hence could not power submersibles.

Or could they? The Reverend George Garrett, an Anglican vicar-cum-engineer, privately built a steam-powered submarine in 1878–1879. Garrett's sub, *Resurgam*, worked around the exhaust issue by making use of reserve hot water tanks. Water heated in *Resurgam*'s boilers while running on the surface retained enough latent heat to power its engines underwater for several hours, albeit at very low speeds. The idea wasn't as far-fetched as it perhaps sounds. The Nordenfelt firm in Sweden, having caught wind of Garrett's sub, built several of their own, along the same principle, at their Stockholm factory in the mid-to-late 1880s. These were serious warships: the larger Nordenfelt submarines, powered by 1,300 hp steam engines, could cruise at fourteen knots on the surface, and underwater at five knots for a distance of twenty miles. More important, Nordenfelt solved the armament dilemma. The Whitehead self-propelled torpedo, now widely available and of proven reliability, seemed to have been made for the submarine. Nordenfelt equipped its first attack submarine with an external torpedo-launching tube, mounted to the bow; later models featured two internal tubes.

The steam engine could work, but it was hardly ideal, and it limited the operational distance of the submarine to the point that it seemed a questionable investment. Even with the Nordenfelt submarines, even with the most careful ventilation, a fair amount of exhaust from burning coal would flood the vessel, rendering it uncomfortable to its crew, at the very least. Submerged running required that fires be extinguished, not a task a submarine commander would relish when faced with the necessity of an emergency dive.

Fortunately there were other options. Working at the same time but independently, Spanish and French engineers had begun to experiment with electric motors in smaller subs. Spanish interest in the submarine abated very quickly, but the French pushed ahead. It helped that the submarine was consonant with prevailing French naval doctrine, heavily influenced by the officers of the *Jeune École* and their predilection for torpedo boats, smaller craft, and stealth. Between 1886 and 1902, French engineers did more to create the modern submarine than anyone else. The sixty-foot long *Gymnote* (1888) relied entirely on electric motors, and it could achieve speeds up to seven knots on the surface and five submerged. As with all the early electric boats, however, range was strictly limited by battery life, and *Gymnote* had no means of recharging batteries on its own. Maxime Laubeuf's *Narval* (1899) solved that problem, and others besides. *Narval* debuted two critical features: a double hull, which improved buoyancy, and an oil-fired steam engine combined with an electric motor. *Narval* could make ten knots on the surface, and more than six submerged. *Narval* even looked like a modern submarine, with four torpedo tubes in the bow and a conning tower amidships. But as revolutionary as it was, three years later it was made obsolete by newer Laubeauf designs. Laubeauf's *Aigrette*-class submarines shed the steam engines and in their place substituted the new oil-fired engine just recently patented by Rudolf Diesel in 1895.

France, by 1902, was years ahead of the rest of Europe, of the rest of the world for that matter, in submarine technology. At the start of the Great War, the French submarine fleet was the envy of the leading naval powers. The French lead was not insurmountable, though, and quickly the other leading navies made great strides to catch up. Britain, Russia, and Italy all had active submarine programs by 1905; even the US Navy, working with Irish-born inventor John Philip Holland through the 1890s, had a functioning gasoline-electric submarine, the USS *Holland*, by 1900.

Of all the greater naval powers, the last to join the game was Germany. Though Germany was at the forefront of naval design at the beginning of the new century, there was little enthusiasm for submarines in the Kaiser's navy. But in 1902, the Krupp shipyards at Kiel hired an Austrian engineer, Raimondo Lorenzo d'Equevilley Montjustin. Montjustin had worked in French shipyards and had seen the Laubeuf submarines up close. When he came to Kiel, he took the lead in Krupp's revitalized submarine program. Within a year, under Montjustin's direction, Krupp was building the *Karp* class of double-hulled, kerosene-electric submarines for sale to Russia. The German naval establishment took notice. Soon Krupp received orders from the German navy, the Kriegsmarine, and in 1906 the first modern German *Unterseeboot*—or U-boat—slid down the ways at Kiel. *U-1*, as the new boat was christened, was far from perfect, with engines that could be neither reversed nor accelerated; it was sufficiently outdated by 1914 that it saw no active service in the Great War. But Germany was closing the technology gap that separated it from France and Britain.

No one, not even the Germans themselves, could have predicted German superiority in submarine warfare during the First World War, or even that submarine warfare would become so prominent a component of naval operations. Submarines were still something of a novelty, and no one as yet had any idea what submarine warships were capable of, what special and so-far undiscerned qualities they might possess, or how they could be assimilated into modern naval warfare. And so there were no set doctrines in 1914, setting out what submarine captains should do or how they should go about doing it. They would have to figure that out as they went along.

BRITAIN AND FRANCE had the largest submarine fleets, and both fleets employed their boats in a variety of ways. Long-range British subs accompanied the surface fleets, while others patrolled regularly along the German North Sea coast; some even entered the Baltic, cooperating on occasion with Russia's small U-boat fleet. Shorter-ranged subs stayed close to the British coastline, acting in a defensive role. British and French submarines were heavily engaged in the Mediterranean and the Adriatic, and they kept up a high profile during the Dardanelles campaign of 1915. There they managed to make some noteworthy kills, like the Ottoman battleship *Barbaros Hayreddin* in 1915, but they did not appreciably sway the course of operations one way or the other.

Much the same could be said of the submarine fleets of the Central Powers. Granted, there were some notable victories early in the war. The German boat *U-9*, in one notable morning in September 1914, torpedoed and sank three British armored cruisers in the North Sea in the space of ninety minutes. The small Austro-Hungarian U-boat service accumulated an impressive record, given its size. Its most enterprising skipper, the commander of *U-5* and *U-14*, sank a total of thirteen enemy ships, including the French armored cruiser *Léon Gambetta*. For this feat, Georg Ludwig, Ritter von Trapp became Austria-Hungary's foremost naval hero—and later gained even greater fame, at least in American popular culture, when the story of his family's flight from the Nazis in the 1930s was immortalized in the American musical and film *The Sound of Music*.

It was the Germans who found a valuable if controversial niche for the U-boat. As the British maritime blockade of German ports tightened, the leaders of the Kriegsmarine set out to use U-boats in a counterblockade of sorts, in the form of an offensive campaign targeting Allied and neutral shipping traveling to and from Britain. This first took shape as policy in February 1915, when the Imperial government officially declared its intention to sink on sight any ship entering the war zone around the British Isles. Unrestricted submarine warfare elicited outrage from the Allies and from neutrals, like the United States, who conducted business with the Allies on a regular basis. Indeed, the infamous torpedoing of the Cunard liner *Lusitania* and the American ship *Nebraskan*, both in May 1915, turned American popular opinion against Germany and nearly brought the United States into the war.

For a while, the Germans eased up, fearful of an American intervention. Besides, the policy wasn't accepted universally in Germany; the practice of sinking noncombatant vessels without warning crossed a threshold of moral repugnance that some in the highest circles of the Imperial government simply could not bring themselves to accept. But in early 1917, compelled by desperation, the German government tried it again. This time it did indeed backfire, as the United States issued its formal declaration of war in April 1917.

But in the meantime, the German U-boats caused a great deal of damage. In the five-month period between October 1915 and February 1916, German U-boats sank 209 Allied vessels, totaling more than half a million tons. Between October 1916 and January 1917, German U-boat attacks claimed 757 ships for a total of over 1.3 million tons. It got worse once unrestricted submarine warfare recommenced in January 1917. Then the kills really racked up: 520,412 tons in February 1917; 564,497 tons in March; 860,334 tons in April. In 1918, from the beginning of the year until the Armistice in November, German subs claimed 2.75 million tons of shipping.

Losses on that scale were too great to bear for very long. Fortunately for the Allies, there were ways of defending against U-boat attacks, and techniques of anti-submarine warfare were already familiar to the navies of the world before 1914. Chain barriers, suspended from floating booms in the water around surface vessels riding at anchor, gave some protection against torpedoes, and giant underwater nets were a commonly employed measure to keep subs out of harbors and inlets, where ships were most vulnerable to attack. Fragile and unarmored, submarines running on the surface were highly vulnerable to even relatively small-caliber deck guns. Armed merchantmen, called Q-ships in the British service, took advantage of this. Carrying their armament as discretely as possible, Q-ships often relied on decoy merchant vessels to lure submarines into attacking from the surface, where they could be counterattacked and sunk with gunfire.

Of course, a submerged sub was not vulnerable to gunfire, and before the Great War began the British (and others) were already developing underwater explosives specifically designed for use against submarines. Hence the depth charge, a high-explosive bomb that could be rolled off the deck of a surface vessel over a submerged submarine, and detonated by a hydrostatic "pistol" triggered by water pressure at a specific depth. Depth charges didn't see a lot of action, claiming only a handful of subs during the Great War; in the world war to come they would hit their stride. And aircraft proved to be an effective instrument of anti-submarine warfare—spotting surfaced submarines from the air and occasionally bombing them—but only against submarines working close to the coastline. By far, the most effective countermeasure deployed against submarines was the convoy. Unescorted merchant vessels were the U-boat's principal prey, but once the Allies started providing destroyer escorts to shepherd groups of merchant ships through the more dangerous sea-lanes, U-boat commanders could no longer torpedo merchantmen with impunity.

The technology of the U-boat itself advanced, too. The submarines of 1914 were sophisticated machines, and they had come a long way from the primitive steam-powered submersibles of the 1880s and 1890s. Diesel-electric propulsion remained the gold standard for wartime submarines, and though performance definitely improved over the course of the war, submarines of the Great War were never especially swift, with surface speeds around twelve to sixteen knots, and around six knots when submerged and running on electric motors. Although there were some unusual experiments with submarine design—both the British and the Germans worked on aircraft-launching subs—submarines tended to fall into one of three basic types. Smaller coastal subs (like the German *UB-III* class) were designed to operate close to port on very short cruises, displaced two hundred to seven hundred tons, and had six to ten torpedo tubes, bow and stern. Oceangoing submarines (for example, the German *U-93* class), of closer to a thousand tons displacement, had ten to sixteen torpedo tubes and were intended for somewhat longer voyages. Finally—exclusive to the German navy—were the so-called cruiser submarines, larger U-boats capable of a much greater range. The largest of the cruisers was the German *U-139* class, a truly impressive boat; displacing three thousand tons and at ninety-two meters in length, it was armed with two 150mm deck guns and twenty-four torpedo tubes. Like all the German cruiser subs, *U-139* was designed for a special purpose: to be able to operate on the other side of the Atlantic, off the eastern seaboard of the United States and Canada, where it could wreak havoc with local shipping and bring the war to the enemy.

In the end, the German submarine war was a failure. Thanks to Allied countermeasures—and more than a few accidents—U-boat losses were high: of the 351 boats to see service in the war, 178—more than half—were lost in combat, most of them the victims of mines. German shipyards simply couldn't build new U-boats fast enough to make up for the combat losses, and the high frequency

Plate 23. The German U-boat *Deutschland*. *Deutschland* was originally used as a merchant submarine, but shortly before America's entry into the First World War in 1917, *Deutschland* was commissioned as *U-155*, part of the *U-151* class of large submarines. A so-called "cruiser submarine," *U-155* was capable of long-distance oceanic travel, and in 1917–1918 it operated off the Azores, the Canadian Maritimes, and New England. Image: NH 43611 courtesy of the Naval History & Heritage Command.

of losses caused morale among the boat crews to plummet months before the war's end. And in the sense that the U-boat campaign contributed directly and significantly to the American intervention in 1917–1918, it was a strategic disaster, resulting in Germany's final defeat in the fall of 1918.

But Germany's submarine war was a highly instructive failure. The high losses in boats and crew for the Kriegsmarine were cold comfort for the Allies. German and Austro-Hungarian U-boats, mostly the former, claimed a grand total of nearly thirteen *million* tons of Allied and neutral merchant shipping over the course of the war, plus 119 Allied warships sunk. The warship losses were alarming, but the civilian sinkings were more disturbing. Until near the end of the war, the Germans were sinking British cargo vessels faster than British shipyards could turn out replacements. The lesson, for all participants, was clear: if the Germans had had more submarines, if the Germans had pressed a little harder, then maybe, just maybe, the U-boat fleet alone could have brought Britain to its knees.

That recognition was not enough to convince the naval establishments of the victorious powers to shift their resources from surface to undersea warfare. For most naval officers of flag rank and higher, faith in the dominance of the gun-bearing battleship remained strong, the product of more than four centuries of war at sea. That the dreadnoughts and superdreadnoughts of the great surface fleets—the focus of nearly all prewar naval planning and the consumer of the lion's share of military expenditures—would play such a subdued role in the Great War, when so much was expected of them, did not change the long-standing assumptions about the conduct of war at sea. Once the great fleets started to rebuild again, in the 1920s and 1930s, battleships and cruisers, differing only by degrees from their *Dreadnought*-era predecessors, would take pride of place at the front of the fleet and the top of the budget.

But the Great War demonstrated, to those who would listen and see, that there was great potential in innovations like the U-boat, and that in the next great war the big-gunned battleship might prove to be an auxiliary vessel and not the star of the fleet. Indeed, the submarine was hardly the only threat to the battleship's long-standing supremacy. Naval warfare was poised on the cusp of a revolution of its own, a revolution that would fundamentally alter the nature, scope, and application of sea power. The submarine was indeed part of that revolution. Another component, of even greater import, was a technology that was just at that moment coming into its own. For the future of sea power would become inextricably intertwined with a new weapon and a new dimension of war: the airplane, and the control of the skies.

CHAPTER 15

THE EMERGING TECHNOLOGIES: AIR AND ARMOR

For each revolutionary new weapon or article of military gear that emerged during the industrial age, there were hundreds more that were workable and adequate but not destined to have an appreciable impact on the conduct of war; and for each of those there were thousands of examples of the ridiculous, impractical, or useless. Whether a newly invented military technology fit into the first or second category depended less on brilliance or engineering sophistication, and more on whether it fit a current need, whether its martial benefits justified the cost of adopting it, or whether it introduced an entirely new dimension to warfare. This is why the first category—the tools of war that shaped the conduct of war—includes both the Maxim gun and the Linnemann entrenching tool. The Maxim was one of the great mechanical marvels of the late 1800s; the Linnemann tool was a small shovel, albeit a very well-designed shovel. But both filled a pressing need and continued to do so for years after their introduction, and both machine gun and spade certainly influenced the way that armies have fought ever since.

Most new or newish weapons of the First World War would fall into the second category—serviceable, adequate, but nothing more than that. Some of them might come as a surprise. For this category would include a number of the truly iconic weapons of the Great War, weapons that have become emblematic of the horrors of war in the age of mechanized death. The flamethrower was one of these. The modern flamethrower, which uses an inert propellant gas (like nitrogen) to project a steady, focused stream of thickened fuel toward a target at close range, appeared right before the war. The German army adopted a *Flammenwerfer* shortly before the outbreak of the war, and first used it in combat in 1915. It was a brutally effective weapon, useful for clearing out trenches and bunkers. In confined spaces, like bombproof bunkers, the intense jet of flame quickly consumed all available oxygen, and was as likely to kill by asphyxiation as by burning. The thought of dying in such a horrific and painful way filled soldiers who faced the flamethrower with abject terror. Much like the pike, the bayonet, even the machine gun, the flamethrower did not have to kill anyone to achieve its objective. The mere sight of the weapon was enough to shatter the morale of all but the steadiest veterans.

But flamethrowers had significant limitations. The fuel and propellant tanks, usually worn on the back of the soldier operating the *Flammenwerfer*, were necessarily small for portability's sake, strictly limiting the time the weapon could be operated without refueling. Because the weapons were so dreaded, flamethrower-wielding soldiers—highly visible at a distance—were favorite targets for snipers. But for all the terror it caused, there was nothing decisive about the flamethrower. Speculative history is always a dangerous enterprise, to be sure, but it's difficult to imagine that the First World War would have turned out any differently had flamethrowers been entirely absent from combat, or if they had been used in greater numbers. The weapon only served to add to the ghoulishness of modern combat and the misery of the fighting man at the front.

The same could be said of gas warfare, though it might seem like heresy to say so. The use of poison gases in First World War combat was far more pervasive and widespread than the use of the flamethrower. Though the Hague Conventions of 1899 and 1907 sought—unsuccessfully—to ban the use of poison gas in warfare, neither the Allies nor the Central Powers exhibited any reluctance to deploy it, in hopes that it could break the tactical stalemate that was already evident on the Western and Eastern Fronts at the end of 1914. The Germans were, as in so many things, the pioneers here, first deploying chlorine gas against French colonial troops near Ypres in April 1915. The Allies soon followed suit. The primary challenge in using gas was, predictably, delivery. Projecting the heavier-than-air toxins via long tubes was an early solution, but a tricky one, entirely dependent on the whims of the wind. A momentary shift in wind direction could push the clouds of poison gas away from their intended target and back into the faces of the attacker. By 1916, the preferred, and safest, way to carry out a gas attack was via artillery. Specially designed gas shells used a tiny bursting charge, just enough to crack the body of the shell and allow the gas to seep out. In this way, gas could be delivered with considerable precision, right in front of or directly into enemy trenches.

The physical damage and human suffering wrought by the common battlefield toxins were hideous beyond imagination; the psychological effect was even greater. Chlorine, the first gas to be used in any quantity, could destroy the lining of the lungs if inhaled; phosgene, harder to detect, also caused suffocation, and was the deadliest of the gases used during the Great War. Mustard gas, the kind most frequently encountered in the last two years of the war, was rarely fatal, but it caused painful burns on exposed skin and long-term, chronic respiratory ailments. Perhaps most insidious of all were gases like chloropicrin, which could get through most gas masks, cause immediate vomiting, and compel soldiers to remove their masks. Such irritant gases sound more annoying than dangerous, but it was when the irritants were used together with a more damaging gas—like mustard—that they showed their worth, because the irritants made it almost impossible for soldiers to restrain themselves from ripping off their masks while in the presence of the deadlier companion gas.

Gas was a constant and unavoidable part of every combat soldier's life in the First World War, at least on the larger fronts in Europe. The gas mask was one of the most vital pieces of a soldier's personal equipment. The belligerent powers, especially Germany and France, devoted huge sums to the development of gas warfare. Europe's most accomplished chemists—including Nobel laureates Fritz Haber (Germany) and Victor Grignard (France)—devoted their wartime careers to the technology. The gas-mask-wearing soldier became one of the most enduring images of the war, a symbol of the dehumanizing and impersonal nature of the conflict in Europe—just as the line of wrecked humanity in John Singer Sargent's painting *Gassed*, or the soldier "flound'ring like a man in fire or lime" in Wilfred Owen's "Dulce et Decorum Est," came to represent the obscenity of that war.

Those fortunate—or unfortunate—enough to survive a gas attack could bear the burden of permanent disfigurement, or compromised lung function, or the prospect of a significantly shortened life. But for all the effort devoted to it, and for all the suffering it caused, gas was not decisive in any way. Though it may have affected the conduct of the war, sometimes, at the operational level, it would be a major stretch to argue that the use of poison gas influenced the outcome of the Great War. As horrible as it was, as many ethical questions as it raised, as much fear as it inspired, poison gas was not a significant weapon.

Flamethrowers would make a reappearance in the next war, and beyond. German and American armies in particular would find them highly useful for clearing heavily reinforced bunkers. American, German, and British tanks were sometimes equipped with flamethrowers mounted in their turrets as their primary armament. Though all the major combatants in the Second World War were prepared for gas warfare, with gas masks remaining standard issue equipment for all personnel for the first two or three years of the conflict, its use in military operations was essentially nil.

From the First World War there also emerged a fourth category of new technologies, innovations that didn't quite fit under any of the other three labels: weapons that were novel, still very much in their infancy, but that held much promise of accomplishing great things in the future. They were not yet sufficiently sophisticated to shape the conduct of war in 1914–1918, but were sophisticated enough to ensure their survival and development after the Armistice. For the Great War was also a testing ground for two brand-new, and very different, military machines, machines that would take warfare in directions that nobody could have foreseen in 1914: the warplane and the tank.

AVIATION WASN'T EXACTLY new in 1914, or even in 1903. That was the year when Wilbur and Orville Wright performed their first powered flight, brief though it was, at Kitty Hawk, North Carolina. Two years later, the Wrights took to the skies in their vastly improved Wright Flyer over their hometown and workplace of Dayton, Ohio, for a flight that lasted a full twenty-four miles. Soldiers and scholars of war observed with keen interest, for some of them had been thinking about war from the air for several decades. Long before the Wrights pioneered powered flight, balloons had found a niche in warfare. The French revolutionary government had created a military balloon unit, the Aerostatic Corps, in 1793, and until its disbandment in 1799 the Corps' balloon-borne aerial observers carried out occasional reconnaissance for French armies. In the American Civil War, Thaddeus Lowe's short-lived US Balloon Corps made a few reconnaissance flights, and again in the Spanish-American War the US Army used balloons for observing the enemy.

There was only so much that could be done with balloons, which were either tethered and stationary or subject to the caprices of the wind, so by the 1880s aspiring aviators were already looking into new, and more flexible, kinds of flight. The most famous of these was the early German aviator Ferdinand, Graf von Zeppelin, whose experiments with dirigibles—airships, often rigidly structured, that were capable of powered, directed flight—gained international acclaim . . . and concern. As the French, Italian, and German armies all invested in powered dirigibles, a few more visionary military minds began to see vast potential for wartime use. Dirigibles—or zeppelins, as they came to be known almost universally—would not only be handy for reconnaissance. Their mobility and range meant that they could fly over enemy military forces and attack from above, and from altitudes that were safely out of range of contemporary firearms. And if they could fly over enemy forces, there was nothing to stop them from flying over enemy population centers. The notion was sufficiently alarming to make military aviation a subject of heated debate at the 1899 Hague Conference, which ultimately imposed a five-year moratorium on the "discharge of any kind of projectile or explosive from balloons or by similar means," a full four years before the first powered flight in an airplane.

But the resolution of the diplomats at The Hague was not enough to dampen interest in aerial warfare. With dirigibles, Germany led the way. By 1912, the German army had an impressive fleet of several types of airships, ranging from small, tethered observation balloons to the first huge zeppelins such as the LZ-4 (1908), which on its first voyage covered 350 kilometers in twelve hours. Military exercises to try out the new weapons and tactics, and to show them off to the world, became common occurrences in the first decade and a half of the twentieth century, and the German army was not shy about testing the zeppelins' potential use as bombers. That was a terrifying thought to anyone living outside of Germany: the possibility that these gigantic airships could travel hundreds of miles and bomb helpless civilians with impunity, and there was nothing that could be done to stop them.

If the zeppelin was all the rage in 1908, the airplane wasn't far behind. In America, the Wright brothers didn't encounter much enthusiasm for their invention, but in Europe—where Wilbur made a sales tour in 1908—they found their audience. Soon, Europe had its own crop of devoted pilots—men such as Henri Farman and Louis Blériot—and in August 1909 France hosted a week-long aviation meet at Reims, with hundreds of pilots and their planes showing off to a million entranced spectators.

That intense popular enthusiasm was one of the things that so firmly set aviation apart from other incipient military technologies: its distinctly civilian origins. There were flying clubs all over Europe within months of Wilbur Wright's visit, and the men who could afford to participate in the sport—for that is how it was seen—were invariably rich, young, and well connected. The partnership between the budding aviation arms of the major European armies and civilian flying enthusiasts paid rich dividends. Civilian pilots were eager to share their experiences test flying new aircraft designs. And aviation made for good public relations. Like battleships, aircraft were crowd-pleasers, and aviation shows drew enormous crowds. Voluntary cash donations to the budding military aviation services became a popular way for ordinary folks to give voice to their nationalistic fervor.

It was one thing to speculate on all the marvelous things that aircraft might accomplish in modern combat; it was another thing altogether to actually integrate airpower into established patterns of warfare. In the entire history of war to that date, there was nothing even vaguely like aviation to which aviation could be compared.

Whether or not they knew what to do with aircraft, all the major armies were quickly building up their air services after 1910, bolstered by nationalism and civilian support. So as Europe edged closer and closer to a general war before 1914, airpower—as far as it was understood at the time—was ready for its stage debut . . . sort of. Prior to the Great War, military aircraft had put in an appearance in three minor wars of the early 1910s, but it was their role in the Italian–Turkish conflict over Libya (1911–1912) that attracted the most international attention. The Italian air arm, some nine aircraft plus a handful of balloons and dirigibles, went to Libya with the Italian land forces. That autumn they scored some notable firsts: the first aerial reconnaissance mission by airplane, the first combat photoreconnaissance flight, the first aerial bombing run, the first aviator wounded in combat. And with the help of Guglielmo Marconi himself, the Italians even managed the first ground-to-air wireless radio transmission.

Foreign observers watched the one-sided air war—one-sided because the Turks did not have an equivalent air arm—with great interest, but the Italian successes did not strike them as having lived up to the hype. One military correspondent noted, with tangible disappointment, that "war has not been revolutionized." But for more imaginative observers, or those who were already inclined to see great things in aviation's future, the Italian war in Libya was nothing short of a revelation. Among them was an obscure Italian staff officer named Giulio Douhet, who announced in 1912: "A new weapon has come forth, the sky has become a new battlefield."*

Overall, the aerial experience of the Libyan war, and of the two Balkan Wars of 1912–1913, encouraged proponents of military aviation, and in turn encouraged government investment in expanding military air services. On the day the First World War began, the European air fleets were substantial: the German army had 232 aircraft in combat-ready condition, Russia 190, France 162, while Britain, Austria-Hungary, and Italy each had around 100. The United States, the birthplace of both powered flight and aerial photography, could claim 8.

Those first military aircraft from the beginning days of the Great War were impressive machines, given the fact that sustained powered flight had been possible for only a decade at that point. When compared to the general state of aviation technology at the end of the war, four years later, they were hopelessly primitive. The Blériot XI, for example, was still quite modern in 1914. Designed by Louis Blériot and Raymond Saulnier, and first flown in 1909, it was the plane that Blériot himself flew across the English Channel that very same year. Its basic features were typical for that generation of aircraft: the fuselage was essentially a box-girder design, made from wood, partly covered in fabric; a twenty-five hp rotary engine was mounted in front, with the cockpit situated immediately behind; instead of ailerons on the trailing edges of the wing

---

*As quoted in Lee Kennett, *The First Air War 1914–1918* (New York: The Free Press, 1999), p. 18.

surfaces, as in more modern aircraft, lateral control came from wing-warping, meaning that the pilot twisted the trailing edges of the wings via a cable-and-pulley arrangement. Its top speed—a world record in 1910, achieved with a more powerful engine—was about sixty-eight mph.

What is most remarkable about the aircraft of the First World War is the fast pace at which they were improved upon. Here we see the research-manufacturing network, established earlier in the Industrial Revolution—the partnership between military institutions, industry, engineers, and the "end users" themselves, the pilots—at its most productive to date. Armies—the first air services were considered to be attached and subordinated to ground forces—were hungry for technological improvements that might give them an edge over their enemies, no matter how fleeting. Industrialists were likewise eager for contracts. And though aerodynamics, as a science, was but imperfectly understood, all the major powers were fortunate enough to have at their command the services of scores of brilliant engineers. Men such as Anthony Fokker, Igor Sikorsky, Herbert Smith, and Geoffrey de Havilland took to the new technology of flight and made astonishing advances under great pressure, and in record time.

The constant demands for improvements came from the pilots themselves, who knew their lives depended on the efficacy of their machines, and also knew—better than anyone else—what kinds of improvements would help them most. Complicating the evolution of the warplane during the Great War was the fact that so much recently invented technology was being rushed into production before it was adequately tested. Many, possibly most, of the results were positive anyway, thanks to the overall high level of talent among aviation engineers. One of the outstanding examples of artificially sped innovation was the American-built Liberty engine, designed by a group of engineers in a Washington, DC, hotel room over a period of six days, built and tested two months later, and in full production a month after that. And, miraculously perhaps, it worked. The Liberty went on to power many Allied aircraft during the last year of the war, including the De Havilland/Airco DH.4 and the Bréguet 14 light bomber, and it was still in active use well into the 1930s. The Liberty engine was one of the success stories. Not all high-pressure innovations-on-demand that were pressed into service turned out quite so well.

What drove that need for improvement at such a frenetic pace was the need for sheer power. Military aircraft evolved in many ways during the course of the Great War. Later planes had more accurate instruments, such as altimeters, tachometers, and air-speed indicators; and hinged control surfaces—ailerons and elevators—replaced the wing warping found on the first generation of aircraft. But in the main, pilots demanded more capabilities: more power, more speed, faster climb rates, the ability to dive steeply without ripping off the wings, the ability to operate at higher and higher altitudes. Plus they needed aircraft that could carry more: greater bomb payloads, more machine guns and ammunition, photographic equipment, wireless transmitters and receivers, bigger fuel-loads for greater range.

The aviation engineers of 1914–1918, brilliant though they were, were severely handicapped by an imperfect command of aerodynamics, which was quite a new field of study. Beyond the basics of lift and drag, they did not entirely understand the physics of flight, and they learned about the stresses that flight put on aircraft largely through trial and error. It would not be until the 1920s that aviation became more of a scientific pursuit and less of a craft trade. Still, the success of those early aviation engineers in improving aircraft flight performance is nothing short of breathtaking. Their options were limited. There was little they could do to make the first warplanes more streamlined, for the early designs required lots of bracing and cables, all of which added considerably to drag, as did fixed landing gear. Nor was it possible to lighten aircraft beyond a certain point. First World War aircraft were very light to begin with, their fuselages and wings constructed from heavily varnished cloth stretched over and around wooden frames, and once you got to a certain point in lightening the frame you only made it impractically fragile. The only real way to make aircraft that were faster and able to carry more stuff was to make the engines bigger and more powerful.

By 1918, the typical warplane in any of the major air services—British, French, German, Austro-Hungarian, Italian—might have looked externally much like its 1914 forebears, but it bore no resemblance at all in terms of performance. The wooden frames and cloth skins remained, although the Junkers firm in Germany introduced a working (but little used) fighter plane with an all-metal airframe in 1916. Biplanes continued to predominate, even at war's end. Monoplanes (aircraft with a single fixed set of wings) were commonly regarded as more fragile, a prejudice largely confirmed by the record of Anthony Fokker's stunningly modern Fokker D.VIII monoplane fighter, which outperformed nearly all of its contemporaries in speed and climb, but which earned an unenviable reputation for shedding its wings in a steep dive. Sesquiplane aircraft (a biplane whose lower set of wings was no more than half the surface area of the top set), like the wonderfully maneuverable Nieuport scouts, suffered from the same failing. Three-wing airplanes, or triplanes—such as the 1916 Sopwith "Tripe" (Britain) and the 1917 Fokker Dr.I (Germany), the fighter made famous by the "Red Baron" Manfred von Richthofen—could boast enhanced climbing ability, but exhibited greater drag than biplanes.

The typical warplane of 1918 was also a tractor, meaning that the engine was mounted in the nose of the aircraft, and the propeller in front of the engine, so that it *pulled* rather than *pushed* the plane. The alternative design, commonly called a pusher, was also quite common earlier in the war. British and French engineers favored the pusher configuration, for it did offer some genuine advantages. The pilot's or observer's view—unobstructed by the engine block, propeller, or exhaust manifolds—was unparalleled, and the pusher design made gun placement a simple matter. But because there had to be an open space between propeller and tail, they were by their very nature frail craft.

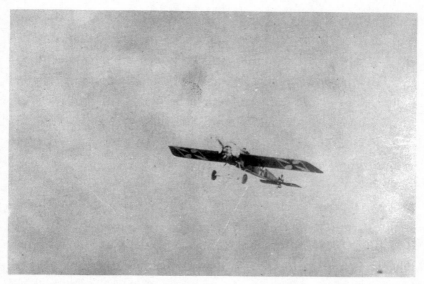

Plate 24. Fokker Eindecker in flight. The Eindecker was the first war-plane to use Anthony Fokker's machine-gun synchronizer. As spindly as it may have looked, for a while in 1915–1916, the Eindecker was the terror of the skies over the Western Front.
Photo courtesy of the Air Force Museum of New Zealand, photo no. MUS9503521a.

The most obvious difference between the aircraft of 1914–1915 and 1917–1918 was in their power plants. Here the automotive industry, which was moving along a parallel path, was especially helpful. Some of the biggest names in automotive design, such as BMW, Mercedes, Rolls-Royce, Packard, Cadillac, and Lincoln, branched out into aviation during the war. The power plants on 1914 aircraft were typically rotary engines, meaning that the crankshaft remained stationary when running while the crankcase and cylinders revolved around it; rarely did they exceed power ratings of 25 to 50 horsepower. Rotary engines persisted to the end of the war, though the bigger they got the less suitable they became, because rotary engines exert a gyroscopic effect on an airplane in flight, giving the plane a tendency to roll to one side. With larger, more powerful rotaries, such as the 110 to 160 horsepower engines used on the famous Sopwith Camel fighter, that effect could be quite dangerous. Increasingly, though, in-line, liquid-cooled piston engines replaced the rotaries, and they were much more powerful. The final power plants in what was arguably the best-designed fighter plane of the war, the German Fokker D.VII biplane, were BMW and Mercedes high-compression engines capable of producing 180 to 200 horsepower. Aircraft engines had effectively quadrupled in power in less than four years.

MILITARY AVIATION IN the First World War was pioneering in its purest form. The technology of flight was, clearly, still in its infancy when war broke out in Europe; that the belligerent powers were prepared to use airplanes in combat from the very beginning of the war seems almost inconceivable. Even though the reality of powered flight was not so novel then, even if it had been a better-established technology, it was still not proven what roles airplanes could actually fill. The range of experience accumulated in the Libyan and Balkan wars was so limited that it was not of much practical use to pilots, and the first attempt at writing a textbook for military flyers—Giulio Douhet's *Il dominio dell'aria* (*The Command of the Air*), written immediately after the war in Libya— contained a great deal of speculation.

Some theorists conjectured that the war in the skies would be somehow analogous to war at sea, that the vast expanse above could only be rightly compared to that of the oceans, and that someday in the not-too-distant future, armadas of airborne battleships and cruisers would dominate this third realm. To others, perhaps more pragmatically, the new air fleets were more like cavalry, performing the most vital duties that cavalry had traditionally done, only better: reconnaissance, scouting, and raiding. It was not for nothing that the language of the early air forces borrowed so heavily from the language of mounted warfare. Basic units of warplanes became squadrons; even the names of ranks, like *Rittmeister*—usually the commander of a cavalry company in the German service—reflected this intentional evocation of gallantry and freedom of movement.

And as with cavalry, there was an overall perception, within the armed forces as with the public at large, that there was something dashing and noble about aerial soldiering, a quality that made flying a plane superior to commanding foot troops on the ground. To fly was inherently noble.

But it didn't take too long for the early air services, their pilots and commanders, to work out their primary roles, once they knew from practical experience what they could accomplish with their aircraft. By the time the war ended in 1918, the airplane had come to play four complementary but distinct roles. Italian pilots had already carved out two of these roles in Libya; the other two emerged as the warplane evolved in the first half of the Great War.

Without a doubt, the first and most important role of the air forces in the First World War was that of reconnaissance and observation. Though the least glamorous—and likely the most dangerous—form of aerial service, it was nonetheless aviation's most solid, enduring, and valuable contribution to the ground war. What the Italians learned in 1911–1912 proved to be doubly applicable in 1914–1918. Even on the Western Front, where the war on the ground bogged down in 1915, aerial reconnaissance was still the surest way to detect the kind of unusual enemy activity that presaged major offensives. Photo reconnaissance became a part of daily routine for specially designated observation squadrons, just as daily analysis of aerial photography became routine for staff officers.

Early in the conflict, it became clear that reconnaissance missions required a minimum of two men per aircraft. The pilot had his hands full with the operation of the aircraft, and though he might be able to make note of something unusual, he certainly could not operate a camera or make a detailed report. A second crewman, a specially trained observer, would have to handle the reconnaissance itself, including operating the aerial camera and any communications equipment on board. As the skies became a more hostile environment, the observer also took on the role of gunner, operating a machine gun on a flexible, rotating ring mount, to defend the plane from aerial attack while the pilot attempted evasive action. The reconnaissance plane thus emerged as a specialized type, typified by the German AEG, LVG, Rumpler, and Roland machines, and the British B.E.2 and R.E.8. In its most common form, it was a two-seater tractor biplane, with the pilot sitting in front of the observer.

Perhaps even more valuable than photoreconnaissance was artillery observation, which made use of the same kind of aircraft, but differently equipped. Indirect artillery fire had become the common tactic of field artillery after the Russo-Japanese War, and it didn't take an extraordinary mind to grasp the possibilities that aerial observation offered, or the challenges it presented. An aerial observer, whether in a stationary balloon or in an airplane, had a much better view of the battlefield than a forward observer on the ground, and the immediate threat to his existence was nowhere near as profound.

The potential hitch, though, was entirely a matter of communications, at least for observation aircraft. An observation balloon, tethered in place behind friendly lines, could easily communicate via field telephone or wired telegraph, or even visual communications in a pinch. But aircraft couldn't be tethered, and therefore a wired connection was impossible. The simplest low-tech solution would be for the pilot to land his aircraft and convey his observations directly to the gun crews on the ground—hardly a satisfactory or efficient procedure. Marconi's wireless telegraphy, though, equipped observation aircraft with a powerful tool, allowing aerial observers to transmit map coordinates and target data directly to artillery commanders on the ground.

Even as aircraft evolved into more sophisticated machines, there was still room for older, simpler technologies, and in the world of aerial reconnaissance that meant balloons. The nascent European air services continued to develop and maintain inventories of balloons and dirigibles alongside their rapidly growing fleets of aircraft. Most numerous were the tethered "kite" balloons, like the German *Drachen* (dragon). Kite balloons were much simpler in construction than their zeppelin contemporaries, being little more than simple cloth bags filled with hydrogen. But they were deceptively sophisticated, designed to be aerodynamically stable even when buffeted about by winds. They were tethered to the ground behind friendly lines but close to the front, and an observer or two stood watch in a basket or cupola suspended from the balloon's underbelly. From here, the observers could watch for enemy movements or direct artillery fire, cabling their instructions to the ground via a wired connection.

As observation points, the kite balloons were probably even better suited for artillery spotting than powered aircraft. But they were shockingly vulnerable. They were regular targets for enemy artillery fire and irresistible temptations for fighter pilots. Balloon-busting was a specialized and dangerous skill, not to be taken lightly, but for those fighter pilots brave enough to take it on, downing balloons wasn't terribly difficult; a few incendiary rounds fired from an aircraft-mounted machine gun would rip the fabric open and ignite the hydrogen. In such emergencies, balloon crewman had at least one advantage that their pilot comrades did not. They customarily wore parachutes, another recent invention, and while the early parachutes did not guarantee a safe (or even nonfatal) landing, they at least gave balloon-men a fighting chance.

The reconnaissance squadrons did not produce any heroes or household names—the only reconnaissance pilots who made it into newspaper headlines were either those who became famous fighter pilots (like Richthofen) or those who were shot down by famous fighter pilots—but reconnaissance aircraft and equipment were the major priority when it came to personnel training and equipment allocation. It's estimated that, midway through the war, the British air service committed about two-thirds of its available resources to artillery spotting.

The second established role for military aviation was bombing. This, of course, was a well-worn trope in the popular "war of the future" literature that seemed to be everywhere in Europe at the turn of the century: that once humankind learned to fly,

Plate 25. Royal Aircraft Factory R.E.8. Observation/artillery-spotting aircraft were the workhorses of the early aviation units, and the R.E.8 was the workhorse of the British observation squadrons in 1917 and 1918. Ungainly and unpopular with its crews, the R.E.8 was nonetheless typical of the breed: slow (top speed of 103 mph, or 90 knots) and stable. The pilot sat in the forward cockpit, the observer/gunner in the rear. Armament included one forward-firing Vickers machine gun and one or two Lewis guns mounted on a rotating ring arrangement in the observer's cockpit.

Photo courtesy of the Air Force Museum of New Zealand, photo no. MUS95179.

via airplane or zeppelin, it would only be a matter of time before someone decided that it would be a good idea to drop explosives from above. The delegates at The Hague in 1899 were all agreed on that. The Italians had tried their hand at aerial bombing in the Libyan war, with results that were inconclusive but not bad enough to discourage further experimentation.

The leaders of the European air arms in 1914 had every intention of using aircraft as weapons, and as bombers in particular. But technology had not yet caught up with the notion. Most aircraft circa 1914 were not capable of the task: they did not have the power to lift flight crew and significant bomb loads off the ground, let alone ascend to a decent altitude. And if there was one thing that aerial combat in the Libyan and Balkan wars taught aviators, it was that aircraft flying under one thousand feet were highly vulnerable to artillery and machine-gun fire from the ground. Bombing would also require a whole new set of apparatus, including bomb racks, bomb-release mechanisms, and bombsights. None of these items had been designed yet, and since the early observation planes did not allow for heavy payloads, the very first bombing runs were executed with light bombs—roughly the size of a light artillery shell—or hand grenades, dropped manually from the aircraft by the observer; this was not a technique calculated to be very effective.

The obvious choice for a bombing platform, then, was the dirigible airship, the zeppelin. The German air service had already experimented extensively with zeppelins as bombers for several years before the beginning of the war, and they had some idea of how it could be done. And zeppelins had just about every physical advantage over airplanes: they could carry much heavier cargoes, could fly for much greater distances, and could tolerate much higher altitudes than airplanes. Zeppelins, however, did not do very well in combat areas. They were too vulnerable to fire from ground troops, their vast bulk and slow speed making them easy targets. The Germans lost three zeppelins over the Western Front during the first month of the war alone. French attempts at deploying dirigibles were equally disappointing, mostly because French troops—who assumed that every dirigible was a German zeppelin—would shoot at every airship they saw, friendly or hostile.

For long-range targets with thinner ground defenses, though, the dirigible airship was very effective. Soon the zeppelin became a bomber of cities and other civilian targets. Here the Germans had a tremendous advantage, for Paris and London were well within range of their zeppelin hangars, while the largest German cities were not easily reached from British or French airfields. German zeppelin raids against London managed to rack up a startling record of success, pulling off a total of fifty-four bombing raids, mostly by night, on London and its environs between 1915 and 1918. Until the autumn of 1916, the zeppelins could move freely in British air space unopposed, as it took the panicked British time to find suitable countermeasures. By then, though, the combination of searchlights, densely layered antiaircraft batteries, and fighter planes firing incendiary ammunition began to inflict crippling losses on the German attackers, and the age of the zeppelin bomber came to an end.

In the meantime, aircraft were developing to the point where they could take over from the zeppelins, and their pilots were learning, through trial and error, the art and science of aerial bombardment. Two-seater observation planes, equipped with underwing bomb racks and primitive bombsights, doubled as attack aircraft, and as their power plants and airframes evolved, so too did their carrying capacity. Bombsights did not improve much over the course of the war, but through frequent practice bomber pilots were learning their craft and compensating for the inadequate targeting equipment with instinct. By 1915, the major air commands were drawing up printed instructions and official tactical doctrines. Bombers approached their targets in formation rather than in an inchoate mass. To many commanders on the ground, bomber squadrons were an extension of artillery. The bombers, then, were sent to hit the kinds of targets ordinarily reserved for the big guns, but that were far enough behind enemy lines where artillery could not reach. Ammunition trains, supply and ammo dumps, critical road junctions—these were the preferred targets of the bomber squadrons.

For all that accumulated experience, the results overall were, in a word, disappointing. Individual bombs were not big, and it took a direct (or nearly direct) hit to do any real damage to a target. And such hits, even when bombs were dropped from modest altitudes, were rare. Over a period of sixteen weeks in the spring of 1915, for example, French and British bomber squadrons on the Western Front carried out a total of 141 bomb attacks on railway stations behind German lines. Only three could be counted as successes.

Such a failure rate could not have been anything but discouraging, given the time, money, effort, and blood that the air services had invested in aircraft and aircrews. What kept bombing alive was the fact that sometimes the bombers scored breathtaking victories. During the battle of Messines (June 1917), for example, German bombers hit and destroyed a British ammunition train, disrupting Allied logistics and effectively silencing British artillery batteries in the area for three hours.

The main flaw of the light bombers—observation planes employed in a bombing role—was their capacity. Bigger bombs, and more of them, would go a long way toward compensating for the inaccuracy of bomb placement. Engineers were already attacking the problem. Even before the war, Giovanni Caproni (Italy) and Igor Sikorsky* (Russia) were working, independently, on large biplanes with multiple engines mounted on the wings. The German aircraft industry followed suit early in 1915, and by the end of 1916 had introduced the first practical *Großflugzeug*—"large aircraft"—designed specifically for bombing and no other purpose. Organized in heavy bomber units, these first Gotha bombers—popularly named after the town where they were built—began to take the place of zeppelins in the spring of 1917, making both day- and nighttime raids on British towns with unsettling regularity. German engineers didn't stop with twin-engine Gothas, designing and producing the so-called *Riesenflugzeug*, or "giant airplane." These behemoths, most of them sporting four large engines, played virtually no role in the war whatsoever. Most did not make it past the prototype stage, and very few were completed before the Armistice in November 1918; the only model that saw any significant service was the Zeppelin-Staaken R.VI, a freakishly large craft with a wingspan of over 138 feet.

---

*This was the very same Igor Sikorsky, born in Ukraine, who would emigrate to the United States in the midst of the Russian Revolution. In the US he pioneered vertical flight, designing some of the earliest helicopters, and establishing, at Stratford, Connecticut, one of the most successful aviation firms in American history.

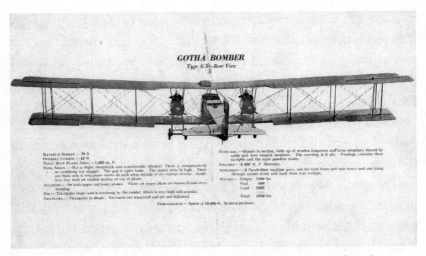

Plate 26. Gotha G.V bomber. This rear view of the German bomber gives some idea of its scale; its fuselage was over 40 feet in length, its wingspan measuring nearly 78 feet. It carried a crew of three to four men—pilot, forward gunner, one or two rear gunners. Its two water-cooled, 260-hp Mercedes engines could push it along at speeds up to 87 mph; much slower than contemporary fighters, of course, but its three Parabellum machine guns had a wide field of fire, and the bomber could fly as high as 21,000 feet—above the service ceiling of most Allied fighters of its day. The G.V and its predecessors, notably the Gotha G.IV, conducted most of Germany's bombing raids against British and French civilian targets.

Courtesy National Archives, photo no. 17342191.

The purpose-built bombers and the reconnaissance planes used as bombers shared two common weaknesses: they were slow and not easily maneuverable. Steadiness was an asset for bombers, to be sure, as it was for observation and photoreconnaissance craft, but it made them vulnerable to fire from the ground. And those shortcomings made them even more susceptible to attacks from aircraft designed explicitly to prey on slower-moving planes: the fighters.

This was the third role played by aircraft in the Great War: attacking and shooting down enemy aircraft. It was also a new role for military aviation, one that hadn't been anticipated before the Great War. At the very beginning of the war, aircrew from opposite sides rarely made an effort to interfere with one another when their paths crossed aloft. To be an airman, after all, was to be gallant and chivalrous, an attitude exaggerated by the perceived link to cavalry and the noble birth of so many early pilots. It wasn't long, though, before pilots and observers began to take weapons with them in the air, mostly handheld firearms—rifles, pistols, and civilian shotguns. And once pilots discovered the superior flight characteristics of single-seat scout (or fighter) aircraft, they sought out slower enemy planes as targets.

The machine gun was a natural choice for aerial armament, for it combined the ballistics of a rifle with the shotgun's ability to spread projectiles over a broad area. Providing the observer in a two-seater with a machine gun was a simple proposition. Machine guns could be made lighter simply by removing the water jacket or converting it into a barrel shroud, for the colder temperatures at higher altitudes were sufficient for keeping the barrel cooled; simple pivot-mounts—or, better, rotating ring mounts—allowed the observer a broad field of fire. But for a single-seater, the only logical place to mount a machine gun was in the front of the aircraft, pointing forward, so that the pilot only had to guide the nose of the plane so that it pointed at his target—aiming the weapon by aiming the plane, in other words. But if most scouts were tractor planes, with the propeller in front, how could that be done without shooting the propeller off?

There were solutions, most of them not very satisfactory. One common approach was to mount the machine gun atop the upper wing on a biplane, so that it fired over the propeller arc. It wasn't easy to aim, since the gun sat several feet over the cockpit, and clearing a jam or reloading would require a death-defying feat of agility and flying skill. The pilot would have to stand upright on his seat while he tinkered with the gun, the plane flying—hopefully—level. Still, French pilots seemed to do fairly well with the arrangement, which was common on the famously nimble Nieuport 11 and Nieuport 17 scouts, as it was on Britain's ungainly Martinsyde G.100 "Elephant."

Another solution was to use pusher airplanes instead of tractors. With the propeller and engine in the rear, the pilot had a clear field of fire in his front, and to the sides, too. The earliest British fighters were pushers, notably the two-seater F.E.2 and Vickers F.B.5 (the "Gun Bus"), and the single-seater Airco DH.2. They performed a valuable service, as fighters and as light bombers. A number of British pilots would achieve ace status, meaning that they were credited with at least five confirmed kills, in the DH.2, and did not have significant German competition until 1916. Still, tractor planes— faster, more maneuverable, less fragile—were preferable to pushers.

French and German engineers were coming close to finding a solution. Their ideas centered mostly on synchronization, linking the firing of the machine gun to the mechanical operation of the motor: when the propeller blade was in front of the machine-gun's muzzle, an interrupter would prevent the gun from firing. But until the spring of 1915, a solution eluded both the French and the Germans. It proved to be so difficult a challenge that the French aviation pioneer Raymond Saulnier gave up on synchronization entirely, in favor of a more direct, even primitive method: understanding that only about one bullet in ten would actually strike a spinning propeller, Saulnier mounted steel wedges on each propeller blade to act as deflectors. When the propeller blade crossed a bullet's path, the bullet hit one of the deflectors and ricocheted harmlessly off. Or almost harmlessly.

The Saulnier method was hardly ingenious. The steel wedges compromised the propeller's effectiveness; the impact of the bullets on the deflectors put additional and dangerous stresses on the crankshaft; and the pilot had the unnerving experience of having his own bullets ricochet toward his face. But it actually functioned, and when a hotshot young Paris car dealer turned pilot named Roland Garros went aloft in a plane equipped with the Saulnier deflector and a Hotchkiss machine gun, he made history. Flying his Morane-Saulnier Type L monoplane over the Western Front on 1 April 1915, Garros spotted a German two-seater observation plane, gave chase, lined up his plane's nose with the enemy, and brought it down with a few bursts from his machine gun. Over the next two weeks he claimed two more German planes, and for a short time in the spring of 1915 Garros was the terror of the skies. His career came to an abrupt halt, only a couple of weeks after his first victory, when a forced landing behind German lines led to a long stint in a prisoner of war camp.

The Germans now had Saulnier's deflector device, triggering a lot of premature enthusiasm, but the experts at *Idflieg*—the general staff of the army air service—knew that the Saulnier device wouldn't work for them. For one thing, German rifle bullets were harder than French rifle bullets, likely to wreak havoc with the deflectors. And their own engineers were close to a solution. Most promising was the research of young Anthony Fokker and his firm in the city of Schwerin in Mecklenburg. Fokker, the most famous aviator in the Netherlands, had just celebrated his twenty-fifth birthday when Garros was captured. A high-school dropout and engineering prodigy, Fokker had built his first airplane when he was twenty-one; at twenty-two, he had set up his first aircraft factory in Germany. He was temperamental, brusque, a sloppy workman, but his brilliance was undeniable, and when the Kaiser's government commandeered his Schwerin factory after the outbreak of war in 1914, Fokker agreed to stay on as director.

Fokker proved to be an invaluable asset to the German air service, designing some of the most effective warplanes of the entire war: the awkward-looking but surprisingly lethal monoplane, the *Eindecker*, the plane with which legendary aces Oswald Boelcke and Max Immelmann learned their trade; the Dr.I triplane, favored by "Red Baron" Richthofen; and the phenomenal D.VII biplane, possibly the best fighter of the war. But Fokker's greatest contribution—to the German war effort and the history of firepower—was not an airplane but a mechanism that first saw the light of day mere hours after Roland Garros was taken prisoner.

Fokker and his team had been working independently on the synchronization problem, but their solution—just now taking shape in the spring of 1915—was not dissimilar to Saulnier's original design. The Fokker synchronizer did not operate on the principle of interruption; the propeller, in other words, did not stop the gun from firing. Fokker went in the opposite direction: with his synchronizer, the propeller would fire the gun. The propeller shaft powered a cam, which in turn thrust back an operating rod to fire the gun, but timed in such a way that the rod went back only when the propeller blades were out of the line of fire.

Fokker's synchronizer worked far better than Saulnier's deflector shields; that it worked at all put it head and shoulders above all competing designs. Late in May, young Fokker gave *Idflieg* a personal demonstration, after mounting a gun on a Fokker monoplane. Within weeks, Fokker was fitting the synchronizer to one plane after another, and that summer the "Fokker scourge" began. German *Eindeckers* with Fokker's new device made short work of Allied observation planes, and the French and British squadrons had little with which they could fight back.

But by the spring of 1916, the war in the air settled down into a war of attrition, much like the war on the ground, with neither side gaining a lasting, clear advantage over the other. The British and French—and the Russians, too, for the air war was not restricted to the Western Front—countered with their own fighters: first with pusher biplanes, such as the multigunned two-seater F.E.2 series and the single-seater DH.2, then with tractor aircraft using their own gun-synchronization systems. Over the next two years, the major opposing air services, at least on the Western Front, had something like parity, with neither side gaining long-lasting advantages over the other. Steadily, though, the quality of fighter planes improved, and though there were exceptions, the "standard" fighter at war's end was a wood and fabric tractor biplane armed with two forward-firing machine guns, capable of airspeeds over one hundred mph. There were differences between them, but the primary fighters at war's end—the German Fokker, Albatros, and Pfalz scouts; the French (and American) Nieuport and SPAD; the British S.E.5 and Sopwith fighters—were quite similar in performance.

Plate 27. Albatros D.Va. The Albatros D.Va was one of the most commonly encountered German scouts—or fighter planes—of 1917–1918, and its performance was fairly typical of the type in the last year of the Great War. Its high-compression, 180-hp Mercedes engine allowed it to achieve speeds of up to 116 mph. Like most scouts at the end of the war, it carried two forward-firing machine guns, synchronized to fire through the propeller arc.

Photo courtesy of the Air Force Museum of New Zealand, photo no. ALB920382B035.

Military pilots in the Great War pioneered a fourth role as well, what today would be called close support. There was little formal coordination of air and ground operations during the greater part of the war, as generals were just starting to grasp the possibilities that airpower offered. But in 1917, German commanders on the Western Front began to experiment with the use of air forces to support ground offensives, suppressing enemy infantry and artillery prior to ground assaults through a combination of strafing (machine-gun fire at ground targets) and light bombing. The technique yielded some impressive results in the fighting around Cambrai (November

1917), and *Idflieg* poured more resources into close support. Ultimately, the Germans developed specially designed ground-attack planes, like the Halberstadt CL.II and CL.IV, heavily armed, short two-seaters with powerful motors, that performed as well as most single-seat fighters of the time. The Allies, notably the British, followed suit, but here the Germans excelled. The experience would prove invaluable in the war to come.

THE POPULAR PERCEPTION of aviation, predictable given the mania for all things related to powered flight before 1914, was enormously positive. The popular press in all the combatant nations played a role in shaping that perception, routinely lionizing fighter pilots above all military heroes, and giving the war in the air a veneer of glamour and grace. The reality, of course, was far different. While aviation personnel were spared the stultifying drudgery and mud and filth of life in the trenches, a military pilot's life was typically unenviable and short. The early military aircraft were unadorned with creature comforts, or even modern flight instruments or protection from the elements, and they did not even admit room for that most recent and most welcome of aviation inventions, the parachute. The pilot of a fatally crippled plane, if he could not glide safely to a landing, faced the choice of either jumping to his death or crashing with his aircraft. Unreliable engines, combined with abbreviated training programs, meant that a distressingly large number of young pilots died in accidents early in their careers. It has been estimated that the average life expectancy for a British pilot in 1918 was little more than eighteen flying hours, or roughly three weeks. Few of the much-lauded fighter aces survived the war, and nearly all of them died at a very young age. Oswald Boelcke and Manfred von Richthofen, two of the highest-scoring pilots on the German side, were each hardened veterans when they died at age twenty-five; Albert Ball, one of the most prolific British aces, was twenty at the time of his fatal crash in 1917.

Yet by war's end, and undoubtedly well before that, military aviation had proven its worth. No discerning military observer would have argued against it, and indeed after 1918 it was no longer possible to consider going to war without an air service. Whether or not airpower had a measurable impact on the conduct of military operations over the four previous years was almost immaterial; combat pilots had learned, through hard and bloody experience, what kinds of roles aircraft could and could not play in war, and the basic parameters of those roles. Even if long-range strategic bombing claimed only the tiniest fraction of the number of lives that it would in the next world war, it still demonstrated how air forces could bring war directly to the civilian population and disrupt life behind the lines. The late-war appearance of close-support aircraft and tactics gave a hint of what could be done if fighter-bombers could be coordinated with ground troops, a notion whose full potential would be revealed to the world two decades later in the German blitzkrieg.

The only substantive question arising from the air war of 1914–1918 was just *how* vital airpower was—or could be. Was it simply an additional dimension to combat, and auxiliary to ground and possibly naval forces, and thus properly subordinated to commanders on the ground or at sea? Or was it a different kind of combat altogether, mostly separate from surface warfare, deserving of its own command structure independent of armies and navies? Was there, as Douhet had predicted, a chance that maybe the aerial theater would be *the* vital and decisive combat arena, and that wars in the future could be fought entirely in and from the skies?

AIRPOWER HAD ACCOMPLISHED something big in the Great War; it waited only for better planes and more time to plan and organize. The same could not be said, however, about the other emerging technology of the Great War: the armored fighting vehicle. The tank was unquestionably an invention of the First World War. It made its first appearance in that war, fought its first battles in that war, and launched the careers of the men who would emerge as the prophets and masters of armored warfare in the war to come. But if one were to weigh the performance of tanks in combat solely on their own merits, without reference to what armor would accomplish two or more decades later, then the verdict would have to be negative: tanks achieved little, and were hardly worth the resources put into them.

Tanks were new to war in 1914–1918, but the constituent elements of armored warfare were not. Automobiles and other ground-based motorized vehicles—notably the farm tractor—were part of a well-established family of technologies. Gottlieb Daimler had patented his internal combustion gasoline engine in 1892; Rudolf Diesel's engine dates from 1895. Even the Deeds-Kettering electric autostart ignition, which eventually replaced the hand-crank starter of early automobiles, was commercially available in 1912. And while aviation had a rapidly growing fan base in 1914, automotive culture was far more ubiquitous. Before the Great War began, cars could be found in every city in the world, nearly everywhere in the West, and they were already at the center of a blossoming professional sports scene throughout North America and Europe. Eddie Rickenbacker, the deadliest ace in the American air service, had been a professional race car driver before the United States entered the war, and in this he was not unique.

It's not that motor vehicles didn't play a major role in the Great War. Indeed they did, and while horses and mules still hauled most war-related cargo, including artillery, the Western Allies relied increasingly on trucks for their transportation needs. The French had trucks operating in and around the combat zones on the Western Front throughout the war, and by war's end the major combatants altogether had pressed nearly a quarter million trucks into service. The motorcycle, also a sophisticated and reliable machine by 1914, had begun to supplant the horse for the vital and demanding job of dispatch riding.

Using motor vehicles *in* combat and using them *for* combat were two different things. Still, it had occurred to army officers around the world that cars and trucks could serve as weapons carriers, and therefore as weapons themselves, before 1914. Most armies, major and minor, had toyed with the adoption of armored cars in the early years of the century. The Italians had used them in the Libyan war with Turkey, and they were a common sight in the Great War. Lightly armored against small-arms fire, fast, usually armed with a machine gun or two, armored cars could be quite useful. They acted as modern cavalry to conduct reconnaissance and escort motorized convoys, and in some theaters of the war—for example, Palestine, where British troops used them en masse like battle cavalry—they proved to be invaluable tactical assets. But wheeled vehicles tended to perform poorly on broken ground, or on heavily worn and pitted roads, limiting their usefulness.

Tempting as it might be to look for one, there is no straight developmental line from armored car to tank. The second did not evolve from the first, and indeed the tank—when compared to most weapons technologies of the early twentieth century—developed in a haphazard way. The tank is a perfect example of a weapons system born and bred in the midst of an active war, a desperate solution to a desperate situation, namely the tactical stalemate that gripped the Western Front from 1915 on. The technology of the armored fighting vehicle also evolved independently and in several places at once, with little international cooperation. And the role it was anticipated to play was vague and poorly defined from the outset, with little notion of how it could actually be deployed in combat, or how it would work alongside conventional ground forces. For the British and French military establishments, who pioneered and explored the idea more than anyone else, the tank had one purpose and one purpose only: to punch through heavily fortified enemy lines.

In Britain, that prospect alone was attractive enough to earn it much support, no matter how half-baked that idea appeared to be at first blush. Among the earliest advocates of the tank were the indefatigable and omnipresent Sir Winston Churchill, then First Lord of the Admiralty, and an army engineer named Ernest D. Swinton. Both Swinton and Churchill were drawn to the same recent invention: the tracked farm tractor. Farm tractors—high torque, low speed vehicles designed to pull heavy equipment over rough or mucky ground—had been a feature of commercial farming in the United States and Britain for several decades. Originally steam-powered, later employing gasoline engines, most tractors were wheeled vehicles.

But a decade before the war, two firms on opposite sides of the Atlantic—Holt in the US, Hornsby in the UK—independently invented tracked tractors. At that time, British army leadership didn't see a potential use for the slow-moving vehicles, but once the war began they changed their tune. Tractors clearly would come in handy for dragging heavy artillery pieces across muddy, shell-pocked terrain. The British army purchased some American-built Holt tractors for that very purpose, and the sight of them in action made a deep impression on both Swinton and Churchill. Both men wondered the same thing, independently: Could a tractor be turned into an offensive weapon? Could it be armed and armored, and sent at the enemy by the hundreds, to roll over all obstacles—shell craters, trenches—in its path? Could it crush barbed wire and disperse the enemy, preparing the way for an assault?

With the enthusiastic backing of both Sir Winston and Swinton, and motivated by the tactical stalemate in France and Belgium, the British military gave the idea a shot. The project moved quickly. The first prototype tank, an armed tractor built by William Foster & Company, made its public debut at the end of 1915; the second, battle-ready prototype performed for a group of generals and the entire Cabinet in February 1916. It was an impressive sight. This second prototype, called Mother, looked nothing at all like modern tanks. It did not ride on its treads; rather, the treads wrapped all the way around the left and right sides of its thirty-two-foot body, which resembled a stretched out, squashed rhombus. From each side protruded a small armored gun emplacement, called a sponson. One can only imagine how jarring its first appearance must have been to the distinguished guests at its first trials. "The signal was given," Swinton recalled, "and a species of gigantic cubist slug slid out of its lair and proceeded to rear its grey hulk over the bright-yellow clay of the enemy parapet." Only a few days after the demonstration, the British government put in huge orders for the machine, ultimately commissioning 150. The new tank, officially called the Mark I, weighed in at a whopping thirty-one tons. The Mark I was almost the spitting image of Mother but was produced in two main variants: "female" tanks carried six Vickers machine guns; "male" tanks carried four machine guns, plus two six-pounder quick-firing naval cannon in the sponsons.

The British would improve continuously on the Mark I through the course of the war. The most common version, the Mark IV, went into production in May 1917. The final version, the Mark V, featured major upgrades in armor, engine, steering, and transmission but was fundamentally the same tank. Though these, the descendants of Swinton's Mother, were perhaps the best-known and most effective heavy tanks of the war, they were not alone. The French developed their own armored behemoths at roughly the same time that the Mark I made its way to the production line, and with roughly the same end in mind: as an offensive weapon, or more correctly an offensive auxiliary, that prepared the way for infantry assaults by crushing barbed-wire obstacles, crawling over trenches, blasting through enemy defenses. The French high command, notably General Joseph Joffre, was desperate to find a way to break free from the constraints imposed by trench warfare. When an artillery officer proposed, late in 1915, the use of armed and armored tractors for the job, Joffre was all ears. His engineers got right to work, and by September 1916 the first French landships were ready for action.

The two basic French models, the Schneider CA1 and the St. Chamond, were less stable and more ungainly than their British counterparts, perhaps reflecting the rush to get workable tanks into production. The St. Chamond was instantly recognizable for its prominent overhang in the front, where the tank's hull protruded well in front of the treads, rendering it highly unsuitable for traversing trenches. The French designers were less interested in the tank's stability or agility, and more concerned with its firepower. Unlike the Mark I and its descendants, both the Schneider and the

Plate 28. A British Mark IV (male) tank passing by a column of captured German soldiers, October 1918. The Mark IV tank, the most common model in Britain's considerable heavy tank fleet in 1916–1918, came in two variants: "Male," armed with two six-pounder cannon and three Lewis machine guns; or "Female," with five Lewis guns only. Britain's heavy tank program was the most successful of the First World War.
Courtesy National Archives, photo no. 4550828.

St. Chamond relied on a single large gun, a 75mm field gun, for their armament.

For the Germans, the tank was almost an afterthought. German generals did not quite see the utility of the thing—not because they were shortsighted, but because they recognized the very real limitations of the early tanks, and so they focused their attentions elsewhere. Research on tanks in the German army appears to have been perfunctory, with little enthusiasm behind it, and that lack of enthusiasm showed in the final product of German tank design. The *Sturmpanzerwagen* (armored assault vehicle) A7V was without a doubt the most ridiculous armored fighting vehicle design to make it to production during the Great War. Twenty-six feet in length and eleven high, it resembled a barn mounted on undersized treads. The driver and commander sat atop the monstrosity in a vulnerable armored cupola, while the rest of the eighteen-man crew worked the engines and the armament—a single 57mm cannon in the bow, and six rifle-caliber Maxim guns mounted along the sides and rear.

The British heavy tanks were undoubtedly superior to the French and German models, but only by degrees. All the heavy tanks were merely different shades of mediocre. They suffered from a laundry list of mechanical issues, which were mostly the same from tank to tank. All were seriously underpowered and very heavy, and hence slow: the French Schneider's seventy hp engine gave it a top speed of 3.7 mph; the A7V, the fastest of the lot, had two one-hundred hp engines, which could push its thirty-three-ton bulk along the road at a blistering 8 mph. Such speeds were only attainable on level, undamaged road surfaces. On cratered, pockmarked battlefields, the maximum speed would be much lower, and of course the early engines and transmissions were likely to break down at the slightest provocation. Steering was clumsy at best; on the British heavies before the Mark V, four "gearsmen" operated the two tracks individually, slowing down or stopping either tread to make the vehicle turn. Maximum range for the heavies averaged around twenty to thirty miles before they emptied their fuel tanks.

Operating conditions for those unwise enough to volunteer for tank service were well-nigh unbearable. Armor was light, varying between less than half-an-inch thick (on the British Mark IV) and just over an inch (on the German A7V). For most tanks—though not all—the armor plate was sufficient to repel rifle and machine-gun bullets—that is, until 1917, when the Germans introduced a steel-core, armor-piercing rifle bullet. None of the tanks of the Great War was artillery-proof. A single round from even the lightest field guns, even at long range, would easily penetrate the hull of any tank of the period, exploding inside the hull and killing the crew. Even putting the terrors of combat to the side, the tanks were beyond torturous to operate. They were hot and poorly ventilated, with little or no consideration given to the comfort of the crew. On the St. Chamond and the A7V, the powerplants were mounted, exposed, inside the main compartment, which was dangerous for all sorts of reasons, but an immediate hazard because of the clouds of exhaust that would fill the tank while in operation. A7V crews would become physically ill from their overexposure to carbon monoxide while driving their tanks. Even in the best of circumstances, when not under fire, the interior of a tank in operation would be stiflingly hot, reeking of sweat and engine fumes and vomit, and the crew would have been in constant fear of becoming stranded in no-man's-land due to mechanical failure. It's a wonder that tank crews were able to function at all.

And yet function they did, after a fashion. Since there was no firm notion of how they would be used in battle—unlike in aviation, where at least the bombing and reconnaissance roles were established and planned-for from day one—tank commanders made up tactics as they went along, and the second half of the war was a prolonged experiment in armored warfare. Swinton envisioned tanks being used in swarms, closely coordinated with infantry and cavalry, to overwhelm enemy defenses in massive combined-arms assaults. They should not, he argued, "be used in driblets," individually or in small groups, where they could be easily neutralized; moreover, it was vital that the tank commanders be in constant communication—via wireless or field phone—with the infantry units following them, the artillery units to the rear, and the other tanks. But Swinton seems to have been alone in devoting so much thought to tank tactics. Indeed, despite the generally welcoming attitude toward armored fighting vehicles in the British and French armies, nobody took the new combat arm very seriously. The first British tank crews received some rudimentary training on two prototype tanks in England, but they were given no instruction in elementary tactical skill, like map reading or signaling.

Still, the tanks went into battle, and their pioneers—the British—were the first to use them, during the Somme campaign in the summer and autumn of 1916. Sir Douglas Haig, commanding

British forces in France, turned to the tanks in desperation after two months of fruitless attacks caused immense Allied casualties with little to show for it. Early in the morning hours of 15 September 1916, thirty-five Mark Is, with their half-trained crews, rolled forward from their departure points behind British lines. Their appearance was indeed a shock to the defending Germans, and all but four made it across the first line of German trenches. But they were spread out, their overall impact was consequently diluted, and the whole episode simply confirmed the German belief that tanks were an interesting novelty and nothing more, frightening at first but easily dispelled with a few carefully aimed shots from a field gun.

In all fairness the Germans were entirely right to think so. As Swinton had pointed out, tanks needed to be employed en masse, and in close cooperation with infantry and other units, to have an impact at all; their unimpressive debut at the Somme was due as much to their failure to concentrate and coordinate as it was to their mechanical fragility, inadequate armor, and unimpressive armament. To their credit, British and French commanders learned from their mistakes and, instead of ditching the idea altogether, invested more time, effort, and research into improving both tanks and tank tactics. More rigorous training regimens, combined with the formation of special tank units, meant more capable tank crews led by junior officers who were both enthusiastic and deadly serious about their new profession. Some of the best minds in the British army, notably the soon-to-be-famous military scholar J.F.C. Fuller, bent their minds toward the task of drafting armored combat doctrine.

The approach was successful, and Allied use of tanks in combat was far more effective from 1917 on. But better training and better tactics didn't necessarily translate into victory, or compensate for the tank's mechanical shortcomings. When the French Fifth Army lunged forward on the very first day of the notorious Nivelle Offensive in April 1917, the 128 Schneider tanks that spearheaded the assault made little or no difference. Their crews found it all but impossible to cross the broken ground of no-man's-land, and many of the tanks simply broke down.

In the British attack on Cambrai (November–December 1917), tanks gave a somewhat better account of themselves. Four hundred tanks, most of them the improved Mark IVs, lurched forward at the outset of the offensive, massed together and under the command of their own officers. The effect was dramatic. The fleet of tanks, belching black exhaust as they surged toward the German lines, easily broke through the German defenses, crushing barbed-wire obstacles into the ground and allowing the British infantry to pour through behind them. Within a single day they had punched a hole five miles deep into the German lines. The breakthrough was dramatic, but predictably fleeting. The attack bogged down as German resistance stiffened and reinforcements arrived to plug the gaps in the German lines. And there was no tank reserve to follow up on the initial successes. Most revealing was the condition of the tanks at the end of the day: about half were out of action, knocked out by artillery fire, stuck in trenches and abandoned by their crews, or—most common—broken down due to engine and transmission failures.

Still, tanks had accomplished something at Cambrai, even if that something did not amount to much of anything in the long run. The British and French stepped up armor production, and when the United States entered the war in mid-1917, the Americans also entered the race to build an Allied tank armada. The Germans would never come close to the Allies in sheer number of tanks, or in the sophistication of tank design or of tank tactics, nor did they try. The sum total of their inventory in the Great War was around thirty-five tanks, fifteen of which were captured British tanks. The British, by contrast, built over 1,200 Mark IVs alone. On both sides, the emphasis was on what were already being called heavy tanks, like the Mark IV, the Schneider, and the A7V, but well before the end of the war, all four of the "tank armies"—British, French, German, and American—had begun to experiment with light tanks.

Light tanks, with smaller crews, smaller armament, and thinner armor, were not meant to serve in the same role as the heavies.

The French, who were most enamored of the concept, intended the light tanks to act as infantry tanks, accompanying infantry on the attack and covering them with machine-gun fire. To the British, the ideal employment of light tanks was as cavalry tanks, literally a replacement for cavalry; capable of moving faster than men on foot, they were intended to exploit breakthroughs made by heavy tanks and infantry.

The first light tanks appeared in the field in 1917. The British version, the Whippet, was a lightly armored, machine-gun-carrying tractor capable of attaining speeds up to eight mph—twice the speed of most heavy tanks. The Germans were so impressed with the Whippets they captured that they attempted to copy the design, but their better armored, more heavily armed prototype never made it into production. But the most impressive model, and arguably the most important tank of the First World War, came from France. Disappointed with the lackluster performance of the awkward Schneiders and St. Chamonds, the French army refocused its efforts on light tanks in the summer of 1916.

The winning model was a two-man tank built by carmaker Renault, officially known as the FT-17. The FT-17 couldn't have inspired much confidence when it first appeared. The driver sat in the front of the tank, his torso covered only by a pair of steel doors; the gunner stood in the center of the vehicle, his head and upper body encased in a manually operated gun turret. Inside the turret was a single gun, loaded and aimed and fired by the gunner alone; most of the Renaults carried a Hotchkiss light machine gun, but some were equipped with a short-barreled, lightweight 37mm cannon. There was no other armament, no machine-gun muzzles poking out from all sides of the tank as there were on the heavies. The turret was the distinguishing feature of the FT-17, the one feature that set it head and shoulders above all other armored fighting vehicles of the Great War, and indeed the only significant feature that would survive to influence all tank design from that point forward. The FT-17 was the most common tank of the First World War, and one of the most common of the century. The French built

Plate 29. The French FT-17. The FT was the most common (and most successful) light tank of the Great War. The two-man tank mounted either a Hotchkiss machine gun or a light 37mm cannon in its small, rotating turret. Both American and French forces used the FT—in this case, American, bearing the markings of the 347th Tank Battalion of the American Expeditionary Force, in the fighting around St. Mihiel in September 1918. American factories in Cleveland and Dayton, Ohio, also turned out an American copy of the tank, the US M1917 Six-Ton Tank, but few if any rolled off the assembly line in time to take part in the war. Image: Library of Congress http://hdl.loc.gov/loc.pnp/ppmsca.53570 (accessed 22 February 2021).

over three thousand before the war was over; the Americans, who adopted it in a slightly revised form as the Six Ton Tank M1917, produced nearly a thousand, though very few if any actually found their way to France before the 1918 Armistice.

Such numbers were telling: the light tank was eclipsing the heavy tank. Easier and cheaper to manufacture than the heavies, faster and more maneuverable on the ground, the light tanks made possible the swarm tactics that Swinton and Fuller advocated. As the Whippets and FT-17s went into mass production, the character and scope of tank battles shifted accordingly. The great Western Front battles of 1918 all featured Allied tanks in their hundreds, invariably employed as auxiliaries to infantry assaults. That April witnessed the first tank-on-tank combat in history. As part of their spring offensive, the Germans sent thirteen of their massive but mostly harmless *Sturmpanzerwagen* A7V tanks in a push toward Amiens; the British, catching wind of the attack, sent twenty tanks out to greet them. Near the village of Villers-Bretonneux, portions of those forces clashed: three A7Vs on the German side, three Mark IVs and seven Whippet light tanks on the British. The brief clash was anticlimactic: two Mark IVs retreated, one A7V was abandoned by its crew; the Whippets attacked some nearby German infantry and lost nearly half their number in the process.

AT WAR'S END, the Renault FT-17 was the most advanced tank in the world. Not only the Americans, but the Japanese and even the Russians copied the design, too. The redoubtable Renault would manage to make a showing in nearly every major conflict of the twentieth century. Of course, within a few years of the Armistice, the FT was hopelessly outdated. Advances in the automotive industry would bring forth more powerful engines and more robust transmissions, so that—mechanically as well as externally—motor vehicles of the 1930s bore very little resemblance to their forebears of the 1910s. That in itself was something advocates of armored warfare could celebrate, for there were no defects more obvious in the tanks of the Great War than speed and mechanical reliability. But the rebirth of armored fighting vehicles in the decade before the outbreak of the Second World War in 1939 owed to more than just improved powertrains. In the interwar period, especially in the 1930s, military leaders would find a new and promising role for combat vehicles. European armies would turn once again to the tank, and from the first day of the first campaign of the next war, the tank would play a pivotal, even decisive, role in combat.

And that is a curious thing, curious that the tank survived at all. Military aviation, the other cutting-edge technology of 1914, had proven itself in the Great War. The wide-scale use of the warplane confirmed the promise that the early aviators saw in it, as planes proved their worth in a multitude of roles—including a couple of roles, like close support, that even the visionary prophets of air-power hadn't foreseen. There was no doubt that military aviation had justified the resources put into it, and only a fool would have suggested ignoring it after 1918.

Armor was a different matter altogether. Tanks had no appreciable impact on the outcome of the Great War or even on the way in which armies fought. Their presence in individual battles did not count for much, except in the short term, as at Cambrai. True, Germany did not maintain a viable tank arm, and Germany lost the ground war, but then there is no correlation between the two things; Germany's defeat in 1918 had nothing to do with its dearth of tanks. But if Germany had neglected its air service in the same way, and the disparity in airpower between the opposing sides had been as great as it was for armor, things might have turned out much differently. It's hard to believe that the German war machine would have performed anywhere near as well as it did without the enormous asset of its air forces. The warplane, in short, proved itself to be useful in the First World War. The tank did not.

But a handful of leaders on both sides, mostly young, were able to look past the tank's considerable shortcomings and see potential that wasn't immediately apparent to everyone. One was an American lieutenant colonel, founder of the US Army's Light Tank School and commander of its 1st Tank Brigade, a young and spare Californian named George S. Patton Jr.; another was an even younger French infantry captain, a scholar of military history and a tactical iconoclast, one Charles de Gaulle; a third was a book-ish British infantry officer, repeatedly wounded and gassed at the Somme, named Basil Liddell Hart; and a fourth was Hart's later mentor J.F.C. Fuller, who had assisted in planning the tank assault at Cambrai. What makes these men remarkable was not only that they were the ones—alongside the German prophets of armor, Os-wald Lutz and Heinz Guderian—who wrote the rules of armored warfare going into the Second World War, but also that they saw a reason to do so. In the lurching, slow and fragile fighting vehicles of the Great War, these men saw a technology that—with a little patient nurturing—would come to change everything about the conduct of war on land.

Book IV

THE TWILIGHT OF FIREPOWER, 1918-1945

CHAPTER 16

THE LESSONS
OF THE GREAT WAR

There had never been anything like the Great War, and there never would be again. The world war to come would transcend it in nearly every measurable way; it would shatter more lives, kill infinitely more soldiers and civilians, do more to shake up the prevailing world order and redraw the map not only of Europe—which it left a smoking ruin—but of the world, as well. But the First World War was the more shocking of the two, because it had no antecedent. The First World War made the Second World War possible, and may have even made the Second inevitable. But it also made the Second World War *thinkable*. But there was nothing even vaguely like the First World War to which it could be compared; indeed, nothing that happened before 1914 would prepare Europe or the world for the cataclysm that was to come. Everything distinctive and disturbing about the First World War was brand new: the massive armies and fleets, the prospect of death delivered from the air and from beneath the waves, the mechanization of killing.

That deadly novelty wasn't just a matter of popular perception. The Great War was, objectively regarded, immense. With armies numbering not in the tens or hundreds of thousands, but in the *millions*, the material demands of war strained the institutions of life to the limit, in a way not seen in Europe before, not even in the darkest days of the Thirty Years' War. The combatant nations were hard-pressed to supply even the most basic, low-tech needs of the fighting forces—things like rations, fodder, draft animals, clothing, shoes, and personal gear. As the Russian war effort in 1914–1917 so eloquently demonstrates, not all the combatants succeeded in accomplishing even that much.

The new technology amplified those pressures. The profusion of motor vehicles and naval vessels—whether powered by oil, diesel, or gasoline—translated into an unslakable thirst for fuel. Rapid-fire weapons meant more ammunition, and unlike in the age of the muzzleloader, that ammunition—precision-made to fine tolerances—could not be manufactured in impromptu laboratories with minimal equipment and semiskilled labor. Even the most thoroughly industrialized economies could barely keep up with the demand. During the artillery bombardment that preceded the Battle of the Somme in the summer of 1916, around 1,400 British guns fired a total of 1.74 million shells at the German positions—over 10 percent of Britain's total production of artillery shells the previous year, and 1 percent of its aggregate output over the course of the war—in a single week. Factories back home couldn't keep up with such a manic production schedule indefinitely. As industrialized as Britain was, it still leaned heavily on foreign imports, especially from the then-neutral United States, whose factories churned out rifle cartridges and artillery shells by the millions for Britain and Russia.

For the first time, too, armies and navies had to divert a fair proportion of their manpower from the battlefield to supporting roles. Prior to the end of the nineteenth century, support troops were virtually unknown in Western armies. All soldiers were assumed to be combat soldiers and were trained as such. Certainly, small numbers of soldiers might be detailed for support duties—as teamsters, for example, or farriers or cooks—but the ratio of noncombat to combat personnel was negligible. The industrialization of war at the turn of the century demanded a significant investment in noncombat labor. The technology itself required it, especially in communications and transportation: working in railyards and depots, laying track, maintaining rolling stock, keeping motor vehicles up and running, setting up and protecting telegraph and telephone lines. Combat troops still made up the bulk of the personnel in combat formations—a typical infantry division in the American army in France was about 80 percent combat troops—but the proportion of noncombatant soldiers had risen steeply overall. Just over 50 percent of the American forces in France were combat troops, about 40 percent worked in logistics and supply, and most of the remainder consisted of headquarters staff.*

SCALE MATTERED IN tactics and the art of war, too. Because the land forces in particular were so much larger than any ever encountered before in Western warfare, the basic parameters of battle were drastically altered. Combat took up much more space, for one thing; battles of the Great War were fought across wider fronts, and those fronts tended to be deeper as well, with multiple reserve trenches behind the front lines, and support units behind them. The rhythm of battle changed, as well. Nineteenth-century (and earlier) battles were measurable and discrete occurrences. They had well-defined beginnings and endings; most likely they would last a day, perhaps two or three, and when they were over the armies would disengage and that was it. Battles in the First World War, especially on the Western Front from 1915 on, rendered that definition irrelevant. If we consider battles to be more or less continuous combat over a given patch of ground, battles in the First World War were long, drawn-out affairs, lasting not days but weeks or even months. The Somme in 1916 was a battle: the artillery bombardment that came before the first infantry assault lasted the better part of a week; the bloody first assault was only a day; but the Battle of the Somme lasted for nearly four and a half consecutive

---

*John McGrath, *The Other End of the Spear: The Tooth-to-Tail Ratio (T3R) in Modern Military Operations* (Fort Leavenworth, KS: Combat Studies Institute Press, 2007), pp. 12–20.

months. The battle of the Meuse-Argonne, widely considered to be the biggest and bloodiest battle in American military history, consumed six weeks. What were considered battles in the First World War were more comparable in duration to what would have been called campaigns in earlier conflicts.

An interesting side effect of this rewritten definition of battle is that it makes the assessment of combat lethality, or the effectiveness of individual weapons, highly problematic. It is tempting, and common, to think of the Great War as uniquely bloody, and that it was the weapons and the generals that were largely to blame. This, in fact, has become one of the most persistent beliefs about the First World War: that the leaders of the armies, especially on the Western and Eastern fronts, were collectively not up to the task of fighting a modern war with the terrifying new weaponry that emerged after 1870. Unable to comprehend the killing power of machine-gun fire and high-explosive shell, or just unwilling to adapt, these be-monocled, unimaginative generals were enmired in Napoleonic tradition that was painfully irrelevant on the modern battlefield. According to this line of thinking, the gallant but hapless common soldiers were "lions led by donkeys," the donkeys in question being their generals, who sent their men "over the top" in futile frontal bayonet charges against entrenched enemies because they couldn't grasp the implications of the new firepower.*

---

*One variant of this argument, first advanced by military historian Jay Luvaas and recently reiterated by Drew Gilpin Faust, contends that European tacticians' deliberate snubbing of the American experience of trench warfare during the Civil War—especially in the fighting around Petersburg—was a big mistake on their part, for their ignorance of trench warfare made possible the dreary slaughter on the Western Front in 1915–1918. It's an odd argument, given that European soldiers had been combining field fortifications with firepower since at least the time of Bicocca, and they had plenty of contemporary examples of modern firepower and trench warfare in their own direct experience, such as in the 1877–1878 siege of Plevna, or in the 1904–1905 siege of Port Arthur. Jay Luvaas, *The Military Legacy of the Civil War: The European Inheritance* (2nd edition, Lawrence: University of Kansas Press, 1988); Drew Gilpin Faust, "Two Wars and the Long Twentieth Century," *The New Yorker*, March 13, 2015. For an important

The Lessons of the Great War

On the whole, it's a heavily flawed and (mostly) demonstrably wrongheaded argument. The truth is that the 1914 generation of weapons, of all types, was potentially deadlier than its predecessors. In land warfare, the sheer volume of firepower that repeating rifles, machine guns, and quick-firing artillery could generate, not to mention the greater range and power of those weapons, could not help but have an effect on battlefield tactics. But the carnage of the First World War, such as it was, did not come about because European commanders were unaware of the lethality of the weapons their troops employed. They had seen magazine rifles, machine guns, and high-explosive shell at work in the Russo-Japanese War—and elsewhere besides—and so there were no big surprises there. A vast body of professional literature, full of realistic assessments of new weapons technologies, was similarly at their fingertips. In the Great War, it was not the weapons themselves, or their performance, that presented thorny tactical problems for battlefield commanders. Rather it was the combination of new, powerful, and complicated weapons and the armies themselves—gigantic hordes of half-trained citizen-soldiers—that made combat in the Great War seem so bloodily indecisive. Modern weapons plus huge half-amateur armies made for a dangerous mix.

Far from mindlessly applying outdated tactics to the twentieth-century battlefield, commanders tried to find the best methods for using the new weapons in combat, and for countering those same weapons in enemy hands. That's not to say that there weren't incompetent, negligent, or ignorant generals, or that the First World War was not unimaginably bloody and tragic; there's no way of getting around the fact that the war destroyed both a way of life and an entire generation of young men. But the challenge of making war with huge armies that were armed with the most modern

---

corrective to the assertions of Faust and Luvaas, see: Hugh Dubrulle, "The Military Legacy of the Civil War in Europe," *Essential Civil War Curriculum,* July 2018 (https://www.essentialcivilwarcurriculum.com/assets/files/pdf/ECWC%20TOPIC%20Military%20Legacy%20Essay.pdf, consulted December 2020).

FIREPOWER

weaponry was both very new and very daunting, and generals had to learn as they went along. The Great War, then, was more of an experiment, or an enormous amalgam of smaller experiments, in the art and science of war, performed at a critical and unique juncture in the history of the West.

Take the example of one of the most notorious days of slaughter in the entire Great War: 1 July 1916, the first day of the British attack at the Somme. The British commanders on that day knew full well what they were up against; their close, painstaking coordination of artillery bombardment and infantry assault shows that they were not mindlessly sending their men "over the top" because they couldn't think of a better solution, or because they still doubted the efficacy of the machine gun. Instead, they were experimenting with a new and well-reasoned tactic, based on their understanding of small arms and artillery firepower. As it turned out, that tactic didn't work as planned, and tens of thousands of British soldiers paid the price for the failed experiment. But the slaughter was most certainly *not* the result of ignorant or sociopathic leadership.

That assault at the Somme, and many other battles besides, highlighted one of the most important lessons that students of the military art drew from the Great War: the great importance of tactical coordination, and of the battlefield communications necessary to foster that coordination. If infantry and artillery were to work together on the assault, whether that involved a massive pre-assault pummeling of enemy lines or a creeping barrage, the artillery had to be able to communicate instantly with its observers and the infantry commanders. Combined arms approaches, perfectly timed, were the wave of the future, and the Great War made that plain. Close support from aerial forces, already part of operations on the Western Front in the last year of the war, would be even more dependent still on planned coordination and instant communication.

That degree of communication and coordination held the key to a more fluid kind of warfare in the future, the kind that ground commanders in the Great War yearned for, the kind of warfare that the German *Stoßtruppen* seemed to hint at. German and Russian assault tactics, as honed by Hutier, Brusilov, and others, also showed the importance of mobile firepower in modern warfare. French, British, German, and American efforts to build a workable light machine gun came from this recognition. So, too, did the late-war German use of the earliest submachine guns. Consequently, tactics and technology in the 1920s and 1930s would move forward with these tactical concerns in mind.

To the open-minded observer, the Great War also hinted at the future role of mechanization. For all the trucks and motorcycles that cluttered the roads behind the lines on both sides of the Western Front, the Great War was still a draft animal's war. Horses and mules provided most transport; trucks were not reliable or powerful enough to be depended on in unfavorable weather or road conditions, nor were there enough of them to fill the transportation needs of any of the major combatants. But anyone could see that there would be a role for motor vehicles to fulfill in the next war, when—one hoped—they would have more powerful engines and more robust transmissions. The tank, too, though not a success story in 1916–1918, performed well enough to convince a few ambitious and thoughtful officers that in the mobile warfare of the future, tanks would take the place of cavalry.

The lessons of war at sea were less clear. The investment poured into the construction of dreadnoughts and battlecruisers in the decade before the war—disproportionately heavy in comparison to expenditures on land forces—hardly seemed justified after the unimpressive performance of the great battle fleets in 1914–1918. It wasn't that the capital ships proved to be disappointing from a technological point of view; rather, it was that they hadn't actually accomplished very much. Besides Jutland and a handful of smaller battles, there were no battleship-on-battleship engagements, and only Jutland could be considered a fleet action in the old style. For all their cost and technical sophistication, the great ships had done very little.

Sea power itself had not diminished in importance; that much had not changed. Control of the seas was as vital as ever, especially so as the Old World became more and more dependent on the resources of the New. The flow of raw materials, manufactured goods, and troops across the Atlantic was of crucial importance to the survival of the Allied powers, and interdicting that maritime lifeline was equally important to the survival of Germany and its allies. And that was where smaller warships came in: submarines to intercept commerce and sow fear, destroyers and other escort vessels to protect cargo vessels and troopships from submarines. For some more conservative navy men, the submarine inspired fear and revulsion in equal measure, the latter amplified by Germany's U-boat war on civilian shipping. But overall the submarine proved its worth. It wielded a power, ton for ton, that the capital ships simply couldn't match: the power of small, inexpensive, easily replaced vessels with small crews to send the mightiest battleships to the bottom. Alone among the more influential technologies of the new century, the submarine did not exclusively favor large and powerful nations. Any nation with a couple of seaports and a modest shipbuilding industry could build a fleet of submarines to defend its coasts or to ravage enemy shipping. The First World War taught that lesson; it would not soon be forgotten.

In that sense—that modern technology actually offered some options to smaller or middling states—naval warfare was the exception. The greatest and most sobering lesson of the First World War, when it came to technology, had more to do with economics than with the tactical implications of the weapons themselves. At war's end, the only participants left standing were those that possessed a major industrial base: Britain, France, the United States, Germany, and to a lesser extent Italy. True, the Ottoman Empire and Austria-Hungary lasted up to the very end, but mostly because they both had been propped up by German military and financial support. A whole host of factors drove Russia from the war, most famously the October 1917 revolution, but the Russian wartime economy had already been failing for quite some time when Lenin returned to stir up trouble in his homeland. In the end, the most important factor in Allied victory in 1918 was productive superiority, and the final blow to German hopes was the active intervention of the world's leading industrial economy: the United States of America. America's decisive role in the closing months of the war had nothing to do with superior generalship or better weapons. It was instead the prospect of facing overwhelming American manpower and industrial power that forced the German government to seek terms in November 1918.

The Great War had become a war of attrition, and the takeaway was as obvious as it could be: industrial power was military power, and the capacity to manufacture munitions in quantity was of greater import than the sophistication of those munitions.

THAT LESSON WOULD be borne out again, in even more pronounced fashion, in the world war to come. More so than the Great War, the Second World War was a struggle between massive wartime economies. More so than in the Great War, in the Second World War victory ultimately went to the two greatest, strongest, most resilient economies in the world: those of the new superpowers, the United States and the Soviet Union. That is not to disregard the very important roles played by the other major combatants allied with the US and the USSR, most notably Britain and the Commonwealth countries. Britain and the Commonwealth nations, after all, stood alone against the Nazi juggernaut from the fall of France in 1940 to Hitler's invasion of the Soviet Union a year later, and had no powerful allies in the West until America entered the war in a significant way, well into 1942. Nor is it to dismiss the very impressive if flawed wartime economies of Hitler's Germany and Tojo's Japan. Neither observation changes the fact, though, that Allied victory came largely from the combined industrial might of America and Russia, and the inability of the Third Reich and its allies, primarily Italy and Japan, to keep up.

That same rule would apply to weapons technology, as well. There is little doubt that the Second World War witnessed a great many surprising leaps forward in weapons technology, and in technology in general. There is also little doubt that Nazi Germany deserves the lion's share of credit for most of those leaps forward. In jet propulsion (and jet aircraft), in rocket technology, in small arms and artillery and armor and submarines—German engineers were either significantly ahead of their Allied counterparts or completely in a class of their own. Even in the ultimate technological innovation of the war, the harnessing of the power of the atom, German scientists came frighteningly close to beating the Allies. It is not at all empty speculation to consider how far German scientists and engineers might have advanced in the technology of death had the Reich not been under constant attack from the air in 1943–1945, nor to recall that the war was hard-fought and a close scrape. But in the end, Soviet and American weapons—often inferior to their German analogues—prevailed, because the Russians and the Americans could manufacture those weapons in staggering quantities and the Nazi war machine could not. When it came to weapons in the Second World War, good enough was good enough, as long as there were enough.

Of course, there was much more to weapons development in the Second World War than a simple matter of quantity versus quality. During the 1920s and 1930s, Western military establishments (and outliers such as Japan)—partnered, as before, with industry, scientists, and engineers—sought to incorporate the tactical lessons of the Great War into the next generation of martial weapons. They did so under unenviable circumstances; unlike in the decades before 1914, the interwar years were mostly lean ones for armies and navies. Besides the all-too-brief (and half-hearted) interest in international disarmament, the economic malaise of the 1920s and 1930s occasioned a great deal of belt-tightening in Europe and the United States. Military budgets were radically pared back, and that meant that weapons production would be, too. After all, the First World War bestowed upon the Western world a vast quantity of surplus weapons and ammunition. Some of it would be destined for the scrap heap, but much of it—especially small arms and artillery—was perfectly serviceable and not likely to obsolesce soon.

But even severely constrained military budgets did not prevent soldiers and engineers from exploring the takeaways of First World War combat and applying them to weapons. The need—or, rather, the intense craving—for tactical mobility in ground combat was paramount. The 1916 Brusilov offensive and the 1918 *Kaiserschlacht* showed that that kind of warfare was possible, that war was not condemned to be forever trench-bound, and so weapons designers made portability the primary consideration when experimenting with new small arms. The other priorities were the emerging technologies of the Great War, notably the warplane and the tank. Military aviation had proven its worth in the Great War, and during the 1920s and 1930s pilots and engineers would successfully expand its utility. Armored fighting vehicles, still quite novel and unimpressive in 1918, would advance to the point in 1939 that the tank, like the warplane, became an indispensable asset to conventional armies.

In all these areas, the period 1918–1939 was not marked by the same kind of abrupt and unsettling change as the years 1870–1914 had been. Certainly the differences between a fighter plane in 1918 and its equivalent twenty years later, or between a Gotha biplane bomber and a Boeing Flying Fortress, merit the label "revolutionary." But in the main, the basics of weapons types, and their essential attributes, remained remarkably similar from one world war to the next. Machine guns of the Second World War were, mostly, better than machine guns of the First World War, but not by much; most infantrymen went into battle in 1939 with rifles of 1914–1918 vintage, perhaps smaller or lighter or with improved sights, but functionally the same. Even the warplanes and tanks of the Second World War, while far superior to their Great War predecessors, had evolved in ways that were fairly predictable, the results of improved motors, transmissions, suspensions, and airframes. There is more a technological continuum connecting the two world wars than there is a technological break separating them.

In the main, what would distinguish the interplay of weapons and warfare in the Second World War from the earlier conflict was not the weapons themselves, but their coordinated use: coordination between service branches and coordination between weapons types. Hence, the tactics of blitzkrieg, the German army's approach to mobile warfare, as evidenced in Hitler's invasions of Poland (1939), the Low Countries and France (1940), and the Soviet Union (1941). Those tactics first showed the efficacy of combining mechanized infantry, armor, and close-support aircraft, using radio communications to synchronize their movements and respond to changing conditions on the battlefield as they arose. The ground war in Europe came to be characterized by this very approach, in slightly different forms. The Russo-German war of 1941–1945, and the Anglo-American operations against German and Italian forces in North Africa, Italy, France, and finally Germany, all reflected this new dynamic. So, too, did the Allied campaigns against Japan in the Pacific, to which was appended the added complication of coordinating land and sea forces in the longest amphibious conflict known in human history.

The naval war of 1939–1945, on the other hand, would mark a significant departure from 1914–1918. The disappointing performance of capital ships, the dreadnoughts and the superdreadnoughts, did not dampen enthusiasm for the turreted battleship, which would continue to be the obsession of naval architects the world over during the interwar years. Granted, battleships and other big-gunned surface vessels would play a role in the Second World War, and not a trivial one. But the principal locus—or loci—of naval warfare in the Second World War was not with the battleships and battlecruisers. In the Atlantic, much as in the Great War, the real war was between Axis U-boats and Allied convoys. In the Pacific, the aircraft carrier came to replace the battleship as the core of the big fleets, and naval operations were principally air operations, carried out via floating steel airbases. In both theaters of combat, as on land, coordination—especially between air, surface, and subsurface units—was key.

All these new roles and new modes of making war were reflected in the technology of weapons. Nowhere was the yearning for mobile warfare so evident as in the standard-issue weapons of the ordinary foot soldier.

CHAPTER 17

PORTABLE FIREPOWER

O n top of the big, difficult, and painful lessons taught, harshly, by the Great War, there emerged from the combat experience of 1914–1918 a host of microlessons about the impact of the new technology. For small arms, the principal takeaways were not earth-shattering, but they were pressing enough to influence firearms design for decades to come. One lesson, for example, had to do with old quandary over the relative merits of long range, high accuracy, and rate of fire. Up to 1914, tactical experts had assumed that the much-increased range of rifles—a consequence of the invention of smokeless powder in the 1880s—would lead to a corresponding increase in the distance at which infantry engaged in battle. In short, longer-ranged weapons would make longer-ranged firefights. This turned out not to be the case in 1914–1918. Exchanges of rifle fire at modest ranges, say between the front lines of two opposing trench systems, were common if largely ineffectual, and firefights at very close ranges (around one hundred meters or less) were even more common. But long-range firefights were rare, even if the rifles of the post-1886 generation were theoretically capable of great accuracy and killing power at extended distances. As infantry officers had known for a long time, rate of fire was the decisive, critical quality of small arms in combat.

Rate of fire—and portability. Another telling lesson of ground combat in the First World War was the desirability of maneuver.

438

The slow-paced, high-cost-for-minimal-gain nature of fighting, prevalent on the Western Front especially, was not something that field commanders desired, though many had resigned themselves to it. Battlefield experience, however, such as the German and Allied offensives in the West in 1918, showed that tactical stalemate was not inevitable, and that it was indeed possible to conduct a more fluid war of maneuver. Those offensives, like Brusilov's two years earlier, featured artillery in a leading role. Nonetheless, successful assault tactics depended heavily on infantry and mobile firepower. Mobility was in fact the byword after 1918, and the quest for tactical mobility was the driving force in the development of new rifles and machine guns in the Second World War and beyond.

THE MACHINE GUN would become so closely associated with the Great War that it—like poison gas and the tank—would come to symbolize the vast impersonal slaughter of modern warfare, the mechanization of death. Though already widely in use before 1914, combat in the Great War proved its worth beyond a shadow of a doubt, and before the war was over the machine gun was an established fixture in infantry arsenals worldwide. There was no denying its value. Its properties transcended mere killing; as the concept of the "beaten zone" revealed, machine-gun bullets didn't have to hit anyone to serve a vital tactical purpose.

The machine gun, in the form that it was most frequently used in 1914–1918, was tailor-made for static warfare and poorly suited to maneuver. Most of the commonly encountered varieties—Maxim, Vickers, Schwarzlose, Browning—were portable only in the sense that it was indeed possible to carry them. But as they tipped the scales at one hundred to two hundred pounds assembled, they were not easily moved. A three-man crew could manhandle a water-cooled machine gun once the gun was broken down: one man carried the gun itself—a German MG 08 Maxim weighed just under sixty pounds, without water, mount, or ammo—while another carried the mount (eighty-five pounds for the MG 08), and a third lugged ammo and water. If the crewmembers were well trained and in good physical condition, they could keep up with the infantry over short distances, setting up and taking down the gun in seconds. But it could not be fired while in movement, and it was not transportable enough to fight as part of infantry units except when the gun was dug in.

That's where the light machine gun (LMG) came in. The LMG would be one of the more high-profile trends in small arms design during the interwar period. The species was not unknown during the Great War, when the need for a portable automatic weapon quickly became apparent. The Danish Madsen, the Hotchkiss "Portative" machine rifle, the Lewis gun, the Browning Automatic Rifle (BAR)—all were put to use in increasing numbers, especially in the closing campaigns in the West. The Germans also tried to convert the solid, reliable MG 08 Maxim into an LMG by adding a pistol grip, a shoulder stock, and a bipod, but at a hair under forty pounds it was only notionally "light."

The performance of these early LMGs, on the whole, was markedly inferior to that of the heavy guns. The heavies were rugged and solidly built. They cooled easily, too. Big, spacious receivers allowed air to circulate freely around the action, and made clearing a jam a simple task. Water-filled cooling jackets, as long as they were kept full, prevented barrels from overheating, allowing for sustained fire.

The LMGs didn't have these features, a necessary sacrifice to keep weight to a minimum. Most of them were gas operated, less reliable and less robust than the recoil-operated Vickers and Maxim guns. Just a speck or two of dirt in the gas port would be enough to put a gun out of action, and the gun might have to be disassembled and cleaned thoroughly for it to be restored to working order. Gas-operated guns had more moving parts and were more delicate. Air-cooled barrels, a universal feature of the new LMGs, were unsatisfactory when compared to water-cooled ones. When air-cooled guns were used to arm aircraft, that was a different matter. Machine guns mounted on a fighter plane would be kept cool by the constant flow of cold air (at high altitudes) over and around the barrel. Not so on the ground, in infantry use. Plus ammunition supply was an issue. Most of the heavy guns were belt-fed, using fabric ammunition belts holding two hundred rounds or more each, but long ammo belts were difficult to handle on the move, and so the LMGs relied on detachable magazines. Magazines could be easily carried in a pouch, and it took no more than a couple of seconds for a gunner (or his assistant) to drop an empty magazine and replace it with a fresh one. But the trade-off was capacity. The top-mounted magazine of the Lewis gun held forty-seven rounds, the box magazines of the Madsen and BAR held twenty. Even if air cooling worked better, sustained fire was physically impossible with an LMG.

The downsides of the LMG were reduced reliability and firepower; the payoff was portability. So long as a light machine gunner fired conservatively, in brief, rapid bursts, he would minimize the chance of overheating and make his limited ammunition supply last longer. And the greater portability gave the machine gun a promising new role to play. Among other things, it meant that machine guns could be used *offensively*, moving forward with advancing infantry. The Japanese had used their French Hotchkiss guns in this way during their war with Russia in 1904–1905. The French tactic of *feu de marche*, "walking" or "marching fire," was predicated on the widespread use of LMGs. The standard French LMG, the much-disliked M1915 CSRG Chauchat, was intended to fill that very role.

The quest to restore mobility to land warfare meant that LMGs were very much in demand, both during and after the First World War. But the war did not allow much latitude, or time or resources, for any of the combatant armies to experiment with new designs, and the catastrophic postwar economic downturn made extensive research unlikely. Some of the earliest LMGs of the interwar period were inspired by thrift, half-baked attempts to save money by repurposing older weapons to newer standards. In the newly born Soviet Union, for example, the Red Army experimented with ways of transforming the beefy Maxim into something a little more portable—in one case, by simply cutting ventilation baffles into the steel water jacket to facilitate air circulation.

But there was a clear path forward, and it came from America, or rather from the fecund genius of John Browning. His Browning Automatic Rifle (BAR) was arguably the best LMG to emerge from the Great War. In rugged reliability, weight, and rate of fire, it stood head and shoulders above its contemporaries. At twenty pounds, it was lighter and handier than the Lewis gun, simpler and cheaper to make than the Madsen. Though capable of fully automatic fire, it was meant to be used differently, to fill in the gap between a machine gun and a bolt-action rifle. And it required only one man to operate it. Its integral bipod steadied it when fired from a prone position, but it was just light enough that it could be fired from the shoulder or hip.

The BAR set the tone for what followed. It stayed on in American service, in both the Army and the Marines, through the Second World War and the Korean conflict. The BAR had its adherents in Europe, too. The FN manufactory in Belgium produced it under license for the armies of Belgium and Poland, and even the Chinese Nationalist Army adopted it. Most of the Western armies adopted native designs, and the majority of them didn't stray far from the BAR's basic characteristics. The French FM24/29, the British Bren gun, the Czech vz.26 and vz.27 (upon which the Bren was patterned), the Finnish Lahti-Saloranta M26, even the Soviet DP-28 and the odd, spindly Italian Breda M30, were all more similar to the BAR than they were different from it. All were gas-operated, all weighed around twenty pounds, all had shoulder stocks, and nearly all were intended to be used as rifles.

These were the most common automatic weapons when the next world war broke out in the late summer of 1939. Most armies held on to their earlier, heavier models, but the LMG had become the centerpiece of the new basic tactical unit: the rifle squad. Building on the experience of the late-war shock offensives, tactical doctrine during the 1920s and 1930s emphasized smaller infantry units to facilitate movement and encourage individual initiative. The most elementary infantry unit was the squad, roughly a dozen men commanded by a senior NCO or a junior lieutenant. The majority of men in a squad were ordinary riflemen; sometimes there were specialists attached to the squad, such as a sniper or a rifle-grenadier, the latter armed with a grenade-launcher attachment for his service rifle. But every squad—with the exception of specialty units, such as heavy machine-gun or mortar units—had at least one machine gunner and an assistant gunner, with the rest of the squad assisting in carrying extra ammunition for the LMG.

One major power, or aspiring major power, didn't exactly follow the automatic rifle/LMG trend as represented by the BAR and its contemporaries. Germany was not in a position to conduct extensive arms research after 1919. Political upheaval and worldwide economic distress would have made it difficult to invest in new weapons anyway, but the main reason was that Germany was not allowed to do so. The restrictions imposed by the punitive Versailles Treaty in 1919 not only eliminated Germany's air forces, gutted its navy, and cut its army down to the size of a border gendarmerie, but it also put a tight lid on weapons development and manufacture within Germany's borders.

When it came to automatic weapons, those restrictions were quite sharp: Versailles limited German machine-gun inventories to 792 water-cooled machine guns and 1,134 LMGs, and outright forbade the future manufacture or development of sustained-fire weapons on German soil. Those restrictions would become irrelevant when Adolf Hitler, who didn't care all that much what the Western democracies thought of a reinvigorated German military, proclaimed himself *Führer* in 1934, scrapping the peace terms shortly thereafter. But until German rearmament became official, the interwar Weimar government (1919–1934) and its army, the Reichswehr, had circumvented the involuntary disarmament by making clandestine arrangements with foreign governments and foreign industrial concerns. The amicable Rapallo Treaty (1922) with the pariah Soviet state granted Germany testing and training facilities deep within Russia, in exchange for the Soviets gaining access to Germany technology. German arms manufacturers simply worked on, and manufactured, their designs abroad.

Germany already had light machine guns, principally the chunky and awkward MG 08/15, and a more conventional LMG, the so-called "Dreyse" MG 13. The air-cooled MG 13 was more than adequate, and with its pistol grip, detachable twenty-five-round box magazine, and shoulder stock, it fit right in with the other LMGs of the interwar period. But the ordnance experts in the Reichswehr were aiming for something else entirely, a kind of machine gun that transcended—quite literally—the distinction between light and heavy machine guns. The Germans called this ideal type the *Einheitsmaschinengewehr*, or "universal machine gun." A universal machine gun would be substantial and durable enough to function as a sustained-fire weapon, taking the place of the old water-cooled Maxim, but light enough to serve as a squad light automatic, and—with specialty mounts and feed mechanisms—could also be adapted for aircraft uses, and even aboard naval vessels, tanks, armored cars, and other vehicles. The MG 13 was almost a step in that direction, but a more promising design was already in the works when the Reichswehr adopted the MG 13 in 1930.

At the Rheinmetall factory in Düsseldorf, a design team led by arms engineer Louis Stange collaborated on a new model LMG that Rheinmetall hoped to sell to the Reichswehr. Stange called it the MG 30, and it didn't look anything like a BAR. It didn't even look like a rifle. It was sleek and black and futuristic, with a buttstock shaped like a fishtail, and a box magazine that jutted out from the left side of the receiver. Its two-position trigger allowed it to be fired either in semiautomatic mode (one shot per trigger pull) or full auto. The Austrian and Swiss armies adopted the unconventional design, and Rheinmetall purchased the Swiss gunmaker Waffenfabrik Solothurn so the MG 30 could be manufactured abroad, bypassing the Versailles treaty restrictions. The Reichswehr, satisfied with the MG 13, turned it down.

But others in Germany saw great promise in the Stange machine gun, and an engineer at Mauser, Heinrich Vollmer, thought it worth improving upon. Vollmer's machine gun kept the basic appearance and action of the MG 30, but a whole host of innovative new features transformed it into a gunner's dream, including a feed mechanism that could handle both long ammo belts and an attached magazine, and a quick-change barrel, so that the gunner could quickly and safely remove a hot or malfunctioning barrel. Vollmer's mounting system permitted the gun to be fired from a lightweight bipod for infantry use, or from a special flexible mount called a lafette, which could be set up in several configurations—including for use as an antiaircraft gun. At just twenty-seven pounds, Vollmer's machine gun was slightly heavier than the BAR but two pounds lighter than the MG 13, and its firing characteristics were superior to anything then in service anywhere. Even though it was air-cooled, the quick-change barrel allowed something very much like sustained fire, and the weapon fired from an open bolt—meaning that the action remained open between shots, allowing fresh air to circulate inside the action and cool the weapon much faster. Its cyclic rate, about eight hundred to nine hundred rounds per minute, was half again as high as the MG 13 and roughly double that of the BAR.

After Hitler came to power, the new, reborn German military establishment, the Wehrmacht, jumped on the Vollmer gun, formally adopting it as the MG 34. It went into full production in 1939, and rolled off the assembly line fast enough to equip much of the Wehrmacht when it surged into Poland later that year. It would go on to serve in Hitler's legions in all theaters of the war as the basic squad-level LMG, the principal weapon on armored cars, and the secondary weapon on tanks. It was, however, a finely engineered and expensive weapon, and though it remained in service to the end of the war, it was officially replaced by an improved wartime model, the notorious MG 42. Easier and cheaper to manufacture than the precision-built MG 34, the MG 42 was made largely from stamped sheet metal parts; and with an astonishing cyclic rate of 1,200 rounds per minute it produced almost half again as much firepower as its predecessor. The MG 42 was, like the MG 34, used as a universal machine gun, and it was demonstrably better than anything the Allies had. Its unique sound when firing, the result of spitting out twenty rounds per second, earned it the American sobriquet of "Hitler's buzzsaw," and soldiers who faced it in combat sometimes compared its chatter to the sound of cloth ripping.

The MG 34 and the MG 42 were the future of conventional automatic weapons. Though they represented German superiority in technology, they were clearly not enough to make up for other deficiencies in the German war effort in the Second World War. But the Allies—principally the Americans and the Soviets, who had stuck with their antiquated, Great War–era machine guns—still recognized that they had much to learn from the Germans.

While a "universal" machine gun could serve in many roles, it could not possibly serve in all, and it was a mark of the machine gun's maturity and manifest usefulness that specialized automatics

Plate 30. A German machine-gun crew in France, June 1944, with the MG 34. Germany's first "all-purpose" or "universal" machine gun, the MG 34 was air-cooled and thus easy to overheat, but it was also equipped with a quick-change barrel, so that overheated barrels could be swapped out for cool barrels to avert mechanical malfunction.

Image: Bundesarchiv, Bild 101I-721-0386-15 / photographer: Jesse.

began to appear in the interwar period. One was the "heavy" machine gun—heavy because of its caliber, not the weight of the weapon itself. The "heavy" machine guns of the Great War were rifle-caliber weapons, meaning that they fired conventional rifle ammunition. That meant, in 1914–1918, roughly .30-inch caliber (or between 7.62mm and 8mm), except for the Italians and the Japanese, who had a predilection for smaller calibers. A .30-caliber bullet worked just fine on human targets, or on soft targets like wood-and-fabric aircraft. But against metal airframes, or armored vehicles, those bullets did little damage. Incendiary bullets could take down hydrogen-filled observation balloons, but there was only so much incendiary compound that could be crammed inside a slender .30-caliber bullet.

Hence the heavy machine gun. Designs appeared as early as 1918–1919. One of the first, and the most enduring, was yet another contribution from the prolific John Browning: the .50-inch caliber M2 (1919), immortalized by American soldiers in every war since then as the Ma Deuce. Its high-velocity, large-caliber bullet made the M2 ideal for all sorts of applications, ranging from the auxiliary armament on American tanks to the basic machine gun on most American warplanes.

The Ma Deuce was only the beginning. By the onset of the Second World War, most of the great and middling powers had adopted heavy machine guns, especially for aircraft and antiaircraft applications.

THE GREAT WAR was the first truly high-tech war, and as such it put to rest all sorts of myths and false assumptions about the role of modern technology in warfare. One was the notion that deadlier weapons would make wars shorter and more humane, because civilized nations would not possibly continue to fight for long when the human costs were so high. Today, that conviction strikes us as naïve, laughable, and obscene, all at once, because we know it to be tragically false; we know the slaughter that actually ensued in 1914–1918. But in the West at the turn of the century, the almost childlike faith in the benign nature of technological progress and the goodness of science made it seductive.

In the nuts-and-bolts world of tactics, the Great War slew even more fantasies about the nature of war in the new century. Of those, none was more enduring than the myth of long-range combat.

That boundlessly optimistic faith in the precision of military rifles is readily seen in one specific feature of those rifles: the rear sight. Since the first rifle-muskets went into service in the 1850s, rifled military weapons featured sights that—while they couldn't be adjusted laterally—were at least graduated for distance. The American M1861 Springfield rifle-musket had a three-leaf rear sight, each leaf of a different height, corresponding to the greater elevation of the muzzle required for long-distance shooting. The shortest leaf was intended for targets at around one hundred yards or less, the second for around three hundred yards, and the third for five hundred. These were not precise at all, but they offered the soldier a general guideline for how much to elevate the muzzle so that its bullet would hit a distant target rather than plunging harmlessly to the earth well short of it.

The rear sights of First World War rifles, by contrast, were far longer, and were graduated at one-hundred-meter (or yards, or *arshins* in Russia) intervals up to exceedingly long ranges. The rear sight of the German service rifle, the *Gewehr* 98, was marked out to two thousand meters. The sheer ridiculousness of this notion—that a soldier, without using a telescopic sight, could see a man-sized target two kilometers away, much less stand a chance of hitting it—should be obvious. And yet it wasn't obvious in 1914, not to those advocates of marksmanship training who truly believed that infantry firefights would take place with the armies barely within view of each other.

Successful trench assault tactics, instead, emphasized melee, usually within the confines of the trench itself. In this environment, the standard infantry rifle was close to useless. Its rate of fire was too slow; it was too long and awkward for hand-to-hand combat. The German *Stoßtruppen* who spearheaded the German assault units in 1918 equipped themselves from a different kind of arsenal altogether. Short carbines were favored over standard infantry rifles. Fighting knives, nail-studded cudgels, sharpened entrenching spades, grenades, and pistols were the preferred weapons of the trench-raider.

The pistol was ideal in the confines of the trench, where its limited range and mediocre accuracy weren't major concerns. The ballistic properties of the pistol and its cartridge were almost irrelevant in these conditions; what mattered most were its portability, its hitting power—its capacity to kill or disable a man with a single shot, usually more a function of bullet mass than of velocity—and a high rate of fire. Revolvers worked just fine, and they were rightly considered to be the sturdiest, most reliable repeating pistols of the era. But if given the choice, most soldiers would opt for something a little more state of the art: a semiautomatic, or autoloading, pistol.

Ever since Hiram Maxim patented his first machine-gun design, firearms engineers had been looking for ways to make that kind of firepower more compact. The first semiautomatic pistols made their debut on the European civilian market in the early 1890s; within a decade or so, they had begun to replace revolvers as the primary pistols in most Western armies. While revolvers were robust and simple, less likely to malfunction than automatics, the latter had some big advantages: rate of fire, lighter trigger pull, speed of loading. Revolvers had to be reloaded by inserting each cartridge, individually, into empty chambers in the cylinder, while with most semiautomatics the user had only to eject an empty magazine and insert a fresh one.

Many of the earliest automatic pistols of the era used recoil-powered actions, variations on the kind of action that Hiram Maxim designed for his machine gun: the backward motion of the free-floating barrel did the work. The pioneering Borchardt C-93 (1893) and the Schwarzlose M1898 operated on this principle, as did the more famous Luger and Mauser pistols. Others employed a much simpler action, popularly known as blowback. In a blowback action, the spent case flew back from the chamber after firing, extracting and ejecting itself; the same energy powered a slide mechanism that slammed back, and was then driven forward by a spring, the slide cocking the hammer and chambering a fresh round from the magazine in the process. Blowback actions were too weak to handle the high chamber pressures made by rifle cartridges, but for most pistol cartridges they worked just fine.

It was indeed possible to make a fully automatic pistol. The army of Austria-Hungary issued one of its main sidearms, the M1912 Steyr-Hahn, in fully automatic form in 1916. Similar alterations were made to Luger and Mauser pistols, too, including the well-known *Schnellfeuer* (quick-fire) variant of the "broomhandle" Mauser pistol. None of them proved to be satisfactory for any foreseeable purpose, and their shooting qualities left much to be desired. In recoil-operated pistols, like the Luger and the *Schnellfeuer* Mauser, the cyclic rate of fire could go as high as eight hundred to one thousand rounds per minute—way too high, and because pistol magazines rarely held more than ten rounds, that kind of speed made a fully automatic pistol useless. Plus, a high rate of fire made it difficult to control the weapon. When a pistol unleashed a torrent of bullets at twice the speed of a Maxim, it invariably resulted in muzzle climb—the tendency of the muzzle to rise during firing, caused by recoil and the motion of the bolt or slide slamming rearward as it cycled. Larger magazines helped, as did attaching a shoulder stock, which allowed the firer to brace the weapon against the body. But there was still no perceived niche that a high-speed, fully automatic pistol could fill.

Still, a more practical small automatic was gradually emerging, not exactly a machine rifle and not exactly a machine pistol, either. In Italy, the army took a light machine gun made for aircraft armament, the Villar-Perosa, and made it into an infantry weapon. The Villar-Perosa was a truly odd gun, firing pistol ammunition and using an unconventional double-barrel configuration, and it made a terrible aerial machine gun. But reduced to a single barrel and given a shoulder stock, it worked pretty well as a light automatic for land use. The Germans had better luck. Hugo Schmeisser, one of the many brilliant engineers in Germany's pool of weapons talent, set to work with a design team at Theodor Bergmann's rifle factory in 1915 to make a miniature automatic. They had a working prototype within a year, but the German high command turned it down. Not because there was anything wrong with the design; the German generals actually found the Schmeisser-Bergmann gun quite impressive. It was just that they couldn't think of a purpose for it. New weapons needlessly complicated supply issues, which were complicated enough as it was.

But when the German army premiered its new assault tactics in 1917, Hugo Schmeisser's odd little weapon finally seemed to have a purpose. It went into production early in 1918, and the first production run of what was officially dubbed the *Maschinenpistole* 18 (or MP 18) found its way into the hands of frontline troops that spring, just in time for the *Kaiserschlacht*.

The Schmeisser-Bergmann MP 18 is not remarkable in appearance. It resembles a short, stubby carbine, with a very ordinary wooden shoulder stock. Its squat barrel is surrounded by a barrel jacket, a tube of thin steel perforated with small holes, designed to improve air circulation and keep the barrel cool. On the left side of the breech, just opposite the ejection port, an oddly shaped magazine—the Germans called it a *Trommel*, or "drum"—juts out at an awkward angle. But inside, the gun was all brilliant simplicity itself. Schmeisser used a blowback system, not rugged but rugged enough to handle German 9mm pistol ammo, and the gun had a relatively low rate of fire, around five hundred rounds per minute. It weighed in at eleven pounds, heavier than a Mauser rifle but much lighter and handier than the MG 08/15 light machine gun. The weapon proved to be a hit with those soldiers lucky enough to be issued one, and it was feared by Allied troops who encountered it. It was more effective than anything, except possibly hand grenades, at clearing an enemy trench. The MP 18 was quite accurate, too, but even if it hadn't been it wouldn't have mattered, for its role was to spray bullets in confined spaces at very short range.

After the war was over, the MP 18 proved itself in another, un-looked-for capacity. As Germany devolved into civil war in the early, troubled years of the Weimar Republic, MP 18s went into action in the hands of the paramilitary *Freikorps* units against the Spartacist rebels and other leftist forces. In the brutal, house-to-house fighting that took place in the streets of German cities, the machine pistol quickly showed its superiority to conventional rifles and machine guns.

The MP 18 was the first practical model of an entirely new type of specialized small arm. The Germans persisted in calling that type the machine pistol, and not without reason, for it used pistol ammunition and had the ballistic properties of a pistol. But the anglophone term for the new infantry weapon more accurately re-flected its value in combat: the submachine gun. The Allies were late to the game, too late to use submachine guns in World War I, but they instantly recognized the worth of the Schmeisser-Bergmann. A retired American ordnance officer, John Taliaferro Thompson, was an engineer at the Remington factory during the war. He had been working on his own design for a blowback semiautomatic rifle, without much luck—no matter what he tried, a blowback action would not stand up to high-powered rifle cartridges. But he found much better results with the standard American automatic pistol round, the beefy .45-caliber ACP (Automatic Centerfire Pistol) cartridge, so Thompson changed his plans accordingly. Soon his hoped-for auto-rifle became a handheld machine gun firing a pistol cartridge—a submachine gun, in other words, although the term wasn't in common use as yet. Thompson's "Annihilator," later officially called the Thompson Submachine Gun, M1919, did not attract any military sales.

In the immediate aftermath of the Great War, generals saw the submachine gun in much the same way they saw the tank: as a clever response to a peculiar set of circumstances, namely trench warfare, but it was by nature a transient solution. The trench war-fare of the Great War was widely regarded as an aberration in the history of warfare, unlikely to be repeated. Since no one seemed able to envision a use for submachine guns outside of trench raiding, it followed that an investment in their further development wouldn't be a wise one. Besides, these were lean years, and whatever funds the military establishments of the West had at their disposal would be dedicated to improving warplanes, light machine guns, and those technologies that would assuredly find a place in the wars of the future. There was a certain amount of snobbery involved, too; even as the profession of arms had accepted the airplane and the machine gun as legitimate, among some more conservative officers the conviction still prevailed that the submachine gun was not a serious weapon.

In America, a flourishing civilian market for the weapon emerged during the interwar decades. Though John Thompson had pictured his invention in the hands of American doughboys, clearing German trenches of jackbooted Huns—Thompson, in fact, had originally advertised his gun as the "Trench Broom"—it instead found a home much closer to home. Shortly after the M1919 Thompson hit the American market, gangsters and street thugs eagerly took up the "tommy gun," which gave them an unbridgeable advantage over police still armed with revolvers. Law enforcement came to favor the Thompson in response.

Even with minimal official interest, the submachine gun survived. Most of the major armies—with the single and unusual exception of Britain—experimented with them, if in a very low-key way, during the interwar period. In the 1930s, a second generation of submachine guns emerged, somewhat improved from their first-generation forebears, and the universal trend toward rearmament in the middle of the decade helped to accelerate the further development of the weapon. Most of the second-generation sub-guns—like Italy's MAB38A Beretta, the Soviet PPD series, and the Finnish KP31—superficially resembled the Schmeisser guns, heavily built with wooden stocks and shrouded barrels. But unquestionably the best of the lot was a radical departure: the German Schmeisser. Not designed with an eye toward the aesthetic qualities of the era, the Schmeisser MP 38 and MP 40 were decidedly futuristic looking. They used no wood at all in their construction, with Bakelite substituted for wood in the grips and forestock. A folding steel shoulder stock, which could be unlocked and tucked under the body of the gun, made the new German guns lighter and handier.

The submachine gun was still, in this incarnation, an elite weapon, as it had been in the Great War, a specialized weapon for specialized troops. The German MP 38, for example, was originally to be issued to tank crews and other soldiers for whom a full-sized infantry rifle was not a practical option. No one would have given serious thought to substituting them for bolt-action rifles, not as a general-issue weapon. The quality of the firearms themselves reflected that elite status. The pre-1939 submachine guns were well-designed, finely produced weapons, with milled steel parts and finishes of the highest quality. Accuracy was as much prized as rate of fire, and many of the early submachine guns had adjustable tangent rear sights to allow for midrange fire. They required, in short, much more labor to manufacture than conventional infantry rifles, and they cost substantially more, too.

But as the new realities of combat in the Second World War became apparent, so too did the virtues of the submachine gun. Its handiness made it a convenient choice for soldiers who spent much of their time in confined spaces, and for infantry NCOs and junior-grade officers who needed more firepower than a service pistol could provide. But there was so much more to this small weapon, and as it had proven itself in trench fighting in 1918, it shone again in close quarters combat in 1939–1945.

The submachine gun, in short, transitioned from a precision instrument—a specialized weapon finely crafted to narrow tolerances—to its reincarnation in the midst of war: a cheap, disposable, ugly, but brutally effective mass-produced firearm. The pioneers here were, perhaps oddly, Britain and the Soviet Union. Both were motivated by desperation. The British army had adopted the Thompson before the war, in modest quantities, but it was an expensive firearm, and once the United States entered the war late in 1941 the American-made trench broom was essentially unavailable. At the same time, the perceived need for close-quarters weapons swelled. The retreat of the British army from France in the late spring of 1940 and the resulting fear of imminent German invasion after the evacuation at Dunkirk prompted the British armed services to invest in submachine guns for home defense. The Royal Navy and the Royal Air Force (RAF) went in one direction, adopting the Lanchester, a close copy of the German MP 28, in itself a somewhat improved MP 18. The army went in a radically different direction.

The Lanchester, like the German weapons that inspired it, was a beautifully crafted weapon. Not so the army submachine gun. A design team at the Royal Small Arms Factory, Enfield, came up with the initial design for a simplified, much less expensive automatic. It was known, officially and unofficially, as the Sten, named after two of its principal designers and their employer (Shepherd, Turpin, Enfield). The Sten resembled no gun that had ever come before. It had neither the oiled-wood-and-burnished-metal charm of the Bergmann-inspired guns, nor the chilling deadly elegance of the MP 38. The Sten wasn't milled from solid steel, but was instead fashioned from stamped steel components. Its skeletal steel shoulder stock was welded to a body that more resembled a length of muffler-pipe than a conventional receiver. The trigger guard was angular and awkward; even the trigger itself was a blocky and thick piece of cut sheet steel. The thirty-two-round stick magazine jutted from the left side of the receiver at a right angle. The sights were so rudimentary as to be almost pointless. Early models had a tendency to jam frequently. The Sten was ugly and inaccurate, and its critics despised it—but it could spray bullets at a five-hundred-rounds-per-minute cyclic rate, and any modestly equipped machine shop could build it. It was cheap and, for the most part, it worked. Its manufacture required less time and fewer materials than a conventional bolt-action rifle. The Sten, in short, signaled that the submachine gun *could* be a mass-issue weapon, not subordinate to the bolt-action rifle but its equal.

The British army did not go quite that far. The Sten was common enough, to be sure, and during the course of the war the British shipped it clandestinely by the tens of thousands to resistance movements and partisan groups across Europe. But it was never a general-issue weapon, and to the war's end the British army favored the tried-and-true, bolt-action Lee-Enfield rifle, now a half-century old.

The Russians, though, *did* go that far. The Red Army did embrace the submachine gun as the equal of the rifle. For all its many flaws, for all the disruptions caused by Josef Stalin's prewar purge of suspected dissidents in the officer corps, the Red Army was making some bold moves in weapons design. Right up to the moment when Hitler betrayed his erstwhile ally Stalin and sent his legions rolling across the frontier onto Russian soil in June 1941, the Soviets were turning out truly remarkable firearms prototypes. It helped, of course, that the forced industrialization of the Communist state brought forth a cadre of gunsmiths and firearms engineers, some of the most talented of the century: Georgy Shpagin, Vasily Degtyaryov, Sergei Simonov, Fedor Tokarev, Alexey Sudayev, and the larger-than-life Mikhail Kalashnikov. But their main focus was on automatic rifles and machine guns. Submachine guns were almost an afterthought.

That is, until 1939–1940, when the Red Army crashed across the Russo-Finnish border to start the Winter War, Stalin's blatant attempt to conquer Finland. Despite the huge disparity in resources between the Soviet Union and the small, newly independent Nordic state, the Finnish army did remarkably well, holding off the vastly superior Red Army for a full two months before finally giving in to the inevitable. It was a humbling experience for the Soviets, who had plenty of armor, heavy artillery, and air support, while the Finns had virtually none of those things.

One of the many lessons that the Soviets took away from the Winter War was the importance of close-range automatics. The Finns made much heavier use of their KP31 submachine guns than the Russians did of their PPD models, and in close combat the difference was telling. It wasn't that the KP31 was superior to the well-made PPD; it was merely a matter of numbers. The Finns regarded their KP as a general-issue weapon, while for the Soviets the PPD was still an auxiliary.

But the Soviets learned from the Finns, and before 1940 was over their engineers were hard at work on new, *cheaper* submachine guns that could be produced quickly and in quantity. Two significant models emerged. Georgy Shpagin's PPSh-41 premiered in late 1940 and went into production the following year. Externally, it closely resembled the old PPD, with a wooden stock and a drum magazine reminiscent of the Thompson's, but most of the metal parts were stamped rather than milled. It was reliable and tough, as Russian weapons tend to be, and while it was made with

Plate 31. German soldier aiming his *Sturmgewehr* 44, the world's first assault rifle. The *Sturmgewehr*, which combined all the best features of an infantry rifle, light machine gun, and submachine gun, was arguably the most versatile infantry weapon of the Second World War; but like so many other German "wonder-weapons," it appeared too late in the conflict to make a meaningful difference.
Image: Bundesarchiv, Bild 146-1979-118-55.

sloppy tolerances and poor finishes, the PPSh could suffer almost infinite abuse and still function fine. With a cyclic rate in excess of one thousand rounds per minute, it was also one of the fastest automatic weapons of the age, but its capacious seventy-one round magazine compensated for the rapid ammo expenditure.

The PPSh was an elegant work of art when compared to its comrade, the PPS. Designed by Alexey Sudayev, the PPS was a product of the epic—and horrific—872-day siege of Leningrad (1941–1944); the scarcity of supplies and skilled labor inspired and guided the design. Sudayev's intention was to create a sub-gun that could be turned out faster than even the PPSh, and in just about any workshop capable of light machining and welding. The result was similar to the Sten: brutal-looking, crude, all parts save the plastic grips made from stamped steel. It consumed half the steel used for the PPSh, and took half the time to make. Its lower rate of fire made it easier to control than the PPSh, too. The PPS was Soviet weapons engineering at its best: not pretty but impossible to destroy; nearly impossible to jam, even when filthy, combining frugality and functionality in better balance than any of its contemporaries.

As the Great Patriotic War against the Hitlerite invaders dragged on, the Red Army came to rely more and more on the PPSh and the PPS, to the point that the sub-guns actually began to rival, even replace, the standard Mosin-Nagant infantry rifles. Soon the Soviets were sending into combat entire rifle squads armed with submachine guns, with rifles slipping into the auxiliary role. When Soviet and German infantry are compared rifle-squad by rifle-squad, the Germans had an advantage in medium- and long-range firepower, as the MG 34 and MG 42 all-purpose machine guns easily outclassed the Soviet Maxim and the DP light machine gun. But in short-range firepower the Soviets had the edge, and that was owed to their submachine guns. In the Red Army, the submachine guns themselves became powerful political symbols after the war. The PPSh came to represent virtuous resistance against fascism, the resilience of the Motherland and the native genius of the people; it's no accident that statues of Red Army *frontoviki*, defiantly brandishing the PPSh, adorn war monuments throughout the lands of the former USSR and its satellite states. The PPS became a symbol, too, but an unfortunate one. The siege of Leningrad was an embarrassment to Stalin, and the PPS was a reminder of the city's suffering and of its self-reliance. Though perhaps the best submachine gun of the Second World War, the PPS quietly disappeared from Soviet service after the end of hostilities.

No other major army went to the lengths the Soviets did to put the submachine gun at the center of infantry tactics. The Germans came close, though. Submachine guns were so commonly used by the Wehrmacht that wartime production of the MP 38 and MP 40 couldn't possibly keep up with the demand, and—as with nearly every other kind of equipment—the German war machine relied heavily upon antiquated and captured foreign weapons to make up the difference. None of the other Allied powers viewed submachine guns as anything more than secondary weapons. But the technology, and the emphasis on function over form with an absolute and utter disregard for aesthetics, spread and prospered. Even the United States, which had in the Thompson an excellent submachine gun, shifted production to a weapon more like the Sten and the PPS. The US M3 submachine gun, known semi-affectionately to its GI users as the Grease Gun for its obvious similarity to an auto mechanic's tool, became the predominant American sub-gun long before the war ended in 1945.

The submachine gun was better suited than the conventional infantry rifle to the most commonly encountered tactical situations in the Second World War. Especially in 1944–1945, much of the ground fighting—on the Eastern Front, in Italy, in France, in the Low Countries, even in the Pacific theater—was done at close range, where the sub-gun worked to best advantage. And yet, outside of the Red Army, it still remained a specialized weapon; close-range firefights, contrary to the prognostications of soldier-scholars, were not obsolete, but that hardly meant that infantry would *only* fight at close range. There was still very much a need for long-range weapons, and the submachine gun did not address that need.

Could there be a middle way? Could there be a universal infantry longarm, one that could deliver the submachine gun's rate of fire, retain its handiness, and yet still be competitive at longer ranges? There actually was, and it was already beginning to make its appearance in the middle of the Second World War.

THE AVERAGE RIFLEMAN went to war in 1939 with a rifle that was functionally identical to the one his father fought with in 1914: a bolt-action rifle with an integral magazine that held five to ten rounds of high-velocity, smokeless, centerfire ammunition. Hitler's Wehrmacht selected as its main service rifle the Kar98k, a shortened version of the *Gewehr* 98 of the Kaiser's army. The Russian long rifle, the M1891 Mosin-Nagant, was shortened, given improved sights, and reborn as the Soviet M91/30. The British SMLE (No. 3 Mk. 1) of the Second World War is almost indistinguishable from the SMLE No. 1 Mk. 3 of the First World War. Just about every major army in the world clung to unaltered or slightly modified versions of its Great War rifles. Even the new armies of the 1920s—those of Poland, Czechoslovakia, and Hungary, for example—took advantage of the massive arms surplus after the First World War and armed their soldiers with cast-off German, Russian, or Austrian weapons.

But if light machine guns and submachine guns were readily available in 1939, and if the new tactics were centered on rapid-fire weapons and mobility, then why didn't the major armies make an effort to rearm all their soldiers, or most of them, with automatics? Perhaps they could have, and there were undoubtedly good reasons to do so, but the reasons against doing so were more compelling. Cost, for one: machine guns were much more expensive to manufacture than bolt-action rifles, and the cheap, sheet-metal submachine guns of the PPS-PPSh generation hadn't been invented yet. European national armories and arms manufacturers already had the machinery in place to make conventional rifles, so starting the production lines rolling again was a relatively simple matter. War surplus abounded, rifles by the millions, rifle cartridges by the tens of millions, and in the cash-strapped interwar period that was reason enough to stick by the older weapons. Big-ticket items like warplanes and battleships were a higher priority, consuming what little discretionary funds were available. In both Britain and the United States, weapons experts recommended new, ballistically superior ammunition, and rifles to fire that ammo. But military authorities nixed the idea in both cases, because when there were so many rounds of the old rifle ammunition gathering dust in arsenals, and it would have been the height of fiscal profligacy to adopt a new rifle and a new cartridge for general issue. The major armies had gone down that road in the years before the Great War, and no one was prepared or inclined to revisit that.

Plus bolt-action rifles had some laudable characteristics. They were sturdier than machine guns, easier to keep clean, nearly idiot-proof. Soldiers were notorious for failing to keep their weapons clean; bolt-action rifles were forgiving of that neglect, but automatics as a rule were not, the lighter gas-operated guns being the most finicky of all. Automatics were significantly heavier, and most of the light machine guns took two men to operate effectively. During the Great War, the task of keeping up with the demand for rifle ammunition had presented a tough challenge, even for the more industrialized powers, but the universal use of fully automatic weapons would increase ammunition consumption exponentially. Or so it was believed.

Still, the notion of a special battle rifle, semi- or fully automatic but just as handy and reliable as a bolt-action, had its prophets and adherents during and after the Great War. The technology was there; the trick, as with light machine guns, was to keep the weight reasonably low and the action robust. John Browning had already patented autoloading shotguns and rifles for the sporting market, as had Winchester, and in 1908 a Mexican general named Manuel Mondragón designed a gas-operated semiautomatic military rifle that fired a standard-issue Mauser cartridge. Mauser came out with a semiautomatic carbine for the German army in 1916; the French, still trying to make the tactic of "marching fire" work, introduced its own gas-operated rifle, the RSC-17, the following year. All were clever designs, and all shared the same basic flaws: they were fragile, expensive, easily fouled by dirt, and needed frequent cleanings. In the muddy trenches of the Western Front in the First World War, the latter issues were a serious demerit.

During the interwar years, the United States and the Soviet Union made the biggest strides in this particular direction. Even under the budget crunch that followed on the heels of the postwar depression, the US Army considered several semiautomatic rifle prototypes during the 1920s and 1930s. It ultimately settled on a gas-operated rifle put forward by John Garand, a government engineer at Springfield Armory, in 1936. The Soviets were working with similar ideas, and followed the Garand with one of their own, Fedor Tokarev's SVT-38, in 1938.

As the world drew near to the brink of war once again at the close of the 1930s, two major armies—the American and the Soviet—had taken a bold step. It turned out to be a smart move for the Americans and an abortive one for the Soviets. A revised and improved version of Tokarev's rifle, the SVT-40, had gone into mass production mere months before the German invasion in June 1941, and the Soviet high command determined that under the circumstances it would be prudent to halt production of the SVT and return to the trusty old Mosin-Nagant. Production of the American Garand, now officially called the M1, on the other hand, was already in full swing when the Japanese attack on Pearl Harbor propelled the United States into the war. As with any weapon, it's difficult to assess the role that the Garand played in American victory in Europe and the Pacific, but it's clear that it gave the GI a measurable advantage over his Axis counterparts. Even if American machine guns were inferior to German ones, the difference in potential firepower between a semiautomatic Garand and a bolt-action Mauser was enough to compensate for it.

The semiautomatic battle rifle caught on quickly in the Second World War. The Germans, too, started working on such a rifle themselves, though why they waited until after the outbreak of war to do so is puzzling. The German results were surprisingly unimpressive, given how successful their arms industry had been with machine gun and submachine gun designs. The first attempts, introduced by Walther and Mauser in 1941, were overly complicated and unreliable when compared to the Tokarev and Garand rifles. German soldiers campaigning in Russia encountered the Tokarev rifles, and promptly fell in love with their rugged simplicity. Tokarevs became a prized possession for those Germans lucky enough to capture one. Inspired by the SVT, Walther modified its 1941 model, and the result—the G43—was a great improvement over the earlier German rifles. Still, it appeared too late to be produced in significant numbers; less than half a million came off the production lines by war's end. The only major combatant to rely mostly on a semiautomatic rifle, then, was the United States.

The Garand was a very good rifle. General George S. Patton, with a generous dash of hyperbole, called it "the greatest battle implement ever devised." The Garand undoubtedly gave American troops a great advantage in firepower, especially over their Japanese foes, who relied less heavily than the Germans did on automatic weapons to augment their infantry firepower at the squad level. But other, even more effective weapons were already in development, and not in the United States. The next step in the evolution of the infantryman's weapon was the select-fire rifle. From the standpoint of engineering, a select-fire rifle is no more challenging to design than a semiautomatic rifle or a light machine gun, because it simply combines the two: a select-fire rifle can be fired either in autoloading (semiautomatic) or full-automatic modes, converting the rifle from one to the other usually by flipping a switch. Some submachine guns (like the Soviet PPSh) and light machine guns (like the German MG 34) already had something very much like this feature. The later models of the BAR were, technically, select-fire rifles, although the Browning's weight and bulk really put it in the LMG category. In 1936, prior to the introduction of the Tokarev autoloading rifles, the Soviets adopted what was perhaps the first general-issue select-fire rifle. Sergei Simonov's pioneering AVS-36, at 9.5 pounds, was half the weight of the BAR. But it had its quirks and faults, like most lightweight automatics. It fouled too easily and was difficult to maintain in the field. Relatively few were made.

Then the Germans took a crack at it. The result was one of the most visually striking weapons of the Second World War, as futuristic in appearance as the MG 34. The FG 42—*FG* stood for *Fallschirmjägergewehr*, or "paratrooper rifle"—was designed in response to Luftwaffe's request for a light automatic suitable for airborne use. The gas-operated FG was one of the most sophisticated rifle designs of the Second World War, incorporating such advanced ergonomic features as a sharply sloped pistol grip and a "straight-line" recoil configuration, which put the line of recoil (that is, the longitudinal axis of the bore) directly in line with the shoulder stock, making the weapon easier to control in full-auto mode. The FG was brilliant, but not practical, especially with regard to its cost. Such a fine weapon could not possibly be made cheaply enough to become standard issue.

All the early select-fire weapons, including the FG 42, shared a major flaw in common: comfort, or rather discomfort. All of them, like LMGs, fired ordinary rifle cartridges: American-made BARs fired the US .30-06 round, like the Garand; the AVS chambered the venerable and punishing Russian 7.62×54mmR cartridge; the FG 42 fired the same 7.92×57mm Mauser cartridge as the German Kar98k bolt-action. These were powerful rounds, designed to be able to hit and kill at two kilometers distance. They were products of the 1890s, after all, when the belief in long-range firefights was at its peak. Because they were powerful, they produced brutal recoil. They put a lot of stress on complex automatic firing mechanisms; worse, they put a lot of stress on the rifleman's shoulder, and when fired in the full-auto mode they were hard to control.

A solution was already in the works as early as the Great War. In 1918, a German staff officer on ordnance duty made what was then a radical suggestion. As he knew from practical combat experience, infantrymen never engaged in firefights at distances greater than eight hundred meters, and usually at much closer ranges. There was no earthly reason to have a rifle that could kill human targets at double or triple that range, except perhaps for specially trained snipers. Instead, he proposed an intermediate cartridge, with a propellant charge smaller than what was used in conventional rifle rounds. The intermediate cartridge would save on propellant *and* on brass, because less propellant meant a shorter cartridge case; since the individual rounds would be lighter, soldiers could carry more ammunition. The lighter ammunition would produce less recoil, definitely a boon for smaller or less muscular riflemen. And all this with no appreciable diminishment in combat performance. It was a brilliant idea, but it was also too radical for 1918. The proposal was quickly shot down. Understandably so, for what army, in the middle of a war and fighting for its life, would want to introduce a new cartridge and complicate both manufacturing and supply?

The idea caught on among firearms engineers, though, and throughout the 1920s and 1930s German gunmakers in particular experimented with reduced caliber intermediate cartridges. And as the Wehrmacht became bogged down in its bloody struggle with the Red Army after 1941, the idea took on new life. The Kar98k, a bolt-action, was too slow, and submachine guns weren't very effective past one hundred meters. The Germans had already devised a universal machine gun. What about a universal infantry rifle, something to fit the gap between bolt-action and sub-gun?

Hugo Schmeisser and the Walther firm both submitted prototype rifles to the Waffenamt, the German office of armaments, which in turn took ideas from both designs and made its own. It was called, tentatively, the MP 43. But that name wouldn't do, and for reasons that had more to do with politics than anything else. Hitler often couldn't resist the temptation to meddle in weapons technology, and usually not for the better. The Führer was suspicious of new rifle designs; he initially opposed the notion of an intermediate cartridge, and didn't see the need for a new submachine gun—after all, that's what an MP was. At one point, Hitler ordered the MP 43 project shut down completely. But the rifle's superior qualities shone through, and field trials in 1943 elicited a uniformly enthusiastic response from combat commanders.

The statistics spoke for themselves. Though at just over ten pounds, the MP 43 was a tad heavier than the general-issue Mauser rifle, it was worth the extra weight, with a cyclic rate of around five hundred rounds per minute when in full-auto mode. As a selective-fire rifle, it could be switched from full-auto to semiauto with the flick of a switch mounted conveniently over the trigger assembly. Its detachable magazine held thirty rounds of the new intermediate 8mm *Kurz* ("short," 7.92×33mm) cartridge. In full-auto mode, the MP 43 produced the firepower of a submachine gun but with much greater accuracy and range, and a lot less recoil than regular infantry rifles. It was deadly accurate well beyond six hundred meters when fired in semiautomatic mode. It could do everything, in short, that an infantry rifle, submachine gun, and LMG could do, without notable compromises. And it, like the FG 42, incorporated all sorts of revolutionary external features, too, including an infrared aiming device code-named Vampir—the world's first functional night-vision scope.

The MP 43 was clearly superior to any other infantry rifle in use, anywhere in the world, and Hitler's generals demanded it. Hitler was impressed with it, too, and agreed; it went into full production in the spring of 1944. The intention was that the MP 43 would replace the Kar98k as the basic infantry firearm, but of course by the time the factories started turning it out in quantity it was already too late. It saw a fair amount of service in the little time that it had left, and not quite half a million had been produced by war's end. Interestingly, the designation MP 43 (or MP 44, its first official designation after it was approved) didn't stick for long. Either because Hitler demanded it, or because the bureaucrats at the Waffenamt hoped to gain the Führer's support, this remarkable longarm was redubbed the StG 44.

After the war, Allied arms experts would turn up their noses at the German hybrid. Its receiver was too delicate, some said; it was too expensive to be considered as a general-issue rifle; its cartridge was not powerful enough to launch a rifle-grenade. But others, chiefly the Soviets, saw in the German rifle the future of infantry small arms. It gave the rifleman unprecedented firepower. No conventionally armed infantry unit could possibly stand up to a rifle squad equipped with StG 44s and light machine guns capable of sustained fire. The new rifle's name says it all, hearkening back to the old but not obsolete idea of "marching fire." For StG stood for the newly coined German term *Sturmgewehr*—"assault rifle."

That term *assault rifle* carries a lot of baggage. But seen from a strictly military standpoint, the assault rifle, starting with the *Sturmgewehr*, was truly revolutionary. Arguably, it represents the last revolutionary advance in the evolution of martial small arms. Regardless of the doubters, the StG quickly spawned imitators even before the Second World War drew to a close. The Soviets were already searching for a handier general-issue weapon to replace the somewhat outdated Mosin-Nagant M91/30 rifle. Though one of the solutions was to simply shorten the M91/30 to carbine length—the 1944 model bolt-action carbine with folding bayonet was the result—their firearms engineers were also at work on an intermediate cartridge. The result was the short 7.62×39mm round, comparable to the German 8mm *Kurz*, and weapons to fire it: the semiautomatic SKS carbine and the RPD light machine gun, both already in the field-testing stage when the war with Germany ended in 1945.

The StG's direct influence was especially apparent in the rifle that replaced the Soviet SKS right after the war. Mikhail Kalashnikov, a Russian firearms engineer who had been experimenting with autoloading rifles and submachine guns, submitted his latest prototype to a design competition in 1946. Though he gave some credit to the American Garand for his inspiration, Kalashnikov borrowed heavily from the StG, and his final design bore an uncanny resemblance to the pioneering German firearm. Kalashnikov won the competition, and a year later it went into production. Kalashnikov's rifle became the general-issue rifle of the Red Army; it went on to arm Soviet-bloc armies, revolutionary movements, guerrilla warriors, and terrorists the world over. The *Avtomat Kalashnikova* model 1947—the AK 47—was not a Second World War rifle. But it was a product of the Second World War, and of the impulse that came from the world wars to give individual soldiers overwhelming and portable firepower.

THE ACHIEVEMENT OF firepower that was both mobile and massive at the same time was the principal distinguishing legacy of infantry combat in the Second World War—the result of the inter-section of technology and tactics after 1918. What's most surpris-ing about that achievement, though, is that it happened without dramatic or revolutionary changes in weapons technology. When it came to infantry combat, the Second World War was fought with weapons that weren't radically different from those of the First, and to an extent it was fought with the same weapons. The most com-mon infantry weapon was, for most combatants, the bolt-action, magazine rifle firing a cartridge designed in the 1890s. Even the weapons that made the infantry firefight unique in 1939–1945 either made their combat debuts in the Great War or were first developed then: the submachine gun, the autoloading infantry ri-fle, the light machine gun, the intermediate rifle cartridge. The main difference between the World Wars in this regard wasn't the appearance of innovative new weapons systems, but the scale in which these weapons were used, and the ways in which infantry tactics took advantage of their performance characteristics.

That's not to say, of course, that there was nothing innovative or superior about the small arms of the Second World War. There were most definitely weapons that stand out as especially effective, or brilliant, or both: the German MG 34 and MG 42, for exam-ple, or the *Sturmgewehr*, or even the American Garand rifle, the only autoloading rifle that was general issue for a major combatant throughout the war. But were any of these so markedly superior that they had a bearing on the outcome of the war? That is, indeed, hard to judge, but it would be difficult to answer that question with a confident and definitive "yes." Clearly, the excellent German automatic weapons did not save Germany from defeat, and it would require a huge logical stretch to make the argument that the US Army prevailed in Europe and the Pacific because of the M1.

In weapons technology, the lesson of the First World War and the post-1870 arms race still very much applied: productive capacity combined with simple, robust designs always trumped sophisticated engineering. As exemplars of finely tuned engineering, the German MP 38 and MP 40 were probably the most impressive submachine guns of the war, and certainly the most beautifully made; but their Soviet analogs, the PPSh-41 and the PPS-43, were as good as, if not better than, the German sub-guns. They were ugly and roughly finished, but they were reliable and tough, and most important they could be made faster and cheaper. Hence, the Soviets could easily issue them by the hundreds of thousands. The American M1, to be sure, was a sophisticated and complicated piece of weapons technology, but the state of American manufacturing was such that factories in the United States could churn them out and keep up with demand, in a way that Germany could not.

Small arms had reached a peak of sorts in 1945, and nearly all the distinguishing elements of firearms technology in 1945 were there in 1939, or even 1919. Much the same could be said of artillery: the artillery of the Second World War was not far removed from its antecedents in the First. The real advances in the tools of land warfare in the war years would come, instead, from the emerging technologies of 1914–1918: the tank and the warplane.

CHAPTER 18

THE BIG GUNS

The Great War was the big gun's big moment. In 1914–1918, it was high explosive, delivered via shell, that was the most prolific killer. However much small-arms firepower had evolved over the preceding decades, casualties attributable to artillery exceeded those credited to small-arms fire by a factor of nearly 3:2. The sophistication and deadliness of artillery had outpaced the development of any other class of weaponry. No single class of weapons had ever been so thoroughly transformed over so compact a span of years as artillery had between 1870 and 1914. The harvest of death in the Great War had borne out the wisdom—or the obscenity—of investing so heavily in artillery technology at the turn of the century. That investment continued to pay off into the decades that followed the Great War. In the Second World War, not only would artillery remain the single deadliest piece of battlefield technology, but one of the most versatile weapons, too. When wedded to the armored fighting vehicle—the tank—the big guns attained a degree of mobility previously unknown in warfare, thereby allowing artillery to become a vital component of the new tactics of movement and maneuver.

WITH THE FIRST World War, artillery had reached a developmental peak of sorts. There was no "revolution" in artillery firepower after 1919 to match the one that had just taken place: the land and sea battles of the Second World War would be fought with the artillery technology of the First. The guns themselves, excepting a few new types of special-purpose artillery, were almost identical to those of 1914–1918 in construction, operation, and performance. Much the same could be said of artillery ammunition, as well.

It wasn't that artillery engineers had run out of ideas, although it is true that interwar innovations in artillery seem like tiny steps when compared to the great leaps of the 1890s, such as high explosive shell and recoil suppression. Unlike in 1870, or even in 1890, by the time of the Great War the technology had made its huge leap forward, and artillery had caught up with science and engineering. Then, too, the harsh fiscal-political realities of the post-Versailles world left their mark. The terms of the Versailles treaty hamstrung German engineers, the postwar economic malaise hindered everyone else, and artillery was a low priority when European and American armies apportioned such meager funds as were allotted them. The nearly unchecked spending on weapons and military materiel, typical of the militaristic age before the Great War, could simply not be repeated.

All that would change in due course. The rise of totalitarian and fascist regimes in Europe and Asia guaranteed the rebuilding of military strengths to prewar levels, an expression of resurgent nationalism, territorial ambition, and fear of Communist revolution. The new militarism of the 1930s prompted a renewed arms race and a surge in weapons development worldwide, at a pace that was even more frenetic than that of the 1890s and 1900s. But even here, artillery took a back seat to high-tech weapons: aircraft, warships, tanks.

Still, there were noteworthy design revisions in the artillery of the interwar period, reflecting both the combat experiences of the First World War and the expectations that military intellectuals had of wars to come. One was the recognition that—however revolutionary the French 75 might have been in 1897—the smaller, lighter, quick-firing field guns were not quite so effective as everyone had anticipated, or as the Russo-Japanese conflict had appeared to predict. German artillery during the Great War was technically inferior to the French guns, but the Germans' early and prescient emphasis on howitzers and heavy artillery gave them an edge. Howitzers, with their bigger bores, shorter barrels, and more plunging trajectories, were better suited for trench warfare; they were more capable than flat-trajectory field guns of dropping their shells into trenches from above. Likewise, the bigger guns—firing larger shells with heavier explosive charges—were more effective than the lightweight French 75 at demolishing field fortifications. The lesson was not lost on the interwar armies, and when rearmament commenced in earnest in the mid-1930s, field howitzers and heavy guns were a production priority. The Soviets, thoroughly overhauling their arsenal even as Stalin purged the officer corps, introduced a 122mm howitzer in 1938, and the Germans followed suit with a 105mm model the next year. Britain and France were latecomers to the game—Britain because of budgetary constraints, France because its generals were overly focused on their Maginot Line and other defensive fortifications. Even the armies of the second-rank powers followed the trend. Czechoslovakia's Škoda works at Pilsen (Plzen) churned out a diverse array of high-quality heavy artillery pieces, including a 100mm field gun and a 100mm howitzer, all of which ended up falling into German hands in 1939 and serving with the Wehrmacht during the war of 1939–1945.

The prevailing trend with the light guns was to go lighter still. The belief that the next major conflict would be a war of movement influenced artillery tactics and weapons as it did those for infantry. The field gun, as it was known in 1918, remained very much in use, with some minor adjustments and tweaks to meet the perceived needs of mechanization: heavy-duty steel wheels with rubber tires, for example, replaced the iron-shod spoked wooden wheels of the previous generation. Even those guns weren't portable enough to suit the prophets of the war-of-movement to come. Small versions of field pieces, often called mountain guns or mountain howitzers, had performed quite well in the Great War. Typically these were lightweight versions of field pieces, easily moved about by a couple of men, sometimes designed to be broken down for easier transport in more difficult or roadless terrain. Their weight made them ideal, too, for use with airborne troops, since unlike most artillery pieces they could be dropped by parachute.

During the 1920s and 1930s, mountain artillery made a resurgence; German, Czech, Soviet, French, and American armies all adopted them. The German Reichswehr secretly developed a series of light field guns, designated as *Infanteriegeschütz*, or "infantry guns." The term was meant to be taken quite literally. Infantry guns were to be assigned, individually, to infantry units, manned by infantrymen, advancing with the infantry on the assault. The only substantial difference between the mountain or infantry guns and their conventional contemporaries was range, and the shorter range of the smaller guns wasn't a big concern. Conventional artillery was better for long-range, indirect bombardment; the mobile infantry pieces, on the other hand, could provide instant and close support for advancing infantry, firing directly on targets identified by the attackers. Long range was not an asset in this context. Thus, also, for mortars. Portable infantry mortars had proven their utility in the Great War. They were inexpensive to produce, light to carry, simple to operate, and—most important—they gave small infantry units instant access to artillery firepower. In the Second World War, the portable mortar would become as vital a piece of infantry equipment as the machine gun and the spade.

There was something vaguely familiar about the new infantry guns. They represented, in fact, a return to a much earlier practice, the battalion pieces of Gustavus Adolphus's army. But if the infantry gun hearkened back to the seventeenth-century battlefield, artillery after the Great War would also be called upon to carry out new tasks and fulfill unaccustomed roles. Anti-tank artillery was one of the new specialty roles; antiaircraft artillery (AAA) was another. The concept of AAA was nearly as old as powered flight itself, and it presented daunting challenges. Machine guns could fill that role well: they could easily be adapted to fire at steep elevations, they were truly portable, and their high rate of fire meant that they could fill a given area of sky with a mass of bullets, since aiming single projectiles at long-distance moving targets was by definition a near impossibility. Mounting a couple of Vickers or Maxim guns in the bed of a truck made for an effective and easily transportable air defense system. But they were only effective against low-flying aircraft, and while rifle-caliber bullets could tear up the wood-and-fabric airframes of the early warplanes, they were not quite so effective against the metal-bodied, armored, faster, more durable aircraft of the 1930s and 1940s. For altitudes higher than a few hundred feet, and to take down modern aircraft, something beefier was required.

The German Krupp firm introduced the first commercially available antiaircraft cannon in 1909; the type caught on, and all the major armies had either purpose-built antiaircraft guns or field guns modified for air defense by the middle of the Great War. The technique wasn't easy, but the ideas behind it were simple. Since precision shooting against fast-moving targets flying thousands of feet above the ground was next to impossible, antiaircraft guns would have to saturate the air around the targeted aircraft with explosions, which meant in turn that the explosions would have to be powerful enough, and dense enough, to damage aircraft with a near miss. These earliest antiaircraft guns were not much different than most field pieces of the time: quick-firing breech-loaders of 3- to 5-inch caliber, lobbing high explosive shell as high as 29,000 feet. Timed fuses made sure that the shells exploded whether they hit a target or not, and did not return to the ground unexploded—a circumstance that could have proven unfortunate for ground personnel and civilians nearby.

The vast improvement in aircraft after the late 1920s triggered a corresponding blossoming of antiaircraft guns. They came in a wide variety of sizes and capabilities, from light, small-caliber auto-cannon like the 40mm Swedish Bofors gun, to the US M1 120mm long-range AA gun. The M1 was a formidable weapon, capable of throwing a fifty-pound high explosive shell up to an altitude of

57,000 feet. The ubiquity of such weapons was a sobering reminder of the importance of aerial warfare. AA guns could be found, quite literally, almost anywhere: clustered in dense rings around major cities, industrial centers, and rail junctions, hundreds of miles behind the lines; on rooftops in cities that were subject to frequent bombings; on the decks of naval ships and even some civilian vessels. Tracer ammunition, first used on a limited basis in the Great War, made it much simpler to aim at distant aircraft; a small quantity of phosphorus or magnesium implanted in the base of the bullet ignited on discharge, leaving a brilliant, brightly colored trail behind it in flight. Proximity fuses, which detonated explosive shells when they were close enough to a metallic target to cause damage, greatly multiplied the efficiency and destructive power of antiaircraft artillery. It was AAA, and not German fighters, which did the most damage to Allied bombers attacking Axis sites on the continent in 1943–1945; bomber crews were invariably greeted with dense clouds of AA fire well before they arrived over a target. It was so common a feature of the Allied airman's existence that the German abbreviation for the weapon became part of everyday idiom the world over: *Fliegerabwehrkanone*—"aerial defense gun"—was shortened to "FlaK," or "flak" in American parlance.

In terms of its overall significance, artillery reprised its performance from the Great War in the Second World War: it was the great reaper of lives, it was highly versatile, and it was utterly indispensable. But it was far more mobile than it had been during the Great War, and by design. Far more so than in the previous conflict, artillery was mechanized. Horse artillery still existed—the German army in particular still relying heavily on draft animals for transport—but the truck and the tractor had begun to take over from the horse and the mule.

True mobility for artillery was already available, however, and it was staring career soldiers and military theorists squarely in the face. It was right there for the taking, for development and expansion, and though many of the former commanders of the armies of 1914–1918 refused to see it, there were a few mavericks who could discern its potential, who were willing to stake their reputations on it as *the* thing that would restore mobility to land warfare. In the two decades following the end of the Great War, the tank would come of age.

THE TANK HAS become, since the Second World War, so firm a fixture in the battlescape, so emblematic of hard-hitting, aggressive, fast-moving warfare, that it is all but impossible to imagine modern war without it. But in 1919, there was little to hint at future greatness for armored fighting vehicles. They were vulnerable, slow, fragile, and unreliable. In the end, they were hardly worth the considerable effort that the British, French, and German armies poured into them.

That makes the triumph of armor in the Second World War all the more remarkable. There were a handful of individuals, in just about every combatant nation, who saw past the comical ineffectiveness of tanks on the Western Front, and pictured what tanks might accomplish if only provided with powerful, reliable engines, robust transmissions, and adequate armor protection. The list of armor advocates in the 1920s and 1930s reads like a roster of the great tacticians of the century: J.F.C. Fuller and Basil Liddell Hart in Britain; Charles de Gaulle in France; Oswald Lutz and Heinz Guderian in Weimar Germany; Kliment Voroshilov and Mikhail Tukhachevsky in the Soviet Union; and Dwight D. Eisenhower and George S. Patton in the United States. They had different ideas about the way tanks should be used in combat, but all of them believed that tanks would be a critical component of modern warfare, and that modern armies would ignore them at their peril. They also believed that tanks would be far less effective operating on their own, and should instead be incorporated into a form of combined-arms approach to tactics, alongside artillery, infantry, and close air support. And because the tank was still an unfamiliar weapon to most soldiers, the advocates of armor also insisted that effective use required an independent tank service, with highly trained personnel and young, open-minded leaders.

But those beliefs didn't matter at first, because few men of influence shared the enthusiasm of the tank advocates. Times were hard, and costly novelties like tanks were a low priority. Yet armor and armored forces still somehow managed to survive the economic malaise of the 1920s. Britain took the lead, as it had in the Great War, primarily because of the dogged interest of its premier arms-maker, Vickers. Vickers turned out prototype after prototype, mostly medium and light tanks. The rest of Europe, which by the 1930s was more receptive to the tank, took a while to catch up. All the powers, great and lesser, got in on the act: Italy, Japan, Hungary, Czechoslovakia, even the United States, where General Douglas MacArthur pushed for the use of light tanks by cavalry in 1931. Throughout the decade, armor was the focus of more funding, more thought, and more experimentation than ever before.

The only thing lacking was a well-defined notion of how to use them in combat, and that was a serious issue. The tank actions of the Great War had been so limited as to provide little instruction, and there was no significant armored combat for nearly two decades after the war. Hence there was no recent experience on which to draw. European military leaders tended to assume that—much as they hoped to be able to restore movement to warfare—the next major war would be similar, tactically, to the war of 1914–1918. Since the main purpose of tanks in the Great War had been breaking through enemy lines, crushing barbed-wire obstacles, and disrupting enemy command and communications preparatory to an infantry assault, the general parameters of tank design in the interwar years centered on this assumption. The heavier machines, with thicker armor and bigger guns, would serve as "breakthrough" tanks, opening up enemy lines to penetration by subsequent assaults. Medium infantry tanks would carry out those assaults, accompanied by swarms of foot troops. Medium tanks would mainly engage enemy tanks, while light (or cavalry) tanks would speed into action after the initial breakthrough, much as traditional cavalry would.

Plate 32. British Light Tank Mark III in Palestine, 1936. The Vickers-built Light Tanks were typical of interwar tank design, which tended to favor small, fast tankettes or "cavalry tanks" over larger designs.
Image: Library of Congress.

Hence the three main categories of tank at the outset of the Second World War: light (cavalry), medium (infantry), and heavy. Light tanks, easier and cheaper to build, outnumbered all other types in 1939. Of the Soviet tank fleet (totaling nearly 23,000 tanks) at the time of the German invasion in June 1941, 2.5 percent were heavy, 5.8 percent were medium, and 91.7 percent were light models. While the British held the lead in the quality of light tanks up to the 1930s, the Soviet BT series—designed in part by American automotive engineer J. Walter Christie—were clearly the best in class, combining the not-insignificant firepower of a 45mm main gun with the astonishing road speed of forty-four mph. Many light tanks carried much lighter armaments, such as the German PzKpfw I (two machine guns) and the PzKpfw II (one 20mm cannon, one machine gun).*

---

*The German label PzKpfw stood for *Panzerkampfwagen*, or "armored combat vehicle." Mercifully, it became common practice to shorten this even further to the simple German word *Panzer*, meaning "armor."

The medium (infantry) tank flourished after the mid-1930s. During the Second World War, the medium tank would become the most plentiful species in combat use—the type embraced such famous models as the American M4 Sherman series, the Soviet T-34, and the German PzKpfw V Panther—but at first its role was only dimly perceived. The best in European service before 1939 was probably the French SOMUA S35. Though technically a cavalry tank, the SOMUA was more heavily armored and armed than most of its larger contemporaries, and it boasted a number of highly advanced features, including self-sealing fuel tanks and an automatic fire-extinguishing system. The SOMUA may well have been the best tank available anywhere in 1940; it was a pity that the French did not have more of them at hand when the Germans attacked that spring.

The heavy tanks were the least practical of the bunch. With the exception of the freakishly long, single-turret French Char 2C, which was ahead of its time when it was first introduced in 1921, heavies were not in style until well into the 1930s. When they did reappear, they were true monstrosities, their bulk reminiscent of the big land battleships of the Great War, but with better power plants, more armor, and bigger guns. And *more* guns, too. Some were multi-turreted, most famously the Soviet T-35. The T-35, which first emerged from Soviet factories in 1933, carried eight or nine guns total—a 75mm cannon, two 45mm guns, and five or six machine guns—in five separate turrets mounted atop the hull. It required a crew of eleven men, and tipped the scales at around forty-five tons. The T-35 was so heavy that its hulking five hundred hp, V-12 engine could not push it any faster than thirty kmh.

The external differences between the scores of tank models that made their debut in the 1930s were considerable, yet they shared notable features. All of them were turreted; the superiority of the 1917 Renault design, allowing a 360-degree field of fire, was universally accepted. Most of the interwar tanks were of riveted construction, meaning that their steel armor was applied with rivets. It was a quick and cheap construction method, to be sure, but testing revealed that welding was a superior way to join steel plates. Riveted armor could be broken apart more easily, and—when hit by an enemy shell—the rivets were likely to shear off and ricochet around the crew compartment, wounding or killing the men inside. Welding was beginning to replace riveting in the latest generation of prewar tanks. So, too, was casting. The French SOMUA was one of the first tanks in general service to have a turret fashioned from a single steel casting. The SOMUA's turret had no seams, and so was inherently stronger than either riveted or welded armor. Turrets grew dramatically in size, to accommodate larger guns and more crew members.

How the tanks would function in war was anybody's guess in 1939. There was, however, lots of inspired speculation. In France, where Germany was assumed to be the once and future enemy, staff officer Charles de Gaulle called for a smaller, more professional, more mechanized army, capable of undertaking rapid preemptive offensives with combined-arms tactics; a highly trained tank corps would be an essential component of de Gaulle's ideal force. But the conservative French army establishment preferred a purely defensive strategy with a mass citizen army, like the one it had raised in the Great War. In this scheme, armor would act as a mobile defensive force only. Britain had been the pioneer of armored warfare in 1914–1918, and in B. H. Liddell Hart and J.F.C. Fuller the British possessed two of armor's most articulate advocates. But the high command favored air and sea power over ground forces, and at the close of the 1930s Britain lagged noticeably behind in tanks.

The Soviet Union, instead, became the foremost practitioner of armored warfare. Having just emerged from the chaos of its own civil war and a brutal war with a newly reborn Poland (1919–1920), the Soviet state produced real visionaries who embraced mechanization and armor both. Among them were Kliment Voroshilov, Josef Stalin's defense commissar, and the young field marshal Mikhail Tukhachevsky. Russia's industrial economy was so thin prior to 1930 that tank warfare really wasn't an option for the Workers' and Peasants' Red Army, but Stalin's first five-year plan (1928)—a radical, brutal, and largely successful attempt to bring Soviet industry up to date—changed all that. National defense took priority over just about everything else, and soon factories all over the USSR were pumping out tanks and other motor vehicles. By the mid-1930s, the Soviets had manufactured well over seven thousand tanks (and many, many more trucks), making possible the mechanized, combined-arms theories espoused by Marshal Tukhachevsky. In Soviet tactical doctrine, massive armor formations were to work together with artillery and air support to break open enemy defenses, which could then be exploited by infantry. There was no question but that the Red Army had the best-developed tank arm in the world. But it soon lost its lead. The mediocre performance of tanks in the Spanish Civil War (1936–1939) cooled much of the Soviet enthusiasm for armor. Stalin's infamous purges of the officer corps, in which much of the best Russian military talent was sacrificed to satisfy the dictator's murderous paranoid delusions, did irreparable harm to Soviet military command. Tukhachevsky was among the victims.

WHILE STILL VERY much under development in the 1930s, the tank matured during the Second World War. No other weapons technology, save that of aerial warfare, evolved so far and so fast during the war years. Tanks that were state of the art in 1939 were obsolete by 1941 at the latest; the main battle tanks of 1945 were far closer—in speed, reliability, and power—to armored fighting vehicles of the twenty-first century than they were to the tanks with which the major powers went to war in 1939–1941. And like military aircraft, the tank revealed a new relationship between combat and military technology. It wasn't just that commanders in the field adapted their tactics to new technology; now technology adapted to tactics, and in very short order, and in the midst of war. The wartime development of the tank demonstrated a responsiveness that was quite new in the history of armed conflict.

In this way, the tank was like the warplane, evolving in real time as circumstances demanded in the short term. But unlike with military aviation, military leaders had no well-formed ideas of how tanks would be used. Warplanes had carved out their niche, or niches, in the Great War; tanks in that war could barely justify their existence. And without a well-defined purpose, tank design in the 1930s was haphazard—except in Germany.

Before 1936, the Soviet Union possessed the best tank army in the world, and even after the purges it remained the most prolific manufacturer of tanks, thanks to Stalin's aggressive and brutal economic policies. After 1936, it was the Germans who put the most thought into armored warfare. Instead of resigning themselves to a trench-bound war in the future, the leaders of the German Reichswehr—notably General Hans von Seeckt—looked for ways to restore mobility. From the promising (if also unsuccessful) *Kaiserschlacht* offensives of 1918, German commanders and tacticians learned the vital importance of coordination between infantry and artillery (and air support). Tanks fit right into this framework. The solution to trench-bound tactical stalemate came from carefully coordinated, focused assaults on a narrow front that used mechanized infantry, tanks, and close air support to overwhelm and punch through enemy defenses, a complex but brilliant approach that came to be known (outside Germany) as blitzkrieg.* Armored forces would play a central, even starring role in these tactics, with the key being continual communication between ground and air units, by means of wireless radio.

German plans for tank production revolved around the projected demands of blitzkrieg. First into production were the light tanks, the Panzer I and II models. The medium Panzer III would act as a breakthrough tank, moving with the mechanized infantry to engage and knock out enemy tanks with armor-piercing ammunition. A heavier tank, the Panzer IV, would use high-explosive shell to take out "soft" targets, like field fortifications and anti-tank

---

*Though the term itself is German, there is little or no evidence that the word *blitzkrieg* was ever embraced by the German military, officially or unofficially, as a label applied to their combined-arms assault tactics during the Second World War.

gun emplacements. Additional support would come from units of a special, tank-like armored vehicle that the Germans called an "assault gun" (*Sturmgeschütz*). The *Sturmgeschütz*, or StuG, did not use a turret, but instead mounted a single forward-firing cannon in a low-profile armored casemate. It would provide direct fire support for the infantry, its heavy armor allowing it to get close to enemy guns. Prior to 1941, the Wehrmacht and its guiding lights, such as Col. Heinz Guderian, did not perceive a need for tanks heavier than the Panzer III and IV models, and shunned the ridiculous land battleships that the Soviets seemed to be so fond of.

In practice, the blitzkrieg didn't work out as expected. The armored divisions of the Wehrmacht were nowhere near as strong or technologically advanced as they were later made out to be. When German troops carried out the annexation of Austria (the Anschluss) in March 1938, the armored column leading the push across the Austrian frontier performed pathetically, with most of its tanks—the bulk of them Panzer Is and IIs—experiencing mechanical failures and breaking down, a major embarrassment to the army and the Führer. Even at the time of the invasion of Poland, a year and a half later, the panzer arm consisted mostly of light tanks, with only a handful of Panzer IIIs and IVs. The Germans were already relying heavily on captured foreign tanks to fill out their ranks, including the high-quality Czech-built vz.35 and vz.38 light tanks.

Even lacking in modern, powerful tanks, the German *Panzertruppen* performed brilliantly. It helped, of course, that the Third Reich's earliest opponents were completely outclassed, and by a wide margin. Poland had a respectable army—not the outdated artifact that popular myth has made it out to be—but Polish armor consisted of a few tankettes (very small light tanks) and French surplus from the Great War. The Danish, Dutch, and Belgian armies, all conquered by the Wehrmacht in that terrible spring of 1940, had nothing larger than armored cars in service.

At the level of strategy, blitzkrieg involved applying overwhelming force, fast and hard, at a weak point in the enemy's defenses, or at least where he was unlikely to expect an attack. At the level of tactics, those attacks combined close air support and artillery bombardment to shake up enemy defenses. Then the panzers advanced with the mechanized infantry to open the breach further.

The critical German advantage was communication. In Poland, but even more so in France the following year, the panzers fulfilled their roles so well because they were continually in touch with one another, with the infantry and artillery, and with the close-support aircraft of the Luftwaffe. German tanks were routinely equipped with wireless receivers and transmitters, and commanders drove special *Panzerbefehlswagen* (armored command vehicle) tanks, stripped of their main armament but equipped with powerful transmitters and elaborate antenna arrays. Panzer commanders in the thick of the action could summon and pinpoint additional air or artillery support immediately, and aerial observers could help direct the battle from their perspective above, all thanks to those radios. No other army—except the French, who were *just* beginning to install radios in their tanks when the Germans invaded in 1940—made similar provisions.

That was the key to German success in those first campaigns of the war: organization and tactics, not technological superiority. The war with Britain and France made the point even more forcefully. British tanks in 1940 (like the ineffectual Mark VIB light tank and the Mark IV "cruiser" medium tank) were, on the whole, unremarkable and mediocre; French armor, tank for tank, was of higher quality than German tanks, the SOMUA in particular. But the French and the British were defeated just the same. Technological superiority did not guarantee victory, and could not make up for inferior organization and tactics.

That's not to say that technological superiority did not count for anything. The Germans learned that bitter lesson the following year, during their invasion of the Soviet Union. By the time the Germans launched Operation Barbarossa in June 1941, their tank production at home had accelerated greatly, and the German *Panzerwaffe* was much better equipped than it had been at the time of

Plate 33. The Soviet T-34. The T-34 medium tank—in this photo, the revamped and improved Model 1941 variant—was one of the most effective and versatile tanks of the Second World War. Note the angled glacis plate—the front of the hull—which made it so resistant to nearly every weapon in the German anti-tank arsenal when Hitler's armies first encountered the T-34 in the summer of 1941.

Courtesy National Archives, image no. 6423170.

the Battle of France. The initial stages of the 1941 invasion showed German armor at its best, as Hitler's legions raced eastward across the steppe, driving the disorganized, dispirited Red Army before them. The Soviet Union had the largest armored force in the world, so the easy German victories in the East were truly startling.

But for German tankers, the first contacts with their Soviet counterparts were also sobering. The war in Russia not only presented new and daunting challenges of supply and logistics—supplying fuel, ammunition, replacement tanks, and spare parts to the panzer divisions scattered across such vast unpeopled distances—but it also forced the Germans to confront an unpleasant and unanticipated fact: the Soviets had better tanks than they did.

Before the war, the tank arm of Stalin's Red Army had focused mostly on light tanks, including the BT series and the British Vickers-inspired T-26. It had also expended considerable resources, unwisely as it turned out, on superheavy tanks like the T-35, slow, heavy, and plagued by irritating mechanical failures. Neither the T-35 nor the light tanks were a match for the improved Panzer IIIs and IVs. But German tank commanders were utterly surprised when they first encountered the latest Soviet tanks, which had just begun to roll off the factory lines in 1939 and 1940: the KV-1 heavy tank and the T-34 medium tank.

In the ways that counted, the T-34 and the KV-1 were superior to anything the Germans had at hand in 1941. The KV-1's thick armor, 90mm on the front and 70–75mm on the sides and rear, was so heavy that the biggest German tank and anti-tank guns could not penetrate it; its 76.2mm main gun was far more powerful than anything in use on a German tank at the time, and it could make quick work of a Panzer IV. The T-34, the product of a design team led by the talented engineer Mikhail Koshkin, was a radical departure from the received wisdom of tank design. Although technically a medium tank, it carried the same big 76.2mm gun as the KV-1, and it had much heavier armor than any other medium tank of its generation. It was quite fast and maneuverable, with a top speed of thirty-three mph, and its unusually wide tracks gave it better traction on soft ground than the narrow treads found on German tanks. The T-34 sported a diesel engine, another wise choice: diesel engines were more fuel-efficient, and diesel fuel is less prone to accidental ignition, a huge advantage for a tank in combat. German tanks, by contrast, invariably used gasoline-fueled internal combustion engines. But by far the most innovative thing about Koshkin's new tank was the shape of its hull. Most tanks of the time were quite square, with front and side plates fastened on at right angles. The T-34 instead had a sloping frontal surface and a turret with curved faces. The slope of the front shield was the key to the T-34's survivability in combat, for an enemy shell hitting the tank head-on would strike it a glancing blow, and was therefore much less likely to penetrate the tank's thick skin.

The Eastern Front, which pitted the two biggest tank armies in the world against one another for the better part of four years, would witness the most intensive armored combat of the war. The terrain was, for the most part, well suited to tank operations; the open, sweeping plains of the steppe were—at least when conditions were dry—the tank's natural habitat. This worked to the advantage of the Wehrmacht in the first few months of the war with Russia, as it swept eastward in pursuit of the retreating—and unraveling—Red Army. The Soviets, predictably, suffered horrendous losses in that first year of what they would come to call the Great Patriotic War, but they also managed to pull off a major off-battlefield victory: they were able to migrate entire industries and populations—some 1,500 factories and ten million civilians—to safety in the east. The German invasion had effectively destroyed Soviet heavy industry, cutting production by half in the last months of 1941, but the migration of the factories saved the Soviet war effort. By the spring of 1942, factory output was again on the rise, and in 1944 the collective production of weapons was at 251 percent of what it had been in 1940. Much of that production was armor. And production, as it would turn out, was key when it came to winning a tank war.

There was much more to combat on the Eastern Front than tank battles, but tanks were an essential component of the Russo-German conflict of 1941–1945. After relying heavily on independent armored units early in the war—and suffering staggering losses in tanks—the Red Army followed the German lead, adopting tactical doctrines that integrated armor, artillery, infantry, and close air support into a smoothly functioning whole. German and Russian approaches to battle, offensive and defensive, were distinctly different, but in this fundamental way they were definitely parallel. On the offensive, for example, artillery and close air support would do the initial heavy work, suppressing enemy artillery and armor; then armor and infantry would advance together, the armor acting primarily as mobile artillery. In Soviet practice, that cooperation was physically very close, as infantry squads rode into battle clinging to the sides of tanks, a tactic known as *tankovyy desant*. As the war wore on, improved anti-tank artillery made things more dangerous for the tank crews, but still the tank remained a crucial component of successful combined-arms operations.

Even if the flow of events on the Eastern Front didn't bear out the optimistic imaginings of the prewar armor advocates—armor had not taken the place of cavalry, and no one used swarms of light tanks to exploit breakthroughs—the sheer quantities of tanks used in the Russo-German conflict were astonishing. At the beginning of the battle of Kursk (July–August 1943), the largest tank battle in history, German forces had nearly three thousand tanks, and the Soviets some five thousand.

The Eastern Front was the focal point of armored warfare in the Second World War; it would also be the epicenter of tank development. The T-34 and the KV-1 forced the Germans to redesign their tanks, including continually up-gunning and up-armoring the Panzer III and IV tanks, the latter serving as the workhorse of the German tank arm. The Wehrmacht also rushed into production entirely new series of tanks to meet the Soviet threat: the Panzer VI, a prewar heavy tank design that would become notorious as the feared Tiger tank, and the Panzer V series, better known as the Panther. The Tiger, though slow and ungainly, was heavily armored, enough to resist all but the luckiest shots from the heaviest Allied tanks, while its big 88mm gun could punch through the armor of nearly any opponent. Despite some initial mechanical issues, the Panther—fast, heavily armored, heavily armed—turned out to be the T-34's superior, and the best medium tank of the war.

In general, though, the evolution of German tank design was erratic, chaotic, and time-consuming. Nearly all the many upgrades that were applied to the basic models were responses to problems revealed in battle with the Russians—for example, the addition of more armor or the upgrading of the main gun. Others were more trivial, but together they meant that there were several versions of each basic model in service at the same time, which could prove to be a logistical nightmare. The quickly obsolescing Panzer III came in no fewer than a dozen variants, the Panzer IV in ten. The Soviets, having settled, wisely, on the T-34 and the KV-1 as their primary tanks, introduced very few upgrades, and those were substantial. The ubiquitous T-34 went through a grand total of five upgrades. The final wartime model, the T-34/85, had an 85mm gun, giving it firepower that rivaled the Panther and the Tiger.

The experience on the other fronts, in tactics and technology, was mostly similar if smaller in scale. Of course, armor didn't work everywhere, because not all kinds of terrain were traversable by tank. Fascist Italy had not invested heavily in armor development before the war because its Alpine frontier did not favor tank use. Tank warfare was noticeably subdued in the Pacific war; though American forces did use armor against the Japanese, the logistics of island-hopping made tank transport somewhat more challenging, and the relatively few tanks fielded by the Japanese army were distinctly inferior to even the most vulnerable American light tanks.

The Anglo-American war against Germany and Italy was a different story altogether, far more like the Russo-German war but on a smaller scale. Both the British and American armies in North Africa quickly learned the value of integrating armor into larger combined-arms units and using combined-arms tactics, rather than relying on tanks to carry out important operations on their own. Erwin Rommel, one of the more talented of Hitler's generals, developed his own brand of combined-arms offensive tactics, involving aggressive preparatory bombardments by artillery and anti-tank guns, followed by tanks advancing under cover of artillery fire. Even the Italian army, which did not invest heavily in tanks, developed a blitzkrieg-like fire and movement tactical doctrine, though the inadequacy of Italian tanks, the lack of radio communications, and the absence of close air support severely limited their effectiveness. By the time of the Normandy landings in June 1944, American and British forces were quite accustomed to seamlessly integrated air-armor-artillery-infantry operations, though their successes in France, the Low Countries, and finally Germany in 1944–1945 probably owed more to their command of the air than to any special merits of their armored forces.

It should be noted that British and American tanks did not quite meet up to the standards set by the Germans and the Soviets, which is surprising given that America led the world in heavy industry and Britain had once been the locus of innovation in armor. The British army lost much of its heavy equipment in the aftermath of the Dunkirk evacuation in 1940, and afterward produced a limited number of very conventional cruiser and heavy tanks. When the United States went to war at the end of 1941, most of its tanks were light models, the M3 and M5 series, not capable of going toe to toe with any German battle tank. It was the main American battle tank, the M4 Sherman and its variants, that would become the general service tank of the Allies fighting in Italy and France in 1943–1945. Even the British came to rely on their own versions of the Sherman. The earliest Shermans did just fine against Japanese tanks in the Pacific theater, but against German tanks of a similar class—like Panzer IVs and Panthers—they stood at a distinct disadvantage. The Sherman was faster and more maneuverable, but the Panther's sloping frontal armor was far superior, and its high-velocity 75mm main gun could easily penetrate the Sherman's hull.

The tank was not the only species of armored fighting vehicle to take part in the Second World War. Armored cars, though not capable of going up against actual tanks, still found plenty of uses, from reconnaissance to behind-the-lines operations against partisans. Most armies adopted some kind of "self-propelled artillery" or assault guns, such as the German StuG, to provide close fire support for advancing infantry. Another specialized type to see extensive service was the tank destroyer, a vehicle designed to combine the heavy hitting power of a heavy tank with the mobility of a lightweight. They were not meant to engage tanks in prolonged firefights, but to hit hard and fast, and then retreat quickly out of range. A defining characteristic of most tank destroyers was that they were turretless, with the main gun mounted atop the chassis in a fixed position; the arrangement allowed them to carry a much larger gun than a conventional tank of similar size. It also meant that they were cheaper to build. The Germans and the Soviets had an affinity for the type. For the Wehrmacht, building tank destroyers was a matter of frugality, as they were often made by repurposing older German or captured foreign tank chassis; hundreds of older Panzer Is and IIs, and even Panzer IVs, found new life by being converted to turretless *Jagdpanzer* or *Panzerjäger* (tank hunters).

TANKS, AND ARMORED fighting vehicles in general, proved to be highly versatile weapons, in ways not foreseen in the interwar period. They could be used to clear minefields; heavy rollers, attached to an outrigger on the bow of a tank, would detonate mines at a safe distance in front of a tank. Tanks could be equipped with flamethrowers substituted for their main guns, or with rocket launchers mounted atop the turret. Armor evolved as a combat branch, too, equal to infantry and artillery, with its own tactical doctrines and organizational norms. In guerrilla warfare behind the lines, such as the German war against Soviet, Polish, and Ukrainian partisans, Wehrmacht and police units found that even outmoded light tanks, useless on the modern battlefield, were effective against lightly armed irregulars. Few weapons of the Second World War went through so thorough a transformation as the tank.

Out of the flurry of wartime technological innovations in armor, out of the bewildering variety of tank types that made their appearance in the Second World War, a couple of general trends emerged. One was the overall move from lighter to heavier tanks. Interwar advocates of armor had envisioned tanks taking over the role of cavalry, and of mobile field artillery, too, notions that were almost Napoleonic. Tanks were, after all, meant to embody the spirit of motion and maneuver that Western generals craved after the stultifying tactical experience of the Great War. But from the moment that German tank crews first encountered the T-34 and the KV-1 in Russia, the dominant design impulse moved in the direction of *bigger*. Contrary to the predictions of the armored warfare theorists of the 1920s and 1930s, tanks tended to engage more with other tanks than they did with enemy infantry or fortifications. Every tank, then, became a tank destroyer, and tank design had to accommodate those requirements. As tanks became more resistant to artillery fire, through the application of ever-thicker armor, it became necessary to equip them with larger and higher-velocity guns and bigger chassis and turrets to accommodate larger guns and larger shells, as well as more powerful engines, tougher transmissions, and more resilient suspensions, which were needed to handle the extra weight.

Hence, on the Eastern Front, the Russian KV-1 and T-34 begat the German Tiger and Panther. But the trend didn't end there. Even while the Tiger was fresh off the production line, another German heavy tank was in the works. In the summer of 1944 it went into action as the Tiger B, though the Germans casually referred to it as the *Königstiger* (Bengal Tiger), which the Americans translated incorrectly as "King Tiger." With a massive turret and thick armor, the Tiger B weighed in at nearly seventy tons. Allied tankers unfortunate enough to encounter a Tiger B in the wild noted that their own shells could barely dent the surface of the monster tank. German assault guns and tank destroyers followed the same trend, culminating in the seventy-two ton *Jagdtiger* (Hunting Tiger), with armor up to 250mm thick and wielding a 128mm gun. Fortunately for the Allies, the giant tanks suffered from a slew of mechanical issues, and both were fuel-hungry at a time when Germany's need for fuel was most desperate.

That trend wasn't exclusively German. By war's end, the four major Western combatants had all committed to it. In the Red Army, the up-gunned KV-85 replaced the venerable KV-1, and in 1944 the tanks of the new IS series made their first combat appearance. The IS, named for the Boss himself (Iosef Stalin), featured a

Plate 34. The German Tiger B. Perhaps the most famous heavy tank of the Second World War: the German *Panzerkampfwagen* Tiger *Ausf.* (version) B, sometimes referred to as the Tiger B or Tiger II. It was significantly bigger and heavier than its better-known predecessor, the *PzKpfw* VI Tiger, weighing nearly 77 short tons as compared to the Tiger's 63, and it packed a powerful 88mm gun. Fortunately for the Allies, the Germans manufactured fewer than 500 before the war ended, and the usual list of troubles—interruptions in manufacturing thanks to Allied strategic bombing, fuel shortages, unreliable transmissions and motors—crippled those units that did make it to the field. In this photo, American GIs in Belgium are examining a Tiger B knocked out by Allied air support in January 1945. The unofficial German designation for the Tiger B was *Königstiger*, which Americans incorrectly translated as "King Tiger"; the German term instead means "Bengal tiger."
Courtesy National Archives, photo no. 193707728.

unique swept-hull design and a flattened turret that set the style for the great Soviet tanks of the Cold War period. Even the Americans got in on the game, introducing their forty-six-ton M26 Pershing heavy tank right before the conclusion of hostilities in Europe in the spring of 1945. The heavy tank, an outlier at the beginning of the Second World War, was fast becoming the main, all-purpose battle tank of the world's major armies.

The emergence of the heavy battle tank was perhaps the most important legacy of the war for armor. The most important lesson of the war was the significance of productive capacity over technological sophistication. Other areas of military technology, like the submachine gun, bore this out, too, but in tanks this basic truth was especially visible. For all their faults, wartime German tank designs were among the best, if not *the* best, in the world. Certainly German tanks were thoroughly designed, with much attention paid to detail. Soviet tanks, on the other hand, bore all the hallmarks of hurried manufacture: rough exterior finishes, unimaginative paint jobs (in contrast to elaborate German camouflage color schemes), spartan accommodations for the crew, with little regard for comfort or ergonomics. And the main Anglo-American-Commonwealth tank of the war, the Sherman, was unquestionably inferior to comparable German tanks in nearly every regard except speed.

Yet the Soviet and American tanks prevailed. Fuel supply had something to do with it, as did air supremacy; nothing crippled German armor in France after D-Day more than petrol shortages and Allied fighter-bombers. But the biggest advantage enjoyed by the Allies in the tank war was the industrial support behind their armored forces. The collective output of American and Soviet heavy industry swelled during the war, while factories in Germany and German-held lands shrank as Allied bombing campaigns took their toll. Political interference made things worse. Hitler's personal involvement in weapons development wasted incalculable time, resources, and manpower on fanciful weapons projects. It was Hitler who insisted on the production of supertanks, vehicles that made the already impractical heavies—like the Tiger B—look like toys by comparison. The Panzer VIII *Maus* (Mouse), a 188-ton tank armed with both 128mm and 75mm guns in one enormous turret, almost made it into production in late 1944—the Soviets captured the sole surviving prototype at war's end. The 1,000-ton *Landkreuzer* (Land Cruiser) P.1000 *Ratte* (Rat) was so cartoonishly big that how anyone ever took it seriously strains credulity. Its main armament was two 280mm naval guns in one turret, *plus* one 128mm gun (the same as the main gun for the *Jagdtiger* and the *Maus*), and a bunch of 20mm autocannon and machine guns mounted in smaller turrets. The whole monstrosity would have used eight twenty-cylinder marine engines, and even if it had become operational, there wasn't a road, bridge, or railcar in Europe that could have borne its weight. But Hitler was Hitler, and if he wanted to waste valuable time and resources on this ridiculous fantasy, then it would be done. Germany's enemies had their fantasy weapons, too, but none even approached the *Ratte* for sheer idiocy.

The tanks that prevailed in the Second World War were the simple, the adequate, the reliable, the mass-produced, and the easily repaired or quickly replaced. That, of course, is not to diminish the excellence of the T-34, or the somewhat lesser excellence of the Sherman. The T-34 was superior to most of its enemy counterparts, the Sherman close to (but not quite) equal to its more commonly encountered foes, such as the later PzKpfw IV models. But Soviet and American industry were geared up for wartime production in a way that the German command economy was not, and by focusing on efficient manufacturing of tanks that were good enough, the Soviets and the Americans were able to overwhelm German armored forces with sheer numbers—numbers that grew over the course of the war as German tank numbers dwindled and production levels shrank.

WHILE THE PREFERRED way of dealing with tanks was using other tanks, or tank destroyers, the growing prominence of armored fighting vehicles in modern warfare demanded tank-killing methods that foot troops could employ. Here, as in so many realms of martial technology, the Germans were ahead of the curve. This should come as no surprise; in the Great War, the Allies had a lock on tank warfare, and so the Kaiser's army was compelled to find ways of countering Allied superiority in armor as early as 1916. An ordinary fieldpiece would do the trick, since the armor on most

Allied tanks was not enough to repel a shell fired at medium range from a 77mm German field gun. But field guns were not always available, so more portable countermeasures were called for. One solution was to bundle several German stick grenades together so that they would detonate simultaneously. If carefully placed, the improvised anti-tank grenade was sufficient to damage an engine or sever a tread, disabling the tank.

Another early solution was the anti-tank rifle, another German first. Early in 1918, the Mauser rifle works introduced the *Tankgewehr* (tank rifle), a single-shot bolt-action firing a powerful 13.2mm cartridge. The *Tankgewehr*'s steel-core, armor-piercing bullet could easily penetrate the light armor of Allied tanks, but it would take a very lucky shot to hit a crewman or damage the internal parts in a way that would neutralize the targeted tank. And the recoil, which could break a man's collarbone, was forbidding. Still, the idea survived into the beginning of the Second World War: the British Boys rifle, the German *Panzerbüchse*, the Finnish Lahti, and the Soviet PTRS and PTRD were all standard-issue weapons for the first two or three years of the war. By 1941, anti-tank rifles were next to worthless, as their bullets could not possibly penetrate the armor on modern medium and heavy tanks.

Until the end of the Second World War, the most effective anti-tank weapon was the anti-tank gun. Like the infantry guns adopted by most armies in the 1920s and 1930s, light anti-tank guns were portable and easy to operate, and meant to be used by infantry. As tanks grew in size and their protective armor thickened, the light guns lost their effectiveness, and anti-tank artillery grew in response. The only effective anti-tank guns at war's end were the very same guns that were mounted on the heavy tanks and tank destroyers. Typical of the breed, and without a doubt the most famous, was Germany's versatile FlaK 18 and the weapons that followed it in series. The FlaK 18, an 88mm high-velocity cannon, was designed—paradoxically—as an antiaircraft gun. At this role it excelled, but when the Wehrmacht's conventional anti-tank guns proved incapable of stopping Soviet T-34s, the 88 was pressed into service as an anti-tank weapon. Even at ranges as great as two miles, the German 88 could destroy the formidable armor of a T-34.

Anti-tank weapons required specialized ammunition. High explosive shell worked well against softer targets, and of course in an antipersonnel role, too. But against truly thick steel armor, high explosive by itself couldn't do much more than superficial damage. Besides, ideally, for a shell to truly cripple a tank, it needed to penetrate first, then explode once inside the tank, rather than explode against the exterior. For the most part, tank crews and anti-tank gunners relied on armor-piercing high explosive (APHE) shells against armored vehicles. The body of the shell itself was made from highly alloyed steel, so as to render it harder than the armor itself; a delayed percussion fuse meant that it would explode shortly after hitting its target, allowing it a fraction of a second to penetrate before detonation.

Midway through the Second World War, a new and terrifying tank-killing weapon came into common use. As early as the 1880s, German scientists discovered the phenomenon, later called the Munroe effect: if an explosion were funneled through a constricted space, its impact would be amplified many times over. The military implications were obvious, and even before the Great War there were experiments with "shaped charges" in high-explosive artillery shells, using a hollow, cone-shaped cavity in the nose of the shell to concentrate the explosive energy. Interest faded after 1918, but in the 1930s physicists and ordnance experts in the USSR, the USA, Britain, and Germany revisited the design of anti-tank ammunition. By 1941, the new anti-tank shell, commonly called high explosive, anti-tank (HEAT), had made its battlefield debut. The HEAT round drastically increased the effectiveness of anti-tank artillery, but it was soon discovered that HEAT technology could be used without cannon, in more portable anti-tank weapons.

Britain introduced the PIAT (Projector, Infantry, Anti Tank), essentially a handheld mortar that flung a 2.5-pound HEAT round, in 1942; in the same year, the US Army adopted its iconic

M1A1 Rocket Launcher, informally called "bazooka" because of its resemblance to a musical instrument invented by a popular American comedian. The most effective of the handheld anti-tank weapons were German: the two-man *Panzerschreck* (tank terror), a rocket launcher like the bazooka, but which fired a much more powerful explosive charge; and the more commonly used *Panzerfaust* (tank fist). The *Panzerfaust* was like nothing else. It was a single-use weapon, consisting of a finned rocket bearing a shaped charge, mounted in a simple steel tube with rudimentary sights. It was lightweight and simple to use—its brief instruction "manual" was printed on the weapon itself, a great boon to the first-time user—and it was devastatingly effective. Fired at close range, say under one hundred meters, the shaped-charge projectile could burn its way through 140mm to 320mm of steel armor, enough to penetrate the hull of any tank in Allied service. The Allies learned to fear the *Panzerfaust*, and to use it, too, whenever they could get their hands on it, for it was far better than the PIAT or the bazooka. The *Panzerfaust* was the ancestor of a whole slew of more sophisticated, handheld rocket launchers—such as the Soviet RPG series and the American M72 LAW (Light Anti-tank Weapon)—later in the century.

The anti-tank weapons of 1944–1945 were highly effective, affordable, easily transported and mass-produced, and they required next to nothing in terms of training. A single soldier with a *Panzerfaust* could take out a medium tank just as readily as a much larger anti-tank gun could, at a fraction of the cost. This gave rise to an interesting counter-phenomenon to the exclusionary effect of high tech in twentieth-century warfare.

Only nations with thoroughly industrialized economies, and therefore with a great deal of heavy manufacturing and access to steel and other vital raw materials, could field a tactically significant tank force. Tanks and warplanes and capital ships made a nation powerful, but only powerful nations could afford them in the first place. The number of such nations was decreasing over time, not increasing, and after the Second World War only the

United States and the Soviet Union really met those qualifications. The *Panzerfaust* and its descendants, the RPG and the LAW, gave smaller, weaker armies—the armies of lesser nations, or partisans, or non-state actors—the ability to resist much larger, more powerful armies, without needing armor of their own. Nearly every conflict of the later twentieth century, major or minor, from Vietnam to Afghanistan, would have looked much different without the abundant presence of handheld anti-tank weapons.

Still, the proliferation of cheap, portable anti-tank weapons did not, and would not, render the tank obsolete. The Second World War marks the point where armored forces became a permanent and integral part of a modern army, on an equal footing with infantry and artillery. Of the two emerging technologies to survive the Great War, the warplane and the tank, the warplane was the one that advanced the most in sophistication during the Second World War. But the tank advanced the most in overall importance. Nobody doubted the efficacy of aircraft for military purposes, not in 1920 nor in 1930, and there already existed a realistic and detailed idea of the roles that military aviation would play in the next war.

Not so the tank. No one could say for sure, before 1939, what tanks could do, and no one knew even whether they would ever figure as anything more than an auxiliary arm, subordinate to artillery and infantry. Very quickly, though, sometime between the Nazi invasion of Poland and the invasion of the Soviet Union, armor showed what it could do. Just as quickly, all the prewar doubts about the efficacy of armor dissipated. A tank could take artillery to places where field artillery ordinarily could not go, but armor had become something more than just unusually mobile artillery. It had come into its own as a combat branch, capable of undertaking tasks that no other branch or weapon could do.

The big guns—whether mechanized, tank-borne, or horse-drawn—dominated the battlefields of the Second World War as they had in the First, perhaps even more so. Artillery, including the tank-mounted variety and portable mortars, was still the great harvester of lives, taking credit for between half and two-thirds of all ground combat casualties in 1939–1945; in contrast, small arms fire accounted for roughly a quarter of battlefield casualties. Artillery had become a dynamic asset, able to go places that it never could before. Thanks to tanks and mechanized transport, artillery could move with infantry on the assault; it could even spearhead assaults. Artillery had also become more flexible tactically, taking on new roles, perfecting old ones. Antiaircraft artillery, a novelty in the Great War, proved to be the most effective defense against aerial attack in the Second World War. Artillery gave an army long-distance firepower, such that it could concentrate massive, overwhelming destructive force on targets that were well out of the reach of infantry, even well out of sight.

But in the Second World War, another weapon—another combat branch, another mode of fighting—rose up to rival artillery for its long-reaching, hard-hitting might. The warplane, whose principal value had previously come from its ability to act as the eyes and ears of ground forces, would in 1939 come into its own as a long-range weapon of enormous power.

CHAPTER 19

AIRPOWER

Tanks were a hard sell after 1918. Aircraft, on the other hand, were not. There was no need to convince any responsible military man that aerial forces had been indispensable in the Great War, and that their role would only grow with time. Aviation technology had come a long way just during the course of the relatively short conflict. Airplanes had just transcended novelty status in 1914; by 1918, they were serious instruments of war. If tanks hadn't existed during the Great War, it's hard to see how their absence would have changed the basic parameters of combat. But if military aviation had not existed, then the Great War would have looked much different, and *might* have ended differently, too.

Military aviation had caught the popular imagination, too, the one aspect of the war that didn't seem dark, gloomy, or hopeless. The leading aces—men like Georges Guynemer, Albert Ball, Billy Bishop, Mick Mannock, the Richthofen brothers, Eddie Rickenbacker, Frank Luke, Oswald Boelcke—were the war's dashing champions, the darlings of the daily press, and their exploits lent some small measure of nobility to an otherwise brutal and ugly struggle. But for all their fame, the fighter pilots probably contributed the least to the war in the air. The main roles, the truly vital ones, that aviation played in the Great War were also the most prosaic: reconnaissance, artillery spotting, bombing, close tactical support.

501

To contemporaries, though, bombing was the future. No one would argue that aerial bombing won the war, or that it even contributed to victory in any significant way. Bombs of the period were too small to cause much damage, and the aircraft too underpowered to carry substantial payloads. Even the infamous Gotha raids on Britain in 1917–1918, as terrifying as they were, did not exact a great toll in lives. It was the *idea*, and the possible future reality, of aerial bombing, rather than the actual experience of bombing, that made the practice so alluring to the prophets of airpower in the 1920s and 1930s. Maybe the Gotha raids had been almost harmless, but what would happen once bombers were faster, bigger, and capable of carrying larger bombs and more of them?

Those questions—and the highly optimistic answers to them—were the subject of most brainstorming about the concept of airpower and its future in the interwar period. The most eloquent advocate of airpower was Giulio Douhet, the pioneering, maverick father of Italian air forces in the First World War. Douhet's firm belief, as expressed in his 1921 book *Il dominio dell'aria* (*The Command of the Air*), was that airpower was the ultimate kind of military force. The vastness of this "third dimension" meant that it was fruitless to try to defend against attack from the air, and that bombers would soon render armies and navies obsolete. By bombing strategic resources—transportation hubs, communications centers, factories, government facilities—a nation making aggressive use of airpower could hobble an enemy's ground forces almost instantly. Targeting civilians in major population centers was, in Douhet's mind, an even more effective means for destroying enemy morale and bringing about the complete collapse of the enemy's infrastructure. If nothing else, a hard-pressed civilian population would compel their political leaders to capitulate.

Like the techno-prophets before the First World War, Douhet genuinely believed that his variety of airpower would ensure short, relatively humane wars. Civilian populations would not, could not, hold up for long under the strain of frequent bombings, firestorms, and clouds of poison gas, and so wars would end after very little actual bloodshed. Only the long-range heavy bomber could achieve that result.

Douhet's ideas about what today we would call strategic bombing found a sympathetic audience worldwide. It helped that the advocates of airpower circa 1920 actually had a voice and a measure of influence. It helped, too, that the aviation arms of the world's leading military powers were in the process of becoming independent or nearly so: Britain's Royal Air Force (RAF) in the spring of 1918, the US Army Air Corps (USAAC)—under Army control but commanded directly by a single general—in 1926. The established leaders in those air commands were, for the most part, senior leaders from the Great War, enthusiastic proselytizers of Douhet's gospel. In Britain, the top man was Hugh Trenchard, who like Douhet believed passionately in the strategic imperatives of long-distance bombing. Trenchard was almost single-handedly responsible for the RAF's continued independence in the face of deep budget cuts in the early 1920s, and for Britain's refusal to agree to international limitations on bomber aircraft. When, in November 1932, former (and later) Prime Minister Stanley Baldwin spoke before Parliament against unilateral disarmament, he uttered a famous sentiment that came straight from Trenchard's thoughts. "The bomber will always get through," he said. "The only defence is in offence."

In the United States, it was the loud, brash, utterly self-confident Billy Mitchell who took up Douhet's mission. William Lendrum Mitchell had been the senior American air commander in France at the close of the Great War, and though his abrasive personality did not endear him to his superiors in the War Department, he remained in the leadership of the (now demobilizing) American air forces in peacetime. Mitchell advocated, ceaselessly, for a truly independent air force and greater investment in naval aviation. His ideas met with stiff opposition—including from the then assistant secretary of the Navy, Franklin Delano Roosevelt—but nothing he said created as much of a stir as his insistence that airpower was superior to sea power—in particular, that bombers could sink even the largest and most powerful battleships afloat, and do so with impunity. This latter assertion he demonstrated, rather graphically, with two test bombings held jointly by the Army and Navy in 1921. Using Martin twin-engine biplane bombers carrying bombs as large as two thousand pounds, Mitchell's aircrews managed to sink several armored naval vessels sacrificed for the test, including the captured German battleship *Ostfriesland*. Though the tests earned Mitchell much notoriety, they also bolstered the arguments in favor of strategic bombing and won a great deal of support from the American public, which warmed to Mitchell's rebellious, irreverent personality as much as it did to the dramatic end of the *Ostfriesland*.

Plate 35. Billy Mitchell's bombing demonstration, 1921. Following up on his dramatic sinking of the captured German battleship *Ostfriesland* off the Virginia Capes (July 1921), Billy Mitchell sank the old American pre-dreadnought USS *Alabama* in a separate demonstration in September 1921. Here a Martin NBS-1 bomber—a twin-engine biplane, much like the heavy bombers of the Great War—scores a hit on *Alabama* with a white phosphorus bomb.

Image: NH57483 courtesy of the Naval History & Heritage Command.

The technology of aviation did not keep pace with the demands that the airpower advocates were heaping upon it. As impressive as Mitchell's bombing demonstrations were, the target ships didn't fight back, and certainly the idea of fighting wars with massive air fleets of multi-engine bombers wasn't feasible in 1921, or in 1939 for that matter, even if the funding had been readily available. The technology just wasn't there. For most of the 1920s, "modern" military aircraft didn't evolve much beyond what they were at the end of the Great War. The typical fighter plane of the 1920s remained a wooden-frame, fabric-skinned biplane armed with two light machine guns firing through the propeller arc, equipped with fixed landing gear and minimal instrumentation. The typical bomber was nearly indistinguishable from the giants of 1917–1918, and therefore had neither the range nor the payload capacity to make Douhet's dreams a reality. Small wonder, then, that airships still weren't off the table, because although slow they could at least carry large bombloads over long distances. But they, too, fell out of favor during the 1930s, due to a series of fatal accidents, including the loss of US Navy airships *Shenandoah* (1925), *Akron* (1933), and *Macon* (1935). These three separate accidents alone, with an aggregate death toll of eighty-nine, went a long way toward proving their vulnerability.

The stagnancy in aircraft design wasn't intentional. The basic construction of most First World War aircraft inherently constrained performance. Fabric-covered, wooden-framed fuselages could not bear much stress. This, in turn, limited the size and power of aircraft engines. Moreover, biplane designs were subject to more drag than single-wing, or monoplane, models. Over the course of the Great War, German scientists had already begun to develop solutions to these structural problems. With the aid of men like Ludwig Prandtl, a pioneering scholar of aerodynamics, the German aircraft industry made great advances in wing and fuselage design. The Germans were years ahead of the Allies in their understanding of theoretical aerodynamics, and in applying science to what Allied aircraft makers saw primarily as engineering problems.

Among the critical German innovations were new construction methods, including the monocoque fuselage and the stressed-skin wing. Most aircraft of 1914–1918 were built by stretching heavily treated fabric over rigid, skeletal wooden or tubular steel frames. The fabric skin filled a purely aerodynamic function; the wooden frame absorbed the stresses of flight. In monocoque and stressed-skin construction, by contrast, a rigid skin—plywood at first, then aluminum alloys—was the main structural element; the skin, and not an internal frame, was the principal load-bearing structure. The chief advantages over conventional framed aircraft were greater structural strength and reduced weight. First used by the French right before the outbreak of the First World War, German engineers integrated it into several Pfalz and Roland warplanes by 1918. Prandtl's pathbreaking research in airfoil design also yielded the surprising discovery that thicker wings, if shaped to the proper profile, produced less draft than the thinner wings in common use.

After the war, American and British aviation experts began to appreciate the German advances, and Prandtl's ideas gained widespread circulation. In the United States, the recently created National Advisory Committee for Aeronautics (NACA), under the direction of Johns Hopkins physicist Joseph Ames, pushed for the advancement of aviation science.

The blossoming of the science of flight yielded practical dividends almost immediately. When it came to military aviation, the greatest advancement was what has been called the monoplane revolution. A detailed understanding of flight physics, occasioned by the rapid emergence of aerodynamics as a field of academic inquiry in the 1920s and 1930s, resulted in a much different kind of airplane. Streamlined metal-skinned fuselages replaced boxy wood and fabric; spinning-cylinder rotary engines gave way to fuel-injected, liquid-cooled inline models or air-cooled, fixed-cylinder radials; retractable landing gear replaced fixed; variable-pitch propellers took the place of fixed blades; the monoplane replaced the biplane. The new planes were tough enough to handle the truly massive motors that rolled off the production lines at Pratt &

Whitney and Rolls-Royce; the new understanding of the relationship between drag, lift, power, and speed assured a level of performance that the aces of the Great War could never have imagined.
The difference in performance between state-of-the-art aircraft in
1919 and in 1930 was like night and day. The Royal Aircraft Factory S.E.5a, one of the fastest fighter planes of the Great War, could
coax 138 mph out of its 150 hp, eight-cylinder engine. By the mid-
1930s, sporting monoplanes were easily capable of reaching speeds
approaching 300 mph.

Shrinking defense budgets in the 1920s meant that the impetus
for this progress came from the civilian market. Most of the major
European states had viable aircraft manufacturers, but the leaders
were Britain and, above all, the United States. Very few Americans
could afford to travel by air, but the mere prospect of air travel was
so glamorous and thrilling that it caught the popular imagination.
Aviation pioneers such as Amelia Earhart and Charles Lindbergh
became national heroes, and Americans followed their exploits
with rapt attention. Lindbergh's famous 1927 transatlantic flight
in his *Spirit of St. Louis*, which demonstrated that even vast oceans
could now be bridged by air, excited ordinary folk as much as it did
the most zealous advocates of airpower. Hollywood fueled the aviation mania. In American film, air travel came off as romantic and
fashionable, and the only truly popular war films to come out of
American studios were about fighter pilots. After 1918, few Americans reflected on their experience in the Great War in sentimental
terms, but they could thrill to the daring and chivalric exploits of
Errol Flynn and Basil Rathbone in *Dawn Patrol*, or immerse themselves in the elaborately choreographed dogfight scene in Howard
Hughes's *Hell's Angels*. America was home, in military historian
Jeremy Black's words, to a powerful "aviation cult."[*]

Commercial investment in aviation technology brought flight
closer to the lives of ordinary people. Delivery of mail by air grew

---

[*] Jeremy Black, *Air Power: A Global History* (London: Rowman & Littlefield, 2016), p. 66.

to be a common phenomenon, a major boon for remote rural and frontier communities, while heavy bombers converted to passenger liners took to the skies as early as 1919. In Canada, the usefulness of aircraft in mapping remote regions, or even for fighting forest fires, quickly became evident. Often war is the driver of technological developments that change civilian life in a big way, but in the case of interwar aviation it was civilian demand that did the most to advance aviation technology.

Yet war was never far from the thoughts of aviators, engineers, and manufacturers. During the 1920s, though there were few "hot" wars big enough to employ large air forces, military aviation still found outlets. The British government found that airpower added another dimension to the maintenance of its empire. The RAF took part in bombing raids in Afghanistan in 1919, against the "Mad Mullah" Sayyid Mohammed Abdullah Hassan in Somaliland in 1920–1921, and helped to uphold British imperial interests in India and Iraq. France, the United States, and the Dutch similarly found airpower useful as a means for cowing resistance within the colonial spheres of influence they had carved out for themselves. And air travel meant that administrators and government officials could be transported quickly and quietly to distant colonial outposts.

The rearmament programs of the 1930s accelerated the modernization of the world's air fleets before the Second World War. The aggressor states of the 1930s—Italy, Germany, Japan—made airpower a central pillar in their bids for rearmament and in their approaches to grand strategy. For Germany, the reincarnation of its earlier Luftstreitkräfte as the Third Reich's new air force, the Luftwaffe, in 1934–1935 was as much an expression of nationalist pride and resolve as anything else. Few of the disarmament clauses of the Versailles peace stung so bitterly as the dissolution of Germany's air forces—arguably the best in the world—in 1919. The creation of the Luftwaffe helped to recapture some of that lost pride, and the birth of the Luftwaffe in turn scared Germany's rivals and enemies into following suit.

The timing of the rearmament was almost perfect, because by the 1930s the practical performance of modern aircraft was just beginning to approach the standards that Douhet and his disciples demanded. The Douhet school revered strategic bombing above all forms of military force. Modern aircraft—larger, more power- ful, capable of carrying heavy loads over distances as great as the breadth of the Atlantic—could vastly outperform the Great War generation of bombers. Here Britain and the United States led the way, especially in the design of heavy bombers. The Martin B-10, first delivered to the US Army Air Corps in 1933, was a milestone in bomber technology: an all-metal monoplane with a three- or four-man crew, the B-10's twin Wright Cyclone 9 engines could

Plate 36. The Boeing B-17F Flying Fortress, one of the two main Amer- ican heavy bombers of the Second World War. This B-17F is taking off on a test flight at Boeing's factory in Seattle, Washington.
Image: Library of Congress.

drive it along at speeds up to a jaw-dropping 213 mph, while carrying more than a ton of bombs. A mere four years later, Boeing made the first deliveries of its Flying Fortress, the B-17. The Fortress, a true heavy bomber with four big Curtiss-Wright Cyclone engines, could carry up to four tons of bombs and move at a maximum speed of 287 mph. The other major American heavy bomber of the Second World War, the Consolidated B-24 Liberator, joined the American air fleet shortly before the United States went to war in 1941.

During the late 1930s and through the war years, the United States was the primary maker of large four-engine bombers. Though favoring smaller, twin-engine medium bombers, the RAF also turned out substantial numbers of four-engine Avro Lancaster and Handley Page Halifax heavies by the end of the war. Interestingly, despite the universal respect for Douhet's ideas, a respect that sometimes bordered on mania, none of the other major air forces expended much effort or resources on the big planes. Germany, Italy, and Japan all focused more on medium bombers. The workhorses of the German blitzkrieg—the Heinkel He 111 (1935), the Dornier Do 17 (1937), and the Junkers 88 (1939)—were all twin-engined, slower and carrying smaller payloads than the Flying Fortress.

The new generation of medium and heavy bombers was, for a short while, superior to anything else in the sky, at least in terms of speed. One of the most notable things about the Martin B-10 was that it could fly faster than any fighter, or pursuit, aircraft in American service at the time of its adoption. The German Do 17, likewise, had been designated a fast bomber, an impression that its oddly slender fuselage—the Do 17 was often called the *fliegender Bleistift*, or "flying pencil"—appeared to substantiate. This quality was consonant with the convictions of Douhet's disciples, of Hugh Trenchard, and of all the proponents of bombing: that the bomber would *always* get through. A bomber that could out-speed and evade enemy pursuit planes was just what airpower advocates had prayed for. Defensive armaments were therefore a secondary consideration. Though powered gun turrets were already available by the mid-1930s, very few of the early bombers made much use of them. The Martin B-10 carried only three light machine guns; the Do 17 had six, aimed in several directions but all concentrated around the cockpit. The American heavy bombers, the B-17 and the B-24, stood out precisely because they were so heavily armed. The B-17 carried no fewer than thirteen heavy guns, .50-caliber Brownings, including two each in powered turrets on the belly and dorsal positions. But that kind of armament wasn't considered entirely necessary, not if the bomber could outrun the fighter. And if the bomber couldn't outrun the fighter? Well, clearly, a bomber with thirteen heavy machine guns could take care of itself.

It wasn't long into the Second World War when air service leaders were disabused of that notion. By the time that the Wehrmacht surged over the Polish border in 1939, fighters could easily outrun bombers. The development of fighter, or pursuit, aircraft was almost as impressively rapid as that of the bomber. The monoplane revolution of the early 1930s had made an entirely different kind of fighter possible, and by 1935–1937 all the major air forces (and some of the lesser ones, too) had entire squadrons of fast, powerful pursuit aircraft.

In Britain, the evolution of the fighter plane was remarkably rapid. The primary RAF fighter in 1931 was the Hawker Fury, a sleek, all-metal biplane, and the first British fighter to pass the 200-mph speed threshold. Four years later, in 1935, the Fury gave way to the slightly faster Gloster Gauntlet (top speed 230 mph); two years after that, Gloster's improved biplane, the Gladiator, replaced the Gauntlet. Officially adopted by the RAF early in 1937, the Gladiator was a distinct improvement on its predecessors, with an enclosed canopy and a top speed of over 250 mph. But it was still a biplane, and there were already superior fighters in the works before the Gladiator found its way to British airfields. In the autumn of 1937, only a few months after the introduction of the Gladiator, Hawker's vastly better monoplane was on its way to equip RAF fighter squadrons. This plane, the Hurricane Mk 1, boasted a top speed of 348 mph. And even the Hurricane would be bested soon. In the summer of 1938, less than a year after the Hurricane's debut, the RAF received its first production orders of the Supermarine Spitfire Mk 1, which was slightly faster and nimbler than the Hurricane. In the space of less than a year (1937–1938), the RAF service fighter had evolved from a 250-mph biplane with two light machine guns to a 360-mph monoplane with six.

The same kind of progression was evident in all the other major air arms. When Adolf Hitler openly discarded the Versailles settlement in March 1936, Germany's main fighters—the Arado Ar 64 and the Heinkel He 51—were biplanes; two years later, Willy Messerschmitt's masterpiece, the Bf 109, was first delivered to Luftwaffe fighter squadrons. The Bf 109, which in its many variants was a formidable opponent for even the best Allied fighters of

Plate 37. A Hawker Hurricane of 488 Squadron, Royal New Zealand Air Force, 1942. The Hurricane was part of the "monoplane revolution" of the 1930s, which witnessed profound improvements in the performance and armaments of fighter aircraft.

Photo courtesy of the Air Force Museum of New Zealand, photo no. PR8367.

the Second World War, would go on to set the record—at nearly thirty-four thousand planes—for being the most heavily produced fighter aircraft in history. France had the Dewoitine D.520 and the Morane-Saulnier M.S.406; the Soviets, the pudgy but surprisingly fleet Polikarpov I-16. The US Army Air Corps went through a rapid succession of metal-bodied monoplane fighters in the 1930s, starting with the cartoonish Boeing P-26 "Peashooter" in 1932 (two .30-caliber machine guns, top speed 234 mph) and ending in 1939 with the Curtiss P-40 Warhawk (six .50-caliber machine guns, top speed 334 mph).

The members of this latest generation of monoplane fighters were not at all identical; some were clearly better than others. But as a group they exhibited notable advantages over their early 1930s predecessors besides raw speed. The most obvious of these was in armaments. One of the greatest benefits conferred by all-metal, stressed-skin wings was their capacity to house guns and ammunition. The best fighters of the Great War, and most fighters before 1935, carried their guns—usually no more than two, and usually no bigger than .30-inch caliber—in or around the engine compartment, synchronized to fire straight ahead through the propeller arc. This made it possible for the pilot to clear a jammed gun, something that was often accomplished with several sharp blows from a mallet. Better armaments were available after the Great War: more reliable, larger-caliber machine guns like the .50-caliber Browning M2 and the 13mm German MG 131, and autocannon firing small (15–20mm caliber) explosive shells. The heavier wings of the new monoplanes could accommodate the weight of these bigger guns and their ammunition load, and they were resilient enough to withstand the shock and heat that came from their firing. Firing from the wings meant that the guns did not have to be synchronized with the propeller, and therefore could generate much higher rates of fire—nine hundred rounds per minute, for example, for the MG 131.

The third major category of combat aircraft to evolve during the interwar period was the close-support, or ground-attack, planes.

These came in several varieties, though some subtypes were more widely accepted than others. They all had their origins in the close-support fighters of the Great War, principally the German Halberstadt CL.II and CL.IV, fast but stoutly built two-seaters designed to strafe trench-bound troops and drop small bombs. The close-support aircraft of the 1930s were somewhat more sophisticated, built more like heavy fighters. The most common, and early on the most popular, subtype was the dive-bomber.

Dive-bombing, as a tactic, emerged from tentative experiments during the closing months of the Great War. It was not a simple technique, for piloting a plane almost straight down to a fairly low altitude, dropping its payload, and then pulling out of the dive made great demands on both pilot and aircraft. It was very hard on wings, especially on those of the wood-and-fabric era, and the g-forces involved in pulling the plane out of a steep dive were enough to cause the pilot to black out at the most inopportune moment. But when done properly, it yielded impressive results. Since no one had yet devised an effective bombsight, diving the plane straight toward the target delivered bombs as precisely as could be done. The plane itself acted as the bombsight.

The dive-bomber filled a role that conventional medium and heavy bombers were not capable of filling. It promised the precise delivery of explosives on small targets: troops and vehicles on the battlefield, trenches, communications bunkers, and ships at sea, for it was extraordinarily difficult to land bombs on a target as narrow as a fast battleship moving at flank speed. As with fighters, the earlier designs were biplanes, usually two-seaters, with the second crew member manning a rearward-facing machine gun to protect the plane from attacks from behind. The Ernst Heinkel firm developed what was probably the first purpose-built dive-bomber in 1931: the Heinkel He 50 in the Luftwaffe (which was the basis for the Aichi D1A in the Imperial Japanese Navy, both biplanes). But monoplanes were far better equipped to withstand the stresses of the vertical dive, without the biplane's disconcerting tendency to shed its wings. Before the Second World War began, monoplane dive-bombers had mostly replaced the early 1930s biplanes in land-based squadrons and on aircraft carrier decks around the world.

For the Americans and the Japanese, two of the most active practitioners of dive-bombing, the dive-bomber was first and foremost a carrier-based naval plane, the familiar examples being the Douglas SBD Dauntless (US, 1940) and the Aichi D3A "Val" (Japan, 1938). But by far the most recognizable dive-bomber was also the most advanced when it joined the Luftwaffe in 1936. The Junkers-built Ju 87 was officially known by its class name, *Sturz-kampfflugzeug* (dive-bomber), abbreviated simply to Stuka. The Stuka included all the design elements that came to distinguish the dive-bomber, such as extraordinarily robust construction and fixed landing gear. As part of the new generation of ground-attack craft, the Stuka also had dive brakes—extra flaps mounted on the underside of the trailing edge of each wing, extended when going into a dive to increase drag and slow the diving craft to a manageable speed. The Stuka also introduced a new and brilliant feature: a mechanism for automatically pulling the plane's nose up at the end of a steep attack dive, so that if the pilot blacked out from the high g-forces the bomber could still recover itself rather than burrowing itself into the ground nose-first. The most memorable thing about the German dive-bomber, according to those unlucky enough to be attacked by one, was the "Jericho trumpet," propeller-driven sirens attached to the fixed landing gear, which gave an unearthly shriek when the plane went into a dive.

Besides these most common types of combat aircraft—medium and heavy bombers, fighters, ground-attack aircraft—there were a variety of non-combat types, such as photoreconnaissance and cargo transport planes for example, and a few combat varieties that never completely caught on. One of the latter was the torpedo bomber. Torpedo bombers had been around since before the First World War; a torpedo launched from a British Short 184 floatplane sank an Ottoman ship in August 1915, the first successful employment of the weapon. In 1917, the British introduced the first purpose-built torpedo bomber, the Sopwith T.1 Cuckoo. Not surprisingly, it was the larger naval powers that invested the most in the development of the concept, with Britain, Japan, and the United States taking the lead. Unlike the dive-bomber, the torpedo bomber didn't have any special design requirements, other than an ability to fly level and steady at low altitudes, and to carry an aerial torpedo of two thousand pounds or more. To ensure that the torpedo hit the water as gently as possible, attack runs by torpedo bombers had to be done "low and slow," so high speed was not so important a requirement. By 1939, the three big navies all had torpedo bombers in quantity: the ungainly Douglas TBD Devastator (US, 1937), the Japanese Nakajima B5N "Kate" (1937), and Britain's Fairey Swordfish (1936). The Swordfish, an open-cockpit biplane, was a true anachronism, but it was still credited with two of the most famous torpedo attacks in history: the November 1940 attack on the Italian fleet at Taranto, and the sinking of the German battleship *Bismarck* in May 1941.

MANY OF THESE technologies, and the tactics that went with them, were put to the test shortly before the outbreak of the Second World War. While tanks went into action in the summer of 1939 virtually untested except in harmless and not very informative peacetime maneuvers, there were several instances in the interwar period when the major air forces did a shakedown cruise of sorts— and when foreign observers could watch them and take notes, just as they had in the Russo-Japanese War.

The lessons learned in combat in the 1930s were instructive but not clear-cut, and often very surprising. Two of the most closely watched aerial campaigns of the decade were the Italian invasion of Abyssinia (Ethiopia) in 1935 and the Japanese invasions of China (1931, 1937). In both cases, aerial bombing against civilian targets, while causing substantial damage and loss of life, was not sufficient to break popular morale and bring about a quick end to combat—a direct challenge to the bold assertions of the Douhet school of air supremacy. But airpower *did* help both Italian and Japanese ground forces achieve their objectives much more easily than would have been the case without air support. In 1937, China—unlike Abyssinia—had an air force of its own, supplemented by auxiliary pilots and aircraft borrowed from the Soviet Union, but the superior Japanese air forces dominated the skies and the battlefield below.

Much more specific examples and lessons came in Europe's biggest, and most troubling, conflict of the 1930s, the Spanish Civil War. Spain itself did not have an air force worthy of the name. Instead, interested outside parties—Hitler, Mussolini, and Stalin—supplied the hardware and often the pilots, too. For all three, whatever their political motivations for inserting themselves into Spain's domestic tragedy, the war presented an unparalleled opportunity to try out both frontline aircraft and untested prototypes in combat conditions, for combat pilots to experiment with tactics, and for the air forces to develop something like a doctrine. It was generally understood among aviation experts that air superiority was desirable, that bombing civilian populations might end wars quickly, and that air forces could coordinate with operations on the ground . . . but what, precisely, did any of that actually look like?

Aerial operations in the civil war yielded lots of clues. A successful airlift of twenty thousand rebel troops from Morocco to the Spanish mainland in late 1936, using a small fleet of German Ju 52 transport planes—the first airlift in military history—demonstrated that command of the air sometimes trumped command of the sea. During the battle of Guadalajara (March 1937), Soviet fighter pilots—on the side of the loyal Republicans—defeated their Italian opponents and then proceeded to destroy advancing Italian ground troops with bombs and machine-gun fire. In a matter of hours, the Soviet planes had obliterated a thousand Italian vehicles and claimed some 2,500 casualties, a grim but eloquent demonstration of the power of close air support. And this power was demonstrated in bombing raid after bombing raid after bombing raid, like three days of bombing by Italian and Nationalist planes over Barcelona (March 1938), and the raid that came to symbolize the wanton cruelty of modern warfare, the German-Italian attack on the Basque town of Guernica, in April 1937.

The air war in Spain seemed to dissipate the fevered dreams of the Douhet school. The bomber did not always get through; enemy fighters, it was soon discovered, could make short work of unescorted bombers. Strategic bombing might kill innocent civilians in their thousands, and arouse international outrage—Western newspapers and their readers sputtered in helpless anger over the story of fifty girls killed by incendiary bombs while they worked in a candy factory in Guernica—but it did not necessarily crack civilian resolve. If anything, it seemed, the bombing of civilian targets hardened popular resolve to resist, which negated the very core of Douhet's arguments. German, Italian, and Russian pilots learned, too, how very effective ground support could be if carefully planned and directed. These three air forces in particular would focus their attention in the next war on their ground-attack role and de-emphasize strategic bombing.

THE SECOND WORLD War was an air war. Ground operations stole public attention, then and now, and many of the truly iconic moments from the 1939–1945 war involved ground combat: the Normandy landings in 1944, the urban fighting in Stalingrad, the raising of the American flag at Iwo Jima. But just as many of those iconic moments centered on the command of the air, and even the Normandy, Stalingrad, and Pacific campaigns would have looked much different without the aerial component. Without the waves of Stukas spearheading German ground assaults as the Wehrmacht brought the blitzkrieg to Poland, the Low Countries, and France; without the Battle of Britain and the Blitz; without the destruction of American battleships at Pearl Harbor and of Japanese carriers at Midway, and—above all—without the terrible and defining climactic moments at Hiroshima and Nagasaki, the Second World War simply would not have been what it was.

It was an air war in the sense that the air itself was a major theater of combat, and that the most devastating blows were struck from the skies—the Allied strategic bombing campaign against German industry and infrastructure, for example, and American air attacks on the Japanese mainland. It was an air war in that every aspect of ground and naval operations was shaped by matters related to airpower, and that "mastery of the air," or the failure to achieve it, could determine the outcome of campaigns. It was an air war also because of the support role that air forces played, from airlifting supplies to isolated forces to transporting commanders quickly and stealthily to dropping airborne ground troops (more or less) precisely where they were needed. It was an air war in that aircraft brought the war directly to civilians, via bombing of non-military targets, and it was an air war because the manufacture of aircraft was probably the most demanding (and prolific) industry in all of the major warring powers.

One of the most notable features of military aviation in the Second World War was its remarkable responsiveness and flexibility—in technology and in doctrine. Aviation was no longer a novelty, but it was still quite novel; its leaders and pioneers were neither tradition-bound nor even especially conservative. There were no traditions to break, and military aviation was thus inherently revolutionary. Experiences drawn from the regional conflicts of the 1930s gave some idea as to what could be expected in a large-scale air war; the intensity and scale of the 1939–1945 conflict, right from the start, corrected and expanded upon those lessons. Almost as important, the technology responded, too, much faster than had been the case historically in wartime. New designs and features, even entirely new aircraft, all emerged to meet new challenges and take up unanticipated roles.

IN AERIAL WARFARE, the greatest takeaway from the interwar period was the utter necessity of making provisions for tactical air support. In Spain, specialized close-support aircraft—the German Ju 87A Stuka and the aesthetically unappealing Italian Breda Ba.65—performed well. The experience confirmed what German aviation experts had already assumed. German leaders during the

Weimar period, such as General Hans von Seeckt, viewed trench warfare on the Western Front as a historical anomaly, not likely to be repeated again; they fervently believed that the next war would be one of lightning-fast offensives and constant movement, favoring mechanized forces. Airpower would be a vital component of any kind of combined-arms tactics.

The invasion of Poland in September 1939, the opening act in the Second World War, showed just how much the Germans had learned. Airpower was an integral part of every aspect of *Fall Weiss*, the first example of what observers would soon call "lightning war"—blitzkrieg. To be fair, it should be pointed out that the Luftwaffe had not quite reached the level of technological sophistication that its leaders, especially Hitler's air marshal Hermann Göring, had hoped for before going to war. Production of the latest aircraft—the Bf 109 fighter, the twin-engined Bf 110 heavy fighter,

Plate 38. The *Stuka*. An icon of the blitzkrieg era: the Junkers Ju 87D *Stuka* (the accepted abbreviation for *Sturzkampfflugzeug*) dive-bomber/close-support plane, here photographed flying over the Russian front in 1943.

Image: Bundesarchiv, Bild 101I-634-3856-34.

the Dornier and Heinkel medium bombers, and the Stuka—was barely keeping up with demand, and the Luftwaffe continued to field a considerable number of obsolete planes. And it wasn't as if Poland was defenseless. Its monoplane fighters were out of date, to be sure, but Poland still had a competent air force, and a well-armed, one-million-man army to boot.

Even so, the Germans overwhelmed Poland with astonishing speed, and the Luftwaffe deserves much of the credit. Aerial reconnaissance units provided the Wehrmacht with detailed intelligence of Polish defenses and troop dispositions. Swarms of German fighters established air superiority in days and destroyed the Polish air force in less than two weeks, much of it while Polish planes were still on the ground. Stukas and their biplane predecessor, the Henschel Hs 123 dive-bomber, pounded enemy ground targets relentlessly. The Poles learned to fear the telltale sounds of a coming attack, the unnerving shriek of the Stuka's sirens and the roar of the Henschel's massive radial engine.

But most important was the coordination between individual air units, and between air and ground formations. Special air liaison officers rode in command vehicles with the mechanized columns on the ground. Linked by wireless radio to the air units, they could direct close support to precisely where it was needed. The larger bombers, the He 111s and Do 17s, hit key transportation and communications targets, focusing on rail facilities and government buildings. German forces could have defeated Poland even without the support of the Luftwaffe, but the Luftwaffe made that defeat quick, resounding, one-sided—and terrifying.

As revolutionary as the blitzkrieg in Poland was, it still had to evolve, in tactics and in technology. German air superiority alone was enough to destroy the Danish and Norwegian air forces, such as they were, when the Wehrmacht invaded the Scandinavian kingdoms in April 1940. German deployment of airborne infantry in both invasions also helped to speed the defeat of Denmark and Norway. In the latter case, German airpower effectively negated British attempts to aid Norway by sea. The following month, the

Luftwaffe struck decisively again, quickly neutralizing Dutch and Belgian air forces, and again German airborne troops played a major role. The glider-based assault on the Belgian fort at Eben Emael has to rank among the most dramatic airborne operations in all of the twentieth century.

Only with the invasion of France, which occurred simultaneously with the assaults on the Low Countries in May 1940, did the Luftwaffe encounter—courtesy of the RAF and the French Armée de l'Air—anything even vaguely close to being its equal. But even the British and French air arms were not close enough. There were a few bright spots for the Allies, to be sure. Many of their fighters, notably the Hawker Hurricane and the Dewoitine D.520, could hold their own in combat against Bf 109s and Bf 110s, and British pilots in particular took a respectable toll of German aircraft—more, in fact, than the Luftwaffe could really afford to lose. Neither the French nor the British had close-support aircraft that could compare with the Stukas and the Henschel biplanes, and German antiaircraft batteries made quick work of slow—and often misemployed—Allied bombers. Just in the first three days of the invasion, German flak took down half of the entire British bomber force in France.

The German air war over France was, much like the invasion itself, a stunning, overwhelming success—costlier, perhaps, than Berlin would have liked, but a success nonetheless. The German victory had less to do with better technology, though, than it did with organizational superiority. As in Poland, the Luftwaffe and the army worked together seamlessly to destroy targets on the ground or in the air in short order. The RAF, overall, performed well, especially its fighters. But the French simply failed—not out of cowardice, as has often been alleged in American popular culture, but because they lacked everything the Germans had built up in combined-arms tactics. French ground and air commanders were barely on speaking terms—they were not at all accustomed to coordinating air and ground operations—and French air forces were shockingly inactive.

France was, on the whole, an easy target. Things would not be so simple after 1940 for the Luftwaffe, and as Germany faced more formidable opponents, the technology of the blitzkrieg was already obsolescing. The first stages of the German invasion of Russia in 1941 went smoothly enough. The Red Air Force was deficient in tactics, organization, and trained aircrews. The Luftwaffe made short work of it, destroying thousands of Soviet warplanes on the ground while suffering insignificant losses. German fighters, bombers, and close-support planes were able to hit ground targets virtually unopposed. But after the initial German gains in the summer of 1941, the tactics of blitzkrieg were no longer novel; the basic concept behind it—the coordination of massive air strikes with the movements of mechanized ground forces—became the norm. On the Russian front, both Soviet and German armies made liberal use of ground-attack aircraft. The Stuka, slow and vulnerable, was already obsolete by the time Hitler launched his prolonged aerial campaign against Britain in 1940, easy prey for British fighters. But in Russia the Stuka found renewed life as a highly successful tank killer, carrying a high-velocity 37mm anti-tank gun under each wing. The Soviet Ilyushin Il-2 *Sturmovik* performed much the same role. And after Allied forces finally established a toehold in Nazi-occupied France on D-Day, 6 June 1944, American and British ground-attack planes and fighter-bombers helped speed the advance of ground troops into the bocage country of Normandy and beyond. Although the Americans did not have a specially designed ground-attack plane, bigger fighters—like the beefy Republic P-47 Thunderbolt, with eight wing-mounted machine guns and capable of carrying heavier ordnance—excelled at interdicting German rail traffic, subduing even the largest German tanks, and making it very dangerous for enemy supply columns to travel by road. Increasingly, the P-47 and its British counterparts, including the Hawker Tempest and the Hawker Typhoon, made use of wing-mounted rockets.

STRATEGIC BOMBING HAD made a less than stellar showing in the Spanish Civil War, but it returned with a vengeance in the

Second World War. Conditions for a bombing war, though, were somewhat different after 1939 than they were only a few years before, when the new generation of fast monoplane bombers seemed to prove Hugh Trenchard's point about the bomber always getting through. By 1939, fighters were much faster than bombers, and the half-dozen or so machine guns typically mounted as defensive armament on most bombers were not up to the task of fending off fighters.

And antiaircraft defenses gained another big edge over bombers in the late 1930s: radar. The notion of an early warning system to detect the approach of enemy aircraft was not new. In the Great War, the British had built a series of concrete "sound mirrors," large concave blocks pointed seaward, which with the aid of a stethoscope-like device could pick up the drone of aircraft engines from miles away, and even allow the operator to determine the direction of approach. Radar marked a significant improvement over this. The use of radio waves to detect distant objects had been the subject of experiments almost from the beginning of the century. By 1935, the British Air Ministry had adopted radar as part of an integrated, expansive early warning system, which was partially built by the time the war began. So when Hitler set his sights on Britain after the fall of France in the summer of 1940, the British were ready to deflate the hyperbolic claims of the Douhet school.

Britain's integrated, radar-based early warning system meant that Luftwaffe bombers could be spotted as far away as *100 miles*, with the detection transmitted to a central intelligence unit and analyzed there, and instructions given to the defensive fighter squadrons to respond immediately. Britain, in fact, had all the advantages. While the Bf 109 was a close match for the British Spitfires and Hurricanes in dogfighting ability, the German fighter was notoriously short-ranged and could not engage in combat for more than a few minutes after it reached Britain's shores from German bases in occupied France. The Bf 110 was too sluggish to dogfight. German bombers—notably the Stuka and the He 111—were easily shot down by British pilots, and were practically defenseless if unescorted by their own fighters. The Luftwaffe was already suffering from materiel and manpower losses incurred during the battle of France, while the British had lost comparatively fewer pilots and planes. German attacks did little to slow British manufacturing, including the production of replacement aircraft. Perhaps most telling, the continuous German bombing of civilian targets, in London and elsewhere, did little to dampen popular ardor for the war with Germany. The collective experience of suffering through the Battle of Britain and the Blitz, if anything, stiffened British popular resolve to fight and rallied citizens behind Winston Churchill and his government. The Luftwaffe did not entirely give up on strategic bombing after the Blitz, and indeed its regular bombings of Soviet-held towns in 1941–1944 killed about as many Soviet civilians as the much more notorious Allied bombings of German-occupied Europe did.

The Allied experience of strategic bombing was somewhat different in scale, purpose, and results. The Soviets were not a part of the Allied bomber offensives; they were uncomfortable with bombing civilian targets, and anyway the Red Air Force had chosen to focus on close support—undoubtedly a wise setting of priorities given the nature of the land war on the Eastern Front. After initially spurning attacks on civilian populations in favor of explicitly military targets, the RAF changed its tune early in 1942, when British raids on German towns and facilities began in earnest. The US Army Air Force (USAAF), which started to establish bases on English soil that same year, joined in shortly afterward. By the spring of 1943, a coordinated Anglo-American bomber offensive was underway, and it did not let up for the remainder of the war in Europe. British four-engine bombers, Avro Lancasters and Short Stirlings, hit German targets at night, when defensive fighter cover was thinner; American B-17s and B-24s did daylight raids, when their Norden bombsights—perhaps the most important technological advance in bombing at the time—were effective.

The damage done to German industry, supply, and communications was both big and almost immediate—that much the airpower advocates of the Douhet school were right about. A series of Allied bombing raids over Hamburg in the summer of 1943 (24 July–3 August) resulted in more than forty thousand civilian deaths and nearly as many wounded. Industrial sites—arms factories, foundries, chemical plants, oil refineries—were the most common targets; collateral civilian casualties could be heavy, but often civilian casualties were the intended goal. The mix of high explosive bombs with incendiaries was especially potent, and the resulting loss of life was almost beyond belief. During the six-month period between July 1944 and January 1945, the Germans lost an average of thirteen thousand civilians to Allied bombing raids every month.

Was the Allied bomber offensive a success? Three-quarters of a century later, that's still not an easy question to answer. If it broke the German will to fight, it wasn't enough to shorten the war. It may not have even reduced German industrial output, which seems to have remained steady in the last two years of the war. But without a doubt, a few specific industries were hit hard, and seriously crippled, as a direct result of the bombing. A few tank models experienced major service disruptions on account of the raids, and production of Germany's revolutionary late-model U-boats also practically came to a halt. Most serious of all were the resulting shortages in fuel oil, thanks to heavy raids on refineries. Few things hampered German ground operations in the last nine months of the war as did fuel shortages. And the insatiable demand for defensive weaponry to protect German urbanized areas and factories diverted valuable assets—fighter planes and antiaircraft artillery in particular—away from the fighting in Russia and France to the German heartland.

Because the stakes were so high, the Allied air war against Germany forced defenders and attackers alike to adjust their tactics and technology to the changing demands of the aerial battlefield. The advantage in the bomber war over Europe, at first, lay with the defenders; the big bombers did indeed get through, but at a prohibitively high cost. Flak claimed many, to be sure, but in the early stages of the air war the real threat came from the German fighters.

The later models of the venerable Bf 109 and the new Focke-Wulf FW 190 were at least as good as the main Allied fighters in 1943–1944, and the FW 190 was probably more maneuverable, more robust, and faster than any of them. The big four-engine bombers were relatively well defended with heavy machine guns covering most approaches, but they were still easy prey for the German fighters that inevitably swarmed them.

Allied fighter escorts would have been a great asset, but the main American fighters—the twin-engine, twin-boomed Lockheed P-38 Lightning and the Republic P-47 Thunderbolt—while excellent warplanes, did not have the range necessary to accompany bombers from their bases in England to German targets and back again. The RAF's heavy bombers, conducting their raids at night, were somewhat less plagued by German interceptors, but the American bomber formations would have to go it alone, unescorted, on the most dangerous part of the trek into the heart of the Reich. The introduction of the North American P-51D Mustang, late in 1943, tipped the balance in favor of the American daylight bombers. Besides being a fast and nimble fighter that was superior to most of its German counterparts, the Mustang could—with the addition of external fuel tanks—escort the B-17s and B-24s for the duration of their long and dangerous journey. By the last year of the war, the Luftwaffe was suffering dire shortages of aircraft, pilots, and fuel, thanks in part to aggressive Allied fighter sweeps that ranged ahead of the bombing attacks, and German aerial resistance weakened drastically.

NO VARIETY OF military aircraft evolved so much during the course of the Second World War as did the fighters. The difference in performance between the best fighters of 1939–1940 and those of 1945 was almost as great as that between fighters before and after the monoplane revolution. Even those models that had been around since before the war, like the Bf 109, went through so many iterations, so many gradual improvements, that it's hardly fair to compare their 1939 and 1945 versions.

To be sure, there were some types of fighters that were failures from the very start. At the outset of the war, the idea of a "heavy fighter" gained some currency. The Germans, who invested in the concept more than most, referred to such a plane as a *Zerstörer*— "destroyer." These multi-seat fighters were bigger, had heavier armaments, and usually featured one or two rearward-facing machine guns on flexible mounts. The Messerschmitt Bf 110 was probably the most widely used: two engines, a three-man crew, four machine guns, and two 20mm autocannon mounted in the nose. Because it had bigger fuel tanks than its smaller cousin, the Bf 109, it boasted correspondingly greater range. But as an intermediate between a fighter and a light bomber, it wasn't particularly good at either. In the Battle of Britain, it could not compete with the infinitely more agile Spitfires and Hurricanes. Britain's original heavy fighter, the Boulton Paul Defiant, was even less successful; externally, it looked much like a conventional single-seat fighter, except that it was a two-seater and had no forward-firing armament at all. All four of its machine guns were housed in a rotating turret situated behind the pilot. It was an imaginative concept, to be sure, but dreadfully unsuccessful, and when Defiants tangled with Messerschmitts the British plane inevitably came up short. Some of the heavy fighters, though, like the Bf 110, found renewed life in another capacity: as night fighters. The capacious airframe of the Bf 110 allowed plenty of space for a radar array in the nose, and in this capacity—as an interceptor targeting Allied bombers flying unescorted night raids over German territory—the Bf 110 came into its own.

The drive for continual refinement and improvement, the same impulse that repurposed the Bf 110 from a mediocre day fighter into an excellent night fighter, also transformed what was theoretically possible in the 1930s into reality by 1943. The evolution of the jet engine, and of jet aircraft, is one of the best examples of this modern dynamic in military technology. Though the subject of intense interest since even before the advent of powered flight, a working turbojet engine was not available until right before the Second World War. British engineer Frank Whittle and his team developed a functional turbojet in 1937; working parallel to Whittle—and influenced by him—was a German engineer, Hans von Ohain. Ohain's turbojet, though postdating Whittle's, was the first to be attached to an airplane. Ernst Heinkel incorporated Ohain's engine in his He 178, the first jet aircraft to take to the skies, which made its first successful flight on 27 August 1939— five days before the Second World War began.

British and German engineers raced to get a jet fighter into production, and once again the Germans won the race. The twin-engine Me 262 *Schwalbe* (Swallow), first test-flown in 1941, entered active service with the Luftwaffe in April 1944. It instantly out-classed every fighter in every air force worldwide. Once airborne it was without peer. Its 560 mph top speed, about 120 mph faster than the P-51D, meant that no Allied fighter could possibly catch it; its armament of four 30mm autocannon could chew up a B-17 in seconds. And the Me 262 was just the start. Late-war German aircraft design was a marvel of ideas that would have seemed far-fetched just a decade earlier, now brought to glorious life. There was the Arado Ar 234 *Blitz*, a twin-engine, jet-propelled medium bomber with a top speed of 460 mph; the Heinkel He 162 *Volks-jäger*, a sleek single-engine turbojet fighter, constructed mostly from wood; and the weird little Messerschmitt Me 163 Komet, a rocket-powered interceptor that could climb to thirty-nine thousand feet in less than four minutes after take-off.

As with most of the better sort of Nazi "wonder weapons," the brilliance of their design and their enormous combat potential were offset by the difficulties that arose because of their late arrival. The overall success of the Allied strategic bombing campaign over German-occupied Europe ensured that manufacturing any of these pioneering new warplanes, let alone developing and testing them, would be a prospect fraught with much danger and frequent work stoppages, compounded by the chronic shortage of fuel. At war's end, the surprisingly large number of He 162s and Ar 234s were largely idle, grounded for the most part for lack of fuel. For that, the Allies had much reason to be thankful. The appearance of any or all of these warplanes, in operational condition and in large numbers, only a couple of years before, would have substantially complicated the task of achieving air superiority in European skies—or, perhaps, rendered that goal impossible. Once again, manufacturing capacity won out over technological superiority.

Whether the new German warplanes were successes or failures ultimately didn't matter. Of course they had their teething issues: The Junkers Jumo 004 turbojet engines, used on both the Me 262 and the Arado *Blitz*, were prone to frequent flameouts and required lots of care. The *Komet*, for all its astonishing climb rate, only had fuel for about eight minutes of flight time, after which the pilot had to finish his mission while making a gliding descent. And all the German jet planes were slow to take off and hence vulnerable before they reached altitude, so Allied pilots learned to "bounce" them while they were still in their initial climb.

These were comparatively minor issues, often the result of production compromises in the resource- and labor-starved Reich, and would have been quickly cleared up had the Nazi war machine had the luxury of time or safety. The teething problems were immaterial; the new German warplanes represented the dawn of a new era and the next great leap forward in the technology of war in the air. Little more than a decade before, the biplane with synchronized machine guns had reached its evolutionary zenith, to be replaced by the all-metal, piston-engine monoplane. Now the piston-engine fighter, too, had evolved as far as it could, and the descendants of the Me 262, Ar 234, and He 162 would replace it. The age of the jet warplane had begun.

More than any other combatant nation in the Second World War, Germany had transformed the technology and tactics of aerial warfare. The Luftwaffe had pioneered close-support tactics in the blitzkrieg; it excelled at the use of radar-equipped night fighters to defend ground targets from enemy bombers; it introduced the first practical jets and used them successfully in combat. No other air force could make the same boasts. German research scientists and aviation engineers—more correctly, now, aerospace engineers—also broke new ground in another kind of aerial warfare, one that was still just a Vernesque fantasy in the years before the war but would become a frightening reality in the last few months of the conflict.

As the ebb and flow of the war turned against Nazi Germany in 1943–1944, Hitler and his generals turned to increasingly desperate means of breaking the Allied will to fight on. One manifestation of this was the Führer's ready embrace of "vengeance weapons" (*Vergeltungswaffen*), designed to take the war to Allied civilian populations just as Allied bombers were raining death daily (and nightly) on German population and industrial centers. The two most notable of the vengeance weapons had been in development since the first days of German rearmament and of the Reich itself. At a top-secret research site in Peenemünde, on Germany's wind-swept Baltic coast, a young Wernher von Braun and his engineering team experimented with liquid-fueled rockets; at the same time, another design team, including the engineers and academics Paul Schmidt, Robert Lusser, and Georg Hans Madelung, were hard at work developing a pulse-jet "flying bomb." The weapons that emerged from these two research programs were both similar and very, very different. The first into production was the flying bomb, christened with the official name Vergeltungswaffe 1, or V-1. The V-1 was, in essence, a cruise missile, guided by gyrocompass, capable of bearing a one-ton high explosive warhead for nearly 160 miles at 400 mph. Sent aloft from mobile launchers or static launch sites in northern France, or even carried by medium bombers and launched in the air, the V-1s could easily hit population centers in Britain. Cheap and easy to build, the Germans sent nearly 7,000 of them against British targets, with more than 2,300 hitting London alone.

Wernher von Braun's project, which came to fruition as Vergeltungswaffe 2, or V-2, served much the same purpose as the simpler, cheaper V-1. Like the V-1, the V-2 could reach London from occupied France; also like the V-1, it packed around a ton of high explosive. But there the similarity ended. The V-1's speed topped out at around 400 mph, and therefore it could be intercepted by Allied fighters or be taken down by antiaircraft artillery. The V-2, powered by an ethanol-fueled rocket engine that used liquid oxygen as an oxidizer, could reach speeds of over 3,500 mph, soaring to an altitude of *fifty-five miles* when in long-range flight. The V-2, in short, was the world's first ballistic missile. Fortunately for Britain, it was also prohibitively expensive, and by the time it was operational in September 1944, manufacturing it—let alone launching it—was an increasingly difficult proposition thanks to Allied dominance of the skies.

As with the jet warplanes, the fact that the V-1 and the V-2 did not reverse the tide of the war, did not compel Britain to surrender, did not fulfill Hitler's fantastical hope that terror weapons would allow his Thousand Year Reich to live to see another year, almost doesn't matter. What mattered was this: that Germany had developed the means to drop bombs on the enemy without risking aircraft or flight crew, and that—in the V-2—it had developed the means to attack enemy civilian populations directly with almost no chance of the enemy detecting the attack, and even less chance that the enemy could do anything about it.

MILITARY AVIATION IN the Second World War more than fulfilled the promise it appeared to hold in the First. It had, in fact, transcended that promise. Airpower did not progress exactly the way Douhet and his ilk had predicted. Clearly there was a lot more to the Second World War than the clash of air forces. The bomber did not always get through, as thousands of downed aircrews could attest. Nor did unrelenting, intensive bombing bring civilian populations to their knees.

But airpower accomplished so much more, much of it unanticipated by the Douhets and the Mitchells and the Trenchards of the interwar period. Airpower helped to meet the goals of ground commanders in a way that would not have been readily apparent in 1917–1918. Tactical air support, especially if combined with command of the air over the battlefield and linked to ground forces via wireless, helped restore mobility to the battlefield.

Aviation also highlighted the central importance of industry, and of economic factors, in modern warfare. Of course, the same could be said about any one of a number of weapons technologies in the Second World War. Steady supply and robust manufacturing trumped brilliance of design. Victory went to the nation with the strongest economy, the most resilient manufacturing base, and not necessarily to the best engineers and the most forward-looking technology. Airpower, in turn, could damage industry to the point that waging war became more and more difficult, even if the civilian will to resist proved to be unbreakable.

But airpower was not restricted to the land war. It also extended the striking power of navies many times over. Indeed, the warplane changed what it was that navies did. Thanks to airpower, the aircraft carrier would take the place of the battleship, and the age of the gun-carrying capital ship would come to an end.

CHAPTER 20

THE TWILIGHT OF
THE BATTLESHIP

T he Great War was full of hard lessons. It was also, from a
purely military standpoint, full of imaginative solutions to
ancient problems, of ways and modes of combat that only a generation before would have been written off as pure fantasy. Sometimes, though, those innovations did not readily fit into traditional
patterns of warfare, and that constrained their potential, even as
Europe geared up again for war in the late 1930s. Nowhere did
conservative minds dominate the conversation about military reform so thoroughly as they did in naval warfare. The Great War
revealed much about the new face of combat at sea in the twentieth century, but few men of influence would assimilate or accept
those lessons.

Chief among those lessons was this: the age of the dreadnought
was over. It was over almost as quickly as it had arrived, and it
had been unimaginably expensive. The diminishment of the dreadnought must have been a difficult notion to swallow, and on its
surface it must have seemed counter-rational. The naval arms race,
in which the competition had been as much about technology and
design as it had been about quantity and raw tonnage, peaked with
the launching of HMS *Dreadnought* in 1906, and that naval race
in turn had done much to bring the European nations to the brink

of war in 1914. Pound for pound, the major European powers invested more in naval construction than they did in any other area of defense spending; until 1914, the very idea of cost cutting in navies would have been thought ludicrous, even dangerous. Navies got what they wanted and needed, most of the time, even if what they wanted and what they needed weren't the same, regardless of whether or not there was a payoff in sight.

For all the expense and energy they consumed, the great Western navies accomplished relatively little in the Great War—or, more correctly, their contribution to the war was not what naval leaders and their governments had anticipated in 1914. Not even close. Prior to the outbreak of war, the understanding had been universal: ships would function in combat much as they had since the seventeenth century. True, they could move much faster than their sail-driven predecessors; their guns could fire at much greater distances, more accurately, and cause much more destruction. There would be changes in combat due to, among other things, the availability of reliable submarines and marine torpedoes. But the ultimate expression of battle at sea, the means by which one navy would assert its mastery over another, was still assumed to be the clash between enemy battle fleets made up of dreadnoughts and heavier cruisers—big ships carrying big guns, squaring off against one another in line-of-battle as battle fleets had done since the very first ships of the line. That's what the dreadnought was, after all: the modern incarnation of the first-rater. The sweeping technological changes that followed one upon another between 1860 and 1914 did not, in the eyes of mainstream naval establishments, change the role of the battleship.

The First World War did not prove them wrong. Not exactly. The capital ships of 1914–1918 were not useless by any means. The British fleet successfully blockaded German ports throughout the war, and Germany suffered profoundly from the resulting cut off of maritime trade, a factor that contributed mightily to its internal collapse and final defeat in 1918. Dreadnoughts and cruisers fought a limited number of fleet actions, with Jutland (May–June 1916) taking pride of place. Naval power was absolutely critical to Allied operations in the Bosporus in 1915, and ship-to-shore artillery fire was a major component of Allied attempts to wrest Gallipoli from Turkish hands.

But the performance of the capital ships did not bear out the wisdom of the investment made in naval technology and construction. Instead, the big trends in naval warfare after 1918 would move in two different directions. The first—and most predictable—of these trends was the ascendancy of the submarine. No naval vessel of the Great War had accomplished more than the submarine, especially in German service. The second trend, less visible in 1918 than the first, was the rise of the aircraft carrier and the merger of airpower with sea power. Much of the Second World War at sea—one might argue the most important parts of the naval war—would be fought below the surface and in the sky.

THOUGH NAVAL AIRPOWER was still very much in an experimental stage when the Great War came to an end, the submarine was already an established technology, and no one doubted the potentially devastating power of U-boats. It was no accident that the Versailles treaty explicitly prohibited Germany from having or building any. Indeed, the British delegation at the Washington Naval Conference (1921–1922)—that thorough if ultimately doomed attempt to reduce the world's biggest battle fleets and prevent future naval arms races—had sought to ban submarines outright, for everyone. But the collective focus of the world's big fleets, and of the admirals and politicians who guided them, remained firmly planted on the big-gun battleships.

The outbreak of war in 1914 slowed naval construction and development in the West. France, Germany, Italy, Austria-Hungary, and Russia all put an end to new construction once hostilities began. Britain continued to build, and in fact turned out one of the most influential designs of the half-century: HMS *Hood*, predecessor of the "fast battleship" type that dominated naval shipyards worldwide in the 1930s.

The two most active shipbuilding nations of the Great War were newcomers, and they reflected the way in which the European conflict was already shaking up the pre-1914 balance of power. In 1916, Japan announced its intention to build and maintain a large fleet of battleships and battlecruisers, and the United States immediately followed suit. A new naval arms race was afoot, and like the early Anglo-German naval race it moved disturbingly fast. Japan had, by 1921, put two new battleships into service, laid down two more, and was working on four battlecruisers; eleven battleships and six battlecruisers were under construction in American yards. The British, alarmed at the prospect of being out-shipped and out-gunned, also got in on the competition.

But for all the dangerous, seductive allure of an arms race, the world—the West in particular—was not ready for another war, nor did it want one. Disarmament, international and universal, had been foremost among Woodrow Wilson's Fourteen Points, the American president's outline of how he wanted the European war to end and somehow justify the terrible sacrifice that war had demanded. It was not all that popular a stance with Wilson's European allies, who insisted upon the disarmament of the Central Powers but at the same time were reluctant to let down their guard. Still, the notion of disarmament resonated with the American public, which was eager to withdraw from further international commitments and not pleased with the Wilson administration's naval expansion program.

The result was a series of naval conferences and resulting treaties, all intended to avert a naval arms race while still allowing the larger naval powers to maintain fleets that were consonant with their legitimate security needs. The Washington Naval Conference and Washington Naval Treaty (1922) were the first, bringing together diplomats from the five nations with the largest navies: Britain, the United States, Japan, France, and Italy. Germany and the Soviet Union, the two pariah states, were deliberately excluded. Follow-on agreements signed at Geneva (1927, 1932) and London (1930, 1936) further refined the Washington settlement. Together, the naval agreements set a ceiling on the total tonnage of capital ships each navy could keep, following the ratio 5 (Britain): 5 (United States): 3 (Japan): 1.75 (France): 1.75 (Italy). The Washington treaty proclaimed a ten-year "holiday"—a moratorium—on the construction of new capital ships. It also strictly limited the size and armament of battleships, battlecruisers, and aircraft carriers, the latter still very much a novelty in 1922. The Geneva and London agreements did the same for cruisers, destroyers, and submarines.

The treaties had their intended effect—at first. To meet the cap on aggregate tonnage, the signatory nations scrapped a fleet's worth of existing capital ships, and even more ships that were still under construction. The United States sold thirty large warships for scrap immediately after the signing of the 1922 treaty. And ships constructed in accordance with treaty guidelines were, on average, smaller than the superdreadnoughts of the Great War. The new capital ships incorporated significant design compromises, as their weight limitations precluded the use of all the advancements in armor, guns, propulsion, and hull design that naval architects would have preferred. These "Treaty battleships" were more lightly armored, with larger but fewer guns, and not as fast as they could have been.

Still, few of the participating naval powers were all that keen to reduce their fleets or to rely on smaller, weaker battleships, and they went out of their way to find loopholes that might allow them to expand instead—observing the letter, but not the well-intentioned spirit, of the disarmament treaties. The ten-year construction holiday was easily bypassed, for the treaties did not attempt to regulate the improvement of existing dreadnought-era battleships; all of the treaty navies took the opportunity to upgrade armaments, add additional armor, and convert coal-burning power plants to modern oil-fired engines.

The naval treaties of the 1920s and 1930s might have prevented or at least slowed a potentially explosive arms race, but they also spurred experimentation, testing, and innovation like nothing before, as naval establishments and naval architects sought to circum-vent the treaty restrictions through improved technology. Even Weimar Germany, though not party to the Washington treaty and its successor agreements, was still prohibited by Versailles from building warships of greater than ten thousand tons displacement. These constricted options encouraged creative solutions. The Germans invented an entirely new category of big-gunned ship, the pocket battleship, that packed a powerful armament, substantial armor protection, and high-speed engines into a compact package that displaced only slightly more than the Versailles-imposed limit. When the treaties, like all the serious and well-intentioned attempts to promote disarmament in the interwar period, came crashing down, the naval powers were ready and waiting to implement a whole host of technological improvements in the next generation of super-superdreadnoughts.

That moment was coming soon. Hitler announced the unilateral rearmament of the Nazi state in March 1935; Britain and France, fearing an impending war of German aggression, were no longer inclined to limit their own fleets. When the treaty signatories met for the final time, at London late in 1935, Japan withdrew and Italy declined to sign on. The naval arms race was set to begin anew.

The new generation of capital ships, those laid out in the late 1930s and into the beginning of the Second World War, were markedly different from both the lighter Treaty-era warships and the pre-1914 dreadnoughts and superdreadnoughts. Unrestrained by arbitrary design parameters, the major naval powers jumped feetfirst into new construction programs, building ships of all sizes and classes at a fevered pace.

The top contender, a new kind of dreadnought known informally as the fast battleship, combined more efficient and powerful engines, bigger guns, and heavier armor on all surfaces—including the deck, to guard against plunging shells. The British battleship *King George V*, one of the first warships of the rearmament era, displaced nearly thirty-seven thousand tons, with a belt of fourteen-to sixteen-inch armor around its hull and gun turrets, and five- to six-inch armor covering the main deck. Its three turrets—one quadruple-gun turret each fore and aft, and a superturret with two guns mounted behind and above the bow quadruple—carried a total of ten 14-inch guns; it could slice through the water at twenty-nine knots. The pride of the German fleet, the battleships *Bismarck* and *Tirpitz*, each carried eight 15-inch guns as their main armament, and though displacing forty-two thousand tons they could still cruise at a respectable thirty knots. Japan beat the rest in sheer size, its *Yamato* and *Musashi* each displacing nearly sixty-five thousand tons, with the main armament of nine 18-inch guns housed in three triple turrets. Though later to the game, the United States quickly caught up with its rivals even before the Japanese attack on Pearl Harbor in December 1941 compelled its entry into the Second World War. Its six fast battleships of the *North Carolina* and *South Dakota* classes were built closely to Treaty specifications, around thirty-five thousand tons displacement and with nine 16-inch guns, but the later *Iowa*-class fast battleships, laid down in 1939 and 1940, were ten thousand tons heavier and could still manage to reach speeds up to thirty-five knots.

Cruisers, heavy and light, far outnumbered battleships in the construction programs of the late 1930s; the United States alone launched sixty-seven cruisers (of four different classes) between 1938 and 1945. Destroyers outnumbered cruisers by a large margin. The type had proven itself supremely useful during the Great War, especially in the American and British fleets, which came to depend on the light, fast warships as the principal platform for anti-submarine warfare and a key component of any transatlantic convoy. Apart from some minor details, these lithe workhorses were quite similar from navy to navy, and represented a significant improvement on the destroyers of the First World War. Most mounted five or six light-caliber guns, 5-inch or 6-inch, in single-gun turrets; most had several torpedo tubes, as well. Typically, destroyers of the Second World War could slice through the waves at speeds as high as forty knots.

These ships—battleships, cruisers, destroyers, and other light craft such as corvettes—were the heart and soul of the major fleets of 1939–1945. In essence, they were not too far removed from the primary warships of the age of sail, little more than a century before. True, the technology was profoundly different, but the purpose of these ships was precisely the same as that of warships in the age of Nelson: to overwhelm and destroy enemy craft with artillery fire. The artillery-based warship remained the principal focus of naval architects and the makers of naval policy, the established expression of sea power.

The Second World War would be fought and won, in large part, at sea. Britain's survival depended on a reliably safe sea route to North America, guaranteeing a supply lifeline to Canada and the United States; even the Soviet Union needed the Lend-Lease lifeline. The biggest operations of the war in the Western theater after 1940—in North Africa, Sicily, Italy, and Normandy—all commenced with naval operations. The entirety of the US-Japan war of 1941–1945 was an oceanic conflict. But for the most part, big-gun capital ships would play a supporting role. In all the oceans of the world, two unconventional kinds of warships would dominate the conduct of naval operations. The Second World War may have witnessed the apogee of the big-gun battleship, but in reality it was the war of the aircraft carrier and the submarine.

THE IDEA OF using a naval vessel as a takeoff and landing platform for aircraft—to use a ship as a floating, moveable aerodrome—is nearly as old as powered flight itself. In November 1910, only months after the Wright brothers returned to the States from their triumphant tour of Europe, American aviator Eugene B. Ely took off from the US Navy cruiser *Birmingham* in his Curtiss biplane. It was a hair-raising feat, to be sure; the impromptu wooden runway, built out over *Birmingham*'s bow, was less than sixty feet long, and when Ely's plane left the deck it dropped so low that it actually skimmed the surface of the water. But Ely coaxed his machine upward, made good his escape, and flew off to make a safe landing ashore. A couple of months later, in January 1911, Ely repeated his performance, this time from a similar runway set up on the armored cruiser *Pennsylvania* in San Francisco Bay, and, far more astounding, Ely managed to land his plane on the same platform, stopping the aircraft by means of weighted ropes stretched across the runway. Hooks attached to the plane caught on several of the ropes, slowing the Curtiss machine down and finally bringing it to a halt—the very first arrester-gear landing.

In the US Navy, though, this was viewed as nothing more than an entertaining novelty, a typical stunt performed by a show-off civilian pilot. It was not that the Navy, or other navies worldwide, had no interest in aviation. Rather, they saw the future of naval aviation—whatever that was—in the use of seaplanes rather than with conventional aircraft launched from floating airfields. The British navy took the prospect a little more seriously, experimenting with shipborne aircraft before the Great War. Early in the conflict, the Royal Navy (RN) outfitted several civilian vessels with flight decks, and even while the war was on it continued to explore the concept. The RN converted a light cruiser, the *Furious*, into a carrier by removing turrets fore and aft, and adding two flight decks, one over the bow, one over the stern. The arrangement, with two flight decks separated by the ship's superstructure, proved to be a failure. But it was an instructive failure: it taught that, in order to be effective, future carriers would have to have one long, uninterrupted flight deck. This would be the noteworthy feature on Britain's next carrier, HMS *Argus*, a converted passenger liner, the first flush deck carrier. By war's end, the Royal Navy had four aircraft carriers afloat.

Even though naval aviation hadn't really proven itself yet, the notion was a powerful one, and it caught on. Carriers were the subject of much discussion at the Washington Naval Conference, with the final treaty limiting carriers to twenty-seven thousand tons displacement and armament no larger than ten 8-inch guns—with a loophole that discounted carriers of less than ten thousand tons, and designated current carriers as "experimental." A carrier race took off almost immediately. Britain, despite its promising early lead, stepped back, its ambitions temporarily halted when control over naval aviation was taken from the Admiralty and given to the independent Royal Air Force. The RAF had little interest in giving up precious resources for naval fliers, not when the most ardent proponents of airpower had come to the conclusion that aerial bombing would soon render navies obsolete and impotent. Turf battles like these were common enough in the time of the World Wars, as conservative military institutions tried to fit new weapons, tactics, and branches of service—tanks, warplanes, submarines—into existing infrastructures, often with crippling results. The RAF-RN competition over the naval air service undoubtedly set Britain back several years behind the two powers that quickly overtook its lead: the United States and Japan.

Both Japan and the United States embraced the aircraft carrier right after the conclusion of hostilities in 1918. Their initial, tentative efforts were not especially impressive: Japan's *Hosho* (1919), displacing 7,500 tons, and the American *Langley* (1922), a converted collier. Paradoxically, the Washington Naval Treaty unintentionally encouraged investment in larger carriers. By a special provision of the treaty, Britain, the United States, and Japan were each allowed to save two capital ships that had been condemned to the scrap heap and convert them instead into aircraft carriers. Hence the American carriers *Lexington* and *Saratoga*, and the Japanese *Akagi* and *Kaga*, all former (or uncompleted) battlecruisers. These were modern fleet carriers: armored, liberally armed with 8-inch guns and smaller antiaircraft guns, and fast. The *Kaga* could cruise at speeds up to thirty-one knots, the *Lexington* at just over thirty-three knots. All were "island" carriers, meaning that the ship's compact superstructure, including the bridge, was located on an "island" along one side of the ship, so as to allow for a clear airstrip from stem to stern.

The mania for carriers was not universal. Britain waited until after 1935 to beef up its carrier fleet, but neither the French, nor the

Plate 39. The American aircraft carrier USS *Saratoga* (CV-3). *Saratoga* was initially intended to be a battlecruiser, but in 1922 the decision was made to convert it to a carrier, and *Saratoga* was commissioned in 1927. It survived the Second World War only to end its days as a target ship in atomic bomb testing at Bikini Atoll in 1946.

Image: NH 82117 courtesy of the Naval History & Heritage Command.

Italian, nor the German fleets evinced anything more than casual interest. Those fleets were focused on battleships and battlecruisers. The Americans and the Japanese, though, kept at it, with construction taking off after the expiry of the Washington Naval Treaty and the failure of the 1936 London agreement. In the late 1930s, Japan launched the *Soryu-*, *Hiryu-*, and massive *Shokaku*-class carriers; the Americans rolled out the modest-sized *Yorktown*-class carriers, the larger *Essex*-class ships, and a series of light carriers. More US carriers were on the way, their keels already laid down in American shipyards, when carrier-based Japanese planes attacked the American naval base at Pearl Harbor in December 1941, inaugurating an entirely new era in naval warfare.

IF DREADNOUGHTS ACHIEVED very little in the First World War, the battleships of the Second World War did even less to earn their keep. Though the Second World War surpassed the First in virtually every way, especially in matters of scale, there was no fleet action between 1939 and 1945 that could compare to the expansive but very traditional fight at Jutland in 1916. That's not to say that the battleship was useless, that it made no difference at all. There were ship-on-ship engagements in all theaters of the war at sea, some of them of no small strategic significance: the battle of the Denmark Strait and the subsequent hunt for—and sinking of—the German super battleship *Bismarck* in 1941; a handful of sharp skirmishes between Allied and Italian ships in the Mediterranean; the British and American actions against the Vichy French fleet in North Africa, culminating in the American attack on Casablanca in November 1942; the clash at Surigao Strait (October 1944), part of the battle of Leyte Gulf, the largest naval engagement of the war and the last battleship-on-battleship fight in history.

But given the size of the combatant fleets in the Second World War, the number of capital ships in service, and the perceived importance of sea power, the frequency of ship-on-ship combat was actually quite low. The true capital ship of the war was, instead, the aircraft carrier. The carrier, and not the battleship, quickly became the core of the great fleets, just as naval actions became synonymous with air battles. The bigger carriers could move just as fast as battleships and battlecruisers. Battleships and battlecruisers served the carriers, and not the other way around.

In the Atlantic, Britain's carriers gave the Royal Navy an unbridgeable advantage over the Germans. In the Mediterranean theater, biplane Fairey Swordfish torpedo bombers, launched from the carriers *Illustrious* and *Eagle*, carried out the daring and devastating raid on the Italian fleet as it lay at anchor at Taranto in November 1940. Swordfish from *Ark Royal* located, and then helped to sink, the German battleship *Bismarck* in 1941. In the Pacific, the carriers truly ruled. Most of the major naval engagements there, notably the critical Battle of Midway (June 1942), were fought between fleets that never actually made visual contact, but instead attacked each other at a distance with torpedo bombers and dive-bombers, with fighter aircraft escorting friendly bombers or intercepting enemy aircraft. Naval aircraft were vital, too, for conducting strikes against enemy ground installations, and for providing close support in amphibious operations.

In all these regards, the carrier proved itself to be a demonstrably effective instrument of sea power—one might say *the* effective instrument. The toll that carriers exacted in ships sunk or damaged beyond repair far exceeded anything that other surface vessels were able to achieve. Japanese carrier-based dive-bombers sank the British cruisers *Dorsetshire* and *Cornwall*, plus the old carrier *Hermes*, in the Indian Ocean in April 1942. Two months later, at Midway, American naval aviators destroyed all four of the Japanese fleet carriers, while the Japanese sank one of the American carriers; in the June 1944 Battle of the Philippine Sea, the Americans took out nearly all of what was left of Japan's once-proud carrier fleet. And it was from the flight deck of USS *Hornet* that Jimmy Doolittle's band of raiders took off in sixteen B-25B Mitchell medium bombers to bomb Tokyo for the first time in April 1942.

The twist, of course, is that the use of carriers was as much an expression of airpower as it was of sea power, a sign that mastery of the air was now more important than nearly any other consideration in achieving victory at sea. The unique contribution of the aircraft carrier was to make airfields portable, and to bring them to just about anywhere on the globe.

As a type, the aircraft carrier evolved little during the Second World War. Their technological limitations, aside from speed, were almost irrelevant. The real limitations on carriers as combat weapons were the aircraft themselves, for inferior aircraft constrained the striking power of the carrier. Witness, for example, the sad fate of American torpedo bombers at Midway. The Douglas TBD Devastator, the standard American torpedo bomber in 1942, was state of the art when it first took to the skies in 1935. Seven years later, though, it was comparatively poorly armed, slow, and vulnerable.

Plate 40. The new face of naval warfare in 1942—the carrier war. Here a pair of American dive-bombers, the Douglas SBD Dauntless, approach the burning Japanese carrier *Mikuma* during the Battle of Midway (June 1942).
Image: 80-G-17054, courtesy of the Naval History & Heritage Command.

The vast majority of them attacking the Japanese carriers at Midway were easily shot from the sky by Japanese fighters—notably the agile and heavily armed Mitsubishi A6M2 "Zero"—or by antiaircraft fire from the surface vessels, without inflicting any noteworthy damage on the Japanese ships themselves. Carrier construction, though, was a high wartime priority for the three major carrier navies. It had to be; as powerful as they were, aircraft carriers were highly vulnerable to attack, and carrier losses were accordingly high. Britain and the United States managed to keep up with the demand for replacement carriers. Japan did not.

THE SUBMARINE HAD proven its worth in the Great War, and then some. Submarines had everything to recommend them.

They were inexpensive and quick to build, they required very small crews, and they were deadly against surface vessels. As a class, submarines claimed more tonnage sunk than dreadnoughts or battlecruisers, and at a tiny fraction of the investment in time, resources, cash, and manpower. All the naval powers used them, but none to greater effect than Imperial Germany. Before the war, Germany had trailed behind Britain and France in submarine development and manufacturing, but in very short order it put together an excellent submarine fleet. Nothing came closer to bringing Britain to the breaking point during the Great War than the U-boat war against Allied and neutral shipping in the North Atlantic and the North Sea. On the other hand, nothing contributed more to America's entry into the war in 1917—one of the key factors assuring German defeat—than the Kriegsmarine's practice of unrestricted U-boat warfare.

Those lessons were very much on the minds of naval leaders in Britain, France, Italy, the United States, and Japan after the Treaty of Versailles was signed. They admired Germany's success, yet they recoiled in horror at the loss of innocent civilian lives that inevitably accompanied U-boat commerce-raiding. The former Allies were therefore eager to assimilate German technology without adopting German ethics. Germany's U-boat fleet, now captured, was divided as spoils of war among the five major naval powers, who studied the German boats intently. But the roles they expected their new submarine fleets to play were, by and large, the same as those they had anticipated in 1914: fleet operations, reconnaissance, and offensive stealth operations against enemy warships.

In the basics, like propulsion, the submarines of the interwar period were very similar from nation to nation: they used diesel engines when cruising on the surface and battery-powered electric engines when running submerged, with the batteries recharging while the diesel engines were in use. Cramped engine compartments limited the size and power of marine diesels, and so maximum speeds were modest when compared to most surface warships. Submerged submarines moved slowly—rarely more than around four to six knots.

A few truly odd types of submarines were in service before 1939. Several navies experimented with a variety known as the cruiser submarine, which the Germans had used with some success in the Great War. Cruiser submarines were larger than fleet submarines, and they were intended to operate independently at great distances from home waters. A common feature of the cruiser subs was an oversized deck armament. Nearly all submarines had a couple of light guns, usually a machine gun and a quick-firing cannon, mounted externally on the deck, but the cruisers carried much heavier guns. Some of the cruisers were ridiculous, reminiscent of the huge multi-turreted tanks of the 1930s. The French cruiser sub *Surcouf* (commissioned 1934) boasted an armored turret with two 8-inch cannon—effectively a gun turret from a heavy cruiser—mounted forward of the conning tower. The British "submarine-monitor" *M1*, designed and launched late in the First World War, carried a 12-inch gun on deck.

But for the most part, submarines of the interwar generation fell into one of three categories: larger fleet submarines to accompany battle fleets, capable of long voyages; smaller coastal submarines of shorter range, meant for sorties close to shore; and midget submarines, with one- or two-man crews, for short-range attacks on anchored fleets.

The German fleet had the simplest, and most successful, submarine fleet of them all. It was a late starter in the interwar period, thanks to the Versailles treaty, which forbade submarine use or construction in Germany. The Weimar government found ways to skirt around the treaty. Krupp worked closely with a Dutch firm, in Dutch shipyards, to experiment with new submarine types and to manufacture them for export—in the process, covertly designing the prototypes for what would become Germany's wartime submarine fleet. Production went into overdrive the moment Hitler went public with his intention to rearm the Reich. By the beginning of the war in 1939, the reinvigorated Kriegsmarine already had a respectable U-boat fleet. The Germans continually upgraded their sub models during the war, as combat conditions revealed shortcomings in performance. But nearly all German submarine operations fell to three basic U-boat types, all developed before the outbreak of war: the Type II, a small, no-frills, short-range coastal sub; the Type VII, larger and faster, the workhorse of the German wolf packs; and the Type IX, a long-range, oceangoing attack boat.

A major upgrade to the Type VII and Type IX boats was the addition of the snorkel, an invention appropriated from the Dutch navy after the conquest of the Low Countries in 1940. The snorkel was an extendable ventilation pipe that, when raised, allowed the sub to exchange stale air for fresh even while submerged. With the snorkel, a U-boat could run its diesel engines for limited stretches of time while below the surface, charging its batteries and supplying the crew with breathable air at the same time.

The war beneath the waves in 1939–1945 was much bigger than in the Great War. There were more participants, each with bigger fleets: Britain, Italy, Japan, the United States, the Soviet Union, and of course Germany all had respectable submarine forces. And because the later subs had greater range, the action spread all over the globe. The British waged a submarine offensive against Norwegian and Swedish ore shipments to Germany, and a more productive campaign against German and Italian shipping in the Mediterranean, complicating the logistics of Axis operations in North Africa. Italian subs hunted in the Mediterranean and even in cooperation with German subs in northern waters. The two most active theaters were in the North Atlantic, pitting German wolf packs against Allied convoys traveling between the Americas and Europe, and in the Pacific.

German and Italian U-boats racked up an impressive tally of kills just before and just after the American entry into the war. During the period from June 1940 to February 1941, Axis submarines claimed some 2.3 million tons of Allied ships, and in July

1942–March 1943 they destroyed a further 4.5 million tons. The dangers of U-boats lurking throughout the Atlantic, sometimes within sight of the Atlantic coast of the United States, compelled the Allies to rely, religiously, on heavily escorted convoys. The increasing sophistication of anti-submarine warfare made those convoys quite effective, swiftly constricting German U-boat attacks by late 1943. The Allies held a measurable technological edge in anti-submarine warfare: long-range aerial patrols from coastal airfields; the ready availability of escort carriers, which could provide continuous aerial surveillance and attack capabilities even while far away from shore; improved depth charges.

ASDIC sonar may have been the most important addition to the anti-submarine warfare toolkit. First explored by the British near the end of the Great War, ASDIC gave escort destroyers the ability to track submarines, even when submerged, even on the darkest of nights. Anti-submarine projectors gave surface warships the ability to throw high-explosive shells at targeted submarines ahead of the ship's course.

In terms of its overall impact on the course of the war, no submarine force was more successful than the American sub fleet in the Pacific, even if the quality of American torpedoes left much to be desired. American subs, mostly large fleet types, were of high quality. They were without a doubt the most comfortable submarines in existence at the time, boasting comparatively spacious sleeping quarters and even air-conditioning. American skippers had also learned a great deal about U-boat warfare from their German foes, employing wolf-pack formations when attacking Japanese shipping. It helped, too, that the Japanese, strained for ships and resources, did not employ any kind of convoy system to protect their merchant vessels until late in the war, and even then not very well. In 1944–1945, American submarines inflicted terrible losses on Japanese ships; two-thirds of all Japanese merchant shipping lost during the war, some 4.8 million tons, is credited to American submarines. American subs sank Japanese ships faster than Japanese shipyards could build replacements. The contribution of the

US Navy's underwater fleet to American victory in the Pacific, in other words, was invaluable.

Yet it was the Axis powers, and not the Americans, that made the great leaps forward in submarine technology. German and Japanese torpedoes were far superior to those of their enemies. The primary American submarine-launched torpedo, the Mark 14, was woefully inadequate. It could travel as far as 4,500 yards at forty-six knots, or 9,000 yards at thirty-one knots, and its 643-pound high-explosive warhead was triggered by either a contact "pistol" or a magnetic one, which detonated when the pistol detected a change in magnetic field. The magnetic pistol was notoriously unreliable, often detonating before the torpedo was anywhere near the target, and the torpedo as a whole was unstable. The Mark 14 had a disturbing tendency to drop a few meters below its intended depth when fired, often cruising harmlessly under the keel of the targeted ship. Sometimes it went forward in an unintentional circular pattern—even to the point of returning to hit the sub that fired it.

Japanese and German torpedoes, on the other hand, were marvels of modern engineering. German torpedoes, such as the common-place G7e series, were all electric-drive rather than steam-propelled, and so left no telltale trail of bubbles and hence were almost impossible to spot. During the course of the war, German engineers developed all sorts of brilliant features: torpedoes that could be set to run zigzag or figure-eight patterns, making it difficult to evade them even if spotted; acoustic homing torpedoes, which "locked in" on the sound of churning propellers. The Japanese Type 93 torpedo, available in 1933, was probably the most advanced in the world in its time. It carried a half-ton high-explosive warhead and was propelled by a compressed oxygen engine, making for higher speeds and vastly superior range—eleven miles at forty-nine knots, or twenty-two miles at thirty-six knots. This gave even small surface ships the ability to strike and sink battleships well out of range of retaliatory gunfire.

No single innovation in submarine warfare, though, could match the pinnacle of German U-boat technology, the Type XXI and Type XXIII *Elektroboote* (electric boats). Most submarines of both World Wars were, technically speaking, submersibles rather than true submarines: surface travel was their normal mode, even for boats equipped with snorkels, and underwater performance was markedly inferior to surface running. The Germans turned this around with the introduction of the Type XXI in 1943. Everything about the Type XXI was new, from its powerful diesel-electric propulsion system to its streamlined, knifelike hull profiles. Its maximum surface speed wasn't extraordinary—about sixteen knots, just slightly less than that of the fast Type IX boats—but its submerged speed was almost beyond belief: seventeen knots conventionally, and right around six knots when employing its electric "creep" motors in silent-running mode. Even without the creep motors, the Type XXI was much quieter than any other sub of the time. It was faster submerged than many surface ships, and it could remain submerged much longer than any other submarine: about seventy-five hours, taking a mere five hours to recharge batteries if the snorkel were deployed. Both the Type XXI and its smaller coastal cousin, the Type XXIII, were meant to operate submerged most of the time, surfacing only rarely.

Had the *Elektroboote* been built in greater numbers before the end of the war, it might well have altered the course of the Battle of the Atlantic. The Type XXI, with a range of over fifteen thousand nautical miles, could prowl and hunt in the Atlantic, as far from home as the American coast, with ease. Difficult to detect and chase, in greater numbers it could have wreaked havoc with transatlantic shipping, effectively shutting down the American-Canadian supply line to the European theater. But it wasn't built in larger numbers because it appeared so late and, mostly, because the priorities of Hitler's command economy were so chaotic and counter-rational. Like so many revolutionary German innovations—the assault rifle, night-vision optics, the Panther and the Tiger B, the Ar 234 and the Me 262—it made little difference in the end, because German industry could not make enough of it when it was needed, and German political oversight so bungled production that the truly effective weapons systems did not have much of an impact on actual operations. Though both World Wars were high-tech conflicts, pioneering technology and unreliable manufacturing lost out to good-enough technology backed by strong, resilient industrial economies.

IN THE HISTORY of naval warfare, the Second World War represents both a conclusion and a transition. Even if the naval leaders of the 1920s and 1930s did not, or would not, see it, the day of the battleship was over in 1918. The big-gun artillery warship proved to be useful in the Second World War, but mostly in secondary roles, and as an auxiliary to the *real* capital ships of 1939–1945: the aircraft carrier, the submarine, and the destroyer. The battleship could provide mobile and massive firepower when it was needed for offshore bombardment in support of amphibious operations, but it was never indispensable. The carriers, on the other hand, were indispensable, and submarines dominated another realm of sea warfare in which battleships had no place except as prey. The gun was fading from prominence, and the priorities of engineering and technology now lay in other directions.

EPILOGUE

Early on the morning of 6 August 1945, an American heavy bomber—a B-29 Superfortress christened *Enola Gay*—released a single bomb over the city of Hiroshima, Japan. The bomb detonated at 1,900 feet, and the massive explosion that ensued leveled much of the city below, incinerating both buildings and people. The immediate death toll from that single bomb was at least 66,000—later reaching about 150,000—with countless others wounded. Three days later, another B-29 from the American airbase on Tinian, this one dubbed *Bockscar*, dropped a second bomb over the seaport of Nagasaki, with similarly horrifying results. Japan surrendered the following day, and the Second World War came to a close.

The atomic bombs dropped on Hiroshima and Nagasaki were nothing like any weapon ever used in warfare up to that point. The bombs were the product of an intensive and top-secret research program, pursued by Allied scientists, overseen and driven by the American government, to create an atomic weapon capable of ending the war in a single blow. They had worked in great haste, for this was an arms race like no other. Germany, and Japan too, were pursuing the same goal, so the stakes of this particular competition were truly existential. The Americans got there first.

In one way, the atomic bomb attacks on Hiroshima and Nagasaki were logical next steps in the evolution of war, points along an already established continuum. The early advocates of airpower, like Giulio Douhet, envisioned a time when bombers alone would win wars by destroying population centers, industrial targets, and government infrastructure. Strategic bombing campaigns, and not battles on land or at sea, would determine the outcome of international conflicts. Hiroshima and Nagasaki seemed to be precisely what Douhet had been talking about, the ultimate expression of this kind of airpower. Whether the bombings ultimately spared lives or made warfare somehow more civilized or humane, as Douhet and his ilk liked to think they would, remained to be seen.

At the same time, the event was also an abrupt and jarring break with the past. No matter the short-term strategic consequences of the atomic bombings, there's no denying that the destruction of Hiroshima and Nagasaki is a watershed moment, marking the passing of one era and the dawning of another—and not just in terms of warfare and weapons. Seen from any perspective, the world looked like a much different place after the bombings, to the point that it's all but impossible to picture the order of things post 1945 had there been no atomic bombs. The Soviet-American rivalry and the Cold War, the political paroxysms of Europe and Asia and Africa and the Americas, the innumerable small wars fought in the wake of decolonization, the civil unrest, the cultural and social upheaval—all the momentous disorder that would characterize the world in the three-quarters of a century following 1945—none of these things would have unfolded in quite the same way without the foreboding presence of nuclear weapons and the possibility of mutually assured destruction. All of it grew from that single breathtaking demonstration of the power of the atomic bombs in 1945, the only time nuclear weapons have been used in combat.

In the admittedly narrow world of military technology and the conduct of war, the fiery climax of the Second World War also marked a clear and distinct break with the past. The atomic age had begun; the age of the gun was over.

That's not to say that firearms were obsolete, or that they had lost their martial purpose. Far from it. In the late Middle Ages and the

Renaissance, gunpowder weapons did not immediately and completely supplant older, less sophisticated weapon types. Longbows and crossbows held on tenaciously for some time after the musket and the arquebus had made themselves permanent fixtures in land warfare; bladed weapons survived well into the modern age, and not merely for ceremonial purposes. The bayonet—little more than a substitute for the pike—remains in common use. Similarly, since 1945 conventional ground warfare still involves the use of firearms and therefore the application of firepower, as it has for centuries. Infantry, artillery, and armor all have roles to play, and the tactics of land warfare—while evolving to meet new weapons and new modes of combat—bear more resemblance to the fighting methods of the Second World War than the fighting methods of the Second World War do to those of the previous century.

Nuclear weapons, on the other hand, fulfill a different role altogether. Most of the world's larger militaries have stockpiled quantities of tactical nuclear weapons—battlefield weapons like artillery shells and rockets and smaller airborne bombs—that substitute nuclear warheads for high explosive. But overall there has been a great reluctance to use them, mostly for fear of needlessly escalating conflict. Nuclear weapons, for the most part, are strategic weapons, intended to strike directly at the heart of a nation's military and economic power, and while they have changed overall patterns of war, peace, and diplomacy, they have not seriously altered the way in which armies and navies fight one another.

Indeed, as the nature of organized violence has mutated in the post-1945 world, firearms—especially handheld firearms—have enjoyed greater prominence. So many conflicts of the past seventy-five years have been either wars fought between smaller states (the Iran-Iraq War of 1980–1988, for example) or "irregular" actions: regional proxy wars in which global superpowers—the United States, China, the Soviet Union, and its post-Communist successor state—have inserted themselves (the Korean War, the several wars fought in Vietnam) or undeclared wars fought between states and nonstate actors, like, most recently, ISIS and al-Qaeda. Small-unit actions, fought in broken terrain or urban environments, favor the use of rifles, machine guns, and other highly portable weapons. Here the formerly exclusionary character of weapons technology has undergone a definite shift, and perhaps something close to a full reversal. In the high-stakes arms race leading up to the First World War, the rapidly increasing sophistication and complexity of small arms—and of weapons in general—effectively sidelined all but the greater industrial powers of the West. But the arms race eventually solved that problem for smaller states and lesser powers. Massive buildups during the World Wars and the ensuing Cold War had the unintended result of generating truly gigantic quantities of military surplus, glutting the international arms market with inexpensive but effective modern weapons, mostly of Russian, German, or American manufacture. Any state, no matter how poor, could easily acquire serviceable assault rifles, machine guns, handheld anti-tank weapons, and plenty of ammunition with which to feed them. Cheap small arms, in short, now acted as a leveler, putting significant, modern military firepower into the hands of impoverished states, revolutionaries, and terrorists.

The mere fact that fifty-year-old surplus Kalashnikov assault rifles could compete with more up-to-date weapons speaks volumes about the pace of technological change in firearms technology since the Second World War: it has slowed almost to a crawl. It's not that the development of firearms and associated technologies has stagnated. Design trends that had their roots in the Great War continued to guide the evolution of small arms, artillery, and armor in the decades after 1945. In small arms, most of these trends stemmed from the old impulse to make firepower more portable: lighter but robust machine guns, intermediate cartridges, and smaller calibers, the further tuning of the assault rifle—descendants of Germany's pioneering StG 44—that would become the standard infantry weapon. Optical sighting devices, including night-vision apparatus, have become considerably more sophisticated since the Germans introduced the Vampir device in the Second World War. Artillery has benefited from more sophisticated projectiles: guided (or "smart") shells; rocket-assisted projectiles for extended ranges; fin-stabilized projectiles, which when fired from a smoothbore barrel are more accurate than conventional ammunition fired from a rifled barrel; and a whole host of new kinds of armor-piercing ordnance. Tanks and other armored fighting vehicles incorporate the improved artillery and vastly better power plants, transmissions, and suspensions, so that tanks as powerful as the heavies of 1945 can zip along faster than the fleetest light tanks of the Second World War.

But in their basics, the weapons of conventional land warfare after 1945 have not departed drastically from their Second World War forebears. The basic principles of semi- and fully automatic small arms, of the centerfire cartridge with smokeless powder and a jacketed bullet, of quick-firing artillery with recoil suppression, are fundamentally the same today as they were in 1945, and in some cases as they were in 1914. There has been no revolution in small arms or artillery to match those of 1870–1918 and 1930–1945. Only in military aviation and naval architecture can it be said that the weapons technologies of the post-9/11 world are markedly different from those of 1945, but even in those areas the underlying parameters of technological development were discernable at the end of the Second World War. The massive, turreted, all-big-gun battleship of the post-Dreadnought era was already a relic when the Second World War ended. The future belonged, instead, to the aircraft carrier and the submarine, and to smaller, faster craft armed with guided missiles rather than monstrous rifled cannon. With military aviation, the jet age was already underway as the Second World War drew to a close. In both realms, at sea and in the air, the prevailing technologies had moved entirely away from firearms. Within a couple of generations after 1945, neither warplanes nor warships were, first and foremost, flying or floating gun platforms.

That was what heralded the passing of the age of the gun: not that firearms had fallen into disuse, but that after 1945 they were no longer front-and-center in military technology. Firearms were, and are, no longer the focal point of weapons engineering; they are no longer carefully guarded state secrets the way they once were; they no longer precipitate panicked arms races. Not unimportant by any stretch, but not nearly so central to organized violence as they once were.

But during the half-millennium that preceded the Second World War, firearms were the most important weapons in existence. They were nearly synonymous with weapons technology. Though continually evolving, firearms were the pinnacle of achievement in weapons engineering, just as firepower was the most important consideration in the conduct of war. Firearms were the principal determinant of tactics in a way that no other family of weapons had been before. Everything about naval combat during the age of the gun revolved around the properties of the ship-killing ship, armed with cannon. Military engineering, especially the art and science of fortification, was similarly guided and constrained by the nature of siege artillery. Though land battle, in the time of the Renaissance and the Reformation, involved a balanced combination of firepower and shock, ultimately it was firepower that prevailed; it was firepower that was cultivated by soldiers and tacticians. The tactics of land warfare, when stripped down to their most fundamental elements, were a simple matter of finding the best and fastest way to direct the greatest possible weight of firepower on the enemy. This basic truth was as vital to small-unit infantry firefights of the Second World War as it was to the more formal linear battles of the eighteenth century.

And tactics were only the beginning. The mass use of firearms in war conditioned logistics and supply; the expertise demanded by firearms promoted professionalism and permanence in armies and navies. The integration of firearms into Western warfare was in large measure responsible for the internal configuration of military establishments, their rank structures, their notions of command and subordination and discipline, even the complex relationship between military institutions and the civil societies from which they emerged. Weapons development in the age of the gun not only responded to shifting currents in international relations, it even caused those currents to shift, so much so that the patterns of war and peace in the West were in part shaped by rapid advances in firearms technology and the frenetic arms races that came from those advances. If warfare created the modern state, then it was firearms that created modern warfare.

NOTES

SOURCES FOR CHAPTER 1

There's a wealth of recent published works on the concurrent rise of siege artillery and artillery fortresses, thanks to an excellent and prolific community of medieval and Renaissance historians who have openly embraced the history of weapons in warfare, notably Kelly DeVries, Simon Pepper, and Bert S. Hall. I have particularly relied upon Brenda J. Buchanan, ed., *Gunpowder: The History of an International Technology* (Bath: Bath University Press, 1996); Buchanan, ed., *Gunpowder, Explosives and the State: A Technological History* (Aldershot, UK: Ashgate, 2006); Tonio Andrade, *The Gunpowder Age: China, Military Innovation, and the Rise of the West in World History* (Princeton: Princeton University Press, 2017); John M. Patrick, *Artillery and Warfare during the Thirteenth and Fourteenth Centuries* (Logan, UT: Utah State University Press, 1961); Kelly DeVries, *Guns and Men in Medieval Europe, 1200–1500: Studies in Military History and Technology* (Aldershot, UK: Ashgate, 2002); Brett D. Steele and Tamera Dorland, eds., *The Heirs of Archimedes: Science and the Art of War through the Age of Enlightenment* (Cambridge: MIT Press, 2005); Bert S. Hall, *Weapons and Warfare in Renaissance Europe: Gunpowder, Technology, and Tactics* (Baltimore: Johns Hopkins University Press, 1997); Georg Ortenburg, *Waffe und Waffengebrauch im Zeitalter der Landsknechte* (Koblenz, DE: Bernard & Graefe, 1984); Simon Pepper and Nicholas Adams, *Firearms & Fortifications: Military Architecture and*

Siege Warfare in Sixteenth-Century Siena (Chicago: University of Chicago Press, 1986); Christopher Duffy, *Siege Warfare: The Fortress in the Early Modern World 1494–1660* (London: Routledge and Kegan Paul, 1979); John Norris, *Early Gunpowder Artillery c. 1300–1600* (Ramsbury, UK: Crowood, 2003); Robert Douglas Smith and Kelly DeVries, *The Artillery of the Dukes of Burgundy, 1363–1477* (Rochester, NY: Boydell, 2005); J. R. Hale, *Renaissance War Studies* (London: Hambledon, 1983); J. E. Kaufmann and H. W. Kaufmann, *The Medieval Fortress: Castles, Forts, and Walled Cities of the Middle Ages* (Conshohocken, PA: Combined Publishers, 2001).

SOURCES FOR CHAPTER 2

On early European navies and sea power, including the political impact of the emerging state fleets, I have relied heavily upon Carla Rahn Phillips, *Six Galleons for the King of Spain: Imperial Defense in the Early Seventeenth Century* (Baltimore: Johns Hopkins University Press, 1986); John F. Guilmartin Jr., *Galleons and Galleys* (London: Cassell, 2002); John F. Guilmartin, *Gunpowder and Galleys: Changing Technology and Mediterranean Warfare at Sea in the 16th Century* (Cambridge: Cambridge University Press, 1974); Jan Glete, *Warfare at Sea, 1500–1650: Maritime Conflicts and the Transformation of Europe* (London: Routledge, 1999). On the technical details of maritime construction, ship design, and armament: Colin Martin and Geoffrey Parker, *The Spanish Armada* (Manchester: Manchester University Press, 2002); Angus Konstam, *Sovereigns of the Seas: The Quest to Build the Perfect Renaissance Battleship* (New York: John Wiley and Sons, 2008); Donald McIntyre and Basil W. Bathe, *Man-of-War: A History of the Combat Vessel* (New York: McGraw-Hill, 1969); Peter Marsden, *Mary Rose, Your Noblest Shippe: Anatomy of a Tudor Warship* (Portsmouth, UK: Mary Rose Trust, 2009); Björn Landström, *Regalskeppet Vasan från början till slutet* (Stockholm: Interpublishing, 1980); Frank Howard, *Sailing Ships of War, 1400–1860* (London: Conway, 1979); Peter Goodwin, *The Construction and Fitting of the English Man of War, 1650–1850* (Annapolis: Naval Institute Press, 1987); Richard Endsor, *The Restoration Warship: The Design, Construction, and Career of a Third Rate of Charles II's Navy* (Annapolis: Naval

Institute Press, 2009); Angus Konstam, *Renaissance War Galley, 1470–1590* (Oxford: Osprey, 2002); Robert Gardiner, *Cogs, Caravels and Galleons* (London: Conway, 2000); Gardiner, *The Line of Battle: The Sailing Warship 1650–1840* (London: Conway, 2004).

SOURCES FOR CHAPTER 3

On the relationship between technology, tactics, and the conduct of war, see Kelly DeVries, *Infantry Warfare in the Early Fourteenth Century: Discipline, Tactics, and Technology* (Woodbridge, Suffolk, UK: Boydell, 1996); F. L. Taylor, *The Art of War in Italy, 1494–1529* (Cambridge: Cambridge University Press, 1921); Charles Oman, *A History of the Art of War in the Sixteenth Century* (London: Methuen, 1937); Bert S. Hall, *Weapons and Warfare in Renaissance Europe: Gunpowder, Technology, and Tactics* (Baltimore: Johns Hopkins University Press, 1997); Georg Ortenburg, *Waffe und Waffengebrauch im Zeitalter der Landsknechte* (Koblenz: Bernard & Graefe, 1984); Siegfried Fiedler, *Kriegswesen und Kriegführung im Zeitalter der Landsknechte* (Koblenz, DE: Bernard & Graefe, 1985); Werner Hahlweg, *Die Heeresreform der Oranier und die Antike* (Osnabrück, DE: Biblio Verlag, 1940); J. W. Wijn, *Het krijgswezen in den tijd van Prins Maurits* (Utrecht, NL: Hoeijenbos, 1934); Olaf van Nimwegen, *The Dutch Army and the Military Revolutions, 1588–1688* (Rochester, NY: Boydell and Brewer, 2010); René Quatrefages, *Los tercios españoles (1567–1577)* (Madrid: Fundación Universitaria Española, 1979); Ignacio and Iván Notario López, *The Spanish Tercios 1536–1704* (Oxford: Osprey, 2012); Keith Roberts, *Pike and Shot Tactics 1590–1660* (Oxford: Osprey, 2010). Though there are lots of English-language books on early firearms, Germany-speaking Europe has had a long tradition of exceptionally well-researched, well-written, scholarly literature on firearms history. A couple of the best: Moritz Thierbach, *Die geschichtliche Entwicklung der Handfeuerwaffen* 2 vols. (Dresden: Carl Höckner, 1886); Arne Hoff, *Feuerwaffen: Ein waffenhistorisches Handbuch* 2 vols. (Braunschweig: Klinkhardt & Biermann, 1969); Peter Krenn, *Gewehr und Pistole* (Graz: Landeszeughaus, 1990). On the pike: Hugo Schneider, "Der Langspiess," *Schriften des Heeresgeschichtlichen Museums in Wien, Band 7. Der Dreissigjährigen Krieg: Beiträge zu seiner Geschichte* (Vienna:

Heeresgeschichtliches Museum, 1976), pp. 7–24. A truly remarkable, and sadly overlooked, book on weapons performance in the age of the smoothbore musket is B. P. Hughes, *Firepower: Weapons Effectiveness on the Battlefield, 1630–1850* (London: Arms & Armour Press, 1974).

SOURCES FOR CHAPTER 4

In addition to the sources already listed for Chapter 3—most notably, B. P. Hughes's *Firepower*, Thierbach's *Handfeuerwaffen*, and Hoff's *Feuerwaffen*—I based most of this chapter on material from Brent Nosworthy, *The Anatomy of Victory: Battle Tactics 1689–1763* (New York: Hippocrene, 1990); Ilya Berkovich, *Motivation in War: The Experience of Common Soldiers in Old-Regime Europe* (Cambridge: Cambridge University Press, 2017); David Chandler, *The Art of Warfare in the Age of Marlborough* (London: Batsford, 1976); Christopher Duffy, *The Military Experience in the Age of Reason* (New York: Atheneum, 1988); Guy Chet, *Conquering the American Wilderness: The Triumph of European Warfare in the Colonial Northeast* (Amherst: University of Massachusetts Press, 2003); Robert S. Quimby, *The Background of Napoleonic Warfare: The Theory of Military Tactics in Eighteenth-Century France* (New York: Columbia University Press, 1957). There are many good studies of individual armies that touch on the relationship between weapons technology and tactics. Among them are: Matthew H. Spring, *With Zeal and with Bayonets Only: The British Army on Campaign in North America, 1775–1783* (Norman: University of Oklahoma Press, 2008) and Christopher Duffy, *The Army of Frederick the Great* (New York: Hippocrene, 1974). There is also a substantial collector literature for the period, at least for small arms, and while collector books tend to be very detailed and technical, they're the next best thing to examining small arms from the period close-up in a museum collection. Here are a few representative examples of the best for the eighteenth century: Jim Mullins, *Of Sorts for Provincials: American Weapons of the French and Indian War* (Elk River, MN: Track of the Wolf, 2008); R. R. Gale, *A Soldier-Like Way: The Material Culture of the British Infantry 1751–1768* (Elk River, MN: Track of the Wolf, 2007); Erik Goldstein and Stuart Mowbray, *The Brown Bess* (Woonsocket, RI: Mowbray, 2010); Bill Ahearn, *Muskets of the Revolution and the French & Indian Wars* (Lincoln, RI: Mowbray, 2005); De Witt Bailey, *Small Arms of the British Forces in North America 1664–1815* (Woonsocket, RI: Mowbray, 2009).

SOURCES FOR CHAPTER 5

There is a vast, illuminating, and contentious literature on the military revolution in early modern Europe. An anthology edited by Clifford Rogers—*The Military Revolution Debate: Readings on the Military Transformation of Early Modern Europe* (Boulder, CO: Westview, 1995)—is absolutely essential reading; the contributions by Clifford Rogers, Jeremy Black, Geoffrey Parker, and David Parrott are especially noteworthy. Rogers's volume also includes the complete text of the lecture that started it all, Michael Roberts's "The Military Revolution, 1560–1660." Also see Andrew Ayton and J. L. Price, *The Medieval Military Revolution: State, Society and Military Change in Medieval and Early Modern Europe* (London: Tauris, 1995); Geoffrey Parker, *The Military Revolution: Military Innovation and the Rise of the West, 1500–1800* (Cambridge: Cambridge University Press, 1988); David Eltis, *The Military Revolution in Sixteenth-Century Europe* (London: Tauris, 1995); David Parrott, *The Business of War: Military Enterprise and Military Revolution in Early Modern Europe* (Cambridge: Cambridge University Press, 2012); Jan Glete, *War and the State in Early Modern Europe: Spain, the Dutch Republic and Sweden as Fiscal-Military States* (London: Routledge, 2001). Perhaps the best overviews of the period in its entirety are Jeremy Black, *European Warfare, 1494–1660* (London: Routledge, 2002); and Lauro Martines, *Furies: War in Europe, 1450–1700* (New York: Bloomsbury, 2013). On parallel developments in the non-Western world, see Frank Jacob and Gilmar Visoni-Alonzo, *The Military Revolution in Early Modern Europe: A Revision* (London: Palgrave MacMillan, 2016).

SOURCES FOR CHAPTER 6

To say that the literature on Revolutionary and Napoleonic warfare is vast would be an understatement; there is somewhat less on warfare in the early industrial age. For general overviews of land warfare in the period, I have relied mostly on Hew Strachan, *European Armies and the Conduct of War* (London: Routledge, 1983) and William McElwee, *The Art of War, Waterloo to Mons* (Bloomington: Indiana University Press, 1974). For the Napoleonic age, see Gunther E. Rothenberg, *The Art of Warfare in the Age of Napoleon* (Bloomington: Indiana University Press, 1978); Rory Muir, *Tactics and the Experience of Battle in the Age of Napoleon* (New Haven, CT: Yale University Press, 1998); Brent Nosworthy, *With Musket, Cannon and Sword: Battle Tactics of Napoleon and His Enemies* (New York: Sarpedon, 1996); Siegfried Fiedler, *Kriegswesen und Kriegführung im Zeitalter der Einigungskriege* (Bonn, DE: Bernard & Graefe, 1991). A special mention should be made of Dennis Showalter's excellent *Railroads and Rifles: Soldiers, Technology, and the Unification of Germany* (Hamden, CT: Archon, 1975), whose significance extends far beyond the narrow topic indicated in the title.

SOURCES FOR CHAPTER 7

Thanks almost entirely to the vast ocean of books on the American Civil War, there's a good selection of quality books on martial small arms of the period—and their manufacture, qualities, and performance in combat. For an overview of European military muskets and rifles of the period, see Thierbach, *Die geschichtliche Entwickelung der Handfeuerwaffen*, and Hoff, *Feuerwaffen*, cited in Sources for Chapters 3 and 4. Some of the more recent, and more specific, arms books also contain valuable information about the design, testing, and manufacturing process at national armories and in privately owned factories. Here are a few: Howard L. Blackmore, *British Military Firearms, 1650–1850* (London: Herbert Jenkins, 1961); Dr. C. H. Roads, *The British Soldier's Firearm, 1850–1864* (London: Herbert Jenkins, 1964); Erich Gabriel, *Die Hand- und Faustfeuerwaffen der Habsburgischen Heere* (Vienna: Österreichischer Bundesverlag, 1990) (on Austrian arms); Jean Boudriot and Robert Marquiset, *Armes à feu françaises, modèle règlementaire, 1833–1861, chargement bouche et percussion* (Paris, 1967); Kent W. Johns, *Springfield Armory Infantry Muskets 1795–1844* (Woonsocket, RI: Andrew Mowbray, 2015); Peter A. Schmidt, *U.S. Military Flintlock Muskets and Their Bayonets: The Early Years, 1790–1815* (Woonsocket, RI: Andrew Mowbray, 2006);

Notes

Giles Cromwell's *The Virginia Manufactory of Arms* (Charlottesville: University Press of Virginia, 1974) is a wonderful look into the workings of an early nineteenth-century arms factory. For an accurate assessment of the rifle-musket in the American Civil War, see the excellent book by Earl J. Hess, *The Rifle Musket in Civil War Combat* (Lawrence: University Press of Kansas, 2008); Brett Gibbons, *The Destroying Angel: The Rifle-Musket as the First Modern Infantry Weapon* (privately published, 2019), presents a more positive view of the weapon. On the development of the expanding bullet, see Dean S. Thomas, *Round Ball to Rimfire: A History of Civil War Small Arms Ammunition* (Gettysburg: Thomas Publications, 1997); Brett Gibbons, *The English Cartridge: Pattern 1853 Rifle-Musket Ammunition* (privately published, 2020); on the impact of the Dreyse, see Dennis Showalter, *Railroads and Rifles: Soldiers, Technology, and the Unification of Germany* (Hamden, CT: Archon, 1975); and Gordon A. Craig, *The Battle of Königgrätz: Prussia's Victory over Austria, 1866* (Philadelphia: University of Pennsylvania Press, 1964)—one of the best battle-studies ever written. One of the best arms studies ever written concerns—naturally—one of the most important firearms ever devised, the Dreyse: Rolf Wirtgen, *Das Zündnadelgewehr: Eine militärtechnische Revolution im 19. Jahrhundert* (Herford, DE: E. S. Mittler, 1991).

SOURCES FOR CHAPTER 8

Perhaps because artillery pieces aren't "collectible" in the way that small arms are, the technical literature on early-to-mid-nineteenth-century artillery is comparatively thin, apart from contemporary technical papers and patent documents. Fortunately, America's combined fascination with weaponry and the history of its Civil War means that there is at least a respectable body of work dealing with Civil War guns of all sizes, much of it germane to general artillery trends of the period. On the Paixhans shell-guns, see: Henri-Joseph Paixhans, *An Account of the Experiments made in the French Navy for the Trial of Bomb Cannon, etc.* (Philadelphia: Dorsey, 1838); J. A. Dahlgren, *Shells and Shell-Guns* (Philadelphia: King & Baird, 1856). On the *Princeton* tragedy and the Ericsson/Stockton guns, see Lee M. Pearson, "The 'Princeton' and the 'Peacemaker': A Study in Nineteenth-Century Naval Research and Development

Procedures," *Technology and Culture*, 7 (Spring, 1966), pp. 163–83. On the general development of mid-nineteenth-century (and earlier) artillery and ammunition, see Antoine-Félix Aloncle, *Renseignements sur L'Artillerie Navale de L'Angleterre et des États-Unis* (Paris: Librairie Maritime et Scientifique, 1865); Warren Ripley, *Artillery and Ammunition of the Civil War* (New York: Promontory, 1970); James C. Hazlett, Edwin Olmstead, and M. Hume Parks, *Field Artillery Weapons of the Civil War* (Newark: University of Delaware Press, 1988); H. Müller, *Die Entwickelung der Feld-Artillerie in Bezug auf Material, Organisation und Taktik, von 1815 bis 1870* (Berlin: Robert Oppenheim, 1873).

SOURCES FOR CHAPTER 9

The history of the transition from the all-wooden, sail-powered warship to the iron and/or steel-hulled battleship doesn't attract as much attention as the periods before and after do—except, of course, for the naval operations of the American Civil War. Excellent overviews of the period are to be found in Donald MacIntyre and Basil W. Bathe, *Man-of-War: A History of the Combat Vessel* (New York: McGraw Hill, 1969); David Ross, *Great Warships from the Age of Steam* (New York: Metro Books, 2014); R. Gardiner, ed., *Steam, Steel and Shellfire: The Steam Warship 1815–1905* (London: Conway, 2001); Lincoln Paine, *Warships of the World to 1900* (New York: Mariner, 2000). On early marine engine technology, see Basil Greenhill, *The Advent of Steam: The Merchant Steamship before 1900* (London: Conway, 1993). On the American ironclad tradition, see William N. Still, *Iron Afloat: The Story of the Confederate Armorclads* (Columbia: University of South Carolina Press, 1971); James McPherson, *War on the Waters: The Union and Confederate Navies, 1861–1865* (Chapel Hill: University of North Carolina Press, 2012); Richard Snow, *Iron Dawn: The Monitor, the Merrimack, and the Civil War Sea Battle That Changed History* (New York: Scribner, 2016). On contemporary European developments: Andrew Lambert, *Battleships in Transition: The Creation of the Steam Battlefleet, 1815–1860* (London: Conway, 1984); Andrew Lambert, *HMS Warrior 1860: Victoria's Ironclad Deterrent* (Annapolis: Naval Institute Press, 2010); James Phinney

Baxter, *The Introduction of the Ironclad Warship* (Cambridge: Harvard University Press, 1933).

SOURCES FOR CHAPTER 10

On the basic trends in warfare at the turn of the century, see, inter alia: Hew Strachan, *European Armies and the Conduct of War*, and William McElwee, *The Art of War, Waterloo to Mons*, both listed in the sources for Chapter 6. On the political, diplomatic, and fiscal background of the European arms race, see the excellent overview by David G. Hermann, *The Arming of Europe and the Making of the First World War* (Princeton: Princeton University Press, 1996); Jari Eloranta, "From the Great Illusion to the Great War: Military Spending Behaviour of the Great Powers, 1870–1913," *European Review of Economic History* 11 (2007): 255–283. On the exploration of new weaponry in the Russo-Japanese War, which is covered in the next four chapters, see Great Britain, War Office, *The Russo-Japanese War: Reports from British Officers Attached to the Japanese Forces in the Field* 3 vols. (London: HMSO, 1908); François Oscar de Négrier, *Lessons of the Russo-Japanese War* (London: Hugh Rees, 1906); US War Department, *Reports of Military Observers Attached to the Armies in Manchuria during the Russo-Japanese War* 5 vols. (Washington, DC: GPO, 1906–1907).

SOURCES FOR CHAPTER 11

Here, again, readers wanting further details about the development of the modern magazine-fed rifle and its ammunition have to rely primarily on collectors' literature; though weapons technology is central to the common narrative of "deadly modern weapons, outdated tactics" commonly connected with the Great War, academic histories don't offer much of a detailed examination of the capabilities of those weapons. Here are some of the best collector books: Roy M. Marcot, *Spencer Repeating Firearms* (Woonsocket, RI: Andrew Mowbray, 2002); Wiley Sword, *The Historic Henry Rifle: Oliver Winchester's Famous Civil War Repeater* (Woonsocket, RI: Andrew Mowbray, 2002); Ian V. Hogg and

John S. Weeks, *Military Small Arms of the 20th Century* (Iola, WI: Gun Digest Books, 2000); John Walter, *Allied Small Arms of World War One* (Ramsbury, UK: Crowood Press, 2000); John Walter, *Central Powers' Small Arms of World War One* (Ramsbury, UK: Crowood, 1999); Luke Mercaldo, *Allied Rifle Contracts in America* (Greensboro, NC: Wet Dog Publications, 2011); Robert W. D. Ball, *Mauser Military Rifles of the World* (Iola, WI: Gun Digest Books, 2011); Paul S. Scarlata, *Mannlicher Military Rifles* (Lincoln, RI: Andrew Mowbray, 2004); Stuart C. Mowbray and Joe Puleo, *Bolt Action Military Rifles of the World* (Woonsocket, RI: Mowbray, 2009); Paul S. Scarlata, *A Collector's Guide to the German Gew. 88 "Commission" Rifle* (Woonsocket, RI: Mowbray, 2007); Ian Skennerton, *The Lee-Enfield: A Century of Lee-Metford and Lee-Enfield Rifles and Carbines* (privately printed, 2007); Jean Huon and Alain Barrellier, *Le fusil Lebel* (Chaumont, FR: Crépin-LeBlond, 2015); Melvin M. Johnson and Charles T. Haven, *Ammunition: Its History, Development, and Use, 1600 to 1943* (New York: Morrow, 1943). On the performance of modern rifles on the battlefield, see William McElwee, *Art of War, Waterloo to Mons* (Bloomington: Indiana University Press, 1974); David G. Hermann, *The Arming of Europe and the Making of the First World War* (Princeton: Princeton University Press, 1996); Quintin Barry, *War in the East: A Military History of the Russo-Turkish War 1877–78* (Havertown, PA: Helion, 2012); Bruce Menning, *Bayonets before Bullets: The Imperial Russian Army, 1861–1914* (Bloomington: Indiana University Press, 1992); F. V. Greene, *The Russian Army and Its Campaigns in Turkey in 1877–1878* (New York: Appleton, 1879).

SOURCES FOR CHAPTER 12

There are tons of coffee-table books on machine guns—some of them, admittedly, very thoroughly researched—but few serious studies. James H. Willbanks, *Machine Guns: An Illustrated History of Their Impact* (Santa Barbara, CA: ABC-CLIO, 2004) is a good introduction, as is John Ellis, *The Social History of the Machine Gun* (Baltimore: Johns Hopkins University Press, 1975). I have also relied upon David A. Armstrong, *Bullets and Bureaucrats: The Machine Gun and the United States Army, 1851–1916* (Westport, CT: Greenwood, 1982); George M. Chin, *The*

Machine Gun 3 vols. (Washington, DC: US Department of the Navy, 1951); Gerald Prenderghast, *Repeating and Multi-Fire Weapons* (Jefferson, NC: McFarland, 2018); Anthony Smith, *Machine Gun: The Story of the Men and the Weapon That Changed the Face of War* (New York: St. Martin's, 2003); Roger Ford, *The Grim Reaper: The Machine-Gun and Machine-Gunners in Action* (London: Sidgwick & Jackson, 1996); Ian V. Hogg, *Machine Guns* (Iola, WI: Krause, 2002). On individual weapons: Dolf L. Goldsmith and R. Blake Stevens, *The Devil's Paintbrush: Sir Hiram Maxim's Gun* (Toronto: Collector Grade Publications, 1989); Paul Wahl and Donald R. Toppel, *The Gatling Gun* (New York: Arco, 1965); John M. Browning and Curt Gentry, *John M. Browning: American Gunmaker* (New York: Doubleday, 1964); Martin Pegler, *The Vickers-Maxim Machine Gun* (Oxford: Osprey, 2013). But topping them all is perhaps one of the most remarkable and insightful books about the history of a single weapon type ever written: Paul Cornish, *Machine Guns and the Great War* (Barnsley, UK: Pen and Sword, 2009).

SOURCES FOR CHAPTER 13

In addition to the general works on weapons and tactics cited previously, such as Hew Strachan's *European Armies and the Conduct of War* (London: Routledge, 1983) and William McElwee's *The Art of War, Waterloo to Mons* (Bloomington: Indiana University Press, 1974), I have relied on the following: Bruce I. Gudmundsson, *On Artillery* (Westport, CT: Praeger, 1993), probably the best single volume on modern artillery; W. Heydenreich, *Das moderne Feldgeschütz* 2 vols. (Leipzig, DE: G. J. Göschen, 1906); Friedrichfranz Feeser, *Artillerie im Feldkriege* (Berlin: Mittler, 1930); Shelford Graham and Dominick Bidwell, *Fire-Power: British Army Weapons and Theories of War, 1904–1905* (Boston: Allen and Unwin, 1985); Paul Strong and Sanders Marable, *Artillery in the Great War* (Barnsley: Pen & Sword, 2011); Georg Bruchmüller, *Die deutsche Artillerie in den Durchbruchschlachten des Weltkrieges* (Berlin: Mittler, 1922); Eric Brose, *The Kaiser's Army: The Politics of Military Technology in Germany during the Machine Age, 1870–1918* (Oxford: Oxford University Press, 2001); Dale Clarke, *British Artillery 1914–18: Field Artillery* (Oxford: Osprey, 2004); Dale Clarke, *British Artillery 1914–19:*

Heavy Artillery (Oxford: Osprey, 2005); Lieutenant S. Gore-Brown, *The Prussian Artillery in the Campaign of 1866* (Solihull, UK: Helion, 2009); H. Müller, *Die Entwickelung der Feld-Artillerie in Bezug auf Material, Organisation und Taktik, von 1815 bis 1870* (Berlin: Robert Oppenheim, 1873); Gordon L. Rottman, *The Hand Grenade* (Oxford: Osprey, 2015). On "breakthrough" tactics in the Great War, see Bruce I. Gudmundsson, *Stormtroop Tactics: Innovation in the German Army, 1914–1918* (New York: Praeger, 1989).

SOURCES FOR CHAPTER 14

Battleships have *almost* as dedicated a fan base as firearms, and the popular literature on the Royal Navy in this period is especially rich. For this chapter, I have mainly consulted: Donald MacIntyre and Basil W. Bathe, *Man-of-War: A History of the Combat Vessel* (New York: McGraw-Hill, 1969); D. K. Brown, *Warrior to Dreadnought: Warship Development, 1860–1905* (Annapolis: Naval Institute Press, 1997); Norman Friedman, *Fighting the Great War at Sea: Strategy, Tactics and Technology* (Annapolis: Naval Institute Press, 2014); Robert Gardiner, ed., *The Eclipse of the Big Gun: The Warship, 1906–45* (London: Conway, 2001). There are exceptional overviews of the prewar naval arms race and the surface campaign that led to Jutland in two fascinating books by Robert K. Massie: *Dreadnought: Britain, Germany, and the Coming of the Great War* (New York: Ballantine, 2002) and *Castles of Steel: Britain, Germany, and the Winning of the Great War at Sea* (New York: Random House, 2003). On technological developments in individual navies, see John Jordan and Philippe Caresse, *French Battleships of World War One* (Barnsley, UK: Seaforth, 2017); Aidan Dodson, *The Kaiser's Battlefleet: German Capital Ships, 1871–1918* (Annapolis: Naval Institute Press, 2016); Nicholas Wolz, *From Imperial Splendor to Internment: The German Navy in the First World War* (Annapolis: Naval Institute Press, 2015); Vincent P. O'Hara, W. David Dickson, and Richard Worth, *To Crown the Waves: The Great Navies of the First World War* (Annapolis: Naval Institute Press, 2013). On the U-boat war: Hans Joachim Koerver, *The Kaiser's U-Boat Assault on America: Germany's Great War Gamble in the First World War* (London: Pen & Sword, 2020); Richard

Compton-Hall, *Submarine Boats: The Beginnings of Underwater Warfare* (London: Conway, 1983); Richard Compton-Hall, *Submarines at War 1914–1918* (Penzance, UK: Periscope Publishing, 2004); Kelly K. Lydon, *The U-boats of World War I* (West Barnstable, MA: New England Seafarer Books, 1997); Jak Mallmann Showell, *The U-Boat Century: German Submarine Warfare 1906–2006* (Annapolis: Naval Institute Press, 2006). On the warships of the lesser naval powers, see the articles in Bruce Taylor, ed., *The World of the Battleship: The Design and Careers of Capital Ships of the World's Navies 1880–1990* (Annapolis: Naval Institute Press, 2018).

SOURCES FOR CHAPTER 15

The air war of 1914–1918 has—like the navies of the period—the great blessing of an extensive literature, much of it in English. Here is a selection of the works upon which I relied most: Lee Kennett, *The First Air War: 1914–1918* (New York: Free Press, 1991); James Hamilton-Paterson, *Marked for Death: The First War in the Air* (New York: Pegasus, 2017); James Streckfuss, *Eyes All Over the Sky: Aerial Reconnaissance in the First World War* (Oxford: Casemate, 2016); John H. Morrow Jr., *The Great War in the Air: Military Aviation from 1909 to 1921* (Washington, DC: Smithsonian Institution Press, 1993). There are innumerable books on individual models of most known warplanes of the Great War, including the excellent little volumes published by Osprey, Aeronaut, and Squadron Signal.

Armored warfare in the Great War, as might be expected, has been more poorly served by historians. I have consulted Bryan Cooper, *Tank Battles of World War I* (Barnsley, UK: Pen & Sword, 2015); Craig Moore, *Tank Hunter: World War One* (Stroud, UK: The History Press, 2017); Michael Foley, *Rise of the Tank: Armoured Vehicles and Their Use in the First World War* (Barnsley, UK: Pen & Sword, 2014); Tim Gale, *The French Army's Tank Force and Armoured Warfare in the Great War: The Artillerie Spéciale* (Burlington, UK: Ashgate, 2013); Dale Wilson, *Treat 'Em Rough: The Birth of American Armor, 1917–20* (Novato, CA: Presidio, 1989); David J. Childs, *A Peripheral Weapon? The Production and Employment of British Tanks in the First World War* (Westport, CT:

Greenwood, 1999); Douglas Orgill, *Armoured Onslaught: 8th August 1918* (New York: Ballantine, 1972); Heinz Guderian, *Achtung-Panzer! The Development of Tank Warfare* (London: Cassell, 1999); J.F.C. Fuller, *Tanks in the Great War, 1914–1918* (London: John Murray, 1920); Steven J. Zaloga, *German Panzers 1914–18* (Oxford: Osprey, 2006); Steven J. Zaloga, *French Tanks of World War I* (Oxford: Osprey, 2010).

Finally, on gas warfare in the Great War, see L. F. Haber, *The Poisonous Cloud: Chemical Warfare in the First World War* (Oxford: Clarendon, 1986); Simon Jones, *World War I Gas Warfare Tactics and Equipment* (Oxford: Osprey, 2007).

SOURCES FOR CHAPTER 17

On machine guns, see the sources cited for Chapter 12, but especially the studies by Willbanks, Ellis, Chin, and Anthony Smith. See also the source by Ian V. Hogg and John S. Weeks cited in Chapter 11. Also, Folke Myrvang, *MG-34–MG-42: German Universal Machineguns* (Cobourg, ON: Collector Grade Publications, 2002); Chris McNab, *Soviet Submachine Guns of World War II: PPD-40, PPSh-41 and PPS* (Oxford: Osprey, 2014); Frank Iannamico, *American Thunder: Military Thompson Submachine Guns* (Henderson, NV: Chipotle Publishing, 2015); Ian V. Hogg, *Submachine Guns* (London: Greenhill Books, 2001); Frank Iannamico, *Blitzkrieg: The MP40 Maschinenpistole of World War II* (Henderson, NV: Chipotle Publishing, 2016). On the evolution of the battle rifle: Bruce N. Canfield, *The M1 Garand Rifle* (Woonsocket, RI: Andrew Mowbray, 2013); D. N. Bolotin, *Soviet Small-Arms and Ammunition* (Hyvinkää: Finnish Arms Museum Foundation, 1995); Peter J. Senich, *The German Assault Rifle, 1935–1945* (Boulder, CO: Paladin Press, 1987). On the origins and development of the assault rifle, see: C. J. Chivers, *The Gun* (New York: Simon & Schuster, 2010).

SOURCES FOR CHAPTER 18

There are *many* good books on tanks, tank operations, and tank technology during the Second World War; there are somewhat fewer on artillery. Hew Strachan provides a truly brilliant overview in *European*

Armies and the Conduct of War (London: Routledge, 1983), especially in relating the use of armor to the mobilization of the Russian, French, German, and British economies in wartime. I have also made use of, among others: Tim Bean and William Fowler, *Russian Tanks of World War II: Stalin's Armored Might* (St. Paul, MN: MBI, 2002); Peter Chamberlain and Chris Ellis, *British and American Tanks of World War Two* (London: Cassell, 2002); Peter Chamberlain, H. L. Doyle, and Thomas L. Jentz, *Encyclopedia of German Tanks of World War Two* (New York: Arco, 1978); Terry J. Gander, *Anti-Tank Weapons* (Marlborough, UK: Crowood, 2000); Ralph Riccio, *Italian Tanks and Fighting Vehicles of World War 2* (London: Pique, 1975); Spencer C. Tucker, *Tanks: An Illustrated History of Their Impact* (Santa Barbara, CA: ABC-CLIO, 2004); Bryan Perrett, *Tank Warfare* (London: Arms and Armour, 1990). On artillery, Bruce I. Gudmundsson's *On Artillery* (New York: Praeger, 1993) is still the best and most insightful survey of artillery technology and tactics in modern warfare. See Gudmundsson's extensive bibliography for further reading. On the artillery arms of the individual combatants, see Ian Hogg, *German Artillery of World War Two* (London: Arms and Armour, 1975); Ian V. Hogg, *British & American Artillery of World War Two* (New York: Hippocrene, 1978).

SOURCES FOR CHAPTER 19

The air war of 1939–1945 is perhaps better served than any other subtopic of World War II history, with the likely exception of the D-Day invasion. The best survey of the war in the air remains Richard Overy, *The Air War 1939–1945* (New York: Stein and Day, 1980). Three well-done broader surveys, which include detailed discussions of the interwar period and the debates over airpower, are Stephen Budiansky, *Air Power: The Men, Machines, and Ideas That Revolutionized War, from Kitty Hawk to Gulf War II* (New York: Viking, 2004); Jeremy Black, *Air Power: A Global History* (London: Rowman and Littlefield, 2016); Horst Boog, ed., *The Conduct of the Air War in the Second World War* (Oxford: Berg, 1992). On strategic bombing and its origins, see Richard Overy, *The Bombing War: Europe 1939–1945* (London: Penguin UK, 2014); Neville Jones, *The Beginnings of Strategic Air Power: A History of the British*

Bomber Force, 1923–1929 (London: Frank Cass, 1987); Thomas Wildenberg, *Billy Mitchell's War: The Army Air Corps and the Challenge to Seapower* (Annapolis: Naval Institute Press, 2013). On close air support: Richard P. Hallion, *Strike from the Sky: The History of Battlefield Air Attack 1911–1945* (Washington, DC: Smithsonian Institution Press, 1989); Peter C. Smith, *The History of Dive-Bombing* (Barnsley: Pen & Sword, 2007).

SOURCES FOR CHAPTER 20

Many of the works consulted for Chapter 14 are pertinent here as well: Donald MacIntyre and Basil W. Bathe, *Man-of-War: A History of the Combat Vessel* (New York: McGraw-Hill, 1969); Robert Gardiner, ed., *The Eclipse of the Big Gun: The Warship, 1906–45* (London: Conway, 2001); Bruce Taylor, ed., *The World of the Battleship: The Design and Careers of Capital Ships of the World's Navies 1880–1990* (Annapolis: Naval Institute Press, 2018). See also: N.J.M. Campbell, *Naval Weapons of World War Two* (Annapolis: Naval Institute Press, 1985); Norman Friedman, *British Naval Weapons of World War Two* (Annapolis: Naval Institute Press, 2019); Norman Friedman, *Naval Firepower: Battleship Guns and Gunnery in the Dreadnought Era* (Annapolis: Naval Institute Press, 2008); David K. Brown, *The Grand Fleet: Warship Design and Development, 1906–1922* (London: Baker & Taylor, 1999); John Jordan, *Warships after Washington: The Development of the Five Major Fleets, 1922–1930* (Annapolis: Naval Institute Press, 2011); John Jordan, *Warships after London: The End of the Treaty Era in the Five Major Fleets, 1930–1936* (Annapolis: Naval Institute Press, 2020).

INDEX

ethics of weapons technology, 243–244

Ethiopia, Italian invasion of (1935), 516–517

Farman, Henri (Anglo-French aviation pioneer), 385

Farragut, David (US Navy officer), 355

Faust, Drew Gilpin (American historian), 428n

Ferdinand and Isabella of Spain, 31

Ferguson, Patrick (British army officer), 173

feudal system, 20, 22

field gun. *See* artillery

Finland, 442, 453, 456–457, 496

firelock. *See* flintlock

First Schleswig War, *see* Three Years' War

First World War (Great War) (1914–1918). *See also* Versailles, Treaty of
anti-submarine warfare, 540
anti-tank weapons, 495–496
Armistice, 334
arms race, 235–250, 262–263
artillery, 312, 325–326, 328, 331–341, *338*, 470–474
aviation, 331–332, 376, 384–407, *391*, *396*, *400*, *405*, 419–420, 501, 507, 513
causes, 244–245, 252
disarmament, 537
duration of battles, 427–428
earthworks, 332–334, 336–337, 428n

emerging technologies, 380–421

gas warfare, 334–335, 381–383

hand grenades, 341–342, 343

lessons from, 425–439

light machine guns, 307–310, *309*, 440, 442

logistics, 426–427

machine guns, 296, 301–305, 307–310, *309*, 439, 440, 442, 447

military surplus, 434–435, 460–461

mortars, 332–334, 341, 473

motorcycles, 408

nature of war, myths about, 447–448

naval operations, 368–369, 373–378, 431–432, 534–536, 547–548

onset, 244, 281–282

productive capacity, 13, 150, 432–433

rifles, 281–282, 438, 448–449, 461–462

scale of war, 13, 246–247, 425–430

submarine warfare, 369, 373–378, 432, 547–548

support troops, 426–427

tactics, 428–430, 428n

tanks, 407–421, 477

transportation, 408, 431

Fisher, Sir John "Jacky" (British admiral), 361–363, 367

Fitch, James (American inventor), 216

Paul Lockhart is professor of history at Wright State University, where he has taught military and European history since 1989. The author of six books on Scandinavian history and the role of war in history, including *The Drillmaster of Valley Forge* and *The Whites of Their Eyes*, Lockhart lives in Centerville, Ohio.